Human Rights Law

The International Library of Essays in Law and Legal Theory
Series Editor: Tom D. Campbell

Schools

Natural Law, Vols I & II *John Finnis*
Justice *Thomas Morawetz*
Law and Economics, Vols I & II *Jules Coleman and Jeffrey Lange*
Critical Legal Studies *James Boyle*
Marxian Legal Theory *Csaba Varga*
Legal Reasoning, Vols I & II *Aulis Aarnio and D. Neil MacCormick*
Legal Positivism *Mario Jori*
American Legal Theory *Robert Samuel Summers*
Postmodernism and Law *Dennis Patterson*
Law in History, Vols I & II *David Sugarman*
Law and Language *Fred Schauer*
Sociological Theories of Law *Kahei Rokumoto*
Rights *Carlos Nino*
Law and Psychology *Martin Lyon Levine*
Feminist Legal Theory, Vols I & II *Frances Olsen*
Law and Society *Roger Cotterrell*
Contemporary Criminological Theory *Francis T. Cullen and Velmer S. Burton Jr.*

Areas

Criminal Law *Thomas Morawetz*
Tort Law *Ernest J. Weinrib*
Contract Law, Vols I & II *Larry Alexander*
Anti-Discrimination Law *Christopher McCrudden*
Consumer Law *Iain Ramsay*
International Law *Martti Koskenniemi*
Property Law, Vols I & II *Elizabeth Mensch and Alan Freeman*
Constitutional Law *Mark V. Tushnet*
Procedure *D.J. Galligan*
Evidence and Proof *William Twining and Alex Stein*
Company Law *Sally Wheeler*
Privacy, Vols I & II *Raymond Wacks*
Lawyers' Ethics *David J. Luban*
Administrative Law *D.J. Galligan*
Child Law *Harry D. Krause*
Family Law, Vols I & II *Harry D. Krause*
Welfare Law *Peter Robson*
Medicine and the Law *Bernard M. Dickens*
Commercial Law *Ross Cranston*
Environmental Law *Michael C. Blumm*
Conflict of Laws *Richard Fentiman*
Law and Religion *Wojciech Sadurski*
Human Rights Law *Philip Alston*
European Community Law, Vols I & II *Francis Snyder*
Tax Law, Vols I & II *Patricia D. White*
Media Law *Eric Barendt*
Labour Law *David L. Gregory*
Alternative Dispute Resolution *Michael D.A. Freeman*

Legal Cultures

Comparative Legal Cultures *Csaba Varga*
Law and Anthropology *Peter Sack*
Hindu Law and Legal Theory *Ved Nanda*
Islamic Law and Legal Theory *Ian Edge*
Chinese Law and Legal Theory *Michael Palmer*
Russian Legal Theory *W. Butler*
Common Law *Michael Arnheim*
Japanese Law and Legal Theory *Koichiro Fujikura*
Law and Development *Anthony Carty*
Jewish Law and Legal Theory *Martin P. Golding*
Legal Education *Martin Lyon Levine*
Civil Law *Ralf Rogowski*
African Law and Legal Theory *Gordon Woodman and Akintunde Obilade*

Future Volume
Cumulative index

Human Rights Law

Edited by

Philip Alston

Professor of International Law
European University Institute, Florence

NEW YORK UNIVERSITY PRESS
REFERENCE COLLECTION

First published in the U.S.A. in 1996 by
NEW YORK UNIVERSITY PRESS
Washington Square
New York NY 10003

Library of Congress Cataloging-in-Publication Data
Human rights law / edited by Philip Alston.
p. cm. — (International library of essays in law and legal theory. Areas ; 27)
Includes bibliographical references.
ISBN 0-8147-0613-4
1.Human rights. I. Alston, Philip. II. Series.
K3240.6.H8787 1995
341.4'81—dc20 95-22868
CIP

Contents

	cknowledgements	vii
	eries Preface	ix
	ntroduction	xi

ART I THE INTERNATIONAL NORMATIVE FRAMEWORK

1	Bruno Simma and Philip Alston (1992), 'The Sources of Human Rights Law: Custom, Jus Cogens, and General Principles', *Australian Year Book of International Law*, **12**, pp. 82–108.	3
2	Martti Koskenniemi (1990), 'The Pull of the Mainstream', *Michigan Law Review*, **88**, pp. 1946–62.	31
3	Richard Falk (1979), 'Comparative Protection of Human Rights in Capitalist and Socialist Third World Countries', *Universal Human Rights*, **1**, pp. 3–29.	49
4	Theodor Meron (1986), 'On a Hierarchy of International Human Rights', *American Journal of International Law*, **80**, pp. 1–23.	77
5	Oscar Schachter (1983), 'Human Dignity as a Normative Concept', *American Journal of International Law*, **77**, pp. 848–54.	101

ART II UNIVERSALITY IN CULTURAL PERSPECTIVE

6	'Statement on Human Rights' (1947), *American Anthropologist*, **49**, pp. 539–43.	111
7	Fernando R. Tesón (1985), 'International Human Rights and Cultural Relativism', *Virginia Journal of International Law*, **25**, pp. 869–98.	117
8	Jack Donnelly (1982), 'Human Rights and Human Dignity: An Analytic Critique of Non-Western Conceptions of Human Rights', *American Political Science Review*, **76**, pp. 303–16.	147
9	R. Panikkar (1982), 'Is the Notion of Human Rights a Western Concept?', *Diogenes*, **120**, pp. 75–102.	161
10	Rajni Kothari (1987), 'Human Rights – A Movement in Search of a Theory', *Lokayan Bulletin*, **5**, pp. 17–27.	189
11	Bilahari Kausikan (1993), 'Asia's Different Standard', *Foreign Policy*, **92**, pp. 24–41.	201
12	Yash Ghai (1994), 'Human Rights and Governance: The Asia Debate', *Australian Year Book of International Law*, **15**, pp. 1–34.	219

13 Abdullahi Ahmed An-Na'im (1990), 'Human Rights in the Muslim World: Socio-Political Conditions and Scriptural Imperatives', *Harvard Human Rights Journal*, **3**, pp. 13–52. 2

14 R.P. Peerenboom (1993), 'What's Wrong with Chinese Rights?: Toward a Theory of Rights with Chinese Characteristics', *Harvard Human Rights Journal*, **6**, pp. 29–57. 29

15 Karen Engle (1992), 'Female Subjects of Public International Law: Human Rights and the Exotic Other Female', *New England Law Review*, **26**, pp. 1509–26. 32

PART III POLITICAL PARTICIPATION, DEMOCRACY AND HUMAN RIGHTS

16 Jürgen Habermas (1994), 'Human Rights and Popular Sovereignty: The Liberal and Republican Versions', *Ratio Juris*, **7**, pp. 1–13. 34

17 Carlos Santiago Nino (1994), 'Positivism and Communitarianism: Between Human Rights and Democracy', *Ratio Juris*, **7**, pp. 14–40. 35

18 Henry J. Steiner (1988), 'Political Participation as a Human Right', *Harvard Human Rights Yearbook*, **1**, pp. 77–134. 38

19 Thomas M. Franck (1992), 'The Emerging Right to Democratic Governance', *American Journal of International Law*, **86**, pp. 46–91. 44

20 Benedict Kingsbury (1992), 'Claims by Non-State Groups in International Law', *Cornell International Law Journal*, **25**, pp. 481–513. 48

21 Tony Honoré (1988), 'The Right to Rebel', *Oxford Journal of Legal Studies*, **8**, pp. 34–54. 52

22 W. Michael Reisman (1990), 'Sovereignty and Human Rights in Contemporary International Law', *American Journal of International Law*, **84**, pp. 866–76. 54

Name Index 55

Acknowledgements

The editor and publishers wish to thank the following for permission to use copyright material.

American Political Science Association for the essay: Jack Donnelly (1982), 'Human Rights and Human Dignity: An Analytic Critique of Non-Western Conceptions of Human Rights', *American Political Science Review*, **76**, pp. 303–16.

The American Society of International Law for the essays: Theodor Meron (1986), 'On a Hierarchy of International Human Rights', *American Journal of International Law*, **80**, pp. 1–23. Reproduced with permission from 80 *AJIL* (1986). Copyright © The American Society of International Law. Oscar Schachter (1983), 'Human Dignity as a Normative Concept', *American Journal of International Law*, **77**, pp. 848–54. Reproduced with permission from 77 *AJIL* (1983). Copyright © The American Society of International Law. Thomas M. Franck (1992), 'The Emerging Right to Democratic Governance', *American Journal of International Law*, **86**, pp. 46–91. Reproduced with permission from 86 *AJIL* (1992). Copyright © The American Society of International Law. W. Michael Reisman (1990), 'Sovereignty and Human Rights in Contemporary International Law', *American Journal of International Law*, **84**, pp. 866–76. Reproduced from 84 *AJIL* (1990). Copyright © The American Society of International Law.

The Australian Year Book of International Law for the essays: Bruno Simma and Philip Alston (1992), 'The Sources of Human Rights Law: Custom, Jus Cogens, and General Principles', *Australian Year Book of International Law*, **12**, pp. 82–108; Yash Ghai (1994), 'Human Rights and Governance: The Asia Debate', *Australian Year Book of International Law*, **15**, pp. 1–34.

Blackwell Publishers for the essays: Jürgen Habermas (1994), 'Human Rights and Popular Sovereignty: The Liberal and Republican Versions', *Ratio Juris*, **7**, pp. 1–13; Carlos Santiago Nino (1994), 'Positivism and Communitarianism: Between Human Rights and Democracy', *Ratio Juris*, **7**, pp. 14–40.

Cornell International Law Journal and Fred B. Rothman & Company for the essay: Benedict Kingsbury (1992), 'Claims by Non-State Groups in International Law', *Cornell International Law Journal*, **25**, pp. 481–513. Copyright © 1992 by Cornell University. All rights reserved.

Foreign Policy for the essay: Bilahari Kausikan (1993), 'Asia's Different Standard', *Foreign Policy*, **92**, pp. 24–41. Copyright © 1993 by the Carnegie Endowment for International Peace.

Harvard Human Rights Journal for the essays: Abdullahi Ahmed An-Na'im (1990), 'Huma Rights in the Muslim World: Socio-Political Conditions and Scriptural Imperatives', *Harvar Human Rights Journal*, **3**, pp. 13–52. Copyright © 1990 by the President and Fellows o Harvard College. R.P. Peerenboom (1993), 'What's Wrong with Chinese Rights?: Towar a Theory of Rights with Chinese Characteristics', *Harvard Human Rights Journal*, **6** pp. 29–57. Copyright © 1993 by the President and Fellows of Harvard College. Henry J Steiner (1988), 'Political Participation as a Human Right', *Harvard Human Rights Yearbook* **1**, pp. 77–134. Copyright © 1988 by the President and Fellows of Harvard College.

The Johns Hopkins University Press for the essay: Richard Falk (1979), 'Comparativ Protection of Human Rights in Capitalist and Socialist Third World Countries', *Universa Human Rights*, **1**, pp. 3–29.

Lokayan for the essay: Rajni Kothari (1987), 'Human Rights – A Movement in Search o a Theory', *Lokayan Bulletin*, **5**, pp. 17–27.

Michigan Law Review Association for the essay: Martti Koskenniemi (1990), 'The Pull o the Mainstream', *Michigan Law Review*, **88**, pp. 1946–62.

Oxford University Press for the essay: Tony Honoré (1988), 'The Right to Rebel', *Oxfor Journal of Legal Studies*, **8**, pp. 34–54.

Virginia Journal of International Law for the essay: Fernando R. Tesón (1985), 'Internationa Human Rights and Cultural Relativism', *Virginia Journal of International Law*, **25**, pp. 869–98.

Every effort has been made to trace all the copyright holders but if any have been inadvertently overlooked, the publishers will be pleased to make the necessary arrangement at the first opportunity.

Series Preface

The International Library of Law and Legal Theory is designed to provide important research materials in an accessible form. Each volume contains essays of central theoretical importance in its subject area. The series as a whole makes available an extensive range of valuable material which will be of considerable interest to those involved in the research, teaching and study of law.

The series has been divided into three sections. The Schools section is intended to represent the main distinctive approaches and topics of special concern to groups of scholars. The Areas section takes in the main branches of law with an emphasis on essays which present analytical and theoretical insights of broad application. The section on Legal Cultures makes available the distinctive legal theories of different legal traditions and takes up topics of general comparative and developmental concern.

I have been delighted and impressed by the way in which the editors of the individual volumes have set about the difficult task of selecting, ordering and presenting essays from the immense quantity of academic legal writing published in journals throughout the world. Editors were asked to pick out those essays from law, philosophy and social science journals which they consider to be fundamental for the understanding of law, as seen from the perspective of a particular approach or sphere of legal interest. This is not an easy task and many difficult decisions have had to be made in order to ensure that a representative sample of the best journal essays available takes account of the scope of each topic or school.

I should like to express my thanks to all the volume editors for their willing participation and scholarly judgement. The interest and enthusiasm which the project has generated is well illustrated by the fact that an original projection of 12 volumes drawn up in 1989 has now become a list of some 60 volumes. I must also acknowledge the vision, persistence and constant cheerfulness of John Irwin and the marvellous work done by Mrs Margaret O'Reilly and Sonia Hubbard.

TOM D. CAMPBELL
Series Editor
The Faculty of Law
The Australian National University

Introduction

he process of choosing leading essays to include in a collection dealing with human rights aw provides an occasion to reflect on the nature of the relevant body of literature and ence on the field itself. It is one which has a number of characteristics which distinguish not only from other areas of law, but even from the mainstream of international law – e discipline of which it is generally assumed to form part. By the same token, it is by no eans a separate discipline nor even a separate field of inquiry. Rather, it is very much an malgam or mélange which draws upon the resources of other disciplines while at the same me maintaining a rather distant and often only superficial relationship with them.

Before turning to consider briefly the significance of the papers contained in the collection, is instructive to reflect further on the characteristics of the field. The most important and nfluential is surely its novelty or youth. While metaphors can easily be taken too far, not nly to the point of tedium but, more importantly, of inaptness, it seems helpful to pursue he metaphor that international human rights law is in its early adolescence. It has come hrough childhood successfully in the sense that its foundations are clearly established; it has definite personality, albeit one which might yet change dramatically, and the other members f the family are generally supportive although sometimes ambivalent. It has not reached naturity in the sense that it has not yet clearly established the nature of its relationship with ther family members, and it is not altogether clear how it will fare as an adult or what long-erm role it will succeed in carving out for itself.

The emphasis in these readings is on some of the manifestations of this adolescent phase. Iaving come through childhood with confidence and an admirable absence of introspection r self-doubt, human rights law is now confronted by all of the doubts and misgivings ssociated with the critiques of indeterminacy and cultural and other forms of relativism.)bservers, both sympathetic and hostile, are asking it, and it is also asking itself, who it eally is, where it came from and whether it can truly live up to its own original aspirations. 3ut rather than viewing this as a stage which is counter-productive or at worst destructive, his should be seen as a necessary developmental phase and one which, if successfully egotiated, will facilitate the transition to maturity and a renewed self-confidence. That elf-confidence will no longer be of the naive and over-enthusiastic type which is oblivious o other ways of thinking and even blindly self-assertive. It will be a maturity which enables t to see itself as others do, to put things into a broader perspective, to be enthusiastic and ven forceful, but in a measured and mature manner. An alternative road to adulthood is ne which denies the need for such introspection, which assumes that the simplicity and self-onfidence of childhood can simply be carried over into adulthood without fundamental uestioning or adaptation. That is the approach that many human rights proponents, and specially activists, would prefer to follow; if the analogy being drawn is appropriate, owever, it is a short-sighted one.

Some Manifestations of Immaturity

There are three principal ways in which international human rights law is immature. The are: (1) its relationship to its parent discipline; (2) its relative lack of normativity; an (3) its relationship to its inter-disciplinary relatives. The average observer might reasonabl be surprised at the extent of the immaturity in each case, especially given the prominenc which human rights law has achieved in recent decades and the weight accorded to i ostensibly at least, both in international relations and in many domestic legal systems.

1. The Uneasy Relationship of Human Rights Law to its Parent Discipline

Human rights law is, in the main, a creation of international law. While its antecedents li in domestic legal and political developments – among which it is commonplace to refer t the Magna Carta, the French Declaration of the Rights of Man and the Citizen, and the U. Bill of Rights – the process through which an authentic body of human rights law ha emerged at the global level has been very much a top-down rather than a bottom-up one It was the inclusion in the United Nations Charter of a commitment to human rights and th subsequent elaboration of more precisely defined obligations in international law that marke the transition of human rights from a field of philosophical inquiry and moral invocatio and of idiosyncratic domestic laws to its present status.

It is thus all the more surprising that human rights has long had an uneasy, and eve tense, relationship with the discipline which gave birth to it and upon which it continues t rely heavily as it seeks to become more effective and more closely linked to the mainstream Sir Hersch Lauterpacht once characterized international law itself as being at the vanishin point of law, and it is no exaggeration to say that human rights law has long been considere by some international lawyers to be, in its turn, at the vanishing point of international law.

By some indicators this marginality has been greatly reduced in recent years. In 198 Oscar Schachter remarked in his 'General Course' at the Hague Academy of Internationa Law that his many predecessors had devoted remarkably little attention to human right matters as they surveyed the wide sweep of the terrain of international law.[2] But if th Hague General Course can be taken as a reliable barometer of the degree of respectability or even centrality, of an issue within the discipline, human rights could be thought to hav come of age within the past decade or so as scholars such as Louis Henkin,[3] Rosaly Higgins[4] and Thomas Franck[5] have devoted considerable parts of their respective Genera Courses to it.

This development notwithstanding, embracing respectability has not, *per se*, succeede in resolving the paradoxes (or the 'antinomies' to which Schachter referred) that continu to characterize human rights law. Rather than resolving them, much of the analysis i question has been devoted to highlighting them and trying to understand them better. How can a field which attaches so much weight to the consent of states accommodate an agend which is anti-statist in many respects? How can so much be dependent upon 'soft law' norm in a field which has traditionally sought to play down their significance and emphasize tha of treaty-based obligations in practice? How can a field which has long attached grea importance to notions of sovereignty and the *domaine réservé* of states reconcile itself t the inevitable intrusiveness of initiatives not only to promote, but also to protect, humar rights? How can bodies which are composed of states representatives, or of their hand-picked 'independent experts',[6] be expected to uphold the interests of the individual when they clash with the forcefully asserted interests of the state? And how can the genuinely indispensable role of non-governmental organizations in the human rights field be reconciled with a system which generally accords only a very minor role to non-state entities except when their interests coincide with those of states?

One of the principal issues raised by the contributors in the first part of the present volume concerns the sources of international law upon which human rights proponents rely when they invoke the relevant norms against a state in the absence of a clear treaty-based obligation. We shall return to that issue below. But it is appropriate to note in this context that such debates can easily be said to be truly academic, both in the sense of being carried out at a high level of technicality and abstraction and of being largely irrelevant to what is happening in the real world. Certainly the fact that between January 1990 and May 1996 the Convention on the Rights of the Child – containing the most extensive catalogue of human rights ever enshrined in a single United Nations treaty – has been formally accepted (through ratification or accession) by 187 states and that only five remain outside its reach (including the United States, which has signed but shows no inclination to ratify) would seem to argue that the questions raised by scholars are of little practical import. But the paradox is that it is precisely at the moment when human rights law is on the verge of achieving an incontestable dimension of formal universality that its role and status are beginning to attract some of the most sustained and meaningful challenges. This is certainly true in relation to the debate over cultural relativism, as we shall see below. It is true also from the perspective of legal theory.

International lawyers have not succeeded in developing any compelling theory of the place of human rights within any grand design of international law. Many examples could be given, but one will suffice to illustrate the point. If we take Wolfgang Friedmann's oft-quoted characterization of the field of international law as consisting of the law of coexistence and that of cooperation, it is not clear that human rights is an important part of the former. Indeed, there are many 'realists' who do not hesitate to emphasize the extent to which it is inimical in that regard. It is equally difficult to make a concrete case in favour of human rights as an integral part of the law of cooperation. But without seeking to develop this point further, it must be conceded that the quest for a grand theory of human rights is a highly optimistic one, given that there are many who argue that international law not only lacks such a theory for itself, but is incapable of generating or supporting one.

It is instructive in this regard to consider the views expressed by one of the most accomplished and stimulating of critical international law thinkers, Martti Koskenniemi. While he has devoted relatively little of his writing to human rights issues *per se*, his work does reveal a strong scepticism towards some of the claims of human rights proponents and particularly their universalist pretensions. In Chapter 2 in this volume he concludes that the 'justifying rhetoric' of mainstream international lawyers is in disarray:

> positivism is no longer credible, naturalism has long been a closed option, and the different policy-science approaches have, if taken seriously, failed to demonstrate what is specifically 'legal' in them, while their popular versions appear to be thinly disguised rhetoric aimed at furthering political interests.[7]

Challenged to explain what the alternative to these rejected orthodoxies is, Koskenniemi has responded by calling for a 'post-realist, post-formalist international legal culture' which would be 'characterised by a constant movement between distance and intimacy, reflection and engagement'.[8] This alternative seems to be inspired to a significant degree by his concern for the intrinsic indeterminacy of human rights law and especially its pretensions to universalism. The latter, he says, 'sets impossible moral demands on us and ultimately undermines our ability to honour the special obligations we may have towards our communities and the most vulnerable of any communities'.[9] Indeed, far from being in the progressive vanguard, he warns that such uses of international law might turn it into 'the *arrière-garde* defending a totalising uniformity against the pluralism of human experience'.[10] Koskenniemi's critique combines a strong element of relativism, a conviction that human rights norms are especially vulnerable to the critique of being indeterminate, and a rejection of the legitimacy of any project premissed on the validity of supposed meta-norms. His critique is incisive and, in the absence of effective refutation, a potentially devastating one. This Introduction is not the place to attempt a detailed refutation, but it is appropriate to underline the need for a more sustained engagement with the critique itself on the part of proponents of human rights law.

2. *The Relatively Under-Developed Normative Dimensions of Human Rights Law*

Again it is Koskenniemi whose writings have best served to highlight the paradox that a normatively immature human rights law might, at least in some respects, be more effective than a mature one in promoting respect for human rights. As he notes in Chapter 2, '[b]y remaining in the periphery, in the field of largely subconscious, private, moral-religious experience that defies technical articulation, human rights may be more able to retain their constraining hold on the way most people, and by extension most states, behave'.[11] Elsewhere he has taken this critique further by suggesting that the use of 'a universalising language of human rights, treaty obligation, legal rules and principles' involves a

> banalisation that makes available all the routine defences, excuses and exceptions and triggers a technical debate which may end up by paralysing our ability to act and undermining our intuitive capability to empathise and thus also the condition for entering into a rudimentary communal relation with others.[12]

This critique follows logically from his assessment of the indeterminacy of human rights norms. He is certainly correct in implying that the content of those norms has tended to remain quite general and that the process of defining it will eventually transform the nature of the enterprise. As long as human rights discourse was used primarily to address egregious violations of norms in relation to which a degree of consensus has long existed, the risks of rupturing that consensus were limited. This would apply, for example, to the rights listed by Steiner in Chapter 18 as being in the first category along a spectrum of rights which represents a sliding scale according to the degree of 'verbal consensus' that he perceives to exist.[13] But, as he also notes, even in relation to rights to physical integrity, views will differ radically as to whether certain forms of treatment are to be considered 'inhuman or degrading' (solitary confinement for prisoners, corporal punishment for school children and some forms of gender discrimination are all contentious practices which might fall within this category).

But it is not at all clear that the movement to accord a more precise normative content to human rights will necessarily extinguish its capacity to inspire or to provide empathy. Koskenniemi approvingly quotes Baumann's assertion that 'when concepts, standards and rules enter the stage, moral impulses make an exit'.[14] It is true that some moral impulses might indeed be stifled or restrained if compelled to meet criteria derived from formally stated human rights norms. But, for the most part, this would seem to be a positive development as long as there are grounds to assume that those norms have themselves emerged from moral imperatives. To the extent that they have not, their effectiveness will be limited.[15] To the extent that they are inadequate to take account of what are perceived to be justified moral impulses to act, they will simply be overridden or transcended, since the dialectical process within the human rights debate is not, and never will be, as stultified as Baumann's statement would seem to suggest in relation to human rights. Moreover, although the international trend is towards the establishment of procedures and mechanisms through which rights can be asserted, and thus their content and applicability contested, it will not be able to succeed, nor indeed should it aspire, to drain the discourse of rights of its capacity to mobilize, to inspire and to exhort. These are essential elements in what has been correctly termed (in a particular context) the 'myth of rights',[16] a concept readily misunderstood.

Cultural relativism is another field in which consideration can be given to the validity of the critique. While there are certainly some instances in which the entry into a debate of the technical dimensions of human rights law may, as suggested, paralyse our ability to act, there are others in which that development would seem to be essential in order to facilitate action. Yash Ghai's analysis in Chapter 12 serves to demonstrate that one of the best ways to counter some of the very vague and imprecise assaults on human rights launched in the name of different cultural values is to subject them to systematic analysis based upon the principles reflected in the established normative framework.

In a separate analysis Koskenniemi has identified three other, closely related impediments to any claim that human rights can form a meaningful basis for social order:

> If we are to define our polity in terms of human rights, we must ascertain the number and content of such rights. If our polity is to be orderly, these rights must form a harmonious whole.[17]

But this quest proves to be predictably futile since he finds human rights to be neither knowable nor harmonious. He finds that 'rights cannot replace the institutions that are needed to enumerate and interpret them';[18] this, in turn, invalidates their claim to normativity. He notes that '[r]ights discourse cannot form a polity because it relies on (conceptually independent) political institutions to define rights'. Since human rights thus 'owe their existence and meaning to decision-making processes ... [t]here is no reason to construe those processes in such a way that one political position would be permanently privileged'.[19] His critique thus identifies three separate flaws in the aspirations of human rights proponents: (1) knowability, (2) harmony and (3) dependence upon institutions.

As to the first, he observes that we cannot know the content of human rights because there is great scope for interpretation and, indeed, for re-interpretation and continuing evolution. This makes us dependent upon institutions, as a result of which the best we can hope for is to know our institutions but never our rights *per se*. As he says, 'we do not know our rights; we create them through our political processes'.[20] But this type of analysis under-estimates the extent to which human rights can provide a meaningful basis for social order without being rigid, absolute or forever enduring. In this sense, rather than expose the futility or fraudulence of rights discourse, Koskenniemi's analysis does little more than highlight the flexibility inherent in the concept and the unavoidability of a dialectical relationship between the norms, which are capable of partly transcending the institutions that gave birth to them, and those very same institutions (or their successors) which seek to exercise responsibility for their elaboration and interpretation. The lack of neatness in the roles played by both the norms and the institutions does not invalidate the enterprise, nor does it necessarily reduce us to the level of a continuing 'conversation', with all of the subjectivity and uncertainty which that image would seem to convey.[21]

For the most part, the process of norm clarification is not one which is dealt with in the present volume, being more appropriately considered in relation to carefully-focused contextual analyses of the various norms.[22] Nevertheless, the part of the collection dealing with democracy and political participation does serve to shed light on the development of norms in relation to what is arguably one of the least consensual areas in human rights. It is a field of endeavour which, over time, will provide a useful context for gauging the strength of Koskenniemi's critique. It is also the area which might potentially be the most vulnerable, or amenable, to that critique.

The requirement that human rights should represent a 'political position [that] would be permanently privileged' reflects an artificial, unjustifiable and even superfluous criterion. The response is perhaps best given by Norberto Bobbio:

> [H]uman rights, however fundamental, are historical rights and therefore arise from specific conditions characterized by the embattled defence of new freedoms against old powers. They are established gradually, not all at the same time, and not for ever. It would appear that philosophers are asked to pass sentence on the fundamenal nature of human rights, and even to demonstrate that they are absolute, inevitable and incontrovertible, but the question should not be posed in these terms.[23]

Koskenniemi's next concern is that rights are not 'mutually exclusive' and that conflicts between them can therefore not be avoided. As he notes, the 'assumption that human rights exist in some pre-established harmony may only be held with a prior commitment to the kind of naturalism that not only defines rights as coterminous with each other, but in doing so, also provides an inherently authoritarian standpoint towards existing conflict'.[24] But this criticism would seem to be unduly focused on conceptions of rights as 'trumps', to use Ronald Dworkin's terminology, although not necessarily the nuanced meaning that he sought to accord the term. Koskenniemi seeks to buttress his point about the disharmony inherent in human rights by reference to Isaiah Berlin's classic work entitled *Two Concepts of Liberty*. But it is Berlin himself who, while conceding the inevitability of disharmony, pleads that this fact alone should not be permitted to inhibit the quest for common values. His typically eloquent statement deserves quoting at some length:

> [O]f course, we must not dramatize the incompatibility of values – there is a great deal of broad agreement among peoples in different societies over long stretches of time about what is right and

> wrong, good and evil. Of course traditions, outlooks, attitudes may legitimately differ; general principles may cut across too much human need... .
> But, in the end, it is not a matter of purely subjective judgment: it is dictated by the forms of life of the society to which one belongs, a society among other societies, with values held in common, whether or not they are in conflict, by the majority of mankind throughout recorded history. There are, if not universal values, at any rate a minimum without which societies could scarcely survive.[25]

As to the critique that we are unduly reliant upon institutions to define the content of ur rights, the process of detailed norm clarification and application, or what Koskenniemi ould characterize as the banalization of human rights, is now well and truly under way rough the work of a variety of judicial and non-judicial bodies at the level of both the nited Nations and the principal regional organizations (notably the Council of Europe and e Organization of American States). There is no doubt that this process has its limits, in e sense that the relevant bodies will always accord a margin of appreciation to practices efended within different states and might on occasion be reluctant to trespass in relation certain matters. Similarly, the possibility exists for governments and communities to ore or less ignore the interpretations adopted by international bodies. But these are, at ast within limits, appropriate safety valves within a system which does not aspire to npose a brutal homogenization of the kind that Koskenniemi would seem to fear.

An important response in this regard is provided by the contribution of Jürgen Habermas Chapter 16. He argues that it is 'not the grammar of legal propositions which is decisive, ut the discursive mode and the procedural setting in which they are explained and stified'.[26] He attaches particular importance to 'the legal institutionalization of those iscursive processes of opinion- and will-formation through which the sovereignty of the eople can be exercised'.[27] In this view the norms and the institutions go together in an ntirely complementary fashion to produce a 'procedural notion of deliberative politics that ields a fuller understanding of how human rights and popular sovereignty mutually pre-ppose each other'.[28]

In essence, Koskenniemi's analysis is a standard post-modernist critique which applies to e field of human rights the consequences of the crisis of legitimation which the post-odernists have rightly insisted we must confront. He is correct in asserting that there are o incontrovertible philosophical foundations upon which human rights law can rest and at it often relies on premises that are by no means politically neutral. But the question is hether the resulting rejection of all mega-norms or meta-narratives leaves us with a viable r acceptable basis upon which to proceed. Shapiro has observed that the rejection of such rgumentation on the basis of its intellectual impurity is the equivalent of suggesting that because there is no single type of foundation on which all buildings ... can be built to last orever, we should henceforth build all buildings with no foundations at all'.[29] They would en collapse, as Shapiro points out. Perhaps the post-modernist reply is that we should efrain from erecting buildings that require foundations. But given the chronic state of uman affairs, abandoning any effort to promote a more morally acceptable world would eem to be a greater evil than risking giving offence to the post-modernists. Questions bout values and the appropriate ends of political activity are both central to our existence nd unavoidable. Failure to address them directly simply means that they will be tackled urreptitiously in ways that are even less objective and less participatory.

3. The Uneasy Relationship between Human Rights Law and its Inter-Disciplinary Relativ

Another sign of the immaturity of human rights law is that, while it draws heavily up disciplines other than law both for its foundations and content as well as for its chances making a significant impact in many areas, it has a very uneasy or tenuous relationsh with those disciplines. Indeed it might even be said that, from the perspective of some the key disciplines upon which it relies, it seems to be counter-intuitive at a number of level Put another way, it might almost be necessary, if experts from some of these disciplines a to be able to take international human rights law seriously, to suspend some of the commonl held assumptions which apply in their fields.

This is a far-reaching point which cannot be sustained effectively within a few par graphs.[30] It must suffice therefore merely to provide a few illustrations. In the realm philosophy, which is assumed by many observers to provide a coherent foundation f international human rights law, the conceptual basis and indeed the very nature of hum rights remain the subject of major controversy. Remarkably few philosophers have ma any sustained attempt to relate their own disciplinary perspectives to that body of law; some of those who have done so have concluded either that there is a fundamental i compatibility between the two endeavours,[32] or that the issue of the international leg consequences is beyond their expertise.[33] It is clear that the catalogue of rights accept internationally is not coherent by the standards of any single philosophical approac Economic and social rights are a key stumbling block in relation to many theories. Similar the difficulties caused by the communitarian challenge to the strongly individualistic foc of many human rights theorists are equally matched by the enthusiastic rejection by oth theorists of any notion of collective rights.[34]

In the realm of economics, a comprehensive listing of books and articles dealing wi rights-based theories or taking the fulfilment of rights as their objective would require ve little space. Amatya Sen has observed that economists generally eschew 'deep normati analysis' and neglect 'the influence of ethical considerations in the characterization of actu human behavior'.[35] Indeed, an analysis of 'economic rights' by many modern economis will be more likely to focus on that very limited array of market freedoms that liber economists hold dear (such as freedom of contract, the right of property and free enterpris than on the traditional 'economic human rights' including the right to work or the right an adequate standard of living.

The situation in relation to anthropology is considered below in the introduction to Pa II of this volume.

It would be unfair, of course, to suggest that the blame for this lack of inter-disciplinarit lies solely, or even primarily, with the practitioners of those various disciplines. Their disda or neglect has been generously reciprocated by those, usually lawyers, who are in the main stream of the debate over human rights law. That is apparent not only from many of th essays reproduced in this volume, but from any broader survey of the literature in the field

Overview of the Collection of Essays

In relation to a collection of essays that purports to capture the most significant writings i this field in recent decades, it is perhaps somewhat surprising that the main theme that brings the collection together concerns the impact of changes that have occurred in the last few years, specifically since the end of the Cold War. While it is now commonplace, even banal, to remark upon the dramatic consequences of the collapse of communism, the movements towards democracy in many parts of the world and the acceleration of globalizing tendencies, the impact of these developments has been far greater in relation to human rights than is generally recognized. For this reason, a particular effort has been made to include in this volume some materials which serve to emphasize the nature and extent of the changes that have occurred in the space of only six or seven years. Until 1988 the Cold War was a constant factor in everything that the international community sought to do in this area. In a bizarre way, which was reassuring to many, the Cold War provided the great advantage of clear and definable limits. Thus, participants in the international human rights debate had a well-honed sense of how far either side (East or West) and their respective Third World allies would go on most issues. The cultural relativism debate was conveniently submerged in the apparently unresolvable ideological struggle; democracy was not a polite topic of conversation, except at a wholly superficial level; humanitarian intervention was able to be contemplated by one or other of the superpowers only within its own self-proclaimed sphere of influence; and the exercise of the right to self-determination leading to the creation of new states was, by mutual agreement, not on the agenda. Albeit in quite different ways, Chapters 3 and 18 by Richard Falk and Henry Steiner both serve to highlight the extent to which the Cold War constituted an inescapable shadow under which the vast majority of pre-1990 literature in this field was written.

The demise of the Cold War thus had a great impact on all of these dogmatic positions, and many more as well. Most importantly, it provided the space and flexibility needed for new vistas to be opened up in the human rights field. Before exploring several of these issues, it should be observed that the end of the Cold War did not, however, prove to be an unqualified good. In certain respects the disappearance of superpower rivalry has removed a major incentive for the sponsorship of initiatives ostensibly designed to develop the human rights regime but primarily motivated by a desire to embarrass 'the other side' or its allies. Many of the finest achievements of the pre-1990's regime had their origins in such exercises.

Part I: The International Normative Framework

The essays in this collection are divided into three parts. The first deals with the international normative framework. Although a sound set of normative foundations is fundamental to the status and effectiveness of the international human rights regime, the centrality of this issue has receded in recent years. This too is largely a function of post-Cold War developments. In particular, the United States has ended its longstanding boycott of the international human rights treaty system which began in the early 1950s when human rights and international machinery to promote them became closely associated in the American polity with the ideological struggle against communism in general and the Soviet Union in particular.[36] The US decision to ratify the Convention on the Prevention and Punishment of the Crime of Genocide in 1984, followed by its acceptance of the Convention against Torture and Other Cruel, Inhuman or Degrading Treatment or Punishment, the International Covenant on Civil and Political Rights and the Convention on the Elimination of All Forms of Racial

Discrimination had a number of consequences for the international regime as a whole as well as for the approach of officials, activists and commentators in the US. It greatly reduced the hitherto rather unnatural interest in, and reliance upon, customary international human rights norms which, in the absence of applicable treaty standards, had been portrayed by many of those concerned as an adequate substitute, both as a justification for the US foreign policy invocation of human rights and for the purposes of evaluating domestic behaviour against international standards. The contributions by Simma and Alston and by Koskenniemi (Chapters 1 and 2) address the issue of the sources of international human rights law, and especially the vexed question of whether customary law is able to provide a sufficient foundation for holding all states internationally accountable for violations of all human rights, regardless of their treaty undertakings.

In Chapter 4, Meron addresses the equally contentious issue of whether any particular set of human rights is hierarchically superior to others. If this is a vexed question for international lawyers, it is even more so for commentators from most other disciplines. It would be possible to identify hundreds of different scholarly analyses which have sought to reach a conclusion as to which rights are superior and to recall but some of the terminology used – central, superior, basic, fundamental, constitutive, prerequisites, inalienable, core, foundational, indispensable, not subject to limitations, etc.[37] Although he acknowledges the benefits of a degree of hierarchy,[38] Meron reaches the almost counter-intuitive, but both legally and empirically defensible, conclusion that '[f]ew criteria for distinguishing between ordinary rights and higher rights have been agreed upon' and that there is 'no accepted system by which higher rights can be identified...'.[39] All rights are thus equally important and any attempt at ranking is doomed to failure. The difficulty inherent in this conclusion is well illustrated by his own earlier statement that the right to life and the right to freedom from torture are 'obviously more important' than other rights.[40]

In addition to capturing the influence of the Cold War over the human rights debate in the late 1970s, Chapter 3 by Richard Falk serves to highlight the structural dimensions of human rights promotion. He laments the fact that 'human rights as a focus of normative concern do not extend their reach to the wider structure of repression allegedly inherent in state power' and commends efforts to reformulate human rights in universalist ways that transcend 'cultural heritage or ideological orientation'. But the main thrust of his analysis is that,

> On balance, it still seems appropriate to argue that, except in very unusual domestic circumstances, socialism is a precondition for human rights in the Third World, whereas capitalism assures their massive denial.[41]

This conclusion reads rather strangely in the 1990s in light of the new orthodoxy of global liberalism and free enterprise. Nevertheless, it provides a useful antidote to that orthodoxy. The 'globalization' caravan that is moving so rapidly across the international landscape rarely pauses to take account of its distributional consequences either between or within states, and yet there are sound reasons to conclude that it is a promoter of even greater inequalities than currently exist.[42]

Chapter 5 by Schachter is notable as a contribution by an international lawyer who acknowledges the lack of a coherent philosophical foundation for international human rights law and looks instead to the concept of 'human dignity' to provide a normative basis. In this sense, the essay provides a bridge between the discussions of legal norms in Part I of this volume and the challenge of cultural relativism dealt with in Part II. His paper is also noteworthy for his reluctance to extend human rights into the private sphere, a reluctance widely shared only a decade or so ago but which has now been largely replaced by a realization that the requirement of a clear 'public' dimension leads to an unduly narrow sphere of influence for human rights norms.[43]

Part II: Universality in Cultural Perspective

Recent years have witnessed a radically increased awareness of the importance of cultural values within the overall international human rights framework. This new awareness has served not only to emphasize the potential benefits of a more culturally sensitive approach, but has also highlighted the potential misuse of cultural concerns to undermine both domestic and international efforts to promote respect for human rights. The first chapter in Part II provides a salutary reminder that such concerns were present right from the start of the enterprise of trying to develop an international approach to human rights. In it, the Executive Board of the American Anthropological Association seeks to reconcile an obvious desire not to stifle the efforts which were already underway in the UN Commission on Human Rights to draft a statement with universalist reach (or at least pretensions) with their own clear misgivings as to the intrinsic limitations of such a quest. Their resulting ambivalence is well captured in the following excerpt:

> Standards and values are relative to the culture from which they derive so that any attempt to formulate postulates that grow out of beliefs or moral codes of one culture must to that extent detract from the applicability of any Declaration of Human Rights to mankind as a whole.[44]

The Statement concluded that any such Declaration would need to be 'of worldwide applicability' which meant that it 'must embrace and recognize the validity of many different ways of life'; it should also explicitly recognize 'the right of men to live in terms of their own traditions'.[45] In a number of respects, however, such formulae do no more than re-state the challenge. They certainly do not provide a recipe by which it can be resolved.

The nature of the cultural relativist 'threat' to universal human rights standards is best understood in the light of the relationship between the two dimensions over recent decades. The post-World War II international human rights regime has reflected a determined, and often single-minded, commitment to universality on the part of most of its key players. They include the treaty drafters, those responsible for the implementation of the norms at the international level, as well as the most active proponents of the norms among the ranks of non-governmental organizations. Appropriately, this approach has also drawn strong support from the ranks of those victims of oppression living under regimes that have sought to challenge the universality of the norms which they stand accused of violating. Indeed it is difficult to see how the human rights movement could have survived as well as it did, from its emergence in the 1960s as a force to be reckoned with through to the 1980s, had a significantly different approach been adopted. Moreover, it was not without support from anthropologists. Thus the American Anthropological Association's 1947 Statement can be contrasted with the conclusions reached in 1983 by one American anthropologist, Elvin Hatch, who argued that relativism had 'fallen on hard times':

> First, it has been the experience of most anthropologists that non-Western peoples (and especially the Third World nations) want change, at least to some extent; second, it is clear that they are often disadvantaged if it does not come; third, anthropologists by and large have altered their thinking about the relativity of material interests and improvement: most today consider these to be general values that can be applied throughout the world.[46]

Despite the confidence of these conclusions – and they are mirrored in the legal field by Tesón's contribution in Chapter 7 – the increasing success of the human rights movement by the 1990s, especially in terms of breaking down defences based on notions such as state sovereignty and domestic jurisdiction, and the increasingly effective threat that it poses to governments which had assumed that they could remain immune to international scrutiny and accountability, has endowed relativist arguments with at least two newly important constituencies. The first consists of those who are supportive of the overall enterprise, but who insist on the need for far greater cultural sensitivity than has hitherto been demonstrated.

Thus, for example, An-Na'im has argued elsewhere that the drafting process involved in developing international human rights norms cannot be regarded as having produced universal consensus. This is in part due to the fact that persons and countries from the South have been disadvantaged in the process of drafting international human rights instruments. Firstly, such treaties are negotiated by government officials who are more concerned with the interests of government than with the attitudes of the populace. Secondly, the negotiators from the South have, broadly speaking, been latecomers to the norm-setting process and do not have the material and human resources of countries of the North. They might also have lacked 'alternative positions to present since their national constituencies did not have the chance to articulate different proposals out of their indigenous experiences and in response to the realities of their own contexts'.[47]

But despite these historical shortcomings and the inherent difficulty of reconciling different cultural values and experiences, An-Na'im does not conclude that 'the project of normative universality ... should be abandoned because of the difficulty of cross-cultural communication and understanding'. Rather, his objective is 'to emphasize the need to take that difficulty into account in seeking to achieve normative universality...'.[48] He suggests that, instead of accepting a false universality, norms should be developed through a process of dialogue occurring within countries. Such dialogue will, over time, help to mediate cultural and contextual differences and thereby produce common standards. In Chapter 13 he concedes that there are clear inconsistencies between Islamic law, in the form of the Shari'a, and international human rights law. He argues that rather than rejecting the Shari'a, those who advocate a different approach should put forward alternative interpretations of the Qur'an and Sunna. He acknowledges that there will be strong resistance from some quarters to such an approach, but places great faith in what might be achieved through an effective process of internal dialogue.

Peerenboom also concludes that any Chinese approach to human rights will, at least within the foreseeable future, not be in accord with the strong liberal individualist model favoured by many in the West. He concludes that 'rights in China will be viewed as a 'oduct of Chinese culture, traditions, and historical and economic conditions'.[49] He entifies eight characteristics of 'Chinese rights': contingency; communitarian, at least in eory; inspirational rather than legal; relational; a preference for informal means of conflict solution; an emphasis on economic rights; an instrumental approach concerned with societal armony, and an emphasis on the interests of the collectivity.

The second constituency favouring a more cultural relativist approach consists of those overnments which would like (for various, often selfish and culturally manipulative, easons) to discredit the human rights concept. Thus in the lead-up to the 1993 World uman Rights Conference, Amnesty International, along with various other groups, sounded arm bells, warning *inter alia* of 'a backtracking on the ideals of universality'. Some oservers suspected that these fears had been realized in the Bangkok Declaration, adopted the World Conference Regional Preparatory Meeting in April 1993, in which the Asian ates recognized 'that while human rights are universal in nature, they must be considered the context of a dynamic and evolving process of international norm-setting, bearing in ind the significance of national and regional particularities and various historical, cultural d religious backgrounds'. While that statement was open to competing interpretations, okespersons for the South did little to discourage negative assessments of its intent through omments such as the following:

> Cultural relativity keeps many countries in the South from embracing total equality for women... . Similarly, the primacy placed upon the importance of the individual or complete freedom of the press cannot be accepted completely in the South, which places a far greater emphasis on the well-being of society. Finally the developmental approach in the South would frown upon absolute priority being given to civil and political liberties if they come in the way of satisfying the basic needs of the people. In sum, therefore, we have recognized that while constantly upgrading human rights, the countries of the South, rather than aping Northern models, must work out their own norms and standards suited to their social, cultural and economic conditions. [50]

In the context of such attitudes, cultural considerations are only one aspect of a range of actors invoked to justify an *à la carte* approach which would clearly undermine any ternational consensus worthy of the name. At the end of the day, however, the World onference on Human Rights adopted an unequivocal statement to the effect that '[t]he niversal nature of [all human rights and fundamental freedoms] is beyond question'. While ome of the wording of the Bangkok Declaration found its way into the Vienna declaration, was accorded a rather different thrust in the following formulation:

> While the significance of national and regional particularities and various historical, cultural and religious backgrounds must be borne in mind, it is the duty of States, regardless of their political, economic and cultural systems, to protect all human rights and fundamental freedoms.[51]

Chapter 11 by Kausikan was written after the Vienna Conference and constitutes a nuanced nd sophisticated formulation of the argument that Asia must interpret human rights norms the light of its own 'Asian values', resulting in a very different approach to that advocated y the West (by which he almost invariably means the United States) and even to that eflected in the Universal Declaration of Human Rights. This analysis is tackled on its wn terms in Chapter 12 by Ghai who challenges both the authenticity and logic of the laim to a coherent and genuinely shared set of 'Asian values'.

One of the most consistent threads that links many of the concerns about relativism is th status of women within traditional cultures. Chapter 15 by Karen Engle exposes some the complexities that determine the extent to which feminists should rely upon positiv formulations of rights or seek to move outside and beyond formal legal structures in ord to press their claims within society.

Part III: Political Participation, Democracy and Human Rights

The third and final focus of this collection of readings is on democracy and politic participation. Again we are dealing with issues with which international human rights la in its pre-1989 infancy was barely able to cope. It was not sufficiently mature or independe to be able to examine the democratic legitimacy of the governments who were, in effec its parents and guardians. It was feared that any such scrutiny or questioning might provok an angry parental response which would lead to disciplinary measures. Human rights la would thus be further constrained and would be forbidden to venture into new areas whic even bordered upon the issue of democracy. In the post-1989 era, however, it has develope sufficient self-confidence and maturity to be able to insist that such matters cannot simpl be excluded from the agenda. The adolescent is beginning to assert its right to challenge th nature of its relationship with its parents and to insist that even a matter of great sensitivi and intimacy needs to be confronted. That is not to say that the parents (governments in th case) will react benignly or will voluntarily agree to the wishes or demands of the chil Indeed, a struggle at one level or another is likely to ensue as different roles evolve.

In this respect the selections in this collection reveal a notable contrast between th cautious approach adopted by Henry Steiner in his 1988 analysis of the extent to whic political participation has developed, or matured, as a human right (Chapter 18) and, i the warm glow of the immediate post-Cold War context, the enthusiastic embrace by Thoma Franck of an 'emerging right to democratic governance' (Chapter 19). The remaining paper in Part III deal with the options available to those whose right to political participation i their own community is denied. In such circumstances a claim to self-determination is ofte put forward and, more often than not, is interpreted as implying the right to form a separat state. Benedict Kingsbury seeks to develop a general international normative framework t cover the various contexts in which claims by non-state groups are made against the state Tony Honoré examines what happens when the avenues provided by human rights ar exhausted and the individual or group in question perceives no alternative but to rebel Finally, Michael Reisman argues that sovereignty, in the sense of the popular will expresse through free, fair and monitored elections, should be upheld through international action including intervention if necessary.

Had this collection been produced in the early rather than the mid-1990s, it woul appropriately have included a substantial collection of essays, in addition to that by Reisman dealing with the issue of humanitarian intervention, broadly defined to include all forms o forcible intervention aimed at promoting respect for human rights. The role of the Securit Council would have been prominent. But that is now barely relevant. If one might ventur to make a prediction, despite the inevitably hazardous nature of such activity in this domain it is that an unwillingness on the part of powerful states to intervene generally in defenc of democracy and human rights is part of a long-term trend.

One final note is appropriate: matters relating to the right to development have been omitted here because of the extensive treatment they have received in a companion volume.[52] Similarly, matters relating to the role of institutional actors in the human rights field have been excluded. Despite their dominance of the literature, they are usually of relatively ephemeral relevance and thus not appropriate for inclusion in a volume such as this.

Notes

1 See, e.g. Alfred Rubin (1990), 'Are Human Rights Legal?', *Israel Yearbook on Human Rights*, **20**, p.45.
2 Oscar Schachter (1991), *International Law in Theory and Practice*, Dordrecht: Martinus Nijhoff, p.330 ('In looking back over the previous General Courses in the *Recueil*, I have noted that my predecessors have rarely given more than passing consideration to the subject of human rights').
3 Louis Henkin (1995), *International Law: Politics and Values*, Deventer: Martinus Nijhoff, chaps. X–XII.
4 Rosalyn Higgins (1994), *Problems and Process: International Law and How We Use It*, Oxford: Clarendon Press, chaps. 6–7 ('[I]t is from his own government that an individual often most needs protection. It is clear that classical international law has relatively little to offer in this regard'; *ibid.*, p.95).
5 Thomas M. Franck (1995), *Fairness in International Law and Institutions*, Oxford: Clarendon Press, chaps. 4–5.
6 This is the official term used in relation to the members of the various treaty bodies such as the Human Rights Committee, and of the Sub-Commission on Prevention of Discrimination and Protection of Minorities.
7 Martii Koskenniemi (1990), chap. 2 of this volume, p.47.
8 Martti Koskenniemi (1996), 'International Law in a Post-Realist Era', *Australian Year Book of International Law 1995*, **16**, p.1 at p.19. He notes that he thinks of international law not 'as the application of one unified method on the world but as social practice and a professional culture, a conversation about the right thing to do in particular circumstances, constantly harking back to the political, the intimate and the subjective'. *Ibid.*, p.17.
9 *Ibid.*, p.19.
10 *Ibid.*, p.18.
11 *Ibid.*, note 7 *supra.*, p.47.
12 *Ibid.*, note 8 *supra.*, p.14.
13 Henry Steiner (1988), chap. 18 of this volume, p.388.
14 Koskenniemi, note 8 *supra*, p.14.
15 See generally Philip Alston (1984), 'Conjuring Up New Human Rights: A Proposal for Quality Control', *American Journal of International Law*, **78**, p.607.
16 Stuart Scheingold (1974), *The Politics of Rights: Lawyers, Public Policy and Political Change*, New Haven: Yale University Press.
17 Martii Koskenniemi (1991), 'The Future of Statehood', *Harvard International Law Journal*, **32**, p.397 at p.399.
18 *Ibid.*
19 *Ibid.*, pp. 399–400.
20 *Ibid.*, p.399.
21 See note 8, *supra*.
22 This endeavour is most productively undertaken in relation to the European Convention on Human Rights. For the two best works in that regard see D.J. Harris, M. O'Boyle and C. Warbrick (1995), *Law of the European Convention on Human Rights*, London: Butterworths; and J.G. Merrills (1993), *The Development of International Law by the European Court of Human Rights*, Manchester: Manchester University Press, 2nd ed.
23 Norberto Bobbio (1996), *The Age of Rights*, Cambridge: Polity Press, p. xi.

24 Martti Koskenniemi (1991), note 17 *supra*, p.399.
25 Isaiah Berlin (1988), 'On the Pursuit of the Ideal', *The New York Review of Books*, 17 March p.11 at p.18.
26 Jürgen Habermas (1994), chap. 16 in this volume, p.354.
27 *Ibid.*, p.355.
28 *Ibid.*
29 Ian Shapiro (1990), *Political Criticism*, Berkeley: University of California Press, p.14.
30 For an initial attempt to highlight some of the deficiencies in this regard, see Philip Alston (1988), 'Making Space for New Human Rights; The Case of the Right to Development', *Harvard Human Rights Yearbook*, **1**, p.3.
31 The exceptions include Henry Shue (1980), *Basic Rights: Subsistence, Affluence and U.S. Foreign Policy*, Princeton: Princeton University Press; James W. Nickel (1987), *Making Sense of Human Rights: Philosophical Reflections on the Universal Declaration of Human Rights*, Berkeley University of California Press; and Norberto Bobbio (1996), note 23 *supra*.
32 Maurice Cranston is a notable example. See Maurice Cranston (1967), 'Human Rights: Real and Supposed', in D.D. Raphael (ed.), *Political Theory and the Rights of Man*, Bloomington: Indiana University Press, p.42.
33 Carol C. Gould (1988), *Rethinking Democracy: Freedom and Social Cooperation in Politics, Economy and Society*, Cambridge: Cambridge University Press ('[H]uman rights properly ought to be internationalized... . On some interpretations this has already been accomplished... . However, this is a matter of some dispute, since on a common reading of the international agreements, these are agreements by the signatories to enact and enforce these rights nationally.' *Ibid.*, p.318.
34 Cf. Amitai Etzioni (1993), *The Spirit of Community: Rights, Responsibilities and the Communitarian Agenda*, New York: Crown; and Rhoda Howard (1995), *Human Rights and the Search for Community*, Boulder: Westview Press, Howard identifies four 'variants of communitarianism' as presenting the principal 'theoretical challenges in the 1990s to the UN principles of international human rights'. They are 'traditionalism, reactionary conservatism, left collectivism, and status radicalism'. *Ibid.*, p.2.
35 Amartya Sen (1987), *On Ethics and Economics*, Oxford: Blackwell, p.7.
36 Natalie Hevener Kaufman (1990), *Human Rights Treaties and the Senate: A History of Opposition*, Chapel Hill: University of North Carolina Press.
37 For an overview of some such efforts, see Richard Falk (1979), chap. 3 of this volume.
38 Theodor Meron (1986), chap. 4 of this volume, p.98.
39 *Ibid.*
40 *Ibid.*, p.80.
41 Richard Falk (1979), chap. 3 of this volume, p.60.
42 Andrew Hurrell and Ngaire Woods (1995), 'Globalisation and Inequality', *Millenium: Journal of International Studies*, **24**, p.447.
43 See generally Andrew Clapham (1993), *Human Rights in the Private Sphere*, Oxford: Clarendon Press.
44 'Statement on Human Rights', chap. 6 in this volume, p.114.
45 *Ibid.*, pp.114–15.
46 Elvin Hatch (1983), *Culture and Morality: The Relativity of Values in Anthropology*, New York: Columbia University Press, pp.127–8.
47 Abdullahi An-Na'im (1994), 'Cultural Transformation and Normative Consensus on the Best Interests of the Child', in Philip Alston (ed.) (1994), *The Best Interests of the Child: Reconciling Culture and Human Rights*, Oxford: Clarendon Press, p.62 at p.65.
48 *Ibid.*, p.67.
49 R.P. Peerenboom (1993), chap. 14 in this volume, p.317.
50 Remarks by Satish Chandra in (1993), *The South and Human Rights*, Geneva: Special N60 Committee on Development, p.8 at 9.
51 UN Doc. A/CONF. 157/24 (1993), Part I, para. 5.
52 Anthony Carty (1992), *Law and Development*, Aldershot: Dartmouth.

Part I
The International Normative Framework

[1]

THE SOURCES OF HUMAN RIGHTS LAW:

CUSTOM, JUS COGENS, AND GENERAL PRINCIPLES

BRUNO SIMMA*

AND

PHILIP ALSTON**

1. Introduction

The question of the sources of international human rights law is of major significance. As international human rights endeavours expand their scope and their reach, and as their potential ramifications become greater, the need to ensure that the relevant norms are solidly grounded in international law assumes increasing importance. The last few years have witnessed an ever-expanding number of contexts in which those norms are being invoked. International development assistance has become far more human rights-conscious than was the case a decade ago, labour rights issues are intruding further and further into the international trade regime, and the very legitimacy of governments is being regularly assessed on the basis of their compliance with international human rights norms. What then are the sources of the norms that are being invoked?

In many situations treaty law provides a solid and compelling legal foundation. But despite a steady increase in the number of States Parties to international treaties in recent years, reliance upon treaties alone provides an ultimately unsatisfactory patchwork quilt of obligations and still continues to leave many States largely untouched. Thus treaty law on its own provides a rather unsatisfactory basis on which to ground the efforts of international institutions whose reach is truly universal, such as the General Assembly and the Commission on Human Rights. The prospects for developing an effective and largely consensual international regime depend significantly on the extent to which those institutions are capable of basing their actions upon a coherent and

* Professor of Law, Law School, University of Michigan.

** Professor and Director of the Centre for International and Public Law, Australian National University.

generally applicable set of human rights norms. Reliance upon treaty law is likely to be even less rewarding in relation to domestic legal argumentation in the courts, legislatures and executives of countries which have ratified few if any of the major international treaties.

There is thus a strong temptation to turn to customary law as the formal source which provides, in a relatively straight-forward fashion, the desired answers. In particular, if customary law can be construed or approached in such a way as to supply a relatively comprehensive package of norms which are applicable to all States, then the debate over the sources of international human rights law can be resolved without much further ado. Given the fundamental importance of the human rights component of a just world order, the temptation to adapt or re-interpret the concept of customary law in such a way as to ensure that it provides the 'right' answers is strong, and at least to some, irresistible. It is thus unsurprising that some of the recent literature in this field, especially but not exclusively that coming out of the United States, is moving with increasing enthusiasm in that direction.[1]

But while largely endorsing the result that is thereby sought to be achieved, we have considerable misgivings about the means being used. In particular, we believe it to be important to pose two questions. The first is whether this effort to revise or 'up-date' custom does fundamental and irreparable violence to the very concept? As Jennings noted almost a decade ago, much of what many modern commentators characterise as custom "is not only not customary law: it does not even faintly resemble a customary law".[2] The second is whether it is a necessary step in order to reach the desired goal, or whether there are other approaches to the issue of sources which enable us to achieve the same objective while maintaining the integrity of the concept of custom relatively intact?

2. Treaties: A Brief Digression

Before turning to the question of which basic rules of human rights law may be considered part of customary international law it is appropriate to note, by comparison, that human rights law-making by way of treaties, and the legal characteristics of such treaties, appear to be more or less uncontroversial. The qualification 'more or less' seems apposite in view of the fundamental tensions inherent in the very concept of sovereign States agreeing to expose to international accountability an issue that a few decades ago they regarded as the core of their *domaine réservé*, as a result of which it would be unrealistic to expect human rights treaty law to operate in exactly the same way as other international treaties. As Jack Donnelly has observed, the international human rights regime, even though strong on promotion, is extremely weak on what a

1 See below notes 6-11 and accompanying text.

2 Jennings RY, "The Identification of International Law", in Bin Cheng (ed), *International Law, Teaching and Practice* (1982) p3 at 5.

lawyer would consider enforcement or remedies.[3] This characteristic has led to some controversy as to whether, and if so to what degree, human rights treaties might be considered 'softened', 'defused', or 'decoupled' from the body of general international law, with the result that the only means of securing compliance with human rights treaty obligations would be the machinery, if any, embodied in or attached to those treaties themselves.[4]

To pursue this issue further would take us too far afield from our focus of concern. But in leaving human rights treaty law let us just suggest that if, for systemic or regime reasons, we really consider human rights treaties to be different from 'normal' international treaties, we should, for those very reasons, approach the question of the existence, or rather, the viability, of an extensive *customary* law of human rights with equal caution.

3. The Significance of Different Approaches to Sources

Caution is far from being a characteristic of much of the contemporary human rights literature. Perhaps this has to do with the fact that "human rights lawyers are notoriously wishful thinkers", as John Humphrey once observed.[5] However this may be, it appears that a majority of authors today take the view that international human rights obligations incumbent upon States may, and actually do, also derive from customary international law. This thesis is presented with varying degrees of sophistication. There are writers who state flatly that the entire *corpus* of international human rights law, or, to be slightly more specific, the substance of the 1948 Universal Declaration of Human Rights, is now to be regarded as customary law in its entirety.[6] A recent variation on this approach is that, in order to accomodate all of the desired human rights principles, a "modernized view of customary international law" should be applied.[7] That view would accord "the ability to create custom" to non-state

---

3 Donnelly J, "International Human Rights": A Regime Analysis" (1986) 40 Int'l Org 599, 633–636.

4 See Simma B, "Consent: Strains in the Treaty System", in Macdonald RStJ and Johnston DM (eds), The *Structure and Process of International Law: Essays in Legal Philosophy, Doctrine and Theory* (1986) pp485, 500–502; "Self-contained Regimes" (1985) 16 Netherlands YBIL 111, 129–135 (with further references).

5 Humphrey JP, "Foreword", in Lillich RB (ed), *Humanitarian Intervention and the United Nations* (1973), VII.

6 See eg Humphrey JP, "The Universal Declaration of Human Rights: Its History, Impact and Juridical Character", in Ramcharan BG (ed), *Human Rights: Thirty Years After the Universal Declaration* (1979) pp21, 37; Sohn L, "The Human Rights Law of the Charter" (1977) 12 Texas Int LJ 129, 133 ;McDougal MS, Lasswell H and Chen L, *Human Rights and World Public Order* (1980) pp273–274, 325–327; D'Amato A, *International Law: Process and Prospect* (1986) pp123–147.

7 Gunning I, "Modernizing Customary International Law: The Challenge of Human Rights" (1991) 31 Virginia JIL, 212, 213.

actors such as international organizations and "certain non-governmental organizations [that] have a distinct, measurable impact on international affairs".[8]

Then there are more moderate, "middle-of-the-road" views, like those of the new *Restatement*[9] or of Oscar Schachter[10] (if this distinction makes sense, given the important contribution of the latter to the former), according to which something like a "hard core" of human rights obligations exists as customary law today. The recent book by Theodor Meron on our topic can be regarded as elaborate and carefully-reasoned support for the *Restatement* view without challenging in any significant way its theoretical foundation.[11] And, finally, there are voices which affirm that nowadays certain obligations to respect and ensure human rights derive from "general" international law,[12] without being specific about the source from which such general international law is supposed to flow.

Against the proponents of a broad-based customary (or, at least, general) international law of human rights stands an embattled group of writers who declare themselves unable to verify the presence of (what they perceive to be) the prerequisites of customary law in a large part of a field so torn by ideology and politics, and so replete with hypocrisy, double standards and second thoughts. Antonio Cassese, for instance, an author certainly not to be accused of avoiding pronounced humanitarian stands, remains firm that "in formal terms, [the Universal Declaration] is not legally binding, but possesses only moral and political force".[13] Some authors even consider it dangerous "to denaturate the practice-oriented character of customary law by making it comprise [in the human rights field] methods of law-making which are not practice-based at all", to quote van Hoof.[14]

Perhaps at this point one might ask what is the practical relevance of all this? In view of the paramount importance of human rights treaties, does it really matter whether, beyond these treaty instruments, there exists an extensive customary, or some other general, international law of human rights?

The answer is, of course, that it matters a great deal – for reasons probably more closely related to domestic law than to international legal issues proper. With regard to domestic law implications, a growing number of modern

8 Ibid 221–222.

9 American Law Institute, *Restatement (Third) Foreign Relations Law of the United States* (1987), § 702; Vol 2, 161. See also Henkin L, "The International Bill of Rights: The Universal Declaration and the Covenants", in Bernhardt R and Jolowicz JA (eds), *International Enforcement of Human Rights* (1987) pp 1,6.

10 Schachter O, "International Law in Theory and Practice: General Course in Public International Law", 178 *Recueil des cours* 21, 333–342 (1982–V).

11 Meron T, *Human Rights and Humanitarian Norms as Customary Law* (1989).

12 See eg Verdross A and Simma B, *Universelles Völkerrecht: Theorie und Praxis* (3d ed 1984) sec. 1234.

13 Cassese A, *International Law in a Divided World* (1986) p299.

14 van Hoof GJH, *Rethinking the Sources of International Law* (1983) pp107–108.

constitutions not only incorporate customary international law automatically as part of the law of the land but also grant it a rank superior to that of domestic statutes. On the other hand, with very few exceptions, contemporary constitutions put treaties on the same footing as statutes in this respect.[15] As a consequence, international human rights prescriptions derived from customary law, or, in the language of Art. 25 of the German Basic Law, from a general rule (or principle) of international law, would be protected against derogation by a conflicting domestic statute much more effectively than provisions of human rights treaties. Apart from such worst-case scenarios, customary or general international law is allowed by modern constitutions to have a persuasive normative impact on municipal law. To return to Art. 25 of the *Grundgesetz*, for instance, the German Constitutional Court ruled in 1987 that German courts and authorities are, by virtue of Art. 25, prevented from interpreting and applying any German domestic law in such a way as to violate the general rules of international law.[16]

In an important Australian High Court case, in which state action aimed at preventing expanded Aboriginal land ownership was struck down as being contrary to the applicable international human rights norms, three of the four judges in the majority were prepared to rely upon customary international law as the source of the relevant norms.[17] In the United States, we have witnessed the emergence of the famous *Filartiga* jurisprudence[18] - one of the few more likeable facets of the omnipresent tendency of U.S. courts to usurp jurisdiction beyond limits - or at least, what most lawyers abroad would consider to be such limits.

For a foreign observer not accustomed to having to squeeze unwritten international law through a constitutional needle's eye, as prescribed in the *Paquete Habana* case,[19] in order to prepare it for consumption by domestic courts, the readiness of U.S. courts - as well as of the Carter Administration and many American international lawyers serving as *amici curiae* - to view official torture, arbitrary detentions, disappearances and summary executions as violations of customary international law without feeling any particular need to engage in much serious debate about the prerequisites of that source, is striking,

---

15 See generally Verdross and Simma, note 12 above, secs. 848-866.

16 75 BVerfGE 1, 19.

17 *Koowarta v Bjelke-Peterson and ors*; *Queensland v The Commonwealth* (1982) 153 CLR 168, 220-221 *per* Stephen J; 234-236 *per* Mason J and 238-242 *per* Murphy J. For an analysis see Byrnes A and Charlesworth H, "Federalism and the International Legal Order: Recent Developments in Australia" (1985) 79 AJIL 622.

18 *Filartiga v Pena-Irala* 630 F. 2d 876 (2d Cir. 1980). For a recent overview and analysis of the decisions based on the Alien Tort Statute of 1789 see Burley AM, "The Alien Tort Statute and the Judiciary Act of 1789: A Badge of Honor" (1989) 83 AJIL 461.

19 *The Paquete Habana* 175 US 677 (Sup Ct 1900), 20 Sup Ct Rep 290, 44 L Ed 320.

to say the least.[20] Given the highly desirable nature of the policy goal of the *Filartiga* jurisprudence, and in view of the formidable array of authorities apparently accepting its approach with respect to custom (or lack of it) as now reflecting the received wisdom, one inevitably hesitates to tamper with it on more or less 'academic' grounds. In many respects, what we observe in action here is essentially a concerted effort by American judges and activist human rights lawyers to compensate for the abstinence of the United States *vis-à-vis* ratification of international human rights treaties.[21] We will turn to another aspect of this phenomenon later.

In addition to its important domestic law ramifications, the question of the existence *vel non* of human rights obligations arising from customary international law is also of considerable relevance on the plane of inter-State relations. Thus for example, less than two-thirds of the U.N. Member States are parties to the two International Human Rights Covenants; and participation in most other human rights treaties is even more limited.[22] With only a limited number of ratifications or accessions being added to that list every year in the case of the Covenants, a certain plateau seems to have been reached. The existence of a wide range of customary law obligations (or, let us say, obligations under general international law) *erga omnes* in this field would mitigate the negative significance of this fact. The existence of such obligations would probably entitle all States – not just the parties to human rights treaties *inter se* – to apply remedies or countermeasures at least in cases of gross and persistent breaches of such obligations.[23] It may appear doubtful, however, whether States which prefer to abstain from joining human rights treaties will, at the same time, pursue activist international human rights policies going so far as to resort to effective countermeasures. But again, the practice of the United States is said to provide examples to the contrary.[24] Perhaps this is another reason why the thesis

20 On *Filartiga* and related issues see: Symposium, (1981) 4 Houston JIL 1; "Federal Jurisdiction, Human Rights, and the Law of Nations: Essays on Filartiga v Pena-Irala" (1981) 11 Georgia JIL & Comp. L. 305; Blum J and Steinhardt R, "Federal Jurisdiction over International Human Rights Claims: The Alien Tort Claims Act after Filartiga v Pena-Irala" (1981) 22 Harvard ILJ 53; Lillich RB, "The Role of Domestic Courts in Enforcing International Human Rights Law" (1980) 74 ASIL Proceedings 20; Gerstel D and Segall A, "Conference Report: Human Rights in American Courts" (1986) 1 American U. JIL & Policy 137; and Burley AM, note 18 above.

21 For a "pessimistic assessment of the role of international human rights treaties in the United States legal system" contrasted with a "somewhat more optimistic outlook about the potential effect of customary international human rights law" see Lillich, "The United States Constitution and International Human Rights Law" (1990) 3 Harvard Human Rights Yearbook 53.

22 See U.N. Centre for Human Rights, *Human Rights: Status of International Instruments as at 31 March 1991*, U.N. Doc. ST/HR/ note 5 above.

23 See eg Verdross and Simma note 12 above sec. 1343; *Restatement* note 9 above, sec. 703; Vol 2, 175.

24 See eg Carleton D and Strohl M, "The Foreign Policy of Human Rights: Rhetoric and Reality from Jimmy Carter to Ronald Reagan, (1985) 7 Hum Rts Q 205; and see,

endorsing the existence of a customary law of human rights is so popular among American international lawyers.

In any case, the purpose of this brief analysis has been to demonstrate that a discussion of whether such obligations do indeed exist, amounts to more than an exercise in esoterics. Let us turn, then, to the question of the viability, so to speak, of a *customary* law of human rights. What makes this issue so controversial and confused is, in our view, the fact that the international human rights movement's quest for additional sources finds its favorite candidate, customary international law, in the midst of a profound identity crisis.[25]

4. The Identity Crisis of Customary Law

According to the traditional understanding of international custom, the emphasis was clearly on the material, or objective, of its two elements, namely State *practice*. Customary international law was generally considered to come about through the emergence of a general (or extensive), uniform, consistent and settled practice, more or less gradually joined by a sense of legal obligation, the *opinio juris*. However, practice had priority over *opinio juris*; deeds were what counted, not just words. What international courts and tribunals mainly did in fact was to trace the subjective element by way of discerning certain recurrent patterns within the raw material of State practice and interpreting those patterns as resulting from juridical considerations. The *Lotus* judgment of the Permanent Court seems to be a perfect illustration of such an inductive approach to custom.[26] Viewed from this angle, *opinio juris* was an elusive and rather ephemeral creature – so much so in fact that two of the most prominent publicists of the first half of our century, Kelsen and Guggenheim, tried in their earlier writings to dispense with *opinio juris* altogether and instead saw customary international law arising from State practice alone.[27]

Rules of customary law thus firmly established through inductive reasoning based on deeds rather than words may have been, and still are, limited in scope, but they had, and continue to have, several undoubted advantages. They are hard

in particular, United States trade legislation which authorises the President to impose a variety of sanctions against any U.S. trading partner which he deems to be engaging in the systematic denial of "internationally recognized worker rights" : s 301 of the Omnibus Trade and Competitiveness Act of 1988, Pub. L. No. 100–418, 102 Stat. 1107 (1988), s 301 codified at 19 USCA s 2411(a). See generally Lawyers Committee for Human Rights, *A Report on Legal Mechanisms to Protect Worker Rights* (mimeo, 1991).

25 For a brilliant overview and extensive discussion see Koskenniemi M, *From Apology to Utopia: The Structure of International Legal Argument* (1989) pp342–421. See also Cassese A and Weiler JHH (eds), *Change and Stability in International Law-Making* (1988).

26 *The Lotus Case*; *France v Turkey* (1927) PCIJ Ser A, No 10.

27 Kelsen H, "Théorie du droit international coutumier" (1939) 1 *Revue internationale de la théorie du droit, Nouvelle Série* 253; Guggenheim P, "Les deux éléments de la coutume en droit international", in *La technique et les principes du droit public: Etudes en l'honneur de Georges Scelle* (1950), Vol 1, p275.

and solid; they have been carefully hammered out on the anvil of actual, tangible interaction among States; and they allow reasonably reliable predictions as to future State behavior. They constitute the type of international law that Kelsen must have had in mind when he expressed his *grundnorm* in the formula: "states ought to behave as they have customarily behaved".[28] In other words, what is happening in this process of inductive reasoning is to look into the past to identify customary patterns of State practice and then to turn this empirical result into a normative projection for the future.[29]

So much then for the old-style of practice-based custom, *la coutume sage*. Then followed the stage of *la coutume sauvage*:[30] a product grown in the hothouse of parliamentary diplomacy and all too often 'sold' as customary law before actually having stood the test of time. What is customary about this cultured pearl[31] version of customary law is not (at least, not necessarily) its consistent application in actual State practice but the fertilizing role it plays through proclamation, exhortation, repetition, incantation, lament. For some writers, practice no longer has any constitutive role to play in the establishment of customary law; rather it serves a purely evidentiary function. After all, the only task practice ever had to perform, the 'modernists' would say, was to bring consent or *opinio juris* to the fore; and now that we have all these international bodies, and above all the U.N. General Assembly, generating an almost permanent, intensive flow of communications, consent and *opinio juris* can manifest themselves more or less instantly and without the help of a vehicle as cumbersome and demanding as actual State practice.[32]

For other writers, it is the notion of "practice" itself which has undergone a dubious metamorphosis. It has changed from something happening out there in the real world, after the diplomats and the delegates have had their say, into paper practice: the words, texts, votes and excuses themselves.[33] The process of customary law-making is thus turned into a self-contained exercise in rhetoric. The approach now used is *deductive*: rules or principles proclaimed, for instance, by the General Assembly, as well as the surrounding ritual itself, are taken not only as starting points for the possible development of customary law in the

---

28 Kelsen H, *Principles of International Law* (1952) p418.

29 As Judge VM Koretsky put it in his Dissenting Opinion to the *North Sea Continental Shelf* judgment, custom "turns its face to the past": ICJ Rep 1969, p 3, at 156.

30 See Dupuy RJ, "Coutume sage et coutume sauvage", in *La communauté internationale. Mélanges offerts à Charles Rousseau* (1974) p75.

31 This phrase was coined by Abi-Saab G, "La coutume dans tous ses états où le dilemme du développement du droit international général dans un monde éclaté", in *International Law at the Time of Its Codification. Essays in Honour of Roberto Ago* (1987), Vol I, p61 ("des perles de culture").

32 See eg Bin Cheng, "Custom: The Future of General State Practice in a Divided World" in Macdonald and Johnston note 2 above, 513, and the further references in Verdross and Simma, note 12 above sec. 566 note 45.

33 See eg Akehurst M, "Custom as a Source of International Law" (1974–75) 47 British YBIL 1, 53.

event that State practice eventually happens to lock on to these proclamations, but as a law-making process which is more or less complete in itself, even in the face of contrasting 'external' facts. This new, radical customary law has lost the element of retrospection; if its protagonists look back at the past it is a look back in anger, full of impatience with the imperfections and gaps of the old rules. Such impatience also extends to the processes of treaty-making, a field in which delay or a lack of consent simply cannot be argued away by theoretical constructs. Thus the flight into a new, "progressive", more or less instant custom.

The elevation of the Universal Declaration of 1948 and of the documents that have built upon its foundations to the status of customary law, in a world where it is still customary for a depressingly large number of States to trample upon the human rights of their nationals, is a good example of such an approach.

[We are taking a short-cut here. In treating this issue many writers start by dealing with the question of whether certain resolutions, or declarations, of the U.N. General Assembly may have a law-making function. We do not need to go into this point because the vast majority of commentators agree that such resolutions may indeed set in motion, influence, or become part of, the process of custom-building,[34] and that is where we meet again].

5. Different Views on the Customary Status of Human Rights Norms

We have already mentioned the view according to which the Universal Declaration has now acquired customary law status *en bloc*. That some of the voices to this effect sound from within the U.N. human rights "establishment" should not be surprising. To cite a particularly striking example, the Commission on Human Rights' Special Rapporteur on the situation in Iran, Mr. Galindo Pohl, arrived at the following conclusions:

> The rights and freedoms set out in the Universal Declaration have become international customary law through State practice and *opinio juris*. Even if the strictest approach is adopted to the determination of the elements which form international customary law, that is, the classical doctrine of the convergence of extensive, continuous and reiterated practice and of *opinio juris*, the provisions contained in the Universal Declaration meet the stringent standards of that doctrine. Of course, they also meet the more liberal standards of contemporary doctrines on the constitutive elements of international customary law.[35]

34 For a recent review of the literature see Sloan F, "General Assembly Resolutions Revisited", (1987) 58 British YBIL 39.

35 "Report on the human rights situation in the Islamic Republic of Iran by the Special Representative of the Commission, Mr. Reynoldo Galindo Pohl, appointed pursuant to resolution 1986/41, U.N. Doc. E/CN.4/1987/23, para.22. It is perhaps symptomatic of the reluctance, or perhaps even the inability, of U.N. organs to grapple with complex theoretical issues, that the Commission fully endorsed (by way of taking "note with appreciation") "the report of the Special Representative and the conclusions and recommendations contained therein" (CHR Res. 1987/55 of 11 March 1987, para. 1) without any significant discussion on the issue of the status of

Turning from United Nations to academic circles, Lung-Chu Chen, a follower of Myres McDougal's New Haven approach, in his evaluation of the new *Restatement*'s provisions on the protection of persons, considers quite categorically that the Universal Declaration's "frequent invocation and application by officials, at all levels of government and in many communities around the world" have conferred on it "those expectations characteristic of customary international law".[36] Similarly, K.M.G. Nayar, writing in the *Harvard International Law Journal* in 1978, argued that the entire Universal Declaration had become part of customary international law.[37] His view was subsequently cited with approval by Judge Kaufman in the *Filartiga* case.[38] Reference might also be made to John Humphrey's view that the Universal Declaration is now "part of the customary law of nations and therefore binding on all States".[39]

Other voices are more clearly aware of the discrepancies between what is said to have become custom and what the facts tell us. Thus, in a Special Issue of the U.N. *Bulletin of Human Rights*, published on the occasion of the 40th anniversary of the Universal Declaration, Alexandre Kiss enquires "whether the assertion that a customary rule of international law exists [i.e. in the human rights field] can be rebutted by evidence of *contrary acts* or by the affirmations of States which do not accept these rules of international law".[40] While he then goes on in some detail to affirm the obvious, namely, that States do not tend to oppose the principles proclaimed in the Declaration explicitly, he draws no conclusions whatsoever from his own admission that, "unfortunately, in every day life violations of these rights and freedoms nevertheless occur".[41] Rather,

---

the Universal Declaration. See U.N. Doc. E/CN 4/1987/SR.56/Add. 1, paras. 10–37. At its 1988 session the Commission specifically endorsed "the conclusion of the Special Representative that the obligations acquired by the Islamic Republic of Iran as a State Member of the United Nations and as a party to the two International Covenants on Human Rights are fully binding and do not admit exceptions on account of constitutional problems, rules and regulations of municipal law, or cultural or historical background". Commission on Human Rights resolution 1988/69, 6th preambular paragraph.

36 Chen LC, "Restatement: Protection of Persons" (1989) 14 Yale JIL 542, 546–547. See also McDougal M, Lasswell H, and Chen L–C, *Human Rights and World Public Order* (1980) pp273–274, 325–327. For a recent Soviet voice to this effect see Kartashkin VE, "The Universal Declaration and Human Rights in the Contemporary World" (1988) 39 Soviet YBIL 39 (English summary at 50).

37 Nayar KMG, "Human Rights: The UN and US Foreign Policy", (1978) 19 Harv ILJ, 813, 816–817.

38 Note 18 above, 883.

39 Humphrey J, "International Bill of Rights: Scope and Implementation" (1976) 17 Wm Mary LR 527, 529.

40 Kiss A, "The Role of the Universal Declaration of Human Rights in the development of international law", U.N. Centre for Human Rights, *Bulletin of Human Rights: Special Issue: Fortieth Anniversary of the Universal Declaration of Human Rights* (1988) pp47, 48 (emphasis added).

41 Id.

what matters under these circumstances is that "quite certainly no State, even the most tyrannical, would wish to proclaim to the whole world in that way its contempt for values recognized as fundamental by all nations".[42] What Kiss seems to be saying is that, if a rule or principle is universally proclaimed and recognized, evidence of its violation is simply irrelevant. We will return to the implications of this view later.[43]

The most sophisticated line of argument in favor of a customary law of human rights based on the Universal Declaration is to be found in the Reporters' Notes on §§ 701 and 702 of the new *Restatement*[44] and, with even greater subtlety, in Oscar Schachter's magnificent 1982 Hague General Course,[45] to which we now turn.

At the outset, Schachter admits that our question "cannot readily be answered on the basis of the *usual* processes of customary law formation",[46] because here one just does not come across the material that is normally considered to constitute State practice accompanied by *opinio juris*. Rather, Schachter proposes to rely on different kinds of evidence in the human rights field, including the incorporation of human rights provisions in many national constitutions and laws; frequent references in U.N. resolutions and declarations to 'duties' arising out of the Universal Declaration; resolutions of the U.N. and other international bodies condemning human rights violations as breaches of international law; statements by national officials criticising other States for serious human rights violations; the famous dictum of the International Court in the *Barcelona Traction* Case;[47] and, finally, some judgments of domestic courts that refer to the Universal Declaration as a source of standards for judicial decisions.[48]

Schachter acknowledges that the weight of all these materials cannot be assessed as evidence of custom without considering actual practice, and that human rights infringements are "widespread, often gross and generally tolerated by the international community".[49] Unlike many others, Schachter does not want to minimise the significance of this negative practice. Rather, he draws a distinction between different provisions of the Universal Declaration. In the case of some rights (freedom of expression, equality between men and women, and the right to work, are given as examples), State behavior clearly does not comport with the claim that they constitute international custom. On the other hand, he continues, there are provisions that clearly do have a strong claim to the status of customary law. In his view, "[t]his can be shown not so much by

42 Ibid p49.

43 See text accompanying notes 68–76.

44 See note 9 above.

45 See note 10 above.

46 Id 334 (emphasis added).

47 ICJ Rep 1970, p33.

48 Note 10 above, 334–335.

49 Ibid 335.

applying formal criteria of customary law as by considering conduct that has been universally condemned as violative of the basic concept of human dignity".[50] This criterion leads Schachter to the cases enumerated in § 702 of the *Restatement*: slavery, genocide, torture, mass killings, prolonged arbitrary imprisonment, and systematic racial discrimination, or any consistent pattern of gross violations of internationally recognised human rights.

Schachter draws attention to the fact that in these cases there is a difference in intensity and depth of the attitudes of condemnation. In the case of torture, for instance, even if it takes place in many countries, it is almost always contrary to national law and is not legitimised as State policy. "Hence, when violations of these strongly held basic rights of the person take place, they are to be regarded as violations, not as `State practice' that nullifies the legal force of the right".[51] According to him, it is also important to consider whether conduct which is the subject of criticism is defended by the perpetrators as legitimate or is instead denied on factual grounds, because in the latter event, one may plausibly infer that the State accepts the principle involved. Finally, he considers the relative intensity of the criticism of infringements of some human rights to be pertinent.[52]

Other commentators, although espousing a comparably careful approach in relation to satisfying the requirements of custom, have been prepared to extend Schachter's list even further. Richard Lillich, for example, has suggested that the right to equality before the law and to non-discrimination (equal protection) as stated in articles 7 and 26 of the Universal Declaration of Human Rights is (provided that their content is interpreted in a "properly limited" way) part of customary law.[53] In addition, while suggesting that the right to free movement within a State is not yet part of customary law, he concludes that "both the right to leave and the right to return seem well-established in conventional and perhaps even customary international human rights law".[54]

Theodor Meron has proposed an even more extensive list of customary norms, although he also leaves open the possibility that the source of some of them might instead (or perhaps as well) be found in general principles of law. His list includes the right of self-determination, the right to humane treatment of detainees, the prohibition of retroactive penal measures, the principle of *ne bis in idem* (the right not to be tried or punished again for an offence for which one has already been convicted or acquitted)[55] and various due process rights including:

---

50 Ibid 336.

51 Id.

52 Ibid 338.

53 Lillich R , "Civil Rights" in Meron T, (ed), *Human Rights in International Law: Legal and Policy Issues* (1984) Vol 1, 115, 133.

54 Ibid, 151.

55 Meron, note 11 above, 97 and 134.

the right to be tried by a competent, independent and impartial tribunal established by law, the right to presumption of innocence, the right of everyone not to be compelled to testify against himself [sic] or to confess guilt: the right of everyone to be tried in his or her presence and to defend himself or herself in person or through legal assistance of his or her own choosing, the right of everyone to examine witnesses against him or her and the right to have one's conviction and sentence reviewed by a higher tribunal according to law.[56]

These various approaches, as well as that of the *Restatement*, seem to warrant a number of comments both in terms of human rights policy and of the doctrine of customary law. With regard to the first aspect, it is noteworthy that in these views there is a remarkable correlation between the norms identified as customary rules, and the range of rights which has been incorporated into the U.S. Bill of Rights. This correlation may, of course, be considered to be coincidental. Alternatively, it might be seen as a tribute to the foresight and perceptiveness of the drafters of the U.S. documents or as a reflection of the dominant influence of American values in the world. It is also possible, however, to view it is an instance of what might be termed normative chauvinism, albeit of an unintentional or sub-conscious variety.[57] We have already mentioned that the *Restatement*'s list in § 702 concludes with the category of "a consistent pattern of gross violations of internationally recognised human rights". The interpretation which the *Restatement* applies to this category is a particularly striking instance of assuming that American values are synonymous with those reflected in international law. The following examples of rights which are covered by this clause are cited in the commentary to the *Restatement*: systematic harrassment, invasions of the privacy of the home, arbitrary arrest and detention (even if not prolonged); denial of fair trial in criminal cases; grossly disproportionate punishment; denial of freedom to leave the country; denial of the right to return to one's country; mass uprooting of a country's population; denial of freedom of conscience and religion; denial of personality before the law; denial of basic privacy such as the right to marry and raise a family; and invidious racial or religious discrimination.[58]

The right to freedom from hunger, the right to adequate housing, the right to access to basic health care, the right to freedom of association, the right to form trade unions and the right to primary education are all excluded from this

56 Ibid 96–97.

57 It is appropriate here to note the comment made by Koskiennemi in a review published after the first draft of the present Article had been presented. He opines that Meron's discussion of customary law norms, note 11 above, "is more intended to show American lawyers how to plead when pressing a human rights case in American courts than to reveal much about international law". Koskiennemi M, "The Pull of the Mainstream" (1990) 88 Mich LR 1946 at 1951.

58 See note 9 above.

listing.[59] The *Restatement*'s reasoning is all the more questionable since the wording of the clause is taken directly from a U.N. procedure (under Economic and Social Council Resolution 1503)[60] which the U.N. has clearly stated to be equally applicable to economic, social and cultural rights as to civil and political rights.[61]

The end result of the *Restatement*'s analysis is, at best, suspiciously convenient. The great majority of rights considered important under U.S. law, as well as virtually every right which recent U.S. governments have been prepared to criticize other governments for violating, are held to be part of customary international law. By contrast, none of the rights which the U.S. fails to recognise in its domestic law, is included. In the final resort it must be asked whether any theory of human rights law which singles out race but not gender discrimination, which condemns arbitrary inprisonment but not capital punishment for crimes committed by juveniles or death by starvation and which finds no place for a right of access to primary health care, is not flawed in terms both of the theory of human rights and of United Nations doctrine.

But the suggestion of sub-conscious chauvinism must not be permitted to conceal the genuinely important point that emerges in this context. That is that, as appealing as Schachter's more sophisticated and more nuanced approach to the issue of the evidence of State practice may be, it still leaves us with an excessively flexible, and thus inevitably rather subjective, set of criteria. The relative intensity of criticism test would surely yield dramatically different results when viewed from the perspective of many Third World diplomats or jurists than from that of their Western, or more particularly American, counterparts. Moreover, at least for the foreseeable future, the evidence that will be called in support of any particular application of the test will be almost exclusively Western in origin except for the evidence produced on those occasions on which Third World governments have been encouraged to pronounce themselves in a United Nations or related forum. And, in those latter cases we are taken back to that school of thought which is prepared to accept diplomatic pronouncements as sufficient evidence for the existence of a customary rule of law. Thus the practical result, at least, of Schachter's relative intensity test may not differ significantly from that yielded by applying virtually the same criteria as those which he had seemed unwilling to accept.

But leaving aside this practical result and returning from policy to the theory of the sources of international human rights, the line of reasoning to be found in the *Restatement* and in Schachter's Hague Lectures is probably as persuasive as any attempt to anchor such rights in customary law can possibly be. Nevertheless

59 For an instructive critique, partly along similar lines, see Murphy D, "The Restatement (Third)'s Human Rights Provisions: Nothing New, But Very Welcome" [1990] The Int'l Lawyer 917.

60 ECOSOC Res. 1503 (XLVIII) of May 27, 1970, 49. U.N. ESCOR Supp. (No. 1A), pp. 8-9, U.N. Doc. E/4832/Add.1 (1970).

61 CHR Res. 5 (XXXIII) (1977).

even such high-powered arguments cannot entirely dispel doubts as to whether custom really is an adequate means for embedding fundamental human rights obligations in general international law. Is it wise to disregard the usual processes and the formal criteria for customary law, as Schachter in effect proposes, or at least to bend these prerequisites very considerably, in order to reach a certain policy result, however desirable it may be? Can we really put customary law on a "sliding scale", as Kirgis has suggested,[62] and put less emphasis on what States actually do, the more generally accepted a principle or rule appears to be? In Kirgis' view, which is similar to that of Kiss, the basic rule is that "the more destabilising or morally distasteful the activity – for example, the offensive use of force or the deprivation of fundamental human rights – the more readily international decision makers will substitute one element for the other [i.e. state practice and *opinio juris*], provided that the asserted restrictive rule seems reasonable".[63] But this reasoning would seem to be a case of arriving at the wrong conclusion for the right reasons. Kirgis suggests that "the Universal Declaration of Human Rights has come to be regarded as an authoritative articulation of customary international law, at least with respect to the most fundamental rights, no matter how widespread or persistent the nonconforming state conduct may be".[64] He defends this result on the grounds that "the alternative would be an international legal order containing ominous silences – where treaty commitments cannot be found – concerning the ways in which states impose their wills on other states or on individuals".[65] Leaving to the concluding part of our paper the question of whether there would in fact be an "ominous silence" if this radical approach to custom is not accepted, it is surely open to doubt whether the concept of custom should be so fundamentally re-shaped in a manner which disregards its intrinsic limitations (and some would say, virtues) in order to accommodate a desired (and highly admirable) policy outcome.

This observation leads us back to what we called the present "identity crisis" of customary law: the de-emphasising of material practice as a constitutive element combined with the tendency to "count" the articulation of a rule twice, so to speak, not only as an expression of *opinio juris* but also as State practice itself. In its *Nicaragua* judgment, after paying lip-service to the classic view,[66] the International Court of Justice also submitted to this current trend of de-emphasising practice in favor of *opinio juris* and looking to soft law emanations

62 Kirgis F, "Custom on a Sliding Scale" (1987) 81 AJIL 146.

63 Ibid 149.

64 Id 147–148.

65 Id 148.

66 *Military and Paramilitary Activities in and against Nicaragua (Nicaragua v U.S.A.), Merits*, ICJ Rep 1986, p14 at 97–98: "The mere fact that States declare their recognition of certain rules is not sufficient for the Court to consider these as being part of customary international law. Bound as it is by Article 38 of its Statute, to apply, *inter alia*, international custom as 'evidence of a general practice accepted as law', the Court may not disregard the essential role played by general practice".

for determining the content of the subjective element. It is astonishing how readily the Court accepted the consent of the parties to certain General Assembly resolutions and other soft law instruments as the manifestation of an appropriate *opinio juris*, without looking for positive evidence of "external" State practice in conformity with these positions.[67]

In another paragraph of the *Nicaragua* judgment, the Court attempted to come to terms with the problem of inconsistency between practice and *opinio juris* – as we have seen, the major argument against the credibility of an extensive customary law of human rights. In such a case, says the Court, in order for customary law to survive, it is sufficient that the conduct of States should be consistent with such rules in general. Instances of State conduct inconsistent with a rule should generally have been treated as breaches of that rule, not as indications of the recognition of a new rule.[68]

In our view, this is a statement valid in those cases in which State practice and *opinio juris* have had a chance to establish themselves solidly in an initial, formative stage. The argument appears to us much less convincing, however, in instances where the inconsistency between words and factual behavior has been glaring from the very beginning.[69] This point deserves to be re-emphasised because it seems decisive. It makes a big difference whether we are in the presence of a case where customary law has been gradually built up, through State practice of the traditional material kind and where subsequent instances of inconsistent conduct occur, or whether claims to the existence of a rule of customary law are voiced amidst – or against – a real world which all too often continues to behave as if it were totally unimpressed by such claims.

Our reservations in this regard are shared by a report of the Committee on the Formation of Customary Law established by the American Branch of the International Law Association ("ILA"). In addressing the role of practice, the Committee considers that where the rule in question is neither old nor established, the approach of looking first to articulated rules and only secondly to practice in support of those rules, coupled with a broader definition of, and diminished requirements for practice, may result in a sort of "instant" customary international law of dubious relationship to the actual behaviour and interests of States.[70] Now, if one assumes that the advance of "soft custom", as we could call it, will continue, or even accelerate, the *Restatement*'s line of thought might soon not have to disregard any formal criteria but would rather blend perfectly with a new general theory of customary law-making. Whether such a development will be as beneficial for custom as for human rights, is open to doubt.

---

67 Ibid 99–104.

68 Ibid 98.

69 *Semble* van Hoof (note 14 above) 108 note 423.

70 Committee on the Formation of Customary International Law, American Branch of the International Law Association: "The Role of State Practice in the Formation of Customary and *Jus Cogens* Norms of International Law" (January 19, 1989) 7.

98 Australian Year Book of International Law

Our own view would be that, instead of further manipulating the established concept of customary law based on an effective requirement of concrete practice, we ought to look for a different – and less damaging – way to explain the legal force of universally recognised human rights. If state conduct is to be entirely disregarded, as some authors suggest may be necessary at least in extreme cases, it would seem more logical and potentially more persuasive to proceed on the basis of some alternative theory of state obligation in the human rights field.

Before turning to such alternatives, let us just say that, if we were really to insist on discovering extensive *customary* law in the field of international human rights, we might well find the most convincing evidence, in full conformity with the established criteria, in a different direction. At the level of universal international law, international concern for human rights and the generally accepted *droit de regard* in this respect have developed over more than four decades through the activities of the U.N. General Assembly, the Commission on Human Rights and a number of other U.N. bodies, on the modest "hard law" basis of a few very generally worded Charter provisions. It is here that the decisive human rights bridgeheads in areas of formerly unfettered domestic jurisdiction of States have been achieved: by a literal avalanche of General Assembly resolutions, through decisions of the Human Rights Commission and its Sub–Commission, through public debate of gross human rights violations or confidential responses to petitions within the Resolution 1503 procedure; by means of country–oriented or thematic reports by Special rapporteurs and their acceptance by the bodies mentioned, through the initiation of sanctions against particularly grave breaches, and so on. In the resolutions and debates of these institutions and organs, the standards contained in the Universal Declaration are consistently and routinely cited as being applicable to all States. We are on safe ground in considering this very *droit de regard*, entitling the U.N. itself to respond to gross violations of human rights in these various ways, to be firmly established in customary international law.[71] Proof of this can be seen, for instance, in the reactions by target governments to the application of the Resolution 1503 procedure; as Tolley has shown in his analysis of the work of the Human Rights Commission, by virtue of their regular participation such governments tacitly acknowledge that any alleged gross violations of human rights norms require some response.[72] This achnowledgement would be even more firmly entrenched if, as we have advocated elsewhere, the 1503 procedure is given a much more significant public dimension than it has at present.[73]

Further, it is now widely accepted that the issue of severe human rights violations may also be taken up in various other multilateral contexts as well as in bilateral inter–State relations, for instance within the framework of the "Helsinki process", without encroaching upon the *domaine réservé* of the

71 *Semble* Müller C, *Die Menschenrechte als außenpolitisches Ziel* (1986) pp115–117.

72 Tolley H, Jr. *The U.N. Commission on Human Rights* (1987) pp124–133.

73 Alston P, "The Commission on Human Rights" in Alston P (ed), *The United Nations and Human Rights: A Critical Appraisal* (forthcoming 1992).

sovereign States addressed. There is no doubt in this regard that intensive State practice has indeed been joined by *opinio juris* and thus has led to firmly established customary international law.[74]

Before leaving the *droit de regard* it is appropriate to ask whether the range of norms which can appropriately be the subject of the scrutiny or *regard* is limited in some way – to customary norms, for example. In our view its scope is comprehensive and embraces all of the dimensions of international human rights law. It thus takes full account of customary norms, norms based on authentic interpretation, and general principles and extends also to soft law norms. This is borne out by the range of norms regularly used by the U.N., the Commission on Security and Co-operation in Europe and other bodies and in which the vast majority of States have acquiesced.

If we compare these – relatively – uncontroversial instances of customary law-making *lege artis* with the mode of recognition of certain substantive human rights obligations, we see that the former can be derived from constant interaction, from claims and tolerances as to what sovereign States can do to *each other*, or in other words how far they can go, unilaterally or in an organised way, out of their concern for human rights. The performance of most substantive human rights obligations, on the other hand, lacks this element of interaction proper; it does not "run between" States in any meaningful sense. Thus, one reason why the claims to the existence of such a number of substantive human rights obligations under customary law remain unconvincing, and even do violence to some degree, to the established formal criteria of custom, can be seen in the fact that an element of interaction – in a broad sense – is intrinsic to, and essential to, the kind of State practice leading to the formation of customary international law. If we review successful as against unsuccessful candidates for norms with customary law status, we could conclude that the processes of customary international law can only be triggered, and continue working, in situations in which States interact, where they apportion or delimit in some tangible way. But, at least in most cases, this is not what happens when a consensus about substantive human rights obligations, to be performed domestically, grows into international law.

One further point warrants consideration in this context. How can we distinguish, in practice, between the performance of customary law obligations operating purely at the domestic level, such as in the case of human rights, and internationally concordant domestic behaviour followed for reasons other than a sense of international legal obligation, such as driving on the correct side of the road?[75] The answer is because of that very sense of *international* legal

74 For a recent confirmation of this approach see the views submitted in the form of a draft resolution on "The Protection of Human Rights and the Principle of Non-Intervention in Internal Affairs of States" submitted by the *Institut de Droit international* to the U.N. Commission of Human Rights in 1990, U.N. Doc. E/CN.4/1990/NGO/55, English text in (1989) 27 *Archiv des Völkerrechts* 230.

75 On this general issue see Simma B, *Das Reziprozitätselement in der Entstehung des Völkergewohnheitsrechts* (1970) pp36–37 note 88.

obligation present in the case of human rights but absent in the other. What this means, however, is that the existence *vel non* of a rule of international customary law not requiring interaction, and not really running between States, can only be ascertained by finding expressions of a respective international *opinio juris*. Thus, as a matter of logic, such an *opinio juris* would remain the only relevant element; domestic practice would simply not matter anymore. But such a result would overstretch the limits of even the most lenient, or "progressive", theory of customary law.

None of this is to suggest that there are no human rights norms that are capable of satisfying the appropriate criteria for the creation of customary international law. Indeed it may well be that, in relation to many of the rights contained in the *Restatement* list, a strong case could be made which also takes careful account of the concerns expressed above. The point that we wish to make, however, is that the resulting list will inevitably be rather brief and will certainly constitute an unsatisfactory or inadequate basis on which to achieve many of the goals appropriately sought by the strongest proponents of international human rights law.

6. The 'Authoritative Interpretation' Approach

Let us now turn to the first of two alternative approaches used to arrive at human rights obligations under international law independently of specific treaties. It consists of treating the Universal Declaration and the body of soft law built upon it as an *authoritative interpretation* of the obligation contained in Articles 55 and 56 of the U.N. Charter according to which "all Members pledge themselves to take joint and separate action in cooperation with the Organization" in order to achieve "universal respect for, and observance of, human rights and fundamental freedoms for all without distinction as to race, sex, language or religion". This approach appears to have been supported by the Carter Administration[76] and has been put forward by several leading academic commentators.[77]

In our view, the authoritative interpretation approach appears to rest on somewhat more solid legal foundations than the customary law approach. Indeed, there are strong grounds for arguing that States Parties to the Charter, having in good faith undertaken treaty obligations to respect 'human rights', are subsequently bound to accept, for the purposes of interpreting their treaty obligations, the definition of 'human rights' which has evolved over time on the

76 Under President Carter, the U.S. Government acknowledged the obligatory character of the Charter's human rights provisions and appeared to accept the Universal Declaration as an authoritative interpretation of those provisions. See eg "Address by President Carter to the United Nations General Assembly" (1977) 76 Dept. of State Bull. 332; and Vance C, "Human Rights and Foreign Policy", id, 505.

77 See Sohn L, "The New International Law: Protection of the Rights of Individuals Rather Than States" (1982) 32 Amer Univ LR 1, 17; and Buergenthal T, "International Human Rights Law and Institutions: Accomplishments and Prospects" (1988) 63 Washington LR 1.

basis of the virtually unanimous practice of the relevant organs of the United Nations.[78] This view has been reinforced by the approach adopted by the Inter-American Court of Human Rights which has stated that the member states of the Organization of American States are, in effect, bound by the American Declaration of the Rights and Duties of Man as an authoritative interpretation of the human rights referred to in the OAS Charter.[79] Nevertheless, at a certain point there must be limits to this approach which would require an individuated analysis in order to determine whether *all* of the rights in the Universal Declaration, as well as the new rights such as the right to development which the U.N. has subsequently proclaimed, can be said to fall within the ambit of the original Charter provision.

Where does such a cautious approach lead us? Do we, by doubting the adequacy or viability of the customary law of human rights advocated by so many voices and, by limiting the scope of the authoritative interpretation approach, negate the possibility or existence of a general international law in this area? For some writers, like Professors Watson, Lane, Weisburd or, more recently, Rubin, there is indeed no alternative to this conclusion.[80] We see things differently, however. In the first place, as noted above, it may well be possible to justify the proposition that a limited range of norms satisfies the relevant criteria. In the second place, and more importantly, the latter school of thought does not, in our view, sufficiently appreciate the potential inherent in the international law-making process. For its adherents, international law does not extend beyond treaties and custom. In contrast, it is proposed to examine some suggestions that were put forward recently and which seem rather attractive - partly so because some of them coincide with what Professor Alfred Verdross and one of the present authors have written quite a while ago, alas, in German.[81]

---

78 In the early years after the adoption of the U.N. Charter and The Universal Declaration, a lively debate over this issue took place. Among those who rejected the approach, see Hudson M, "Charter Provisions on Human Rights in American Law" (1950) 44 AJIL 543; and Kelsen H, *The Law of the United Nations* (1950) p110. In support, see: Jessup P, *A Modern Law of Nations* (1948) 4; and Lauterpacht H, *International Law and Human Rights* (1950) p166.

79 "Interpretation of the American Declaration of the Rights and Duties of Man Within the Framework of Article 64 of the American Convention on Human Rights", Advisory Opinion OC-10/89 of July 14, 1989, para. 43. (1990) 29 Int'l Legal Materials 379 at 389.

80 Watson JS, "Legal Theory, Efficacy and Validity in the Development of Human Rights Norms in International Law", [1979] U of Illinois L Forum 609; Lane E, "Demanding Human Rights: A Change in the World Legal Order" (1978) 6 Hofstra LR 269; "Mass Killing by Governments: Lawful in the World Legal Order?", (1979) 12 NYU JIL and Politics 239; Weisburd AM, "Customary International Law: The Problem of Treaties" (1988) 21 Vanderbilt J of Transnational L 1. The last-quoted contribution led to a veritable *dialogue des sourds* on the nature and formation of customary law between Professors D'Amato and Weisburd; see D'Amato, "Custom and Treaty: A Response to Professor Weisburd", ibid 459. See also Rubin A, "Are Human Rights Legal?", (1990) 20 Israel Yearbook on Human Rights 45.

81 See Verdross and Simma note 12 above, secs. 526, 602, 606, 639.

In the Report of the Committee on the Formation of Customary Law established by the American Branch of the ILA, to which reference was also made earlier, (entitled "The Role of State Practice in the Formation of Customary and *Jus Cogens* Norms of International Law"),[82] the authors share our concerns about the contemporary movement in the direction of minimising the role of State practice in the formation of customary international law, or by adjusting its definition.[83] In assessing the relevance of State practice for the formation of unwritten international law, they draw attention to the third source mentioned in Art. 38 of the Statute of the International Court, namely "the *general principles of law* recognised by civilized nations".[84] Admittedly, the dominant view understands this concept in a narrow sense, as referring to legal principles developed *in foro domestico*. But, as many writers have pointed out in various contexts, there is no necessity to restrict the notion of 'general principles' in this way.[85] For the drafters of the Statute the decisive point was that such principles were not to be derived from mere speculation; they had rather to be made objective through some sort of general acceptance or recognition by States.[86] Such acceptance or recognition, however, may also be effected on the *international* plane. The emphasis on acceptance *in foro domestico* was simply caused by the necessity to validate general principles in a reliable way; it cannot be read as closing the door to alternative means of objective validation.

7. Using 'General Principles'

Such new means are available today: general principles can now be accepted in an international setting. Principles brought to the fore in this 'direct way', so to speak, would (and should) then percolate down into domestic fora, instead of being elevated from the domestic level to that of international law by way of analogy. Of course, if we perceive customary international law to be derived not only from a generalisation of State practice but from the express articulation of rules in, for example, declarations of the General Assembly, the concept of custom will be difficult to distinguish from that of general principles recognised internationally in the first instance. The Report, however, pleads in favour of keeping the two notions separate on the ground, among others, that the concept of a "recognised" general principle seems to conform more closely than the concept of custom to the situation where a norm invested with strong inherent authority is widely accepted even though widely violated.[87] The example that

82 See note 70 above.

83 Ibid 1, 6 *et seq*.

84 Ibid 8 *et seq*.

85 For an overview of theoretical opinions see Vitanyi B, "Les positions doctrinales concernant le sens de la notion de 'principes généraux de droit reconnus par les nations civilisées'", (1982) 86 *Revue générale de droit interntional public* 48.

86 On the drafting history of Art. 38 (1)(c) of the Statute see, eg van Hoof, note 13 above 136–139; Herczegh G, *General Principles of Law and the International Legal Order* (1969) pp11–33.

87 Note 70 above, 10.

the Report primarily has in mind here is the prohibition on the threat or use of force, but it may be that internationally recognized human rights are even more pertinent.

The prohibition against the threat or use of force and fundamental human rights prescriptions share another important characteristic. They both belong to the body of international *jus cogens*. We must emphasise that what is referred to here are *fundamental* human rights, of the type considered earlier in connection with the list set up by the *Restatement*. We would certainly hesitate to claim the peremptory nature of the entire body of today's human rights and humanitarian law lock, stock and barrel.[88]

According to the Report, it is not clear whether such peremptory international law has significance outside treaties.[89] In contrast to this hesitancy stands the opinion of the International Law Commission that "[i]t is not the form of a general rule of international law but the particular nature of the subject matter with which it deals that may... give it the character of *jus cogens*".[90] We submit that the latter view (certainly held by the majority of commentators) is correct. In any case, the U.S. Report follows it implicitly by undertaking a comparison of the conditions which have to be met for the formation of customary law on the one hand and of *jus cogens* on the other.[91] We have already dealt with the prerequisites of custom. With regard to peremptory rules, the emergence of such norms presupposes their acceptance and recognition by the international community of States as a whole as norms from which no derogation is permitted and which can be modified only by subsequent norms of general international law having the same character, to quote the definition used in Art. 53 of the Vienna Convention on the Law of Treaties. If we compare the interpretations given to the term 'international community of States as a whole' with the prerequisites for 'general practice' eventually leading to the formation of custom, we are safe in concluding that the threshold requirement for the emergence of *jus cogens*, namely the generality, or universality, of acceptance *and* recognition, is set at least as high as that necessary for the development of general (or universal) customary law.[92]

According to the Report, it is doubtful whether rules of *jus cogens* can ever meet this generality-of-practice criterion.[93] Settled practices of States as regards *jus cogens* are elusive to grasp, mainly because most, if not all, rules of *jus cogens* are prohibitive in substance; they are rules of abstention.[94] How does one marshal conclusive evidence of abstentions? Abstentions *per se* mean

88 See in general Schachter note 10 above, 339–342; Meron T, "On a Hierarchy of International Human Rights" (1986) 80 AJIL 1.

89 Note 70 above, 15.

90 (1966) 2 Yearbook of the International Law Commission 248.

91 Note 70 above, 15–16.

92 See Verdross and Simma note 12 above sec. 530.

93 Note 70 above, 16.

94 Ibid 17.

nothing; they become meaningful only when considered in the light of the intention motivating them. Consequently, fundamental importance must be attached to *opinio juris* when one considers a customary rule of abstention.[95] This of course is exactly what the International Court indicated in its *Nicaragua* judgment. In fact, as noted earlier, the Court went to the extreme in minimising the role of actual State conduct in regard to non-use of military force. As the Report correctly observes, the *Nicaragua* Court really had no other choice because if it had insisted on the criteria of State practice established in its own earlier jurisprudence, it would have been unable to sustain the rule.[96]

Indeed, the situation with regard to non-use of force bears a striking similarity to the position of States with respect to human rights. While principles of behavior are generally recognised and maintained, tangible State conduct frequently does not live up to these promises. Perhaps, as the Report suggests, the *Nicaragua* Case tells us that the general practice of States is simply irrelevant in regard to peremptory rules; only *opinio juris* matters.[97] But how is this assumption to be reconciled with the exigencies of customary law? According to the Report, the truth of the matter may very well be that *jus cogens* is not international custom as defined in the ICJ Statute at all. The customary law-making process may be unable to provide logical and sound devices to identify peremptory norms of abstention.[98] Such norms do not (and simply cannot) result from a gradual accretion of State practice eventually accepted as law. Rather, what we witness here is the express articulation of principles in the first instance, *ab initio* or progressively being "accepted and recognized" as binding and peremptory by the "international community of States as a whole". This process does not - or not yet - lead to the emergence of customary law but to the formation of "general principles of law recognized by civilized nations" in the sense of Article 38 of the ICJ Statute.

So much then for the Report of the American ILA Committee. Maybe it goes too far in denying in such categorical terms the possibility that *jus cogens* rules might emerge in the customary law mode. But still it seems that the Report's line of argument provides a more plausible explanation of how substantive human rights obligations may be established in general international law, than that offered by a strained, or even denaturated, "new" theory of custom. The value of the Report lies not so much in its originality of thought as in the convincing, clear and matter-of-fact way in which it reconciles the mainstream, positivist, theory of sources with earlier views expressed by international lawyers of the natural law school. To mention just two examples of such natural law recourse to general principles, Professor Verdross claimed as early as 1935 that general

---

95 Id.

96 Ibid 18.

97 Ibid 19.

98 Ibid 20.

principles could trump rules based on treaty or custom.[99] And, in his Dissenting Opinion to the 1966 *South West Africa* judgment, Judge Tanaka of Japan had no doubt that the law concerning the protection of human rights belonged to *jus cogens*, and that, "[a]s an interpretation of Article 38, paragraph 1(c), ... the concept of human rights and of their protection is included in the general principles mentioned in that Article", although, in his view, this provision did not require the consent of States as a condition of the recognition of general principles.[100]

In contrast to such natural law views, the recourse to general principles suggested here remains grounded in a consensualist conception of international law.[101] Consequently, what is required for the establishment of human rights obligations *qua* general principles is essentially the same kind of convincing evidence of general acceptance and recognition that Schachter asks for – and finds – in order to arrive at customary law.[102] However, this material is not equated with State practice but is rather seen as a variety of ways in which moral and humanitarian considerations find a more direct and spontaneous "expression in legal form".[103]

Turning from possible doctrinal views to the jurisprudence of the International Court of Justice and reviewing those judgments in which human rights issues have been addressed,[104] we see that the Court, too, has unambiguously accepted that the obligation to respect fundamental human rights is an obligation under general international law. However, in none of these cases does the Court expressly speak of customary international law in this regard. Indeed a close reading might even give rise to the impression that the Court has rather carefully avoided the use of this notion. Thus in the *Corfu Channel* Case the Court spoke of "obligations...based...on certain general and well-recognized

99 Verdross A, "Les principes généraux du droit dans la jurisprudence internationale", 52 *Recueil des Cours* 204–206 (1935 II).

100 ICJ Rep 1966, p4 at 298.

101 Cf. the line of reasoning in the U.S. Report (note 70 above) just described as well as Verdross and Simma (note 12 above). Note also the view that "[t]he obligation to respect human rights is a general principle of law recognised by all civilised nations". Bossuyt M, "The UN and Civil and Political Rights in Chile" (1978) 27 ICLQ 467.

102 See the text preceding note 48 above. See also the observation by Van Boven that: "[i]t is, in terms of human rights law, difficult to draw a dividing line between the concepts of customary law and of general principles of law. It would seem that they substantially overlap...". Van Boven TC, "Survey of the Positive International Law of Human Rights", in Vasak K and Alston P (eds), *The International Dimensions of Human Rights* p87 at 107, Vol 1 (1982). Van Boven's approach differs somewhat from that suggested herein by virtue of his characteristion of general principles as "fundamental or suprapositive norms which lie at the basis of the whole human society". Id.

103 To use the phrase coined by the International Court of Justice in the 1966 *South West Africa* judgment: ICJ Rep 1966, p4 at 34.

104 See in general Rodley NS, "Human Rights and Humanitarian Intervention: The Case Law of the World Court" (1989) 38 ICLQ 321.

principles", among them "elementary considerations of humanity".[105] In its advisory opinion on *Reservations to the Genocide Convention* the ICJ observed that "the principles underlying the Convention are principles which are recognized by civilized nations as binding on States, even without any conventional obligation".[106] We are all familiar with the distinction drawn in the *Barcelona Traction* judgment between mere bilateral obligations and the obligations of a State towards the international community as a whole. Such obligations *erga omnes* were seen as deriving, *inter alia*, "from the principles and rules concerning the basic rights of the human person".[107]

In the *Tehran Hostages* Case, the Court stated that "[w]rongfully to deprive human beings of their freedom and to subject them to physical constraint in conditions of hardship is in itself manifestly incompatible with the principles of the Charter of the United Nations, as well as with the fundamental principles enunciated in the Universal Declaration of Human Rights".[108] And finally, in its *Nicaragua* decision the International Court evaluated certain activities of the U.S. on the basis of "fundamental general principles of humanitarian law", referring to its *Corfu Channel* dictum.[109] The least one can deduce from this choice of words is that if another case involving human rights issues, perhaps even more centrally, was brought before the Hague Court tomorrow, the Court would adhere to the tendency described by acknowledging fundamental human rights prescriptions as binding and part of peremptory international law without going into details about their formal source, but rather stressing their inherent authority and universal recognition.

In any case, the jurisprudence of the International Court cannot be read as lending support to the customary-law-of-human rights school. The same is true of the jurisprudence generated by decisions of high-ranking domestic courts outside the U.S. in human rights matters. Thus, the German *Bundesverfassungsgericht*, in a decision rendered in 1977, considered a minimum standard of human rights to be part of "general international law",[110] while the *Bundesverwaltungsgericht* considered grave infringements of human rights, such as official torture, to be prohibited by "general principles of international law".[111] The Swiss *Bundesgericht* has viewed the prohibition of torture as a rule of *jus cogens*.[112] None of these decisions spoke of customary law in this regard.

---

105 ICJ Rep 1949, p4 at 22.

106 ICJ Rep 1951, p15 at 23.

107 ICJ Rep 1970, p3 at 32.

108 ICJ Rep 1980, p3 at 42.

109 ICJ Rep 1986, p14 at 113–114.

110 46 BVerfGE 342, 362; *semble* 60 BVerfGE 253, 303–304.

111 (1985) 45 *Zeitschrift für ausländisches öffentliches Recht und Völkerrecht* 88.

112 (1983) 39 *Annuaire suisse de droit international* 281–282.

8. Conclusion

To sum up then, the international protection of human rights has extended the scope of international law beyond hitherto accepted 'natural' boundaries. In the development of this new human rights law, international treaties certainly play the most obvious role and give rise to the least jurisprudential difficulties. However, in human rights as in any other branch of the law, participation in treaties is at the discretion of States, the substance of the relevant treaties is often unsatisfactory and sometimes there simply is no treaty around. Thus the need for additional sources of international human rights law.

The mainstream position, particularly in the United States, satisfies its appetite by resorting to a progressive, streamlined theory of customary law, more or less stripped of the traditional practice requirement, and through this dubious operation is able to find a customary law of human rights wherever it is needed. Against this tendency, we have sought first of all to ascertain on the basis of the human rights activities of States and international organisations those processes which may be considered as leading to the emergence of 'hard' customary law, conforming to traditional kinds of evidence. As the outcome of such processes we identified a general *droit de regard* in response to gross infringements of human rights and a correlative inroad into national sovereignty. As ways to ground substantive obligations to respect human rights in positive international law, we then sketched two approaches which are considered to be more acceptable under the premises of consensual international law-making. The first one arrives at general human rights obligations by treating the Universal Declaration of 1948 and the body of soft law following up and building upon it as an authoritative interpretation of the human rights provisions of the U.N. Charter. The second approach attempts to accommodate this very consensus within the triad of Article 38 of the ICJ Statute by regarding it as a "modern" method of articulating and accepting general principles of law. Admittedly, general principles have not fared too well as a source of international law, mainly due to their natural law flavour and the uncertainties surrounding the ways in which they are to be established and applied. But the acceptance of principles in the human rights field does not share this aleatory element: it is a decidedly *consensual* process, giving "a sufficient expression in legal form"[113] to the underlying humanitarian considerations. International law has grown to encompass the protection of the human person spontaneously rather than out of a habit; in the development of human rights law principles have always preceded practice. Finally, law-making through international acceptance of general principles appears to be much better suited than customary law to meeting the requirements for the formation of *jus cogens*.

Throughout this paper we have sought to follow a strictly consensualist line of argument. Whether human rights need such backing from State practice and

---

[113] Note 103 above.

consent in order to be valid[114] is a different question. Louis Henkin said it well in his 1989 General Course at the Hague Academy:

> [P]rinciples common to legal systems often reflect natural law principles that underlie international law. ... [I]f the law has not yet developed a concept to justify or explain how such general principles enter international law, resort to this secondary source seems another example of the triumph of good sense and practical needs over the limitations of concepts and other abstractions.[115]

---

114 See Koskenniemi note 25 above, pp 350–362 for an analysis of natural law elements in doctrine and ICJ jurisprudence on sources of international law.

115 Henkin L, "International Law: Politics, Values and Functions: General Course in Public International Law", 216 *Recueil des cours* 61–62 (1989–IV).

[2]

THE PULL OF THE MAINSTREAM

Martti Koskenniemi *

HUMAN RIGHTS AND HUMANITARIAN NORMS AS CUSTOMARY LAW. By *Theodor Meron.* Oxford: Clarendon Press. 1989. Pp. xi, 263. $55.

I

Ever since the Grotian tradition became little more than an object of ritualistic invocation in keynote speeches at conferences of learned societies, international lawyers have had difficulty accounting for rules of international law that do not emanate from the consent of the states against which they are applied. In fact, most modern lawyers have assumed that international law is not really binding unless it can be traced to an agreement or some other meeting of wills between two or more sovereign states. Once the idea of a natural law is discarded, it seems difficult to justify an obligation that is not voluntarily assumed.

Simultaneously, however, it has been evident that if international law consisted only of formalized meetings of will called treaties, it would not seem very important. Nor would it then contain many of those norms that most lawyers believe are crucial for the functioning of the present international system (such as sovereignty, nonintervention, etc.). A thoughtful commentator once noted: "[O]ne can have a very fair idea of international law without having read a single treaty: and . . . one cannot gain any very coherent idea of the essence of international law by reading treaties alone."[1]

The matter is particularly important in regard to norms intended to safeguard basic human rights and fundamental freedoms. If the only states bound to respect such rights and freedoms are the states that have formally become parties to the relevant instruments — and even then only within the scope of their often compromised wordings and multiple reservations — then many important political values would seem to lack adequate protection. It is inherently difficult to accept the notion that states are legally bound not to engage in genocide, for example, only if they have ratified and not formally denounced the 1948 Genocide Convention. Some norms seem so basic, so important, that it is more than slightly artificial to argue that states are legally bound to comply with them simply because there exists an

* Counsellor (legal affairs), Permanent Mission of Finland to the United Nations, and member of the Finnish Foreign Service since 1979. Diploma in Law 1983, Oxford University; Doctor of Laws 1989, Turku University, Finland. — Ed.

1. C. PARRY, THE SOURCES AND EVIDENCES OF INTERNATIONAL LAW 35 (1965).

agreement between them to that effect, rather than because, in the words of the International Court of Justice (ICJ), noncompliance would "shock[ ] the conscience of mankind"[2] and be contrary to "elementary considerations of humanity."[3]

Professor Theodor Meron's book, *Human Rights and Humanitarian Norms as Customary Law,* places itself squarely within this problem: To what extent are states bound by humanitarian or human rights norms regardless of treaties, by way of customary law? The subject, an important one, is situated in a theoretical mine field. Although it seems clear that not all international law can be based upon agreement, it seems much less clear what else, then, it may be founded upon. Basic questions arise about the legitimacy of applying norms that are based on something other than voluntarily concluded agreements. A Grotian lawyer would not, of course, perceive a great difficulty. He would simply say that some norms exist by force of natural reason or social necessity. Such an argument, however, is not open to a modern lawyer or court, much less an international court, established for the settlement of disputes between varying cultures, varying traditions, and varying conceptions of reason and justice. Such conceptions seem to be historically and contextually conditioned, so that imposing them on a nonconsenting state seems both political and unjustifiable as such.

It is, I believe, for this reason — the difficulty of justifying conceptions of natural justice in modern society — that lawyers have tended to relegate into "custom" all those important norms that cannot be supported by treaties. In this way, they might avoid arguing from an essentially naturalistic —and thus suspect — position. "Custom" may seem both less difficult to verify and more justifiable to apply than abstract maxims of international justice.

Besides treaty and custom, the Statute of the ICJ in paragraph 1 of article 38 (the provision usually held to contain the authoritative statement of the sources of international law) also lists the "general principles of law recognized by civilized nations" as well as, in a secondary fashion, teachings of publicists and judicial precedent.[4] At first blush,

2. Reservations to the Convention on the Preservation and Punishment of the Crime of Genocide, 1951 I.C.J. 15, 23 (Advisory Opinion of May 28).

3. Corfu Channel (U.K. v. Alb.), 1949 I.C.J. 4, 22 (Apr. 9).

4. Paragraph 1 of article 38 of the Statute of the International Court of Justice states:

> The Court, whose function is to decide in accordance with international law such disputes as are submitted to it, shall apply:
>
> (a) international conventions, whether general or particular, establishing rules expressly recognized by the contesting States;
>
> (b) international custom, as evidence of a general practice accepted as law;
>
> (c) the general principles of law recognized by civilized nations;
>
> (d) subject to the provisions of Article 59, judicial decisions and the teachings of the most highly qualified publicists of the various nations, as subsidiary means for the determination of rules of law.

STATUTE OF THE INTERNATIONAL COURT OF JUSTICE art. 38, para. 1.

the category of "general principles" would seem a suitable candidate for arguing about human rights or principles of humanitarian law. But the ICJ, for one, seems never to have made express reference to general principles. For most modern lawyers, and the World Court, international law consists, for all practical purposes, of only two sorts of norms: treaty norms and custom. All nonwritten norms — whatever their basis, character, or significance — are routinely treated as customary. As a result, as a judge at the ICJ has noted, much of what we tend to call custom "is not only *not* customary law: it does not even faintly resemble a customary law."[5]

Professor Meron follows this strategy. Although he accepts the category of "general principles" as a valid way to argue about human rights and humanitarian norms, he does not use this argumentative tack. Nor does he examine whether, or to what extent, such norms might be valid as natural law. His reason for so doing is clearly stated: he wishes to "utilize irreproachable legal methods" to enhance "the credibility of the norms" for which he argues (pp. 81, 246). The assumption here is that to argue in terms of general principles or natural justice is to engage in a political debate and to fall victim to bias and subjectivism. Following his rationalistic credo, Meron hopes to base human rights and humanitarian norms on something more tangible, something that jurists can look at through a distinct (objective, scientific) method and thus ground their conclusions in a more acceptable way — a way that would also better justify their application against nonconsenting states.

The starting point — hoping to argue nontreaty-based human rights and humanitarian norms as custom — however, does not fare too well in Professor Meron's careful analysis of pertinent case law and juristic opinion. He accepts the orthodox "two-element theory" of custom (*i.e.*, for custom to exist, there must be both material practice to that effect and the practice must have been motivated by a belief that it is required by law (p. 3)), yet case law contains little to actually support such a theory, although passages paying lip service to it are abundant. Thus, his analysis of the judgement by the ICJ in the *Nicaragua* case,[6] in which the Court inquired, *inter alia*, whether articles 1 and 3 common to all four of the Geneva Conventions of 1949 had "crystallized into" custom, concludes by noting the Court's "complete failure to inquire whether *opinio juris* and practice support the crystallization of articles 1 and 3 into customary law" (p. 36).

Meron's unwillingness to inquire into a nonwritten law which might not be "custom" in the sense of the two-element theory is sur-

5. Jennings, *The Identification of International Law*, in INTERNATIONAL LAW, TEACHING AND PRACTICE 3, 5 (B. Cheng ed. 1982).

6. Case Concerning Military and Paramilitary Activities in and Against Nicaragua (Nicar. v. U.S.), 1986 I.C.J. 14 (June 27).

prising. The results of his analysis of the pertinent ICJ practice would seem to compel him to abandon or at least completely revise the traditional view of custom. Should "custom" perhaps be thought of in terms of some deeper historical necessity, for example, as many nineteenth-century international jurists argued?[7] But no such radical revision is proposed. Meron's analysis complies with the orthodox approach — however much Meron is led to conclude that legal practice does not support it.

It often seems that Meron's analysis and criticism of the ICJ's method for "finding" customary law leaves little ground for Meron himself to stand on. Sometimes Meron notes that his own "preferred indicators" for determining when a human rights norm is to be valid as custom would be whether it is repeated in instruments and confirmed in national practice (in particular, in national laws) (pp. 93-94). Yet, there is no study of national laws in the book. In another place, Professor Meron stresses that "*Opinio Juris* is thus critical for the transformation of treaties into general law" (p. 53; footnote omitted), although he does not explain how courts might ascertain the presence of this "subjective element" without making presumptions on the basis of material practice. Yet, he also holds that the ICJ has made "only perfunctory and conclusory references to the practice of states" (p. 42) and he argues that only "limited significance" is given to the two elements and that the burden of proof for establishing custom in the human rights field is lighter than usual (p. 113). Sometimes he throws the orthodox theory completely overboard by concluding that, for important human rights norms, "[t]he 'ought' merges with the 'is' " (p. 42); that the "derivation of specific rules from general principles . . . is an important process in the development of customary humanitarian law" (p. 68); and that "the central source for the rules [for internal armed conflicts] will be the principles of humanity" (p. 74).

These results are clearly correct. And yet, they are also threatening by focusing attention away from "rigorous" tests of pedigree to uncertain and controversial moral principles. It is somewhat disappointing that so much analysis seemed necessary when the conclusion would have been available from a number of important studies on the practice of the ICJ and its predecessor.[8] It appears to be the case that the Court has "instituted a system of decision-making in which the legal conclusion reached is determined by the application of rules of

7. *See, e.g.*, Vinogradoff, *Historical Types of International Law*, in 1 BIBLIOTHECA VISSERIANA 1 (1923).

8. *See, e.g.*, C. JENKS, THE PROSPECTS OF INTERNATIONAL ADJUDICATION 264 (1964); M. SØRENSEN, LES SOURCES DU DROIT INTERNATIONAL 108-11 (1946); Haggenmacher, *La doctrine des deux éléments du droit coutumier dans la pratique de la cour internationale*, 90 REVUE GÉNÉRALE DE DROIT INTERNATIONAL PUBLIC 5 (1986); Virally, *The Sources of International Law*, in MANUAL OF PUBLIC INTERNATIONAL LAW 116, 133-35 (M. Sørensen ed. 1968).

law largely treated as self-evident."[9] Meron's book would have been a more important contribution to human rights law if, instead of arriving where most thoughtful scholars have arrived on the subject for the past forty years, it had attempted an analysis of what makes a norm binding even absent a basis in treaty, if not the practice and the *opinio.* But there is no analysis of the political right in the book, no "derivations" from general principles or from principles of humanity, and no attempt to take the Court's departures from orthodox custom seriously.

Although Meron does not analyze the various general theories of international custom (and no such analysis is really needed), he does review the arguments used by lawyers seeking to make treaty-based human rights norms binding on nonparties. The four principal argumentative strategies claim that a norm is binding for nonparties if (1) it can be deduced from the provisions — in particular articles 55 and 56 — of the United Nations Charter; (2) it is supported by a general (even if perhaps not unanimous) consensus; (3) it has become a "general principle of law" in the sense of article 38 of the Statute of the ICJ; or (4) it has been tacitly accepted by nonparties as well (pp. 81-106). Of these, Meron concentrates on the last two, which he thinks are the most likely to succeed.

The category of "general principles," it must be noted at the outset, does not signify for Professor Meron what is signified to the drafters of the ICJ Statute — particularly Baron Descamps.[10] General principles are not natural or even quasi-natural principles but generalizations from municipal jurisprudence (pp. 88-89). But one wonders whether this is really the secret of their apparent relevance. Given that it is practically impossible to collect representative data of such jurisprudence, and given that only a minority of countries apply a *stare decisis* system, the usefulness of this approach seems doubtful. For a continental lawyer — such as this author — using basically American and British cases to argue for general principles is a questionable strategy. It is true that analyzing American cases — as Meron has done — is a useful tool for illustrating the structure of typical argumentation in human rights as in other cases. But I would be very hesitant to imply that the arguments by U.S. courts in, for instance, the much-debated *Filartiga v. Peña-Irala*[11] and *Tel-Oren v. Libyan Arab Republic*[12] cases possess any formal authority in determining the obligations of other states. Perhaps this is not what Meron

9. Kearney, *Sources of Law and the International Court of Justice*, in 2 THE FUTURE OF THE INTERNATIONAL COURT OF JUSTICE 610, 653 (L. Gross ed. 1976).

10. *See* ADVISORY COMMITTEE OF JURISTS, PROCÈS-VERBAUX OF THE PROCEEDINGS OF THE COMMITTEE 293 (1920).

11. 630 F.2d 876 (2d Cir. 1980).

12. 726 F.2d 774 (D.C. Cir. 1984).

implies. Maybe he merely intends to show the typical (natural!) way in which the relevant norms (prohibition of torture and terrorism) are applicable. But, in that case, he should have considered those arguments on their merits, not merely described their use in U.S. courts. Yet the book contains no such discussion. One is left with the feeling that Meron's very discussion — informative though it is — is more intended to show American lawyers how to plead when pressing a human rights case in American courts than to reveal much about international law.

The other strategy recommended by Meron as an "effective means for expanding the universality of international human rights" (p. 89) — arguing on the basis of tacit acceptance ("acquiescence") — is a strategy much used in international litigation.[13] Using it for the purposes he intends, however, meets with the difficulties any consensualism is bound to confront. First, it contains the unpleasant implication that people have human rights only so far as actually accepted by states. It thus leaves the door open for a state to come up with evidence actually denying its intent to be bound by others' treaties. Second, and relating to the first point, it meets with difficulties of proof. If a state denies that it has consented to a human rights norm embedded in a treaty to which it has refrained from being a party, how can we justifiably claim to know which norms that state has consented to *better* than the state itself does? The very assumption that we could seems odd. It provides a justification for overruling a state's express report about its will — in this sense it is a Hobbesian argument which posits the arguer in the place of Leviathan. It also destroys the liberal justification for relying on consent — and the justification for basing social order on a popular vote — in the first place: Why do this if someone else (we) can know better?

In fact, arguing from tacit consent tends to be a camouflage for arguing from a conception of justice, most frequently from the principle that legitimate expectations should not be ignored. It is not really — despite appearances — a consensual argument at all.[14] This is the lesson of the judgment by the ICJ in the *Nuclear Tests* cases,[15] in which the court held France bound by certain statements made by its president and foreign minister despite other evidence that France never intended to assume a legally enforceable obligation. This result, however, is not a conclusion about someone's consent, but an extrapolation of what seems just or, as the Court here put it, in accordance

13. *Cf.* M. Koskenniemi, From Apology to Utopia: The Structure of International Legal Argument 284-341 (1989).

14. *Cf.* C. Pateman, The Problem of Political Obligation: A Critique of Liberal Theory 15-17, 81-98 (2d ed. 1985).

15. Nuclear Tests (N.Z. v. Fr.), 1974 I.C.J. 457 (Dec. 20); Nuclear Tests (Aus. v. Fr.), 1974 I.C.J. 253 (Dec. 20).

with the good faith principle.[16] Therefore, it is hardly consistent with the orthodox theory of customary law, nor, for that matter, with the assumptions of legal objectivity behind liberal legal theory.

Throughout the book one has the impression that whenever Meron states that some humanitarian or human rights principle is a part of customary law, the conclusion does not really follow from the arguments, but instead existed in Meron's head even as the arguments were chosen. This feeling is in no way diminished by the fact that he continually changes the types of arguments he puts forward to support his conclusions. Sometimes he relies quite openly on a shared intuition between the reader and himself. The feeling is, in other words, that Professor Meron has quite strong opinions about which norms should be included among those that are binding even beyond specific treaties,[17] and that he uses whichever arguments are available to support them.

This is intended less as a criticism than a point of reflection. Might it not be that the certainty we have of the illegality of genocide, or of torture, or of depriving ethnic wholes the right of self-determination, is *by itself sufficient reason* to include those norms in international law? What does it add to such certainty if we find, or do not find, a precedent, a state, or the United Nations General Assembly, saying the same? Very little, I feel.

My point is as follows: In his wish to look for "irreproachable legal methods" to argue for the validity of nontreaty norms, Professor Meron has tried to rely on the traditional two-element theory of custom — the material practice and the *opinio juris*. His hope was that these would provide a noncontroversial litmus test that would finally convince everyone of the certainty of his conclusions. As Meron himself shows, however, this test is in fact relatively useless. It is useless, first, because the interpretation of "state behavior" or "state will" is not an automatic operation but involves the choice and use of conceptual matrices that are controversial and that usually allow one to argue either way. But it is also, and more fundamentally, useless because we do not wish to condone anything that states may do or say, and because it is really our certainty that genocide or torture is illegal that allows us to understand state behavior and to accept or reject its legal message, not state behavior itself that allows us to understand that these practices are prohibited by law. It seems to me that if we are uncertain of the latter fact, then there is really little in this world we can feel confident about.

16. Nuclear Tests (Aus. v. Fr.), 1974 I.C.J. at 268.

17. Meron's list includes the prohibition of torture and racial discrimination, and the minimum guarantees for humane treatment found in article 3 of the Geneva Conventions. *See* pp. 46-47 (his list of customary standards in Geneva Convention No. IV); pp. 94-98 (his list of general human rights norms).

In other words, finding juristic evidence (a precedent, a habitual behavior, a legal doctrine) to support such a conclusion adds little or nothing to our reasons for adopting it. To the contrary, it contains the harmful implication that it is *only* because this evidence is available that we can justifiably reach our conclusion. It opens the door for disputing the conclusion by disputing the presence of the evidence, or for requiring the same evidence in support of some other equally compelling conclusion, when that evidence might not be so readily available.

It is, of course, true that people are uncertain about right and wrong. The past two hundred years since the Enlightenment and the victory of the principle of arbitrary value have done nothing to teach us about how to know these things or how to cope with our strong moral intuitions.[18] But one should not pretend that this uncertainty will vanish if only one is methodologically "rigorous." If the development of the human sciences has taught us anything during its short history, it is that the effort to replace our loss of faith in theories about the right and the good with an absolute faith in our ability to understand human life as a matter of social "facts" has been a failure. We remain just as unable to derive norms from the facts of state behavior as Hume was. And we are just as compelled to admit that everything we know about norms which are embedded in such behavior is conditioned by an anterior — though at least in some respects largely shared — criterion of what is right and good for human life.

II

There is little else to be said about Professor Meron's discussion in Parts I and II of the book dealing with the customary law character of humanitarian and human rights norms. The discussion is balanced and the conclusions are usually intuitively acceptable. They are not so, however, because Meron succeeds in showing how well they correspond to state practice, but because they, for the most part, appear reasonable and coincide with our moral imagination. For example, he discusses at length whether a provision in a treaty allowing reservations — or not allowing them — is relevant in determining the customary character of that provision. Meron concludes, correctly, that these facts may have some probative value although they remain unreliable as rules for determining whether the respective provision might be valid as custom (p. 24). The point I want to make here is that the contextual assessment that ascertains the customary character of a provision cannot be fitted within any rigid "method" for finding custom in every case. It is a practical matter (in the sense of being related to normative *praxis*) that requires making contested, political evalua-

18. *Cf.* A. MacIntyre, After Virtue: A Study of Moral Theory (2d ed. 1984).

tions. It is not a rule-determined activity but one which gives meaning to rules (namely rules concerning reservations, consent, and *jus cogens*) and which therefore remains external to them.

Meron also discusses the transformation of treaties into custom with particular reference to norms enshrined in the 1949 Geneva Conventions and the 1977 Additional Protocols. He considers, for example, whether practice by treaty parties constitutes relevant "practice," the effect of occasional deviations and possible reactions to them, and the scope of the relevant practice by nonparties. But his framing of the problem is notoriously problematic. A treaty may be evidence of custom (in the sense that it shows the importance of a norm to its parties) or evidence of the absence of custom (otherwise we must remain puzzled about the need to conclude the treaty in the first place).[19] Professor Meron is aware of these — and other — paradoxes, but his discussion does little more than lay them in the open. At a significant place in his argument, he contends that "[b]oth scholarly and judicial sources have shown reluctance to reject conventional norms whose content merits customary law status as candidates for that status . . . " (p. 57). This, he adds, "may reflect the strength of moral claims" for their application (p. 57). Again, this seems quite correct but is simultaneously puzzling if one remembers Meron's insistence on the "two-element" method. Again, one seems drawn into a contextual assessment of the political significance of the treaty.

Consider, for example Professor Meron's account of how the United States determined which of the rules in Protocol I to the Geneva Convention (which the United States has not ratified) had customary law character. The determination, it seems, was "guided both by considerations of [the United States'] own military interests and by policy and value judgments" (p. 68). Meron should take this as an affirmation that such factors do indeed play a role in this determination, yet he does not. At least he should list this finding among the state practices he uses to draw consequences from.

III

Lawyers — and international lawyers are no exception — often assume that the core of law consists of norms enforced by sanctions. There may even be some doubt about whether norms alone, without some regime for enforcing them, can properly be called legal norms at all. As is well known, this point is frequently asserted to deny the

19. Thus, in Libyan Am. Oil Co. v. Government of the Libyan Arab Republic, 20 INTL. LEGAL MATERIALS 1, 72-73 (1981), the Arbitrator regarded lump sum agreements whereby less than full compensation was paid as evidence of custom which did not provide for full compensation in nationalization cases. However, lump sum agreements were treated as conscious *departures from* a customary standard of full compensation by the Iran-United States Claims Tribunal in Sedco, Inc. v. National Iranian Oil Co., 25 INTL. LEGAL MATERIALS 629, 633 (1986).

"legal" character of intersovereign law.[20]

If international lawyers have had some trouble convincing critics about the legal character of their law in the absence of effective sanctions, they have experienced even more difficulty when arguing for the "hard law" character of international human rights norms. Therefore, the third, and longest, part of Professor Meron's book — discussing the international responsibility of states for violations of human rights standards — seems of paramount importance for human rights lawyers (pp. 136-245). If human rights are really connected with a regime of international accountability, then they might emerge from their association with "soft" ethico-political principles onto the level of hard law.

This part of Meron's book is divided into eleven sections, which deal with most of what are usually thought of as central issues in the international law of responsibility. Professor Meron discusses, *inter alia,* problems relating to attribution of responsibility (private acts/state responsibility), the application of the domestic remedies rule with respect to citizens and foreigners, the relevance of the problematic distinction between obligations of conduct and of result, the usefulness of the notion of obligations *erga omnes,* the distinction between international crimes and delicts, exceptions to the responsibility rule (state of necessity), and modalities for realizing responsibility (national vs. international enforcement).

Here, too, the discussion is balanced and methodologically "rigorous" and one finds little substantive disagreement with Meron's conclusions. He argues that international human rights norms are hard law, just as any other international norms, being connected with an identical accountability regime. The main problem here relates to Meron's admission that "[d]ue to the scarcity of practice . . . our discussion will frequently be largely theoretical" (p. 137). This admission detracts somewhat from Meron's wish to show that human rights norms are "hard law," enforceable — and actually enforced — by national and international courts and mechanisms. To speak of a regime may even seem somewhat grandiose in view of the virtual absence of relevant practice outside of specific treaties, such as the European Convention on Human Rights (1950) and its American counterpart (1970) as well as the International Covenant on Civil and Political Rights (1966). As Meron notes, a general regime exists nowhere apart from the drafts and reports of the International Law Commission, the United Nation's main body for the codification and progressive development of international law. These drafts and reports are not classifiable as custom by any classical test, yet, according to Meron, they still "give a useful indication of customary law" (p. 137). For all practical

20. *See, e.g.,* F. Hayek, The Road to Serfdom 173 (1950).

purposes, his discussion uses those materials as if they contained an authoritative statement of custom.

The International Law Commission (ILC) has discussed international responsibility for most of its forty-three-year existence. Its current project, begun in 1969, contains a repository of valuable materials on the matter. These materials can — and should — be used in any discussion concerning the law of responsibility. But the fact that the materials are only drafts and reports, that the project itself is far from finished, and that it is the subject of much academic as well as diplomatic controversy shows that one is moving here among a host of uncertainties.

This may explain why much, if not most, of Meron's discussion not dealing with the views of the ILC on particular matters concentrates on the application of human rights treaties by organs established in them. The lengthy, handbook-like section on "mapping recourse options" for addressing breaches (pp. 136-54) is almost exhaustively concerned with treaty-based remedies. These remedies are, of course, generally inapplicable to breaches of customary norms (unless the customary norm is included or interpreted into the respective instrument). In any case, the jurisdiction of the treaty bodies is based on the acceptance of their jurisdiction by the parties. Nevertheless, and despite any doctrinal problems this may involve, the practice of these bodies does have relevance for the interpretation and application of general human rights norms as well. To this extent, Professor Meron's approach seems justified. One would, perhaps, have only hoped for a discussion of the basis on which such generalizations are made — particularly in view of the recognized under-utilization of the treaty mechanisms for state complaints, which seems to indicate that pleading human rights cases is not "business as usual" among states.

Outside the practice of the European Convention, there are no cases in which a state has filed a complaint within a supervisory body under the relevant provisions of the political covenant, the racial discrimination convention (1966), or the torture convention (1984). The complete nonuse of the state complaint procedure in these treaties, and the virtually complete absence of practice concerning international accountability for human rights violations does make it problematic to argue that such accountability exists as matter of customary law — unless, of course, "custom" is understood as a modern code word for something politically compelling.

Meron's discussion of imputability follows closely the work of the ILC in this field. He accepts the Commission's conclusion that both authorized as well as unauthorized acts by state organs create responsibility (pp. 156-59). Though this is clearly correct as a matter of policy (it being otherwise virtually impossible to establish responsibility), it is doubtful whether many states will accept this conclusion — particularly because he also concludes that states are directly responsible for acts of even minor officials (pp. 158-60). The latter point is affirmed by a large jurisprudence concerning acquiescence or estoppel, for instance, in which the acts, statements, or silence by minor officials have sufficed to bind the state.[21] Indeed, were this otherwise, many of those whose rights are constantly violated by officials in the regular police force, for instance, would have no remedy. The combined conclusion — that states are responsible even for nonauthorized acts of minor officials — though evidently tempered by the exhaustion-of-local-remedies rule is perhaps inevitable if one wishes to have an effective accountability system for violations of human rights. Still, one wonders whether such a principle can in any near future become anything close to effective reality.

Meron shares the classical view that responsibility in relation to acts of private persons is connected to the state's duty of care (due diligence) (p. 171). Responsibility is triggered if the state failed to take preventive measures. What such measures might be is determined by a "reasonable person" standard and necessarily varies from case to case and probably also from country to country.[22] That there is something of a double standard favoring economically worse-off countries seems today quite clear.[23] The broad standard set down by the Inter-American Court of Human Rights in the *Velásquez-Rodríguez* case[24] is probably close to the customary one, as noted by Meron. However, it is uncertain to what extent the jurisprudence of the European Court can be argued to support a customary standard. Here the European Court has repeatedly noted that states that are parties to the European Convention must legislate to give effect to its provisions. It does not seem possible to draw the analogy that states should also legislate to give effect to the uncertain and varying customary standard of due diligence.

One might be prompted to ask, however, whether "due diligence" is a proper concept within which to grasp the evolving law of state responsibility at all. It bears a relationship to fault liability which is today widely criticized. The construction of the due care standard may often take place with little or no concern to whether state organs actually knew about a violation or had any chance of preventing it.

21. *See, e.g.*, Temple of Preah Vihear (Cambodia v. Thailand), 1962 I.C.J. 6, 25 (June 15); Cahier, *Le comportement des états comme source de droits et d'obligations*, in RECUEIL D'ÉTUDES DE DROIT INTERNATIONAL EN HOMMAGE À PAUL GUGGENHEIM 237 (1968).

22. *Cf. Affaire des biens Britanniques au Maroc Espagnol*, (U.K. v. Spain), 2 R. Intl. Arb. Awards 615, 644 (1925).

23. *See, e.g.*, Fitzmaurice, *The Future of Public International Law and of the International Legal System in the Circumstances of Today* in LIVRE DU CENTENAIRE 1873-1973: EVOLUTION ET PERSPECTIVES DU DROIT INTERNATIONAL 198, 232 (1973); G. DE LACHARRIÈRE, LA POLITIQUE JURIDIQUE EXTÉRIEURE 63 (1983).

24. Velásquez Rodríguez Case, 28 INTL. LEGAL MATERIALS 291 (Inter-American Court of Human Rights, July 29, 1988) (1989).

The presumption of knowledge, based on territorial control — as constructed by the ICJ in the *Corfu Channel* case,[25] for example — comes very close to an objective responsibility which is triggered by many considerations, among which subjective "fault" in some agent may be only a minor concern. As is clear to anyone having read the statements by state representatives at the Sixth Committee of the UN General Assembly when it undertakes its annual discussion of the ILC topic "Liability for Injurious Consequences of Acts not Prohibited by International Law" — a topic introduced in 1980 and discussed each autumn since — no-fault liability (notwithstanding terminology and the somewhat painful attempts to distinguish between "liability" and "responsibility" in international law) has never come close to receiving the consent of states. But consent, too, may be a relatively minor matter here.

In fact, Meron comes close to adopting this view in his discussion of the relationship of "obligations of means" and "obligations of result" (pp. 182-88). He concludes that most human rights obligations are, or can be conceived of as, obligations of result (pp. 184, 188). Clearly, for the reality of those obligations, this is the only acceptable conclusion — though many would not accept it.[26] But it also brings in a nonfault-related standard and it renders largely superfluous any inquiry into whether anyone has acted with due diligence. It may be in order not to impose a pure no-fault standard on states that Meron still contends that "[o]bligations of means and obligations of result do not compete with, but complement, one another" (p. 184). Such a "combination" might leave it open to argue in terms of due diligence after all, and thus escape from the consequence, so hard to accept by states, that they might be responsible for some act or event which they had no practical means of preventing.

There is virtually no discussion of the customary status or responsibility attached to economic, social, and cultural rights in the book. While one can appreciate the difficulties that such a discussion would create, reference to the problem might still have been appropriate, at least in the present context. It seems that a state's obligations relating to economic, social, and cultural rights — whatever their basis — cannot easily be construed in terms of obligations of result. As often observed, these rights are "programmatory" in some way that is difficult to define precisely but which clearly implies that the state has an obligation to act, instead of an obligation to achieve a result.

The discussion concerning the highly problematic conceptions of norms *erga omnes* brings in very little that would alleviate the intuitive feeling that what is at issue here is simply a political evaluation of the importance of some norms (or compliance with them) vis-à-vis others.

25. Corfu Channel (U.K. v. Alb.), 1949 I.C.J. 4, 18-22 (Apr. 9).

26. *See, e.g.*, P. Reuter, Droit international public 37 (5th ed. 1976).

(The same can be said of any attempt to distinguish between international crimes and other, "ordinary" offenses.) As Meron correctly notes (p. 210), the distinction, as it appears in ILC drafts, is based on the (naturalistic) assumption that such crimes could be distinguished by their content. This leaves us with very little in the event of inevitable disagreement about such content. Making a preference between two assumptions about the intrinsically heinous character of some act is inevitably a political choice. It is uncertain whether the results of that choice, if made, for instance, through a majority decision at the United Nations, would be very appealing to human rights lawyers.

Meron's discussion of *erga omnes* norms takes up the (highly inconclusive) practice of the International Court of Justice in this respect. He notes that the Court's distinction in the *Barcelona Traction* case,[27] between "basic rights of the human person" and "ordinary" human rights norms is both "conceptually difficult" and "politically contentious" (p. 192). Referring to the U.S. *Restatement of Foreign Relations Law*[28] as well as to draft article 5 of the Second Part of the ILC draft on state responsibility (p. 198) (which establishes the law of human rights as an "objective regime," extending the definition of "injured states" in cases of human rights violations to include all states), he concludes that all relevant human rights norms should be seen as norms which are valid *erga omnes* — *i.e.*, owed not to any particular state but to the international community as a whole. As a result, he asserts, such norms should be capable of being invoked by any state regardless of the usual jurisdictional rule that permits only a state against which or against whose national a violation has taken place to appear as plaintiff (pp. 196-99).

It is difficult to imagine another conclusion on this matter that would be more morally compelling and further removed from the realities of international life than this. It is, to say the least, quite impossible to justify such a view by reference to any international custom — if by "custom" one means something even remotely connected with an *opinio juris* plus generally conforming practice. States simply do not, in any manner which could be termed "customary," take up violations of human rights in other countries. Neither has judicial practice in any way formally overturned the dictum of the ICJ in the *South West Africa* cases, according to which *locus standi* is not constituted by the fact that all states have an interest in "humanitarian matters."[29] Though Meron does argue that "international practice" supports his conclusion (p. 199), he does not mention even one incident of state practice to this effect. The only "practice" he cites is the relevant ILC

27. Barcelona Traction (Belg. v. Spain), 1970 I.C.J. 4, 32 (Feb. 5).

28. RESTATEMENT (THIRD) OF THE FOREIGN RELATIONS LAW OF THE UNITED STATES § 703 (1987).

29. South West Africa Cases (Ethiopia v. South Africa), 1966 I.C.J. 4, 34 (July 18).

draft. Perhaps for this reason, Meron retreats somewhat from his conclusion by noting that "customary law" is "not yet settled" on whether the right to take up violations wherever and against whomever they might take place is restricted only to gross and systematic violations (p. 199). One is left wondering what type of evidence would go to settle the matter. Two facts seem pertinent. On the one hand, states do not grant each other the right to complain to judicial bodies about domestic human rights violations regardless of the nationality of the victims. On the other hand, they do make political protests every now and then, and these are made selectively, based on such factors as political alliances and controversies, inclinations of domestic audiences, and the like.

It would be difficult to accept that states could not criticize or take up in international organs the plight of people struggling against repeated human rights violations, regardless of considerations of nationality or geography. The practice of UN organs, for example, has witnessed a marked reduction in the use of the reservation of matters on "domestic jurisdiction" in article 2(7) of the UN Charter.[30] But it is one thing to note and applaud this development and another to argue that states have generally the *right* to ask for judicial determination of the conformity of a practice in some state with a customary standard of human rights. If there existed consensus about a basic customary standard, this suggestion would perhaps not seem too objectionable. In view of the extreme variations of political culture, and economic and technological capacity, however, as well as the range of plausible interpretations about the content and application of any potential basic standard, my fear is that such *actio popularis* would simply mean an attempt to enforce judicially a set of Western values. I have little doubt that strong ethico-political necessities require international lawyers, and others, to condemn oppressive social practices, wherever they might occur. Such practices should be taken into international fora, discussed there, and hopefully eliminated sooner rather than later. But I would hesitate to affirm a right of *actio popularis,* with all that this implies about the finality and enforcement of the judgment, the creation of a legal culture of pleading human rights in other countries, and other issues. Such an attempt at a shortcut to a world state would too easily become an apology for imperialism.

Similar problems arise in Professor Meron's discussion of the state of necessity and other causes for departing from the assumed customary standard. On the one hand, there exists some practice under the political covenant on this matter, but it is doubtful whether this practice may be generalized as customary. On the other hand, any acceptable conclusion should provide for a set of core rights — however they

30. For a detailed analysis, see M. RAJAN, THE EXPANDING JURISDICTION OF THE UNITED NATIONS (1982); M. RAJAN, UNITED NATIONS AND DOMESTIC JURISDICTION (1958).

are characterized — from which states may not derogate. What these latter norms might be raises the issue of *jus cogens,* a Latin code phrase for making the political distinction between important and less important rights. Meron does not discuss the problem of how (*i.e.*, by what "method") to recognize *jus cogens.* But the expressions he uses ("categorical rules," "decisive importance of certain norms and values" (pp. 221, 222)) are far removed from any assumption that these norms might be recognizable by the orthodox twin criterion of custom. The point is that this is a matter of political value: if you and I believe something is so important that it can in no circumstance be derogated, then surely this conviction *is* deeper and more forceful than any conviction about legal validity created by any formal test, and we will feel fully justified in enforcing it as law (if that is the sensible way to enforce it).

IV

Professor Meron's work is a solid piece of writing within the mainstream of international legal scholarship. He has taken up an issue which has surprisingly long been neglected by publicists, and he arrives at substantively consoling conclusions: Indeed, some human rights and humanitarian norms may be argued as custom; indeed, these norms may be linked with a regime of responsibility for violations of the respective rights. The conclusions in each specific problem area are just as unsurprising in their final vindication of liberal intuitions. Indeed, which rights are customary is less a matter of formal tests of legal validity than a deference to their ethico-political importance; indeed, "elementary considerations of humanity" and "basic rights of the human person" receive legal protection regardless of whether lawyers come up with any number of precedents to support them; indeed, the more shocking the violation, the more open is the law for allowing responsibility to be triggered. Would any other conclusion have been acceptable, or possible?

Throughout the book, Professor Meron stresses the importance of backing his conclusions with "irreproachable legal methods" (p. 81). He stresses the need for "greater analytical rigour on the part of human rights lawyers" (p. 247). His concern is, obviously, the relative exclusion of human rights specialists from the center of international legal debate — an exclusion grounded in what for the mainstream analytical jurists has appeared to be their uncritical enthusiasm over certain ethico-political principles of doubtful juristic value and their sloppiness in the face of orthodox rule-identification criteria.[31]

31. A similar concern has been expressed by some political theorists who have wished to develop a more analytical (*i.e.*, substantively empty) approach to current international human rights discourse. Especially relevant is J. DONNELLY, UNIVERSAL HUMAN RIGHTS IN THEORY AND PRACTICE (1989).

Clearly, Meron has succeeded in showing that human rights can be argued just as technically as maritime delimitation. One may ask, however, whether this is not in some way a mixed blessing. For it may be argued that the justifying rhetoric of the mainstream is in disarray: positivism is no longer credible, naturalism has long been a closed option, and the different policy-science approaches have, if taken seriously, failed to demonstrate what is specifically "legal in them," while their popular versions appear to be thinly disguised rhetoric aimed at furthering political interests. By becoming more mainstream, human rights lawyers may gain in academic or diplomatic prestige. But they will also face the danger of losing their critical teeth and finding themselves discussing analytic distinctions whose one social function is the legitimation of oppressive practices through the strategy of the exception: once you define a right, you delimit it. And once you delimit it, you offer a formally valid argument for someone to deny that right.

Here is a final paradox: late-modern legal, social, and linguistic theory has taught us that rules, whether extracted from behavior or texts, are of necessity indeterminate. Thinking of human rights in terms of legal rules will extend indeterminacy into those rights as well. The secularization of human rights rhetoric involved in its becoming mainstream, then, may not be the best way to protect human rights. By remaining in the periphery, in the field of largely subconscious, private, moral-religious experience that defies technical articulation, human rights may be more able to retain their constraining hold on the way most people, and by extension most states, behave.

[3]

SYMPOSIUM
Human Rights: Economic and Political Development in the Third World

Comparative Protection of Human Rights in Capitalist and Socialist Third World Countries

RICHARD FALK

Albert G. Milbank Professor of International Law and Practice and Director of the American participation in the World Order Models Project (WOMP). Author of numerous books and articles, he is currently working on a series of related essays dealing with human rights.

This article is a revised form of a paper presented at the 1978 Annual Meeting of the American Political Science Association. Revisions reflect the helpful comments of several friends and colleagues, especially those of Eqbal Ahmad and Michael Doyle.

In the economic policies of the government, one finds not only the explanation for its repressive crimes, but also a greater atrocity which punishes millions of human beings with carefully planned misery...
'Open Letter' by Rodolfo Walsh to the Argentinian junta

With colonialism gone, the separate states of Africa and Asia have moved in diverse directions. The states of Latin America, despite some notable differences in terms of formal status, ethnic identity of ruling elites, and resource endowments, share sufficiently their national challenge and international difficulties to deserve to be joined with the states of Africa and Asia in a single inquiry into "the Third World." Formal independence has not, in many of these instances, brought the blessings expected. New forms of external control and influence have emerged, both more subtle and, possibly, more disruptive, perceived collectively under the vague label of "neocolonialism." Perhaps more disturbing is the degree to which Third World peoples in this period celebrated for the collapse of colonialism have found themselves yoked to new forms of internal oppression, in some instances far more terrifying and comprehensive than anything they had experienced at the hands of foreign masters.

UNIVERSAL HUMAN RIGHTS, Vol. 1, No. 2, Apr-June 1979
0163-2647/79/0400-0003$5.00/0

Another source of disappointment was the American role in the decolonialization process. The United States, with its own war of independence and liberal tradition, might have exerted a benign influence on the transition to independence. Instead, geopolitics intruded to place the United States on the colonial side of the struggle, and afterwards, in the postcolonial settings of Asia and Africa and in Latin America, the United States engaged in interventionary diplomacy generally on behalf of authoritarian political solutions that were, in many instances, more inconsistent with the realization of human rights than other plausible options.

This trend toward oppressive rulership is evident in all parts of the Third World. Its perception is usually interpreted, by way of an ideological filter, as "socialist" (or "communist") or "capitalist." In both sets of cases the realities of oppression are evident, as is the characteristic tendency to enlarge the role of military influence and technique in the administration of power. Militarized politics is the most characteristic expression of oppressive rule in the Third World.

A focus on human rights represents an attempt to specify the standards of nonoppressive rule as an entitlement of all peoples, whatever their stage of development, cultural heritage, ideological persuasion, or resource base. In effect, the claims embodied in human rights take precedence over the prerogatives of state sovereignty, and acknowledge the oneness of the human family as a normative premise.

The developmental crunch in the Third World has generated a wide array of authoritarian political solutions. These solutions invariably violate prevailing conceptions of human rights, although to different degrees. The central argument of this essay is that the economic premises of authoritarian solutions are an important, although not necessarily in each instance a decisive, determinant of the degree of authoritarian severity. Socialism and capitalism, although each is manifest in a variety of forms, provide the ideological underpinnings for the principal choice between developmental options. Comparing the record of socialism and capitalism with respect to the protection of human rights seems like a useful way to consider whether there are any systemic regularities that flow from a given ideological orientation.

The choice of ideological labels raises some difficulties. It would be possible to categorize regimes by the simple "left"/"right" distinction. However, the ideological leanings of these regimes are better understood if directly identified with attitudes toward economic policy, the role of the market, of private enterprise, and of developmental priorities. Here, the affinities of Third World regimes are generally clearly drawn from "Marxist-Leninist" roots or from some adaptation of capitalism, although the latter orientation is not generally proclaimed as such. It is sometimes contended that the term "fascist" covers one or another form of authoritarian rule.[1] Some Third World governments that possess a capitalist attitude toward development disguise it for public relations

1. See A. James Gregor, *The Fascist Persuasion in Radical Politics* (Princeton University Press, 1974); Eqbal Ahmad refers to authoritarian/capitalist regimes as partaking of "developmental fascism"; for a useful review of the question of labeling see Herbert Feith, "Repressive-Developmentalist Regimes in Asia: The Search for Hope," World Order Models Project discussion paper, Poona, India, July 1978.

reasons beneath a socialist rhetoric. Some Western ideologues prefer to call these "left" regimes "communist" rather than "socialist." The issue of nomenclature should be faced in a rigorous fashion at some point, but it is not important for the analysis that follows here.

On balance, "socialism" and "capitalism" seem like the most convenient noninflammatory ways to emphasize the links between authoritarian and development choices in the Third World.

The position taken here is that there are distinct virtues and vices attributable to capitalism and socialism in the context of Third World countries. The relative importance of these virtues and vices is difficult to assess—how does one rate, for instance, the greater economic equity of socialist systems against the greater cultural openness of capitalist systems? There is no satisfactory way to objectify such analyses. I arrive at the uncomfortable conclusion that the human rights records of both socialism and capitalism are so poor in the Third World at this point that it is quite unconvincing to insist that one approach is generically preferable to the other. This conclusion is so uncomfortable because it seems clear that only socialism has the capacity to deal with mass poverty in the short run, and surely economic deprivation is a key element of human rights. However, the transition costs of moving to socialism have turned out to be so heavy, the absence of any tradition of checks and balances or pluralist politics and culture have made the administration of power in socialist states so totalitarian, and the effectiveness of control has been so great as to make popular control over a socialist state so difficult to exert that we cannot conclude, with confidence, that a given Third World society is better off "socialist." In effect, my position is that socialism *as applied* to date in the Third World deprives it of the moral advantage associated with socialism *as theory* or as an ideological perspective.

Surely, capitalism is not attractive, in general, from a human rights viewpoint for a Third World country. Its capital-intensive approach to development does not generally improve the relative or absolute poverty of the masses. The productive process, oriented around profits and foreign exchange earnings, tends to satisfy the cravings of the rich rather than the needs of the poor. In addition, when the masses are poor and excluded from the gains of the economy, as is the case in Third World capitalist economies (with some minor exceptions having special explanations), then a *structural* tendency to repress exists. There is no way to assure long-term stability in such a societal setting except by intimidating and repressing those who are victimized by it. Thus, while socialism cannot be preferred, given its record, capitalism is a recipe for doom, unless the country is exceptionally endowed with resources, including skills and leadership abilities, and even then, as the case of Iran illustrates, the results of a capitalist orientation may be national disaster.

In effect, from an ideological perspective, socialism is the preferred system for a Third World country, but its record in practice is too poor at present to support the preference. From the viewpoint of human rights the prescriptive challenge is to reconstruct socialist practice so as to achieve greater overall protection of human rights, or alternatively, to comprehend at the level of theory the consistent betrayal in practice of socialist ideals.

Even without the developmental crunch, we would expect to encounter widespread repression in the Third World. Indeed, the integration of society by the bureaucratic state is itself coercive to a degree. In the circumstances of many Third World countries, lacking a recent tradition of political competition, the mere structure of state power creates a strong disposition toward repression, especially given the diversity of antagonistic ethnic elements contained within many Third World state boundaries. And yet, the whole point of the socialism/capitalism debate is the contention that some forms of repression are better than others in terms of the stakes, as well as the identity and proportion of winners and losers. The deep structure of oppression is important to appreciate, if only to undergird an inquiry into reasonable expectations for human rights goals. Other structural explanations of repression will be mentioned, as well. "Intermediate" structural explanations place weight on the international system, making the propensity to repress at the state level a consequence of patterns of transnational domination (e.g. imperialism, neocolonialism) at the global level. Finally, manifest structural explanations of repression place weight on the pathological makeup of those who emerge as the primary leaders of a modern state, given the competitive struggle for dominance within political elites.

This article proceeds as follows. It considers, first, the structural explanations of repression associated with statism, and refers briefly to those associated with imperialism and personal pathology. Secondly, it seeks to put the Third World human rights situation in the context of the debate between socialism and capitalism. Thirdly, it tries to identify a conception of human rights that follows from this concern, as well as from a diagnosis of Third World priorities and trends. And fourthly, it briefly illustrates the distinctive patterns of human rights failure appropriately associated with socialism and capitalism.

DEEP STRUCTURE

Simone Weil notes "What is surprising is not that oppression should make its appearance only after higher forms of economy have been reached, but that it should always accompany them."[2] In particular, socialism and capitalism as the dominant modes by which "higher forms of economy" are organized have, in this most fundamental sense, been oppressive. As Weil argues in her essay, oppression is associated with the organization of any complex social order, both through its dependence on leadership and bureaucracy to administer an unequal division of labor and by its necessary sponsorship of a dynamic of power by which only a privileged few exert control over the masses, ultimately by reliance on armed might. In this regard, the crystallization of power in the coercive state assures the persistence of oppression in this fundamental sense, and seeks to endow oppression with legitimacy. As Stanley Diamond, Marvin Harris, and Simone Weil each contend, the only instances of nonoppressive social orders are primitive forms of social organization that do not depend upon

2. Simone Weil, "Analysis of Oppression," in George A. Panichas, ed., *The Simone Weil Reader* (David McKay Co., Inc., 1977), p. 131.

or lend themselves easily to coordination of effort and status differentiation. It is significant to note that there is virtually no support in the Third World for a destructuring of state power so as to achieve nonoppressive social orders. Gandhi's original vision of India after independence came closest, perhaps, and yet it never had much of a chance, given the overriding drive to build a modern state that could respond to domestic expectations of economic growth and modernization, as well as protect the autonomy of India against a hostile and unpredictable outside world. At this time, the deep structure of oppression is accepted by most advocates of human rights as an inevitable ingredient of modernism.

Marx clearly perceived the incompatibility between statist organization and liberation, as is evident in his celebrated prediction that the state would wither away in a communist society. However, the failure to address seriously or even to understand the tremendous resistances to the dissolution of the state in the socialist phase of societal evolution has restricted the usefulness of his deeper insight. There is an odd dichotomy in Marxist thought: in the distant postrevolutionary future we have a theory of the non-state; in the immediate postrevolutionary future we are saddled with a theory of the superstate, that is, with a legitimated dictatorship that is regarded as necessarily coercive, operates in a political vacuum, and so is not even ideologically insulated against its own intoxication with power. In country after country during this century, Marxism-Leninism in practice has led to systematic abuse of power, ossified in a variety of bureaucratic centralist governmental forms. In fairness, the ferocity of capitalist responses to socialist triumphs created an unanticipated priority for national security that inevitably hardened the state, and lent credibility to the preoccupation with internal and external enemies.

More modest than Marx, nineteenth-century liberal philosophers who set forth the creed that dominated the bourgeois state of northern Europe and North America were content with the notion of setting up a balance between different parts of government and between the state and its citizenry. Market mechanisms, as well as the sanctity of private property, were intended to create a private realm relatively secure against encroachment by government; the minimum state, rationalized by laissez-faire economics and morality, as well as by a skeptical account of human nature, was conceived to provide sufficient guidance and security for the polity without endangering the autonomy of its citizenry. Here again, however, the prescriptive vision gave way to social forces that have witnessed a steady accretion of state power as vast bureaucratic establishments have arisen, partly to assume the welfare tasks accepted by the political leadership of capitalist societies as the necessary alternative to a revolution from below. Built into the capitalist ethos is an acceptance of inequality, exploitation, and hierarchy, as well as the continuous struggle for power within and among states, necessitating a police system within the state and a war system within the global realm, realities consistent with the maintenance of oppressive structures at all levels of social intercourse.

Doing away with oppression in these fundamental senses seems tantamount to an insistence on doing away with capitalism and socialism as basic modes of social, economic, and political organization. Each of these ideological traditions is challenged on its grounds by antagonistic subtraditions that condemn the corruption of what exists in the name of capitalism and socialism as a betrayal of an underlying libertarian promise. Such libertarian critiques (ultra-individualism on the one side, anarchism on the other) call for revolutionary dissolutions of state power. These critiques are generally dismissed with scorn by mainstream opinion as lacking political credibility as well as lacking any capacity to keep order in the wider and complex social settings of the modern world. Nevertheless, the popular appeal of these radical countertraditions abides, especially in the affluent postindustrial sectors of world society, where it is increasingly understood that the reality of the modern state makes oppression inevitable.

In many African and Asian countries the challenge of state-building after formal independence unleashed dangerous ethnic antagonisms that had been bottled up or used as a divisive tactic during the colonial period. These antagonisms, combined with the drive of ruling groups to build strong states capable of standing on their own, helped produce an authoritarian "fix" in many countries. This "fix" was virtually inevitable in those states where one ethnic group captured all or most state power at the expense of others. Thus, even without the developmental crunch some strong reasons for the spread of authoritarian rule exist.

"Deep structure" also relates to the special overlapping claims of self-determination in which rival nationalities appear to seek exclusive, or at least dominant rights, within a given territorial state. The rival claims of Israeli and Palestinian self-determination, or of white and black claims in South Africa, illustrate this underlying structural situation. In such a situation, the dominant claimant must repress the subordinate or revisionist claimant so as to sustain the structure. The severity of repression reflects the actual and perceived relation of forces, as well as tactical judgments of elites as to the effects of differing techniques for exerting control. The structural basis of repression is reinforced by prevailing Hobbesian views of order that premise effectiveness on physical force and control. As a result, efforts at compromise are generally not made voluntarily, but only under pressures generated by violence. A closed loop of escalating violence is created by the action/reaction dynamics of antagonistic claimants, perhaps broken over time by exhaustion and disillusionment.

In the interim, the dominant elite is faced with a security dilemma. If it softens its approach, it makes itself feel (and quite become) more vulnerable to the destructive impulses of its rivals. If it remains hard, it unwittingly encourages its rivals to rely on brutal means and to seek total victory for itself. The structural quest for state sovereignty at the expense of an alien people seems inconsistent, at once, with either compromise or nonrepressive forms of political order.

In addition to "deep" structure there is an "intermediate" structure of transnational influences that tips the exercise of power at the state level in a repressive direction. The role of multinational corporations, arms sales and training programs, and covert operations all exert an antidemocratic interventionary influence. This feature of politics can be best understood in terms of "spheres of influence," "neocolonialism," and "imperialism," various names for patterns of domination by which rich and powerful elites in the North exert control over political life in the South. The direction of this influence is repressive in the sense that the external elites seek to maintain stability and to keep their dependable friends in power, as well as to assure access to resources, markets, and base rights. Only a dependent national elite or one isolated from nationalist consciousness would accept such an arrangement; its stability depends not so much on legitimacy as on its coercive capabilities to intimidate.

Finally, there is a structural bias toward repressive rule associated with leadership. The struggle to be primary leader in the intense political life of most Third World states seems to emphasize a commitment to nonmoderate forms of competition. The personality type that prevails in such competition tends to be acutely sensitive to the threat of displacement by others who might be equally unscrupulous. Hence, there is little toleration of oppositional activities or dissent. The leader may carry such intolerance to pathological extremes, but it is a pathology that is partially induced by the nature of the power chase in Third World polities.

These elements of deep structure are aggravated in the contemporary period by the character of military technology. The Third World, in particular, is victimized by the dangers of nuclear technology over which it has no control. Superpowers use space and oceans to establish their earth-girdling security systems, and expose the planet as a whole to enormous risks. Also, global patterns of industrialization result in disproportionate claims on energy and other earth resources by non–Third World societies. As well, dangerous environmental hazards result and are "exported" to Third World pollution sanctuaries or are "externalized" to inflict various degrees of harm on the planet as a whole. In addition, the shifting economics of productive enterprise is inducing shifts to more dangerous technologies (e.g., nuclear power). The Third World is a passive participant in the process of technological and lifestyle choice going on in the North and yet will suffer the consequences. To wit, repression as an international structure is real, even if not fully perceived.

At the same time, although deep structure conditions political prospects, it does not preclude certain forms of progress with regard to human rights.

IDEOLOGICAL AFFILIATIONS IN THE THIRD WORLD

The specific identity of a national political system can only be provisionally established by whether it is classified as "socialist" or "capitalist." Such labels may be more or less descriptive of actual patterns of organization and underlying approach to governance. Many governments in the Third World have evolved distinctive economic programs, allowing private economic initiative in some sectors, while reserving others for state ownership. Others have opted for hybrid ideological and political approaches. The declaration of Nigeria's Olusegun Obasanjo that "[n]o African country is about to embrace communism any more than we are willing to embrace capitalism" is also part of the picture.[3] Regardless of their internal development strategy most Third World

3. Quoted from the *Boston Globe*, 25 July 1978, p. 6.

governments seek to project an international image of nonalignment so as to safeguard their political independence and discourage meddling by the superpowers. Third World leaders of almost every persuasion are eager to avoid getting caught in the maelstroms of geopolitics; this preoccupation undoubtedly lay behind General Obasanjo's remark and, more widely, explains the widespread controversy in the Third World over Cuba's African presence, because whatever else, Cuba *is* aligned. Nevertheless, ideological orientation as capitalist or socialist does seem to have a significant bearing on the degree to which the economy and development strategy of a given society will accord priority to meeting the basic needs of its population as a whole. Despite the immense pressure from the United States, recent studies support the view that Cuba under Castro has done exceptionally well by needs criteria, even as compared to Mexico, and despite a host of other economic failures.[4]

We draw a fundamental distinction in this essay between doing away with repression and securing respect for human rights. Neither capitalism nor socialism is responsive to the fundamental challenge of the repressive state, but the enterprise of human rights is more modest, less ambitious in its goals, far less drastic in its diagnosis. The satisfaction of human rights claims does not purport to challenge the legitimacy of statist modes of organization, and in fact is endorsed by governments of all ideological persuasions. Therefore, human rights can, in principle, be realized in any state, whether rich or poor, whether organized along socialist or capitalist lines.[5] Recently, specialists in human rights, sensitive to ideological dualism in our world, have been striving to identify a set of core rights that reflect the professed values of both socialism and capitalism as operative global ideologies, and do give priority to what one, but not the other; ideology regards as important.[6] Such a search for what is mutually compatible does not mean identifying the lowest common denominator acceptable to both ideologies. As "human rights" were formulated initially as a dimension of liberal, capitalist ideology, what has been required is the elimination of those aspects of human rights that pertain *only* to capitalism (e.g., rights to property) while adding those rights that have been protected heretofore only in socialist conceptions (e.g., rights to basic human needs).

Against this background, a capitalist, liberal-democratic undertaking like that of Freedom House, which publishes its annual freedom map, is increasingly scorned as a tool for appraisal because of its ethnocentrism.[7] As Fouad Ajami persuasively argues, any approach to human rights that rates

4. For careful, well-documented comparison see Jorge Dominguez's contribution to the forthcoming 1980's volume on human rights, Jorge I. Dominguez, Nigel S. Rodley, Bryce Wood, and Richard A. Falk, eds., *Enhancing Global Human Rights* (New York: McGraw-Hill, The 1980's Project, 1979).
5. See Eric Lane, "Demanding Human Rights: A Change in World Legal Order," *Hofstra Law Review* 6, no. 2 (1978): 269–95; H. Lauterpacht, *International Law and Human Rights* (1950), on links between Westphalian system and the realization of human rights.
6. For discussion see Dominguez, *Enhancing Global Human Rights;* Fouad Ajami, "Human Rights and World Order Politics," Working Paper no. 4, World Order Models Project, 1978, pp. 1–33; Peter Berger, "Are Human Rights Universal?" *Commentary* 64, no. 3 (Sept. 1977), pp. 60–63.
7. See also careful categorization of forms of repression in Ernest Duff and John McCamant, *Violence and Repression in Latin America* (Free Press, 1976), esp. pp. 24–55.

South Africa higher than Cuba or Tanzania is not worth much. Even President Carter's approach to human rights widens the conception to give lip service to "vital needs" (food, shelter, health care, and education) as one of the three areas within which to assess the human rights record of a particular country.[8] Socialist orientations, then, have attained sufficient legitimacy that even the main capitalist country incorporates their principal tenet into its conception of human rights.

Not only must the conception of human rights be broadened to take account of socialist perspectives, it must also be deepened to include international structural issues. The attempts to achieve a new international economic order are part of the struggle for human rights in the present world setting. Even the notion of "basic needs" can be regressive unless associated with the international, collective expression of economic rights (for countries, as well as for the poor in countries) prefigured in the U.N. Charter of the Economic Rights and Duties of States. Surely part of the squeeze on Third World societies comes from "neocolonial" patterns, as well as from distortions of international economic relationships reflecting longer term differentials of power, wealth, prestige.

It is also increasingly unacceptable to overreact to the socialist critique of Western liberalism by going to the opposite extreme of associating human rights exclusively with basic needs or economic rights, conceived of as the material bases of minimum human existence. In the development debate going on in the Third World there was a widespread tendency some years ago to repudiate the political side of the human rights agenda as formal Western liberalism that is a dispensable political luxury for most Third World societies, and to claim that the only test of satisfactory government performance is a materialistic one. On the one side are the claims of official technocrats that growth measured in terms of GNP is what counts, and on the other side are the claims of disenfranchised intellectuals that satisfaction of basic needs is the proper measure. An extension of this argument contends that human rights in the noneconomic sense are limited in their applicability to the liberal democracies of the advanced industrial countries in the North. The argument is sometimes coupled with the assertion that Third World countries have always been authoritarian, that repression is virtually predetermined by political culture, or that conditions are not yet ripe for the introduction of more moderate governing strategies. The new leader of Bolivia, General Juan Pereda Asbún, announced that he would rule over "a Bolivian-style democracy in which the armed forces ratified the popular decisions." He justified this assertion by saying that a poor country, filled with illiterate peasants, could not "have the same kind of democracy as that experienced by industrialized countries."[9] Similarly, the Shah of Iran often said, in effect, that when the people of Iran began to act

8. Cyrus Vance, "Human Rights and Foreign Policy," *Department of State Bulletin*, vol. 76, 23 May 1977, pp. 505–08; see also manner in which country reports on human rights are organized—"Country Reports on Human Rights Practices," Report of State Department to Congress, 3 February 1978.
9. Quoted from the *New York Times*, 25 July 1978, p. A3.

like the people of Sweden, then he would begin to rule like the King of Sweden. In more recent years, as the severity of repression has increased throughout the Third World, the claim is increasingly accepted by Third World observers that nonmaterial issues relating to measures of repression are crucial to assessing a government's performance, and even its legitimacy. Now, oddly enough, it is only the capitalist exploiters who intimate the nonapplicability of noneconomic human rights criteria to their national situations.

The Cocoyoc Declaration of 1975, an important expression of recent Third World outlook, declares itself clearly:

> Development should not be limited to the satisfaction of basic needs. There are other needs, other goals, and other values. Development includes freedom of expression and impression, the right to give and receive ideas and stimulus. There is a deep social need to participate in shaping the basis of one's own existence, and to make some contribution to the fashioning of the world's future. Above all, development includes the right to work, by which we mean not simply having a job but finding self-realization in work, the right not to be alienated through production processes that use human beings simply as tools.[10]

Even China, originally exempt from criticism except from avid anti-communists, is being evaluated more recently by reference to human rights criteria additional to those associated with its programs to eradicate deep poverty and gross inequality.[11]

It would seem that socialism is *structurally* better adapted to the realization of fundamental human rights than is capitalism, especially in the setting of the Third World. In a world of resource and environmental constraint, of population pressures, and mass poverty amid rising material expectations and dissolving traditional bonds, the adoption of a socialist model of development appears to be a necessary precondition for the realization of human rights, although it is not of course sufficient. Without socialism there is no prospect of rapidly eliminating poverty, achieving relative economic equality, and imposing limited consumption on the rich. Capitalist models of development necessarily produce a privileged elite that appropriates a large proportion of the capital surplus not allocated for further development, and a substantial fraction of that elite may not even be resident in the country. Furthermore, socialist models tend to be based on national economic autonomy to a far greater extent than do capitalist models, as the roles of multinational corporations and international financial institutions are much smaller and more selective, if they exist at all. Especially in Third World country settings where securing the fruits of formal independence against outside encroachment invariably has the status of a fundamental human right of a collective character, a capitalist orientation seems disadvantageous.

Of course, in practice a given socialist Third World country (say, Cambodia) may compile a worse human rights record than a given capitalist country

10. For convenient text see *Development Dialogue*, no. 2 (1974): 88–96; note that rights affirmed here extend beyond what it is reasonable to achieve within the state system.
11. See for example Simon Leys, *Chinese Shadows* (Penguin, 1978); also Donald Zagoria, "China by Daylight," *Dissent* 22 (Spring 1975): 135–47; Susan Shirk, "Human Rights: What About China?" *Foreign Policy*, no. 29 (1977–78): 109–27; Jerome A. Cohen, "Human Rights in China: U.S. Should Press Issues, But Not As Barrier to Ties," *Washington Post*, 23 April 1978, p. D2.

(say, the Ivory Coast). One political scientist recently indicted "liberal journals like the *New York Times*" for spreading the view "that any group calling itself 'socialist' must be an improvement over the 'corrupt' Lon Nol, Souvanna Phouma, and Nguyen Van Thieu." In fact, Professor Lande contends: "How relatively benign they appear in retrospect.'"[12] Nevertheless, the structural argument (in both its national and international aspects) holds. A capitalist-oriented polity cannot begin to achieve human rights (as these will be formulated below) unless the country happens to be endowed with exceptional wealth relative to its population, and even then the record may well be deplorable (e.g., Iran, Singapore). Of course, there are those who dispute this structural argument. Daniel Patrick Moynihan, for instance, argues that capitalist Third World regimes "commit abominations in practice; the Communist countries commit abomination in principle." He goes on: "Anyone who cares about human rights will know what type of abomination is the more destructive of those rights.'"[13]

Mao Tse-tung in an important speech outlining an approach to democratic centralism argued that the problems facing the Chinese government arose from only that four to five percent of the population drawn from "landlords, rich peasants, counter-revolutionaries, bad elements, and anti-Communist rightists.'"[14] The rest of the Chinese population, Mao went on to contend, were on the side of socialism. Of course, socialist rulers have, in practice, alienated a far greater proportion of most socialist societies, although precisely how large a proportion is difficult to assess. Nevertheless, there is, I believe, a deep insight in Mao's assertion that bears on the relative capacity of socialist and capitalist polities to realize human rights in Third World countries. There seems to be little doubt that the domestic component of "the growth dividend" in capitalist Third World countries goes predominantly to the upper ten to twenty percent of the population (as well as to external elites), widening rich/poor gaps, and in most cases deteriorating the real income of the bottom forty percent at least for a period of some decades.[15] In effect, the mass of the population suffers from a capitalist orientation toward development. This orientation can no longer be successfully legitimated by resting the claim of the rich and powerful on some traditional ground of privilege (e.g., caste, vested property rights), or by invoking "trickle down," "expanded pie" imagery. Only repression works. It is functional for a capitalist Third World country, and it generally assumes an acute form because of the depth of poverty, as well as the high ratio of poor to rich in the overall stratification of the population. For this reason, the extent of coercive authority and its duration and severity do not seem as integral for a socialist approach as for a capitalist approach in a Third World country. However, as we shall note later on, the costs of the transition to socialism seem higher in practice than those of the persistence of a capitalist social order,

12. See Carl H. Lande, "Letter to the Editor," *New York Times*, 25 July 1978, p. A14.
13. D. P. Moynihan, "The Politics of Human Rights," *Commentary* 63, no. 4 (April 1977), p. 24.
14. Mao Tse-tung, "Talk at Enlarged Workers Conference of January 30, 1962," released and printed in *Peking Review*, no. 27 (7 July 1978): 13.
15. See for example Irma Adelman, "Development Economics: A Reassessment of Goals," *American Economic Review* 65 (1975): 302–09.

thereby offsetting to a significant extent the humanitarian structural advantage of socialism.

In essence, both socialism and capitalism will be repressive in most Third World contexts because of the developmental squeeze, requiring capital formation to persist under conditions of mass poverty combined with popular expectations of higher living standards. The distributional priorities of socialist states, as well as the absence of any need to produce "profits," make the squeeze, other factors being equal, both less severe and less exploitative. Again the appeal of a clean generalization gives way to some complicating realities. The capital squeeze in socialist Third World societies, although more equitably distributed in its effects, may be more severe than in capitalist societies because of the greater tendency toward self-reliance and the high priority attached to collective goals (e.g., heavy industry, defense capability).

And there is another factor. Capitalist Third World countries display a far lower capacity than do their socialist counterparts to provide jobs for their populations. The crisis of unemployment and underemployment, intensified by the introduction of profit-maximizing, discipline-minimizing capital-intensive technology, constitutes a pervasive failure on the part of capitalist Third World countries for which no relief is in sight. Even a country as relatively prosperous as Mexico now is able to provide jobs for only about half of the six hundred thousand Mexicans added each year to its work force, and this situation is not atypical for capitalist Third World countries.[16] The severity of the employment crisis is hidden to some extent by not counting the grossly underemployed (i.e., the person holding a superfluous part-time job at a tiny salary) in the ranks of the unemployed. If statistics were recalculated to count underemployed, the ranks of the unemployed in Third World capitalist countries would rise to levels between thirty and sixty percent.

There are some factors pointing in the opposite direction. Capitalist polities maintain certain realms of private freedom to a greater extent than do socialist polities. The ethos of the market, the class affinities of intellectuals and bureaucrats, the importance of sustaining ties to the liberal West all tend toward preserving, by and large, some space for cultural freedom and creativity in otherwise repressive Third World societies. Also, capitalist rulers have so far been somewhat less successful in stabilizing their repressive systems of rule than their socialist counterparts, making it easier to sustain some opposition patterns of behavior.

On balance, it still seems appropriate to argue that, except in very unusual domestic circumstances, socialism is a precondition for human rights in the Third World, whereas capitalism assures their massive denial. At the same time, in practice the shift to socialism may entail severe transition costs that outweigh its greater equity of operation once established, and its successful domination of political and cultural space may make it virtually impossible to overcome deformations of socialism once they occur in a given concrete instance.

16. See Philip Russell, "On Mexico," *New York Times*, 20 July 1978, p. 21.

The international dimension of the comparison is also relevant. International capitalism as a mode of organizing the dominant global market makes its own independent, significant contributions to authoritarianism. The role of the United States as the leading imperial actor in the world system uses coercive power to advance capitalist interests, which include biasing developmental patterns in a capitalist direction, by interventionary means if necessary.[17] The Soviet imperial role in Eastern Europe reveals an analogous control process, but the Soviet role in the Third World has, up to this point, been less widely detrimental to the pursuit of human rights than has the American role. This is partly a consequence of the historical circumstance which made the protection of investment, markets, and access to raw materials a vital vested interest for the capitalist West, as exemplified by American leadership, throughout the Third World, and a rallying point of Soviet opposition.

It is possible to draw some preliminary conclusions:

(1) human rights as a focus of normative concern do not extend their reach to the wider structures of repression allegedly inherent in state power or flowing from irreconcilable claims for security and self-determination, nor do they extend to the internal effects of imperialism or of authoritarian personality types to prevail in struggles for political leadership at the state level;

(2) human rights, as a set of limits on the exercise of state power, possess historical origins associated with Western liberal ideology, including the ethos of laissez-faire capitalism, and, as such, generate an appeal that is often suspect in the Third World, although decreasingly so;

(3) reformulations of human rights are seeking to achieve sufficient universality of tone and content to engender respect and legitimacy in all parts of the world, regardless of cultural heritage or ideological orientation;

(4) an acceptable reformulation of human rights in these universal terms will necessarily be eclectic, and will include a synthesis of the equity preoccupations of socialist systems with the liberty preoccupation of capitalist systems (note that capitalist Third World dictatorships tend to preserve some kind of private economic sphere for business enterprise);

(5) nevertheless, the ideological situation is not symmetrical in the Third World, as the objective conditions of mass poverty, aroused expectations, and resource constraints make the adoption of a socialist program of development a virtual necessity except in a few isolated "special cases" (Israel, Kuwait, Taiwan, Venezuela) where affluence or external capital accumulation makes it possible (although not assured) that both the material and nonmaterial elements of fundamental human rights could be realized; therefore, capitalist systems of development should be repudiated per se on human rights grounds, although their performance relative to each other can be assessed;

(6) furthermore, neocolonialist patterns associated with superpower diplomacy, multinational corporations, and international financial institutions reinforce repressive tendencies in Third World capitalist countries to a

17. See R. J. Barnet, *Intervention and Revolution*, rev. ed. (New American Library, 1972); F. Schurmann, *The Logic of World Power* (Pantheon, 1972).

significantly greater extent than do certain analogous international patterns associated with "socialist imperialism";

(7) no clear lines of normative preference can be persuasively drawn. On the domestic scene, transition and termination costs of socialist forms of development may seem, on balance, more severe for the population as a whole, than do the maintenance costs of capitalist forms; in the end, we are left with the requirement of assessing, at a given point in time, the foreseeable costs of alternative paths of development in the concrete circumstances of each country.

FUNDAMENTAL HUMAN RIGHTS

Having specified some ground rules, we can now clarify the content of human rights that will serve as the criteria for assessing the performance of particular governments. The most obvious starting point of inquiry is the substantial body of international law on the subject. Leaving aside the thorny question of whether and to what extent human rights norms are binding on various governments (including the extent to which the obligations imposed depend on expressions of formal sovereign consent), can we rely on the Universal Declaration of Human Rights (along with more detailed, specialized, and treaty-like instruments such as the International Covenants on Economic, Social, and Cultural Rights and on Civil and Political Rights) as an adequate description of what is to be encompassed by "human rights"? After all, the Universal Declaration is the product of intergovernmental negotiation, it has been widely endorsed and invoked as authoritative in all parts of the world, and it is an eclectic instrument that seems reasonably sensitive to the concerns of both socialist and capitalist systems. The same generalizations apply, to a lesser extent, to the subsequent international human rights treaties. There are several difficulties, however, with these "authoritative" formulations that rest on international law:

(1) the type of eclecticism embodied in the documents of international law includes whatever is *vital to either ideology* rather than what is *fundamental to both*; for instance, Article 17 of the Universal Declaration upholds the right of property, obviously inimical to socialist systems, whereas Article 23(1) affirms the right of everyone to work at a job of his or her choice, obviously inconsistent with the operational codes of capitalist systems;

(2) the rights endorsed include those that can be realized only through the dissolution of the coercive sovereign state and the abolition of the war system; for example, Article 28 of the Universal Declaration states: "Everyone is entitled to a social and international order in which the rights and freedoms set forth in this Declaration can be fully realized";

(3) the corpus of international human rights law is too diffuse in coverage to permit a focus on the most serious, pressing, or correctible violations;

(4) some important "fundamental" human rights are omitted, for example, rights to survival associated with ecological balance and threats to use weapons of mass destruction;

(5) the normative foundations of human rights are entrusted too exclusively to mechanisms of negotiability and implementation among governments of

sovereign states; the legitimacy of naturalist, communitarian, and populist assertions should also be incorporated into the basic conception;

(6) the ideological "bias" embodied in international human rights law is somewhat slanted toward the liberal ideas of capitalist society rather than toward the ideas and ideals of socialism, thereby reflecting the relevant weight of the two ideologies in the negotiating setting, and offers no proposals for rectifying the international economic order.

The Carter administration has proposed a more focused conception of human rights, loosely connected with the international legal norms mentioned above, but incorporating also features of a new global consensus that brings vital or basic needs explicitly into the orbit of human rights.[18] This conception of human rights was authoritatively set forth by the American Secretary of State, Cyrus Vance, in his 1977 Law Day address at the University of Georgia. Vance proposed the separation of human rights into three categories:

> First, there is the right to be free from governmental violation of the integrity of the person. Such violations include torture; cruel, inhuman, or degrading treatment or punishment; and arbitrary arrest or imprisonment. And they include denial of fair public trial and invasion of the home.
>
> Second, there is the right to the fulfillment of such vital needs as food, shelter, health care, and education. We recognize that the fulfillment of this right will depend, in part, upon the stage of a nation's economic development. But we also know that this right can be violated by a government's action or inaction—for example through corrupt official processes which divert resources to an elite at the expense of the needy or through indifference to the plight of the poor.
>
> Third, there is the right to enjoy civil and political liberties: freedom of thought, of religion, of assembly; freedom of speech; freedom of movement both within and outside one's own country; freedom to take part in government.[19]

As Vance observed, these rights "are all recognized" in the Universal Declaration, and yet his formulation of the American approach provides a selective focus. In actuality, the potential suspension of foreign military assistance is correlated with "gross violations of internationally recognized human rights" by legislative enactment. "Gross violations . . ." are defined as "torture or cruel, inhuman, or degrading treatment or punishment, prolonged detention without charges and trial, and other flagrant denial of the right to life, liberty, or security of the person." The Carter administration in 1977 actually reduced aid to only three (Argentina, Uruguay, and Ethiopia) of the fifty-seven countries found guilty of gross violations.[20] It is a selective approach, omitting any reference to the Article 23 affirmation of rights associated with work or the Article 27 affirmation of rights connected with cultural and scientific activity. It provides an appealing compromise between a comprehensive approach and an emphasis on a few items that capture popular imagination at the moment. The Carter administration has consistently employed Vance's categorization in discussing human rights and has organized its annual edition of country reports

18. For creative assessment see Lane, "Demanding Human Rights."
19. See Vance, "Human Rights and Foreign Policy," p. 505.
20. See Lane, "Demanding Human Rights," p. 270.

(as required by congressional legislation) around this conception. As a shorthand, considered from a purely intellectual point of view, this conception facilitates communication, understanding, and mobilization, and it aptly confines its goals to the human rights enterprise of reform within the state system.

Nevertheless, the Vance conception has disadvantages. First, its formulation by American officials limits its international authoritativeness, especially in certain sectors of world society where the United States is seen as a principal violator of human rights. Secondly, it leaves out of account, as does the Universal Declaration, critical rights pertaining to ecological balance and freedom from threats of mass destruction. Thirdly, the application of the Carter approach is slanted by anticommunist domestic pressures and by the overriding geopolitical rivalry with the Soviet Union. This impression is confirmed by the concrete application of the Carter approach; for instance, Carter instructed his representatives in international financial institutions last year to vote against loans to Cuba, Cambodia, Laos, Vietnam, Angola, Mozambique, and Uganda, and other "gross violators" of human rights.[21] Fourthly, the Carter approach, as would be expected, is statist in character, resting its claims of right on what governments do.

A quite different approach to human rights is staked out by the Universal Declaration of the Rights of Peoples, adopted in Algiers on July 4, 1976 (called hereafter "The Algiers Declaration"). This declaration was the outgrowth of efforts by the Lelio Basso Foundation for the Rights of People (an Italian private institute) working in cooperation with especially qualified individuals, in a large number of countries, including representatives of National Liberation Movements.[22] The Algiers Declaration affirms the positive activity of the U.N. General Assembly, singling out the Universal Declaration of Human Rights and the Charter on the Economic Rights and Duties of States. The Algiers preamble makes a partisan diagnosis, attributing central responsibility for the denial of human rights to "new forms of imperialism" that have emerged in the postcolonial period "to oppress and exploit the peoples of the world":

> Imperialism, using vicious methods, with the complicity of governments that it has itself often installed, continues to dominate a part of the world. Through direct or indirect intervention, through multinational enterprises, through the manipulation of corrupt local politicians, with the assistance of military regimes based on police repression, tortures and physical extermination of opponents, through a set of practices that has become known as neo-colonialism, imperialism extends its stranglehold over many countries.

And to make its position even clearer the preamble goes on:

> May all those who, throughout the world, are fighting the great battle, at times through armed struggle, for the freedom of all peoples, find in this Declaration the assurance of the legitimacy of their struggle.[23]

The operative provisions emphasize the rights of "peoples" as distinct from "individuals"; there is a greater stress on economic liberation and on cultural

21. *New York Times*, 30 July 1978, sec. 4, p. 4.
22. For discussion and evaluation of Algiers Declaration see Antonio Cassesse and Edmond Jouve, eds., *Pour un droit des peuples* (Paris: Berger-Levrault, 1978).
23. For convenient text see Universal Declaration of the Rights of Peoples, 4 July 1976 (Paris: François Maspero, 1977).

autonomy. In the background of the Algiers Declaration is a preoccupation with those transnational structures of domination (and their domestic collaborators) that preclude genuine political, economic, and cultural autonomy on a national level, and that have been identified above as "intermediate" structure. The Algiers Declaration is distinctive among human rights documents by the degree of emphasis it accords to international structural factors as explanatory of violations of human rights. Article 27 of the Algiers Declaration also declares that "[t]he gravest violations of the fundamental rights of peoples, especially of their right to existence, constitute international crimes for which their perpetrators shall carry personal penal liability." Rights of resistance against internal oppression are also affirmed, including the right "in the last resort" to use force as specified in Article 28. This emphasis on criminal accountability of repressive leaders and on rights of popular resistance is also distinctive in the human rights context.

The Algiers Declaration has several advantages over the Universal Declaration or the Carter approach. First, it extends the coverage of human rights from individuals to peoples and movements. Secondly, its diagnosis and prescriptions pointedly reflect the actual content of Third World concerns, and its promulgation at Algiers gives its existence a more genuine Third World flavor, which is appropriate given the preponderance of peoples and countries in the Third World and their minimal role in earlier formulations of human rights law. Thirdly, it posits a claim that rights can be authoritatively formulated by populist initiative and do not depend upon governmental actions. Fourthly, it assesses the landscape of repression and assigns primary responsibility to the interplay between neocolonialism and struggles for control internal to the Third World, thereby linking up denial of human rights with capitalist dynamics. Fifthly, it introduces ideas of popular rights of resistance and enforcement, and of criminal responsibility, into the corpus of human rights law.

The Algiers Declaration also has several disadvantages or, more aptly, limitations. First, it is incomplete without incorporation of the traditional corpus of human rights, and yet it never sufficiently clarifies its connections with it. Secondly, the legitimacy of a populist norm-generating procedure is highly controversial, and its claims are ignored or dismissed by most governments and many private groups. Thirdly, the content of analysis and prescription is unbalanced to the extent that it virtually overlooks abuses to the rights of peoples emanating from socialist origins. Fourthly, as with other approaches considered, it fails to depict rights relating to environment and to threats of mass extermination.[24] Fifthly, the auspices of the Algiers Declaration are relatively obscure, and funds at its disposal sparse, as compared to principal governments or even the United Nations, and therefore its position on human rights remains relatively unknown.

Various attempts have been made by individuals to focus the human rights struggle by proposing specific formulations. Moynihan, in the course of attacking Carter's approach to human rights for its tendency to avoid the central

24. Algiers Declaration should be read in conjunction with Delhi Declaration on Disarmament and Development, May 1978, also a populist Third World-oriented initiative.

ideological struggle, argues on behalf of an antitotalitarian focus, as the priority element in any adequate conception of human rights. Partisanship is the hallmark of Moynihan's approach, and he resents Carter's attempt to equate the pursuit of economic goals with antitotalitarian ones. Moynihan believes that the socialist countries, led by Soviet armed might, "are the most powerful opponents of liberty on earth," professing "the only major political doctrine that challenges human rights *in principle.*" For this reason, Moynihan believes that overriding attention should be given to the plight of the "billion-and-a-half" persons who "live in totalitarian Marxist states."[25] Moynihan regards the struggle against socialist forms of totalitarianism as being a matter of survival rather than moral preference: *"Human rights has nothing to do with our innocence or guilt as a civilization. It has to do with our survival."* He views the Vietnam defeat in this light, as a setback in the struggle to halt the expansion of totalitarianism: ". . it did not end the expansion of totalitarianism, nor yet the need to resist. If anything, it added enormously to the importance of ideological resistance, and this precisely is the role of 'Human Rights in Foreign Policy.' " For this reason, he connects the American response to the Third World with the willingness of specific governments to join in on the correct side of this struggle: *"The new nations must be made to understand that our commitment to them depends on their ceasing to be agents of the totalitarian attack on democracy."*[26]

Moynihan's approach, although substantively almost opposite from that taken in this paper, is notable in at least one respect. It links the conception of human rights to a value-oriented, explicit politics that is appropriately centered on the ideological tension between capitalism and socialism.

However, such a politicized approach has serious drawbacks. First of all, it chooses sides on a basis that is unconvincing, especially with respect to the well-being of Third World people; it overlooks the achievement of socialist societies in reducing dramatically the incidence of poverty and gross income disparities. Secondly, by mobilizing human rights constituencies around an avowedly anti-Soviet interpretation of the central global struggle, it tends to increase international tensions, thereby contributing to an arms race mentality and quite possibly increasing the risk of general warfare without doing anything appreciable to help human rights in the target societies. Thirdly, Moynihan's approach is completely insensitive about the degree to which American initiatives, direct and covert, have contributed to the rise of totalitarianism in the Third World, or about the seriousness of human rights violations at home, or elsewhere in the capitalist First World. Fourthly, this self-righteous, militantly anticommunist emphasis is extremely unpopular with public opinion in most parts of the world and, thereby, does not possess any capacity to mobilize wider international support for human rights concerns.

Another quite different approach has been advocated by Peter Berger. Berger argues strongly that much of the debate on human rights is flawed by its failure to draw a clear distinction between ethnocentric and "fundamental" human rights; only the latter are sufficiently legitimated by underlying cultural

25. Moynihan, "The Politics of Human Rights," p. 24.
26. Ibid., p. 25.

values to support an international stature. It is necessary, Berger argues, to reject those claims of right that owe their origins to Western values, and, in effect, to ignore even those rights incorporated in international legal instruments that cannot pass the test of cultural resonance. Therefore, Berger excludes from the fundamental category of human rights those associated with either "political democracy" or "economic rights," contending that these are distinctively Western. Berger restricts the scope of human rights as international claims to those "grossest cases" of abuse that infringe the minimal views of decency embodied in every major world cultural tradition:

> Genocide; the massacre of large numbers of innocent people by their own government or by alien conquerors; the deliberate abandonment of entire sections of a population to starvation; the systematic use of terror (including torture) as government policy; the expulsion of large numbers of people from their homes; enslavement through various forms of forced labor; the forced separation of families (including the taking away of children from their parents by actions of government); the deliberate desecration of religious symbols and persecution of those adhering to them; the destruction of institutions that embody ethnic identity.

According to Berger, "in condemning *these* as violations of human rights, we can call upon a consensus far wider than that of Western civilization. That consensus emerges from all the major world cultures—especially in their religious foundations."[27]

Peter Berger's approach has several attractions. First, it anchors the international affirmation of human rights in a universal consensus that allegedly has identifiable indigenous roots in each principal world culture. Secondly, rooting human rights in values rather than norms premises the basis for collective international action on more promising grounds when it comes to mobilizing genuine support. Thirdly, the concreteness of Berger's list of specific abuses has a mobilizing potential that the more abstract designations each lack, and yet it appears to lack the partisanship that mars Moynihan's approach.

Berger's approach is not, however, on balance, very appealing. First, by placing an overriding emphasis on tradition-based cultural values, Berger's "consensus" seems to reject critical elements of an operational consensus emergent in the Third World outlook, especially its emphasis on basic needs, on economic rights and duties of states, and on the campaign against apartheid; as a consequence, contrary to what Berger claims, his approach *appears* to stress only those concerns that currently agitate the West, and possesses the very partisan character it is so preoccupied with avoiding. Secondly, the Berger list omits some critical universal dangers, including those associated with threats of mass destruction and ecological decay, that seem important to include in a contemporary conception of human rights, regardless of whether they pass the cultural resonance test. Thirdly, the Berger list of fundamental human rights makes no assessment of responsibility as between socialism and capitalism for their abridgement, purporting to rest human rights on a basis that transcends this central, ideological fissure, and therefore deprives the domain of human rights of a principal moral and political rationale; in this regard, cultural con-

27. Berger, "Are Human Rights Universal?", p. 62; note that Carter's middle category of "vital needs" is not embraced by Berger's notion of "grossest cases."

sensus as the central tenet of legitimated human rights is insensitive to their potential role on behalf of reformist claims in the international political system. Fourthly, Berger's approach overlooks international factors (e.g., "neocolonialism," interventionary diplomacy) that cause, or at least reinforce, various repressive tendencies, and therefore avoids making structural prescriptions as human rights correctives.

A quite different attempt at a human rights focus is that of Fouad Ajami. He orients his analysis toward the debate about human rights initiated by Carter's approach. He contends that "flawed concepts of human rights" allow the United States to be a human rights champion while at the same time opposing "the New International Economic Order and Third World demands for a fairer distribution of global wealth."[28] Ajami also criticizes Third World leaders who ". . . speak the language of egalitarianism abroad, while they defend systems of acute inequalities within their own boundaries." He regards militarized politics at home as almost invariably leading to severe denials of humane politics, a characterization, he contends, that holds for " 'leftist' Ethiopian soldiers as well as for 'rightist' Brazilian officers."[29] In the spirit of the Algiers Declaration, yet with less partisanship, Ajami's approach to human rights seeks to attribute responsibility for their decline to an interlocked series of domestic and international factors. As a consequence, the political roots of repressive rule give direction to Ajami's views as to what needs to be done.

Perhaps the most original, challenging feature of Ajami's approach is to place emphasis on the link between the war system and human rights. He argues that matters of survival (rather than liberty, or even equity) provide the "domain" within which "the fate of human rights will be determined"; "the nexus of the war system and technology is our principal trap." Against this background Ajami affirms an eclectic conception of human rights that seeks to encompass principal sensitivities involving liberty, equity, and survival without enumerating a long shopping list of human rights issues. Ajami emphasizes four sets of concerns that embody "the maximum feasible consensus at this time":

1. The right to survive; hence the concern with the war system and nuclear weaponry.
2. The right not to be subjected to torture.
3. The condemnation of apartheid; it is accepted that other societies violate racial equality but that South Africa's blatant, officially sanctioned and codified racism is particularly intolerable.
4. The right to food.[30]

The Ajami approach is attractive for several reasons. First, it is encompassing and universalistic, yet focused. Secondly, it is sensitive to the main areas of perceived abuse and danger. Thirdly, it stakes out a progressive position, and

28. See Ajami, "Human Rights and World Order Politics," p. 8.
29. Ibid., pp. 16, 21 respectively; cf. David H. Bayley's more agnostic view of the military in power in *Public Liberties in the New States* (Rand McNally, 1964), p. 3.
30. See Ajami, "Human Rights and World Order Politics," pp. 25, 28–29 respectively.

yet criticizes all sectors of international society without seeking refuge in legalism or moralism. Fourthly, it regards militarization, nuclear weaponry, and threats of mass destruction as core human rights issues. Fifthly, it formulates human rights issues in language that can be translated into political action and goals.

Although I find these positive features generally persuasive, a few reservations about the Ajami approach do exist. Firstly, there is no effort to ground its proposals in the Universal Declaration and other legitimating instruments, although this could easily be done. Secondly, the approach does not focus directly on the link between neocolonial features of the international system and national development impacts on the national level, although the stress on the New International Economic Order (NIEO) could be so interpreted. Thirdly, it doesn't relate the struggle between capitalist and socialist models of development to the prospects for human rights, especially in relation to the rapid alleviation of mass misery in the poor societies of the Third World. Fourthly, its short list of four human rights goals places an emphasis too insufficient on restraining state power to allow it to have a wide appeal at this time.

Jorge Dominguez has attempted to combine the focus of a short list with the coverage of a comprehensive conception. He grounds the content of human rights in the norms of the Universal Declaration on Human Rights, yet he offers an orientation that identifies the most serious violations: "At the top of the hierarchy I would place concern for any identifiable government action that reduces a people's right to life and health. Attention would be focused not only on political massacres, arbitrary action by governments, but also on governments whose identifiable actions aggravate famines and epidemics."[31] The Dominguez image of priority rights is much less crystallized than is the Ajami short list; as such, it leaves more room for interpretative differences. It does encourage an observer to concentrate on specific accomplishments and failures in a given country and, as such, is far more amenable to social science observations or to acceptance by human rights nongovernmental organizations than is the Ajami list. Ajami's list, on the other hand, is more useful for mobilizing change-oriented constituencies, as it is much more responsive to political agendas that dominate international policy-making arenas.

My purpose is intermediate between those of Dominguez and Ajami. I seek a theoretically sound framework for comparison, yet one that yields an understanding that can relate easily to policy debates. At the core of my approach, as has been outlined above, is the conviction that socialism and capitalism are the fundamental approaches to Third World actualities, and that these actualities center on choices of developmental strategy. In the background of developmental choices are some wider issues of world order that also should be brought into the human rights framework, including those relating to cultural autonomy, the war system, and overburdening of the environment.

The content of human rights is obviously controversial. My proposal of five categories draws inspiration from the approaches discussed here. It does not restrict its image of human rights to norms legitimated by intergovernmental

31. See Dominguez, *Enhancing Global Human Rights*.

consent or, even, by United Nations consensus. Populist initiatives (e.g., Algiers Declarations) can also achieve legitimacy. To focus inquiry, reflection, and policy recommendation, five categories of rights are set forth as a proposal to delimit the subject matter of human rights:

1. *Basic human needs:* the rights of individuals and groups to food, housing, health, and education; the duty of governments to satisfy these rights, taking into account resource constraints and natural disasters (e.g., drought, flood);

2. *Basic decencies:* the rights of individuals and groups to be protected against genocide, torture, arbitrary arrest, detention, and execution, or their threat; the duty of peoples and governments and their officials to establish an atmosphere wherein these rights can be securely realized, including the protection of the society against paragovernmental violence of various kinds (e.g., "death squads"), taking into account constraints on governmental capabilities and the threats and tactics relied upon by enemies of the state;

3. *Participatory rights:* the rights of individuals and groups to participate in the processes that control their lives, including choice of political leadership, of job, of place of residence, of cultural activity and orientation; the duty of peoples and governments to uphold these rights in ways that provide individuals and groups with opportunities to lead meaningful lives, including the freedom to participate in procedures for the shaping and execution of norms;

4. *Security rights:* the rights of individuals and groups (including those of unborn generations) to be reasonably secure about their prospects of minimal physical well-being and survival; the duty of governments and peoples to uphold this right by working to achieve sustainable forms of national and ecological security;

5. *Humane governance:* the rights of individuals and groups to live in societies and a world that realizes the rights depicted in 1–4; the duty of individuals, groups, governments, and institutions to work toward this end.

Categories 1–3 are fairly standard. Category 4 speaks to the special circumstances created by nuclear weaponry and other military technology, as well as to the situation created by the scale and character of global industrialization; these concerns are mainly a consequence of what has taken place in non–Third World sectors of world society, yet its effects on the Third World are potentially massive. Category 5 is a kind of world order imperative that implies an inability to achieve human rights in 1–4 without transforming the political order that now exists; as such, it extends the boundaries of human rights beyond those set by the state system with its operative code of sovereignty that limits attention to carefully depicted national territorial limits.

This approach does not purport to achieve a rigorous conception of what is a "right," how "rights" inhere in unborn individuals or in relation to protection from policies that risk nuclear war or environmental harm. A theory of right that rests upon the emerging reality of planetary citizenship needs to be developed as an intellectual foundation for the approach advocated here.

Such an approach loses the specificity of a more legally grounded conception of human rights that assesses whether a claim is a right by whether it is potentially justiciable according to some constituted judicial or administrative procedure. The broader approach is less directed at issues of enforceability than of appraisal, the standards relevant for assessment of how far a given polity realizes the elements, as set forth, of humane governance.

It is also important, especially given the focus of socialism versus capitalism, to have some way of capturing phases of the cycle of political development. To simplify matters, three phases seem crucial: initiation, maintenance, and termination. These phases direct attention at essential aspects of ideologically diverse developmental experiences:

1. *Initiation Phase:* the inception of a political system as socialist or capitalist, and its secure establishment as the stable, dominant order. Here, in general, the initiation costs tend to vary with the degree of societal discontinuity, as well as with the relation of internal forces. Capitalist developmental forms are more continuous with colonialist or dependent status than are socialist forms. Soviet and Chinese initiation costs entailed millions of casualties. The initiation phase may also include a period of civil strife that can involve great suffering and loss of life. The Indochina War, carried on against the French, and then against the Americans, should be understood, in part, as a struggle between socialist and capitalist developmental orientations. Outside capitalist forces greatly magnified the transition costs to socialism in Indochina.

At the same time, the initiation costs in Cambodia, relatively more severe than in either Vietnam or Laos, suggest that factors other than ideological orientation broadly conceived can be significant. The prevailing attitude about the construction of socialism in the aftermath of a devastating internal war is a significant variable in the initiation phase. The behavior of outsiders, especially their adherence to norms of nonintervention, is likely to exert a strong influence on the construction of human rights in the initiation phase. Also significant is the "openness" of the society, its readiness to engage in diplomatic, economic, and cultural contacts with outsiders across ideological battlelines. In this regard, Vietnam seems particularly "open," possibly because it seeks to avoid being squeezed between rival socialist superpowers.

If capitalist developmental forms are reestablished, even after interludes of "soft" socialism, as in Indonesia (1965) or Chile (1973), the initiation costs are also likely to be quite severe, suggesting that the degree of discontinuity may be more telling than ideological identity.

Initiation costs are sometimes minimized by allowing "enemies" to emigrate, especially if their destination is distant. However, if exile communities continue an armed opposition, under the protective cover of a foreign state, then the initiation costs can be high and the phase extended for a longer period. Cuba experienced this pattern, being confronted by enemy exiles given encouragement, protection, resources, military training and equipment, and a political presence by a hostile neighboring superpower, the United States. Naturally, such a climate hardened internal security requirements in Cuba, and may have helped generate an internal security apparatus that would otherwise have evolved differently and played a lesser role. Also, we must assume that the extent of Stalinization of Cuban socialism reflected to some degree the extent of the Soviet presence, which was itself largely a reaction against American anti-socialist hostility.

Thus, we can say that socialist orientations are generally more discontinuous with the socioeconomic structure of a given country, and hence most likely to stimulate an all-or-nothing struggle. This discontinuity is reinforced by the greater tendency for foreign capitalist states, especially the United States, to support the internal capitalist faction by funds, arms, and advice. As a consequence, heavy start-up or initiation costs are associated with the transition to socialism, although most of these costs may be incurred during the armed struggle phase which included an anticolonial rationale. Once socialism is established, then the reestablishment of capitalism will also tend to induce heavy costs during its initiation phase.

Comparing initiation costs of the new order with the maintenance costs associated with the old one is difficult. One observer, for instance, reports thirty thousand deaths in connection with the initiation costs of the Ethiopian socialist regime as of mid-1977, whereas maintenance costs for its predecessor included two hundred thousand victims of the 1972 famine, many of whom might have survived if the ruling elite at the time had acknowledged and competently responded to the problem.[32]

2. *Maintenance Phase:* the maintenance of a stable socialist or capitalist order after it has secured control over the apparatus of state power. Here, no issue of discontinuity is present, although a given political form, whether socialist or capitalist, evolves along a broadly varied path. In this regard, even ultra-stable political systems are experimental, especially in their efforts to generate satisfactory economic policy. Also, political elites factionalize and struggle, at least within limits, for dominance, especially at times of economic crisis and of leadership succession.

In general, after the initiation phase, socialist systems seem stable in the maintenance phase. The programmatic commitments to equity and the elimination of poverty, as well as the capacity to find jobs for virtually everyone and to orient productive output around needs, lead to a condition of mass acquiescence (or subservience). Extreme self-reliance (Cambodia during famine, China after earthquake) suggests that socialist governments may not acknowledge disasters even sufficiently to receive outside help that could mitigate the suffering.

Capitalist maintenance is more problematic. The capitalist approach necessarily slights the well-being of the masses and runs contrary to the Marxist economic and ethical consensus dominant among intellectuals and students in the Third World. Because capitalism emerged often with the help and support of "liberal" Western outlooks, extreme repression was not undertaken, meaning that an opposition persists, and is likely to grow, in the maintenance stage. For these reasons, governments like those in South Korea, Iran, and the Philippines have to sustain high levels of active repression throughout the course of their existence. The class politics of capitalist development means that the masses must be kept actively disorganized and their leaders intimidated.

At the same time, the pluralist character of a capitalist system, with its

32. An observer, "Revolution in Ethiopia," *Monthly Review* 29, no. 3 (July/August 1977): 46–60.

private business and cultural sphere, its nominal consumer and intellectual diversity, makes it easier for an opposition to stay alive and flourish. The totalness of socialist control makes it less necessary to repress, yet the control itself is a form of repression. Cuba and Yugoslavia have shown some limited capacity, especially at certain stages, to combine cultural pluralism with a socialist approach to development.

In general, socialism seems to do better in the maintenance phase with economic rights and with those human rights concerned with the avoidance of extreme abuse of the person, while capitalism seems to do better with respect to preserving some cultural and political space for oppositional tendencies and general creativity.

3. *Termination Phase:* the period during which a political system is discarded and replaced by another. The termination phase is analogous to the initiation phase, calling attention to the dynamics of a transition. Whereas "initiation" is located in time as postcolonial (or post-1945), "termination" is viewed as a subsequent phenomenon in which socialism replaces capitalism or vice versa. Also, initiation refers to the birth process, once a particular elite is established in power, while termination refers to the death throes of a particular system.

The essence of termination is the process of getting rid of an abusive or weak regime. We assume that withdrawal of popular consent, via electoral politics, is rarely sufficient, especially in the case of a socialist governing elite. Experience suggests that it is virtually impossible to get rid of socialist regimes once they have managed to get into the maintenance phase and have adopted a "hard" orientation toward the retention of state power. Outside intervention, as in Iran (1953) or Guatemala (1954) can topple a "soft" socialist or socialist-inclined government rather easily.

By contrast, "soft" capitalist governments cannot survive, and have been steadily superseded by harder ones. The evolution of capitalist governance in South Korea, the Philippines, and Iran is exemplary. With the elaboration of bureaucratic structure, internal security systems, and a militarized form of politics, the "hard" capitalist regimes are also becoming very difficult to terminate, even when exceedingly unpopular.

What is true, however, is that oppositional forces remain active, coherent, in struggle in capitalist instances of authoritarian rule. Enough "space" is maintained because of pluralist pretensions and realities; degrees of factional disagreement as to how much repression is necessary also tend to produce periods of reduced repression. Unlike a socialist conception of total control by the state as integral to class rule, the capitalist conception relates repressive rule more closely to functional necessity; as such, it is more reactive, although its bureaucratic structures have a life of their own.

As yet, we have no experience with the termination of "hard" socialist regimes. The attempts of Eastern European governments to evolve in moderate directions and to break away from Soviet domination suggest the phenomenon. The perception is blurred by the heavy element of Soviet imperial presence, blocking termination initiatives. Also, the Soviet imperial issue establishes a legitimated basis for oppositional tendencies except in the most Stalinized of socialist systems.

The approach advocated, then, would suggest the following matrix:

Phases of governance / Categories of human rights	Initiating Phase	Maintenance Phase	Termination Phase
Basic human needs			
Basic decencies			
Participatory rights			
Security rights			
Humane governance			

A given government could, then, on the basis of available data be rated on a scale of 1–5 for each category in each phase; lack of data would be indicated by the notation "i.d." (insufficient data); nonapplicability of instance by notation "n.a." (not applicable).

SOME REMARKS ON APPRAISAL

Of course, the criteria set forth are difficult to apply. Requisite data are either unavailable or uneven. What data exist are difficult to use in any systematic and objective way. It is an immense task to make a careful appraisal for all Third World countries, requiring a staff of specialists. At the same time, one of the purposes of the framework is to propose an orientation for data collection and evaluation projects.

Obviously, a comparison of countries should be as objective as possible, making it desirable to operationalize criteria of appraisal. At the same time, qualitative considerations are often decisive. For instance, a human rights comparison that overlooked Kathleen Gough's finding that workers in a Vietnamese community are far more satisfied with their lives than workers in an Indian community at a similar socioeconomic level would be deficient.[33] So would one that did not assess the relative degree of cultural vitality operative in a given polity.

At this stage, the evidence available enables only crude forms of comparison with respect to the relative achievement of human rights in particular states at particular times. It heightens sensitivity about broad Third World patterns and trends. One way to proceed is to try out exemplary case studies of national profiles of ideological prototypes: for instance, to describe Brazil, Iran, and South Korea for capitalist variants, and to describe China, Cuba, and North Korea for socialist variants. The hypothesis is that these cases would reveal, in addition to their critical, distinctive features, a patterning of developmental dynamics and human rights that would be more or less played out in other country examples. Such a hypothesis is central to the view that ideological orientation is associated with certain structural patterns. This hypothesis need not be deterministic: variations would emerge (due to resources, quality of leadership), pressures may vary (due to mass consciousness, safety valves for opponents, geographical position, attitudes by external governments), policies may reflect diverse antecedent conditions (due to land tenure arrangements, ethnic diversity and structure, prior degree of industrialization, reliance on foreign skills and capital). Nevertheless, the fundamental argument remains: Authoritarian solutions seem virtually unavoidable in most Third World countries over the period of the next decade or so, although their degree and form of severity will vary greatly. In general, socialist forms of authoritarianism are to be preferred to their capitalist counterparts because of a combination of domestic and international factors that have been indicated above, but not unreservedly.

33. See Kathleen Gough, "The Green Revolution in South India and North Vietnam," *Bulletin of Concerned Asian Scholars* 10 (Jan.-Mar. 1978): 13–23.

[4]

ON A HIERARCHY OF INTERNATIONAL HUMAN RIGHTS

*By Theodor Meron**

I. Introduction

The quest for a hierarchy of international human rights continues unabated, despite the impressive challenge raised by Professor Weil to the notion of "relative normativity" of international legal norms.[1] To illustrate: in *Tel-Oren v. Libyan Arab Republic,*[2] a suit brought under the (First) Judiciary Act of 1789,[3] Judge Harry T. Edwards discussed whether torture, as distinguished from terrorism, "is among the handful of crimes to which the law of nations attributes individual [civil] responsibility."[4]

The International Court of Justice gave currency to the idea of a hierarchy in the *Barcelona Traction* case[5] by suggesting in a famous dictum that "basic rights of the human person" (*droits fondamentaux de la personne humaine*) create obligations *erga omnes.*[6] This dictum was construed by the International Law Commission (ILC) to mean that there is "a number, albeit a small one, of international obligations which, by reason of the importance of their subject-matter for the international community as a whole, are—unlike the others—obligations in whose fulfilment all States have a legal interest."[7]

* Of the Board of Editors. Research for this essay was supported by the NYU Law Center Foundation.

[1] Weil, *Towards Relative Normativity in International Law?*, 77 AJIL 413 (1983).

[2] 726 F.2d 774 (D.C. Cir. 1984).

[3] 28 U.S.C. §1350 (1982) (Alien Tort Claims Act, which provides federal courts with jurisdiction over actions by an alien for a tort committed in violation of the law of nations or a treaty of the United States).

[4] 726 F.2d at 795 (Edwards, J., concurring).

[5] Barcelona Traction, Light & Power Co., Ltd. (New Application) (Belg. v. Spain), 1970 ICJ Rep. 4 (Judgment of Feb. 5).

[6] *Id.* at 32. In *United States Diplomatic and Consular Staff in Tehran (United States of America v. Iran)*, the Court referred to the "fundamental principles enunciated in the Universal Declaration of Human Rights." 1980 ICJ Rep. 3, 42 (Judgment of May 24). In the Advisory Opinion on *Legal Consequences for States of the Continued Presence of South Africa in Namibia (South West Africa) notwithstanding Security Council Resolution 276 (1970)*, the Court stated that the "denial [by South Africa] of fundamental human rights is a flagrant violation of the purposes and principles of the Charter." 1971 ICJ Rep. 16, 57 (Advisory Opinion of June 21).

In a statement on human rights, Secretary of State Kissinger declared that while there will

> always be differences of view as to the precise extent of the obligations of government . . . there are standards below which no government can fall without offending fundamental values, such as genocide, officially tolerated torture, mass imprisonment or murder, or the comprehensive denial of basic rights to racial, religious, political, or ethnic groups. Any government engaging in such practices must face adverse international judgment.

Statement by Sec'y of State Kissinger before the OAS General Assembly, 75 Dep't St. Bull. 1, 3 (1976).

[7] [1976] 2 Y.B. Int'l L. Comm'n, pt. 2 at 99, UN Doc. A/CN.4/SER.A/1976/Add.l (pt. 2).

Extrapolating from *Barcelona Traction* into the field of international criminal responsibility, the ILC adopted[8] on first reading the controversial Article 19(3)(*c*) of the draft articles on state responsibility proposed by the special rapporteur, Professor (now Judge) Ago. Article 19(3)(*c*) provides that an international crime may result, inter alia, from "a serious breach on a widespread scale of an international obligation of essential importance for safeguarding the human being, such as those prohibiting slavery, genocide and *apartheid*." For international crimes, the ILC thus introduced a twofold test relating to the seriousness both of the violation and of the norm.

More recently, in discussing derogations from human rights, a United Nations document spoke of the "intangibility of certain fundamental rights."[9] The UN Secretary-General complained of the denial by South Africa of the "most fundamental human rights."[10] And the authoritative draft *Restatement of the Foreign Relations Law of the United States (Revised)* considers the rules of customary law of human rights listed in section 702 (discussed in section IV below) to constitute *jus cogens.*[11]

Claims of hierarchical status are also raised as to the relationship among rights belonging to the so-called first generation (civil and political rights), second generation (economic, social and cultural rights) and third generation (solidarity rights, e.g., the rights to peace, development and a protected environment).[12] Perhaps because, as Professor Brownlie aptly observes, "there is no Rubicon between law and morality,"[13] in the largely political controversy over the ranking of the several generations of rights (the first two generations represent *lex lata*, the third largely still *lex ferenda*), little attention is paid to the distinction between rights and claims. Yet another priority claim arises in distinguishing between individual and collective rights: the Canadian expert on the UN Sub-Commission on Prevention of Discrimination and Protection of Minorities (Deschênes) recently called for an end to the suppression of individual rights in the name of collective rights.[14]

[8] *Id.* at 73. For the text of Article 19(3)(*c*), see *id.* at 95.

[9] UN Doc. E/CN.4/Sub.2/1985/19, at 6.

[10] UN Press Release (Geneva) No. SG/SM/617, July 24, 1985.

[11] RESTATEMENT OF THE FOREIGN RELATIONS LAW OF THE UNITED STATES (REVISED) §702 comment *l* (1 Tent. Draft No. 6, 1985) [hereinafter cited as DRAFT RESTATEMENT].

[12] *See generally* Sohn, *The New International Law: Protection of the Rights of Individuals rather than States,* 32 AM. U.L. REV. 1, 61–62 (1982). Regarding the interdependence and equal status of human rights, see *id.* at 63. *See also* Alston, *Conjuring up New Human Rights: A Proposal for Quality Control,* 78 AJIL 607, 612 (1984).

[13] Brownlie, *Causes of Action in the Law of Nations,* 50 BRIT. Y.B. INT'L L. 13, 40 (1979).

[14] UN Press Release (Geneva) No. HR/1735, Aug. 7, 1985, at 2. *See generally* Schachter, *International Law in Theory and Practice,* 178 RECUEIL DES COURS 12, 331–32 (1982 V); Humphrey, *Political and Related Rights,* in 1 INTERNATIONAL LAW OF HUMAN RIGHTS: LEGAL AND POLICY ISSUES 171, 171–74 (T. Meron ed. 1984); Shestack, *The Jurisprudence of Human Rights,* in *id.* at 69, 99–101; van Boven, *Distinguishing Criteria of Human Rights,* in 1 THE INTERNATIONAL DIMENSIONS OF HUMAN RIGHTS 43, 53–57 (K. Vasak ed., P. Alston Eng. ed. 1982); Marks, *Emerging Human Rights: A New Generation for the 1980s?,* in INTERNATIONAL LAW: A CONTEMPORARY PERSPECTIVE 501 (R. Falk, F. Kratochwil & S. Mendlovitz eds. 1985); Vasak, *Pour une Troisième Génération des Droits de l'Homme,* in STUDIES AND ESSAYS ON INTERNATIONAL HUMANITARIAN LAW AND RED CROSS PRINCIPLES IN HONOUR OF JEAN PICTET 837 (C. Swinarski ed. 1984); Alston, *supra* note 12.

The increasing use of hierarchical terminology in international human rights merits attention. In addition to its conceptual interest, this development is of practical importance in resolving conflicts between norms. The object of this essay is to examine the significance and implications of the trend towards a graduated normativity in international human rights in regard to two sometimes overlapping notions: fundamental (or basic) human rights and peremptory (*jus cogens*) human rights.

II. Aspects of the Notion of a Hierarchy of Norms in International Law

National legal systems are characterized by a well-established hierarchy of norms. Constitutional provisions prevail over ordinary statutes, the latter prevail over secondary legislation or administrative regulations, and so on. It is therefore only natural that international lawyers, trained in national legal systems, should seek hierarchical principles in the international legal system as well. But in its present stage of development, the international community has no single and supreme legislature whose decrees would prevail over those of subordinate lawmaking bodies. Moreover, such an institution is not likely to be established in the foreseeable future. Nor has customary law filled the gap (consider the various constitutional conventions in the United Kingdom). Except for the emerging rules of *jus cogens* to be discussed later in this essay, only in Article 103 of the Charter of the United Nations (which provides that in the event of a conflict between the obligations of member states under the Charter and their obligations under any other international agreement, their obligations under the Charter shall prevail) is a hierarchical principle of general international law made explicit. Its binding character is explained, as Lord McNair does, by the "constitutive or semi-legislative character"[15] of the Charter.

The supremacy of the Charter, of course, carries implications for other instruments concerned, wholly or partly, with human rights. Thus, in one of its earliest resolutions, the UN Economic and Social Council (ECOSOC) expressed the wish that, "[p]ending the adoption of an international bill of rights, the general principle shall be accepted that international treaties involving basic human rights, including to the fullest extent practicable treaties of peace, shall conform to the fundamental standards relative to such rights set forth in the Charter."[16] The generality of these standards and the resultant difficulty in realizing this *voeu* should in no way detract from its

[15] A. McNair, The Law of Treaties 217 (1961). For a recent discussion of the hierarchical character of Article 103, see Flory, *Article 103*, La Charte des Nations Unies 1371 (J. Cot & A. Pellet eds. 1985).

In the Advisory Opinion on *Reparation for Injuries Suffered in the Service of the United Nations*, the Court stated that the member states of the United Nations, representing the vast majority of the international community, had the power to bring into being an entity possessing objective international personality and the capacity to bring international claims against states not members of the United Nations. 1949 ICJ Rep. 174, 185 (Advisory Opinion of Apr. 11). *See also* UN Charter art. 6, para. 2.

[16] ESC Res. 9, 2 UN ESCOR 400, 401 (1946).

salutary purpose, i.e., the avoidance of normative conflicts, which is particularly important where they cannot be resolved by invoking generally agreed hierarchical principles.

This is not to suggest that, apart from Article 103 of the Charter, hierarchical principles are totally absent from international law. Some such rules have been developed in international organizations and administrations. In the European Economic Community, for example, the Treaty Establishing the European Community (Treaty of Rome) is supreme law; [7] in the United Nations, Staff Rules promulgated by the Secretary-General are subordinate to Staff Regulations (resolutions of the General Assembly); and the latter, of course, are subordinate to the Charter. Nevertheless, despite occasional claims to the contrary,[18] the reach of hierarchically superior instruments adopted within a particular regional or specialized institution is limited to the legal system of the parent organization and should not be confused with *jus cogens.*

Apart from *jus cogens,* whose application in particular cases is made difficult not so much by the continuing doctrinal controversy about the concept itself as by the lack of consensus about the identity of most peremptory norms, some human rights are obviously more important than other human rights. But except in a few cases (e.g., the right to life or to freedom from torture), to choose which rights are more important than other rights is exceedingly difficult. It is fraught with personal, cultural and political bias and, to make matters worse, has not been addressed by the international community as a whole, perhaps because of the improbability of reaching a meaningful consensus. The differences in the social, cultural, political and economic values of states have made it easier to arrive at agreement on a set of rights than on the order of priority to govern them. As Professor Schachter cogently argues, setting up a hierarchy of goals has an attractive simplicity, but "[e]ven the attempt to impose guidelines . . . for relatively well-defined specific situations involves choices among competing values which states are reluctant to make in advance or to abide by in practice."[19] Except, perhaps, in cases where the same control organ is competent to interpret and balance two potentially conflicting norms, the practical consequences of the assessment that right *X* is more important than right *Y* are not clear.[20] The intrinsic value of a particular norm, a necessarily subjective notion, should not be confused with recognized hierarchical principles that have clearly established legal significance.

[17] *See, e.g.,* Arts. 228 and 234, Treaty Establishing the European Economic Community (Treaty of Rome), 298 UNTS 11.

[18] Gormley, *The Right to Life and the Rule of Non-Derogability: Peremptory Norms of Jus Cogens,* in THE RIGHT TO LIFE IN INTERNATIONAL LAW 120, 125–26 (B. Ramcharan ed. 1985).

[19] Schachter, *The United Nations and Internal Conflict,* in DISPUTE SETTLEMENT THROUGH THE UNITED NATIONS 301, 305 (K. Raman ed. 1977).

[20] Resolution of normative conflicts is discussed in T. MERON, HUMAN RIGHTS LAW-MAKING IN THE UNITED NATIONS: A CRITIQUE OF INSTRUMENTS AND PROCESS, ch. IV (Oxford University Press, forthcoming 1986). *See also* Meron, *Norm Making and Supervision in International Human Rights: Reflections on Institutional Order,* 76 AJIL 754 (1982).

III. FUNDAMENTAL RIGHTS

Examination of the Charter of the United Nations (Preamble, Articles 1(3), 13(b), 55(c), 62(2), 76(c)), the Universal Declaration of Human Rights (Preamble, Articles 2, 29(2), 30), the International Covenant on Civil and Political Rights (Political Covenant) (Articles 2(1), 3, 5(1), 5(2)), the International Convention on the Elimination of All Forms of Racial Discrimination (Preamble, Article 1(1)) and the Convention on the Elimination of All Forms of Discrimination Against Women (Preamble, Articles 1, 3) reveals that the terms "human rights," "freedoms," "fundamental human rights," "fundamental freedoms," "rights and freedoms" and, most commonly, "human rights and fundamental freedoms" appear, in general, to be used interchangeably. This practice suggests that there is no substantive or definable legal difference between these terms. In these instruments at least, "human rights" are not inferior to "fundamental" rights and freedoms. They are the same.

The Tentative Proposals for a General International Organization submitted by the United States to the Dumbarton Oaks Conference (1944) referred to "basic human rights," a term that was subsequently replaced by "human rights and fundamental freedoms."[21] Interpreting the latter term, Kelsen found that " 'freedoms' are human rights."[22]

The regional instruments on human rights also do not show that the international community has defined fundamental rights or placed them ahead of ordinary rights. The European Convention for the Protection of Human Rights and Fundamental Freedoms[23] (European Convention) names various rights and freedoms *tout court* in its body, though the title and Preamble refer to "fundamental freedoms." The American Convention on Human Rights (American Convention) speaks of the obligation of the states parties to respect various rights and freedoms, rather than fundamental rights.[24] The African Charter on Human and Peoples' Rights,[25] which has not yet entered into force, mentions fundamental human rights that "stem

[21] L. GOODRICH, E. HAMBRO & A. SIMONS, CHARTER OF THE UNITED NATIONS 373 (1969). In an important study, Professor Sohn has pointed out that the reference to "basic human rights" in the U.S. Tentative Proposals of 1944 was preceded by other references, e.g., that of President Roosevelt in his 1941 "Four Freedoms" message to "four essential freedoms." The United States Bill of Rights of 1942 and the Declaration of 1943 spoke of "human rights." Sohn, *A Short History of United Nations Documents on Human Rights*, in COMMISSION TO STUDY THE ORGANIZATION OF PEACE, THE UNITED NATIONS AND HUMAN RIGHTS: EIGHTEENTH REPORT 44–47 (1968). For discussions at San Francisco, see *id.* at 48–56 and documents cited therein.

[22] H. KELSEN, THE LAW OF THE UNITED NATIONS 29 (1966). Professors Cot and Pellet have observed that little importance should be attached to the distinction between references in the Charter to fundamental human rights and to human rights *tout court*. Cot & Pellet, *Préambule*, in Cot & Pellet (eds.), *supra* note 15, at 1, 14.

[23] 213 UNTS 221.

[24] For the official text, see ORGANIZATION OF AMERICAN STATES, HANDBOOK OF EXISTING RULES PERTAINING TO HUMAN RIGHTS IN THE INTER-AMERICAN SYSTEM 29, OEA/Ser.L/V/II.60, Doc. 28, rev.1 (1983).

[25] *Reprinted in* 21 ILM 58 (1982).

from the attributes of human beings" in its Preamble, but simply rights and freedoms in its body.

Nevertheless, the literature of international human rights demonstrates that some observers believe that there is a substantive difference between fundamental human rights and other human rights. One of these observers, Professor van Boven, alluding to the term "fundamental human rights" in the Charter, emphasizes the "supra-positive" character of such rights,[26] suggesting, perhaps, that they are based on natural law. However, whether this term brings any significance to bear on the question of a hierarchy of norms in positive international law is not clear. The author states that the principle of nondiscrimination on grounds of race has been "upgraded" "on the hierarchical scale of human rights norms," but he qualifies this claim by adding "in so far as there is any such scale."[27] Because it is not certain that the prohibition of some forms of racial discrimination would prevail over other human rights in case of a conflict,[28] can one really speak here of a hierarchical relationship?

The draft *Restatement* contains an important instance of a distinction between fundamental rights and other rights: section 702(g) mentions "consistent patterns of gross violations of internationally recognized human rights" as a violation of customary international law. This formulation results from the grafting of language from United States legislation[29] onto that of ECOSOC Resolution 1503 (XLVIII).[30] Comment *k* to section 702 states that "[w]hile all the rights proclaimed in the Universal Declaration and protected by the . . . Covenants . . . are internationally recognized human rights, some rights are fundamental and intrinsic to human dignity, and consistent patterns of violation of such rights as state policy may be deemed 'gross' *ipso facto.*" Comment *k* thus suggests that when a pattern of violations of certain rights has reached a critical mass, it may be regarded as a breach of customary international law. But would this proposition not hold true also if applied to all internationally recognized human rights, rather than to "fundamental rights" only?

The lack of generally agreed standards makes it extremely difficult to select such fundamental rights. To illustrate: among the fundamental rights listed in comment *k* to section 702 is the right to leave one's country. Nevertheless, this right, considered *ut singuli*, is not listed among the customary human rights in the black-letter text of section 702. This writer agrees with the drafters of the *Restatement* that the right to leave is fundamental. Yet the relativity of our perceptions is emphasized by the fact that in a recent study prepared for the UN Sub-Commission on Prevention of Discrimination and Protection of Minorities, Rapporteur Mubanga-Chipoia, discussing the

[26] Van Boven, *supra* note 14, at 44. [27] *Id.*

[28] *See generally* Meron, *The Meaning and Reach of the International Convention on the Elimination of All Forms of Racial Discrimination*, 79 AJIL 283, 296–305 (1985).

[29] DRAFT RESTATEMENT, *supra* note 11, §702 Reporters' Note 9 (listing examples of relevant U.S. statutes); Schachter, *International Law Implications of U.S. Human Rights Policies*, 24 N.Y.L. SCH. L. REV. 63, 75 (1978); Meron, *Teaching Human Rights: An Overview*, in 1 Meron (ed.), *supra* note 14, at 1, 20 & nn.98–100.

[30] 48 UN ESCOR Supp. (No. 1A) at 8–9, UN Doc. E/4832/Add.1 (1970).

effect of limitation clauses such as that contained in Article 12(3) of the Political Covenant, asks whether the right to leave one's country, which is stated in Article 12(2) thereof, constitutes a right "or is rather a mere human attribute."[31]

In a certain sense, all human rights can be regarded as fundamental, but inconsistent use of the terms "human rights" and "fundamental human rights" may give rise to difficulties in the interpretation of international human rights instruments. For example, Article 2 of the Declaration on the Elimination of All Forms of Intolerance and of Discrimination Based on Religion or Belief[32] prohibits discrimination on grounds of religion or other beliefs by any state, institution, group of persons or person; and it defines intolerance and discrimination based on religion or belief as "any distinction, exclusion, restriction or preference based on religion or belief and having as its purpose or as its effect nullification or impairment of the recognition, enjoyment or exercise of human rights and fundamental freedoms on an equal basis." Assuming that the freedom of religious groups to administer religious law is protected by the principles of the Declaration, restrictions placed by the state upon that freedom would be permissible only if they complied with Article 1(3), which provides: "Freedom to manifest one's religion or belief may be subject only to such limitations as are prescribed by law and are necessary to protect public safety, order, health, or morals or the *fundamental* rights and freedoms of others" (emphasis added). Any limitation not prescribed by law and not considered necessary to protect one of the stated goals would be "discrimination based on religion or belief."

The catalog of limitations tracks the language of Article 18(3) of the Political Covenant and differs significantly from that in Article 29(2) of the Universal Declaration of Human Rights,[33] which served as the original model for this type of clause: while the latter also allows limitations for the purpose of securing due recognition and respect *for the rights and freedoms* of others and of meeting the requirements of the general welfare in a democratic society,[34] Article 1(3) is addressed only to the "*fundamental rights and freedoms* of others" (emphasis added). Was this formulation of Article 1(3) deliberately selected to impose greater limitations on the state's ability to encroach upon freedom of religion? Arguably, this language may limit the state's right to regulate the exercise of freedom of religion, even when such regulation may be justified by other human rights, e.g., the advancement of women's equality, unless, of course, the latter is considered a fundamental right, rather than a right *tout court.* Thus, as a matter of literal construction, invocation of the human rights of others will not suffice; only "fundamental human rights" will do. Does the determination that a right is fundamental *vel non* depend on international conceptions or on the mores and traditions of a

[31] UN Doc. E/CN.4/Sub.2/1985/9, at 5. On the right to leave, see generally Lillich, *Civil Rights*, in 1 Meron (ed.), *supra* note 14, at 115, 151–52.

[32] GA Res. 36/55, 36 UN GAOR Supp. (No. 51) at 171, UN Doc. A/36/51 (1981).

[33] GA Res. 217A, UN Doc. A/810, at 71 (1948).

[34] *See generally* E. Daes, The Individual's Duties to the Community and the Limitations on Human Rights and Freedoms under Article 29 of the Universal Declaration of Human Rights, UN Doc. E/CN.4/Sub.2/432/Rev.2 (1983).

particular national society? If the latter, account must be taken of the deplorable fact that some societies will not yet accept the goal of women's equality as a fundamental right.

The term "fundamental rights," which inspired the development of international human rights, originated in national constitutions,[35] where it continues to be commonly employed. It is in this sense that the Court of Justice of the European Communities spoke of "fundamental rights [which] form an integral part of the general principles of the law" and of "the fundamental rights recognized by the constitutions [of member states]."[36] In national legal systems, fundamental or constitutional rights are characterized by the especially rigorous procedures required for their adoption, amendment or termination, and by their superior position in the hierarchy of legal norms. In case of conflict, a subordinate norm must yield to a constitutional norm and its legal validity may even perhaps be questioned.

None of these characteristics can be found in the notion of fundamental human rights. In its commentary on Article 17 of the draft articles on state responsibility, the ILC has already warned that

> only by erroneously equating the situation under international law with that under internal law . . . some lawyers have been able to see in the "constitutional" or "fundamental" principles of the international legal order an independent and higher "source" of international obligations. In reality there is, in the international legal order, no special source of law for creating "constitutional" or "fundamental" principles. The principles which come to mind when using these terms are themselves customary rules, rules embodied in treaties, or even rules emanating from bodies or procedures which have themselves been established by treaties. Consequently, the view that international responsibility generated by a breach of certain obligations established by those principles is more grave, cannot be justified on the basis of their "origin", but rather by taking account of the undeniable fact that the international community has a greater interest in ensuring that its members act in accordance with the specific requirements of the obligations in question.[37]

While it is true that the determination of the "greater importance" of some obligations should be the function of the international community, as suggested by the ILC, in the absence of effective institutional procedures for making such a determination and given the continued elusiveness of international consensus, the characterization of some rights as fundamental results largely from our own subjective perceptions of their importance. Perhaps they are marked by a special *erga omnes* character, as was suggested by the Court in *Barcelona Traction.* We shall see, however, that the *erga omnes*

[35] *See generally* Schindler, *The International Committee of the Red Cross and Human Rights,* INT'L REV. RED CROSS, No. 208, Jan.–Feb. 1979, at 3, 6.

[36] Hauer v. Land Rheinland-Pfalz, 1979 ECR 3727, 3744–45, 29 Common Mkt. L.R. 42, 64 (1980 III).

[37] [1976] 2 Y.B. INT'L L. COMM'N, *supra* note 7, pt. 2 at 73, 85–86.

character is no longer the exclusive attribute of fundamental rights. Moreover, being *erga omnes* is a consequence, not the cause, of a right's fundamental character. The *erga omnes* criterion is therefore unhelpful for characterizing rights as fundamental or ordinary.

For those fundamental rights which overlap with *jus cogens*, of course, Articles 53 and 64 of the Vienna Convention on the Law of Treaties[38] suggest certain analogies with higher, constitutional norms in national legal systems, but this is because of their being "peremptory" rather than fundamental. While it is true, as the ILC pointed out in its commentary on Article 50 (now 53) of the Vienna Convention on the Law of Treaties, that "[i]t is not the form of a general rule of international law but the particular nature of the subject-matter with which it deals that may . . . give it a character of *jus cogens*,"[39] it is difficult to accept the ILC's suggestion, made in the commentary on Article 17 of the draft articles on state responsibility, that the "process by which [such rules] were created" is irrelevant.[40] Process is relevant for the acceptance of a rule of *jus cogens*, which requires a very large majority of states ("the international community as a whole"), and even more for the establishment of a subsequent norm of general international law having the character of *jus cogens* and modifying an earlier rule of *jus cogens* (*jus cogens superveniens*). Can a subsequent rule of *jus cogens* modifying an earlier rule of *jus cogens* be established through practice and customary law that is in conflict with the earlier rule, or by a general multilateral treaty as suggested by the ILC?[41] What would the significance be of practice or customary law that is being crystallized in conflict with existing rules of *jus cogens*? Neither the scant international practice nor the richer doctrine has given fully satisfactory answers to this question.

If a fundamental right may constitute a peremptory right, the difficulty of identifying fundamental rights gives way to the even greater difficulty of qualifying certain rights as peremptory. Because invalidity of a norm may result from its conflict with *jus cogens*, this qualification is a formidable, even awesome task. For the scholar as well as the practitioner, it requires discharging a heavy burden of proof.

A catalog of "fundamental human rights" can, of course, be established by a future agreement or, perhaps, developed through international practice and jurisprudence. Such a catalog should not be confused with lists of non-

[38] *Opened for signature* May 23, 1969, UNTS Regis. No. 18,232, UN Doc. A/CONF.39/27 (1969), *reprinted in* 63 AJIL 875 (1969), 8 ILM 679 (1969).

[39] [1966] 2 Y.B. INT'L L. COMM'N 169, 248, UN Doc. A/CN.4/SER.A/1966/Add.1.

[40] [1976] 2 *id.*, *supra* note 7, pt. 2 at 85.

[41] [1966] 2 *id.*, *supra* note 39, at 248. Sir Ian Sinclair has questioned the status of a new multilateral treaty which, at the time of its conclusion, would be in conflict with an earlier rule of *jus cogens*. I. SINCLAIR, THE VIENNA CONVENTION ON THE LAW OF TREATIES 226 (2d ed. 1984). But would such a conflict arise where the international community has accepted, through a very large majority's support for a new general multilateral treaty, the formulation of a new rule of *jus cogens*? Would such acceptance not indicate the emergence of a new rule of *jus cogens* and the modification of the previous rule of *jus cogens* even before the entry into force of the new treaty?

derogable rights and their relationship with *jus cogens*, to be discussed later in this essay.

Account must be taken, however, of the following important, but ambivalent, dictum by the International Court of Justice in its Judgment in the *Barcelona Traction* case:[42]

> 33. When a State admits into its territory foreign investments or foreign nationals, whether natural or juristic persons, it is bound to extend to them the protection of the law and assumes obligations concerning the treatment to be afforded them. These obligations, however, are neither absolute nor unqualified. In particular, an essential distinction should be drawn between the obligations of a State towards the international community as a whole, and those arising vis-à-vis another State in the field of diplomatic protection. By their very nature the former are the concern of all States. In view of the importance of the rights involved, all States can be held to have a legal interest in their protection; they are obligations *erga omnes*.
>
> 34. Such obligations derive, for example, in contemporary international law, from the outlawing of acts of aggression, and of genocide, as also from the principles and rules concerning the basic rights of the human person, including protection from slavery and racial discrimination. Some of the corresponding rights of protection have entered into the body of general international law . . . ; others are conferred by international instruments of a universal or quasi-universal character.[43]

The above pronouncement does not make clear, however, whether "basic rights of the human person," which give rise to obligations *erga omnes*, are synonymous with human rights *tout court* or are limited to rights intimately associated with the human person and human dignity and generally accepted, such as the protection from slavery and racial discrimination. Moreover, the distinction between basic rights of the human person and "ordinary" human rights is not self-evident. If the Court intended to set apart the basic rights of the human person, the inclusion of some human rights among them would perhaps depend on their acceptance into the corpus of general international law or on their incorporation into instruments of a universal or quasi-universal character; but a more subjective and difficult characterization would also have to be made, such as the nature of their association with the human person and human dignity.

Elsewhere in the Judgment, an indication can, indeed, be found that the Court intended to distinguish between human rights in general and the basic rights of the human person. The Court emphasized that, in contrast to the European Convention, "which entitles each State which is a party to the Convention to lodge a complaint against any other contracting State for violation of the Convention, irrespective of the nationality of the victim,"[44] "on the universal level, the instruments which embody human rights do not confer on States the capacity to protect the victims of infringements of such

[42] 1970 ICJ Rep. 4, *supra* note 5.

[43] *Id.* at 32.

[44] *Id.* at 47.

rights irrespective of their nationality."[45] The Court seems to suggest that, while basic rights of the human person give rise to obligations *erga omnes* and are appropriate for protection by states regardless of the nationality of the victim, other human rights, or ordinary human rights, can be espoused, under the agreements embodying such rights, only by the state of nationality of the victims.

This pronouncement of the Court will obviously create some perplexity when the need arises to characterize human rights as either ordinary or basic. Most observers would probably agree that protection of the right to life from arbitrary taking and protection of the human person from torture or egregious racial discrimination are fundamental rights. Perhaps they would also agree that the small number (irreducible core) of rights that are deemed nonderogable under both the Political Covenant[46] and the European and American Coventions constitute fundamental, and perhaps even peremptory norms. But that irreducible core comprises four rights only: the right to life and the prohibitions of slavery, torture and retroactive penal measures. The prospects for a consensus reaching beyond these few rights are not immediate. For instance, while for some observers, including this writer, due process rights are fundamental and indispensable for ensuring any other right, for others, the rights to food and other basic needs take precedence. Superficially seductive formulae such as the notion of rights protecting the physical and mental well-being of the human person are not helpful either, because they involve clusters of rights whose components require scrutiny. Would the prohibition of indefinite preventive detention, for example, be considered fundamental?

One point is clear, however. The Court's reference to the body of general international law and to universal or quasi-universal agreements suggests that a fundamental right must be firmly rooted in international law and that mere claims or goals, important as they may be, would not qualify.

Protection from slavery and racial discrimination, the examples of basic human rights mentioned by the Court, may well reflect its conception of norms of *jus cogens*, which it did not explicitly spell out; but rights characterized by an *erga omnes* reach are not necessarily identical with *jus cogens*. Despite a certain overlap, the latter is narrower than the former.

Since the Judgment of the Court, and perhaps under the impact of that Judgment, there has been a growing acceptance in contemporary international law of the principle that, apart from agreements conferring on each state party *locus standi* against the other state parties, all states have a legitimate interest in and the right to protest against significant human rights violations wherever they may occur, regardless of the nationality of the victims. This crystallization of the *erga omnes* character of human rights, rooted in Articles 55 and 56 of the Charter, is taking place despite uncertainty as to whether a state not directly concerned (e.g., in the protection of its nationals), *ut singuli*, may take up claims against the violating state[47] and demand

[45] *Id.*

[46] GA Res. 2200, 21 UN GAOR Supp. (No. 16) at 52, UN Doc. A/6316 (1966).

[47] I. SINCLAIR, *supra* note 41, at 213; Schachter, *supra* note 14, at 196–99, 341–42.

reparation for a breach of international law. However, the general principle establishing international accountability and the right to censure can be regarded as settled law.[48] Thus, while doubts may persist about the appropriate remedies that can be demanded by a third state that does not have a direct interest in the matter, subject to the acceptance by the states concerned of the jurisdiction of a competent tribunal, the *locus standi* of such a third state, in principle, is not questioned.

The most interesting feature of this development is that the growing acceptance of the *erga omnes* character of human rights has not been limited to the basic rights of the human person. Thus, section 703(2) of the draft *Restatement*[49] provides that any state may pursue international remedies against any other state for a violation of the customary international law of human rights. In their notes, the reporters elaborate as follows:

> The customary law of human rights . . . protects individuals subject to each state's jurisdiction, and the international obligation runs equally to all other states, with no one state a victim of the violation more than any other. If there is to be any remedy at all, it must be available equally to all states.[50]

The *erga omnes* character of human rights is also suggested by Article 5(d)(iv) of the draft articles on state responsibility (part 2), proposed by the ILC's special rapporteur, Professor Riphagen, which states:

> For the purposes of the present articles "injured State" means:
>
> . . .
>
> (d) if the internationally wrongful act constitutes a breach of an obligation imposed by a multilateral treaty, a State party to that treaty, if it is established that:
>
> . . .
>
> (iv) the obligation was stipulated for the protection of individual persons, irrespective of their nationality.[51]

While the above provision concerns obligations imposed by treaties,[52] it is

[48] *See generally* Schachter, *supra* note 29, at 66–74; Schachter, *supra* note 14, at 200.

[49] DRAFT RESTATEMENT, *supra* note 11.

[50] *Id.* §703 Reporters' Note 3.

[51] Report of the International Law Commission on the work of its thirty-sixth session, 39 UN GAOR Supp. (No. 10) at 237 n.299, UN Doc. A/39/10 (1984); Report of the International Law Commission on the work of its thirty-seventh session, 40 UN GAOR Supp. (No. 10) at 39, UN Doc. A/40/10 (1985).

[52] UN Doc. A/CN.4/389, at 9 (1985). In 1985, the ILC amended Article 5(d)(iv) of the Riphagen draft, emphasizing that the principle stated in it applied to international customary law as well. The relevant part of Article 5 as provisionally adopted by the ILC reads as follows:

> 2. In particular, "injured State" means
>
> . . .
>
> (e) if the right infringed by the act of a State arises from a multilateral treaty or from a rule of customary international law, any other State party to the multilateral treaty or bound by the relevant rule of customary international law, if it is established that:
>
> . . .
>
> (iii) the right has been created or is established for the protection of human rights and fundamental freedoms. . . .

noteworthy that the distinction between basic rights of the human person and ordinary human rights is not addressed.

In a recent statement, the UN Assistant Secretary-General for Human Rights, Dr. Kurt Herndl, emphasized that one of the accomplishments of the United Nations has been to consolidate the principle that human rights are a matter of international concern that the international community is entitled to discuss.[53] Scholarly writings point in the same direction. Thus, in an important study of international accountability and the right to censure human rights violations, Professor Schachter does not distinguish between the basic rights of the human person and human rights *tout court.* He points out, rightly, that in the absence of specific interests of their own, states tend to focus on censuring violations of "fundamental norm[s] of humanity."[54] This tendency, however, appears to reflect considerations of foreign policy and an assessment of the significance of the breach, rather than a formal distinction between fundamental rights and ordinary rights.

In sum, international practice and scholarly opinion seem to have moved well beyond the *erga omnes* dictum of *Barcelona Traction:* perhaps the distinction between basic human rights and human rights *tout court,* as regards their *erga omnes* character, can no longer be supported. We shall see, however, that despite the acknowledged vagueness of the term,[55] the Institute of International Law has carried the notion of basic rights of the human person even further into the uncertain terrain of *jus cogens.*

IV. *Jus Cogens*

The notion of peremptory norms of international law (*jus cogens*) is stated in Articles 53 and 64 of the Vienna Convention on the Law of Treaties. Article 53 provides as follows:

> A treaty is void if, at the time of its conclusion, it conflicts with a peremptory norm of general international law. For the purposes of the present Convention, a peremptory norm of general international law is a norm accepted and recognized by the international community of

Report of the International Law Commission on the work of its thirty-seventh session, *supra* note 51, at 54. The commentary explained that "[t]he term 'human rights and fundamental freedoms' is here used in the sense which is current in present-day international relations." *Id.* at 58.

[53] UN Press Release (Geneva) No. HR/1733, Aug. 6, 1985, at 2.

[54] Schachter, *supra* note 29, at 70. Principle 2 of the Principles for the International Law of the Future emphasized the duty of each state to "treat its own population in a way which will not violate the dictates of humanity and justice or shock the conscience of mankind." 38 AJIL Supp. 72, 74 (1944). These terms can be traced to the preambular Martens clause to (Hague) Convention (No. IV) Respecting the Laws and Customs of War on Land, with Annex of Regulations, Oct. 18, 1907, 36 Stat. 2277, TS No. 539. *See* Meron, *On the Inadequate Reach of Humanitarian and Human Rights Law and the Need for a New Instrument,* 77 AJIL 589, 593 & n.24 (1983).

[55] *See, e.g.,* Suy, *Droit des Traités et Droits de l'Homme,* in VÖLKERRECHT ALS RECHTSORDNUNG—INTERNATIONALE GERICHTSBARKEIT—MENSCHENRECHTE: FESTSCHRIFT FÜR HERMANN MOSLER 935, 936–37 (R. Bernhardt, W. Geck, G. Jaenicke & H. Steinberger eds. 1983); I. BROWNLIE, PRINCIPLES OF PUBLIC INTERNATIONAL LAW 512 (3d ed. 1979).

> States as a whole as a norm from which no derogation is permitted and which can be modified only by a subsequent norm of general international law having the same character.

The literature on *jus cogens* is rich.[56] For our purposes, only a few observations narrowly focused on human rights are called for.

The principle of *jus cogens,* which restricts the freedom of states to contract and voids instruments that conflict with peremptory norms, has unquestionable ethical underpinnings and unimpeachable antecedents. It may be traced to the distinction in Roman law between *jus strictum* and *jus dispositivum* and to Grotius's references to *jus strictum.*[57] Its moral and deterrent effect is of particular importance in our era, characterized as it is by internal and international violence and frequent breaches of most human rights. But even for those who accept it, as this author does, this principle gives rise to difficult questions.

First, in the contemporary world, what is the relevance of *jus cogens* to agreements implicating human rights? As a matter of fact, states do not conclude agreements to commit torture or genocide or enslave peoples. Many of the examples of *jus cogens* commonly cited in legal literature are really *hypothèses d'école.* Moreover, states are not inclined to contest the absolute illegality of acts prohibited by the principle of *jus cogens.* When such acts take place, states deny the factual allegations or justify violations by more subtle or ingenious arguments. Thus, while the principle of *jus cogens* has moral and potential value, its immediate practical importance for the validity of agreements is still limited. However, when it comes to balancing one human right that has assumed the status of *jus cogens* against another human right that has not gained such exalted status, the concept may be relevant.

A second set of questions stems from the continuing lack of agreement about the peremptory rules themselves. The International Law Commission, which prepared the draft of the Vienna Convention, has prudently refrained from suggesting a catalog of peremptory rules. Few attempts have been made to identify such rules in the field of human rights. Invoking the authority of Professors McDougal, Lasswell and Chen,[58] comment *l* to section

[56] *See* I. SINCLAIR, *supra* note 41, at 203–26, and the literature mentioned in *id.* at 236 n.8; Weil, *supra* note 1; Whiteman, *Jus Cogens in International Law, With a Projected List,* 7 GA. J. INT'L & COMP. L. 609 (1977); Domb, *Jus Cogens and Human Rights,* 6 ISRAEL Y.B. HUM. RTS. 104 (1976); Schwelb, *Some Aspects of International Jus Cogens as Formulated by the International Law Commission,* 61 AJIL 946 (1967); Gros Espiell, *Self-Determination and Jus Cogens,* in UN LAW/FUNDAMENTAL RIGHTS 167 (A. Cassese ed. 1979).

[57] Frowein, *Jus Cogens,* [Instalment] 7 ENCYCLOPEDIA OF PUBLIC INTERNATIONAL LAW 327, 328 (R. Bernhardt ed. 1984).

[58] M. MCDOUGAL, H. LASSWELL & L. CHEN, HUMAN RIGHTS AND WORLD PUBLIC ORDER 338–50 (1980). The authors state that "many of the policies about human rights would appear to be so intensely demanded that they are acquiring . . . not merely the status of 'international concern,' but in addition that of *jus cogens* or of a global bill of rights." *Id.* at 185. They regard the Universal Declaration of Human Rights "as established customary law, having the attributes of *jus cogens.*" *Id.* at 274. They suggest that "the great bulk of the contemporary human rights prescriptions" are identifiable as *jus cogens. Id.* at 345. The view of these learned authors finds

702 of the draft *Restatement*[59] states that the prohibitory rules of customary international law carefully listed in that section constitute *jus cogens* and that an international agreement that violated them would be void. The following prohibitions are so listed: genocide; slavery or slave trade; murder or causing the disappearance of individuals; torture or other cruel, inhuman or degrading treatment or punishment; prolonged arbitrary detention; systematic racial discrimination; and consistent patterns of gross violations of internationally recognized human rights;[60] all of which constitute violations if practiced as a matter of state policy. To this list, one should perhaps add certain norms of international humanitarian law. Considering the difficulties inherent in this subject, it is not surprising that in a study prepared in 1977, Whiteman compiled a significantly different and shorter list of peremptory human rights.[61] Because the prohibition of prolonged arbitrary detention is not mentioned among the nonderogable rights in Article 4 of the Political Covenant, the *Restatement*'s identification of that prohibition as a rule of *jus cogens* creates a particularly difficult problem.[62]

The relationship between *jus cogens* and derogability is an interesting one. The principal human rights instruments (the Political Covenant, the American Convention, the European Convention) contain the same hard core of nonderogable rights, yet different lists of nonderogable rights. Rights that

---

support in the statement of Judge Tanaka that "the law concerning the protection of human rights may be considered to belong to the *jus cogens*." South West Africa (Ethiopia v. S. Afr.; Liberia v. S. Afr.), Second Phase, 1966 ICJ REP. 250, 298 (Judgment of July 18) (Tanaka, J., diss. op.). Also, Verdross argues that "all rules of general international law created for a humanitarian purpose" constitute *jus cogens*. Verdross, *Jus Dispositivum and Jus Cogens in International Law*, 60 AJIL 53, 59 (1966).

Sinclair, who disagrees with the attempts to regard all human rights as *jus cogens*, asks whether rights subject to progressive realization under Article 2(1) of the International Covenant on Economic, Social and Cultural Rights (Economic Covenant) can constitute *jus cogens*. I. SINCLAIR, *supra* note 41, at 217. For the text of the Economic Covenant, see GA Res. 2200, 21 UN GAOR Supp. (No. 16) at 49, UN Doc. A/6316 (1966). For a view that not all human rights are *jus cogens*, see also Schachter, *supra* note 14, at 339; Higgins, *Derogations under Human Rights Treaties*, 48 BRIT. Y.B. INT'L L. 281, 282 (1976–77).

[59] DRAFT RESTATEMENT, *supra* note 11, Reporters' Note 10; *see also* 2 *id.* §331(2) comment *e* and Reporters' Note 4. *See generally* Schachter, *supra* note 14, at 333–38.

[60] A later draft omitted "consistent patterns of gross violations of internationally recognized human rights" from the list of peremptory norms. RESTATEMENT OF THE FOREIGN RELATIONS LAW OF THE UNITED STATES (REVISED) §702 comment *n*, Reporters' Note 10 (Tent. Final Draft, 1985) [hereinafter cited as Tent. Final Draft].

[61] Whiteman, *supra* note 56, at 625–26.

[62] It is suggested that detentions occurring during a time of emergency and that comply with the requirements of Article 4 of the Political Covenant are not arbitrary. Tent. Final Draft, *supra* note 60, §702 Reporters' Note 10. But the requirements of Article 4 are addressed primarily to the conditions for the proclamation of an emergency, not the standards governing detention procedures (due process). The notion of arbitrariness must refer to the character of the procedures of detention themselves, rather than only to the legality of the state of emergency under which they are authorized. Is there not a danger that the suggestion made in Reporters' Note 10 might be invoked to support the claim that every detention that takes place in a time of emergency in compliance with Article 4 is nonarbitrary, despite the prevalence of arbitrary detentions in such situations?

are nonderogable under such instruments are not necessarily *jus cogens* (e.g., the right not to be imprisoned merely on the ground of inability to fulfill a contractual obligation, which is stated in Article 11 of the Political Covenant, or perhaps the more important nonderogable right to participate in government, which is stated in Article 23 of the American Convention) and some of them may not even have attained the status of customary law. Conversely, can a right whose derogation is permitted by a primary international human rights agreement (the Political Covenant) be regarded as *jus cogens* in light of the statement of the principle of *jus cogens* in Article 53 of the Vienna Convention (a norm from which no derogation is permitted)?

The existence of nonderogable rights is cited by some writers as evidence of "at least a minimum catalogue of fundamental or elementary human rights."[63] In an important essay, Professor Suy carries this argument further into the field of the public order of the international community, which is somewhat analogous to *jus cogens*, and to which we shall return later in this essay:

> L'interdiction formelle de toute dérogation nous paraît en effet être un critère objectif permettant d'identifier une règle relevant de l'ordre public de la communauté internationale. En appliquant ce critère, non seulement on sera amené à exclure du champ de cet ordre public tous les droits de l'homme auxquels il est expressément permis de déroger, mais on y fera aussi rentrer toutes les normes auxquelles il n'est pas permis de déroger qu'elles aient trait ou non aux droits de l'homme.[64]

While the first part of Professor Suy's suggestion is perfectly correct, the second is true only with regard to states contractually bound to a particular list of nonderogable rights. Since the reference to the public order of the international community is to general international law, the fact that a particular right is stated in a particular instrument, even one as important as the Political Covenant, is not necessarily conclusive.

While most nonderogable rights are of cardinal importance, some derogable rights may be of equal importance (e.g., due process of law under Article 14 of the Political Covenant). The international community as a whole has neither established a uniform list of nonderogable rights nor ranked nonderogable rights ahead of derogable rights. If a derogable right conflicts with a nonderogable right, the latter will not necessarily prevail, unless, of course, its status as a peremptory norm of general international law is recognized. We shall return to certain additional problems of derogability in our discussion of international public order.

Even a well-established right such as the prohibition of systematic racial discrimination, mentioned in section 702(f) of the draft *Restatement*, presents difficulties when regarded as *jus cogens*. Apartheid, which is mentioned in comment *i* to section 702, is easy to characterize because of its governmental nature and systematic administration, as well as its egregious character. Even apart from apartheid, there is little disagreement with the overall prohibition

[63] Van Boven, *supra* note 14, at 46.

[64] Suy, *supra* note 55, at 938.

of racial discrimination, but the consensus narrows as one moves from the general principle to specific manifestations of discrimination.

These comments are not meant to disparage the ethically important contribution made by the draft *Restatement* to the crystallization, through a proposed list, of the still fluid notion of *jus cogens.* In the long run, such a list may influence the development of the law of *jus cogens,* whose contents will be established through general custom or by universal or quasi-universal agreements.

A recent advisory opinion of the Inter-American Court of Human Rights deals with another important aspect of *jus cogens:* the relationship between derogability and reservations. The Court emphasized that "a reservation which was designed to enable a State to suspend any of the non-derogable fundamental rights must be deemed to be incompatible with the object and purpose of the Convention and, consequently, not permitted by it."[65] Judge (now President) Buergenthal comments that this opinion

> constitutes the first unambiguous international judicial articulation of a principle basic to the application of human rights treaties, that non-derogability and incompatibility are linked. The nexus between non-derogability and incompatibility derives from and adds force to the conceptual interrelationship which exists between certain fundamental human rights and emerging *jus cogens* norms.[66]

While the possibility of conflicts between *jus cogens* norms of human rights and other human rights is largely academic, conflicts may arise between human rights and rules, and especially the implementation of rules, embodied in international agreements governing other matters such as extradition. The *jus cogens* nature of human rights is thus implicated, as the deliberations of the prestigious Institute of International Law (Cambridge, 1983) reveal to interesting effect.

Under the item "New problems of the international legal system of extradition with special reference to multilateral treaties," the rapporteur, Professor Doehring, proposed a draft resolution that provided (Article III(2)): "The invocation of the duty to protect human rights should in any case justify non-extradition, in particular [*sic*—the word "even" would have been preferable] in cases where political persecution does not exist and where thus the granting of asylum cannot be based on that ground."[67] Rather than

[65] Restrictions to the Death Penalty (Arts. 4(2) and 4(4) American Convention on Human Rights), Advisory Opinion No. OC-3/83 of Sept. 8, 1983, Inter-American Court of Human Rights, ser. A: Judgments and Opinions No. 3, para. 61 (1983).

[66] Buergenthal, *The Advisory Practice of the Inter-American Human Rights Court,* 79 AJIL 22, 25 (1985) (footnote omitted). On reservations and *jus cogens,* see generally I. SINCLAIR, *supra* note 41, at 211–12.

[67] 60 Y.B. INST. INT'L L. 214 (1983 II).

In opposing Doehring's proposal, Briggs argued that "the concepts of asylum and human rights were introduced as a sort of unilateral *jus cogens* justifying violation of obligations." *Id.* at 230. McDougal, in supporting the proposal, argued that "for some two hundred years there had been decisions to the effect that the responsibility of the State in respect of the protection of aliens overrode national laws. States could not unilaterally, and *a fortiori* bilaterally, override human rights." *Id.*

merely recommend that states include in extradition agreements provisions stating that if any of their obligations under the agreements conflict with human rights, the latter shall prevail, Professor Doehring's proposal would, in effect, have conferred a hierarchically superior status on human rights *tout court*.

In proposing that the expression "human rights" in the draft resolution be replaced by "basic rights of the human person," Judge Mosler explained that the latter, "though lacking a well-defined content, took account of the dignity of the human person and the needs closely linked with the development of man as a human being." He added that it would not be an exaggeration to state that "the protection that this basic human position justified might prevail over treaties as a norm of *jus cogens*."[68] On the other hand, the expression "human rights" could be interpreted as meaning the United Nations Covenants on Human Rights, at least that on civil and political rights, and even regional conventions. Judge Mosler considered that "obligations to protect human rights as *jus cogens* did not go [so] far. Many of these law-making conventions defined human rights in a precise manner and prevented a wide interpretation of them by making exceptions, for example, for domestic jurisdiction or for measures 'necessary in a democratic society'." Judge Mosler concluded by recommending that the latter type of provision be excluded from Professor Doehring's draft resolution.[69]

Judge Schwebel proposed that the English text of Article III(2) employ the (synonymous) word "fundamental" rather than "basic" to modify human rights,[70] as in the French text (*droits fondamentaux*) of the Judgment in the *Barcelona Traction* case. The text that was eventually adopted by the Institute as Article IV of the resolution reads as follows: "In cases where there is a well-founded fear of the violation of the fundamental human rights of an accused in the territory of the requesting State, extradition may be refused. . . ."[71]

The Institute thus appears to support the proposition that "fundamental human rights" are *jus cogens* and prevail over extradition agreements. We have already discussed the difficulties inherent in defining the content of fundamental human rights. These difficulties are neither resolved nor alleviated by the resolution. If fundamental human rights already constitute *jus cogens*, why does the resolution not employ the term "shall" rather than "may," which would imply a clear duty to accord priority to the norms of *jus cogens*?

To be sure, some human rights that can well be regarded as fundamental have become *jus cogens*. Yet can a whole block of fundamental human rights lacking a well-defined content, as Judge Mosler himself admits, constitute norms that the international community of states as a whole accepts and

It is of interest to note that Frowein and Kühner single out the danger of torture as justifying nonextradition. Frowein & Kühner, *Drohende Folterung als Asylgrund und Grenze für Auslieferung und Ausweisung*, 43 ZEITSCHRIFT FÜR AUSLÄNDISCHES ÖFFENTLICHES RECHT UND VÖLKERRECHT 537 (1983).

[68] 60 Y.B. INST. INT'L L., *supra* note 67, at 234.

[69] *Id.*

[70] *Id.* at 259.

[71] *Id.* at 306.

recognizes as permitting no derogations? Nevertheless, the Institute's resolution promotes valuable ethical considerations and may yet contribute to the crystallization of human rights into *jus cogens* and the development of the notion of fundamental human rights.

Another question crucial to international human rights is whether the concept of *jus cogens* applies only to the law of treaties or whether it extends to other fields of international law, including the unilateral action of states. Since violations of human rights almost always result from the unilateral acts of states, rather than from international agreements, the nontreaty aspect of the problem is far more important than the treaty aspect. Even scholars who reserve *jus cogens* to treaty law tend to agree with the elementary proposition that international public order, public order of the international community and international public policy do not allow states to violate severally such norms as they are prohibited from violating jointly with other states.[72]

The International Law Commission appears to have applied the term "peremptory norms" outside the law of treaties to unilateral state action when it adopted the draft articles on state responsibility.[73] Article 33(2)(*a*) provides that "a state of necessity may not be invoked by a State as a ground for precluding wrongfulness . . . if the international obligation with which the act of the State is not in conformity arises out of a peremptory norm of general international law."[74] In this context, however, peremptory norms may refer to categorical rules of international law, or of international public policy, rather than *jus cogens* (which contrasts with the bulk of the rules of international law, the *jus dispositivum*, from which states are permitted, *inter partes*, to contract out), a concept that resides primarily in the law of treaties. Judge Mosler, who deserves credit for coining the phrase "public order of the international community," characterized such order as

> consist[ing] of principles and rules the enforcement of which is of such vital importance to the international community as a whole that any unilateral action or any agreement which contravenes these principles can have no legal force. The reason for this follows simply from logic; the law cannot recognise any act either of one member or of several members in concert, as being legally valid if it is directed against the very foundation of law.[75]

Obviously, the rationale underlying the concepts of *jus cogens* and public order of the international community is the same: because of the decisive importance of certain norms and values to the international community, they merit absolute protection and may not be derogated from by states, whether jointly by treaty or severally by unilateral legislative or executive

[72] H. MOSLER, THE INTERNATIONAL SOCIETY AS A LEGAL COMMUNITY 19–20 (1980). *Contra* Stein, *The Approach of the Different Drummer: The Principle of the Persistent Objector in International Law*, 26 HARV. INT'L L.J. 457, 481 (1985).

[73] [1980] 2 Y.B. INT'L L. COMM'N 30, UN Doc. A/CN.4/SER.A/1980/Add.1 (pt. 2). *See also infra* note 87.

[74] *Id.* at 33. *See generally* Gaja, *Jus Cogens beyond the Vienna Convention*, 172 RECUEIL DES COURS 271, 296–97 (1981 III).

[75] H. MOSLER, *supra* note 72, at 18.

action. It is in this sense that the International Court of Justice, in *United States Diplomatic and Consular Staff in Tehran*,[76] treated the "imperative character of the legal obligations incumbent upon the Iranian Government."[77]

Elsewhere, we have suggested that even states that are not parties to the Political Covenant may not derogate from categorical or absolute human rights, and that derogations cannot be clearly excessive or arbitrary, or in conflict with other international obligations of the state concerned.[78] Comment *h* to section 711 of the draft *Restatement* contains the intriguing proposition that the derogations permissible during an emergency under the Political Covenant are presumably also permissible under customary law in relation to nationals of other states.[79] Perhaps there is, indeed, some overlap in international law between derogations permitted by Article 4 of the Political Covenant and the customary rules of exception to the law governing state responsibility, such as those based on force majeure, state of necessity or self-defense (draft Articles 31, 33 and 34 of the draft articles on state responsibility). It is not certain, however, that the match of these customary rules with derogations permissible under Article 4 is perfect, or that the scope of the derogations allowed is identical.

If human right *X* is binding on a state not party to the Political Covenant in relation to its nationals or aliens, the derogating state would have to discharge the burden of establishing justifications such as state of necessity, just as if it had breached any other international legal obligation. Where a state cannot successfully discharge such a burden, the principle applies, as pointed out by Professor Marek (who cites Professor Verdross),[80] that a single state is not permitted to derogate from any rule of international law, peremptory or not. The significance of the *jus dispositivum* character of most rules of international law lies in the fact that a group of states, strictly in their mutual relations, may substitute a rule of conventional law for a rule of customary law. The difference between peremptory and other rules of international law is that, in the case of the former, the prohibition of derogations is absolute.

If the rationale underlying the concepts of *jus cogens* and public order of the international community is the same, are the legal consequences of violation also the same? An affirmative answer is suggested by Judge Mosler, who insists that an agreement or unilateral action that conflicts with the public policy of the international community can have no legal force and presumably is void *ipso jure*.

This thesis requires scrutiny. Of course, a conflict between an international agreement and a rule of *jus cogens* nullifies the former. Judge Mosler would find a unilateral act similarly void. A treaty, however, is a creature of international law, while a unilateral state act may be rooted in the national legal system. Depending on the relationship between international law and internal law in the state concerned, it cannot be taken for granted that the unilateral

[76] 1980 ICJ REP. 3, *supra* note 6. [77] *Id.* at 41.

[78] Meron, *supra* note 54, at 601–02 & n.69. [79] DRAFT RESTATEMENT, *supra* note 11.

[80] Marek, *Sur la Notion de Progrès en Droit International*, 38 ANNUAIRE SUISSE DE DROIT INTERNATIONAL 28, 35 (1982).

act would have no internal legal force. Indeed, the possibility of nullity is not even mentioned in Article 33 of the ILC's draft articles on state of necessity. The violating state would incur international responsibility (or perhaps even international criminal responsibility if the principle stated in Article 19(3) of the ILC's draft articles were applied), but the unilateral act itself would probably not be void, at least as regards its consequences under internal law. Professor Marek properly warns against "l'oblitération de la différence entre acte illicite et acte nul."[81]

The appropriate remedy for such a violation of a peremptory norm may therefore be annulment of the unilateral act, rather than nullity *ipso jure*. Third states would have the right and the duty to question the illegal act, and to refrain from recognizing it or giving it legal effect. On the international legal plane, the principle *ex injuria jus non oritur* would thus be followed. Judge Mosler's statement that the unilateral act would have no legal force may have been intended to suggest that the act would not be recognized by third states as valid under international law. It is in this sense that Professor Jaenicke perceives the ramifications of international public order.[82]

These observations may become clearer if viewed against a specific case. The United Nations Report on Protection of Human Rights in Chile (the Ermacora report) discussed a Chilean amnesty decree-law, which had been applied to protect governmental agents responsible for the deaths of detainees.[83] The report argued that Chile was responsible under Articles 29 and 146 of the Convention Relative to the Protection of Civilian Persons in Time of War (Geneva Convention No. IV) of August 12, 1949.[84] It is not our present object to discuss whether this position was correct in law. Suffice it to observe that rather than insist on the nullity of the decree-law, the report recommended that the "amnesty decree-law should not be applied in such a way as to run counter to Chile's international responsibilities, especially in regard to the Geneva Convention."[85]

V. CONCLUSION

The use of hierarchical terms in discussing human rights reflects the quest for a normative order in which higher rights could be invoked as both a moral and a legal barrier to derogations from and violations of human rights. Their introduction into international law was inspired by the national law analogy with its firmly established hierarchical structure. The trend towards the characterization of certain rights as hierarchically superior may also be seen as a response to the proliferation of human rights instruments, sometimes of poor quality and uncertain legal value. When some rights proclaimed

[81] *Id.*

[82] Jaenicke, *International Public Order*, in ENCYCLOPEDIA, *supra* note 57, at 314, 317.

[83] UN Doc. A/34/583/Add.1, at 96 (1979).

[84] *Id.* For the text of Geneva Convention No. IV, see 6 UST 3516, TIAS No. 3365, 75 UNTS 287.

[85] UN Doc. A/34/583/Add.1, *supra* note 83, at 98.

by such instruments are questioned, it is not surprising that attempts are made to upgrade other rights by giving them various quality labels, on the assumption that the authority of the higher right will not be impugned.

One cannot deny that the quality labels are a useful indication of the importance attached to particular rights. They strengthen the case against violation of such rights. Hierarchical terms constitute a warning sign that the international community will not accept any breach of those rights. Historically, the notions of "basic rights of the human person" and "fundamental rights" have helped establish the *erga omnes* principle, which is so crucial to ensuring respect for human rights. Eventually, they may contribute to the crystallization of some rights, through custom or treaties, into hierarchically superior norms, as in the more developed national legal systems.

Yet the balance of pros and cons does not necessarily weigh clearly on the side of the pros. Resort to hierarchical terms has not been matched by careful consideration of their legal significance. Few criteria for distinguishing between ordinary rights and higher rights have been agreed upon. There is no accepted system by which higher rights can be identified and their content determined. Nor are the consequences of the distinction between higher and ordinary rights clear. Rights not accorded quality labels, i.e., the majority of human rights, are relegated to inferior, second-class, status. Moreover, rather than grapple with the harder questions of rationalizing human rights lawmaking[86] and distinguishing between rights and claims, some commentators are resorting increasingly to superior rights in the hope that no state will dare—politically, morally and perhaps even legally—to ignore them. In these ways, hierarchical terms contribute to the unnecessary mystification of human rights, rather than to their greater clarity.

Caution should therefore be exercised in resorting to a hierarchical terminology. Too liberal an invocation of superior rights such as "fundamental rights" and "basic rights," as well as *jus cogens,* may adversely affect the credibility of human rights as a legal discipline.

Removal of the underbrush that clutters the landscape of concepts and nomenclature may make it possible to build a sounder, less amorphous structure of human rights, which should be based on an enlarged core of nonderogable rights. To these ends, the international community should direct its efforts to defining the distinction between ordinary and higher rights and the legal significance of this distinction, steps that would contribute significantly to resolving conflicts between rights. It should also intensify the effort to extend the list of nonderogable rights recognized by the international community of states as a whole. In addition, the ethically important concepts of *jus cogens* and public order of the international community should be allowed to develop gradually through international practice and growing consensus. General acceptance of these concepts would go far towards deterring violations. Finally, the new human rights structure should eventually be secured by international acceptance of binding provisions for the adju-

[86] *See generally* Alston, *supra* note 12; Meron, *Reform of Lawmaking in the United Nations: The Human Rights Instance,* 79 AJIL 664 (1985).

dication of disputes implicating *jus cogens* and public order of the international community.[87]

One day, perhaps, the international community will be able to agree on at least some of these measures. That day, however, is not yet in sight.

[87] The ILC's commentary to draft Article 12(b) on state responsibility (part 2) mentions the reluctance of some members to apply the concept of *jus cogens* outside of the framework of the Vienna Convention on the Law of Treaties. Other members, however, supported the retention of that article. The view was expressed that "a provision relating to *jus cogens* required . . . a procedural provision along the lines of that provided for in the Vienna Convention." Report of the International Law Commission on the work of its thirty-seventh session, *supra* note 51, at 48.

[5]

Human Dignity as a Normative Concept

The "dignity of the human person" and "human dignity" are phrases that have come to be used as an expression of a basic value accepted in a broad sense by all peoples.

Human dignity appears in the Preamble of the Charter of the United Nations as an ideal that "we the peoples of the United Nations" are "determined" to achieve. The words are part of the second paragraph of the Preamble, which reads in full as follows: "to reaffirm faith in fundamental human rights, in the dignity and worth of the human person, in the equal rights of men and women and of nations large and small."

The term dignity is also included in Article 1 of the Universal Declaration of Human Rights: "All human beings are born free and equal in dignity and rights. They are endowed with reason and conscience and should act towards one another in a spirit of brotherhood."

In some subsequent instruments, we find the expression "respect for the inherent dignity of the human person." For example, the International Covenant on Civil and Political Rights provides in Article 10 that "[a]ll persons deprived of their liberty shall be treated with humanity and with respect for the inherent dignity of the human person." A similar provision is found in the American Convention on Human Rights (Article 5).

The International Covenant on Economic, Social and Cultural Rights states in Article 13 that "education shall be directed to the full development of the human personality and the sense of its dignity."

The Helsinki Accords in Principle VII affirm that the participating states will promote the effective exercise of human rights and freedoms, "all of which derive from the inherent dignity of the human person."

References to human dignity are to be found in various resolutions and declarations of international bodies.[1] National constitutions and proclamations, especially those recently adopted, include the ideal or goal of human dignity in their references to human rights.[2] Political leaders, jurists and philosophers have increasingly alluded to the dignity of the human person as a

[1] *See, e.g.*, the ILO Declaration of Philadelphia (May 10, 1944) affirming the right of all persons to pursue their well-being and development "in conditions of freedom and dignity"; the UN Standard Minimum Rules for the Treatment of Prisoners (1955) (Rule 60); the UN Declaration on the Elimination of Discrimination against Women (1967); the UN Declaration on the Use of Scientific and Technological Progress in the Interests of Peace and for the Benefit of Mankind (1975). The latter declaration notes that scientific and technological achievements can be used to the detriment of human dignity.

[2] Article 1 of the German Federal Constitution states: "Human dignity is inviolable. It is the duty of all governmental power to respect and protect it." There is a considerable legal literature in German on this article. For a recent commentary by the President of the German Constitutional Court, see Benda, *Die Menschenwürde*, in Handbuch des Verfassungsrechts der Bundesrepublik Deutschland 107 (1983).

basic ideal so generally recognized as to require no independent support. It has acquired a resonance that leads it to be invoked widely as a legal and moral ground for protest against degrading and abusive treatment. No other ideal seems so clearly accepted as a universal social good.

II. The Meaning of the "Inherent Dignity of the Human Person"

We do not find an explicit definition of the expression "dignity of the human person" in international instruments or (as far as I know) in national law. Its intrinsic meaning has been left to intuitive understanding, conditioned in large measure by cultural factors. When it has been invoked in concrete situations, it has been generally assumed that a violation of human dignity can be recognized even if the abstract term cannot be defined.[3] "I know it when I see it even if I cannot tell you what it is."

In some situations an abstract definition is not needed; but it is not entirely satisfying to accept the idea that human dignity cannot be defined or analyzed in general terms. Without a reasonably clear general idea of its meaning, we cannot easily reject a specious use of the concept, nor can we without understanding its meaning draw specific implications for relevant conduct.

An analysis of dignity may begin with its etymological root, the Latin "dignitas" translated as worth (in French, "valeur"). One lexical meaning of dignity is "intrinsic worth." Thus, when the UN Charter refers to the "dignity and worth" of the human person, it uses two synonyms for the same concept. The other instruments speak of "inherent dignity," an expression that is close to "intrinsic worth."

What is meant by "respect" for "intrinsic worth" or "inherent dignity" of a person? "Respect" has several nuanced meanings: "esteem," "deference," "a proper regard for," "recognition of." These terms have both a subjective aspect (how one feels or thinks about another) and an objective aspect (how one treats another). Both are relevant to our question, but it seems more useful to focus on the latter aspect for purposes of practical measures.

One general answer to our question is suggested by the Kantian injunction to treat every human being as an end, not as a means. Respect for the intrinsic worth of every person should mean that individuals are not to be perceived or treated merely as instruments or objects of the will of others. This proposition will probably be generally acceptable as an ideal. There may be more question about its implications. I shall suggest such implications as corollaries of the general proposition.

The first is that a high priority should be accorded in political, social and legal arrangements to individual choices in such matters as beliefs, way of life, attitudes and the conduct of public affairs. Note that this is stated as a "high

[3] Several judicial decisions have applied the concept of dignity without attempting to define the concept in general terms. *See, e.g.*, the decision of the European Court of Human Rights in Lawless v. Ireland (Merits), 1 EHRR 15, 39 (Judgment of July 1, 1961) (individual op. Maridakis, J.). The courts of West Germany have also handed down several interesting decisions applying the constitutional provision on human dignity. *See* Benda, *supra* note 2.

priority," not an absolute rule. We may give it more specific content by applying it to political and psychological situations. In the political context, respect for the dignity and worth of all persons, and for their individual choices, leads, broadly speaking, to a strong emphasis on the will and consent of the governed. It means that the coercive rule of one or the few over the many is incompatible with a due respect for the dignity of the person. It also means that governments are not to use coercion to impose beliefs and attitudes on those subject to their rule or to extend their authority into areas of human life that are essentially personal and familial. The question of the proper boundaries between the public and the private, and between the sphere governed by the "general will" and that left to the individual remains to be answered in particular cases. But the idea that such boundaries need to be drawn and that an appropriate priority should be accorded to individual choices is not without significance. It clearly runs counter to many existing political ideologies and practices.

The conception of respect for dignity suggested above can also be given more specific meaning by applying it to actions of psychological significance. Indeed, nothing is so clearly violative of the dignity of persons as treatment that demeans or humiliates them. This includes not only attacks on personal beliefs and ways of life but also attacks on the groups and communities with which individuals are affiliated. Official statements that vilify groups or hold them up to ridicule and contempt are an especially dangerous form of psychological aggression resulting in a lack of respect by others for such groups and, perhaps even more insidious, destroying or reducing the sense of self-respect that is so important to the integrity of every human. We can also point to the widespread practice of using psychogenic drugs or other forms of psychological coercion to impose conformity and ideological obedience. These should clearly be seen as violations of the inherent dignity of the person. Put in positive terms, respect for the intrinsic worth of a person requires a recognition that the person is entitled to have his or her beliefs, attitudes, ideas and feelings. The use of coercion, physical or psychological, to change personal beliefs is as striking an affront to the dignity of the person as physical abuse or mental torture.

Our emphasis on respect for individuals and their choices also implies proper regard for the responsibility of individuals. The idea that people are generally responsible for their conduct is a recognition of their distinct identity and their capacity to make choices. Exceptions may have to be made for those incapable of such choices (minors or the insane) or in some cases for those under severe necessity. But the general recognition of individual responsibility, whether expressed in matters of criminal justice or civic duties, is an aspect of the respect that each person merits as a person. It is also worth noting as a counterpart that restraint is called for in imputing responsibility to individuals for acts of others such as groups of which they are members. In general, collective responsibility is a denigration of the dignity of the individual, a denial of a person's capacity to choose and act on his or her responsibility.

We do not by this last comment mean to separate individuals sharply from the collectivities of which they are a part. Indeed, we believe that the idea of human dignity involves a complex notion of the individual. It includes recognition of a distinct personal identity, reflecting individual autonomy and responsibility. It also embraces a recognition that the individual self is a part of larger collectivities and that they, too, must be considered in the meaning of the inherent dignity of the person. We can readily see the practical import of this conception of personality by considering political orders that, on the one hand, arbitrarily override individual choice and, on the other, seek to dissolve group ties. There is also a "procedural" implication in that it indicates that every individual and each significant group should be recognized as having the capacity to assert claims to protect their essential dignity.

We are led more deeply into the analysis of human dignity when we consider its relation to the material needs of human beings and to the ideal of distributive justice. Few will dispute that a person in abject condition, deprived of adequate means of subsistence, or denied the opportunity to work, suffers a profound affront to his sense of dignity and intrinsic worth.[4] Economic and social arrangements cannot therefore be excluded from a consideration of the demands of dignity. At the least, it requires recognition of a minimal concept of distributive justice that would require satisfaction of the essential needs of everyone.

Some would probably go beyond this and contend that substantial equality is a necessary condition of respect for the intrinsic worth of the human person. "Each person is as good as every other" may be inferred as a plausible maxim. In particular, relations of dominance and subordination would be viewed as antithetical to the basic ideal. If this is so, great discrepancies in wealth and power need to be eliminated to avoid such relations. However, the counterargument can be made that such egalitarian objectives cannot be realized without excessive curtailment of individual liberty and the use of coercion. This familiar confrontation of conflicting political philosophies need not be pursued here, but it is worth noting that demands for the respect of human dignity will almost surely lead into the continuing debate between advocates of equality and advocates of freedom.

These observations on the meaning of respect for the inherent dignity of the human being suggest the far-reaching implications of an ideal that has not yet been given substantial specific content. At the same time, our analysis indicates that a determinate core of meaning may be elucidated that is in keeping with widely accepted (though not universally accepted) values. This core of meaning has not been formulated as an explicit definition. To do so would result in another highly abstract formula. What is important is the extent to which the analysis leads to more concrete acceptable norms of con-

[4] Benda considers that the German constitutional provision on human dignity imposes a constitutional duty on the state to protect individuals against material want (*materieller Not*). *See* Benda, *supra* note 2, at 113, 115. The right to public assistance has been linked to Article 1 of the Constitution by the Supreme Administrative Court, No. 55, 1 BVerwGE 159 (1954). There is an old judgment of the Constitutional Court stating that Article 1 standing alone did not impose a duty of protection against material want (No. 22, 1 BVerfGE 97, 104 (1951)), but this opinion does not represent the views held generally today. I am indebted to Professor Stefan Riesenfeld for information on the German constitutional law concerning this point.

duct. I have sought to indicate this in my comments. As a further step in this direction, I shall next suggest some examples of conduct and ideas antithetical to or incompatible with respect for the inherent dignity of the human person.

II. Conduct and Ideas Antithetical or Incompatible with Respect for Inherent Dignity

The following list embraces two categories: one relates to conduct and ideas that directly offend or denigrate the worth and dignity of individuals; the second, to conduct and ideas that are implicitly incompatible with the basic ideas of the inherent dignity and worth of human persons. The line between the two categories is not a sharp one, but the distinction is helpful to the task of identifying relevant factors and to considering how to respond to incompatible acts and attitudes. The examples given are not limited to official acts and statements. Affronts to dignity may come from nonofficial sources. They should not be excluded for that reason, although a different position might be taken if the question were whether such affronts should be grounds for legal action.

(1) Statements that demean and humiliate individuals or groups because of their origins, status or beliefs.

(2) Vilification or derision of beliefs that people hold in reverence. Teaching that particular races, ethnic groups or religions hold "ridiculous" or dangerous views, or otherwise belittling cherished beliefs.

(3) Denial of the capacity of a person to assert claims to basic rights.

(4) Punishment of detained persons by psychological or physical means that are meant to humiliate or ridicule their beliefs, origins or way of life.

(5) Dissemination of negative stereotypes of groups (ethnic, religious, social) and implications that members of such groups are inferior.

(6) Psychiatric treatment that involves coercive means to change beliefs or choices that are lawful.

(7) Restrictions on opportunities and means to maintain family life as, for example, by denying access to family members or requiring members of families to inform authorities of the acts or beliefs of others.

(8) Denial of educational or employment opportunities to persons on ground of their membership in groups or their beliefs.

(9) Restrictions on equal participation in political processes because of beliefs, status or origin.

(10) Degrading living conditions and deprivation of basic needs.

(11) Abuse and insolence by officials, especially to persons suffering from infirmities or social opprobrium.

(12) Medical treatment or hospital care insensitive to individual choice or the requirements of human personality.

III. Human Dignity and Human Rights

The relation of human dignity to human rights is of particular interest to our thesis.

The Helsinki Final Act declares in Principle VII that all human rights and fundamental freedoms "derive from the inherent dignity of the human person." This statement should be understood in a philosophical rather than historical sense. As history, it would probably be more correct to say the opposite: namely, that the idea of dignity reflects sociohistorical conceptions of basic rights and freedoms, not that it generated them. However, as a philosophical statement, the proposition that rights derive from the inherent dignity of the person is significant. It clearly implies that rights are not derived from the state or any other external authority.

One may ask whether a philosophical statement of this broad character has any practical consequence. The answer lies in the degree to which general ideas influence perceptions and attitudes affecting conduct. The general idea that human rights are derived from the dignity of the person is neither truistic nor neutral. It has two corollaries that challenge conceptions prevalent in some societies and ideologies. The first corollary is the idea that basic rights are not given by authority and therefore may not be taken away; the second is that they are rights of the person, every person. It is not unrealistic to assume that ideas of this kind will have a role in challenging existing attitudes. When they are found in official declarations, they become part of the instruments of change, sometimes loudly proclaimed, at other times almost imperceptibly affecting ideas of legitimacy.

There is a further implication to be drawn from the recognition of human dignity as a "source" of human rights. Drawing upon the conception of human dignity and the intrinsic worth of every person, we can extend and strengthen human rights by formulating new rights or construing existing rights to apply to new situations. The analysis of human dignity given earlier is suggestive of such possibilities. As an example, one might suggest that aliens now commonly deprived of rights to take part in civic and political life should as a matter of respect for their worth be given such rights. Other examples might perhaps be inferred from the recognition that vilification and demeaning of group beliefs and aspirations are affronts to dignity and that official behavior involving such vilification or demeaning should be considered as a violation of the rights of the person.

This latter example raises another general question: namely, whether violations of dignity should as a rule be dealt with through legal action and the assertion of rights. I would suggest the contrary. Respect for human dignity may be realized in other ways than by asserting claims of right. In many cases, the application of a "rights approach" to affronts to dignity would raise questions involving existing basic rights such as free speech. In other cases, respect for dignity may be more appropriately and effectively attained through social processes such as education, material benefits, political leadership and the like. Various situations involving apparent violations of dignity may be alleviated by a code of conduct or of good manners such as those followed in some parliamentary bodies or educational institutions. Simply making people aware of language and acts that would be considered disrespectful of the worth of others could have a beneficial effect. Steps may be taken to foster better understanding by those in power and in the information media of the sensitivities of persons and groups to slurs and belittling comment. Informal channels for dealing with alleged affronts to dignity might be more suitable and effective than litigation in many cases. In such areas of public administration as social welfare, health care and prison administration, there is ample room for the elimination of actions that impinge on the self-respect of those in need of aid.

These observations indicate that the central idea of human dignity has a wide range of applications outside of the sphere of human rights. It is therefore of some importance to treat it as a distinct subject and to consider ways that respect for dignity can be fostered through public and private agencies.

OSCAR SCHACHTER

Part II
Universality in Cultural Perspective

[6]

American Anthropologist

NEW SERIES

Vol. 49 OCTOBER-DECEMBER, 1947 No. 4

STATEMENT ON HUMAN RIGHTS

SUBMITTED TO THE COMMISSION ON HUMAN RIGHTS, UNITED NATIONS
BY THE EXECUTIVE BOARD, AMERICAN ANTHROPOLOGICAL ASSOCIATION

THE problem faced by the Commission on Human Rights of the United Nations in preparing its Declaration on the Rights of Man must be approached from two points of view. The first, in terms of which the Declaration is ordinarily conceived, concerns the respect for the personality of the individual as such, and his right to its fullest development as a member of his society. In a world order, however, respect for the cultures of differing human groups is equally important.

These are two facets of the same problem, since it is a truism that groups are composed of individuals, and human beings do not function outside the societies of which they form a part. The problem is thus to formulate a statement of human rights that will do more than just phrase respect for the individual as an individual. It must also take into full account the individual as a member of the social group of which he is a part, whose sanctioned modes of life shape his behavior, and with whose fate his own is thus inextricably bound.

Because of the great numbers of societies that are in intimate contact in the modern world, and because of the diversity of their ways of life, the primary task confronting those who would draw up a Declaration on the Rights of Man is thus, in essence, to resolve the following problem: How can the proposed Declaration be applicable to all human beings, and not be a statement of rights conceived only in terms of the values prevalent in the countries of Western Europe and America?

Before we can cope with this problem, it will be necessary for us to outline some of the findings of the sciences that deal with the study of human culture, that must be taken into account if the Declaration is to be in accord with the present state of knowledge about man and his modes of life.

If we begin, as we must, with the individual, we find that from the moment of his birth not only his behavior, but his very thought, his hopes, aspirations, the moral values which direct his action and justify and give meaning to his life in his own eyes and those of his fellows, are shaped by the body of custom of the group of which he becomes a member. The process by means of which this is accomplished is so subtle, and its effects are so far-reaching, that only after considerable training are we conscious of it. Yet if the essence of the Declaration is to be, as it must, a statement in which the right of the individual to develop his personality to the fullest is to be stressed, then this must be based on a recognition of the fact that the personality of the individual can develop only in terms of the culture of his society.

Over the past fifty years, the many ways in which man resolves the problems of subsistence, of social living, of political regulation of group life, of reaching accord with the Universe and satisfying his aesthetic drives has been widely documented by the researches of anthropologists among peoples living in all parts of the world. All peoples do achieve these ends. No two of them, however, do so in exactly the same way, and some of them employ means that differ, often strikingly, from one another.

Yet here a dilemma arises. Because of the social setting of the learning process, the individual cannot but be convinced that his own way of life is the most desirable one. Conversely, and despite changes originating from within and without his culture that he recognizes as worthy of adoption, it becomes equally patent to him that, in the main, other ways than his own, to the degree they differ from it, are less desirable than those to which he is accustomed. Hence valuations arise, that in themselves receive the sanction of accepted belief.

The degree to which such evaluations eventuate in action depends on the basic sanctions in the thought of a people. In the main, people are willing to live and let live, exhibiting a tolerance for behavior of another group different than their own, especially where there is no conflict in the subsistence field. In the history of Western Europe and America, however, economic expansion, control of armaments, and an evangelical religious tradition have translated the recognition of cultural differences into a summons to action. This has been emphasized by philosophical systems that have stressed absolutes in the realm of values and ends. Definitions of freedom, concepts of the nature of human rights, and the like, have thus been narrowly drawn. Alternatives have been decried, and suppressed where controls have been established over non-European peoples. The hard core of *similarities* between cultures has consistently been overlooked.

The consequences of this point of view have been disastrous for mankind. Doctrines of the "white man's burden" have been employed to implement economic exploitation and to deny the right to control their own affairs to millions of peoples over the world, where the expansion of Europe and America has not meant the literal extermination of whole populations. Rationalized in terms of ascribing cultural inferiority to these peoples, or in conceptions of their backwardness in development of their "primitive mentality," that justified their being held in the tutelage of their superiors, the history of the expansion of the western world has been marked by demoralization of human personality and the disintegration of human rights among the peoples over whom hegemony has been established.

The values of the ways of life of these peoples have been consistently misunderstood and decried. Religious beliefs that for untold ages have carried conviction, and permitted adjustment to the Universe have been attacked as superstitious, immoral, untrue. And, since power carries its own conviction, this has furthered the process of demoralization begun by economic exploitation and the loss of political autonomy. The white man's burden, the civilizing mission, have been heavy indeed. But their weight has not been borne by those who, frequently in all honesty, have journeyed to the far places of the world to uplift those regarded by them as inferior.

We thus come to the first proposition that the study of human psychology and culture dictates as essential in drawing up a Bill of Human Rights in terms of existing knowledge:

1. *The individual realizes his personality through his culture, hence respect for individual differences entails a respect for cultural differences.*

There can be no individual freedom, that is, when the group with which the individual indentifies himself is not free. There can be no full development of the individual personality as long as the individual is told, by men who have the power to enforce their commands, that the way of life of his group is inferior to that of those who wield the power.

This is more than an academic question, as becomes evident if one looks about him at the world as it exists today. Peoples who on first contact with European and American might were awed and partially convinced of the superior ways of their rulers have, through two wars and a depression, come to re-examine the new and the old. Professions of love of democracy, of devotion to freedom have come with something less than conviction to those who are themselves denied the right to lead their lives as seems proper to them. The religious dogmas of those who profess equality and practice discrimination, who stress the virtue of humility and are themselves arrogant in insistence on their beliefs have little meaning for peoples whose devotion to other faiths makes these inconsistencies as clear as the desert landscape at high noon. Small wonder that these peoples, denied the right to live in terms of their own cultures, are discovering new values in old beliefs they had been led to question.

No consideration of human rights can be adequate without taking into account the related problem of human capacity. Man, biologically, is one. *Homo sapiens* is a single species, no matter how individuals may differ in their aptitudes, their abilities, their interests. It is established that any normal individual can learn any part of any culture other than his own, provided only he is afforded the opportunity to do so. That cultures differ in degree of complexity, of richness of content, is due to historic forces, not biological ones. All existing ways of life meet the test of survival. Of those cultures that have disappeared, it must be remembered that their number includes some that were great, powerful, and complex as well as others that were modest, content with the *status quo*, and simple. Thus we reach a second principle:

2. *Respect for differences between cultures is validated by the scientific fact that no technique of qualitatively evaluating cultures has been discovered.*

This principle leads us to a further one, namely that the aims that guide the life of every people are self-evident in their significance to that people. It is the principle that emphasizes the universals in human conduct rather than the absolutes that the culture of Western Europe and America stresses. It recognizes that the eternal verities only seem so because we have been taught to regard them as such; that every people, whether it expresses them or not, lives in devotion to verities whose eternal nature is as real to them as are those of Euroamerican culture to Euroamericans. Briefly stated, this third principle that must be introduced into our consideration is the following:

3. *Standards and values are relative to the culture from which they derive so that any attempt to formulate postulates that grow out of the beliefs or moral codes of one culture must to that extent detract from the applicability of any Declaration of Human Rights to mankind as a whole.*

Ideas of right and wrong, good and evil, are found in all societies, though they differ in their expression among different peoples. What is held to be a human right in one society may be regarded as anti-social by another people, or by the same people in a different period of their history. The saint of one epoch would at a later time be confined as a man not fitted to cope with reality. Even the nature of the physical world, the colors we see, the sounds we hear, are conditioned by the language we speak, which is part of the culture into which we are born.

The problem of drawing up a Declaration of Human Rights was relatively simple in the Eighteenth Century, because it was not a matter of *human* rights, but of the rights of men within the framework of the sanctions laid by a single society. Even then, so noble a document as the American Declaration of Independence, or the American Bill of Rights, could be written by men who themselves were slave-owners, in a country where chattel slavery was a part of the recognized social order. The revolutionary character of the slogan "Liberty, Equality, Fraternity" was never more apparent than in the struggles to implement it by extending it to the French slave-owning colonies.

Today the problem is complicated by the fact that the Declaration must be of world-wide applicability. It must embrace and recognize the validity of many different ways of life. It will not be convincing to the Indonesian, the African, the Indian, the Chinese, if it lies on the same plane as like documents of an earlier period. The rights of Man in the Twentieth Century cannot be circumscribed by the standards of any single culture, or be dictated by the aspirations of any single people. Such a document will lead to frustration, not realization of the personalities of vast numbers of human beings.

Such persons, living in terms of values not envisaged by a limited Declaration, will thus be excluded from the freedom of full participation in the only right and proper way of life that can be known to them, the institutions, sanctions and goals that make up the culture of their particular society.

Even where political systems exist that deny citizens the right of participation in their government, or seek to conquer weaker peoples, underlying cultural values may be called on to bring the peoples of such states to a realization of the consequences of the acts of their governments, and thus enforce a brake upon discrimination and conquest. For the political system of a people is only a small part of their total culture.

World-wide standards of freedom and justice, based on the principle that man is free only when he lives as his society defines freedom, that his rights are those he recognizes as a member of his society, must be basic. Conversely, an effective world-order cannot be devised except insofar as it permits the free play of personality of the members of its constituent social units, and draws strength from the enrichment to be derived from the interplay of varying personalities.

The world-wide acclaim accorded the Atlantic Charter, before its restricted applicability was announced, is evidence of the fact that freedom is understood and sought after by peoples having the most diverse cultures. Only when a statement of the right of men to live in terms of their own traditions is incorporated into the proposed Declaration, then, can the next step of defining the rights and duties of human groups as regards each other be set upon the firm foundation of the present-day scientific knowledge of Man.

JUNE 24, 1947

[7]

International Human Rights and Cultural Relativism

FERNANDO R. TESÓN*

Notre conception des droits de l'homme ne varie pas selon les latitudes ni selon les circonstances.[1]

I. INTRODUCTION

We are witnessing an unequivocal process of universalization of the concern for human dignity.[2] As international law becomes more responsive to the demands for individual freedom, however, it necessarily challenges the validity of certain state practices reflecting geographical and cultural particularities. The tension between national sovereignty and the enforcement of international

---

* Associate Professor of Law, Arizona State University. J.D. 1975, Universidad de Buenos Aires; Licencié en Droit International 1982, Université Libre de Bruxelles; currently S.J.D. candidate, Northwestern University. This article grew out of a presentation delivered to the Conference on Third World Legal Studies at Harvard Law School in December 1983. I am grateful to my colleagues David Kaye and David Kader for their valuable suggestions. The remaining mistakes are only mine.

1. President Francois Mitterand on the eve of his trip to the Soviet Union, Le Monde, May 17, 1984, at 1, col. 5. ("Our conception of human rights does not vary with latitudes or with circumstances.") [trans. by eds.].

2. For a survey of the literature dealing with what has been, in the words of Professor Sohn, a true "human rights revolution," Sohn, The New International Law: Protection of the Rights of Individuals Rather than States, 32 Am. U.L. Rev. 1 (1982), see Vincent-Daviss, Human Rights Law: A Research Guide to the Literature-Part I: International Law and the United Nations, 14 N.Y.U. J. Int'l L. & Pol. 209 (1981); Vincent-Daviss, Human Rights Law: A Research Guide to the Literature-Part II: International Protection of Refugees, and Humanitarian Law, 14 N.Y.U. J. Int'l L. & Pol. 487 (1982); Vincent-Daviss, Human Rights Law: A Research Guide to the Literature-Part III: The International Labor Organization and Human Rights, 15 N.Y.U. J. Int'l L. & Pol. 211 (1982) [hereinafter collectively cited as Vincent-Daviss, Human Rights Law Research Guides].

human rights standards is highlighted when governments point to national cultural traditions to justify failures to comply with international law.[3] States espousing such positions have found invaluable allies not only in Third World writers,[4] but also among certain Western legal scholars,[5] anthropologists, and philosophers.[6]

"Cultural relativism" is not a term of art, nor even a legal term. It has been borrowed from anthropology and moral philosophy, a fact that has several consequences. First, because an intimate link exists between the moral and legal dimensions of relativism,[7] both the philosophical aspects of relativism and the status of that doctrine in positive international law will be discussed. Second, the theory of cultural relativism has several different possible meanings.[8] While the core idea of cultural relativism will be discussed and critiqued,[9] arguments that relativists could or should advance will also occasionally be anticipated, even though such arguments may not yet have been articulated by relativist scholars or governments.

In the context of the debate about the viability of international human rights, cultural relativism may be defined as the position according to which local cultural traditions (including religious, political, and legal practices) properly determine the existence and scope of civil and political rights enjoyed by individuals in a given society.[10] A central tenet of relativism is that no transboundary le-

---

3. See, e.g., the statement made by the Saudi Arabian representative to the United Nations, 32 U.N. GAOR C.3 (43rd mtg.) at 11-13, U.N. Doc. A/C.3/32/SR.43 (1977) (different social, cultural, and political traditions justify different interpretations of human rights).

4. See, e.g., Wai, Human Rights in Sub-Sahara Africa, in Human Rights: Cultural and Ideological Perspectives 1 (A. Pollis & P. Schwab eds. 1979) (claiming that Western-oriented human rights notions embodied in the U.N. Charter and the Universal Declaration on Human Rights may not be applicable in non-Western areas); Mani, Regional Approaches to the Implementation of Human Rights, 21 Indian J. Int'l L. 96, 97 (1981).

5. A recent work by E. McWhinney, United Nations Law Making (1984), bears the following subtitle: Cultural and Ideological Relativism and International Law Making for an Era of Transition.

6. See, e.g., M. Herskovits, Man and His Works 61-78 (1949); E. Westermarck, Ethical Relativity 183-219 (1932).

7. See infra notes 79-84 and accompanying text.

8. See infra notes 85-94 and accompanying text.

9. See infra text accompanying notes 10-13.

10. Many contemporary situations exemplify the tension between domestic cultural imperatives and international norms: mutilation and flogging as criminal punishment (see U.S. Dep't of State, Country Reports on Human Rights Practices 1084 (1981); Marett, Some Medical Problems Met in Saudi Arabia, 4 U.S.A.F. Med. J. 31, 36 (1953)); the circumcision of women (see Dullea, Female Circumcision a Topic at U.N. Parley, N.Y. Times, July 18, 1980, at B4, col. 3.); the subjugation of women (see White, Legal Reform as an Indicator of

gal or moral standards exist against which human rights practices may be judged acceptable or unacceptable.[11] Thus, relativists claim that substantive human rights standards vary among different cultures and necessarily reflect national idiosyncracies. What may be regarded as a human rights violation in one society may properly be considered lawful in another, and Western ideas of human rights should not be imposed upon Third World societies.[12] Tolerance and respect for self-determination preclude crosscultural normative judgments. Alternatively, the relativist thesis holds that even if, as a matter of customary or conventional international law, a body of substantive human rights norms exists, its meaning varies substantially from culture to culture.[13]

The critique advanced here of cultural relativism shall be limited in several important ways. First, the paper will only deal with violations of civil and political rights—the so-called "first generation" rights. Cultural relativism will not be analyzed in relation to other human rights that may be part of international law, such as the socioeconomic or "second generation" rights.[14] Second, cultural

---

Women's Status in Muslim Nations, in Women in the Muslim World 52 (L. Beck & N. Keddie eds. 1978); Marshall, Tradition and the Veil: Female Status in Tunisia and Algeria, 19 J. Mod. African Stud. 635, 632-37 (1981)); and various authoritarian methods of government (see Note, Human Rights Practices in the Arab States: The Modern Impact of Shari'a Values, 12 Ga. J. Int'l & Comp. L. 55, 92 (1981) (Shari'a values established a philosophical foundation for human rights abuses)). All of these examples of contemporary practices, while clearly unlawful by international standards, are defended by some as being required or permitted by cultural traditions. See also the discussion of the Iranian position on human rights in E. McWhinney, supra note 5, at 210.

11. Since the main concern of international human rights is the position of the individual vis-à-vis the government, the expression "human rights practices" encompasses, in addition to governmental acts, actions by groups or individuals that governments tolerate or condone (e.g., religious practices carried out by the clergy and tolerated by the state).

12. See supra note 4.

13. See Pollis, Liberal, Socialist and Third World Perspectives on Human Rights, in Toward a Human Rights Framework 1, 23 (A. Pollis & P. Schwab eds. 1982) (arguing that human rights judgments ought to be determined "by the criteria set by the philosophic/cultural/ideological roots of particular states"); Said & Nasser, The Use and Abuse of Democracy in Islam, in International Human Rights: Contemporary Issues 61 (J. Nelson & V. Green eds. 1980) ("freedom exists in Islam as long as it serves the interest of the community").

14. For a complete though somewhat uncritical account of the evolution and meaning of the different "generations" of rights in the United Nations, see Sohn, supra note 2, and references cited therein. The so-called "third generation" of human rights are the "solidarity" rights. The advocacy of this new set of rights may represent an attempt to use the favorable emotive connections of human rights language to expand the "rights" of the state at the expense of individual rights. Cf. Alston, A Third Generation of Solidarity Rights: Progressive Development or Obfuscation of International Human Rights Law?, 29 Neth.

relativism must be distinguished from the thesis that governments, especially those of the Third World, may suppress, delay or suspend civil and political rights in an effort to achieve a just economic order. While the issue of whether socioeconomic rights should in certain situations have priority over civil and political rights has received a great deal of attention in human rights literature,[15] it differs from the problems raised by cultural relativism *stricto sensu.*[16]

The discussion here will be further circumscribed by two assumptions which have solid foundations in international law. The first assumption is that human rights are a substantive part of international law, not only as a matter of treaty, but also as part of customary law.[17] It follows that arguments premised upon the ex-

---

Int'l L. Rev. 307, 321 (1982) (proponents of such rights have a strong burden of proof to show that they are compatible with and do not devalue existing rights).

15. See Forsythe, Socioeconomic Human Rights: The United Nations, the United States and Beyond, 4 Hum. Rts. Q. 433, 434-45 (1982); Zalaquett, An Interdisciplinary Approach to Development and Human Rights, 4 B.C. Third World L.J. 1, 28-31 (1983). Unlike "solidarity" rights, socioeconomic rights represent a positive force in the fight to enhance human dignity. However, the emergence of socioeconomic rights need not entail the demise or contraction of civil and political rights. It should be noted that authoritarian regimes, whether Marxist or not, invariably defend the priority of socioeconomic rights. See Forsythe, supra, at 434. The U.N. majority appears to take the position that socioeconomic rights deserve as much attention as civil and political rights. See G.A. Res. 34/46, 34 U.N. GAOR Supp. (70th mtg.) at para 4, U.N. Doc. A/Res. 34/46 (1979). The philosophical literature has devoted considerable attention to the priority issue since the publication of John Rawls' A Theory of Justice (1971). Rawls suggests a "lexical" order between civil and political freedoms on the one hand and economic principles of justice on the other. Id. at 243-50. Some of the numerous responses to Rawls' solution of the priority problem include B. Barry, The Liberal Theory of Justice ch. 8 (1973), and Hart, Liberty and Its Priority, in Reading Rawls 230 (N. Daniels ed. 1975).

16. The position that socioeconomic rights should have priority over civil and political rights need not embrace cultural relativism. The relativist thesis states that *cultural* standards—and not economic development or the need to implement distributive justice—determine the extent and nature of human rights. A government that justifies human rights deprivations by appealing to economic priorities may well reject cultural relativism. Some of the arguments marshalled in this article, however, are also directed to the thesis of the priority of socioeconomic rights. See infra notes 121-26 and accompanying text.

17. See H. Lauterpacht, International Law and Human Rights 147-52 (1950) (human rights provisions of the U.N. Charter are binding). Accord Haile, Human Rights, Stability and Development in Africa: Some Observations on Concept and Reality, 24 Va. J. Int'l L. 575, 581 (1984). See also M. McDougal, H. Lasswell & C. Chen, Human Rights and World Public Order 7-27 (1980) (human rights are binding as a result of the *combined* effect of treaties, U.N. resolutions, diplomatic intercourse, and the impressive rise of awareness of the problem in world opinion); D'Amato, The Concept of Human Rights in International Law, 82 Colum. L. Rev. 1110, 1128-49 (1982) (human rights have become part of customary international law through the process of generalization of treaty provisions). On the other hand, some commentators deny that human rights are part of international law. See, e.g.,

clusively municipal nature of human rights law are inconsistent with present international law.[18] The cultural relativist may, but need not, disagree with this assumption. He need only hold that the various freedoms have different meanings when applied to different societies.[19] Some relativists would even agree that a few basic human rights, such as the right to life and the freedom from torture, are absolute in the sense that even cultural traditions may not override them. But relativists do not regard other rights, such as the right to physical integrity, the right to participate in the election of one's government, the right to a fair trial, freedom of expression, freedom of association, freedom of movement, or the prohibition of discrimination, as required by international law.[20] While I assume that the core meaning of international human rights law encompasses rights beyond the right to life and to freedom from torture, I do not attempt to prove this assumption. Rather, my main thesis can be condensed into the following two propositions:

> a) If there is an international human rights standard—the exact scope of which is admittedly difficult to ascertain—then its meaning remains uniform across borders.
>
> b) Analogously, if there is a possibility of meaningful moral discourse about rights, then it is universal in nature and applies to all human beings despite cultural differences.

The second assumption made in this paper is that an obligation in international law indeed exists to respect the cultural identities of peoples, their local traditions, and customs.[21] For example, the

---

Lane, Demanding Human Rights: A Change in the World Legal Order?, 6 Hofstra L. Rev. 269 (1978); Watson, Normativity and Reality in International Human Rights Law, 123 Stetson L. Rev. 221 (1984); Watson, The Limited Utility of International Law in the Protection of Human Rights, 1980 Am. Soc'y Int'l L. Proc. 1.

18. See L. Goodrich, E. Hambro & A. Simmons, Charter of the United Nations 370-78 (1949); M. Rajan, The Expanding Jurisdiction of the United Nations 98-123 (1982).

19. See, e.g., Pollis, supra note 13, at 22-23.

20. See Murphy, Objections to Western Conceptions of Human Rights, 9 Hofstra L. Rev. 433 (1981).

21. See Declaration on Principles of International Law Concerning Friendly Relations and Co-operation among States in Accordance with the Charter of the United Nations, G.A. Res. 2625, 25 U.N. GAOR Supp. (No. 28) at 123, U.N. Doc. A/8028 (1970) ("Every State has an inalienable right to choose its political, economic, social, and cultural systems without interference in any form by another State.") [hereinafter cited as Declaration on Principles].

classical international law on the treatment of aliens has long recognized that Westerners cannot expect to enjoy Western judicial procedures in non-Western states. Arbitral tribunals have consistently refused to accept the claim that partially nonadversary criminal procedures violate the international minimum standard concerning the right to a fair trial.[22]

However, to say that cultural identities should be respected does not mean that international human rights law lacks a substantive core.[23] Such a core can be gleaned from international human rights treaties, both regional and universal,[24] and diplomatic practice, including the relevant practices of international organizations. Indeed, human rights treaties offer a surprisingly uniform articulation of human rights law. They may safely be used as a reference, regardless of how many or which states are parties.[25] The rights, *inter alia*, to life, to physical integrity, to a fair trial, freedom of expression, freedom of thought and religion, freedom of association, and the prohibition against discrimination are all rights upon which international instruments agree. Unless one wishes to give up the very notion of an international law of human rights altogether, these rights should have essentially the same meaning regardless of local traditions.[26]

---

22. Salem Case (Egypt v. U.S.), 2 R. Int'l Arb. Awards 1161, 1197 (1932); McCurdy Case (U.S. v. Mexico), 4 R. Int'l Arb. Awards 418 (1929).

23. Schachter, The Charter and the Constitution: The Human Rights Provisions in American Law, 4 Vand. L. Rev. 643, 652 (1951). Cf. M. McDougal, H. Lasswell & C. Chen, supra note 17, at 5-6 (while different peoples may assert human rights demands in different modalities, a universal insistence on certain basic values exists among all cultures); Kader, Book Review, 1980 Ariz. St. L.J. 815, 825 (1980) ("The challenge confronting the human rights movement . . . is to recognize and take into account the sociopolitical differences in the world and yet to resist the relativism which is incompatible with the promotion of universal standards of human rights.").

24. See, e.g., African Charter on Human Rights and Peoples' Rights, Organization of African Unity, O.A.U. Doc. CAB/LEG/67/3 Rev. 5 (Jan. 1981), reprinted in 21 I.L.M. 58 (1982) [hereinafter cited as African Charter]; American Convention on Human Rights, O.A.S. Off. Records OEA/Ser. K/XVI/1.1, Doc. 65 (1969), reprinted in 9 I.L.M. 101 (1970) [hereinafter cited as American Convention]; International Covenant on Civil and Political Rights, G.A. Res. 2200, 21 U.N. GAOR Supp. (No. 16) at 49, U.N. Doc. A/6316 (1966) [hereinafter cited as U.N. Covenant]; European Convention on Human Rights and Fundamental Freedoms, 213 U.N.T.S. 221, 1950 Gr. Brit. T.S. No. 71 (Cmd. 8969) (1950) [hereinafter cited as European Convention].

25. As of December 31, 1983, 78 states are parties to the U.N. Covenant, 21 to the European Convention, and 14 to the American Convention. The African Charter is not yet in force. For the view that the treaties themselves have created human rights obligations to third parties, see D'Amato, supra note 17, at 1127-49 nn.70-74.

26. A growing number of Third World scholars reject the relativist approach. See, e.g.,

I will argue that cultural relativism cannot be reconciled with the recognition in international law of fundamental rights of the individual. Part II will demonstrate that positive international law does not recognize cultural diversity as a justification for the failure to observe human rights. In Part III, I will argue further that ethical relativism is a philosophically untenable position. Part IV includes a brief exposition on and critique of two by-products of relativism: the elitist and conspiracy theories of human rights. Finally, Part V sets forth some general conclusions.

II. CULTURAL RELATIVISM AND INTERNATIONAL LAW

A. *Cultural Relativism and the Structure of International Law*

Some commentators have argued that in the absence of centralized international organs, one cannot give a manageable core of meaning to international human rights norms.[27] It may be suggested along these lines that, because the uniform meaning of human rights advanced by the universalist thesis can be achieved only in conjunction with international bodies having jurisdiction to decide conflicting claims regarding the observance of human rights, relativism best accounts for the realities of contemporary international society.[28] This is not a negligible argument. While some encouraging steps are being taken, mainly in regional settings,[29] there

---

Eisemokhai, Towards Adequate Defense of Human Rights in Africa, 21 Indian J. Int'l L. 141 (1981) (criticizing the failure of African governments to comply with human rights law); Haile, supra note 17, at 584 (African traditions are not inconsistent with international human rights law). Some African leaders have also taken a less relativistic position, at least with regard to basic human rights. See, e.g., the speech of President Julius Nyerere of Tanzania criticizing African nations that refrained from condemning President Idi Amin of Uganda on the grounds that Amin was black, 1979 Keesing's Contemporary Archives 29670A (1979) ("blackness has become a certificate to kill with impunity").

27. See Watson, Legal Theory, Efficacy and Validity in the Development of Human Rights Norms in International Law, 1979 U. Ill. L.F. 609, 626 (1979).

28. Indeed, centralized systems for the protection of human rights aim to give uniform meaning to basic rights and freedoms in countries with disparate cultural and legal traditions. The system established by the European Convention provides a striking illustration. In the *Sunday Times Case*, the European Court of Human Rights held that the ancient British institution of contempt of court as applied by British courts was inconsistent with the freedom of speech guaranteed by the European Convention. Sunday Times Case, 23 Y.B. Eur. Conv. Human Rights 480 (1980) (Eur. Comm'n on Human Rights).

29. The creation of the Inter-American Court of Human Rights represents a major development in the human rights enforcement area, particularly because countries like Argentina have accepted the jurisdiction of the court. See generally Buerghenthal, The Inter-American Court of Human Rights, 76 Am. J. Int'l L. 231 (1982). The Inter-American Human Rights Commission, although not endowed with judicial power, has considerable political weight.

is no doubt that the lack of centralized, compulsive judicial machinery represents a major weakness of current international human rights law.

This argument, however, is open to two fatal objections. First, it proves too much. The lack of courts and enforcement agencies characterizes international law generally, not just the law of human rights. Therefore, the relativist who leaves human rights out of the scope of international law solely because of the absence of adjudicatory and enforcement mechanisms ultimately must deny the legal character of international law altogether.[30]

Second, this view overlooks the way that international law works. Unlike domestic societies where legislatures, courts, and government agencies create law, law in the international arena results from the subtle interplay of claims, counterclaims, actions and omissions of many international actors.[31] Thus, what nations do and say, even if they sometimes do not believe it, becomes part of the raw material from which international law ultimately springs. This observation rings particularly true in the field of human rights, precisely because of the absence of enforcement and judicial bodies. Soviet-bloc countries, for example, cannot join the critics of the Chilean regime without at the same time opening the door to criticisms of their own human rights abuses.[32] The process thus underscores the role of reason in international law. Contrary to what some realists contend,[33] national interest alone cannot support valid international claims. Instead, as is true in all legal discourse, such claims must be supported by principles that are neu-

---

The same can be said of the U.N. Human Rights Commission, although the primary importance of both commissions stems from their position as forums for the open discussion of human rights situations. Governments attach great importance to the debates before the U.N. Human Rights Commission.

30. Although those who deny the "legal" character of international law can point to such venerable authority as John Austin's The Province of Jurisprudence Determined 201 (ed. 1954), this position has been fully discredited by modern scholars. See, e.g., H.L.A. Hart, The Concept of Law 222-25 (1961).

31. McDougal, Lasswell & Reisman, The World Constitutive Process of Authoritative Decision, in The Future of the International Legal Order 73 (R. Falk and C. Black eds. 1969). The "New Haven" approach can be supplemented with the contributions of modern political philosophy. See generally infra notes 79-120 and accompanying text.

32. All of the Soviet-bloc countries voted in favor of the U.N. Resolution on the Protection of Human Rights in Chile, G.A. Res. 3219, 29 U.N. GAOR Supp. (No. 31) at 83, U.N. Doc. A/9631 (1974).

33. See, e.g., H. Morgenthau, Politics Among Nations 5-12 (5th rev. ed. 1978).

tral to individual interests.[34] No authoritative judicial bodies are needed for this process, though it would be preferable to have them. The decentralized nature of international law does not, therefore, preclude the existence of a universal human rights standard.

B. *Cultural Relativism and the Human Rights Conventions*

Supporters of cultural relativism argue that the theory creates a legal defense to the general duty incumbent upon governments to observe international human rights. One should therefore expect to find a provision to that effect in the international legal materials. Yet, virtually nothing in the human rights conventions suggests that the respect for human rights depends upon, or can be modified by, local cultural conditions. The U.N. Covenant, the American Convention, and the recent African Charter[35] do not acknowledge any right of governments to avoid compliance by alleging the priority of local traditions.

The only apparent exception is article 63(3) of the European Convention, which states that "[t]he provisions of this Convention shall be applied in [colonial territories] with due regard, however, to local requirements."[36] If one reads this provision as supporting cultural relativism, the parties would be exempted from enforcing the human rights guaranteed by the Convention in those colonial territories where "local requirements" conflict with the Convention.

The European Court of Human Rights rejected this interpretation in the *Tyrer Case*, which involved corporal punishment, a local tradition, on the Isle of Man.[37] The court found that the word "requirement" embodied the idea of necessity, and that corporal punishment, no matter how accepted by public opinion and practice or enshrined in the traditions of the Isle, was not necessary to maintain law and order and consequently ran afoul of the Conven-

---

34. The "neutral principles" advocated by Herbert Wechsler in a different context are narrower in scope, since they refer to constitutional review. Wechsler, Towards Neutral Principles of Constitutional Law, 73 Harv. L. Rev. 1 (1959). The concern here, more generally, is with *claims*. The "neutrality" requirement holds even where the principles argued from are incorrect or nonexistent. Cf. D'Amato, supra note 17, at 1125-27 (human rights are entitlements of nations which are universal in nature).

35. See supra note 24.

36. European Convention, supra note 24, art. 63(3).

37. Eur. Ct. Hum. Rts., Tyrer Case, Judgment of 25 April 1978, Series A No. 26.

tion.[38] Further, the court wrote that no local requirement could enable a party to the Convention to make use of a criminal sanction in violation of article 3, which prohibits degrading punishment.[39]

The *Tyrer* opinion thus forcefully supports the idea that human rights are non-negotiable in the sense that not even the force of overwhelming public opinion or state practice may impair them. It also stands for the proposition that international human rights possess a transboundary meaning that cannot be modified or ignored on relativist grounds. The *Tyrer* court noted that article 63(3) of the European Convention,[40] drafted in 1950, had been conceived to meet the European perception about the insufficient degree of civilization of colonial peoples.[41] Although the court did not elaborate on this point, it is doubtful that the relativist interpretation of article 63(3) of the Convention, whereby entire populations are less eligible for protection in the enjoyment of human rights, conforms to the anti-colonialist values embodied in present international law.[42]

In assessing the validity of the relativist doctrine, it is noteworthy that each of the major human rights conventions contains a nondiscrimination clause.[43] The classical interpretation of such clauses holds that a government may not discriminate within its own borders on the basis of race, sex, religion or other impermissible criteria in the enforcement of human rights.[44] The clause is commonly regarded as operating purely within national borders, but a broader interpretation is also possible. The nondiscrimination clause arguably forbids governments to treat individuals in ways that substantially depart from the core of meaning of international human rights law, because such treatment would amount to discrimination vis-à-vis the treatment enjoyed by individuals in other states. In other words, one could argue that an individual's

38. Id. at 18.

39. Id.

40. See supra note 24.

41. "The Court notes, in this connection, that the system established by article 63 was primarily designed to meet the fact that, when the Convention was drafted, there were still certain colonial territories whose state of civilisation did not, it was thought, permit the full application of the Convention." *Tyrer Case*, Judgment at 19.

42. Such a construction would amount to an elitist version of relativism. See infra notes 121-26 and accompanying text.

43. See, e.g., African Charter, supra note 24, art. 2; American Convention, supra note 24, art. 24; U.N. Covenant, supra note 24, art. 26; European Convention, supra note 24, art. 14.

44. See, e.g., Belgian Linguistics Case, 11 Y.B. Eur. Conv. Human Rights 832, 862-69 (1968) (Eur. Comm'n on Human Rights).

entitlement to human rights does not depend on the particular traditions of the state in which the individual is located, that national boundaries do not affect the imperative of nondiscrimination.

The thrust of article 1(3) of the U.N. Charter is no different. It states that a major purpose of the organization is to achieve international cooperation in encouraging and promoting "respect for human rights and for fundamental freedoms *for all without distinction as to race, sex, language and religion.*"[45] To interpret the clause "for all" to mean for all individuals on earth, and not just for all individuals within a given state, surely violates neither the letter nor the spirit of the Charter. Suppose, for example, states A and B conclude a human rights treaty that contains a nondiscrimination clause. It is insufficient to say that *within* state A there should be no discrimination based on sex, race, and the like. The nondiscrimination clause must also be read to have a transboundary dimension. Accordingly, the rights enjoyed by individuals in state A cannot differ substantially in content and scope from those enjoyed by individuals in state B. Otherwise the human rights treaty would be redundant, at least insofar as the principle of nondiscrimination already existed in those states as a matter of municipal or constitutional law.[46]

C. *Cultural Relativism and Self-Determination*

One may object to the foregoing analysis on the grounds that human rights treaties only bind the parties,[47] and that the status of cultural relativism in international law cannot be ascertained from treaty analysis alone. It is therefore necessary to determine whether customary international law supports the claims of the cultural relativists. The principles of self-determination and nonintervention offer, at first glance, possible legal support for the rela-

45. U.N. Charter art. 1, para. 3 (emphasis added).

46. Admittedly, the interpretation of the nondiscrimination clause suggested in the text is a novel one. But if we accept that the international legal system primarily entrusts the application of human rights law to states, and if we further accept that individuals are the beneficiaries of such law, then it becomes clear that violations premised upon cultural traditions represent transboundary discriminatory treatment. To put it differently, the relativist contention that freedom of religion, for example, means one thing in the West and a different thing in the Third World, requires a discriminatory application of human rights law.

47. See, e.g., the statement of the Chilean representative to the U.N. General Assembly Third Committee, 31 U.N. GAOR C.3 (46th mtg.) paras. 1-25, U.N. Doc. A/C.3/31/SR.46 (1976) (rejecting case law under the European Convention, supra note 24, regarding the Emergency Clause as irrelevant to the Chilean situation).

tivist doctrine.[48] A closer consideration of these principles reveals, however, that this support is only illusory.

Ascertainment of the precise contours of the self-determination principle is not easy.[49] In addition to the important anti-colonialist aspect of self-determination,[50] an internal dimension appears to exist as well.[51] Article 2 of the Declaration on the Granting of Independence to Colonial Countries and Peoples[52] ("Declaration of Colonial Independence"), widely regarded as embodying customary law concerning self-determination, provides that "[a]ll peoples have the right to self-determination; by virtue of that right they freely determine their political status and freely pursue their economic, social and cultural development."[53]

Commentators espouse two conflicting interpretations of this clause. The democratic, anti-authoritarian view holds that internal self-determination requires internal democracy and respect for the human rights of all peoples.[54] This thesis finds support in the intent of the framers of the U.N. Charter,[55] and arguably reflects a correct reading of the self-determination principle as agreed upon

---

48. For a brief and lucid account of the role played by self-determination concerns in the development of the Third World's distrust toward the human rights movement, see Nickel, Cultural Diversity and Human Rights, in International Human Rights: Contemporary Issues 43, 43-46 (J. Nelson & V. Green eds. 1980).

49. See generally M. Pomerance, Self-Determination in Law and Practice 1-28 (1982).

50. External self-determination means the right of peoples to decide their international status. It represents an expression of modern anti-colonialist values in the international community. The literature on external self-determination is voluminous. See references in id. at 130-38.

51. See id. at 37 nn.209-11.

52. Declaration on the Granting of Independence to Colonial Countries and Peoples, G.A. Res. 1514, 15 U.N. GAOR Supp. (No. 16) at 66, U.N. Doc. A/4684 (1960) [hereinafter cited as Declaration of Colonial Independence].

53. Id. This provision is echoed by the Declaration on Principles, supra note 21, art. 1 ("all peoples have the right freely to determine, without external interference, their political status and to pursue their economic, social and cultural development"), and by the U.N. Covenant, supra note 24, art. 1 ("All peoples have the right of self-determination. By virtue of that right they freely determine their political status and freely pursue their economic, social and cultural development.").

54. See Moore, Grenada and the International Double Standard, 78 Am. J. Int'l L. 145, 154-56, 165 (1984) (Grenada mission was designed to restore self-determination, in the form of democratic rights, to the Grenadian people); Reisman, Coercion and Self-Determination: Construing Charter Article 2(4), 78 Am. J. Int'l L. 642, 643-44 (1984) ("Ongoing self-determination [works] to increase the probability of the free choice of peoples about their government and political structure."); Rosenstock, The Declaration of Principles of International Law Concerning Friendly Relations: A Survey, 65 Am. J. Int'l L. 713, 732 (1971).

55. See Cassese, The Helsinki Declaration and Self-Determination, in Human Rights, International Law and the Helsinki Accord 83, 84 (T. Buergenthal ed. 1977).

by the European states in the Helsinki Accord.[56] Under this interpretation, the word "freely" means "free from *internal*, as well as from external, interference." The right of self-determination in international law would thus represent an expression of the entitlement of all individuals to democratic representative government and to basic human rights.[57]

The relativist version of the rule embodied in article 2 of the Declaration of Colonial Independence differs radically from the one expressed above. According to this view, internal self-determination represents the flip side of the nonintervention principle: it forbids any state from interfering with the cultural and political choices of autonomous peoples.[58] Self-determination in this sense represents the rights-language version of the duty of nonintervention in internal affairs. People have the right to create whatever form of government they want, no matter how repressive, and human rights claims put forward by other states may not interfere with the fulfillment of this right. Under this view, a people exhausts its right to self-determination when it achieves the status of a sovereign state.[59] Once the people choose a political and cultural system, nothing in international law confers a right to change the system.[60] Under this construction, internal self-determination

---

56. Id. at 99-105.

57. Some Western states defended this position in the negotiations that led to the 1970 Declaration on Principles, supra note 21. The proposals presented by the United Kingdom and the United States suggested that representative government was essential for the realization of the right to self-determination. See U.N. Doc. A/AC.125/L.44, July 19, 1967 (United Kingdom draft); U.N. Doc. A/AC.125/L.32, Apr. 12, 1966 (U.S. draft). In fact, some support for this position may be found in the final wording of the Declaration on Principles, supra note 21, at 123: "[A]ll peoples have the right *freely* to determine, without external interference, their political status and to pursue their economic, social and cultural development." (emphasis added). Arguably, the word "freely" means "without *internal* interference," or else it would be superfluous. Contra Cassese, supra note 55, at 89-90 (Declaration only requires internal self-determination in cases involving racist regimes or foreign domination, in contrast with the Helsinki declaration).

58. See Mojekwu, International Human Rights: The African Perspective, in International Human Rights, supra note 48, at 89 ("Self-determination . . . would involve the right of a people to take into their hands the full responsibility of determining, without coercion, their own political, economic and cultural destiny."). Obviously, "coercion" here means external coercion. Mojekwu's definition clearly tolerates internal coercion, i.e., human rights violations without foreign interference.

59. This is the official position of Soviet-bloc countries. See Poeggel, 1 Volkerrecht (Manual of International Law of the German Democratic Republic) 270 (1973), cited in Cassese, supra note 55, at 85 n.7.

60. The Soviet Union and its allies defended this view during the 1975 Helsinki negotiations. See Cassese, supra note 55, at 99. This position does not simply reflect tactical "power

means that no state may impose a cultural or political system on people living beyond its borders.[61]

However, this version of internal self-determination is at best a misconception, and at worst it can be a rationalization for oppression. First, a contextual interpretation of the Declaration of Colonial Independence yields a very different result. The preamble of the Declaration recalls the commitment of the peoples of the world to "fundamental human rights" and to "the dignity and worth of the human person."[62] The same argument applies *a fortiori* to the self-determination principle embodied in article 1 of the U.N. Covenant,[63] which exactly reproduces article 2 of the Declaration.[64] The relativist interpretation of article 1 grants people "the right to freely . . . pursue their economic, social and cultural development"[65] even where that pursuit would reduce to meaninglessness the remaining fifty-one articles of the Covenant. A more reasonable approach, consistent with sound treaty interpretation, would dictate that the principle of independent cultural development as a part of self-determination be harmonized with human rights law.[66]

Further, the relativist version of internal self-determination often defines the interests of a people in mystical or aggregative terms that ignore or belittle individual preferences. Such mystical definitions may be articulated in the form of axiomatic "true" interests of peoples, as opposed to real or expressed interests.[67] They

---

politics" devices. It is strongly linked to the Leninist conception that the "true" interest of the people can only be expressed by, and result in, the dictatorship of the proletariat. See M. Pomerance, supra note 49, at 40.

61. The proviso "beyond its borders" is crucial, because according to a widespread view, self-determination does not grant rights (of secession or otherwise) to minorities within a sovereign state. See generally Nanda, Self-Determination under International Law: Validity of Claims to Secede, 13 Case W. Res. J. Int'l L. 257 (1981). Thus, many governments (not only those of the Soviet-bloc) hold the inconsistent view that cultural standards determine the scope of human rights, and that minorities within a sovereign state are not entitled to choose their own political institutions and pursue their independent cultural development.

62. Declaration of Colonial Independence, supra note 52, preamble.

63. U.N. Covenant, supra note 24.

64. See supra text accompanying note 53.

65. U.N. Covenant, supra note 24, art. 1.

66. See, e.g., the draft proposed by the Dutch delegation to the Helsinki conference:

> The participating States recognize the inalienable right of the people of every State freely to choose, to develop, to adapt or to change its political, economic, social and cultural systems without interference in any form by any other State or group of States and *with due respect to human rights and fundamental freedoms.*

Doc. CSCE/II/A/8, cited by Cassese, supra note 55, at 96 (emphasis added).

67. See supra note 60.

may also be expressed as a plain rule of political power, whereby those in power automatically are deemed to represent the people, regardless of whether they have been democratically elected and regardless of their human rights record. Consequently, a relativist would maintain that in Pinochet's takeover in Chile or Ho Chi Minh's takeover in Vietnam, the peoples of Chile and Vietnam exercised their right of self-determination, and that the governments so formed are immune from foreign interference even when they deprive people of human rights. It may well be that self-determination, external or internal, exists only as a collective right that can be exercised jointly by individuals.[68] It is equally true, however, that self-determination is a *human* right, not a right of governments, whether they are headed by charismatic revolutionary leaders or military dictators.[69] Therefore, the right to self-determination must ultimately be ascertained by reference to the wishes and rights of individuals.[70] As Professor Schachter has convincingly argued, the concept of human dignity implies that high priority should be given to individual choices in ways of life, beliefs and the conduct of public affairs.[71] This concept, however, simple as it is, clearly contradicts many existing ideologies and political arrangements.[72]

Finally, a consideration of the concerns which prompted the development of the self-determination principle also leads to a rejection of the relativist thesis. The self-determination principle has traditionally been directed against colonialism and various tangible

68. See Dinstein, Collective Human Rights of Peoples and Minorities, 25 Int'l & Comp. L. Q. 102, 103 (1976).

69. Professor Dinstein aptly cautions that "collective human rights retain their character as direct human rights. The group which enjoys them communally is not a corporate entity and does not possess a legal personality." Id.

70. "The state must protect the individual citizen, its units or atoms; *but the international organization also must ultimately protect human individuals, and not its units or atoms, i.e., states or nations.*" 1 K. Popper, The Open Society and its Enemies 288 n.7 (1966) (emphasis added). See also Luban, The Romance of the Nation-State, 9 Phil. & Pub. Aff. 392 (1980) (arguing against the "rights" emphasized by nationalism). Under the relativist version of internal self-determination, the term "state will" does not mean the sum of the individual wills, because then governments would never act against the popular will—which is obviously not the case. "State will," instead, means what the government decides. Relativism asks us to believe that the government necessarily represents the people, and that the government always acts as a surrogate for the "people." The authoritarianism embodied in this notion of "state will" is clearly incompatible with respect for human rights, and must therefore be rejected.

71. Schachter, Human Dignity as a Normative Concept, 77 Am. J. Int'l L. 848, 849 (1983).

72. Id. at 850.

forms of *foreign* domination.[73] It primarily guarantees to people the right to establish their own government and pursue their cultural development without external interference.[74] Yet external pressure for human rights compliance has nothing to do with colonial domination, imperialism and the other evils against which self-determination was conceived. An analysis of the purposive dimension of self-determination, therefore, provides no support for the relativist doctrine.

As to the nonintervention principle, there is broad support today for the proposition that discussing human rights does not amount to "intervention" within the meaning of article 2(7) of the U.N. Charter,[75] unless one takes the position—discarded at the beginning of this study—that human rights are not part of international law.[76] For the relativist, the nonintervention principle and internal self-determination have identical content. Saying that people may choose whatever government they want is the same as saying that other states may not intervene to criticize human rights violations.[77] Thus, *mutatis mutandi*, the same arguments marshalled in the previous paragraphs apply.[78]

In sum, under international law, all individuals, regardless of their state of origin, residence, and cultural environment, are entitled to fundamental human rights. International law does not relieve governments of the obligation to respect these rights simply because a particular right is inconsistent with local traditions.

---

73. See supra note 50.

74. See generally M. Pomerance, supra note 49, at 9-28. The Declaration of Colonial Independence, supra note 52, emphasizes decolonization and independence, which suggests an "externalist" approach to self-determination.

75. See generally R. Higgins, The Development of International Law Through the Political Organs of the United Nations 118 (1963); Gilmour, The Meaning of "Intervene" Within Article 2(7) of the United Nations Charter—An Historical Perspective, 16 Int'l & Comp. L. Q. 330 (1967).

76. Contra Watson, Autointerpretation, Competence and the Continuing Validity of Article 2(7) of the U.N. Charter, 71 Am. J. Int'l L. 60 (1977). Whether international law supports military intervention to protect human rights under certain circumstances is a far more difficult problem. It is the subject of extensive discussion in my forthcoming S.J.D. dissertation, "Humanitarian Intervention in International Law."

77. See Cassese, supra note 55, at 85-86.

78. See supra notes 47-74 and accompanying text. The Argentine military junta used the principle of nonintervention as its main defense against human rights criticisms. The U.S.S.R. also frequently invokes it. Schreman, Gorbachev Meets the Press: A Bantering Style and an Echo of Krushchev, N.Y. Times, Oct. 5, 1985, at 4, col. 2.

III. CULTURAL RELATIVISM AND MORAL PHILOSOPHY

This part of the paper addresses the philosophical status of cultural relativism. After outlining the link between human rights law and moral philosophy, I draw a distinction between several types of relativism. Ultimately, I reject relativism on the grounds that it violates formal and substantive constraints of moral discourse.

A. *Moral Philosophy and Human Rights Law*

The law of human rights borrows its language from moral philosophy. From its inception at the end of World War II, the modern international law of human rights has been indissolubly linked with the moral concerns prompted by the Nazi horrors. The statesmen who drafted the U.N. Charter were motivated in part by the moral imperative to restore human dignity and give it legal status, and indeed that moral concern permeates the subsequent development of human rights law.[79]

At the same time, the framers of the Charter also worried about problems of conflict avoidance, peace, security, and maintaining the balance of power. Paradoxically, while national sovereignty continues to be strongly asserted both inside and outside the confines of the United Nations, human rights law has developed impressively.[80] Indeed, reconciling national sovereignty and the international law of human rights remains one of the central challenges of our times.[81] Despite serious problems of enforcement, the dynamism of human rights groups throughout the world and the pressure exerted on delinquent governments by democratic nations has achieved remarkable results, demonstrating that the belief in human rights is not a mere illusion created by scholars, but an effective and living tool for political reform.[82]

---

79. See Sohn, supra note 2, at 9-14.

80. See Vincent-Daviss, Human Rights Law Research Guides, supra note 2.

81. Cf. Delbrueck, International Protection of Human Rights and State Sovereignty, 57 Ind. L. J. 567 (1982) ("[T]he sovereign states not only are creating the international norms for the protection of human rights, but also are determining the process of their implementation—or nonimplementation—according to their sovereign will. Seen from this perspective, state sovereignty and the international protection of human rights appear to be incompatible.").

82. Sometimes the importance of the pressure exerted by democratic governments is erroneously downplayed. I can personally attest that President Carter's human rights policy saved thousands of lives in Argentina. Human rights organizations also play a significant role, despite justified criticisms of occasional one-sidedness. See generally Weissbrodt, Strategies for the Selection and Pursuit of International Human Rights Objectives, 8 Yale J.

Another reason for focusing on moral philosophy is that the concern for human rights did not grow from a desire to force governments to comply with the law "as it is." The world regards human rights violations as a moral wrong of the most serious nature, and presumably continues to condemn such practices even though technically the accused government has not violated any unambiguous positive international obligation. Given the intimate historical and conceptual connection between international human rights law and morality and the current emphasis of some writers on relativism as a supposed basis of the contemporary world order,[83] it is important to examine the conclusions about cultural relativism that can be gleaned from moral philosophy.[84]

B. *Descriptive, Metaethical, and Normative Relativism*

To analyze the moral status of relativism, several types of relativism must be carefully distinguished.[85] First, different societies have different perceptions of right and wrong. This assertion—which may be called "descriptive" relativism—finds support among anthropologists who consider themselves relativists.[86] Although descriptive relativism has been challenged,[87] its validity may be conceded for the purposes of the present analysis.

The second type of relativism, "metaethical" relativism, asserts that it is impossible to discover moral truth. Metaethical relativism may take the form of a thesis about the meaning of moral terms.[88] The relativist can adopt either some version of emotivism[89] or a

---

World Pub. Ord. 62 (1981).

83. See generally E. McWhinney, supra note 5. While McWhinney's conception of relativism is broader, it encompasses the one treated here.

84. The relevance of moral inquiry to international law depends, of course, upon one's particular theory of the relation between law and morality. However, if the relativist concedes that his theory is not supported by independent moral reasoning, he must conclude that cultural relativism, although technically legal, is immoral, and he is therefore logically committed to the reform of international law in the sense of eliminating the relativist defense.

85. See Brandt, Ethical Relativism, in 3 Encyclopedia of Philosophy 75 (P. Edwards ed. 1967).

86. See, e.g., M. Herskovits, supra note 6, at 61-78.

87. The debate centers on whether *fundamental* diversities of ethical views exist in different societies. See Brandt, supra note 85, at 75.

88. Id. at 75.

89. Emotivism holds that moral propositions are no more than interjections or emotive utterances. See generally, A. Ayer, Language, Truth and Logic (1946); C.L. Stevenson, Ethics and Language (1944).

straight nihilist position.[90] A milder version of metaethical relativism contends that there is no valid *method* for moral reasoning—that is, no method that would have, on moral matters, the same persuasive force as scientific method.[91]

Finally, "normative" relativism asserts that persons, depending on their cultural attachments, ought to do different things and have different rights.[92] This is the version of relativism equivalent to the one discussed in Part II of this study.[93] It should be clear that descriptive and metaethical relativism do not logically entail normative relativism. Descriptive relativism operates at a different logical level than its normative counterpart. The anthropologist or descriptive relativist says that different cultures in fact have different conceptions of morality. The normative relativist asserts that individuals of different cultures have different rights, and that they *ought* to do or to abstain from doing different things. It is therefore perfectly possible for the descriptive relativist to concede that different societies have different social practices and conflicting views about morality and yet consider some practices or views morally preferable to others.[94]

The relationship between metaethical and normative relativism is more complex, but the two theories are still logically distinguishable. The metaethical relativist doubts the possibility of demonstrating the correctness of any particular moral principle. As a matter of moral decision, he may reject normative relativism while denying that any moral principle or system is demonstrably correct. To create a framework within which to make moral judgments, the metaethical relativist nevertheless has an option: he may subscribe to the "reflective equilibrium" method suggested by John Rawls.[95] Rawls devised a framework within which to make

---

90. Nihilism, in this context, holds that moral terms lack any meaning whatsoever.

91. Brandt, supra note 85, at 76.

92. See E. Westermarck, supra note 6, ch. 5; Benedict, Anthropology and the Abnormal, 10 J. Gen. Psych. 59 (1934). Even "relativism" is too charitable a name for this theory, which may properly be called "moral positivism." See the brilliant critique in 2 K. Popper, supra note 70, ch. 12, 392-96.

93. See supra text accompanying notes 10-13.

94. See Douglas, Morality and Culture, 93 Ethics 786 (1983) ("Two conversations are running parallel, one the philosophers', about the rational formulation of ethics, one the anthropologists', about the interaction between moral ideas and social institutions. The conversations, as they are set at the present time, will never converge.").

95. J. Rawls, supra note 15, at 48-51. Of course, the acceptance of reflective equilibrium as a plausible description of moral methodology is completely independent from (a) the acceptance of Rawls' contractarian justification for principles of social justice; (b) the ac-

meaningful moral judgments without encountering the problem of demonstration. He suggests that moral conclusions may be reached by checking one's moral intuitions against one's moral principles with the crucial proviso that both be subject to modification.[96] At the very least, Rawls demonstrates that it is unnecessary to have an infallible method of discovering moral truth in order to speak about the rights all people should enjoy.

C. *Critique of Normative Relativism*

As a moral theory, normative relativism cannot withstand scrutiny.[97] First, its straightforward formulation reflects a fundamental incoherence. It affirms at the same time that (a) there are no universal moral principles; (b) one ought to act in accordance with the principles of one's own group; and (c), (b) is a universal moral principle.[98] David Lyons demonstrated that the typical anthropologists' version of relativism ("an act is right if, and only if, it accords with the norms of the agent's group") does not validate conflicting moral judgments, because each group is regarded as a separate moral realm.[99] Consequently, the incoherence attached to normative relativism springs from the fact that the very assertion of universal relativism is self-contradictory, not from the fact that it validates conflicting substantive moral judgments. If it is true that no universal moral principles exist, then the relativist engages in self-contradiction by stating the universality of the relativist principle.[100] As Bernard Williams observed, this is a "logically un-

---

ceptance of the principles themselves; or (c) the acceptance of his solution to the priority problem. For Rawls' view that "undeveloped" societies may fail to observe human rights in certain situations, see infra note 109.

96. J. Rawls, supra note 15, at 48.

97. Bernard Williams calls relativism "the anthropologists' heresy, possibly the most absurd view to have been advanced even in moral philosophy." B. Williams, Morality: An Introduction to Ethics 20 (1972).

98. Id. at 20-21; Lyons, Ethical Relativism and the Problem of Incoherence, 86 Ethics 107, 109 (1975-76).

99. Lyons, supra note 98, at 109.

100. This problem resembles the one exhibited by ideologism, the theory that everything is ideology, which for some mysterious reason does not apply to itself. This paper will not deal with Gilbert Harman's narrower version of moral relativism because Harman intended for his version to apply only to "inner" judgments, i.e., judgments that someone who had already settled upon a moral code ought or ought not to have acted in a certain way. His theory does not apply to the judgment that a given institution is unjust, which is most relevant for the purposes of this paper. Harman, Moral Relativism Defended, 84 Phil. Rev. 3, 4 (1975). See the critique of Harman's theory by Copp, Harman on Internalism, Relativism and Logical Form, 92 Ethics 227 (1981-82).

happy attachment of a nonrelative morality of toleration or noninterference to a view of morality as relative."[101]

However, this objection over the incoherence of normative relativism is not decisive. Normative relativism can be reformulated to avoid the threat of incoherence as follows: (a) there are no universal moral principles, save one; (b) one ought to act in accordance with the principles of one's own group; and (c) the only universal moral principle is (b).[102] Yet, if the normative relativist is also a metaethical relativist, he cannot justify why (b) is a universal moral principle. If the relativist has a method of discovering universal moral principles—for example, Rawls' "reflective equilibrium" or the utilitarian principle—then it is difficult to see why the only principle yielded by such method would be (b) above. Thus, this new version of relativism avoids inconsistency, but it is epistemologically weak.

A second problem with normative relativism is that it overlooks an important feature of moral discourse, its *universalizability*.[103] Independently of substantive morals, when we talk about right and wrong or rights and duties, and act accordingly, we are logically committed to "act in accordance with the generic rights of [our] recipients as well as of [our]selves," on pain of self-contradiction.[104] This not only means that we cannot make exceptions in our own favor, but also that individuals must be treated as equally entitled to basic rights regardless of contingent factors such as their cultural surroundings. The requirement of universalizability may be thought of as having a logical nature,[105] or alternatively, as be-

---

101. B. Williams, supra note 97, at 21. See also a profound criticism of relativism in B. Williams, Ethics and the Limits of Philosophy, ch. 9 (1985).

102. I am grateful to David Kaye for demonstrating this point to me.

103. The requirement of universalizability is usually traced to IV I. Kant, Critique of Practical Reason § 436 (L. Beck trans. 1949). It has been revived in recent philosopical literature, mainly by A. Gewirth, Reason and Morality (1978) and M. Singer, Generalization in Ethics (1961).

104. A. Gewirth, Human Rights: Essays on Justification and Application 52, 128-41 (1982).

105. See id. at 89; IV I. Kant, supra note 103, § 436 ("All maxims have . . . a form, which consists in universality; and in this respect the formula of the moral imperative requires that the maxims be chosen as though they should hold as universal laws of nature."); M. Singer, supra note 103, at 34 ("The generalization principle . . . is involved in or presupposed by every genuine moral judgment, for it is an essential part of . . . distinctively moral terms."); Frankena, The Concept of Morality, 63 J. Phil. 688, 695-96 (1966). Professor D'Amato makes a convincing linguistic case against relativism, showing that when we ordinarily refer to some conduct as "moral," we usually mean that it is universally valid. Conversely, when we are prepared to be tolerant about some conduct (for example, sexual hab-

ing a requirement of moral plausibility.[106] If the first approach is correct, the relativist simply refuses to engage in meaningful moral discourse. Under the second approach, the relativist endorses the highly implausible position that in moral matters we can pass judgments containing proper names, and that consequently we may make exceptions in our own favor.[107]

The relativist has two responses to the universalizability argument. First, the relativist may argue that belonging to different communities is a morally relevant circumstance.[108] Universalizability, he would argue, is not violated when individuals are situated in different factual conditions. To say that if A ought to do X in circumstances C, then B also ought to do X in circumstances C, presupposes a similarity of circumstances. If such circumstances vary substantially, that is, if cultural traditions, creeds, and practices differ, then we would not violate the universalizability requirement by holding that individuals who belong to different cultures ought to have different basic rights.[109] Sometimes relativists articulate this position in the form of an attack on the assertion of the existence of abstract rights, as opposed to the assertion of concrete rights and duties in materially defined social conditions.[110]

---

its), we regard such conduct as "mores" or "custom," and not as "morality in the stronger sense." D'Amato, Lon Fuller and Substantive Natural Law, 26 Am. J. Juris. 202, 204 (1981).

106. See, e.g., J. Rawls, supra note 15, at 132 (principles apply to everyone by virtue of their being moral persons).

107. See J. Hospers, Human Conduct 276-77, 285 (1972).

108. See the elementary but excellent discussion in id. at 283-90.

109. John Rawls asserts that in societies which have not attained certain minimal material conditions, individuals may be denied human rights. J. Rawls, supra note 15, at 151-52. This seems a surprising statement in the context of Rawls' impressive defense of the "rights" conception of justice. As Brian Barry put it:

> Why this should be so is not at all clear to me. Is there anything in the material condition of, say, a group of nomadic Bedouin eking a bare subsistence from the desert or a population of poor peasant cultivators which prevents them from being able to use personal liberty?

B. Barry, supra note 15, at 77.

In his most recent article, Rawls expressly refused to deal with the issue of whether his theory "can be extended to a general political conception for different kinds of societies existing under different historical and social conditions." Rawls, Justice as Fairness: Political not Metaphysical, 14 Phil. & Pub. Aff. 223, 225 (1985). It would be unfair, however, to charge Rawls with yielding to relativism, since he expressly avoids "prejudging one way or the other." Id.

110. See Tushnet, An Essay on Rights, 62 Tex. L. Rev. 1363, 1364-65 (1984) ("It does not advance understanding to speak of rights in the abstract. It matters only that some specific right is or is not recognized in some specific social setting. . . . In this way rights become identified with particular cultures and are relativized."). Tushnet's article astonishes in several regards. For example, he states that "[t]he use of rights in contemporary discourse

Such arguments are flawed, however, because the fact that one belongs to a particular social group or community is not a *morally* relevant circumstance. The place of birth and cultural environment of an individual are not related to his moral worth or to his entitlement to human rights. An individual cannot be held responsible for being born in one society rather than in another, for one "deserves" neither one's cultural environment nor one's place of birth. There is nothing, for example, in the nature of a Third World woman that makes her less eligible for the enjoyment of human rights (though she may, of course, consensually waive her rights) than a woman in a Western democracy.[111] If the initial conditions are not morally distinguishable, the requirement of universalizability fully applies to statements about individual rights, even where the agents are immersed in different cultural environments.

The relativist's first objection to universalizability also confuses the circumstances in which one learns moral concepts with the *meaning* of those concepts.[112] A person who learns a moral concept (such as that of "wrong") by applying it in fact situations peculiar to his culture, is perfectly able to apply that concept to a set of facts he has never encountered before. As Bernard Williams said in his most recent work:

> The fact that people can and must react when they are confronted with another culture, and do so by applying their existing notions—also by reflecting on them—seems to show that the ethical thought of a given culture can always stretch beyond its boundaries. Even if there is no way in which divergent ethical beliefs can be brought to converge by independent inquiry or rational argument,

---

impedes advances by progressive social forces." Id. at 1364. Such criticism, of course, assumes that it is morally desirable for the "progressive social forces" (whatever that means) to dictate conducts and impose ends and conceptions of moral excellence on other individuals (i.e., on those who presumably would be accused of militating in the ranks of the "regressive social forces"). John Rawls artfully responded to this assertion in an oft-quoted sentence: "Each person possesses an inviolability founded on justice that even the welfare of society as a whole cannot override." J. Rawls, supra note 15, at 3. This is what I mean by "rights" in the "abstract." See also infra text accompanying notes 116-17.

111. One must be careful not to overstate this exception. Dictators typically assert that they represent the people or that they have their support. Even if a particular dictator enjoys popular support, however, such support does not entitle him to oppress dissenters who have not consented to his rule. The majoritarian principle is thus useless when assessing human rights violations. See the discussion in J. Rawls, supra note 15, at 356-62.

112. See R. Trigg, Reason and Commitment 20 (1973).

> this fact will not imply relativism. Each outlook may still be making claims it intends to apply to the whole world, not just to that part of it which is its 'own world.'[113]

By claiming that moral judgments only have meaning within particular cultures, the relativist underestimates the ability of the human intellect to confront, in a moral sense, new situations.

The relativist's second objection to universalizability has a logical nature. As noted above, the relativist may contend that (a) his only principle is that culture determines human rights; and (b), (a) is universal.[114] The relativist thus universalizes a principle. But the requirement of universalizability applies to *substantive* moral statements, which (a) is not. The principle that culture determines human rights is a principle of *renvoi*; that is, it refers us to different normative systems in order to determine the rights of individuals. The principle does not establish rules governing the rights of any particular individual. Universalizability requires that *if* we make a statement about the right of X to freedom of thought, we are committed to grant that right to Y under similar, morally relevant circumstances. Because the relativist principle does not address issues of substantive morality in this respect, it is not susceptible to being universalized in the same way. The violation of universalizability becomes apparent when one translates the relativist principle into substantive moral statements (i.e., X, who lives in culture C1, has the right R; while Y, who lives in culture C2, does not have the right R). In other words, the relativist principle may be regarded as *metamoral*, even where it is asserted as the basis of normative morality.[115]

Third, normative relativism runs counter to the principle that persons have moral worth *qua* persons and must be treated as ends in themselves, not as functions of the ends of others—a non-trivial version of the Kantian principle of autonomy.[116] This principle of moral worth forbids the imposition upon individuals of cultural

113. B. Williams, supra note 101, at 159.

114. See supra text accompanying note 102.

115. The characterization of relativism as metamoral differs from the assertion of metaethical relativism. This part of the paper deals with normative relativism, which does not need support from metaethical skepticism. See supra notes 88-97 and accompanying text. But normative relativism is still not strictly a substantive moral theory. It only tells us where to look for the norms that determine individual rights.

116. See Ping-Cheung Lo, A Critical Reevaluation of the Alleged "Empty Formalism" of Kantian Ethics, 91 Ethics 181, 182 (1980-81). See also Schachter, supra note 71, at 849.

standards that impair human rights. Even if relativists could show that authoritarian practices are somehow required by a community—a claim which in many cases remains to be proven—they would still fail to explain why individuals should surrender their basic rights to the ends of the community. If women in Moslem countries are discriminated against, it is not enough to say that a tradition, no matter how old and venerable, requires such discrimination.[117] The only defense consistent with the principle of autonomy would be a showing that each subjugated woman consented to waive her rights. However, because of the mystical and holistic assumptions underlying relativism, presumably the relativist would not regard such a test as relevant or necessary.

Quite apart from the moral implausibility of normative relativism, it is worth noting the extreme conservatism of the doctrine.[118] Normative relativism tells us that if a particular society has always had authoritarian practices, it is morally defensible that it continue to have them. It works as a typical argument of authority: it has always been like this, this is our culture, so we need not undertake any changes.[119] In the final analysis, normative relativism thus conceived amounts to the worst form of moral and legal positivism:

---

117. For examples see supra note 10.

118. A similar point is made by Amy Gutman in her response to modern critics of liberalism. Gutman, Communitarian Critics of Liberalism, 14 Phil. & Pub. Aff. 308, 309 (1985). As the text demonstrates, anti-liberal theories that emphasize the priority of communal values are necessarily relativist.

119. Tushnet asserts that his radical critique of rights "is a Schumpeterian act of creative destruction that may help us to build societies that transcend the failures of capitalism." Tushnet, supra note 110, at 1363. Tushnet later expressed this idea in relativistic terms: "The critique of rights takes a strong relativist position: it insists that rights-talk is meaningful only when placed within a full social and legal context." Id. at 1394. Thus, relativism to Tushnet is a basic assumption of radical politics, an essential underpinning of left-wing scholarship and politics. Yet nothing is farther from the truth. Relativism is tantamount to moral positivism and to "legalism," two of the most reactionary doctrines in the history of ideas. Tushnet himself seems to realize this. He tells us that "to say that some specific right is (or ought to be) recognized in a specific culture is to say that the culture is what it is, ought to recognize what its deepest commitments are, or ought to be transformed into some other culture." Id. at 1365. Thus, for Tushnet the only way to talk about rights is to *describe* rights as they are recognized by this or that culture. Those are the only *existing* rights. True, he accepts that we can say that this culture "ought to be transformed into some other culture." He thus avoids the charge of moral positivism. But because he has been precluded from even talking about rights in the abstract, he loses the best and most effective philosophical tool for criticizing positive law: the idea that individuals have rights independent of contingent cultural standards. Thus, when criticizing a particular culture, a Tushnet-type relativist may not rely on the proposition that individuals are entitled to some other social arrangement or that their rights have been violated.

it asserts that the rules enacted by the group are necessarily correct as a matter of critical morality.[120] If there is a particularly unfit domain for arguments of authority, it is surely that of human rights.

Admittedly, the force of the moral critique of relativism articulated here depends on the intuitive acceptance of certain moral premises. The relativist can successfully resist the attack by rejecting metaethical relativism so as to avoid logical incoherence, denying that universalizability is an ingredient of moral judgments, and rejecting the principle of autonomy. But this is a high price to pay. Normative relativism would then be a poor and implausible moral doctrine, and it is doubtful that many relativists, upon careful reflection, would accept the harsh implications. Furthermore, cultural relativism as defined in the first part of this article expressly or impliedly assumes the validity of normative relativism. Not only does positive international law fail to provide any basis for the relativist doctrine, but the underlying philosophical structure of relativism also reveals profound flaws.

IV. Two By-Products of Relativism: Elitism and Conspiracy

In this Part I will briefly consider two doctrines closely associated with relativism. The first theory asserts that one can appropriately honor human rights in certain societies, usually the most sophisticated ones, but not in others, on account, for example, of the latter's insufficient economic development. This doctrine, which can be called "elitism," necessarily follows from relativism. The second theory states that the law of human rights results from a conspiracy of the West to perpetuate imperialism. The "conspiracy theory," by contrast, does not follow inevitably from, and is not required by, cultural relativism.

A. *The Elitist Theory of Human Rights*

During the dark years of the military dictatorship in Argentina, one commonly heard many well-intentioned commentators exclaiming: "It is really a shame! Argentina, a country that springs

120. See supra note 92. This indictment only attacks what Professor Carlos Nino has called "ideological positivism," the theory that the norms of a group are necessarily correct as a matter of critical morality. C. Nino, Introduccion al Analisis del Derecho 32-35 (1980). This paper is not concerned with the more fertile concept of "methodological positivism," the theory of the separation between law and morality defended by H.L.A. Hart and others.

from Western tradition, cannot be excused for not respecting human rights." The statement implies that countries that do not spring from a Western tradition may somehow be excused from complying with the international law of human rights. This elitist theory of human rights holds that human rights are good for the West but not for much of the non-Western world.[121] Surprisingly, the elitist theory of human rights is very popular in the democratic West, not only in conservative circles but also, and even more often, among liberal and radical groups.[122] The right-wing version of elitism embodies the position, closely associated with colonialism, that backward peoples cannot govern themselves and that democracy only works for superior cultures.[123] The left-wing version, often articulated by liberals who stand for civil rights in Western countries but support leftist dictatorships abroad, reflects a belief that we should be tolerant of and respect the cultural identity and political self-determination of Third World countries (although, of course, it is seldom the people who choose to have dictators; more often the dictators decide for them).[124]

The position of relativist scholars who are human rights advocates illustrates an eloquent example of concealed elitism.[125] Such persons find themselves in an impossible dilemma. On the one hand they are anxious to articulate an international human rights standard, while on the other they wish to respect the autonomy of individual cultures. The result is a vague warning against "ethnocentrism,"[126] and well-intentioned proposals that are deferential to tyrannical governments and insufficiently concerned with human suffering. Because the consequence of either version of elitism is that certain national or ethnic groups are somehow less entitled than others to the enjoyment of human rights, the theory is fundamentally immoral and replete with racist overtones.

---

121. I am indebted to Professor Guido Pincione from the University of Buenos Aires for our stimulating discussions on this point.

122. See, e.g., Pollis, supra note 13, at 22-23; Tushnet, supra note 110, at 1394.

123. Relativism influenced the British colonial administrators. See B. Williams, supra note 97, at 20.

124. See supra notes 67-72 and accompanying text.

125. See, e.g., Pollis, supra note 13, at 22-23.

126. Id. McWhinney's work is another example of this paradox. See E. McWhinney, supra note 5, at 209 ("eurocentrism").

B. *The Conspiracy Theory of Human Rights*

The final aspect of relativism to be discussed is what Karl Popper might describe as "the conspiracy theory of human rights."[127] This theory asserts that human rights are a Macchiavelian creation of the West calculated to impair the economic development of the Third World. Starting from the Marxist assumption that civil and political rights are "formal" bourgeois freedoms that serve only the interests of the capitalists,[128] the conspiracy theory holds that human rights serve the same purpose in the international arena. It sees them as instruments of domination because they are indissolubly tied to the right to property, and because in the field of international economic relations, the human rights movement fosters free and unrestricted trade which seriously hurts the economies of Third World nations. Furthermore, proponents of the conspiracy theory charge that human rights advocacy amounts to moral imperialism.[129] In short, "the effect, if not the design, of such an exclusive political preoccupation [is] to leave the door open to the most ruthless and predatory economic forces in international society."[130]

The conspiracy theory, however, fails to justify the link between the support for human rights and support for particular property rights or trade policies—a fundamental flaw. The argument made in this paper does not presuppose or imply any position in this regard. Moreover, to claim that civil and political rights must be suppressed as a necessary condition for the improvement of Third World economies grossly distorts the facts. As Louis Henkin put it:

> [H]ow many hungry are fed, how much industry is built, by massacre, torture, and detention, by unfair trials and other unjustices, by abuse of minorities, by denials of freedoms of conscience, by suppression of political association and expression?[131]

The contention that the West imposed human rights on the world and that "poor peoples" do not care about freedom is clearly

127. 2 K. Popper, supra note 70, at 94.

128. See, e.g., Marx, On the Jewish Question, in The Marx-Engels Reader 42 (2d ed. Tucker 1978).

129. For an account of the Marxist critique, see Murphy, supra note 20, at 438-42.

130. E. McWhinney, supra note 5, at 211. Cf. Tushnet, supra note 110, at 1398 (the fact of unnecessary human suffering alone is enough to support the critique of "rights" theory).

131. L. Henkin, The Rights of Man Today 130 (1978).

a myth.[132] First, it contradicts the plain fact that a growing awareness exists in the Third World about the need for reinforcing the respect for human rights.[133] Second, even if, *gratia argumentandi*, some Western plot created human rights philosophy, that fact alone would not necessarily undermine its moral value. Conspiracy theories (such as vulgar Marxism, "ideologism," and Critical Legal Studies) assert that the true explanation of a phenomenon consists of discovering the groups of people or hidden interests which are interested in the occurence of the phenomenon and which have plotted to bring it about.[134] To be sure, conspiracies do occur. As Popper conclusively showed, however, the fact that conspiracies rarely succeed ultimately disproves the conspiracy theory. Social life is too complex and the unforeseen consequences of social action too many to support conspiracy as the explanation of every social phenomenon.[135] Institutions originally designed for a certain purpose often turn against their creators. Thus, even if the law of human rights was originally conceived as an ideological tool against communism, today human rights have achieved a universal scope and inspire the struggle against all types of oppression.[136] In other words, the circumstances surrounding the origins of human rights principles are irrelevant to their intrinsic value and cannot detract from their beneficial features.

V. CONCLUSION

The human rights movement has resisted the relativist attack by emphasizing that social institutions, including international law,

132. Id.

133. Cf. the statement by the All Africa Council of Churches/World Council of Churches (1976), cited by Haile, supra note 17, at 584 (describing the system of checks and balances that prevented gross abuses of human and civil rights in traditional African societies); the statement by the Arab Lawyers' Union at their meeting of December, 1983, reprinted in 9 Hum. Rts. Internet Rep. 564 (1984) ("The basis of the legitimacy of any regime or system of government is related to its effective observance of human rights, particularly those set forth in the Universal Declaration."). See also Nickel, supra note 48, at 45 (human rights appeal to many peoples, not just to Westerners).

134. 2 K. Popper, supra note 70, at 94.

135. Id. at 95.

136. South Africa is a case in point. Maybe in 1948 the framers of the Universal Declaration on Human Rights did not intend for it to apply to the black majority in South Africa. Maybe they thought that democracy "among whites" was enough to comply with the Declaration. The international community has subsequently rejected that interpretation, however, and today the law and philosophy of human rights are the main bases for the claims for freedom by the black majority.

are created by and for the individual. Consequently, as far as rights are concerned, governments serve as but the agents of the people. International norms aim to protect individuals, not governments, by creating concrete limits on how human beings may be treated.[137]

I have suggested that cultural relativism is not, and ought not to be, the answer to human rights concerns. Supported neither by international law nor by independent moral analysis, cultural relativism exhibits strong discriminatory overtones and is to a large extent mistaken in its factual assumptions.

I also demonstrated that regardless of its historical origins, the international law of human rights cannot mean one thing to the West and another to the Third World. International human rights law embodies the imperfect yet inspired response of the international community to a growing awareness of the uniqueness of the human being and the unity of the human race. It also represents an eloquent body of norms condemning the effects of organized societal oppression on individuals. Fortunately, the Third World is now starting to play a role in the process of universalizing human rights. The significance of its new role will increase when governing elites cease to use authoritarian traditions as a shield against legitimate demands for basic human rights.

---

137. For example, the purpose of the prohibition of the use of force, U.N. Charter, article 2, para. 4, is to spare humanity from the horrors of war—to prevent human suffering. Although the Charter articulates the rule as an inter-governmental prohibition, its humanitarian underpinnings should be kept in mind. Governments are thus made responsible for the maintenance of peace as agents of humanity, not merely for their own benefit.

[8]

Human Rights and Human Dignity: An Analytic Critique of Non-Western Conceptions of Human Rights

JACK DONNELLY
College of the Holy Cross

It is regularly argued that human rights are not a Western discovery and that non-Western societies have long emphasized the protection of human rights. Such claims, however, are based on a confusion of human rights and human dignity. A concern for human dignity is central to non-Western cultural traditions, whereas human rights, in the sense in which Westerners understand that term—namely, rights (entitlements) held simply by virtue of being a human being—are quite foreign to, for example, Islamic, African, Chinese, and Indian approaches to human dignity. Human rights are but one way that has been devised to realize and to protect human dignity. Although the idea of human rights was first articulated in the West in modern times, it would appear to be an approach particularly suited to contemporary social, political, and economic conditions, and thus of widespread contemporary relevance both in the West and the Third World.

An intimate link between human rights and human dignity is frequently noted in the literature. For example, the International Covenant on Civil and Political Rights states that the rights enumerated "derive from the inherent dignity of the human person." With respect to other cultures, Abdul Aziz Said argues that "[i]n Islam as in other religious traditions, human rights are concerned with the dignity of the individual." (1979, p. 63) Many authors go so far as to treat human rights and human dignity as essentially equivalent concepts (e.g., Pollis and Schwab 1980, pp. 4, 8; Legesse 1980, p. 132; Harkin 1979, p. 15; Said 1977).

However, it will be argued here that human rights present only one path to the realization of human dignity. Although there are indeed close connections between the two concepts, I shall argue that there are conceptions of human dignity which do not imply human rights, and societies and institutions which aim to realize human dignity entirely independent of human rights. This view, which was once rather common, seems to be ignored or rejected in most of the recent literature specifically devoted to the topic.

The argument that "human rights are not a Western discovery," (Manglapus 1978), that "all societies have human rights notions" (Pollis and Schwab 1980, p. xiv), and that "all societies cross-culturally and historically manifest conceptions of human rights" (Pollis and Schwab 1980, p. 15), is a common feature of contemporary discussions of human rights in non-Western settings. I shall argue to the contrary that most non-Western cultural and political traditions lack not only the practice of human rights but the very concept. As a matter of historical fact, the concept of human rights is an artifact of modern Western civilization.

It does not necessarily follow, however, that human rights are in any important sense arbitrary, wrong, misguided, or in need of basic rethinking. Rather, human rights represent a distinctive approach to the problems of human dignity which deserves to be fully and fairly evaluated on its merits, not its parentage. The historical character of the concept must be taken seriously, but more importantly, we must move beyond a limited genetic perspective to the important substantive issues raised by human rights. In this paper, I attempt to specify the special character of the human rights approach to human dignity, to demonstrate its historical uniqueness, and to begin to explore some of the issues it raises.

Defining the Topic

The Concept of Human Rights. Mention of the Western concept of human rights is likely to raise visions of yet another discussion of the relationship between civil and political rights and social and economic human rights. However, my argument is cast at an entirely different level.

The question, "What are human rights?" generally is taken to be a request for a *catalogue raisonné* of human rights; i.e., a question about the list of valid human rights. For the most part we will not be concerned here with this level of analysis. Instead we will be dealing with the con-

*I wish to thank Hanna Fenichel Pitkin and Ernst B. Haas for their many helpful comments on earlier drafts of this article.

ceptual question: "What is the meaning of 'human rights'?" "What kind of 'thing' is a human right?" rather than "Is this a human right?"

Clearly the two questions are interrelated; one's definition of the concept prescribes the content of one's list. However, in the deviation of a list from the concept, there is a crucial intermediate level that needs to be distinguished by developing further the distinction between concept and list.

Ronald Dworkin distinguishes a *concept*, what something means, from a *conception*, a particular and more concrete specification of that concept. Dworkin argues that such principles as fairness or the constitutional prohibition of cruel and unusual punishment have a settled although rather abstract meaning (the concept), even though what is to be construed as cruel and unusual punishment (the conception) may vary with time and circumstances (Dworkin 1978, pp. 134-6, 226).[1]

With respect to human rights, we can say that at the level of the concept, human rights are rights one has because one is a human being (person); or as the Covenants put it, rights that "derive from the inherent dignity of the human person." The crucial ideas that need to be explicated at the level of conceptions are rights, persons, and (inherent) human dignity; once this is done, it is relatively easy, even if still controversial, to develop a list.

The familiar debates about the priority of civil and political or social and economic rights take place almost entirely at the level of lists and conceptions. I would argue that the concept of human rights as a matter of conceptual logic permits an emphasis on either set of rights, as well as more balanced approaches based on the interdependence or indivisibility of human rights. However, arguments for or against a particular conception of human rights will not be our concern here. Instead I will focus on the concept of human rights, as defined here, and on non-Western approaches to the realization of human dignity, which amount to challenges to the idea that there are rights one has merely because one is a human being.

Defining Human Rights. Human rights are *rights*, not benefits, duties, privileges, or some other perhaps related practice. Rights in turn are special entitlements of *persons*. Although a thorough analysis of rights and human rights is not possible here, at least a brief explanation is required.

Not just any benefit is a right; only those benefits to which one is entitled are, or rather may be, rights. Not even all benefits that another person is obliged to render to one are one's rights. For example, A may be obliged to confer a benefit on B out of considerations of charity, without B having a right to that benefit. Although I am morally obliged to aid the needy, a particular destitute person does not, ipso facto, have a right to my money or even a right to assistance from me. I may be obliged to aid him, but he is not entitled to that aid from me; i.e., he does not have a right to it from me.

The distinction between duty and obligation, the right thing to do, and entitlement, i.e., rights, is crucial. We speak of right in both instances but in quite different senses, which need to be kept distinct.

Elsewhere (Donnelly 1980) I have argued that these two senses of right are marked by different characteristic locutions. The sense involving moral duty or righteousness I have called right in the sense of "right that" as in "It's right that you. . . ." The sense involving entitlement can be called right in the sense of "right to," as in "I have a right to. . . ."

Another way to mark these two senses is by the verbs with which they are used. When we talk of righteousness, the verb characteristically used is to be: It is right for you to help her; What is right here?; It wouldn't be right to leave now. However, when we talk of rights, of entitlements, to be is rarely if ever used. Instead we talk of having or holding rights, and various ways of putting rights to use, all of which are based on possession of that right. Thus we might distinguish these two senses of right as right in the sense of what is right (or right in the sense of being right) and right in the sense of having a right.[2]

Having a right places one in a protected position. To violate someone's right is not merely to fail to do what is right but also to commit a special and important personal offense against the rightholder by failing to give him his due, that to which he is entitled. To violate a right goes well beyond merely falling short of some high moral standard.

Furthermore, rights, especially basic rights, have a special priority where they come into conflict with other action-justifying principles. This is

[1]Pitkin (1972, Chapter VIII, especially pp. 186-192) draws a similar distinction between the substance and the form of a concept, its meaning and its institutionalization. Pitkin's analysis is particularly interesting for her discussion of divergences between form and substance.

[2]This way of making the distinction seems preferable because, for example, when one says "It is right to do x for him," one means right in the sense of 'right that,' whereas when one says "I have a right that you do this for me," the sense intended is right in the sense of right to.

nicely captured in Dworkin's simile of rights as trumps. (1978, pp. xi, 81-105 and *passim*) Rights are not just one type of social or moral goal coequal with others; rather, in ordinary circumstances, rights have prima facie priority over utilitarian calculations or considerations of social policy. In fact, one of the basic purposes of rights would seem to be to insulate right-holders from claims based on such principles, which otherwise would be not only appropriate but decisive reasons for political and even individual action.

However, this priority is only prima facie. Rights are defeasible; i.e., in particular cases they may be justifiably overriden by other rights, considerations of right in the sense of what is right, necessity, scarcity, or some other principle. Nonetheless, it is essential to rights that they have this special status of taking priority over all but the most pressing non-rights demands and interests.

One also can do many things with rights beyond what is available by virtue of right in the sense of what is right. Rights serve as the basis for special claims against those in relation to whom the right is held.[3] One may exercise, assert, claim, press, demand, waive, or transfer rights, as well as put them to many other uses.

Thus rights are under the control of the right-holder, who in large measure manages the use of the right and thereby the consequences of having that right. The right-holder is not only placed in an advantageous position vis-à-vis the obligee; he is placed in charge of the relationship insofar as it is based on his right.[4] The duties imposed by rights not only operate at a different level but in a different way. Both what is demanded of the obligee and how those demands are imposed are crucially different, depending on what sense of right is involved.

It is clear that the Western tradition of natural or human rights, which goes back at least to Locke, has conceived of human rights in this way.[5] In fact it is precisely this conception that distinguishes this modern tradition from the Greek, medieval, and Stoic natural law theories and competing modern theories such as utilitarianism.[6] The guarantees of life, liberty, and property (and increasingly, since the late eighteenth century, beginning with Paine, guarantees of such rights as education and social security) are treated as more than merely right in the sense of what is right, more than simply the righteous demands of God, morality, conscience, or social policy. Rather, they are viewed as the rights of man, as human rights.

Here we will take this tradition to be stipulative of the meaning of human rights. At the very least, this is the sense present in the classic documents and philosophical defenses, as well as in ordinary usage. For our purposes this usage must suffice.

Of course human rights are but one type of rights, namely the rights one holds by virtue of being a person. Not all rights held by human beings are human rights. Legal, contractual, promissory, and constitutional rights are held by human beings without their being necessarily human rights; that is, they are rights of persons without being among the rights of man.

Human rights are conceived as naturally inhering in the human person.[7] They are neither granted by the state nor are they the result of one's actions. In Hart's (1955) well-known categorization, they are general rights, rights that

[3]Claim theories of rights (most notably Feinberg, 1980) usually are distinguished from, and viewed as incompatible with, entitlement theories such as the one presented here. However, a claim theory can be more profitably seen as a complementary approach that highlights different parts of the practice of rights. A crucial element of being entitled to something is being in a position to make claims. However, the claim theorist tends to ignore the fact that there are other sorts of claims than claims to rights. What distinguishes and grounds claims to rights is the special entitlement of the right-holder.

[4]Discretionary exercise of rights is crucial. The best-known account that stresses discretionary control is Hart, 1973. Whether *all* rights share this feature is debatable—e.g., discretionary control of an inalienable right would be in some way limited—but in most standard cases it is central to the rights-based relationship that exists between right-holder and duty-bearer.

[5]I use the two terms more or less interchangably, despite subtle differences in connotation. Defending such a usage, though, is beyond our scope here. However, compare Beitz (1979, pp. 53-61), who argues that a natural rights model of human rights is inadequate, and Bay (1980), who advances an argument for the derivation of rights from needs.

[6]Of course, this is but one tradition of modern Western political thought, as Burke and Bentham, for example, so clearly indicate. There are today, and have been in the past, other Western as well as non-Western approaches to human dignity. In fact I would argue that pre-modern Western political theory lacks the notion of human rights. See Donnelly (1980).

[7]Exactly how nature creates or confers rights is rather obscure, at least in non-theistic theories. Nonetheless, such a natural basis seems essential to distinguish human rights from other types of rights, such as basic constitutional, legal, or moral rights. We should also note, however, that although the moral source of human rights is human nature, their institutionalization is crucial to their effective enjoyment. Therefore, the human decisions underlying this institutionalization and implementation may be seen as, in another sense, the source of the rights.

arise from no special undertaking beyond membership in the human race. To have human rights one does not have to be anything other than a human being. Neither must one do anything other than be born a human being.

Since they are grounded in human nature, human rights are generally viewed as inalienable, at least in the way in which one's nature is inalienable. Inalienability is a particularly difficult concept to analyze. However, at the minimum what is suggested is that in some moral sense one cannot fully renounce, transfer, or otherwise alienate one's human rights. To do so would be to destroy one's humanity, to de-nature oneself, to become other (less) than a human being and thus it is viewed as a moral impossibility.

There is also a strong and quite essential implication that human rights, as a particularly important class of rights, take priority over all but the most serious non-rights demands. If rights in general are trumps, human rights are the honor cards in the suit.

Sometimes this view is expressed in the claim that human rights are absolute. However, this is taking the point too far. For example, an absolute right to liberty would make unjustified even the jailing of criminals. Nonetheless, there are very few circumstances in which human rights might be justifiably overridden. Human rights are relatively absolute, at least in part because their natural and inalienable character is based largely on the attributes and potentials they protect, which are essential to a meaningful and fully human life.

Finally, human rights are conceived as being held primarily in relation to society and particularly to society in the form of the state. As the natural rights of persons, they are seen as logically and morally to take precedence over the rights of the state and society, which are viewed as major contributors to the realization of these rights but also the greatest potential violators of basic human rights.

Non-Western Political Cultures and Human Rights

Having sketched this conceptual benchmark, let us look briefly at the ways in which several traditional cultures and one modern non-Western society have approached the issues we consider in terms of human rights, i.e., the social and political ideals by which these cultures aspire to realize human dignity. In each case I will show that the substantive issues discussed today in terms of human rights, such as life, speech, religion, work, health, and education, are handled almost entirely in terms of duties that are neither derivative from nor correlative to rights, or at least not human rights. These societies recognize that guarantees in these areas are essential to a fully human life and the realization of inherent human dignity. They have elaborate systems of human duties, which are designed for the protection of human dignity. However, human rights are quite foreign to their approaches.

Human Rights in Islam. Numerous authors assert that human rights have an important place in Islam.[8] For example, Abul A'la Mawdudi argues that "Islam has laid down some universal fundamental rights for humanity as a whole, which are to be observed and respected under all circumstances . . . fundamental rights for every man by virtue of his status as a human being" (1976, p. 10). Diplomats as well as scholars have argued that "the basic concepts and principles of human rights had from the very beginning been embodied in Islamic law."[9] Nadvi (1966, pp. 14-15) and Tabendeh (1970, pp. 1, 8) have even claimed that contemporary human rights doctrines merely give recognition to 1400-year-old Islamic ideas, but on examination, these claims prove to be almost entirely without basis.

For example, Khalid M. Ishaque argues that "Muslims are enjoined constantly to seek ways and means to assure to each other what in modern parlance we call 'human rights' " (1974, p. 32). Ishaque admits that "human rights" cannot be translated into the language of the Islamic holy works but nevertheless suggests that something very much like human rights lies at the core of Islamic doctrine. He even lists fourteen "human rights" recognized and established by Islam.

However, when we look at these alleged human rights, we find that virtually all of them are only duties of rulers and individuals, not rights held by anyone. The scriptural passages cited as establishing a right to protection of life in fact are divine injunctions not to kill and to consider life as inviolable. Likewise, the right to justice proves to be instead a duty of rulers to establish justice, whereas the right to freedom is merely a duty not to enslave unjustly. In fact, economic rights turn out to be duties to earn a living and to help to provide for the needy, whereas the right to freedom of expression actually is an obligation to speak the truth; i.e., the right is not even an obligation of others but an obligation of the alleged right-holder! Although Moslems are regularly and forcefully enjoined to treat their fellow men with respect and dignity, the bases for these injunc-

[8]Piscatori (1980) makes a similar argument in the case of Islam. For a brief, more general, discussion along the lines developed here, see Pagels (1979).

[9]Mr. Makki, representative of Oman to the Third Committee of the General Assembly, speech of 25 October 1979, UN document number A/C.3/34/SR.27.

tions are not human rights but divine commands which establish only duties, that is, which deal only with right in the sense of what is right.

In a similar fashion, Majid Khadduri (1946, pp. 77-78) lists five rights held by men according to Islam: rights to personal safety, respect of personal reputation, equality, brotherhood, and justice.[10] Again, what little evidence is presented shows that Islam treated these subjects entirely in terms of right in the sense of what is right.

Khadduri's discussion makes it clear just how far the Islamic precepts he mentions diverge from the notion of human rights. For example, he claims that "human rights in Islam are the privilege of Allah (God), because authority ultimately belongs to Him." This is, quite literally, incoherent: "human rights" that are not rights of human beings but privileges of God. In another vein he argues that "human rights in Islam, as prescribed by the divine law, are the privilege only of persons of full legal status. A person with full legal capacity is a living human being of mature age, free, and of Moslem faith." Human rights, then, would be the privileges of free, male Moslems, not the rights of man qua man. Infidels receive only guarantees of life, property, and freedom of religion, and slaves only a right to life.

Similarly, Abdul Aziz Said claims "to identify precepts that establish human rights in the Islamic tradition" (1979, p. 64). He argues that in Islam, "human beings have certain God-granted rights, and right by definition is the exercise of power" (Said 1980, p. 92).[11] However, he does not present a single piece of evidence in direct support of this claim, whereas the discussion he offers once more demonstrates the absence of the concept of human rights in Islam.

For example, Said lists nine basic precepts regulating the operation of an Islamic political system which it would appear that he takes to be human rights (1979, pp. 65-68). In every case, though, either there is merely a rights-less duty or the rights that exist are not human rights but legal rights, rights held not simply as human beings but as a result of one's legal or spiritual status.[12]

In fact, Said, much like Khadduri, implicitly admits these sorts of counterarguments without seeming to recognize their significance.

> The essential characteristic of human rights in Islam is that they constitute obligations connected with the Divine and derive their force from this connection.
>
> Human rights exist only in relation to human obligations. Individuals possess certain obligations towards God, fellow humans and nature, all of which are defined by Shariah. When individuals meet these obligations they acquire certain rights and freedoms which are again prescribed by the Shariah (1979, pp. 63, 73-74).

In other words, in Islam, in the realm of human rights (read human dignity), what really matters is duty rather than rights, and whatever rights do exist are a consequence of one's status or actions, not one's nature.

There can be little objection to claims that in Islam "it is the state's duty to enhance human dignity and alleviate conditions that hinder individuals in their efforts to achieve happiness" (Said 1980, p. 87). It may even be plausible to argue that "there is no aspect of human need but Islam, in its ethical, social and liturgical precepts, has made provision for it" (Tabandeh 1970, p. 10). Without a doubt the social and political precepts of Islam reflect a strong concern for human good and human dignity, but although such concern is important in itself and would appear to be a prerequisite for human rights notions, it is in no way equivalent to a concern for, or a recognition of, human rights.

Human Rights in Traditional African Societies. "The African conception of human rights was an essential aspect of African humanism." (Asante 1969, p. 74). "It is not often remembered that traditional African societies supported and practiced human rights." (Wai 1980, p. 116). As in the case of similar claims about Islam, such assertions prove to be not only unsupported, but actually undercut, by the evidence that is presented on their behalf.

For example, Dunstan M. Wai, the author of the second quoted passage, continues by writing that "traditional African attitudes, beliefs, institutions, and experiences sustained the 'view that certain rights should be upheld against alleged necessities of state' " (1980, p. 116). Clearly he is confusing human rights with limited government in this claim.

[10]Compare Mawdudi (1976, pp. 17-24), whose "Charter of human rights granted in Islam" (p. 19) is similar in substance and shares the same features as the lists of Ishaque and Khadduri. Compare also Tabandeh (1970), where the approach is the reverse, attempting to show that the rights in the Universal Declaration of Human Rights are anticipated and recognized by Islam.

[11]Exactly what the appended definition of "right" means here is hard to say, but I take it to be something like what I have called here right in the sense of having a right.

[12]Compare Tabandeh (1970, p. 17) who claims that the preferential treatment of Muslims in certain criminal cases is "quite free of difficulty" in terms of human rights because "people who have not put their reliance in conviction and faith, nor had that basic abiding-place nor believed in the one Invisible God, are reckoned as outside the pale of humanity."

There are many bases on which a government might be limited—divine commandment, human rights, legal rights, and extra-legal checks such as a balance of power, to name a few. Simply having a limited government does not in any way entail that one has human rights. Yet Wai and others base their arguments on little more than a demonstration of the existence of limited government.[13]

"There is no point in belaboring the concern for rights, democratic institutions, and rule of law in traditional African politics" (Wai 1980, p. 117). To this we can only add that it is particularly pointless in a discussion of human rights, given the form such concerns took. Even in the many cases where Africans had personal rights vis-à-vis their government, those rights were not based on one's humanity per se but on membership in the community, status, or some other ascriptive characteristic.

Asmarom Legesse argues along similar lines that "many studies have been carried out that suggest that distributive justice, in the economic and political spheres, is the cardinal ethical principle that is shared by most Africans" (1980, p. 127). This is quite true. It is also, once again, irrelevant.

Distributive justice and human rights are quite different concepts. One might have a theory or conception of distributive justice based on human rights, but one might as easily base it on some other principle. Plato, Burke, and Bentham all had theories of distributive justice, yet no one would ever think to suggest that they advocated human rights. Although giving to each his own (distributive justice) will involve giving a person that to which he is entitled (his rights), unless the definition of one's own takes place in terms of that to which one is entitled simply as a human being, the rights in question will not be human rights. In African societies, rights were assigned on the basis of communal membership, family, status, or achievement.

As with human rights in Islam, we see here an attempt to establish that the differences with the West lie only in the words used, not the concepts. "Different societies formulate their conception of human rights in diverse cultural idioms" (Legesse 1980, p. 124). In fact, though, as we have seen, the difference is not simply one of idiom, but one of concept. Although many of the same ideas are valued, the ways in which they are valued are quite different. Recognition of human rights simply was not the way of traditional Africa, with obvious and important consequences for political practice.

Human Rights in Confucian China and Hindu India. The available literature on China and India is of much the same sort. For example, Chung-Shu Lo, after noting that the Chinese language lacked even a term for rights until one was coined in the late nineteenth century to translate the Western concept, nonetheless insists that the absence of the language of rights "does not mean that the Chinese never claimed rights or enjoyed the basic rights of man" (1949, p. 186). However, the evidence presented demands the reverse conclusion.

One wonders how the Chinese managed to claim rights without the language to make such claims. Likewise, the assertion that basic human rights were enjoyed seems implausible. Did the Chinese have these rights, exercise them, assert them, or *only* enjoy them? One suspects the latter, in which case Lo's claim collapses, because of the confusion between enjoying a benefit and having a right. Simply because acts that we would say involved violations of human rights were not considered permissible does not necessarily entail that people were viewed as having human rights.

Lo claims that "the idea of human rights developed very early in China" and he examines one particular human right, the right to revolt, which "was repeatedly expressed in Chinese history" (1949, pp. 186-87). However, the passages he quotes from the classic texts show only that the ruler "has a duty to heaven to take care of the interests of the people." Thus the only particular human right he advances proves not to be a right at all, for a duty of the ruler to heaven is quite a different matter from a right of the people vis-à-vis the ruler.

Shao-Chuan Leng also argues that "Chinese political theory sanctioned the people's revolts against oppressive rulers" (1980, p. 84). However, he fails to show that this sanction was based on human rights. Instead he simply assumes that democracy, in a very loose sense of the term, can be equated with human rights (1980, pp. 82-85). For example, after showing the elitist, hierarchical, and station-based character of traditional Chinese social relations and Confucian political and social philosophy, Leng adds that "there were also democratic traits in Chinese civilization," apparently taking this to be a demonstration of the existence of the concept of human rights (1980, p. 82). We have already discussed this conceptual error above.

As before, the problem lies in a confusion of ethical and political duties with human rights.

[13]See Wai (1980, pp. 115-118), e.g., "This chapter will argue that authoritarianism in modern Africa is not at all in accord with the spirit and practice of traditional political systems," and Legesse (1980, pp. 125-127). For non-African examples, see Said (1979, p. 65) and Manglapus (1978). Most generally, see Pollis and Schwab (1980).

Undeniably there were elaborate duties imposed on rulers. Obligation, though, is only one side of a rights-based relationship. In itself, it does not even suggest, let alone establish, the existence of rights on the part of those in whose interests one is obliged to act. Lo notes that traditional Chinese doctrine is expressed almost entirely in terms of duties of rulers. However, he refers to this only as a "different approach to the problem of human rights" (1949, p. 188). In fact, it is an approach to the problem of human dignity which involves no human rights.

Moving from China to India, particularly traditional Hindu India, one would imagine that there would be no question about human rights being present, given the central place of the caste system. For example, Ralph Buultjens captures nicely the essential implications of the caste system for human rights.

> The essential feature of caste was the assumption that there are fundamental and unchangeable differences in the status and nature of human beings.[14] These differences make it necessary for people to be governed by different norms of behavior appropriate to their station in life. . . . Caste divisions . . . were the framework of society. . . . Progression of birth and rebirth, with different rights attached to each step, enable access to different gradations of rights. The universal application of a common set of rights for all people in a given society, at the same time, is not part of the cosmology (1980, pp. 112-13).

Yet half a page below this clear, if implicit, denial of the presence of the concept of human rights, Buultjens talks of "Hindu orthodoxy, including the more traditional, multidimensional views of human rights" (1980, p. 113). The denial of human rights is thus transformed into a "multidimensional" view! Such uses reduce the term human rights to little more than a fashionable hurrah and need to be vigorously resisted.

The Soviet Union and Human Rights. Moving from traditional to modern non-Western societies, we can consider human rights in the Soviet Union. The differences between the Soviet and Western approaches usually are presented as lying at the level of conceptions and lists and are concerned with the Soviet emphasis on social and economic rights in contrast to the Western emphasis on civil and political rights. However, the differences reach to the level of the concept as well.

Central to the Soviet approach is the fusion of rights and duties. The Preamble of the 1977 Constitution states that the USSR "is a society of genuine democracy, whose political system ensures . . . the combination of real citizen's rights and liberties with their duties and responsibilities to society."[15] Article 59 states that "the exercise of rights and liberties is inseparable from the performance by citizens of their duties." We see this same characterization in semiofficial accounts: "The linkage of rights and duties [is] the special quality of socialist law" (Sawczuk 1979, p. 89); "The most important feature of the Soviet citizen's legal status is the organic unity between their rights and their obligations" (Chkhidvadze 1980, p. 18); and even in human rights activist Valery Chalidze's account of Soviet doctrine (1974, p. 21).

The correlation of rights and duties is a standard topic in the theory of rights. As ordinarily conceived, A's right to x with respect to B implies duties of B with respect to A's having or enjoying x; i.e., A's right entails B's obligation.[16] However, in Soviet doctrine it would seem that A's right to x is correlated with substantively parallel obligations on the part of A.

For example, Article 40 of the Constitution states that "USSR citizens have the right to labor . . . including the right to choice of occupation, type of employment and work. . . ." However, in Article 60, labor is a citizen's duty: "Conscientious labor in one's chosen field of socially useful activity and the observance of labor discipline are the duty of, and a matter of honor for, every able-bodied USSR citizen." Soviet diplomats have been quite open and explicit in noting that "it [is] considered the individual's duty, as well as his right, to work for the benefit of society."[17] How, though, can rights and duties be conceptualized as coincident?

It is sometimes suggested, not just by the Soviets, that this is just the way rights are and work, that the conceptual logic of rights entails that A's rights imply duties for him.[18]

[14]In fact, these differences are so extreme that it would appear that the notion of the human person, which is so central to the concept of human rights, is quite foreign to such a way of thinking.

[15]In the initial public draft of the Constitution, this reads "human rights" in the official English translation. I am unsure what, if any, significance to attach to this.

[16]For a thorough discussion of the correlation of rights and duties, see Donnelly (in press).

[17]Mr. Ivanov, the Soviet representative to the Economic and Social Council Working Group on the Implementation of the International Covenant on Economic, Social and Cultural Rights, UN document number E/1980/WG.1/SR.14.

[18]For recent official diplomatic statements of such a position, see the speeches of the representatives of Rumania, Ecuador, and Iraq to the Economic and Social Council Working Group on the Implementation

> Rights and duties are two facets of the same picture. Whoever demands a right to liberty has to respect a similar right in others which circumscribes his right to personal liberty very considerably. If an individual thinks it his right to be fed and clothed and maintained in proper health and if he has a right to work, it is also his duty to work according to his energies and skill and accept the work which the welfare of the community demands from him. (Hakim 1955, p. 3).

However, these duties, which we certainly do recognize, are not conceived of as arising from the possession of rights, or rather, not from one's own rights.

The duty to respect another person's liberty is imposed on me by his right to liberty, not mine, and he has such a right not because I have a right to liberty but as the result of a particular pattern of distribution of rights. Likewise, I can have a right to work or a right to health care without being under an obligation, as a result of that right, to work for, or to contribute to, the welfare of the community. It may be an unjust or immoral society which gives me such rights without these duties, but that is another matter altogether.

If the logic of rights does not render rights and duties coincident, the only way I can see to accomplish this is to treat rights as social grants. If A (society), having a right to, or control of, x (jobs), transfers x to B (citizens), conditional on B accepting certain parallel or reciprocal duties (work), the right to x would be simultaneously a duty, as a result of the manner in which the right was invested.

Such a transfer may be seen to benefit both parties to the transaction and thus is easily defended. The individual in this situation would benefit from the guaranteed access to suitable rewarding work, whereas society would benefit if all able-bodied citizens worked. The individual would, as a result of the transaction, have a right to a job, coupled with a non-rights-based duty to work, whereas the state would have a rights-based duty to provide jobs and a (contractual?) right to have citizens work in a socially productive field.

Such an analysis is particularly attractive because it is consistent with the basic philosophical and ideological precepts of the Soviet system. The focus is unambiguously social, and the state is given prominence of place, with the individual conceptualized as not actually subsidiary to the state but capable of realization only in his social capacity. This analysis also places the emphasis, as the Soviets always do, on objective and concrete rights, which the individual enjoys only through state agency, rather than subjective, abstract or formal rights inhering in the individual per se.

A full system of such rights would indeed involve the organic unity of rights and duties, and such a system would be full of rights, in the sense of having a right. However, human rights would be entirely absent, for human rights are not grants, either conditional or unconditional, of state or society, but are inherent to man.

Even in the Constitution, the Soviets rather clearly treat rights as contingent on the performance of duties; in Article 59, which states that "the exercise of rights and liberties is inseparable from the performance by citizens of their duties," and in Article 50, where civil rights are held to be granted "in accordance with the people's interests and for the purpose of strengthening and developing the socialist system." As one Soviet commentator has tellingly put it, "the significance and worth of each person are determined by the way he exercises his rights and performs his duties" (Egorov 1979, p. 36).

Economic and social rights as well as civil and political rights are treated as contingent and are forfeited when the duties that accompany them are not discharged. For example, despite the apparently unqualified character of the right to work mentioned in Article 40, jobs in their fields are regularly denied dissidents and Jewish activists, in accordance with Soviet law and administrative practice, on the grounds of the individuals having failed to discharge their social duties. The right to education, according to Article 45, "is ensured by the free nature of all types of education." Nonetheless, emigres may be required to buy back this "free" education as a legal condition of exit.

Admittedly, any right, even a basic right, has its limits which are specified by law. For example, in this country the right to freedom of speech is limited by laws of slander and libel and by the general requirement that the right not be exercised so as wrecklessly to endanger others such as by yelling "Fire!" in a crowded theater. However, one's possession and exercise of a basic human right like the right to freedom of speech are not conditional on accepting either these limits or some parallel duty.

For example, the slanderer is fined for the damage done and yet continues to be able to exercise his right to freedom of speech. As a human or constitutional right in this country, the right to freedom of speech is conceived to be inherent to the individual and independent of his merit or the discharge of civic responsibilities.[19] In contrast,

of the International Covenant on Economic, Social and Cultural Rights in UN documents number E/1980/WG.1/SR.4 and E/1980/WG.1/SR.7..

[19] The connection between human and constitutional rights presents difficult analytical problems that are

the rights of Soviet citizens are treated as grants of the state which are held only contingently. Thus although there are numerous rights held by men and women in the Soviet Union, among these rights are not the "rights of man." Even though there are major substantive parallels between the rights of Soviet citizens and internationally recognized human rights, Soviet citizens do not have and enjoy these rights as human rights, with important practical consequences for the way in which they work.

The Individual, Society, and Human Rights

One of the key differences between the modern Western and the non-Western approaches to human dignity is the much greater individualism of the Western human-rights approach. Rights held by individuals will of course tend to be more individualistic in their operation and effects than group rights or substantively similar non-rights protections because of the special claims justified by rights-based entitlements and the substantial discretionary control of the right-holder. When these rights are at the basic level of human rights, this individualism will be accented by the rarity of the social claims that will justifiably override rights.

Non-Western writers often stress this difference. For example, Asmarom Legesse writes that a

> critical difference between African and Western traditions concerns the importance of the human individual. In the liberal democracies of the Western world the ultimate repository of rights is the human person. The individual is held in a virtually sacralized position. There is a perpetual, and in our view obsessive, concern with the dignity of the individual, his worth, personal autonomy and property (1980, p. 124).

He further suggests the way in which Africans would seek to redress this imbalance.

> If Africans were the sole authors of the Universal Declaration of Human Rights, they might have ranked the rights of communities above those of individuals, and they might have used a cultural idiom fundamentally different from the language in which the ideas are now formulated (1980, p. 129).[10]

Writing from an Islamic perspective, Ahmad Yamani likewise argues that the West "is so overzealous in its defense of the individual's freedom, rights and dignity, that it overlooks the acts of some individuals in exercising such rights in a way that jeopardizes the community" (1968, p. 15).

Throughout the Third World—and for the sake of simplicity and ease of exposition we will focus on the developing Third World in what follows—this general orientation seems to be overwhelmingly predominant. The question, though, is what conclusions are to be drawn from the undeniable fact of such differences and what, as a practical matter, ought to be done about human rights in the face of such fundamental divergences.

Legesse, like many others, argues that "any system of ideas that claims to be universal must contain critical elements in its fabric that are avowedly of African, Latin American or Asian derivation" (1980, p. 123).[11] In practice this would mean the inclusion of group or peoples' rights along with individual human rights. However, the issues at stake in such a move demand a substantive, rather than a geographical, argument.

Human rights, as we have been discussing them, are held by individuals and are exercised primarily in relation to society, usually in the person of the state, against which they are most characteristically claimed.[12] Peoples' rights, though, are held by society (again, usually in the form of the state) and directed against the individual (or other states) in their operation. If social rights and duties are both extensive and take priority over individual rights, as for example in the USSR, human rights are likely to be largely formal in practice. In such circumstances, although one might be said to have a human right, in those instances in which one would be inclined to assert or claim it, namely where the right is threatened,

---

beyond our scope. There certainly is some relationship, at least in most countries. However, the two types are by no means equivalent, and thinking about them as equivalent can lead to serious problems. This is implicitly illustrated in Brown and MacLean (1980), pp. 1-82.

[10]Such an assessment seems to be confirmed by the Organization of African Unity's recent African Declaration of Human and *Peoples'* Rights (my emphasis).

[11]It is ironic that those most attuned to Western neocolonialism and who would correctly reject with contempt an argument that an idea was correct or even applicable because of its Western origin, show the same basic error in such a geopolitical approach to the question of the truth, defensibility, or utility of the (Western) concept of human rights.

[12]The exceptions to this, in the realm of internationally recognized human rights, represent a clear and rather explicit redefinition of the concept along the lines approved of in Legesse's argument. This is particularly evident in the case of the right to self-determination, which is included in the Covenants but not the Universal Declaration, and in the emerging "third generation" of human rights, such as the rights to peace and development (see, e.g., UN documents number E/CN.4/1334 and HR/GENEVA/1980/BP.1-4 and Alston 1980).

challenged, violated, or frustrated, it would be largely useless. One might be said to have the right, but it would not serve as much of a trump, for where one would be likely to want to claim it, the claim would be rather easily overridden by the rights of society and associated individual duties.

In fact, as a practical matter, one would be able to enjoy the right only at the discretion of the state, and yet the state would not be violating one's rights in denying that enjoyment. This approach looks much more like being granted a benefit than having a right. In other words, it would appear as if human rights could be combined with peoples' rights in any substantial way only with great risk to their essential character.

In any case, having that kind of a human right would be rather different from having a human right as that has been interpreted until now. Restoring the balance between the individual and society in this fashion thus comes dangerously close to destroying or denying human rights as they have been understood. Therefore, incorporating Third World views would be likely to have major costs for human rights.

Such costs may or may not be justified. A society which regularly balanced human rights against the rights of society may or may not be preferable to one based on a Western concept of human rights. However, the issue must be addressed in substantive terms, not simply on the basis of anthropological and historical differences.

Here is not the place to assess the relative merits of claims of human and peoples' rights. However, I do want to suggest that writers like Legesse seem to base their proposals on a rather wistful social vision of limited applicability to contemporary circumstances and aspirations.

The social model they seem to have in mind is the small community based on groupings of extended families, the type of community so characteristic of traditional societies, both Western and non-Western. In particular, a relatively decentralized, non-bureaucratic, communitarian society seems to be the ideal.

In such a society, the individual lacks many, if not most, of the rights that are so highly valued in the liberal democratic state. However, he has a secure and significant place in his society and has available a wide range of intense personal and social relationships which provide him important material and non-material support. He also has available regularized social protections of many of the values and interests which in the West are protected through individual human and legal rights. One might argue that introducing individual rights would diminish his prospects for achieving a dignified life worthy of a human being. In any case, such a society is undeniably morally defensible, is in many ways quite attractive, and can be said to protect basic human dignity.

Along somewhat different lines, one might argue that only such a society is defensible in conditions of extreme scarcity (Keenan 1980, pp. 80ff). If extremely limited resources or environmental severity make survival precarious, the individual, in the absence of the close-knit community whose interests take priority, would be doomed to death, if only through accident or disease. Certainly our anthropological evidence suggests that such a communitarian solution appears to be natural to most peoples.

However, if we remove the pressures of necessity and, even more importantly, if we remove the social support and protection provided to the individual by the traditional community, things appear in a different light. Now it would be difficult to justify the continued absence of individual human rights while still having a system that could be said to protect and give prominence to human dignity, in any plausible sense of that term.

Westernization, modernization, development, and underdevelopment—the dominant contemporary social and economic forces—have in fact severed the individual from the small, supportive community. Economic, social, and cultural intrusions into, and disruptions of, the traditional community have removed the support and protection which would "justify" or "compensate for" the absence of individual human rights. These intrusions have created a largely isolated individual who is forced to go it alone against social, economic, and political forces that far too often appear to be aggressive and oppressive. Society, which once protected his dignity and provided him with an important place in the world, now appears, in the form of the modern state, the modern economy, and the modern city, as an alien power that assaults his dignity and that of his family.

In such circumstances, human rights appear as the natural response to changing conditions, a logical and necessary evolution of the means for realizing human dignity. The individual needs the protection of individual rights, barring the implausible, and generally undesired, reemergence of the traditional order. And given the power of modern institutions and the demonstrated inclinations of the individuals and groups that control them, not just any type of individual rights will do, but only rights with the moral force and range of universal human rights. In Marxist terms, the bourgeois economic revolution brings with it the bourgeois political revolution and bourgeois rights; capitalism and industrialization bring in their wake natural or human rights, which represent a major advance in the protection of human dignity in such circumstances.

From this perspective, then, the individualism of human rights appears as a response to objective conditions. Therefore, to rail against the individualism of human rights in the absence of an alternative solution to the very real problems of protecting the individual and human dignity, is at best utopian or shortsighted.

This is admittedly only a functional, rather than a moral, defense of human rights, and a defense based on a limited, largely Western, historical experience. Nonetheless, it does suggest that serious consideration be given to the argument that the underlying concerns and needs in the area of human rights and human dignity are, for objective, historical reasons, essentially the same today in the Third World as they were two or three centuries ago in England and France. This requires, though, that we put aside questions of the origins of concepts, practices, and institutions—not to mention the awarding of credit or praise for discovering them—and focus instead on their applicability to the problems we face today in protecting and realizing human dignity. The real question is whether the concept of human rights has contemporary relevance outside the West.

The Relevance of Human Rights

The claim that the Western concept of human rights is in some way irrelevant to Third World needs is a recurrent theme in the contemporary literature. Adamantia Pollis and Peter Schwab present an extreme version of this argument. They write that "it is evident that in most states in the world, human rights as defined by the West are rejected or, more accurately, are meaningless" (1980, p. 13) and refer to the Western concept as "inapplicable," "of limited validity" and "irrelevant" (1980, pp. 13, 8, 9). These are strong claims. I shall argue that for the most part they are not justified.

Admittedly, human rights are likely to appear to be foreign to the average person in most developing countries. People in these countries may even have the greatest difficulty comprehending what is meant by human rights. However, this is no more evidence that human rights are meaningless than similar difficulties in comprehension are evidence that dharma or tao are meaningless in Iowa or that anti-proton or neutrino telescope are meaningless most everywhere. Pollis and Schwab simply confuse meaning with understanding.

Inapplicable or irrelevant seem closer to what they have in mind. However, even these terms are ambiguous, having at least three important possible interpretations: that human rights objectively have no applicability; that their applicability is not recognized; or that the applicability of human rights is (or would be) rejected. Clearly the differences among these three senses are crucial, and all of them raise serious problems.

Determining the objective relevance of human rights would be a difficult matter. However, it is clear that a simple demonstration that most people in a country have been, and continue to be, unaware of the concept, or that they have adopted alternative mechanisms for realizing human dignity, will not establish that human rights are (objectively) irrelevant. A head count might be part of such a determination, although even that is not obvious. However, it certainly would not be definitive. A positive, substantive, probably even empirical argument would be necessary to establish objective inapplicability.

The two subjective senses of irrelevant raise problems of a different sort. For example, we are forced to ask what weight we ought to give to such subjective decisions and preferences. Also, we need to determine who is to speak for the society, and how, which is especially important given the basic political implications of such decisions.

In answering such questions, we find ourselves faced with at least partially competing intuitions. We must recognize the validity of claims of traditional values and institutions, as well as the rights of modern nations and states to choose their own destiny. At the same time, though, we feel a need to keep these choices constrained within acceptable bounds and reject an anything-goes attitude.

Certainly Louis XIV found the revolutionary rights of man to be inappropriate—and today's historians seem to be not altogether certain that the majority of his subjects, especially those outside of Paris, did not agree with him. More recently, "Emperor" Bokassa and Idi Amin have found human rights concerns to be irrelevant while Pol Pot and his successors alike have determined that human rights are inappropriate to Cambodia's needs and interests. Although there is widespread agreement that these men were and are wrong in their judgments, elucidating the bases for such a conclusion and then applying the resulting principles to less extreme cases raises serious difficulties.

We might begin by suggesting that extreme cases such as Amin or Bokassa can be criticized on the basis of the concept of human dignity alone. The practices of such regimes evidence not an alternative conception of human dignity but the denial of the very concept. For example, killing schoolchildren who protest school rules simply is incompatible with any and all plausible conceptions of human dignity. Although claims of human rights would substantially increase the force of our condemnations of these regimes, we can both forcefully and appropriately condemn such practices on the basis of the concept of human dignity alone.

Problems arise, though, when we are faced instead with competing conceptions of human dignity such as we have been considering here. In such more common cases Pollis and Schwab and many others advocate an attitude of extreme toleration for variations, coupled with an attempt to resolve differences at the international level through compromise or even a lowest-common-denominator solution (1980, pp. 1, 14-17).

However, lowest-common-denominator and compromise approaches seem to assume: (1) that the claim of human rights advocates and theorists that human rights are universal rights is false; and (2) that the human rights approach is not a better one and therefore does not deserve to be more widely or even universally applied. Neither of these assumptions seems obvious, or even correct.

If we are to try to assess whether human rights is a better way to approach human dignity and organize a society, we need to ask, "Better for what?" This is a question of means, not ends. Human rights are not ends in themselves; or rather they are not entirely ends in themselves. Among other things, as we have seen, they are means to realize human dignity. To the extent that they have instrumental value we can, in principle at least, assess their merits largely empirically. I would suggest that for most of the goals of the developing countries, *as defined by these countries themselves,* human rights are as effective or more effective than either traditional approaches or modern non-human rights strategies.

For example, if our concern is with the realization of human dignity, one could argue, along the lines suggested above, that the conditions created by modernization render the individual too vulnerable in the absence of human rights. If the concern is with development and social justice, a strong case might be made that the recognition and protection of human rights will increase participation and therefore popular support and productivity, open up lines of communication between people and government (thus providing greater efficiency and important checks against corruption and mismanagement), spur the provision of basic services through the recognition of economic and social rights, and provide to dispossessed groups regular and important channels for demanding redress. If one is concerned with stability, an argument might be advanced that a regime that violates or does not recognize basic human rights engenders destabilizing opposition, especially where the government is weak and does not have at its disposal substantial, effective modern mechanisms of political repression.

Certainly such suggestions are not even outlines of the arguments that would be necessary to establish such conclusions. However, I think they show that we cannot simply assume that other strategies are as good or as valid merely because they are widely advocated. Furthermore, they suggest most clearly the need to move beyond the level of demonstrating differences in values, which is the level of most current discussion, to assessing the relative merits of competing approaches which, as we have suggested, can be done largely empirically in many instances.

The case against the other assumption of those who would approach differences in ways to realize human dignity by compromise or seeking a lowest common denominator, namely the assumption that human rights are not in fact universal rights, would have to be largely normative. The issue involved here is whether there are human rights, since non-universal human rights simply would not be human rights as they have been conceived even in such documents as the Universal Declaration of Human Rights. The compromise approach thus involves abandoning human rights as we have understood them largely without even presenting arguments.

At the very least it must be noted in response that if we take seriously the idea of human rights, we must recognize them as both a historical product and of universal validity. As the rights of man, as human rights, they cannot be treated as merely a historical product without destroying the concept. In fact, the idea of human rights would even seem to demand of us a concern for their realization universally, even though we know that the concept was first formulated and institutionalized in a particular civilization at a particular time. Such a demand is a difficult one to be sure, but it is one that seems unavoidable if we are not to renounce human rights in the name of avoiding cultural neo-imperialism. And it is not much more difficult than taking seriously any major moral claim, which we know arises out of values that are genetically contingent but which by their very nature must be taken to apply universally or nearly universally.

However, even if, for the sake of argument, we grant the assumption that human rights are not universal, the most important result will be to increase the importance of the questions of relevance and instrumental value we have just discussed. Simply establishing that human rights are not universal would not show that an alternative or competing approach to human dignity is necessarily defensible, let alone preferable. Rather, we would be left with several competing approaches which, unless we accept the crudest sort of value-relativism (e.g., emotivism), not only can but must be evaluated comparatively.

The differences between Western and non-Western approaches to human dignity certainly are large. In fact, one of my major aims here has been to show that they are far greater than seems to be generally recognized in the contemporary literature. However, these differences do not, in themselves, entail the necessity of a laissez faire approach. Neither do they establish the substantive merits of any particular approach, let alone the inferiority of the Western human rights approach.

Conclusion

The belief that there are important practical consequences to the ways in which we think and talk about human rights and human dignity underlies the foregoing analysis, which has attempted to show that there are important differences in approach and that these differences can influence political practice in significant ways. If the alternative approaches to human dignity we have been discussing are accepted as legitimate conceptions of human rights, the practice of human rights is likely to suffer. For example, not only would it become easier for a repressive regime to cloak itself in the mantle of human rights while actually violating them, thereby turning "human rights" into an instrument of oppression rather than liberation, but in those countries with established human rights practices, the conceptual bases of the concept are likely to be eroded, thereby weakening the practice.

Of course, there is nothing inherent in the concept of human rights which assures that it won't, let alone shouldn't, change or evolve. Strong arguments can even be made that it would be desirable to reduce or minimize the place of human rights in political doctrine and practice, or even to replace human rights with entirely different organizing principles.

However, such arguments rarely are made today. Instead, human rights is used as roughly equivalent to "our approach to human dignity" and just about anything that is good or highly valued is transformed into a human right.

As a result, the distinctive and distinctly valuable aspects of a human rights approach are insidiously eroded. Human rights thus are attacked through their apparent advocacy in a covert linguistic operation which is not only particularly difficult to handle but which frustrates rather than encourages the discussion demanded by issues of such importance. Pressing the distinction between human rights and human dignity should not only clarify what is at stake but should improve the general level of discussion and perhaps even improve political practice. Admittedly, it is probably utopian to expect that any of this analysis will have a real effect in more than a handful of instances. Nevertheless, it seems mandatory to perpetuate the discussion if for no other reason than to preserve the human rights approach as a distinctive option; if we lose the concept, we stand in greater danger of losing the practice as well.

References

Alston, Philip. 1980. Peace as a human right. *Bulletin of Peace Proposals* 11:319-30.

Asante, S. K. B. 1969. Nation building and human rights in emergent Africa. *Cornell International Law Journal* 2:72-107.

Bay, Christian. 1980. Peace and critical knowledge as human rights. *Political Theory* 8:293-318.

Beitz, Charles R. 1979. Human rights and social justice. In Brown, P. G., and MacLean, D. (eds.), pp. 45-63.

Brown, Peter G. and MacLean, Douglas (eds.) 1979. *Human Rights and U.S. foreign policy*. Lexington, Mass.: Lexington Books.

Buultjens, Ralph. 1980. Human rights in Indian political culture. In Thompson, K. W. (ed.), pp. 109-22.

Chalidze, Valery. 1974. *To defend these rights: human rights and the Soviet Union*. New York: Random House.

Chkhidvadze, V. 1980. Constitution of true human rights and freedoms. *International Affairs* (Moscow) October 1980:13-20.

Donnelly, Jack. 1980. Natural law and rights in Aquinas' political thought. *Western Political Quarterly* 33:520-35.

______ (in press). How are rights and duties correlative? *Journal of Value Inquiry*.

Dworkin, Ronald. 1978. *Taking rights seriously*. Cambridge: Harvard University Press.

Egorov, A. G. 1979. Socialism and the individual—rights and freedoms. *Soviet Studies in Philosophy* 18:3-51.

Feinberg, Joel. 1980. The nature and value of rights. *Rights, justice and the bounds of liberty: essays in social philosophy*. Princeton: Princeton University Press.

Hakim, Khalifa Abdul. 1955. *Fundamental human rights*. Lahore: Institute of Islamic Culture.

Harkin, Tom. 1979. Human rights and foreign aid: forging an unbreakable link. In Brown, P. G. and D. MacLean (eds.), pp. 15-26.

Hart, H. L. A. 1955. Are there any natural rights? *The Philosophical Review* 65:175-91.

______ 1973. Bentham on legal rights. In A. W. B. Simpson (ed.). *Oxford essays in jurisprudence (second series)*. Oxford: The Clarendon Press.

Ishaque, Khalid M. 1974. Human rights in Islamic law. *Review of the International Commission of Jurists* 12:30-9.

Keenan, Edward L. 1980. Human rights in Soviet political culture. In Thompson, K. W. (ed.), pp. 69-80.

Khadduri, Majid. 1946. Human rights in Islam. *The Annals* 243:77-81.

Legesse, Asmarom. 1980. Human rights in African political culture. In Thompson, K. W. (ed.), pp. 123-38.

Leng, Shao-Chuan. 1980. Human rights in Chinese political culture. In Thompson, K. W. (ed.), pp. 81-108.

Lo, Chung-Shu. 1949. Human rights in the Chinese tradition. In *Human rights: comments and interpretations, a symposium edited by UNESCO*. London: Allan Wingate, pp. 186-90.

Manglapus, Raul. 1978. Human rights are not a western discovery. *Worldview* 4:4-6.

Mawdudi, Abul A'la. 1976. *Human rights in Islam*. Leicester: The Islamic Foundation.

Nadvi, Syed Muzaffar-ud-Din. 1966. *Human rights and obligations (in the light of the Qur'an and Hadith)*. Dacca: S. M. Zahirullah Nadvi.

Pagels, Elaine. 1979. The roots and origins of human rights. In Henkin, Alice H. (ed.), *Human dignity: the internationalization of human rights*. New York: Aspen Institute for Humanistic Studies, and Dobbs Ferry: Oceana Publications, Inc., pp. 1-8.

Piscatori, James P. 1980. Human rights in Islamic political culture. In Thompson, K. W. (ed.), pp. 139-68.

Pitkin, Hanna. 1972. *Wittgenstein and justice*. Berkeley and Los Angeles: University of California Press.

Pollis, Adamantia, and Schwab, Peter. 1980. Human rights: a western construct with limited applicability and Introduction. In Pollis, Adamantia, and Schwab, Peter (eds.), *Human rights: cultural and ideological perspectives*. New York: Praeger, pp. xiii-xvi, 1-18.

Said, Abdul Aziz. 1977. Pursuing human dignity. *Society* 15:34-8.

_____ 1979. Precept and practice of human rights in Islam. *Universal Human Rights* 1:63-80.

_____ 1980. Human rights in Islamic perspectives. In Pollis, A., and Schwab, P. (eds.), pp. 86-100.

Sawczuk, Konstantyn. 1979. Soviet juridical interpretation of international documents on human rights. *Survey* 24:86-91.

Tabandeh, Sultanhussein. 1970. *A Muslim commentary on the Universal Declaration of Human Rights*. London: F. T. Goulding and Company Limited.

Thompson, Kenneth W. (ed.) 1980. *The moral imperatives of human rights: a world survey*. Washington, D.C.: University Press of America for the Council on Religion and International Affairs.

Wai, Dunstan M. 1980. Human rights in sub-Saharan Africa. In Pollis, A., and Schwab, P. (eds.), pp. 115-45.

Yamani, Ahmad Zaki. 1968. *Islamic law and contemporary issues*. Jidda: The Saudi Publishing House.

[9]

R. Panikkar

IS THE NOTION OF HUMAN RIGHTS A WESTERN CONCEPT?[1]

We should approach this topic with great fear and respect. It is not a merely "academic" issue. Human rights are trampled upon in the East as in the West, in the North as in the South of our planet. Granting the part of human greed and sheer evil in this universal transgression, could it not also be that Human Rights are not observed because in their present form they do not represent a universal symbol powerful enough to elicit understanding and agreement?

No culture, tradition, ideology or religion can today speak for the whole of humankind, let alone solve its problems. Dialogue and intercourse leading to a mutual fecundation are necessary. But sometimes the very conditions for dialogue are not given, because there are unspoken conditions which most partners cannot meet. It is a fact that the present-day formulation of Human Rights is the fruit of a very partial dialogue among

[1] This paper is an expanded and revised version of the presentation at the "Entretiens de Dakar," Senegal, to the annual session of the Institut International de Philosophie on *Philosophical Foundations of Human Rights*, a summary of which will appear in the Proceedings.

the cultures of the world. It is only recently that this question has been acutely felt.[2]

I shall not enter into the details of the history of Human Rights, nor into an analysis of their nature. I shall confine myself to the interrogation implied in the title: are Human Rights a universal invariant?

I. The Method of Inquiry

1. *Diatopical Hermeneutics*

It is claimed that Human Rights are universal. This alone entails a major philosophical query. Does it make sense to ask about conditions of universality when the very question about conditions of universality is far from universal? Philosophy can no longer ignore this inter-cultural problematic. Can we extrapolate the concept of Human Rights, from the context of the culture and history in which it was conceived, into a globally valid notion? Could it at least *become* a universal symbol? Or is it only one particular way of expressing—and saving—the *humanum?*

Although the question posed in the title is a legitimate one, there is something disturbing in this formulation as it was given to me. At least at first glance, it would seem to offer only one alternative: either the notion of Universal Human Rights is a Western notion, or it is not. If it is, besides being a tacit indictment against those who do not possess such a valuable concept, its introduction into other cultures, even if necessary, would appear as a plain imposition from outside. It would appear, once again, as a continuation of the colonial syndrome, namely the belief that the constructs of one particular culture (God,

[2] Cf. probably the first Symposium of its kind convened by UNESCO at Bangkok in December 1979, *Meeting of Experts on the Place of Human Rights in Cultural and Religious Traditions*, where nine major schools of religious thought discussed the issue and recognized "that many of them have not paid sufficient attention to human rights... (And that) it is a task of the different religions of the world to deepen and eventually to enlarge and/or reformulate the urgent and important issue of human rights." § 116 g of the Final Report SS-79/CONF. 607/10 of 6 February, 1980. The entire report is worth reading.

Church, Empire, Western civilization, science, modern technology, etc.) have, if not the monopoly, at least the privilege of possessing a universal value which entitles them to be spread over all the Earth. If not, that is, if the concept of Universal Human Rights is not exclusively a Western concept, it would be difficult to deny that many a culture has let it slumber, thus again giving rise to an impression of the indisputable superiority of Western culture. There is nothing wrong in admitting a hierarchy of cultures, but this hierarchical order cannot be assumed as the starting point, nor can one side alone lay down the criteria necessary for establishing such a hierarchy. There is then a prior question implied by asking whether the notion of Human Rights is a Western concept. It is the question regarding the very nature of Human Rights, and it directly submits this notion to cross-cultural scrutiny.

Our question is a case in point of *diatopical hermeneutics*: the problem is how, from the *topos* of one culture, to understand the constructs of another.[3] It is wrong-headed methodology to begin by asking: Does another culture also have the notion of Human Rights?—assuming that such a notion is absolutely indispensable to guarantee human dignity. No question is neutral, for every question conditions its possible answers.

2. *The homeomorphic equivalent*

I was once asked to give the Sanskrit equivalents of the twenty-five key Latin words supposed to be emblematic of Western culture. I declined, on the grounds that that which is the foundation of one culture need not be the foundation for another. Meanings are not transferable here. Translations are more delicate than heart transplants. So what must we do? We must dig down to where a homogeneous soil or a similar problematic appears: we must search out the *homeomorphic equivalent*—to

[3] By diatopical hermeneutics I understand a thematic reflection on the fact that the loci (*topoi*) of historically unrelated cultures make it problematic to understand one tradition with the tools of another, and the hermeneutical attempt to bridge such gulfs. Cf. R. Panikkar, *Myth, Faith and Hermeneutics*, New York, Paulist Press, 1979, pp. 8 sq.

the concept of Human Rights in this case. "Homeomorphism is not the same as analogy; it represents a peculiar functional equivalence discovered through a topological transformation." It is "a kind of existential functional analogy."[4]

Thus we are not seeking merely to transliterate Human Rights into other cultural languages, nor should we be looking for mere analogies; we try instead to find the homeomorphic equivalent. If, for instance, Human Rights are considered to be the basis for the exercise of and respect for human dignity, we should investigate how another culture satisfies the equivalent need—and this can be done only once a common ground (a mutually understandable language) has been worked out between the two cultures. Or perhaps we should ask how the idea of a just social and political order could be formulated within a certain culture, and investigate whether the concept of Human Rights is a particularly appropriate way of expressing this order. A traditional Confucian might see this problem of order and rights as a question of "good manners" or in terms of his profoundly ceremonial or ritual conception of human intercourse, in terms of *li*. A Hindu might see it another way, and so on.

* * *

In order to clarify the question of our title, I shall indicate some of the assumptions on which the notion of Human Rights is based and immediately insert some cross-cultural reflections which will lead us to the *locus*—the context—of the question and the justification for my answer, which I would like to anticipate by means of a simile: Human Rights are one window through which one particular culture envisages a just human order for its individuals. But those who live in that culture do not see the window. For this they need the help of another culture which sees through another window. Now I assume

[4] Cf. R. Panikkar, *The Intrareligious Dialogue*, New York, Paulist Press, 1978, p. xxii. The two words Brahman and God, for instance, are neither analogous nor merely equivocal (nor univocal, of course). They are not exactly equivalent either. They are homeomorphic. They perform a certain type of respectively corresponding function in the two different traditions where these words are alive.

that the human landscape as seen through the one window is both similar to and different from the vision of the other. If this is the case, should we smash the windows and make of the many portals a single gaping aperture—with the consequent danger of structural collapse—or should we enlarge the viewpoints as much as possible and, most of all, make people aware that there are—and have to be—a plurality of windows? This latter option would be the one in favor of a healthy pluralism. This is much more than a merely academic question. There can be no serious talk about cultural pluralism without a genuine socio-economic-political pluralism. This is, for example, what has led intellectual groups in India to ask whether "civil rights" are not incompatible with "economic rights." At any rate, to speak of cultural pluralism within what could be called a paneconomic ideology makes little sense and amounts to treating the other cultures of the world as mere folklore. The example of the notion of dharma from the Indian tradition will offer us a point of reference from which to formulate our conclusion.

II. Assumptions and Implications of the Western Concept

I take the expression "Human Rights" in the sense of the Universal Declaration of Human Rights adopted by the General Assembly of the United Nations in 1948.[5] The Western, mainly liberal protestant roots of the Human Rights Declaration are well known.[6] The Western world has known of the struggle for

[5] I shall capitalize Human Rights when these words have the particular meaning derived from this "Universal Declaration."

[6] The dates to recall are:

10 December 1948	— Proclamation in Paris of the Universal Declaration;
4 November 1950	— Adoption in Rome of the Convention safeguarding Human Rights and fundamental freedom, known as "The European Convention on Human Rights";
20 March 1952	— Adoption in Paris of the first additional Protocol to this Convention;
16 December 1966	— International Covenant on Economic, Social and Cultural Rights; International Covenant on Civil and Political Rights; Optional Protocol (to the latter—not passed unanimously).

Is the Notion of Human Rights a Western Concept?

citizens' rights since the Middle Ages.[7] This struggle for concrete rights, rooted in the practices and value system of a particular nation or country, is felt with greater urgency after the French Revolution.[8] Western Man passes from a corporate belonging in a community of blood, work and historical destiny, based on practically accepted custom and theoretically acknowledged authority, to a society based on impersonal law and ideally free contract, to the modern State, for which explicitly rational norms and duties are required. The problem becomes increasingly acute with the growth of individualism.

This paper assumes knowledge of the history of Human Rights, as well as of the fact that this transition from one form of collective life to another more modern form is said today to have acquired a worldwide character. We would like to concentrate on the more strictly philosophical *assumptions* which seem to be at the basis of the Declaration.

1. At the basis of the discourse on Human Rights there is the assumption of a *universal human nature* common to all peoples. Otherwise, a Universal Declaration could not logically have been

[7] For the astounding documents of the first nine Christian centuries, cf. the collection and translation with insightful introduction by H. Rahner, *Kirche und Staat*, Munich, Kösel, 1961. The first edition, published in 1943 during the Second World War with the title *Abendländische Kirchenfreiheit*, is in itself a document for Human Rights.

Because it is less known than the *Magna Carta* of King John of England in 1215, let us mention King Alfonso IX of León in 1188 with his rights to life, honor, home and property.

Interesting also is the statement and justification of Francisco de Vitoria in 1538: "Cuando los súbditos tengan conciencia de la injusticia de la guerra, no les es lícito ir a ella, *sea que se equivoquen o no*" (emphasis mine). *De los indios o del derecho de la guerra*, II, 23 (Ed. BAC, Madrid 1960, p. 831). ("When its subjects are aware of the injustice of a war, it is not lawful for them to go to it, *whether they are in error or not.*") And the reason he gives is to quote Rom. XIV, 23: "omne quod non est ex fide peccatum est," which he translates "todo lo que no es según *conciencia* es pecado" (*ibid*, emphasis added) The Pauline passage is usually rendered: "Whatever does not come from faith is sin." Vitoria's variation reads: "Whatever is not in accordance with one's *conscience* is a sin." Cf the Thomistic principle that the rational being that is Man has to follow his or her personal conscience in order to act morally.

[8] Just as a memorandum, we may recall:
1689 — Bill of Rights (England)
1776 — Virginia Bill of Rights
1789 (26 August) — Déclaration des droits de l'homme et du citoyen
1798 — American Bill of Rights

proclaimed. This idea in its turn is connected with the old notion of a Natural Law.

But the contemporary Declaration of Human Rights further *implies*:

a) that this human nature must be *knowable*. For it is one thing to accept human nature uncritically or mythically, and another to know it. Otherwise, the Declaration could not speak and legislate about Rights that are universal;

b) that this human nature is known by means of an equally universal organ of knowledge, generally called *reason*. Otherwise, if its knowledge should depend on a special intuition, revelation, faith, decree of a prophet or the like, Human Rights could not be taken as *natural* rights—inherent in Man. This must be a commonly-held knowledge. Otherwise, Human Rights could not be declared universal by an Assembly which does not claim to have a privileged epistemological status. This is made plain by the use of the word "Declaration," which stresses the fact that it is not an imposition from above but a public explication, a making clear of what is inherent in the very nature of Man;[9]

c) that this human nature is essentially *different* from the rest of reality. Other living beings inferior to Man obviously have no Human Rights, and creatures superior to Man are likely not to exist. Man is the master of himself and the universe. He is the supreme legislator on Earth—the question of whether a Supreme Being exists or not remains open, but ineffective.[10]

2. The second assumption is that of the *dignity of the individual*. Each individual is, in a certain sense, absolute, irreducible to another. This is probably the major thrust of the Modern question of Human Rights. Human Rights defend the dignity

[9] The Paris document is a *declaration*, a manifest statement making clear what is already there, an explication (*dēclārāre*, to make clear—from *de-clārāre*. Cf. *clārus*, clear, but also loud (*clamor*)). It is not a law, a superimposition, a human creation, but the recognition or discovery of something intrinsic to the nature of the thing; in this case "the inherent dignity and equal and inalienable rights of all the members of the human family," as the Preamble to the 1948 Declaration says.

[10] This practical a-theism and even practical ignorance of any ulterior philosophical issue or religious factor became patent in the presentation and discussion of the Bangkok Conference mentioned above, let alone in the more official meetings where Philosophy and Religion have hardly a voice.

of the individual *vis-à-vis* Society at large, and the State in particular.

But this in turn implies:

a) not only the distinction but also the *separation* between individual and society. In this view the human being is fundamentally the individual. Society is a kind of superstructure, which can easily become a menace and also an alienating factor for the individual. Human Rights are there primarily to protect the individual;

b) the *autonomy* of humankind *vis-à-vis* and often versus the Cosmos. This is clearly shown in the ironic ambivalence of the English expression, which means at the same time "*Menschenrechte*," "*droits de l'Homme*," and also "*menschliche Rechte*," "*droits humains*" (humane rights). The Cosmos is a kind of understructure. The individual stands in between Society and World. Human Rights defend the autonomy of the human individual;

c) resonances of the idea of Man as *microcosmos* and reverberations of the conviction that Man is *imago dei*, and at the same time the relative independence of this conviction from ontological and theological formulations. The individual has an inalienable dignity because he is an end in himself and a kind of absolute. You can cut off a finger for the sake of the entire body, but can you kill one person to save another?[11]

3. The third assumption is that of a *democratic social order*. Society is assumed to be not a hierarchical order founded on a divine will or law or mythical origin, but a sum of "free" individuals organized to achieve otherwise unreachable goals. Human Rights, once again, serve mainly to protect the individual. Society here is not seen as a family or a protection, but as something unavoidable which can easily abuse the power conferred on it (precisely by the assent of the sum of its individuals). This Society crystallizes in the State, which theoretically expresses the will of the people, or at least of the majority. The idea

[11] Cf. R. Panikkar, "Singularity and Individuality: The Double Principle of Individuation," *Revue internationale de philosophie* XIX, 1-2, No, 111-112 (1975) p. 141-166, where it is argued that the ontic status of human individuals is basically different from that of all other individual entities; in short, that we cannot treat human individuals as we could peanuts or cattle, by a merely numerical individuality.

of an Empire, or a People or a Nation with a transcendent destiny—whose duty it is to carry through the entrusted mission independent of the will of the members of that society—still exists today in some theocratic states, but even most of these try to palliate their messianic vocation by democratic endorsements.

This implies:

a) that each individual is seen as equally important and thus equally responsible for the welfare of society. Hence the individual has the right to stand by his or her convictions and propagate them or to resist impositions against his or her inherent freedom;

b) that Society is nothing but the sum total of the individuals whose wills are sovereign and ultimately decisive.[12] There is no instance superior to Society. Even if there were to exist a God or a superhuman Reality, this too would be filtered through human consciousness and human institutions;

c) that the rights and freedoms of the individual can be limited only when they impinge upon the rights and freedoms of other individuals, and in this way majority rule is rationally justified.[13] And when the rights of an individual are curtailed by "reasons of State," this is allegedly justified by the fact that the State is supposed to embody the will and the interests of the majority. It is interesting to note that the "Universal Declaration" speaks of "freedoms" in the plural and, even more intriguing, of "fundamental freedoms." The individualization does not stop at the individual, but divides this segregated entity even further into separated freedoms.

In enumerating these Assumptions and Implications I do not mean to say that they were actually in the minds of the framers of the Declaration. In fact, there is evidence to suggest that no unanimity could be found regarding the basis of the rights that were being declared. But the Declaration clearly was articulated

[12] "The will of the people shall be the basis of the authority of government;" —Art. 21,3 of the Declaration.

[13] "In the exercise of his rights and freedoms, everyone shall be subject only to such limitations as are determined by law *solely* for the purpose of securing due recognition and respect for the rights and freedoms of others and of meeting the *just* requirements of *morality, public order* and the general *welfare* in a *democratic* society." Art 29,2 (Emphasis of the problematic words added.)

along the lines of the historical trends of the Western world during the last three centuries, and in tune with a certain philosophical anthropology or individualistic humanism which helped justify them.

III. Cross-Cultural Reflections

1. *Is the Concept of Human Rights a Universal Concept?*

The answer is a plain *no.* Three reasons vouch for it.

a) No concept as such is universal. Each concept is valid primarily where it was conceived. If we want to extend its validity beyond its own context we shall have to justify the extrapolation. Even mathematical concepts imply the previous acknowledgment of a limited field defined by the axioms we postulate. Furthermore, every concept tends to be univocal. To accept the possibility of universal concepts would imply a strictly rationalistic conception of reality. But even if this were the theoretical truth it would not be the actual case, because *de facto* humankind presents a plurality of universes of discourse. To accept the fact that the concept of Human Rights *is* not universal does not yet mean that it *should* not *become* so. Now in order for a concept to become universally valid it should fulfill at least two conditions. It should, on the one hand, eliminate all the other contradictory concepts. This may seem improbable, but there is a logical necessity here and, theoretically, it would all be for the best. On the other hand, it should be the universal point of reference for any problematic regarding human dignity. In other words, it should displace all other homeomorphic equivalents and be the pivotal center of a just social order. To put it another way, the culture which has given birth to the concept of Human Rights should also be called upon to become a universal culture. This may well be one of the causes of a certain uneasiness one senses in non-Western thinkers who study the question of Human Rights. They fear for the identity of their own cultures.

b) Within the vast field of Western culture itself, the very assumptions which serve to situate our problematic are not universally recognized. The particular origin of the formulation of Human Rights is sufficiently well known. Probably the most important sources of dissent are three.[14]

i) *Theology*:

Human Rights need to be grounded, says the theological view, in a superior, transcendent and therefore unmanipulable value, whose traditional symbol is God as origin and guarantor of both human rights and duties. Otherwise, they are only a political device in the hands of the powerful. According to this view, the Declaration suffers from a naive optimism regarding the goodness and autonomy of human nature. Moreover, it implies a deficient anthropology, inasmuch as it seems to view the human person as merely a bundle of needs, material and psychological, of which it then proceeds to make an inventory.[15] And finally, in case of doubt or conflict, who is going to decide? Majority rule is only a euphemism for the law of the jungle: the power of the strongest.

ii) *Marxism*:

For the Marxist, so-called Human Rights are merely "*Klassenrechte*," class rights.[16] "There are no rights without duties and no duties without rights." They reflect the interests of a certain class and in many cases only its aspirations. There is no mention of the economic conditions for the effective realization of what are said to be universal human claims. Furthermore, there is something abstract and too general about most of these

[14] We do not include here a fourth source of dissent, namely the *political*, because the argument in such cases bears mainly on different interpretations of facts, emphases and factors other than those related to the nature of Human Rights. Cf. as a single example: *Colloques de Riyad, de Paris, du Vatican, de Genève et de Strasbourg sur le dogme musulman et les droits de l'homme en Islam*, Riyad, Ministère de la Justice; Beirut, Dar Al Kitab Allubhani, 1974; and D. Sidorsky (ed.) *Essays on Human Rights. Contemporary Issues and Jewish Perspectives*, Philadelphia, The Jewish Publication Society of America, 1979.

[15] "Human rights, in short, are statements of basic needs and interests." S.I. Benn, *The Encyclopaedia of Philosophy*, New York, Macmillan, 1967, *sub voce Rights*, speaking about the U.N. Declaration.

[16] Cf. K. Marx, *Zur Judenfrage* I, p. 352.

rights; they are not sufficiently grounded in the material and cultural reality of particular groups. Finally, their individualism is evident. The individual is conceived as being in confrontation with (rather than included in) society, although the latter is said to be the result of freely contracting individuals. Society is not merely the sum total of individuals and it has rights which the individual may not violate. History has transcendent power.

iii) *History*:

"Human Rights" appear to some students of recent history as another example of the more or less conscious domination exerted by the powerful nations to maintain their privileges and defend the *status quo*. Human rights continue to be a political weapon. Human rights were known long ago but only for the nobleman, or the free citizen, or for whites or christians or males, etc., and when they were hastily applied to "human beings" it was often defined just which groups belonging to the race could properly be styled "human." If not all humans had human rights, the claim of human rights on behalf of animals, plants and things would seem and still does seem bizarre, not to say ridiculous, in spite of occasional remonstrances delivered by Societies for the Protection of Animals. Animals and such may very well have rights, but not human ones. And, as we have seen, this particular notion of the "human" has not always been very humane. And who is to speak for the whole? History discloses that only the victors declare and promulgate "rights," which are simply what the powerful consider right at any given time.

c) From a cross-cultural stance the problem appears exclusively Western, i.e. the question itself is at stake. Most of the assumptions and implications enumerated earlier are simply not given in other cultures. Furthermore, from a non-Western point of view the problem itself is not seen as such, so that it is not merely a question of agreeing or disagreeing with the answer. If anything, the problem is that the issue is experienced in a radically different way. A *diatopical* hermeneutic does not deal

[17] "Keine Rechte ohne Pflichten, keine Pflichten ohne Rechte," Marx-Engels, *Werke* XVI, 521 *apud* G. Klaus, M. Buhr, *Philosophisches Wörterbuch*, Leipzig. VEB, 1976, *sub voce Menschenrechte*.

with just another point of view on the *same* problem. At issue here is not simply the answer, but the problem itself.

Now is it possible to have access to other *topoi* so that we may be able to understand other cultures from within, i.e. as they understand themselves? We may not be able to jump over our own categories of understanding, but it may not be impossible to have one foot in one culture and another in a second. Generally, we have only one culture as we have only one mother-tongue—but we may also have a father-tongue. We cannot *a priori* deny this possibility. I recall that, in certain parts of the East, to be illiterate means to know only a single language. It is in dialogue with others that we can encompass our common ground. We may not integrate more than one culture in ourselves but we may open the possibility of a wider and deeper integration by opening ourselves, in dialogue, to others.

The following parallelism may be instructive. To assume that without the explicit recognition of Human Rights life would be chaotic and have no meaning belongs to the same order of ideas as to think that without the belief in one God as understood in the Abrahamic tradition human life would dissolve itself in total anarchy. This line of thinking leads to the belief that Atheists, Buddhists and Animists, for instance, should be considered as human aberrations. In the same vein: either Human Rights, or chaos. This attitude does not belong exclusively to Western culture. To call the stranger a barbarian is all too common an attitude among the peoples of the world. And, as we shall mention later, there is a legitimate and inbuilt claim to universality in any affirmation of truth. The problem is that we tend to identify the limits of our own vision with the human horizon.

2. *Cross-Cultural Critique*

There are no trans-cultural values, for the simple reason that a value exists as such only in a given cultural context.[18] But there may be cross-cultural values, and a cross-cultural critique is

[18] Cf. R. Panikkar, "Aporias in the Comparative Philosophy of Religion," *Man in World*, XIII, 3-4 (1980), p. 357-383.

Is the Notion of Human Rights a Western Concept?

indeed possible. The latter does not consist in evaluating one cultural construct with the categories of another, but in trying to understand and criticize one particular human problem with the tools of understanding of the different cultures concerned, at the same time taking thematically into consideration that the very awareness and, much more, the formulation of the problem is already culturally bound. Our question is then to examine the possible cross-cultural value of the issue of Human Rights, an effort which begins by delimiting the cultural boundaries of the concept. The dangers of cultural westocentrism are only too patent today.

a) We have already mentioned the particular historical origins of the Declaration of Human Rights. To claim universal validity for Human Rights in the formulated sense implies the belief that most of the peoples of the world today are engaged in much the same way as the Western nations in a process of transition from more or less mythical *Gemeinschaften* (feudal principalities, self-governing cities, guilds, local communities, tribal institutions...) to a "rationally" and "contractually" organized "modernity" as known to the Western industrialized world. This is a questionable assumption. No one can predict the evolution (or eventual disintegration) of those traditional societies which have started from different material and cultural bases and whose reaction to modern Western civilization may therefore follow hitherto unknown lines.

Further, the very powerful Declaration of Human Rights also shows its weakness from another point of view. Something has been lost when it has to be explicitly declared. As the Chinese say: It is when *yi* (justice) declines that *li* (ritual) arises.[19] Or as the British and Spaniards repeat: There are things which you take for granted and about which you do not speak. And in some traditional societies, you cannot boast of being noble or a friend of the royal family because the very moment you do so, you lose your nobility and your friendship with the reigning house.[20] When Human Rights are declared, this is a sign that the

[19] *Tao Te Ching*, p. 18.

[20] The *Manavadharmaśastra* (2-4) puts the same idea in a more sophisticated way: To act from a desire for reward is reprehensible. Yet without that desire, no action is possible. Laws are needed to put order into those human actions.

very foundation on which they rest has already been weakened. The Declaration only postpones the collapse. In traditional words, when the tabu of the sacred disappears sacredness fades away. If you have to teach a mother to love her child, something is amiss with motherhood. Or, as some theoreticians of Human Rights have also recognized, the legislation on Human Rights is introduced in order to find a justification for contravening somebody else's freedom. Putting it positively, you need some justification to encroach on somebody's field of activity.

I am not saying this in order to revert to Utopian dreams of an earthly paradise, but just to sound another voice. You may promulgate laws, but you do not declare what is the case—unless it has ceased to be evident; you do not proclaim an "ought" if there are no transgressions at all.

b) We may now briefly reconsider the three assumptions mentioned above. They may pass muster, insofar as they express an authentically valid human issue from one particular context. But the very context may be susceptible to a legitimate critique from the perspective of other cultures. To do this systematically would require that we choose one culture after another and examine the assumptions of the Declaration in the light of each culture chosen. We shall limit ourselves here to token reflections under the very broad umbrella of a pre-Modern, non-Western state of mind.

i) There is certainly a *universal human nature* but, first of all, this nature does not need to be segregated and fundamentally distinct from the nature of all living beings and/or the entire reality. Thus exclusively *Human* Rights would be seen as a violation of "Cosmic Rights" and an example of selfdefeating anthropocentrism, a novel kind of apartheid. To retort that "Cosmic Rights" is a meaningless expression would only betray the underlying cosmology of the objection, for which the phrase makes no sense. But the existence of a different cosmology is precisely what is at stake here. We speak of the laws of nature; why not also of her rights?

Secondly, the interpretation of this "universal human nature," i.e. Man's self-understanding, belongs equally to this human nature. Thus to single out one particular interpretation of it may be valid, but it is not universal and may not apply to the entirety of human nature.

Thirdly, to proclaim the undoubtedly positive concept of Human Rights may turn out to be a Trojan horse, surreptitiously introduced into other civilizations which will then all but be obliged to accept those ways of living, thinking and feeling for which Human Rights is the proper solution in cases of conflict. It is a little like the way technology is often introduced in many parts of the world: it is imported to solve the problems that it has itself created. We have already made reference to this when criticizing the universalization of the concept of Human Rights.

ii) Nothing could be more important than to underscore and defend the *dignity of the human person.* But the person should be distinguished from the individual. The individual is just an abstraction, i.e. a selection of a few aspects of the person for practical purposes. My *person*, on the other hand, is also in "my" parents, children, friends, foes, ancestors and successors. "My" person is also in "my" ideas and feelings and in "my" belongings. If you hurt "me," you are equally damaging my whole clan, and possibly yourself as well. Rights cannot be individualized in this way. Is it the right of the mother, or of the child?—in the case of abortion. Or perhaps of the father and relatives as well? Rights cannot be abstracted from duties; the two are correlated. The dignity of the human person may equally be violated by your language, or by your desecrating a place I consider holy, even though it does not "belong" to me in the sense of individualized private property. You may have "bought" it for a sum of money, while it belongs to me by virtue of another order altogether. An individual is an isolated knot; a person is the entire fabric around that knot, woven from the total fabric of the real. The limits to a person are not fixed, they depend utterly on his or her personality. Certainly without the knots the net would collapse; but without the net, the knots would not even exist.

To aggressively defend my individual rights, for instance, may have negative, i.e. unjust, repercussions on others and perhaps even on myself. The need for consensus in many traditions—instead of majority opinion—is based precisely on the corporate nature of human rights.

A paragraph on language is required here. Each language has its own genius and its own particular way to see the world and even to be it and be in it. But from a cross-cultural perspective, each language has to show the flexibility necessary to incorporate other human experiences. I know that in current English "individual" is synonymous with "person," but this should not prevent me from using these two words in the sense I have suggested, and from recognizing a particular human trend which tends to identify the human being with the most salient features of a gross "individualized" body or at least to inscribe it within that framework. In drawing the distinction between individual and person I would put much more content in it than a French moral philosophy would do nowadays, for instance. I would like to adduce this case as a particular instance of two radically different anthropologies.

iii) *Democracy* is also a great value and infinitely better than any dictatorship. But it amounts to tyranny to put the peoples of the world under the alternative of choosing either democracy or dictatorship. Human Rights are tied to democracy. Individuals need to be protected when the structure which is above them (Society, the State or the Dictator—by whatever name) is not qualitatively superior to them, i.e. when it does not belong to a higher order. Human rights is a legal device for the protection of smaller numbers of people (the minority or the individual) faced with the power of greater numbers. This implies a quantitative reductionism; the person is reduced to the individual and the individual to the basis of society. I may put it more positively by saying that it is the way by which the individual as cornerstone of society is protected, and his or her dignity recognized. In a hierarchical conception of reality, the particular human being cannot defend his or her rights by demanding or exacting them independently of the whole. The wounded order has to be set straight again, or it has to change altogether. Other traditional societies have different means to more or less successfully restore the order. The rāja may fail in his duty to protect the people, but will a Declaration of Human Rights be a corrective unless it also has the power to constrain the rāja? Can a democracy be

Is the Notion of Human Rights a Western Concept?

imposed and remain democratic?[21]

The policy of non-alignment subscribed to by many countries of Africa and Asia here strikes a much deeper chord than possible political opportunism, or just another way of being relevant in the contemporary political scene. It represents precisely this refusal to admit the vision of the world as a function of the just mentioned set of dilemmas represented by the so-called superpowers.

In short, the cross-cultural critique does not invalidate the Declaration of Human Rights, but offers new perspectives for an internal criticism and sets the limits of validity of Human Rights, offering at the same time both possibilities for enlarging its realm, if the context changes, and of a mutual fecundation with other conceptions of Man and Reality.

3. *Should the symbol of Human Rights be a universal symbol?*

It should be noted that I speak here of Human Rights as a symbol which, unlike a concept, is by its nature polyvalent and polysemic.

The answer is yes, and no.

a) *Yes.* When a culture as a whole discovers certain values as ultimate, these values must have a certain universal meaning. Only collective and culturally expressed universal values may be said to be human values. A mere private value cannot be called a *human* value. It is a humane value, but not necessarily a value for every human—as *Human* Rights claim to be. As a matter of fact, Human Rights come as a corrective to the former exclusive rights of the Whites, the Believers, the Rich, the Brahmans and others—without meaning to touch legitimate privileges in the traditional sense of the word. The Declaration of Human Rights must needs be considered, at least in its intention,

[21] A recent example: A Catholic missionary, after over a year of really living together with an Asian tribe and sharing with the people their respective beliefs, thinks that the moment has come for some formal conversions, since they are already practically Christians. He talks matters over with the enthusiasts about Christianity: "Would you like to become officially and publicly Christians? You are already convinced..." *etcetera.* Answer: "No, because some other people in the tribe are not ready." "But it is your *right!*," says the missionary, "you have the *right* to decide by yourselves—all the more since you neither harm nor despise the others." The answer is cutting: "We only have the right to take this step if the whole tribe does it."

as a declaration with universal validity. To say that Human Rights are not universal would amount to saying that they are not human; they would cease to be *Human* Rights. The whole novelty of the Declaration lies precisely here, in the assertion that every human being, by the mere fact of being human, is endowed with inalienable rights that everybody should respect.

In that sense we may have here something rather unique and revolutionary in the Declaration of Human Rights. Here indeed we have the positive side of the individual *vis-à-vis* the person. Every single human being in its individuality, by the very fact of being born, has a dignity and rights equal to any other. It is not one's place in society, or degree of civilization, or intellectual, moral or religious endowments that counts. Certainly, limits will immediately appear: you may be subnormal or abnormal, and not only physically, but also morally—or, others would also add, intellectually or religiously. But the naked fact of being born is the universal symbol on which Human Rights is based. From this point of view, the claim to universality of Human Rights has found a solid basis.

Paradoxically enough, the Christian origin of this belief has been the cause of some of its degradation, i.e. when it became an ideology, a doctrine to serve the interests of one particular group. Everybody is born free and equal; all human beings are equal in the sight of God; every human person has the same rights as any other. Nonetheless, in order to justify the fact that the unbaptized, or the negro or slave or female or whoever, did not have the same rights, one was compelled to claim that they were not fully human beings, as history cruelly witnesses.

b) *No.* Because each culture expresses its experience of reality and of the *humanum* in concepts and symbols which are proper to that tradition and are as such not universal, and most likely not universalizable. This relationship between truth and the expression of truth in concepts and symbols is one of the most central philosophical problems. Truth has the inbuilt claim to be universally valid, here and there, yesterday and tomorrow, for you and for me. Yet my grasping and formulating it cannot sustain the same claim without charging all the others who do not agree with me with stupidity or wickedness. Hence the necessary *via media* between agnostic relativism and dogmatic absolutism. This is what can be called *relativity*.

Our particular case is a typical example of the *pars pro toto*: from the optic of the inside it looks like the whole; from the outside it looks like a part, a fragment. Similarly, Human Rights are universal from the vantage point of modern Western culture, and not universal from the outside looking in. Now, if we take from the inside the *pars pro toto*, are we able to take from the outside the *totum in parte*? Can another culture see in the Human Rights issue a universal language? Or should we say that it is only one way of looking at things, one way of speaking?

The answer which claims to discover the *totum in parte* is appealing, but not convincing. This is the temptation of the intellectual, who senses that any affirmation has the inbuilt tendency to be universally valid—or of the politician who, having neither the time nor the inclination to engage in such reflections, would like to see the *totum* in the *parte* of his party. But then we tend to become the self-appointed judges of all humankind. Now philosophy, being a situated reflection, makes us aware that nobody has direct access to the universal range of human experience. We can only indirectly and through a limited perspective come to know the totality. Even were we to know all the existing human opinions, ours would amount to just another opinion. One cannot view the *totum* except in and through one's own window. This is the case not only because the whole is more than the sum of its parts, but also because that *totum* does not exist independently from the *parte* through which it is seen. It is only seen in and through the respective *parte* and there is no stance from which one could proceed to the integration of all the parts. Co-existence is only possible on a common ground, a *co-esse* recognized by the different parties.

Here lies the crux. We cannot but aim at the *totum*, and yet we often forget that all we see is the *pars* which we then take *pro toto*. If a Christian, to put another example, were to say that Christ is not the universal savior, according to accepted custom he or she would cease to be a Christian. But a non-Christian cannot, and should not, agree with this. It is only in mutual dialogue that their respective views will change or evolve. Christ will be for the Christian the symbol of the totality; for the non-Christian, only the symbol of the Christians.

Myriad examples from the past, especially regarding the West, are all too striking for one not to be wary of the danger of repeating what was done in the name of the one God, the one Empire, the one Religion, and what is nowadays being done under the aegis of the one Science and the one Technology.

In brief, we need a new hermeneutic: the diatopical hermeneutic that can only be developed in a *dialogical* dialogue. This would show us that we must take neither the *pars pro toto*, nor believe that we see the *totum in parte*. We must accept what our partner tells us: simply that we take the *totum pro parte,* when we are aware of the *pars pro toto*; which is obviously what we will retort right back to him. This is the human condition and I would not consider it to be an imperfection. This, again, is the topic of pluralism.

Let us consider now an example of a different perspective without attempting to present any homeomorphic equivalent.

IV. An Indian Reflection

The word "Indian" here has no political connotations. It does not refer to the "nation" with the third largest Islamic population in the world, but to the traditional Hindu, Jain and Buddhist conceptions of reality.

Dharma (*dhamma*) is perhaps the most fundamental word in the Indian tradition which could lead us to the discovery of a possible homeomorphic symbol corresponding to the Western notion of "Human Rights." I am not advancing the idea that dharma is the homeomorphic equivalent of Human Rights. I am only indicating that a reflection at the level of dharma may help us find our footing on a common ground, so that we may know what we are looking for when we set out on our search for "Human Rights" in the classical Indian context.

As is well known, the meaning of the word dharma is multivocal: besides element, data, quality and origination, it means law, norm of conduct, character of things, right, truth, ritual, morality, justice, righteousness, religion, destiny, and many other things. It would not lead us anywhere to try to find an English common denominator for all these names, but perhaps etymology

Is the Notion of Human Rights a Western Concept?

can show us the root metaphor underlying the many meanings of the word.[22] Dharma is that which maintains, gives cohesion and thus strength to any given thing, to reality, and ultimately to the three worlds (*triloka*). Justice keeps human relations together; morality keeps oneself in harmony; law is the binding principle for human relations; religion is what maintains the universe in existence; destiny is that which links us with our future; truth is the internal cohesion of a thing; a quality is what pervades a thing with an homogeneous character; an element is the minimum consistent particle, spiritual or material; and the like.

Now a world in which the notion of dharma is central and nearly all pervasive is not concerned with finding the "right" of one individual against another or of the individual *vis-à-vis* society, but rather with assaying the *dharmic* (*right*, *true*, consistent...) or *adharmic* character of a thing or an action within the entire theanthropocosmic complex of reality.

Dharma is primordial. We cannot hope to understand it if we approach it with moral categories (cf. the case of the *Gītā*) or even epistemological ones. It embraces both the conflict and the resolution; both the ought and the ought not. There is no universal dharma above and independent of the *svadharma*, the dharma which is inherent in every being. And this *svadharma* is at the same time a result of and a reaction to the dharma of everyone else.

The starting point here is not the individual, but the whole complex concatenation of the Real. In order to protect the world, for the sake of the protection of this universe, says Manu, He, Svayambhū, the Self-existent, arranged the castes and their duties.[23] Dharma is the order of the entire reality, that which keeps the world together.[24] The individual's duty is to maintain his "rights;" it is to find one's place in relation to Society, to the Cosmos, and to the transcendent world.

[22] From the root *dhr*, to hold, to maintain, keep together. Cf. Latin *tenere* and English *tenet*.

[23] Manu, I, 31 and I, 87.

[24] Cf. the famous *lokasamgraha* of the *Gītā*, and the well known definition of the *Mahābhārata*: "that which maintains and sustains the peoples." (*Karnaparvam*, LXIX, 59).

It is obvious from these brief paragraphs that here the discourse on "Human Rights" would take on an altogether different character. It would distract us from the purpose of this article to look now for the homeomorphic equivalent of Human Rights in a culture pervaded with the conception of dharma. We adduce this Indian example only to be able to elaborate in a fuller way the question of our title.

Only one submission and one observation may be allowed here so as not to leave this thought incomplete. I submit that the homeomorphic equivalent is *svadharma*, and I make the observation that the homeomorphic equivalent does not mean the corresponding counterpart, as if all that is conveyed by Human Rights is also borne by *svadharma* or *vice versa*. Cultures are wholes, and do not fit into one-to-one correspondences. In order to have a just society, the modern West stresses the notion of Human Rights. In order to have a dharmic order, classical India stresses the notion of *svadharma*.

We shall now attempt to formulate without further development some reactions to the Western discourse on Human Rights from this Indian perspective. We should add immediately that this Indian critique does not imply that the Indian model is better, or that Indian culture has been faithful to its fundamental intuition—as the existence of the outcastes and the degeneration of the caste system sufficiently prove.

In confrontation and dialogue with the Western model, the Indian critique would stress fundamentally that Human Rights should not be absolutized. It would contest that one can speak of Human Rights as "objective" entities standing on their own in isolation from the rest of the Real. This is what seems to be implied in the very first article of the Declaration: "All human beings are born free and equal in dignity and rights. They are endowed with reason and conscience and should act towards one another in a spirit of brotherhood." Particular rights, privileges due to a special position in society, i.e. a relativization of rights does not seem to be compatible with this article.

Developing this point, the Indian vision would insist on the following points among others:

1. Human Rights are not individual Human Rights only. The

humanum is not incarnated in the individual *only*. The individual as such is an abstraction, and an abstraction as such cannot be an ultimate subject of rights. As we have already indicated, the individual is only the knot in and of the net of relationships which form the fabric of the Real. The knots may individually be all the same (either *jīva*, *ātman* or *anātman*), but it is mainly their position in the net which determines the set of "rights" an individual may have. Individuality is not a substantial category, but a functional one. The structure of the universe is hierarchical, but this does not imply that the higher echelons have the right to trample upon the rights of the lower ones—in spite of the dangers of this happening the moment the harmony of the whole is disturbed.

I am not entering into the merits or demerits of this world view. We should however bear in mind that this conception is intimately linked with the conception of karma, and thus should not be evaluated outside its proper context.

2. Human Rights are not Human only. They concern equally the entire cosmic display of the universe, from which even the Gods are not absent. The animals, all the sentient beings and the supposedly inanimate creatures, are also involved in the interaction concerning "human" rights. Man is a peculiar being, to be sure, but neither alone nor so essentially distinct. One could even ask whether there are specific human rights, or if this specificity is again only an abstraction for pragmatic reasons which defeats its own purpose the moment we forget its merely practical character.

Here again, another cosmology and another theology provide the justification for this conception. Whether modern India, accepting and adopting modern science as it is, will be able to maintain this conception for very long is another matter altogether. But we know also about the persistence of mythical patterns.

3. Human Rights are not Rights only. They are also duties and both are interdependent. Humankind has the "right" to survive only insofar as it performs the duty of maintaining the world (*lokasamgraha*). We have the "right" to eat only inasmuch as we

fulfill the duty of allowing ourselves to be eaten by a hierarchically higher agency. Our right is only a participation in the entire metabolic function of the universe.

We should have, if anything, a Declaration of Universal Rights and Duties in which the whole of Reality would be encompassed. Obviously, this demands not only a different anthropology but also a different cosmology and an altogether different theology—beginning with its name. That only human beings and not animals could make this Declaration would invalidate it only to the same extent that the Declaration of Human Rights could be contested because the Nagas and the Masai did not take part in the discussion and framing of the Declaration.

4. Human Rights are not mutually isolatable. They are related not only to the whole cosmos and all their corresponding duties; they form, among themselves as well, a harmonious whole. It is for this reason that a material list of definitive Human Rights is not theoretically feasible. It is the universal harmony that ultimately counts. This is not invalidated by the fact that India, as so many other countries, knows the codification of laws. India suffers, perhaps more than most countries, from legalistic *minutiae*, precisely because no juridical legislation will ever suffice.[25]

5. Human Rights are not absolute. They are intrinsically relative, they are relationships among entities. Moreover, these entities are determined by the relationships themselves. To say that my human value depends on my position in the universe would be a caricature of what has been said if we start by thinking of an individual in itself, whose dignity is then made to

[25] A recent example may illuminate the issue: In July 1981 the Indian nation is in an uproar because some 352 outcastes of the small village of Minakshipuram in Tamilnadu converted to Islam, probably in protest and reaction against their ostracism (to say the least) from the Hindu caste-communities. For our point it is interesting to remark that H.H. Sri Vishveshva Tirtha Swamiji of Pejavar Mutt along with many other Hindu religious leaders can now—for obviously political and opportunistic reasons—raise their voices against untouchability and discrimination without paying attention to the *Manavadharmaśastra* (III, 92, 150, 157; IV, 79, 213; IX, 238-239; etc.) and other sacred Laws sanctioning the system. Cf. the Indian press from May to August, 1981; e.g. *The Hindu* from Madras, May 26; July 15, 16, 18, 28, 29, 30; August 2; etc.

depend on whether he or she is rich or poor, of one caste or another, etc. The classical Indian vision would not subscribe to this—in spite of the failures of the system in the praxis and even the degeneration in time—but it would start from a wholistic conception and then define a portion of Reality by function of its situation in the totality. In a certain sense, the knot is nothing—because it is the whole net.

6. Both systems (the Western and the Hindu) make sense from and within a given and accepted myth. Both systems imply a certain kind of consensus. When that consensus is challenged, a new myth must be found. The broken myth is the situation in India today, as it is in the world at large. That the rights of individuals be conditioned only by their position in the net of Reality can no longer be admitted by the contemporary mentality. Nor does it seem to be admissible that the rights of individuals be so absolute as not to depend at all on the particular situation of the individual.

In short, there is at present no endogenous theory capable of unifying contemporary societies and no imposed or imported ideology can be simply substituted for it. A mutual fecundation of cultures is a human imperative of our times.

The Declaration defends the individual from the abuses of the State or Society. The Indian view would say that we are part of a harmonious whole on pilgrimage toward a non-historical goal. Interactions are the very warp and woof of the universe. Cultural and religious traditions offer a whole that cannot easily be dismembered without doing violence to their insights. Hindu karma outside its context may become fatalistic. Christian charity outside its system may turn oppressive. The universalization of Human Rights is a very delicate question indeed.

V. By Way of Conclusion

Is the concept of Human Rights a Western conception?

Yes.

Should the world then renounce declaring or enforcing Human Rights?

No.

Three qualifications, however, are necessary:

1. For an authentic human life to be possible within the *megamachine* of the modern technological world, Human Rights are imperative. This is because the development of the notion of Human Rights is bound up with and given its meaning by the slow development of that megamachine. How far individuals or groups or nations should collaborate with this present-day system is another question altogether. But in the contemporary political arena as defined by current socio-economic and ideological trends, the defense of Human Rights is a sacred duty. Yet it should be remembered that to introduce Human Rights (in the definite Western sense, of course) into other cultures before the introduction of *technicultur*e would amount not only to putting the cart before the horse, but also to preparing the way for the technological invasion—as if by a Trojan horse, as we have already said. And yet a technological civilization without Human Rights amounts to the most inhuman situation imaginable. The dilemma is excruciating. This makes the two following points all the more important and urgent.

2. Room should be made for other traditions to develop and formulate their own homeomorphic views corresponding to or opposing Western "rights." Or rather, these other world traditions should make room for themselves, since no one else is likely to make it for them. This is an urgent task; otherwise it will be impossible for non-Western cultures to survive, let alone to offer viable alternatives or even a sensible complement. Here the role of a cross-cultural philosophical approach is paramount. The need for human pluralism is often recognized in principle, but not often practiced, not only because of the dynamism which drives the paneconomic ideology, linked with the megamachine, to expand all over the world, but also because viable alternatives are not yet theoretically worked out.

3. An intermediary space should be found for mutual criticism that strives for mutual fecundation and enrichment. Perhaps such an interchange may help bring forth a new myth and eventually a more humane civilization. The dialogical dialogue appears as the unavoidable method.

Is the Notion of Human Rights a Western Concept?

* * *

Perhaps a suggestion here may prove helpful. Playing on the metaphor of the knots (individuality) and the net (personhood) we could probably affirm that traditional cultures have stressed the net (kinship, hierarchical structure of society, the function to be performed, the role of each part in relation to the whole), so that often the knot has been suffocated and not allowed sufficient free space for its own self-identity. On the other hand, Modernity stresses the knots (individual free will to choose any option, the idiosyncracies of everyone, the atomization of society) so that often the knot has been lost in loneliness, alienated by its own social mobility, and wounded (or killed) in competition with other more powerful knots. Perhaps the notion of personhood as the interplay between the knots and the net, as well as the realization that freedom is not just the capacity to choose between given options but also the power to create options, could provide a starting point for the proposed mutual fecundation.

If many traditional cultures are centered on God, and some other cultures basically cosmocentric, the culture which has come up with the notion of Human Rights is decisively anthropocentric. Perhaps we may now be prepared for a cosmotheandric vision of reality in which the Divine, the Human and the Cosmic are integrated into a whole, more or less harmonious according to the performance of our truly human rights.

R. Panikkar
(*University of California, Santa Barbara*)

Lokayan Bulletin, 5 : 4/5, 1987

Human Rights—A Movement In Search Of A Theory

Rajni Kothari

The emerging scenario of the politics of human rights in India is becoming increasingly complicated and problem-ridden. On balance, it does not appear too encouraging at this point in history, given the growing brutalisation of the state in its relationship to civil society as well as the increasing availability of the apparatus of the state to dominant interests keen on maintaining and augmenting levels of oppression and terror. And yet there continue to persist countervailing forces representing and organising the oppressed as integral parts of a larger democratic struggle, often putting the dominant interests and the state structures through which they operate on the defensive. It is not impossible, even in a period of rapid decline of democratic institutions, to build upon these tendencies, to bridge the inevitable gaps and divisions that bedevil diverse 'movements', and to move from a politics of mere protest to one of active resistence and effective challenge to the status quo. But, for this to happen, it is essential to face squarely the ideological confusion in which the different human rights constituencies have landed themselves in and to evolve a *politics* of the movement that goes beyond bold rhetoric and engages various actors in a framework of common endeavour based on shared understanding.

An essential paradox afflicts the human rights scene. On the one hand, everyone associated with this movement or that—women, ecologists, trade unionists, peasantry, tribals, even exponents of state's right's—claims to be struggling for civil liberties and democratic rights. On the other hand, when it comes to the growth of the human rights 'movement', most of these tend to hold back, keen on retaining their specialized identities and afraid of being swamped by a generalised platform or body. In insisting on their diverse specializations, they have pushed human rights activists towards playing a specialized role. Many of the human rights activists have themselves contributed to such an image by insisting that a human rights body should confine itself to fighting against atrocities committed by the state, not in dealing with the sources of these atrocities in the structure of the state and of civil society. While individual activists may involve themselves in political activities, including in party politics, it is not the role of human rights bodies to get so entangled. So both by the reckoning of others and by their own, human rights activists are a breed apart. And, I may add, a breed that is shrinking in number, influence and, to an extent, even legitimacy.

The reasons for the latter are many and most of them somewhat recent. There has taken place an unprecedented polarisation of the Indian society following the rather rapid
18 spread of communalism and the systematic build-up in the media of the 'extremist' and 'terrorist' threat to the country's integrity and unity. This has polarised the human rights community too. Alongside, there has taken place a striking decline in the independence and objectivity of the judiciary and the press, partly due to the overall polarisation of society but partly also due to a more comprehensive conditioning of the middle class mind that anything that appears to weaken the government at the Centre weakens the Indian state, and anything that weakens the state weakens the constitutional fabric of 'democracy'. The paradox is almost tragic: the greater the incidence of oppression, the more widespread the span and location of resistance from civil society, which in turn produces the sense that the state is under attack and must be protected. This in turn is reflected in the fact that increasingly the relevance of human rights activists and organizations is reduced to holding protest meetings and rallies, and to registering and fighting court cases which also amount to little more than protesting, as nothing much comes out of the writs and petitions anyway. This has made the human rights endeavour even more segmented and specialised—reducing it to lawyers and orators—and, given the 'piller to post' nature of the running about that is

involved, has produced a growing state of exhaustion and shrinkage in its composition and character.

The fact that this has also been a period of the rise of a number of social movements and growing challenge to the state does not contradict what has been said above. Rather, it underscores the issues. When institutions get eroded precisely during a time of rising political consciousness and growing demands on the governing structure, the latter take the form of assertion of rights of different segments of the population that are usually aimed against the state, even though (as in the case of women, or the tribals and forest dwellers, or even the dalits) the sources of injustice and exploitation lie in the social structure rather than in the framework of the state. In this lies the ambivalence of the various social movements *i.e.*, while both the volume and the variety of their demands grow, their definition and articulation does not take the form of joining a larger struggle for transforming the state, much less of building a civil society that can limit and control the role of the state. Quite often they are demands advanced to the state, to be conceded by it in the form of administrative actions, or new legislation, or judicial interventions. At other times, these movements are aimed against certain 'tendencies' that are sought to be reversed
through policy prescriptions—such as deforestation, or rape **19**
and dowry deaths, or displacement of tribals that are not properly 'rehabilitated' (the demand being that they be properly rehabilitated). Sometimes the efforts at highlighting and removing injustices may take highly emotive and stirring forms, as in the case of the plight of women *as women* in a male dominated society, and could be backed by large and successful efforts at mobilizing opinion and shaping consciousness. Or there may take place a gradual but continuously growing build-up of opinion on certain forms of destruction, and how little was being done about them, as in the case of the environment movement. Specific cases of this destruction may even be traced to government policies, or the influence of vested interests (like business houses or transnational corporations) on the government. But hardly ever are these conceived as arising out of the role and nature of the state, much less seen as struggles for 'rights' against the state. It is only when the police or some such arm of the state steps in, and the activists are subjected to atrocities of some kind, that the latter start interpreting their struggles as involving 'rights' vis-a-vis the state—and hence definable as human rights struggles. It is this limited, segmented and largely apolitical self-image of these

various constituents of democratic struggle that has prevented them from becoming part of a more comprehensive human rights movement.

The failings of the civil liberties and human rights activists are no less serious. If the activists of other social movements have tended to be rather apolitical, the human rights activists have taken too narrow a view of politics. Two main currents have contributed to the growth of a human rights platform in India in recent years—one emanating from the Emergency period and renewed after 1980 of which PUCL has been the main vehicle, focussing on violation of constitutional rights, and the other (going back long before the Emergency) growing from more radical sections, especially the Marxist-Leninist, focussing on the atrocities committed on the rural poor, and on 'Naxalites'. The two streams have at times come together and at other times stood apart, giving rise to divergence in thinking within each. The coming together has been against the Congress government, particularly during Mrs. Gandhi's regime, but also occasionally against other party governments, in particular against the Telugu Desam and AIADMK regimes in Andhra Pradesh and Tamilnadu respectively. The standing
20 apart has been with respect to the role of violence in the conduct of human rights struggles which has often driven a wedge between the liberals and the Marxists, with the more radical sections of the former broadly going with the latter. Another issue on which both the coming together and the standing apart has taken place is large-scale communal violence, first against the Sikhs and more recently against the Muslims (as also against other 'minorities' like the dalits and the tribals). Some of the most strident, and successful, assertions of the civil liberties movement have been recorded on the latter issue but so have major differences and 'cracks' in the movement.

But, notwithstanding these oscillations between joint action and divergent positions between the liberals and the radicals in the civil liberties movement, their interpretation of human rights has consisted of struggles against the state in respect of violation of constitutional rights and particularly those involving unlawful arrests, police atrocities and 'mafia' operations of ruling parties—broadly in the framework of 'life and liberties' of the people. More indirect violations and longer term infringements of people's rights and intrusions in the framework of civil society, the environmental and life-support system and diverse cultures and their ethnic identities do not normally enter their arena of concerns, except when these take the form of state repression or terror. The increasingly complex and changing nature of the Indian state which is converting in into an agent of large-scale devastations is not their immediate concern. And, finally, there is, as already mentioned, that self-imposed restraint accepted by a majority (though not all) of civil liberties activists that their role is restricted to resisting violations of constitutional rights by the state and not that call for longer term struggles for social and political transformation, either vis-a-vis the social structure or vis-a-vis the state.

Now such a strictly constitutional interpretation of civil liberties and such a self-imposed limitation on the political role of civil liberties and democratic rights organisations would make sense if one were to assume that the traditional instrumentalities of transformative politics—parties, unions, the Left movement—were (a) engaged in transformative politics and (b) worked in concert with human rights organisations when it comes to larger violations of the rights of the opressed and marginalised sections of society. It would also make sense if the nation-state (irrespective of levels of repression vis-a-vis sections of the citizenry) was able to withstand pressures emanating from global frameworks of economic, technological and strategic power, and was able to protect local and national spaces against external 21
encroachments that have resulted in patterns of recolonisation of India's countryside, including massive destruction of the resource base of the people as well as of tribal cultures and the ethnic pride and identity of diverse communities. Lacking either a radical engagement by the parties or a State that acts as a bulwark against externally induced destructions, involvement in a politics of transformation on the one hand and a politics of conserving ecologies, cultures and lifestyles on the other—alongside preserving the dignity and values associated with the feminine gender and ethnicity—must of necessity become the concern of a broadly defined human rights movement. Yet both the definitional and boundary-drawing predisposition of human rights activists and the clever manipulation thereof by party politicians—who have insisted on making the larger political tasks a monopoly of political parties even when they do little about it has rendered the human rights movement in a peculiar self-imposed paradox.

It is the paradox of massive failure in carrying out its defined role of waging a struggle for citizen's rights against an increasingly repressive and militarized state arising out of its refusal to join in the other major struggle that is on the anvil, namely changing the framework and the 'system' within which the political process is carried out. If one realizes some other parameters of the current situation—massive depoliticization through the rise of a technocratic state wedded to world capitalism, major efforts at cooptation of sources of dissent by both international and national agencies, the growth of a 'national socialist' version of Marxism, the rise of a national chauvinist press, and the crystallisation of a mind-set in the elite that thinks of the 'backward' as dispensable—one can begin to fathom the depth of the paradox faced by a movement that claims to fight for and protect the 'rights' of the 'people'.

Let me elaborate on the paradox. Here we have a 'movement' that once occupied a fair amount of public space, at any rate in the minds of the sensitive citizenry, being reduced to a near-collapse. So much violation of human dignity and freedom is taking place all around, so much oppression is taking place every day, and so much is happening even in the limited space defined by human rights activists—in the arena of the state—and there is so little protest, what to speak of determined intervention and action. All round one notices a failure of will, a decline in courage and commitment, a decay in
22 organisational integrity and cohesion. So much so that even when the ultimate in draconian legislations was passed recently in the form of an amendment to the National Security Act, empowering the state—which means the police—to arrest and detain and wrest 'confessions' under duress and then use that as evidence against the persecuted, not only did the political parties do little to stop the measure, there was precious little in the form of organised protest by civil liberties organisations; not even the usual press statements from the liberal intelligentsia. The contrast with the time when the first round of anti-terrorist ordinances was passed in 1984 and 1985, when the PUCL came out with *The Black Laws* and a series of protest meetings and 'anti-repression' conventions were organised round the country, is striking. The same is the case with the ferocious 'riots' in Meerut, the old city in Delhi and elsewhere. The contrast with November 1984 is again striking. That a few valiant souls like Inder Mohan and Madhu Kishwar and her associates from *Manushi* stirred out and spent days meeting the victims of the carnages, or that Mr Vaskar Nandy and his associates have been straining hard to organise a set of conventions against communalism and threats to diversity to reassure the minorities and the dalits and the tribals, that there are still a few of us who stand by them, is indeed heart-warming, but it only further

underlines the depth of the crisis which the civil liberties organisations and the human rights 'movement' finds itself in. The more the proponents of human rights draw circles around themselves by limiting their legitimate activity to fighting abuses by the State and the greater their reluctance to join (if not spearhead) the larger battles for survival of marginalised peoples, and communities and cultures, the more massive is their failure in fulfilling their obligations, even in the limited space defined by them.

Two important reasons lie behind this failure and the general state of institutional decay and paralysis of will, each of which also brings out the conceptual flaws in the human rights movement as it has developed in India. First, it is quite clear that the movement has entered a state of exhaustion. The struggle against the state is becoming an unequal one, constantly frustrating and causing depletion in ranks, in turn leaving the field to an ageing leadership that is still living in the past as far as its grasp of the human rights problematique is concerned. state violence and state terror are on the increase, the judiciary is proving insensitive to real suffering, and middle class opinion (including the bulk of the national Press) is strongly conditioned by the spectre of terrorism and the slogan 23
of national unity in danger. Human rights activists in the various regions have been found to fight increasingly loosing battles, running against impregnable walls erected by a state that is fast being reduced to a police and paramilitary apparatus, are found to be implicated in all manner of harassments and false cases, and are running from pillar to post to get even a fair hearing. The environment in which they function is increasingly inhospitable and the state—and its underworld—is always found to get the better of them. The result is growing exhaustion, cynicism, even defeatism.

The 'flaw' behind this state of affairs lies in a conception of human rights that is essentially state-centred. The very state that the human rights movement is trying to struggle against defines the terms of the latter's thinking and action, and in fact receives further endorsement from it. Organisations of civil liberties and democratic rights have done little to reduce the all-embracing and monopolistic role and character of the modern state. They do expose its misdemeanours and tendentious nature; they bring out its malfunctioning; they occasionally lay bare the interests that shape and influence its behaviour; they unravel its growing militarization and they even occasionally point out its changing character—its growing

centralisation, its subservience to the whims and fancies of a few individuals, and its increasingly dynastic nature seen in the build-up of a personality cult. But they have done precious little in bringing out either the nature of the state's undermining of civil society, or the extent to which the state has become an instrument of national chauvinism on the one hand and arrogant majoritiarianism on the other; even less the manner in which the state has been used for spreading the neurosis about 'national interest' and 'national security' and in the process weakened the deeper roots of national cohesion and cultural integrity. And this when the real threats to the country's democratic survival and plural character—as well as the survival of millions of marginalised men, women, and children—come precisely from both these openly avowed and incipient tendencies. Nor have they even begun to comprehend and work against even deeper ecological and cultural destructions being unleashed by a state that has become an alien presence and is so privy to a global technological design that lies behind both large scale erosion of the natural resource base of the people (and the consequent phenomenal growth of natural disasters' like droughts and floods which are in fact man-made disasters) and the erosion of
24 distinctive cultures, community lifestyles and the role of women in the social and economic process. It is its failure to face up to these contextual crises arising from a development process that is state-centred, that human rights activists seem to operate in a social vacuum and necessarily fail to be come effective.

The second major reason that lies behind the decline and disarray in the human rights movement is in many ways conceptual, and can be traced to the very genesis and historic antecedents of the idea of human rights. Some of the other social movements that also employ the phraseology and rhetoric of 'rights', such as the women's movement, also suffer from the same historic legacy. This is the legacy of universal human rights grounded in the western conception of rights, that is at once grounded in an individualistic ethic and takes as a philosophical given that social formations are homogeneous and hence amenable to universal formulations of individual and community, liberty and democracy. This, in my view, is a basic flaw when it comes to highly diverse, plural and continental size societies like ours that also happen to be predominantly rural. Even the distinction between legal and political rights and social and economic rights that the U.N. Charter talks about fails to get over this negative legacy from the West. The tradition of civil liberties and even of democratic rights is too grounded in this conception of 'universal man', whereas the more powerful assertions of even 'rights' that have occured have been either community based or class based. There is therefore, a hiatus between theory and practice. And yet many of the 'demands' that continue to be voiced are couched in either citizen versus state terms, or in terms of one class of citizens versus another class (not 'class' as a collective category but rather a statistical one).

The classic Liberal idea of basic or fundamental rights enshrined in a written Constitution is, of course of this variety, and is based on the concept of liberty—the traditional freedoms of speech, expression, assembly as well as the rights to life, liberty, property and the like. But even the more egalitarian expressions of human rights, such as are associated with the idea of equality (before law as well as in terms of equality of opportunities) as found in the struggle for fair or equal wages, or equal status or equal access to property rights, also bear the imprint of the individualistic ethic. The typical intervention of civil liberties groups, of protecting individuals and sometimes groups against arrest, intimidation, discrimination and torture derive their sanctions from the same legacy. And so do more
recent accretions to them, such as of the rights of women as **25**
compared to men, and the rights pertaining to treatment within family and other primary institutions. Together they do add up to quite an array of struggles for rights against a large spectrum of abuses of state power or abuses arising from lack of adequate state guarantees against them. And yet they are all too discrete to add up to an organic whole and, furthermore, do not go to the heart of the collective social process that gives rise to them. They sometimes are even liable to miss out the essence for the form. Thus even the more radical of the recent demands coming from feminist circles, regarding ownership rights of women over land in the rural areas (as compared to men), while legitimate in themselves, obfuscate the real issue which consists in increasing marginalisation of women in patterns of land *use* and from the productive process itself as a result of modern farm technology which favours machines over humans and men over women. A conception of rights based on universal norms of freedom, equality, ownership and opportunity ignores historical specificities and community contexts that define human roles and undermine the positioning of less privileged groups in society. It also overemphasizes the role of the state in providing rights as against the basic social structure and the long term forces that shape that structure.

Nowhere has the ahistorical nature of a state-centred and universalist conception of human rights become as manifest as in the relations between ethnicity and the growth of civil society—perhaps the most crucial issue in the texturing of democracy in a country like India. The question of the role of the human rights movement in dealing with the spectre of communalism and increasing communalisation of the political process has remained so undefined, caused so much confusion and has in a sense split the human rights community because of a basic lack of conceptual clarity. The point that communalism (particularly of the minorities, we are told) threatens the unity and integrity of the country is based on an unspoken assumption that the country is co-terminus with the Indian state rather than with the people organized in the form of a civil society. This has happened largely because in India a 'civil society' has not yet emerged (or is confined to the narrow elite strata in a few metropoles) and the only organized form in which castes, communities and tribes are seen to be brought together is the state. The result is that in the absence of a vibrant and self-conscious civil society, the state is found to impinge directly on diverse communities and impose, a
26 centralised and homogeneous structure and culture, forcing in turn the latter to express their voices of protest and dissent in separate, regional and often sectarian and communal forms, both fomented by the agents of the state and provoking a backlash from it on behalf of an imagined majority called the 'Hindus'. The result is a peculiar structure of dualism. It appears to be dualist in communal terms, viz. between the Hindus and the non-Hindus, but is in fact dualist in a much more fundamental sense, namely a division between the state and its agents and the society and its diverse formations. Hence the growing alienation of each of these formations (including several segments among the Hindus) from the state and a growing feeling that, alone and unprotected, and lacking genuine social cohesion in local habitats, each of them will have to fend for itself.

It is important to understand that the Western conception of civil society (which emerged after several centuries of intellectual, territorial and economic struggles) pressumes a homogeneous society and, where a fair degree of homogeneity does not exist, the state was supposed to create it. We face a situation in which such a conception of the state is proving inimical to the very diversity that defines our national identity. (This is beginning to happen in the West too, in societies facing cultural diversity and

ethnic upsurges). With us, the creation of civil society becomes the task facing leaders of diverse social and cultural entities—in cooperation and communion with each other, drawing upon available and still surviving traditions of togetherness, mutuality and resolution of differences and conflict—in short traditions of a democratic collective that are our own and on which we need to build in a changed historical context. This is the basic political task facing Indians—the creation of a civil society that is rooted in diversity yet cohering and holding together. If the human rights movement in India ignores this distinctive historical context and the much more fundamental schisms and sources of destruction that have emerged—ecological, ethnic, gender-based—it is likely to be marginalised and, what is worse, become prey to the very ills that it must come to grips with. But if it comprehends the reality in which it is placed and develops a relevant theoretical perspective, it can become the catalyst of a renewed democratic political struggle, and can draw upon other diverse social movements, citizen initiatives and grassroots awakening into its orbit. For this to happen it will need to give up both its state-centredness and its Western pedigree, become relevant to the fundamental task of
constructing a civil society that is rooted in the unique social 27
and ecological constellation of India, and with this in view, develop a comprehensive strategy. But *first* it must develop a relevant political theory of democratic transformation that can provide the basis for a movement in a radically different social setting than one that obtains in the West. The imported theory of human rights is already proving counter-productive.

[11]

ASIA'S DIFFERENT STANDARD

by Bilahari Kausikan

East and Southeast Asia must respond to a new phenomenon: Human rights have become a legitimate issue in interstate relations. How a country treats its citizens is no longer a matter for its own exclusive determination. Others can and do legitimately claim a concern. There is an emerging global culture of human rights, and a body of international law on human rights has gradually developed, codified in the United Nations Charter, the Universal Declaration of Human Rights, and other international instruments. The United States and many European countries increasingly emphasize human rights in their foreign policies. Of course, human rights are not, and are not likely to become, a primary issue in international relations. Their promotion by all countries will always be selective, even cynical, and concern for human rights will always be balanced against other national interests. Nevertheless, the Western emphasis on human rights will affect the tone and texture of post–Cold War international relations.

In response, East and Southeast Asia are reexamining their own human rights standards. Of the noncommunist states in the region, only Japan, South Korea, and the Philippines are parties to both the International Covenant on Civil and Political Rights and the International Covenant on Economic, Social and Cultural Rights. Seoul and Manila have also accepted the Optional Protocol to the International Covenant on Civil and Political Rights. Tokyo has partially adopted the Western approach to human rights. But there is a more general acceptance of many international human rights

---

BILAHARI KAUSIKAN *is the director of the East Asian and Pacific bureau of the Ministry of Foreign Affairs of Singapore. The views expressed are personal and do not represent those of the ministry.*

norms, even among states that have not acceded to the two covenants or are accused by the West of human rights abuses.

The human rights situation in the region, whether measured by the standard of civil and political rights or by social, cultural, and economic rights, has improved greatly over the last 20 years. As countries in the region become more prosperous, secure, and self-confident, they are moving beyond a purely defensive attitude to a more active approach to human rights. All the countries of the region are party to the U.N. Charter. None has rejected the Universal Declaration. There are references to human rights in the constitutions of many of the countries in the region. Countries like China, Indonesia, and even Burma have not just brushed aside Western criticism of their human rights records but have tried to respond seriously, asserting or trying to demonstrate that they too adhere to international human rights norms. They tend to interpret rather than reject such norms when there are disagreements. They discuss human rights with Western delegations. They have released political prisoners; and Indonesia, for instance, has even held commissions of inquiry on alleged abuses and punished some officials found guilty.

Abuses and inconsistencies continue. But it is too simplistic to dismiss what has been achieved as mere gestures intended to appease Western critics. Such inclinations may well be an element in the overall calculation of interests. And Western pressure undeniably plays a role. But in themselves, self-interest and pressure are insufficient and condescendingly ethnocentric Western explanations. They do less than justice to the states concerned, most of which have their own traditions in which the rulers have a duty to govern in a way consonant with the human dignity of their subjects, even if there is no clear concept of "rights" as has evolved in the West. China today, for all its imperfections, is a vast improvement over the China of the Cultural Revolution. So too has the situation in Taiwan, South Korea, and the Association of Southeast Asian Nations (ASEAN) improved. Western critics who deny the improvements lose credibility.

25.

FOREIGN POLICY

As countries in East and Southeast Asia position themselves more in the international human rights mainstream, they are trying to stake out distinctive positions in line with their own cultures, histories, and special circumstances. Like all states, East and Southeast Asian countries still subordinate human rights to other vital national interests, such as the territorial integrity of the state or the fundamental nature of their political systems. Moreover, the movement toward greater emphasis on human rights is not even. But in that respect the region is no different from the West. Such imperfections are inescapable political realities; it does not advance human rights to ignore the real progress that has occurred in the name of a pristine, but unattainable, ideal.

The diversity of cultural traditions, political structures, and levels of development will make it difficult, if not impossible, to define a single distinctive and coherent human rights regime that can encompass the vast region from Japan to Burma, with its Confucianist, Buddhist, Islamic, and Hindu traditions. Nonetheless, the movement toward such a goal is likely to continue. What is clear is that there is a general discontent throughout the region with a purely Western interpretation of human rights. The further development of human rights there will be shaped primarily by internal developments, but pressure will continue to come from the United States and Europe.

Human Rights as a Tool

Human rights did not evolve in a vacuum. During the Cold War, the Western promotion of human rights was shaped by and deployed as an ideological instrument of the East-West struggle. The post–Cold War human rights dialogue between the West and Asia will be influenced by the power structure and dynamics of a more regionalized world, built around the United States, Europe, and Asia, which is replacing Cold War alliances and superpower competition. Trade and security will, as always, be foremost on the international agenda, and human rights will not be an issue of the first order. But human rights touch upon extraordinarily delicate matters of culture and values.

And human rights issues are likely to become more prominent.

An additional factor affecting the prominence of human rights is that Western governments need no longer be constrained in their efforts to advance their fundamental values for fear of driving countries into Moscow's arms. Even if Western foreign ministries find it imprudent or difficult to shake off ingrained habits of caution, there will be pressure from Western publics, human rights nongovernmental organizations (NGOs) and other interest groups, and the news media to take an active approach. It will be more difficult for Western governments to find politically compelling arguments to ignore human rights violations, particularly in an age when modern communication technologies allow images and information to travel almost instantaneously around the world. Even without popular pressure, some Western governments may find it useful for other reasons to selectively inject a greater human rights component in their relations with East and Southeast Asia. New governments may, for example, trumpet human rights in order to distinguish themselves from their predecessors—early Clinton administration rhetoric being a case in point.

As the external threat to their survival recedes in the post–Cold War world, the United States and Europe are turning to deal with urgent and difficult domestic problems. The West will have less time, attention, and resources to devote to the rest of the world. Yet the United States and several European Community (EC) countries still regard themselves as global powers. It would require a painful redefinition of their identities if they did not seek a voice in the affairs of an economically dynamic region like East and Southeast Asia. They may be tempted, at least on occasion, to employ the rhetoric of human rights as a substitute for policies that would require an inconvenient commitment of resources or attention. Talking about human rights is an easy, cheap, and popular way to exercise influence or maintain the illusion of involvement.

Meanwhile, relations among the United States, Europe, and Asia may lead the West to use human rights as an instrument of economic

FOREIGN POLICY

competition. As American and European apprehensions about their competitiveness rise, the West is emphasizing values like openness and equal opportunity and relating them to broader issues of freedom and democracy. Japan's commitment to such values is already being questioned and its cultural traits criticized as deviations from allegedly "universal" norms. The French prime minister has accused foreigners in Asia with "different values" of undermining France's prosperity.

The lengthening catalogue of rights and freedoms in international human rights law now encompasses such matters as pay, work conditions, trade unions, standard of living, rest and leisure, welfare and social security, women's and children's rights, and the environment. The pressures and temptation to link economic concerns with human rights will certainly rise if economic strains increase. That is not to say that the West is insincere in its commitment to human rights. But policy motivations are rarely simple; and it is difficult to believe that economic considerations do not to some degree influence Western attitudes toward such issues as, say, the prison labor component of Chinese exports, child labor in Thailand, or some of the AFL-CIO complaints against Malaysian labor practices. President Bill Clinton's declared intention to press for human rights in China in return for continuing to grant most-favored-nation trading status to Beijing makes the linkage explicit.

But efforts to promote human rights in Asia must also reckon with the altered distribution of power in the post–Cold War world. Power, especially economic power, has been diffused. For the last two decades, most of East and Southeast Asia has experienced strong economic growth and will probably keep growing faster than other regions well into the next century. Not just Japan, but increasingly also the newly industrialized economies (NIEs), near NIEs like Thailand and Malaysia, and sub-regions such as southern China are considerable forces in the global economy. The economic success of East and Southeast Asia is the central strategic fact of the 1990s. Across the Pacific, power adjustments are already underway.

Of course, the economic growth has not been even. The United States and Europe are still major markets for almost all East and Southeast Asian countries, many of whom remain aid recipients. But Western leverage over East and Southeast Asia has been greatly reduced. The countries in the region are reacting accordingly. Indonesia's response to the Netherlands when the Hague pressed human rights after the November 1991 Dili incident in East Timor was to reject Dutch aid and dissolve the Inter-Governmental Group on Indonesia (IGGI). The World Bank agreed to form a new group, excluding the Netherlands. In July 1992, Portugal vetoed a new ASEAN-EC agreement because of East Timor. The move was unfortunate, but hardly a disaster for ASEAN. For most East and Southeast Asian countries, life without Western aid would be more uncomfortable—but life would go on. It would not cause the crisis that withdrawal or curtailment of Western aid would cause in Africa, Central America, and many South Asian countries. And aid is not just a favor the West bestows on its less-fortunate brethren; it is a policy tool deployed to advance the West's interests.

East and Southeast Asia are now significant actors in the world economy. There is far less scope for conditionality and sanctions to force compliance with human rights. The region is an expanding market for the West. Global production networking makes the region an important source of intermediate goods for Western industry. It is also becoming a source of capital. What hurts East and Southeast Asia will also pain the West. And the growing interdependence within the region and among Asia, Europe, and America will make it difficult to single out any one country for sanction without hurting others, China and Hong Kong being only the most obvious example. That may explain the compromise on East Timor worked out during the October 1992 ASEAN-EC ministerial meeting. The majority of EC countries agreed to regard East Timor as a bilateral problem between Portugal and Indonesia and conduct business as usual with ASEAN.

The United States is the only remaining superpower capable of exercising global leader-

FOREIGN POLICY

ship. Many European countries may well take their cues from how the Clinton administration implements its human rights policies. The United States will be a major influence on human rights debates in the U.N., International Monetary Fund, World Bank, and other international forums. Since most East and Southeast Asian countries regard a continued U.S. presence in Asia as desirable, it is not entirely unreasonable for the Clinton administration to ask that its own interest in promoting human rights and democracy be taken into account in some way. But how it does so is critical.

For the first time since the Universal Declaration was adopted in 1948, countries not thoroughly steeped in the Judeo-Christian and natural law traditions are in the first rank.

A zealous but inexperienced new administration may try to distinguish itself by taking up human rights where the Carter administration left off more than a decade ago, but the problem extends across the political spectrum. Democrats and Republicans share the basic values of a common American political culture. Presidents Ronald Reagan and George Bush did not reject Jimmy Carter's emphasis on human rights. They merely objected to its focus. Reagan and Bush did not dismantle the human rights legislation and bureaucracy created by Carter. They built upon it and focused it more on the anticommunist struggle. That battle is over and the trend, already evident under Reagan and Bush in the attendant strains between the United States and many Asian countries, is away from rights as relatively precisely defined in international law, toward the promotion of hazier notions of "freedom" and "democracy." The human rights apparatus is now even more open to manipulation by competing legislative, executive, judicial, media, and special interests devoted to such transcendent American values.

The operation of the American political process magnifies the scope for disagreement between Asia and the West. Clinton has proceeded more pragmatically than his campaign rhetoric would have suggested. But the president is bound by the language of the laws and restricted by the system. Much American human rights legislation is loosely worded. The ambiguities constitute an invitation to struggle: The proclivity of American politicians to narrow political debate to the dimensions of sound-bites and the propensity for human rights rhetoric to be presented in legalistic and absolutist terms do not make for a nuanced public understanding of complex issues and diminish the room for compromise—the more so since U.S. leverage is limited.

Most of the outside leverage that now exists clearly belongs to Japan, the world's largest aid donor. Although Tokyo has made human rights one of the yardsticks for its official development assistance, it will certainly implement its human rights policies according to its own assessments. Unlike the West, Japan cannot escape the consequences if pressing human rights or forcing the pace of political change in its Asian neighbors leads to instability. Distance makes it easier to be virtuous; proximity makes for prudence. If, for instance, tough sanctions break the grip of the State Law and Order Restoration Council in Burma or the Communist party in China, the results could be violent. If disorder breaks out in Burma or China, it is not the United States or Europe that will pay the immediate price. Is the West prepared to intervene and remain engaged, perhaps for decades, to restore order? China will be a formidable political and economic force by the turn of the century. That does not mean human rights abuses in China must be overlooked. But if the promotion of human rights ignores Chinese realities and interests, expect China to find ways to exert countervailing pressures. And it will have the wherewithal to try to reshape any international order it sees as threatening.

East and Southeast Asia are now capable of exerting considerable influence on the international politics of human rights, and their interests, values, and cultures cannot be disregarded. Most of the region's countries can no longer be pushed or coerced. Unlike Eastern Europe, Russia, or many states of the former Soviet

FOREIGN POLICY

Union, Asians do not wish to be considered good Westerners, even if they are friendly to the West. At least two countries, Japan and China, have the power to make a major impact on the international system.

For the first time since the Universal Declaration was adopted in 1948, countries not thoroughly steeped in the Judeo-Christian and natural law traditions are in the first rank: That unprecedented situation will define the new international politics of human rights. It will also multiply the occasions for conflict. In the process, will the human rights dialogue between the West and East and Southeast Asia become a dialogue of the deaf, with each side proclaiming its superior virtue without advancing the common interests of humanity? Or can it be a genuine and fruitful dialogue, expanding and deepening consensus? The latter outcome will require finding a balance between a pretentious and unrealistic universalism and a paralyzing cultural relativism. The myth of the universality of all human rights is harmful if it masks the real gap that exists between Asian and Western perceptions of human rights. The gap will not be bridged if it is denied.

The June 1993 Vienna U.N. conference on human rights did not even attempt to do so. The West went to Vienna accusing Asia of trying to undermine the ideal of universality, and determined to blame Asia if the conference failed. Inevitably, Asia resisted. The result after weeks of wrangling was a predictable diplomatic compromise ambiguous enough so all could live with it, but that settled very few things. There was no real dialogue between Asia and the West, no genuine attempt to address the issues or forge a meeting of the minds. If anything, the Vienna conference may only have hardened attitudes on both sides and increased the deep skepticism with which many Asian countries regard Western posturing on human rights.

Culture and Human Rights

Most Western governments are well informed about political and economic conditions in East and Southeast Asia. Most therefore try to pursue nuanced policies on human rights. But what Western governments would consider a sophisticated appreciation of the complexities and realistic policies, their publics, media, and human rights NGOs often dismiss as timidity. The Western media, NGOs, and human rights activists, especially in the United States, tend to press the human rights dialogue beyond the legitimate insistence on humane standards of behavior by calling for the summary implementation of abstract concepts without regard for a country's unique cultural, social, economic, and political circumstances. And it is precisely those NGOs and media that are most influential in shaping the public attitudes to which Western governments must respond. In the post–Cold War world, advocacy organizations can be expected to seize the opportunity to push harder.

For many in the West, the end of the Cold War was not just the defeat or collapse of communist regimes, but the supreme triumph and vindication of Western systems and values. It has become the lens through which they view developments in other regions. There has been a tendency since 1989 to draw parallels between developments in the Third World and those in Eastern Europe and the former USSR, measuring all states by the advance of what the West regards as "democracy." That is a value-laden term, itself susceptible to multiple interpretations, but usually understood by Western human rights activists and the media as the establishment of political institutions and practices akin to those existing in the United States and Europe.

There is good reason to doubt whether the countries of the former USSR and Eastern Europe will really evolve into "democracies" anytime soon, however this term is defined, or even whether such a transformation would necessarily always be for the better, given the ethnic hatreds in the region. But the Western approach is ideological, not empirical. The West needs its myths; missionary zeal to whip the heathen along the path of righteousness and remake the world in its own image is deeply ingrained in Western (especially American) political culture. It is entirely understandable that Western human rights advocates choose to interpret reality in the way they believe helps their cause most.

FOREIGN POLICY

But that is not how most East and Southeast Asian governments view the world. Economic success has engendered a greater cultural self-confidence. Whatever their differences, East and Southeast Asian countries are increasingly conscious of their own civilizations and tend to locate the sources of their economic success in their own distinctive traditions and institutions. The self-congratulatory, simplistic, and sanctimonious tone of much Western commentary at the end of the Cold War and the current triumphalism of Western values grate on East and Southeast Asians. It is, after all, a West that launched two world wars, supported racism and colonialism, perpetrated the Holocaust and the Great Purge, and now suffers from serious social and economic deficiencies. It has difficulty competing economically and is unwilling to come to grips with many of its own domestic problems, all too prone to blame others for its own failings, and apparently exhausted of everything except pretensions of special virtue.

The Vienna conference may only have hardened attitudes on both sides and increased the deep skepticism with which many Asian countries regard Western posturing on human rights.

The hard core of rights that are truly universal is smaller than many in the West are wont to pretend. Forty-five years after the Universal Declaration was adopted, many of its 30 articles are still subject to debate over interpretation and application—not just between Asia and the West, but within the West itself. Not every one of the 50 states of the United States would apply the provisions of the Universal Declaration in the same way. It is not only pretentious but wrong to insist that everything has been settled once and forever. The Universal Declaration is not a tablet Moses brought down from the mountain. It was drafted by mortals. All international norms must evolve through continuing debate among different points of view if consensus is to be maintained.

Most East and Southeast Asian governments are uneasy with the propensity of many American and some European human rights activists to place more emphasis on civil and political rights than on economic, social, and cultural rights. They would probably not be convinced, for instance, by a September 1992 report issued by Human Rights Watch entitled *Indivisible Human Rights: The Relationship of Political and Civil Rights to Survival, Subsistence and Poverty*. They would find the report's argument that "political and civil rights, especially those related to democratic accountability," are basic to survival and "not luxuries to be enjoyed only after a certain level of economic development has been reached" to be grossly overstated. Such an argument does not accord with their own historical experience. That experience sees order and stability as preconditions for economic growth, and growth as the necessary foundation of any political order that claims to advance human dignity.

The Asian record of economic success is a powerful claim that cannot be easily dismissed. Both the West and Asia can agree that values and institutions are important determinants of development. But what institutions and which values? The individualistic ethos of the West or the communitarian traditions of Asia? The consensus-seeking approach of East and Southeast Asia or the adversarial institutions of the West? The post-Marcos Philippines—which combines what is probably the most democratic constitution and political institutions in Southeast Asia with mismanagement, lawlessness, and the worst economic record in ASEAN—must at least open to question whether there are valid alternative relationships between civil-political and economic-social rights.

Poverty, insecurity, and instability breed human rights abuses, while wealth creates the stability of Western societies and allows the operation of political institutions that in less-favorable circumstances could lead to disaster. Only America's wealth, for example, allows it to operate a political system that elevates conflict to the status of principle and makes a virtue of a tendency toward paralysis in all but exceptional circumstances. Wealth makes political institutions almost irrelevant to the well-being and happiness of the majority in many Western

FOREIGN POLICY

societies. Many Americans do not even bother to vote and the popular estimation of American politicians is low. Those are among the luxuries that wealth buys. But the costs are already becoming evident.

As the international distribution of power and wealth changes, the West ought to subject itself to a probing and unsentimental analysis. It should ask itself whether many of its persistent problems and its lack of economic competitiveness compared to several East and Southeast Asian countries are not in part due to its tendency to transform every social issue into an uncompromising question of "rights" and place the claims of the individual and special interests over those of society. There are grounds to question whether, viewed against the continuing march of history, the Western type of "democracy" provides optimal societal arrangements or even whether it can endure in its present form.

At any rate, many East and Southeast Asians tend to look askance at the starkly individualistic ethos of the West in which authority tends to be seen as oppressive and rights are an individual's "trump" over the state. Most people of the region prefer a situation in which distinctions between the individual, society, and state are less clear-cut, or at least less adversarial. It will be far more difficult to deepen and expand the international consensus on human rights if East and Southeast Asian countries believe that the Western promotion of human rights is aimed at what they regard as the foundation of their economic success. In fact, many Asians perceive the values and practices insisted upon by Western human rights purists as exacerbating the thorny problems faced by the West.

There is, however, a natural tactical convergence of interests between the Western media and human rights activists and those aspiring Asian elites who are challenging established governments. Such elites seek sympathy and legitimacy abroad by espousing human rights, just as the rhetoric of anticommunism served to gain support in the West during the Cold War and nationalist leaders of an earlier generation employed the ideology of liberalism to undermine the legitimacy of illiberal colonial regimes. Thus the popular image is created of repressive

Kausikan

Asian governments holding down the masses yearning to be free, occasioning cheers when they fail and condemnation when they succeed. Such are, for example, some common popular Western interpretations of events in China in June 1989 and in Thailand in May 1992. Such images are not always entirely wrong, as events in Rangoon in 1988 showed, but they often have a political significance that bears little relationship to their accuracy.

If dramatic scenes of the "Goddess of Democracy"—cleverly modeled after the Statue of Liberty—and students shouting defiance in Tiananmen stirred Western hearts, the emotion obscured the fact that the vast peasantry of China—among the first beneficiaries of Deng Xiaoping's reforms—were largely unmoved. Sympathy for the students came, if at all, after the massacre and probably had more to do with the disproportionate use of force against them than with their ideas. What may have struck a chord with the peasants was not "democracy," but complaints against inflation, corruption, and nepotism. When Westerners cheered the Bangkok crowds that brought down General Suchinda Kraprayoon's government, they forgot that most Thais accepted the previous year's military coup, which Suchinda carried out against the corrupt Chatichai government. The most popular recent Thai prime minister, Anand Panyarachun, was not elected and ruled out his participation in the electoral process. Only six years after Imelda Marcos and her husband's crony Eduardo Cojuangco fled the Philippines in ignominy, both obtained more votes combined in the May 1992 presidential election than Fidel Ramos, whose opposition to Marcos in 1986 tipped the balance in favor of people power.

One explanation of the contradictions in Asian attitudes is that popular pressures against East and Southeast Asian governments may not be so much for "human rights" or "democracy" but for good government: effective, efficient, and honest administrations able to provide security and basic needs with good opportunities for an improved standard of living. To be sure, good government, human rights, and democracy are overlapping concepts. Good

FOREIGN POLICY

government requires the protection of human dignity and accountability through periodic fair and free elections. But they are not always the same thing; it cannot be blithely assumed, as many in the West have, that more democracy and human rights will inevitably lead to good government, as the many lost opportunities of the Aquino government demonstrated. The apparent contradictions mirror a complex reality: Good government may well require, among other things, detention without trial to deal with military rebels or religious and other extremists; curbs on press freedoms to avoid fanning racial tensions or exacerbating social divisions; and draconian laws to break the power of entrenched interests in order to, for instance, establish land reforms.

Those are the realities of exercising authority in heterogeneous, unevenly modernized, and imperfectly integrated societies with large rural populations and shallow Western-style civic traditions. The competing Asian elites who today use human rights rhetoric to advance their causes may find good reason to retain and use such measures if ever they come to power and encounter the realities of governance. Espousing or claiming rights in the midst of political struggle does not mean they will or can be granted once the struggle is won. After all, their predecessors found it prudent to retain colonial laws that had been used against them and that they too denounced as contrary to human rights. Disagreements over human rights may therefore not be resolved even if the current generation of East and Southeast Asian leaders is replaced. The conviction that these countries are inevitably evolving toward Western-style democracy is unwarranted. Greater convergence with the West is possible, but a perfect fit is unlikely.

Room for Debate

For East and Southeast Asia, the challenge will be to devise credible, distinctive, and coherent positions within the parameters of international law on human rights. Most East and Southeast Asian governments sincerely want to protect and advance the human dignity of their citizens, even if they must do so within the constraints of their circumstances. Their good faith is less likely to be questioned if they accept the framework of the two U.N. human rights covenants. Those documents are flexible enough to accommodate a diversity of political institutions, cultures, and traditions. There is sufficient provision for reservation and derogation and room for further interpretation to ensure that special conditions are acknowledged and vital interests need not be compromised. Working within existing international law on human rights will also ameliorate what could otherwise be the overwhelming influence of the area's most powerful states, Japan and China, on the evolution of a regional position.

The challenge for the West is far more difficult because it requires wrenching psychological adjustments. The West must internalize the reality of diversity in all its dimensions and acknowledge that, notwithstanding the existence of a body of international law on human rights, many rights are still contested concepts where a consensus of meaning is coupled with equally important, and perhaps unresolvable, conflicts of interpretation. The West is no more or less special than any other region. It must recognize that the main influence on the development of human rights in East and Southeast Asia will be internal and difficult for the West to reach. Abrasive or ill-considered attempts to influence that dynamic are not only unlikely to succeed but could set back acceptance of human rights by arousing nationalistic responses. Progress will entail eschewing transcendent crusades or dramatic confrontations for patiently and quietly building consensus on modest, specific objectives through a still-evolving process of international lawmaking. The result will not always reflect Western preferences.

Future Western approaches on human rights will have to be formulated with greater nuance and precision. It makes a great deal of difference if the West insists on humane standards of behavior by vigorously protesting genocide, murder, torture, or slavery. Here there is a clear consensus on a core of international law that does not admit of derogation on any grounds. The West has a legitimate right and moral duty to promote those core human

FOREIGN POLICY

rights, even if it is tempered by limited influence. But if the West objects to, say, capital punishment, detention without trial, or curbs on press freedoms, it should recognize that it does so in a context where the international law is less definitive and more open to interpretation and where there is room for further elaboration through debate. The West will have to accept that no universal consensus may be possible and that states can legitimately agree to disagree without being guilty of sinister designs or bad faith. Trying to impose pet Western definitions of "freedom" and "democracy" is an incitement to destructive conflict, best foregone in the interest of promoting real human rights.

The international law on human rights provides a useful, relatively precise, and common framework for the human rights dialogue between West and East. It helps prevent "human rights" from becoming a mere catchphrase for whatever actions the West finds contrary to its preferences or too alien to comprehend. But the implementation, interpretation, and elaboration of the international law on human rights is unavoidably political. It must reflect changing global power structures and political circumstances. It will require the West to make complex political distinctions, perhaps refraining from taking a position on some human rights issues, irrespective of their merits, in order to press others where the prospects for consensus are better.

If, for example, the West protests the murder or "disappearance" of East Timorese, it is likely to get a hearing in Jakarta. The Suharto government would not dispute that such events are wrong, and it has in fact behaved very correctly, punishing the senior military officers responsible for the Dili tragedy. Similarly, the West can legitimately object to the torture or murder of Tibetans or point out defects in the administration of justice in China. If done with patience and finesse, there is some chance of improving conditions as China develops. But to demand independence for East Timor or Tibet is an entirely different matter. It is a fantasy to believe that any Indonesian or Chinese government would do anything but reject that outright, no matter what the West does. And it is not self-evident that the cause of human rights will really be advanced if China or Indonesia, both of which contain a diversity of ethnic groups, disintegrates under such centrifugal pressures, generating instabilities across the region. It is immoral for the West to give East Timorese or Tibetans false hope by encouraging wild dreams of self-determination. Better to help the East Timorese and Tibetans improve their lot within the existing system.

Unfortunately, it is not obvious that Western governments are free to adopt such hard-headed policies of political triage. It goes against the most deeply held Western notions of human rights: individualism, the idea that rights are held against the state, the primacy of civil and political rights, and universalism. It will be complicated by the temptation to use human rights to pursue other interests. And it raises difficult questions about the role of human rights NGOs in mobilizing public and media pressures on Western governments to take action. Precisely because they are advocacy organizations, NGOs must adopt a strident, adversarial stance; they are impatient of nuance; they must define issues in stark moral outline; and they are usually quick to dismiss interpretation and exception as self-serving. For them, to do otherwise is to risk diminishing their influence and lose public support in a maze of moral ambiguities and contradictions.

Yet it is only through such thickets of compromise, contradiction, and ambiguity that further progress on human rights can be made. Those in the West concerned about human rights in East and Southeast Asia, therefore, must be asked a simple question: Do you ultimately want to do good, or merely posture to make yourselves feel good?

[12]

Human Rights and Governance: The Asia Debate

Yash Ghai[*]

I. The International Context of Human Rights and Democracy

The history of human rights is ancient but its contemporary salience can be traced to the establishment of the United Nations and the proclamation by its General Assembly of the Universal Declaration of Human Rights in 1948. Since then the United Nations and related agencies have concluded a number of conventions to implement the provisions of the Universal Declaration by elaborating detailed formulations of specific rights and establishing some machinery for their supervision. Much of this work was done in committees of officials and did not, for the most part, attract much public attention. There were undoubtedly differences among groups of countries on the scope of particular rights, the priorities among them, and the extent of their enforceability. These were resolved within the committees and did not engage great public interest (even in the highly controversial instance of the right to development). However, in the last few years questions of human rights have achieved a high salience. This has revealed considerable differences among governments and intellectuals on the understanding, scope and importance of human rights.

There is broad agreement that a key purpose of society is to ensure the dignity of the human person. For many people, human dignity is to be secured through the protection of human rights. Others have different views on how to achieve this aim, but all would concede some role for human rights. However, there is no general agreement on the nature of human rights. The conception of

---

* Sir YK Pao Professor of Public Law, University of Hong Kong. This paper draws upon my two previous papers, "Asian Perspectives on Human Rights" (1992) and "Human Rights and Governance in Asia" (1994). The first paper was presented at a conference on Human Rights of Migrant Workers organised by the Scalabrini Migration Centre in Manila. It was also tabled at a workshop on Human Rights and Governance in Asia organised by the Asia Foundation in Manila in March 1993. The second paper was written at the request of the Asia Foundation as a record of my reflections on the discussions at the workshop. It was subsequently used as a background paper for an Asian Foundation sponsored dialogue on the same subject between Asia scholars and senior officers of the Clinton Administration and the United States Congress in Washington in June 1994. The present paper reflects also on the Washington discussions. I am grateful to the participants of all these meetings for their thoughtful and stimulating contributions. An earlier version of this paper appeared as an occaisional paper of the Asia Foundation. The author is grateful to the Hong Kong Research Grants Council for support of his work on human rights.

the basis of human rights has varied from time to time, and from place to place. For a long time in the West, the belief that rights were derived from a divine ordering held sway, but it gradually gave way to the notion that rights originated from and were a response to the very nature of man. In that sense they are inherent and inalienable. This secularisation of the source of human rights arose under certain social and economic conditions which are said to mark the rise of market economic systems and consequently to emphasis individualism. In one way, it could be argued that basing human rights on the nature of man (and these days we must concede, woman) should lay the foundations for a universal regime. Unfortunately, this has not been the consequence—for a variety of reasons, it would seem. At first the attacks came from those who believed that these rights, associated with the market, served merely to strengthen the dominance of one social class over others, and to result in the misery of the general public. It was also perceived that the "man" of the market system is acculturated in its peculiar values and dynamics, "disembodied" from the community. In societies where the dominance of the market over culture and community has not taken place or is incomplete, this view of human rights does not command universal acceptance. Similarly where the sway of religion or tradition is strong, the secular basis of human rights affects their acceptability, for which they must draw from the orientation of a particular religion or tradition. The difficulties of establishing political order and political authority in several regions of the world have also brought into question the utility of norms that detract from the power of the government.

Differences over perceptions and status of human rights are not new. After the somewhat uneasy consensus over the Universal Declaration of Human Rights, serious conflicts emerged which were responsible for protracted negotiations over the instruments that were to implement the Declaration as well as for the fact that a truce was possible only through the bifurcation of rights into civil and political on the one hand, and economic, cultural and social on the other—with separate Covenants for each. The West conceived of rights largely as political, while the socialist States provided the impetus for economic and social rights. At the heart of the controversy was the role of the market in the organisation of the economy and the distribution of resources. The interesting point about contemporary controversies about human rights is that all the major contestants are committed to the market (the opponents of the market get little hearing now). The basis of differences has changed—an aim of this Paper is to explore what that is.

These contemporary differences have been highlighted by the context in which human rights have now achieved salience. An important aspect of that context is the collapse of the communist regimes in Europe, which removed the Cold War agenda and introduced space for discussions of liberty and freedom. The West took the opportunity to develop another agenda centring around human rights and democracy. This interest coincided with the growth of highly visible international non-governmental organisations (NGOs) which assumed a major responsibility for the scrutiny of the record of individual countries on human rights. The link of human rights to democracy was established through the work of international aid agencies, particularly the World Bank and the United States Agency for International Development, which made "governance" a central feature of their development assistance. Good governance was largely equated with democratic institutions and practices (including transparency of policy-making and administration).

There are other aspects of the post-Cold War context which bear upon human rights. The collapse of the communist systems was attributed largely to the inefficiencies of command economies, and while a few years previously there was much talk of the crisis in capitalism, there was now a surge in the legitimacy of markets. Much effort has gone into the establishment of markets in Eastern Europe and formerly communist States in Asia; indeed a veritable and diverse profession has developed around this enterprise. In some respects these efforts represent an extension of privatisation and structural adjustment policies that had been adopted by or imposed on various States in Africa, Asia and Latin America, the effect of which was to diminish the economic role of the State. The marketisation of domestic economies was paralleled by the globalisation of capital, markets and services, as national barriers to investments and trade were removed (under pressure from world economic institutions). The thrust of globalisation came largely from the West, and served to increase its economic influence and hegemony over the rest of the world.[1] But it was presented, instead, principally in terms of the virtues of entrepreneurship, economic rationality and an efficient legal regime marked by security, predictability and transparency. The links of these developments to human rights were sought to be established through claims of increased choices for investors, consumers and workers, the restrictions on State power and the emergence or strengthening of civil society. So democracy, marketisation of economies, the promotion of human rights and the emergence of civil society were declared to be all of a piece.

The result of the approach of the West was to bring out clearly the implications of the human rights work steadily (and indeed sometimes obscurely, as with the Convention on the Rights of Migrants) developed through the United Nations and its agencies. It brought to the fore the responsibility of the international community for the protection of human rights everywhere, and thereby highlighted the ways in which national sovereignty has been qualified by the UN Charter and the human rights conventions. Relations between a State and its nationals were no longer a matter merely for that State; some fundamental norms of that relationship (enacted at an exponential rate, some claimed) were now defined in international law, and subject not only to the scrutiny of the international community but also to its sanctions. International relations themselves are increasingly mediated through human rights discourse and practice. Aid conditionalities, unthinkable a decade ago, have become

1 The globalisation of capital and markets should minimise rather than increase tensions between the West and the successful economies of East Asia. They enhance the interests and stakes of each side in the success of the other, and alliances are forged increasingly on transnational class lines than national. The international rhetoric of confrontation hides this emerging transnational identity.

common place. The legitimacy of international involvement was heightened not only by the moral authority of human rights and the collapse of political regimes associated in many minds with their denial, but also by the willingness of several countries to accept international assistance for establishing human rights and democracy (for example, Eastern Europe, Russia, Nepal, Cambodia, and South Africa) and considerable public support in many countries for such intervention in their own case. Further support for the emphasis on human rights and good governance was secured through arguments about their link to sustained economic and social development. However, not all governments have taken kindly to the internationalisation of human rights and democracy, although many of them are unable to carry their opposition to it to international fora because of their fragile political and economic systems and the dependence on external donors. Several Asian countries, particularly in South-East and East Asia, have offered a spirited rebuttal of this internationalisation.[2] They resent the interposition of the international community (and particularly the hegemony of particular countries within it) in their relations with their citizens, in an ever increasing number of areas. They also resent the leverage it has given these other countries (and international institutions) over their policies, and see the new approach as attempts to undermine their moral authority, disrupt their political stability, and retard their economic progress. Rather than, as in some other regions, withdraw from the debate, they have sought to provide an alternative framework for the discourse of human rights and democracy.[3]

Secure in the economic success of their policies which owe little to democracy or human rights, they contest the claims of the positive links between democracy (and human rights) and economic development. Another plank in their argument is that most of the rights which the West is purveying are "Western" in origin, oriented towards an individualistic society and therefore inappropriate to Asia where the values of communal action are highly prized. Furthermore, the priorities as between different human rights vary from country

---

2 In this paper I sometimes refer indiscriminately to "Asian governments". Clearly not all governments subscribe to views that I attribute to "governments". So that my position is not misunderstood, I should say that my paper does not deal with the Middle East. It is also useful to try to make distinctions as among clusters of Asian governments. Issues and politics in South Asia (India, Pakistan, Nepal, Sri Lanka and Bangladesh) are often different from that in East Asia (China, Japan, North and South Korea, Taiwan, and Vietnam). The former are more plural with specific parliamentary traditions underpinned by ethnic politics, while the latter are influenced by Confucianism and a measure of authoritarianism. But even this broad generalisation needs to be qualified. since Japan may be said to have shed authoritarianism some decades ago, while Singapore could be included for this classification with East Asia, and Malaysia with South Asia. See Richard Cullen, "Protecting Individual Rights: East Meets West" (mimeo, 1994).

The politicisation of the discourse of human rights, along the North-South divide, has nevertheless resulted in a certain closing of ranks, and the more vocal of the governments are able in regional and international meetings to muster a show of solidarity on the basis of their own doctrines, as was demonstrated in the pre-Vienna regional meeting in Bangkok in 1993.

3 Perhaps the most articulate statement of this position is Kausikan, "Asia's Different Standard" (1993) 92 *Foreign Policy* 24.

to country, and certainly in their own States, the priority must be given to economic and social rights. On a more doctrinal but basic level, they challenge the legitimacy of international involvement in human rights and national political systems on the argument that the fundamental principle of international law and relations is State sovereignty (to which belong these questions). They also accuse the West of hypocrisy, since it has long been engaged in violations of human rights, from slavery to colonialism, and the current decline of moral authority and public order in its own States.

The politicisation of human rights that has followed their internationalisation raises acute questions of theory and practice. What is the basis for international action on human rights? What justifies political and economic conditionalities? What abuses are inherent in conditionalities? How does one check these abuses, particularly those of "double standards" and "double speak"? Why should a State's competence to deal with its citizens be circumscribed by reference to human rights or governance? At the heart of this debate lies the nature of human rights and the source of their authority. Are human rights determined by the culture or economic development of a country, contingent on history, or do they represent universal values true for all time and places? Stemming from considerations of theory and strategies, are some rights more basic than others? How do civil and political issues relate to economic and cultural rights? Is there a sequence in the development and achievement of human rights? How do human rights, the rule of law, and democracy relate to each other? How are human rights and democracy linked to economic and social development? What is the role of civil society? These are in fact extraordinarily hard questions, to which political theory does not provide ready answers. Yet some resolution of these questions is essential to place current international debates within a more rational, objective and consensual framework. The Vienna World Conference on Human Rights failed to resolve these issues, despite a "consensus" document. Consensus was achieved by genuflections to a series of contradictory positions, rather than an engagement with and the reconciliation of issues that divided them. The politicised environment of human rights discourse is not particularly conducive to a productive discussion of these issues. It is important to recall that these issues pre-date the North-South divide; and for a long time have been the basis of great controversy in Western political and social thought.

II. Asian Perspectives on Human Rights

As a backdrop to an exploration of some of these issues, I review the principal perspectives on human rights in Asia. In contemporary debates, it is generally assumed that there is one Asian view of human rights, and that it is opposed to the traditions of individual human rights that first developed in the West. It is easy to believe that there is a distinct Asian approach to human rights because some government leaders speak as if they represent the whole continent when they make their pronouncements on human rights. This view is reinforced because they claim that their views are based on perspectives which emerge from the Asian culture or religion or Asian realities. The gist of their position is that human rights as propounded in the West are founded on individualism and therefore have no relevance to Asia which is based on the primacy of the community. It is also sometimes argued that economic underdevelopment renders most of the political and civil rights (emphasised in the West) irrelevant in Asia. Indeed, it is sometimes alleged that such rights are dangerous in view of fragmented nationalism and fragile Statehood.

It would be surprising if there were indeed one Asian perspective, since neither Asian culture nor Asian realities are homogenous throughout the continent. All the world's major religions are represented in Asia, and are in one place or another State religions (or enjoy a comparable status: Christianity in the Philippines, Islam in Malaysia, Hinduism in Nepal and Buddhism in Sri Lanka and Thailand). To this list we may add political ideologies like socialism, democracy or feudalism which animate peoples and governments of the region. Even apart from religious differences, there are other factors which have produced a rich diversity of cultures. A culture, moreover, is not static and many accounts given of Asian culture are probably true of an age long ago. Nor are the economic circumstances of all the Asian countries similar. Japan, Singapore and Hong Kong are among the world's most prosperous countries, while there is grinding poverty in Bangladesh, India and the Philippines. The economic and political systems in Asia likewise show a remarkable diversity, ranging from semi-feudal kingdoms in Kuwait and Saudi Arabia, through military dictatorships in Burma and formerly Cambodia, effectively one party regimes in Singapore and Indonesia, communist regimes in China and Vietnam, ambiguous democracies in Malaysia and Sri Lanka, to well established democracies like India. There are similarly differences in their economic systems, ranging from tribal subsistence economies in parts of Indonesia through highly developed market economies of Singapore, Hong Kong and Taiwan and the mixed economy model of India to the planned economies of China and Vietnam. Perceptions of human rights are undoubtedly reflective of these conditions, and suggest that they would vary from country to country.

The official view

Perceptions of human rights are reflective of social and class positions in society. What conveys an apparent picture of a uniform Asian perspective on human rights is that it is the perspective of a particular group, that of the ruling elites, which gets international attention. What unites these elites is their notion of governance and the expediency of their rule. For the most part, the political systems they represent are not open or democratic, and their publicly expressed views on human rights are an emanation of these systems, of the need to justify authoritarianism and occasional repression. It is their views which are given wide publicity domestically and internationally.

The unity of governments is more apparent than real. Although the Bangkok Declaration[4] was endorsed by all the Asian governments at the April 1993 Asian regional preparatory meeting for the Vienna World Conference on Human

4 The Declaration has been published in the (1993) 57(3) *Law and Society Trust Fortnightly Review* 1 (1 May 1993).

Rights, some of them have a firm commitment to human rights and their record is better than one might expect from their endorsement of the Declaration. India is one example. Along with some other States, it is committed to human rights by its constitutional instruments, has a strong and independent judiciary, and despite problems and setbacks tries hard to maintain human rights. Nor is their adherence to traditional values and rules absolute; the Indian Constitution prohibits many traditional and religious practices like the discriminatory and degrading treatment of lower castes and provides for an equal treatment of women with men.[5] The reason for presenting a united front is not unconnected with a perceived North-South confrontation (as is evident from the Bangkok Governmental Declaration, which stressed the need to avoid the application of "double standards" in the implementation of human rights and its "politicisation").[6] Asian governments feel that since the end of the Cold War, the West has focused its attention on what it perceives to be the "undemocratic" nature of Third World polities. In Africa and Latin America the concern with human rights is seen to be an instrument for the establishment or strengthening of the market, in an attempt to restrict the interventions of the State in economic relations. In Asia, however, the key economies are heavily market oriented, and for the most part are successful. Even China is now turning to the market, which is widely credited for China's economic success. So the emphasis on human rights is not necessary as a spur to the market (and indeed, as I explore later, the relationship between the market and human rights is problematic).

Some Asian governments consider that the Western pressure on them for an improvement in human rights is connected with the project of Western global hegemony. This is to be achieved partly through the universalisation of Western values and aspirations, and partly through the disorientation of Asian State and political systems (and the consequent negative effect on their burgeoning economies). They have fashioned their response accordingly.

I turn first to "official" views of human rights of a number of influential Asian countries (Singapore, China, Malaysia, Indonesia). These views have developed primarily in response to two contingencies: the imperatives of control, and confrontation with Western pretensions. They are therefore formulated somewhat defensively. It also means, because they arise in the context of an engagement and a debate with the West, that they are formulated in universalistic terms, in the usual discourse of human rights. Several ingredients constitute the official view I am discussing. One which flows directly from both the contingencies is the assertion of "domestic jurisdiction" over human rights. Human rights are encapsulated within State sovereignty; the national treatment of human rights is no concern of other States or the international community. Self-determination, a concept which has been used to advance claims of human rights, is regarded as irrelevant to independent States.

---

5 Indian Constitution, see articles 14 and 17, and the Directive Principles of State Policy (particularly articles 42, and 46) which set a wide agenda of social reform consisting largely of attacks on traditional values and practices.

6 Note 2 above, para 7. These differences dominated the World Conference on Human Rights in Vienna, June 1993.

In its "White Paper" *Human Rights in China* (1991), the Chinese Government stated that "Despite its international aspect, the issue of human rights falls by and large within the sovereignty of each state".[7] The Chinese delegation to the UN Commission on Human Rights at its meeting in February 1993 urged that the World Conference in Vienna should

> reiterate the principle of State sovereignty contained in the UN Charter and international law which is basis for the realisation of human rights. Only when the state sovereignty is fully respected can the implementation of human rights be really ensured.[8]

This is also pre-eminently the position of the other countries mentioned above.

Another element in the official view is the relativity of rights, determined by the economic, political and cultural circumstances of each country. The Bangkok Governmental Declaration "recognises that while human rights are universal in nature, they must be considered in the context of a dynamic and evolving process of international norm-setting, bearing in mind the significance of national and regional peculiarities and various historical, cultural and religious backgrounds".[9] This stance reflects the position in the Chinese White Paper which states that "the evolution of the situation in regard to human rights is circumscribed by the historical, social, economic and cultural conditions of various nations, and involves a process of historical development. Owing to tremendous differences in historical background, social system, cultural tradition and economic development, countries differ in their understanding and practice of human rights.[10] "The Chinese use this framework to establish the priority of social and economic rights in their country, and much of the Paper is taken up with an account of the ending of pre-Communist regime practices of feudalism and other forms of human exploitation and the steady progress since in nutrition, education, health, the position of women and the disabled. Other countries too have used the state of national economic development as explanations for the failure fully to guarantee the complete range of human rights ("to eat their fill and dress warmly were the fundamental demands of the Chinese people who had long suffered cold and hunger").[11]

There are two major implications of this relativist position on human rights. The first relates to the conditions for political stability, and the other to the primacy of economic development. The implications of the first represent restrictions on civil and political rights. A forthright statement of this position is to be found in pronouncements of the Singapore Government following the detention of various social workers and activists in May 1987. I quote here from one such statement (dated 24 June 1987, and addressed by the then Minister for

---

7 *Human Rights in China* (1991). The Paper was published by the State Council to refute the charges of human rights violations in China. The quotation occurs ibid, p 11.

8 Statement by Mr Zhang Yishan, UN Doc E/CN. 4/1993/ SR 25, p 2 (17 Febuary 1993).

9 Note 7 above, para 8 at n 1.

10 Ibid, p 2 at n 2.

11 Ibid, pp 4–5 at n 5.

Home Affairs, Mr Jayakumar, to United States Congressmen who had written to complain about the detentions). It contrasted the "resilience and cohesiveness" and shared values of the nation of the United States (which presumably makes possible the tolerance of human rights) to the fragility and heterogeneity of Singapore.

> We are vulnerable to powerful centrifugal forces and volatile emotional tides. Like many other developing countries, Singapore's major problem of nationhood is simply to stay united as one viable nation. ...In our short history, Singapore has repeatedly encountered subversive threats from within and without. ...To combat these threats to the nation, the usual procedures of court trials, which apply in Singapore to most criminal cases, have proved totally inadequate. The very secrecy of covert operations precludes garnering evidence to meet the standards of the criminal law for conviction. In many cases of racial agitation, the process of trial itself will provide further opportunity for inflammatory rabble rousing. ...Singapore cannot be ruled in any other way...Preventive detention is not a blemish marring our record; it is a necessary power underpinning our freedom.

(Another aspect of the Singapore by-passing the formal legal system, with its guarantees of openness and fairness, not discussed in the Minister's statement, is the taped and doctored "confessions" extracted from the detainees under coercion, and then shown on the national television as proof of guilt and calculated to destroy their credibility and dignity.) These remarks were directed at a justification of administrative powers of detention without any kind of trial, but similar arguments have been used to justify other curtailments of civil rights, like the right to associate and assemble, of peaceful marches, of speech and expression. The Chinese Paper says that the people's right to subsistence will be threatened in the event of social turmoil or other disasters, and that it is the fundamental wish and demand of the Chinese people and a long-term, urgent task of the Chinese Government to maintain national stability and concentrate their efforts on developing productive forces.[12]

The economic backwardness of Asia has been used to establish the primacy of economic development over human rights. The argument is, in part, that civil and political rights are neither meaningful nor feasible in conditions of want or poverty. Therefore the first priority of State policy must be to promote economic development. It is implied that economic development may well require restrictions on human rights, both to provide a secure political framework in which it can be pursued and to remove obstacles in its way (for example, through forced movement of people from lands required for "development"). Economic backwardness is also used to establish the priority as between different kinds of rights, in which civil and political rights occupy a lowly position (in part a response to an argument that human rights are indivisible, and all of them enjoy an equal status).

---

12 Ibid, p 8. There is of course no easy way to find out what the people of China want since there are no truly representative bodies or a free press—a point I return to later to establish the link between political rights and social rights.

The emphasis these governments purportedly place on economic development has led them to support the right to development. This right is a matter of considerable contention internationally, with developing countries arraigned on the side supporting it, and most developed countries united in their opposition to it. It certainly does not have the quality of other kinds of rights, which inhere in individuals or groups and for the most part are entitlements against the State. Nevertheless, the General Assembly of the United Nations adopted, in the face of abstentions by most Western States, a Declaration on the Right to Development on 4 December 1986.[13] The Declaration ties the realisation of human rights in the developing countries to international economic aid for them and gives to "peoples" (presumably meaning "States") the right to "participate in, contribute to, and enjoy economic, social, cultural and political development, in which all human rights and fundamental freedoms can be fully realised". In return for these, several concessions are made in emphasising the indivisibility of rights and the claims of individuals to full participation in development and in the fair distribution of the benefits resulting from it.

The Declaration is a fuzzy document, trying to be all things to all persons. So while there are sections of it which can be used to advance the (more traditional) cause of human rights, the gist of it seeks to establish reason for the failure of the realisation of human rights in the international economic and political systems (including encroachments on the principle and practice of self-determination), while affirming that the primary responsibility for human rights are vested in States as part of their sovereignty. In other words, the rich countries must provide economic assistance to the poor countries, but must not question their human rights situation. (The Western riposte to the Declaration has been a massive imposition of political conditionalities on economic assistance and indeed, in the case of China, on economic relations and cooperation).

The Declaration is also an attempt to provide an alternative framework for the international discourse on human rights. It shifts the focus from domestic arenas (where most violations of human rights take place) to the international, and takes attention away from specific rights, for example, speech, assembly, social welfare to an ambiguous portmanteau right of development, for which in the nature of Third World affairs, the State must take the responsibility in defining and implementing it. Through the Declaration, Asian governments seek to promote the ideology of developmentalism which justifies repression at home and the evasion of responsibility abroad.

Another Asian initiative in changing the framework for the discourse on human rights is even more fundamental. The approaches discussed so far have taken the Western discourse as the main framework and have advanced qualifications to it or provided justifications for derogation from its values. Some governments have put forward the argument that the cultural matrix,

---

13 The Declaration is reprinted in, United Nations, *Human Rights: A Compilation of International Human Rights Instruments*, vol 1 (1994), p 548. I have criticised the Declaration in Ghai, *Whose Human Right to Development?* (1989).

within which relations between individuals and the State are embedded, is fundamentally different in Asia from that in the West. This matrix governs the nature and salience of human rights. This approach has been taken up aggressively in Singapore and Malaysia (less so in China, where the government's residual loyalty to Marxist thought is inconsistent with the adoption of this cultural approach, especially since so much of it is based on semi-feudal thought in Asia).[14]

I take as the basis of my discussion of this point an official 1991 statement of the Government of Singapore, *Shared Values*.[15] The context of this White Paper is a concern of the Government that the cultural values of its people are under attack from foreign ideas and values. It poses the rhetorical question, "Can we build a nation of Singaporeans, in South-East Asia, on the basis of values and concepts native to other peoples, living in other environments?" It goes on, "If we are not to lose our bearings, we should preserve the cultural heritage of each of our communities, and uphold certain common values which capture the essence of being a Singaporean".[16] It then finds certain perceptions and values which are common to the different ethnic communities of Singapore and which also distinguish them from society in the West. The key section of the Paper is devoted to a discussion of the relationship between the individual and society. Disputing the proposition that values are universal and common to all mankind, it states that there is a major difference between Asian and Western values in the balance each strikes between the individual and the community; Asian societies emphasise the interests of the community, while Western societies stress the rights of the individual. The Singapore society has always weighted group interests more heavily than individual ones. "This balance has strengthened social cohesion, and enabled Singaporeans to pull together to surmount difficult challenges collectively, more successfully than other societies. An emphasis on the community has been a key survival value for Singapore".[17] The core values of the Asian society are identified as placing society above self, upholding the family as building block of society, and resolving major issues through consensus instead of contention. There is a strong element of Confucianism in this elaboration, although the Government denies that the values it propagates are purely Confucian. It, however, picks up an element of Confucian teaching as particularly relevant to Singapore. "The concept of government by honourable men (*junzi*), who have a duty to do right for the people, and who have the trust and respect of the population, fits us better than the Western idea that a government should be given as limited powers as possible, and should always be treated with suspicion unless proven

---

14 This sentence was written in 1993. As I revise it, today's *People's Daily*, 19 September 1994, (Beijing) starts the rehabilitation of Confucius, in several articles extolling the virtues of Confucianism as an aid to political stability and economic development.

15 Singapore Government, *Shared Values*, Cmd 1 of 1991 (Government Printers).

16 Both these quotations appear at ibid, p 1, and are taken from a presidential address to Parliament, January 1989.

17 Ibid, p 5 at para 26.

otherwise".[18] The supremacy of political authorities is emphasised by the first of the Shared Values, "Nation before Community". Another aspect of Asian values, implicit though not explicit in the Paper, is the importance of duty as a counterpoint to right. The cohesion of society as well as the fulfilment of the individual is secured through a chain and hierarchy of duties. (The primacy of the notion of duty is emphasised elaborately both in the Chinese and Indian Constitutions.)[19]

The individual does not disappear altogether as a bearer of rights in the Singapore Paper. However, characteristically the concern with the individual is expressed more in terms of the obligations of the community to look after its less advantaged members. (In Singapore there is a twist to this, in that the "community" in question is the ethnic community of the individual, not the State, "to avoid the dependent mentality and severe social problems of a welfare state as experienced in many developed states",[20] laying the foundations of a kind of community corporatism in the wake of declining popularity of the ruling party, showing how much these questions are viewed in that country from the perspectives of governance and management).

Cultural "embededdiness" is not the only justification for this view of the relationship between the individual and the community and the interposition of the family. It is said to be also rooted in more pragmatic considerations. The White Paper hints at this, but it has been developed elsewhere. In at least South-East Asia, there is a strongly held view that an authoritarian political system is the secret of its economic success, and the frequent Singaporean mocking of the democratic efforts of the Philippines (with a rather inefficient economy) is advanced as proof of it. But there is also the belief that it is not the individual but the family (tied into a network of clan associations and relationships) which has been at the forefront of the phenomenal economic success of the region. There appears to be the view of a significant number of people (primarily but

---

18 Ibid, p 8 at para 41.

19 Chapter 2 of the Chinese Constitution is entitled "The Fundamental Rights and Duties of Citizens". Article 42 states that Chinese citizens have the right as well as the duty to work and article 46 says that they have the duty as well as the right to receive education. Other duties include safeguarding the "unification of the country and the unity of all its nationalities" (article 52); abiding by the Constitution and the law, keeping of State secrets, protection of public property, observing labour discipline and public order, and respecting social ethics (article 53); safeguarding the security, honour and interests of the motherland and a prohibition against acts detrimental to the security, honour and interests of the mother land (article 54); and to pay taxes (article 56). Article 55 states "the sacred duty of every citizen of the People's Republic of China to defend the motherland and to resist aggression" as well as to "perform military service and join the militia in accordance with the law".

The Indian Constitution requires citizens, *inter alia*, to abide by the Constitution, protect the sovereignty, unity and integrity of India, to promote harmony and the spirit of common brotherhood amongst all the people of India, and to renounce practices derogatory to the dignity of women, and to safeguard public property and abjure violence (article 51-A).

20 Ibid, p 7 at para 38.

not only, among the business community as is well evidenced in the debates in Hong Kong) that this combination of authoritarian rule and family and kinship networks lies at the root of economic success.[21] This model (which reverses the normal understanding of the relationship between the market, individualism and the rule of law) is seen to be threatened by democracy and human rights. Hence democracy and human rights are not high on many people's agenda.

Other voices

There are other Asian voices as well. There are, admittedly somewhat muted or censored, the voices of the oppressed and the marginalised. There are the passionate voices of indigenous peoples whose cultures are destroyed by governments which claim to be the custodians of Asian cultures; they speak in a language which finds few resonances even in the West (because their language is threatening to the system of the market). There is the voice, rising in density, of the middle classes, with a stake in affluence whose new found prosperity and economic enterprise shows to them the virtues of the legal protection of property and the rule of law. There are the strident voices of ethnic minorities who seek collective autonomies which challenge the governments' claims of political monopoly and State sovereignty. An important and articulate group are intellectuals who are alienated from the State, and for the most part are not apologists for the regime. Intellectuals respond to and engage in international debates; and like the NGOs they form networks with their counterparts in other parts of the world.[22] Like the NGOs they have a commitment to human rights and democracy (even in China there is a growing and vibrant academic community with a keen interest in human rights and constitutionalism).[23] They are less ready to accept Western conceptions in totality, and attempt to relate questions of human rights to specific national conditions.

I have space only to discuss the views of the NGOs which provide the most consistent and coherent alternative view of human rights to that of governments. An authoritative statement of the position of Asian NGOs was issued on 27 March 1993 on the occasion of the Asian intergovernmental conference on human rights preceding the Vienna World Conference.[24] It endorsed the view that human rights are universal, and are equally rooted in different cultures. While it supported cultural pluralism, it condemned those cultural practices which derogate from universally accepted human rights. Since in its view human

---

21 I have reviewed this literature (and examined its implications for the centrality or otherwise of the rule of law) in "Capitalism and the Rule of Law: Reflections on the Basic Law" in Wacks RI (ed), *Legal Theory: China, Hong Kong and 1997* (1993), p 343.

22 For a view of leading Indian intellectuals see Baxi, "The Right to be Human" (1986) 13(3) *India International Centre Quarterly*; Kothari S and Sethi H (eds), *Rethinking Human Rights: Challenges for Theory and Action* (1989); Baxi U, *Inhuman Wrongs and Human Rights* (1994), p 123.

23 For a succinct summary see Chen, "Developing Theories of Rights and Human Rights in China" in Wacks RI (ed), *Hong Kong, China and 1997: Essays in Legal Theory* (1993).

24 Note 4 above.

rights are of universal concern and universal value, it does not regard the advocacy of human rights as an encroachment upon national sovereignty. Indeed it recommends international cooperation and solidarity for the promotion of human rights, as a refutation of claims of national sovereignty over human rights issues. The NGOs signatories of the statement support the principle of the indivisibility and interdependence of human rights.

If in these perspectives the views of the NGOs are at variance with those of governments, there is some common ground on other points. The NGOs attribute the poor state of human rights to the international economic order, whose reform through structural changes as well as the adoption of a Convention on the Right to Development, they urge. Unlike the governments, they see a much closer connection with domestic oppression and international exploitation, in the collaboration of local economic and political elites with multinational corporations and aid agencies. Unlike the governments, they are critical of the consequences of the market system. They share with governments the desire to establish a broad framework for the analysis of human rights, but their framework (unlike that of governments which is informed by a statist view of development) is suffused with notions of social justice, eradication of poverty through equitable distribution of resources and the empowerment of people, especially women and other disadvantaged communities. The NGOs also part company from governments in their assessment of the state of human rights, which they find marked by massive and terrible violations of these rights and pervasive lawlessness on the part of State authorities. They deplore the militarisation of their governments and societies which is a primary cause of these violations. Their prescription for the ills of their countries is thorough going democracy and an unambiguous recognition and enforcement of human rights

III. A Critique of Governmental Perspectives

Asian governments are right to insist that human rights must be located within the social and economic conditions of specific societies. So called universal human rights of the West have evolved over a long period of European history, responding to the changing configurations of power and the tasks of each epoch of history. Claims of universality and indivisibility of rights are hard to sustain in the face of the West's history of the oppression of its own people and of others, with slavery which once enjoyed religious approbation, abuse of child labour, the exploitation of colonies and the other depredations of imperialism and racism. Nor is the process of the development of rights complete. Social welfare rights were acknowledged only in this century, and the appalling degradation of the environment has now set the stage for a new conception of rights and responsibilities, in which the community will have to be accorded a key position as a bearer of rights as well as duties. There is no reason why contemporary concerns and fads in the West should define the parameters of international discourse in, and aspirations, of human rights.

That is, however, not to say that the framework adopted by Asian governments is justifiable. I start with one element of that framework, religion, which has played a less important part in East Asia than in South and West Asia, but which is nevertheless supposed to give a uniform and distinctive character to Asian perspectives on human rights (although the invocation of religion is somewhat ambiguous since it is also argued that all religions are based on essentially the same values, and provide a common foundation for the primacy of human rights).

Religion

An immediate difficulty facing an exploration of the question whether a distinctive Asian perspective on human rights emerges from the religion of its people is that there are numerous religions in Asia, including all the world's major ones. Assuming that religion does indeed influence a people's perception of human rights, then one would have to concede that there would be a plurality of perspectives, not one. Even if we concede that for our inquiry what matters are "Asian" religions (Hinduism, Islam and Buddhism plus the influential set of beliefs represented by Confucianism), as reflecting more accurately Asian pre-dispositions, they too vary in their beliefs and values. Nor does the same religion manifest itself uniformly in its discourse about human rights at all times and in all countries. Buddhism is militant and aggressive in Sri Lanka, asserting ethnic and religious superiority of one section of the population, while elsewhere, as in Cambodia, it has been a force for peace and the protection of the rights of all communities. Hinduism was once seen as tolerant and non-proselytising, providing a constitutional basis for secularism in India; today many of its adherents are militant and attack beliefs and institutions of other religions. The Hinduism of Nepal is more syncretised than of modern India, able to co-exist and even assimilate with other religions. In many East Asian countries, all religions seem to be mediated through Confucian thought and values, detracting from the specificity of the religion.

In many places religion takes its coloration from politics, woven into the apparatus of the State or claiming a special eminence in its affairs. While Western States separated State and religion (whatever the influence of religion on human rights), the contemporary tendency in many parts of Asia (particularly South Asia) is to connect religion with State. In some instances this has served to diminish the scope for human rights. Sometimes religion acts as a conservative force, at other times it is a major factor for change (and the same religion can play these opposite roles if we compare Christianity in Latin America with that in Europe).[25]

---

25 A strategic question is how far one should use religion to legitimise rights. Religions can lend themselves to alternative propositions. Texts of most religions can be mined for contradictory interpretations. In the circumstances, is it best to separate the discourse of human rights from religion? One answer is no, on the assumption that since Asian people rely on religion for spiritual sustenance and sometimes political authority, rights should be anchored in religion. This may also counter the argument that human rights are foreign constructs by providing an autochthonous base for them in Asian beliefs and values.

As to whether religions can provide a basis for a universal or pan-Asian regime of rights, it is always hard to say what the essence of a particular religion is, but it would seem that different values are enshrined in different religions. Some like Hinduism have sanctified social and caste distinctions, and others like Confucianism, established a social and political hierarchy. Nor is equality the hallmark of Islam, for despite its ideals, its practices cleaved to a tribal and unequal society of its origin. Christianity justified slavery for centuries, and Christian-based Western political systems did not accommodate the equal rights of blacks and women until this century. Not all Asian States (including the largest of them) encourage the holding or the exercise of religious beliefs (preferring, as in China, to base the source of rights in popular sovereignty). Religions would not appear, therefore, to hold the key to universalism. Indeed most religions in some sense deny the claims of equality: traditionally, Hindus found people of other religion polluting, and most other religions have a notion of the "non-believer" to whom an inferior status is accorded in both religious and secular systems. Nor does religion provide a basis for a distinctive Asian perspective on human rights.

Culture

If an interest in religion is frequently motivated by the wish to find common roots for human rights, culture is explored to explain diversity and specificity. As noted above, some Asian governments claim that their societies place a higher value on the community than in the West, that individuals find fulfilment in their participation in communal life and community tasks, and that this factor constitutes a primary distinction in the approach to human rights. The Western pre-occupation with individualism is explained by the alienation resulting from its economic system which has sapped the vitality of the community, and forced introspection on individuals as a means towards their identity. This argument is advanced as an instance of the general proposition that rights are culture specific.

The "communitarian" argument is Janus-faced. It is used against the claim of universal human rights to distinguish the allegedly Western, individual-oriented approaches to rights from the community centred values of the East. Yet it is also used to deny the claims and assertions of communities in the name of "national unity and stability". It suffers from at least two further weaknesses. First, it overstates the "individualism" of Western society and traditions of thought. Even within Western liberalism, there are strands of analysis which assert claims of the community (for example, Rousseau); and most Western human rights instruments allow limitations on and derogations from human rights in the public interest, or for reasons of State. Western courts regularly engage in the task of balancing the respective interests of the individual and the community.[26] Within liberal societies there are nuances in the approach to and the primacy of human rights, as becomes evident when one examines the differences among the United States, Canada, France and the United Kingdom.

26 See for example, Kymlicka W, *Liberalism, Community, and Culture* (1989).

Furthermore, liberalism does not exhaust Western political thought or practice. There is social democracy, which emphasises collective and economic rights, and Marxism, which elevates the community to a high moral order, is also reflective of an important school of Western thought. There is much celebration in Western political thought of "civil society".[27]

Secondly, Asian governments (notwithstanding the attempt in the Singapore Paper to distinguish the "nation" and the community) fall into the easy but wrong assumption that they or the State are the "community".[28] (A similar conflation occurs in the African Charter of Human and Peoples' Rights.)[29] Nothing can be more destructive of the community than this conflation. The community and State are different institutions and to some extent in a contrary juxtaposition. The community, for the most part, depends on popular norms developed through forms of consensus and enforced through mediation and persuasion. The State is an imposition on society, and unless humanised and democratised (as it has not been in most of Asia), it relies on edicts, the military, coercion and sanctions. It is the tension between them which has elsewhere underpinned human rights. In the name of the community, most Asian governments have stifled social and political initiatives of private groups. Most of them have draconian legislation along the lines of the British colonially inspired Societies Act[30] which gives the government pervasive control over civil society. Similarly rights to assemble and march peacefully have been mortgaged to the government. Governments have destroyed many communities in the name of development or State stability, and the consistent refusal of most of them to recognise that there are indigenous peoples among their population (who have a right to preserve their traditional culture, economy and beliefs) is but a demonstration of their lack of commitment to the real community. The vitality of the community comes from the exercise of the rights to organise, meet, debate and protest, dismissed as "liberal" rights by these governments.

---

27 See Cohen J and Arato A, *Civil Society and Political Theory* (1992).

28 Although, as I argue that the lip service to the "community" is hypocritical, the real "community" which motivates politicians is parochial and clannish, pursuing its selfish interest at the expense of other communities, and is the basis of public corruption and graft—and therefore nothing to be proud of. An interesting light on "community" occurred in Hong Kong in April 1994, when two shoppers beat up a shop assistant, while her colleagues watched but did nothing to defend her. However, she bore no grudge against them saying, "Even though I have known them for a long time what difference does it make? You cannot expect someone to help you. I am not their relative". (*Eastern Express*, 11–12 June 1994).

See Siu-kai Lau, "Utilitarianistic Familism: The Basis of Political Stability" in King A and Lee R (eds), *Social Life and Development in Hong Kong* (1981).

29 The African Charter was adopted in Nairobi in June 1981. Its preamble refers to the "values of their historical tradition and the values of African civilisation which should inspire and characterise their reflection on the concept of human rights and peoples' rights".

30 Typically such legislation provides that a society has to be registered before it can operate. The government has the discretion to refuse to register a society and to de-register it. It has the power to seek information from the society about its membership, finances and other affairs, and to control or prohibit political links with outside bodies.

Nor is the tight regulation of society as in China and Singapore particularly Confucian. Confucius argued against reliance on law or coercion, and advocated a government of limited powers and functions.[31]

Another attack on the community comes from the economic, market oriented policies of the governments. Although Asian capitalism appears to rely on the family and clan associations, there is little doubt that it weakens the community and its cohesion. The organising matrix of the market is not the same as that of the community. Nor are its values or methods particularly "communitarian". The moving frontier of the market, seeking new resources, has been particularly disruptive of communities which have managed to preserve intact a great deal of their culture and organisation during the colonial and post-colonial periods. The emphasis on the market, and with it individual rights of property are also at odds with communal organisation and enjoyment of property (and a further irony is that Asian leaders who allege their allegiance to communal supremacy and values are among the most ardent opponents of a Marxism that espouses the moral worth and authority of the community). Market policies have relied greatly on multi-national capital and corporations, which have brought new values and tastes, and are increasingly integrating their economies and elites into a global economy and culture. Indeed, it is these very considerations which prompted the Singapore White Paper, but the contradictions of official policies largely escaped its authors. It totally ignored the impact, indeed the onslaught, of modern technologies on traditional communities.

A final point is the contradiction between claims of a consensus and harmonious society, and the extensive arming of the state apparatus. The pervasive use of draconian legislation like administrative detention, disestablishment of societies, press censorship, and sedition, belies claims to respect alternative views, promote a dialogue, and seek consensus. The contemporary State intolerance of opposition is inconsistent with traditional communal values and processes. Contemporary State processes in Asia are less hospitable to community politics than the much derided adversarial processes of the West, which at least ensure a hearing for all parties.

Thoughtful Asians, who concede many of the above criticisms of a "communitarian" approach, nevertheless hold on to some important distinctions between the West and Asia, which they consider are rooted in culture. There is first the distinction between duties and rights. An aspect of this is the tendency in the West towards formalism, the transformation of values as legal rights, and the consequent emphasis on the rights and prerogatives of an individual. Based on a theory of competition and suspicion of authority, this leads to demands rather than concessions, to confrontation rather than reciprocity and accommodation. An emphasis on duties on the other hand leads to honour and

31 As with religion, Confucianism has been used for political purposes so that its essence has become somewhat obscure. It is undisputed, however, that Confucius was against tough laws and strong punishments, believing in the virtue of rulers and their sense of duty. See Rubin V, *Individual and State in Ancient China* (1976), and Van der Sprenkel S, *Legal Institutions in Manchu China* (1962), esp Chapters 2 and 3.

peace, as well as stability. It is argued that the rights-based emphasis leads to the impoverishment of society, so that in the search for the protection of the citizen against the State, the community collapses and non-State actors become the principal source of oppression and insecurity (making it unsafe to be on the streets of major metropolises after sunset). There is also the danger in formalisation of values as "rights" that the form may elude substance (so that the satisfaction of formal criteria hides realities that deny the values; as Professor Mazrui once said, the West may have abolished child marriages, but the number of teenage pregnancies and one parent families has vastly increased).

However, in the hands of an intolerant government, the concept of duties can become a justification as well as an instrument of authoritarianism. This is perhaps not inherent in the notion of duties because duties are also laid upon rulers (in the best Islamic and Confucian traditions), and indeed the notion of duty can be truly revolutionary. In practice, however, this is not how it often is, duties vary from person to person (persons at the top of the hierarchy having rights and those at the lower reaches, duties), reminiscent of feudalism. The emphasis on the fulfilment of duties, frequently betokening social, economic or political subordination, tends towards conservatism and the perpetuation of inequalities—antithetical to the claims of equitable development advanced by many Asian governments. Furthermore, the conflation between the State and community serves to strengthen the tentacles of the government over society. The notion of duties transferred from the community to the State changes its nature from inter-citizen obligations and responsibilities to the much more problematic case of State-citizen relations. The West has, to some extent, separated civil society from the State, creating a "neutral" public area and space for communities (from which of course the commanding heights of the State may be controlled), while in Asia the tendency is towards the convergence of the two, regarded perhaps as necessary for the legitimacy of the State[32] but ultimately destructive of the community.

Even if we were to concede that Asian cultures or religions are distinctive and that these colour the perception and reality of rights, it is not clear why the global debate has taken the opposition of political and civil rights ("Western") versus economic and social rights ("Asian"). Why should the communitarian approach suggest that economic and social rights are more important than political? It may be argued that traditionally, communities were hierarchically organised and that its cohesion depended on duties. But the communities were even less concerned with "development" which is undoubtedly more of a foreign concept than fair or accountable administration or harmony within the community. If human rights do not follow from Asian cultures, then neither does economic development. The same can be said of "Asian" religions, which are stereotyped as other worldly (like most religions), more concerned with

---

32 The argument here is that in non-Western States, legitimacy does not come from the rule of law, constitutionalism and the neutrality of State institutions, but from their association with religion and culture—which in the mostly heterogenous States, means the culture and religion of the majority community. See for example, Tiruchelvam, "Development and the Protection of Human Rights" (mimeo. 1993).

salvation in the next world than economic prosperity in this. Ethics are more important than power, and asceticism and austerity are values approved by most of these religions. Apart from the somewhat ambiguous position of Confucianism (which is mistakenly today regarded as development oriented rather than as preserving the status quo as traditionally regarded), there is little in "Asian" religions to support a privileged position for economic development. It is interesting that the most influential Christian church in Asia is Catholicism rather than the Weberian, development driven Calvinism or a variant of it! Asian governments are therefore on shaky ground when they invoke tradition to justify the primacy of development. If economic rights are seen to flow from "communal" or "collective rights" there is a misapprehension, for these rights are normally attributed to individuals, not groups (collective rights being associated with "solidarity" rights to a clean environment, property as commons, and a measure of equity, which are anathema to at least some Asian prime ministers).

If there is no substantial basis in community, culture or religion for economic and social rights, then why do Asian governments place such rhetorical emphasis on them? They sometimes say that civil and political rights are meaningless if the people are poor and illiterate. There is of course considerable truth in this, but there is reason to be sceptical about the sincerity of the governments for they have done little to establish economic rights or promote civil rights in countries which have achieved great economic success. The more plausible reason is that the talk of economic and social rights is diversionary, an attack on civil and political rights. Governments are anxious to minimise challenges to their authority or legitimacy, which means (as it seems to them) the suppression or emasculation of political opposition. A preference for economic rights might also arise from the consideration that it is much harder to hold governments accountable for them. They are for the most part, matters more of standards than precise rules and entitlements, their enforceability is problematic and they are widely regarded as contingent on resources. In fact these governments dislike talk of economic and social rights, except when engaged in global debates (many of them do not like talk of any rights). It is not easy to establish how civil and political rights threaten economic and social rights. The juxtaposition these governments play upon domestically is not between these different rights, but between civil and political rights and *economic development*. It is economic development, not economic rights, that they emphasis. They are, however, content to seek economic rights of *States*, the so-called developing States (as in their advocacy of the right to development). It is of course easy to understand why governments want economic development; it increases State resources, enables governments to establish larger armies, enhances the status of their leaders, and secures the support of the populace.

I conclude this section by reference to another distinction that is seen to flow from cultural differences—the role of the family (as that suggests an appropriate approach to study of human rights). It is frequently said that the bedrock of Asian societies is the family, and it has become fashionable to ascribe social problems in the West to the breakdown of family life. It is claimed for Asia that mutual responsibilities within the family provide for the welfare of its members, ensure traditions of respect and rectitude, and promote social stability and economic development. The conversion of values into individual rights undermines the basis of family solidarity. However, countries which are not known for their practice of individual rights have found that the family may well be weakening under the pressure of other social and economic changes. A particular irony is that a legislator in Singapore, known to enjoy government support, recently introduced a bill to give parents the right to sue their children for maintenance (and the children the defence that the parents mistreated them when they were young!). It is hard to imagine that such a bill would achieve its objective of maintaining family solidarity!

The concern with the erosion of family values is instructive in a number of ways. At one level, it minimises the Asian claim for cultural distinctiveness and therefore relativity of rights. At another level, it provides another basis for relativity. Societies are constantly changing, and with economic and social changes, there are also changes in the perception of what is important and valuable to a community or a group. In other words, an assessment of the priorities in human rights alters with the underlying economic transformations. The West too has had its "communitarian" phase (and the community is still important there) and the family is even now cherished, even if old solidarities are beginning to dissolve under economic pressures. Asian governments which cheerfully and sometimes aggressively espouse "Western" notions of development and the market, find that they can no longer ward off its child, human rights.

The above analysis suggests that a useful perspective on human rights is drawn from history: the (dialectical) unfolding of rights, and representing social achievements. This in turn suggests that the development and understandings of rights are contingent on a variety of factors, moral ideas as well as material conditions, and that differences in their perception are attributable to them rather than to any inherent ideas of culture or community. This approach does indeed provide a basis for reconciling so called "Western" and "Eastern" perceptions of human rights. In my view this provides a better basis for global debates on this subject. The notion that distinct "Western" and "Asian' perspectives exist is inaccurate, ahistorical, and leads to unfruitful polarities (ignoring, for example, that the West also has a notion of duty (limitations on rights/freedoms)). Equally it distorts the debates on human rights, by suggesting that the key conflict is between the East and the West, rather than that it is within each. It detracts from the relevance and urgency of human rights discourse in Asia, the keen debates on the appropriate models for representation, governance and accountability, and equity. Asian intellectuals and activists need to rescue the debate from the present sterile phase to place it at the centre of national and regional politics.

If human rights have to be located in their social and economic contexts, what are the appropriate features that constitute the context for them in Asia? If one may generalise (keeping in mind the simplification that this may involve), the following specifics of the Asian situation stand out. The first point is that the function of human rights (and discourse on them) in Asia is quite different from that in the West. Human rights in the West have responded to the configurations of power and economic relationships as they have evolved over a long period. They are consequently consistent with the patterns and structures of authority, and people's aspirations as well as expectations. There are no serious competing paradigms of political organisation. The role of human rights is to fine tune the administrative and judicial system and fortify rights and freedoms that are largely uncontroversial. In Asia, on the other hand, human rights have a transformative potential. They are a constant challenge to vested interests and authority in societies riven by enormous disparities of wealth and power, with traditions of authoritarianism and the helplessness of disadvantaged communities, of militarisation and the conjunction of corrupt politicians and predatory domestic and international capital. Human rights are therefore a terrain for struggle for power and the conceptions of good society. It is for this precise reason that Asian governments have engaged in the debate with the West; the real audience are their own people.

The second point is that there are massive violations of human rights in Asia, of the rights of women and children, of lower castes and otherwise disadvantaged communities, of ethnic minorities, and of workers. Violations range over the whole conspectus of human rights; civil and political rights, as well as cultural, social and economic; there are mass killings and widespread disappearances; torture; wide displacements of communities from their traditional abode; arbitrary detentions and extensive censorship of thought and expression. The State is a major culprit, brutalising whole populations, but massive violations also take place in and through civil society, sometimes with the connivance of the State, and frequently reflecting feudalistic and patriarchal dimensions of culture. Social conflicts, particularly those stemming from ethnic or caste differences, have politicised and militarised civil society in many States. These developments should caution us against over-romanticisation of civil society (which in India, for example, is a major source of the oppression of millions of people, through murder and rape, bonded labour, and a web of discriminatory and punitive customs and practices).[33]

The third point is that despite these violations, human rights consciousness is low. Explanations for this paradox may lie in the weight of oppression over centuries, a fatalistic acceptance of one's miseries, and obstacles placed in the way of those who would seek to make explicit to the downtrodden the causes of their oppression. It certainly lies in the ethnic divisions of societies; ethnic consciousness can dull human rights consciousness, distinguishing us from

---

33 The framers of the Indian Constitution were well aware of these problems of civil society. Article 15 declared illegal discriminations on ground, *inter alia*, of caste, in, for example, access to wells, tanks, bathing ghats, roads and other places of public resort. Article 17 abolished untouchability and its practice in any form. Article 23 prohibited traffic in human beings and forced labour, particularly the traditional form of bonded labour known as "begar". There are various laws at the central and State levels to implement these provisions, particularly the Civil Rights Act 1955 (expanded and renamed as the Scheduled Castes and Scheduled Tribes (Prevention of Atrocities) Act in 1989). Despite these attempts, the social and economic position of these disadvantaged communities shows little improvement.

"others" and facilitating justifications for their oppression. A major challenge to human rights workers is undoubtedly this ethnic consciousness which compels a perception of outsiders as less than human. Another cause of low human rights consciousness may be widespread poverty. Poverty is a great cause of the denial of human rights. The international system refuses to accept this reality—for largely political reasons. It refuses to acknowledge that poverty destroys human dignity; and without human dignity there can be no human rights; or indeed the capacity to challenge the system of oppression.

Thus economic development is undoubtedly important. But not just any kind of economic development. Economic growth must be accompanied by a wide measure of egalitarianism, the protection of the rights of workers, particularly migrant workers, and democratic practices at work places. Nor must economic growth be undertaken at the expense of land, customs and autonomy of long settled communities. Unless these and other community concerns are safeguarded in the process of economic growth, development is perverse and adds to the violation of human rights and dignity.

A further point about human rights in Asia is that challenges to their violations are not individual based, but group or class based. This is particularly the case in multi-ethnic States. The protection of human rights is therefore pursued through the group. This fact, and the fact that the State is a major violator of human rights, suggests strategies that are different from the traditional Western approaches which are legalistic and court centred. Asian strategies cannot realistically be court centred, however favourably the judiciaries may be disposed towards human rights (and for the most part they are not). Human rights conscientisation and mobilisation based on connections between them and their oppression are a fundamental starting point (connections which neither local governments or the West are anxious should be made).

Nor must the terrain of struggle be purely domestic. Despite the resistance of governments, the realisation of human rights in each country is intimately tied to wider global forces (particularly in the contemporary world wide pursuit of marketisation). Even today many governments in the Third World are surrogates for external economic and political interests, and it is necessary to take the battle to the homelands of these interests, just as it is necessary to recruit foreign interests to put pressure on domestic governments which deny their people the right to participate in decisions affecting their own destiny.

For Asians concerned with the welfare and dignity of their fellow citizens, the right strategy should embrace the universalism and indivisibility of human rights. The implication of universalism and indivisibility is that human rights can no longer be seen in national terms or responsibility or as contingent on particular economic systems. They raise global issues which highlight the responsibility of people in one State to peoples in others. They imply that consumers in the rich Western countries owe a duty to present generations in other parts of the world and to future generations everywhere. They necessitate the closure of the armaments industry. They require a more equitable international economic system. They import a more democratic international system. Consistent with the dominant role of human rights in history, they raise a truly revolutionary agenda, sufficient to discomfort the West.

IV. Theoretical Issues

The polemics between the "West" and "Asia" on human rights has stimulated the search for a consensus on the importance as well as the scope of rights. One strategy has been to find agreement on the source of rights, but as pointed out above, this has not been promising. Another is to see if there can be a consensus on the purpose of human rights, at least at a very general level. One aspect of this approach has been to try to identify rights which form a "core" that all cultures and jurisdictions would subscribe to—the obvious candidates are the right to life, the prohibition of slavery, and the prohibition of torture—but beyond that, lists tend to diverge.[34] Equally, while every one would subscribe to the view that a primary purpose is to ensure the "inherent dignity" of a person, dissent starts with attempts to draw out its implications. Since it is assumed that the West regards civil and political rights as central to human dignity and Asia accords economic and social rights that primacy, much effort has been expended on the reconciliation of these types of rights. The Vienna Conference formulation was that "rights are indivisible"—but the riders that followed it demonstrated that priorities may need to be established and that these varied from place to place. I discuss this issue later in this section, for in my view it shows not only the scope of disagreement, but also a certain kind of consensus. Indeed I would argue that there is a measure of hypocrisy in the polemics between the West and the part of Asia I am discussing. The United States has cordial relations with the States which are the most outspoken proponents of the Asian position (and also some of them with a poor record of human rights)—Indonesia, Malaysia, Singapore, and occasionally and in the past, Thailand and South Korea. The United States provides security for them both through its own troops and the sale of arms (there are willing donors and willing recipients). There are extensive economic and trade relations between them. There is, in practical terms, very little disagreement on the agenda of the government of these States. The sincerity of the commitment of both parties to human rights has to be judged in this context of cordiality and fundamental common purpose.

(a) Conditionalities

How far should (in this instance) Western countries specify conditionalities on their aid or economic relations with other (in this instance) Asian countries? What is the justification for conditionalities? What are the dangers in conditionality? How effective are they?

The justification goes to the nature of the responsibilities of the international community for human rights, and here we have a confrontation between those who argue that contemporary international law has brought human rights within

34 Even the avoidance of pain, which one might suppose is a basic human instinct, does not hold in all cultures—forms of self-immolation or self-injury are practised as expressions of dissent or mourning, etc.

the jurisdiction of the international community, and those (which includes most Asian States) believing that they remain securely within national sovereignty. From these perspectives, one difficulty is that conditionalities are rarely imposed by the international community. They are imposed by a State or an association of like minded States, which clearly affects their legitimacy. As national or regional initiatives they do not of course require to be justified by a rule of international law on human rights; they are within the sovereignty of the donor/trading State.

The justification for conditionalities weakens if there is no agreement on the universality of rights. To those who believe in relativities, this may seem merely another form of cultural imperialism. They may also be seen as economic imperialism, for they have frequently embodied requirements of privatisation and de-regulation, and the general strengthening of the market mechanism, generally under the rubric of good governance. If conditionalities are not controlled by generally accepted norms, there is the danger of "reverse" conditionalities, instances of which are provided by economic boycotts or threats of them by Malaysia against the United Kingdom and Australia (if the latter did not curb the freedom of the press in their countries to criticise the policies of Malaysia or to make allegation of corruption against its leaders). Indonesia too has practised similar conditionalities in its relations with Australia (and recently against the Philippines in relation to the 1994 Manila conference on East Timor).

Justification may also depend on the kind of conditionalities. The earlier instances of conditionalities, particularly in Africa, related to the restructuring of the economies of the recipient States which involved privatisation, liberalisation and the reduction or elimination of the State provision of welfare services. Subsequent conditionalities related to the respect for human rights and the establishment of democratic practices. Political conditionalities may be easier to justify in that they reinforce internationally agreed norms of governance—human rights and self-determination. They also increase the options and self-expression of the people of the recipient States, and for that reason one welcomes them. Economic conditionalities, however, represent a more fundamental invasion of State sovereignty (for there are no international norms on how an economy should be organised) and they also close options for governments and people—and hence are undemocratic. There is thus a basic contradiction between political and economic conditionalities.

Conditionalities raise other kinds of problems as well. There is the danger of "double standards" in a dual sense; the standards or human rights practices of the "donor" may be little better than that of the recipient, and the donor may pick and choose States for conditionalities, further politicising the practice of conditionality. The United States, "the mother of all conditionors", is particularly vulnerable to these temptations; its record of connivance in the massive violations of the rights of the Palestinian people by Israel, and its active engagement in the destabilisation of democratic orders in many parts of the Third World being particularly despicable. Political conditionalities (for example, regarding good governance) are particularly offensive when the "donor" engages in activities in the recipient country which are inconsistent with the conditionalities (forcing the recipient into a kind of schizophrenia)—a ready example (of widespread practice of Western States and corporations) is the deal made by the United Kingdom Government for the financing of a dam in Malaysia if Malaysia would purchase arms from the United Kingdom (not only is this corruption but also forcing the purchase of arms runs counter to the policy of the West to penalise such purchases).[35] Conditionality may threaten consistency in another sense; a State may decide that its national interests no longer lie in maintaining conditionality, and may abandon it after having initiated it (as with the recent United States decision on the Most Favoured Nation status for China). A country's foreign policy is determined by many considerations, largely of its own self-interest, and therefore human rights are unlikely to be an important or consistent factor. A change of policy may raise a particular moral problem; an important casualty of this change may well be human rights activists in the "recipient" country who have staked a great deal (personally and otherwise) on continued support from abroad.

For the above reasons, conditionalities are not often effective—even if they lead to some temporary improvements. Those who impose and those on whom conditionalities are imposed are generally anxious to return to normal relations, and are therefore astute to find an improvement even if such a conclusion cannot be supported by the evidence. Conditionality can also backfire if the local government decides to whip up anti-foreign sentiments on its basis—as it may frequently suit its purposes. They engage the State and civil society institutions in a human rights dialogue with the donors, rather than with their own people. They may also sharpen polarities which are unlikely to be productive (and which may weaken the capacity of the imposing State to achieve progress through other means).[36] Smaller and weaker countries are more likely to be subjected to conditionalities (as the reversal of United States policy towards China demonstrates).

Although sometimes conditionalities may be necessary (especially if a government, with a poor human rights, is particularly intransigent, there is

---

35 See the resolutions of the European Community and the Council of Europe reprinted in DANIDA. *Human Rights and Democracy: Perspectives for Development Co-operation* (1993).

36 Mr John Shattuck, the Assistant Secretary of State and the highest ranking United States official with responsibility for human rights, described human rights conditionality as a "blunt weapon" in his defence of the reversal of the United States position on China, at an Asia Foundation Washington meeting (June 1994). He explained that it prevented the United States from having normal relations with China and precluded the use of other methods and instruments for change in China's human rights pressure. However many people have interpreted the reversal of the United States policy as kowtowing to American business, and regard with distaste the unseemly haste with which Secretary for Commerce Ron Brown rushed to China with a coterie of business people to sign up several lucrative contracts.

The episode illustrates another danger with conditionalities: the reversal caused much confusion and was widely seen as a signal to human rights activists in China and elsewhere not to depend on the United States for support.

evidence of widespread dissatisfaction with the regime by the public, and there is multi-lateral support for the conditionalities), dialogue or other forms of "constructive engagement" are preferable—at least in the initial stages.

(b) Political and civil rights versus economic and social rights

The controversy over the priority of these two types of rights is not new. Representing a clash between "liberalism" and "Marxism", it dominated the drafting of the International Bill of Rights, and resulted in a bifurcation of rights into two covenants (the International Covenant on Civil and Political Rights, and the International Covenant on Economic, Social and Cultural Rights). The ideological context of the controversy has, however, changed. By and large the market provides the matrix for the proponents on both sides. For example, while the Soviet Union was firmly opposed to the right to property (which does not feature in the Covenants), Asian governments (including China now) are wedded to it. The difference between the two sides lies in the vision of the market. In Western theory the market is autonomous, and the safeguarding of that autonomy requires a number of civil and political rights (property, freedom of movement, association and organisation, expression and an independent and rational legal order). The control of the State (which provides the legal and administrative framework for the market) by the ruling group comes from its prior dominance in civil society (emphasising yet again the importance of civil rights). Asian markets are organised in a much more authoritarian and rapacious manner; there is wide scale corruption; the State, more autonomous of social forces than in the West, is a means to control over economic resources and civil society; and many are still at the "primitive accumulation" stage. Administration is more important than the law; and the imperatives of control override those of economic rationality.

Although both the West and the Asian States are committed to the market, there is competition between them for the national or regional dominance of world markets. Just how the market is organised may affect the interests of the States differently. The West has an interest in equalising the conditions of competition and in the opening up of markets, while Asian States are concerned with twin objectives—of increasing competitive edge and political control. It is thus easy to understand why the West would want to emphasise transparency, accountability, functioning legal codes and courts and a narrowing of the role of the State. It is equally easy to see why Asian States would resist these, using the shibboleths of economic, social and cultural rights. Culture becomes particularly functional as both providing a moral and popular mode of differentiating the East from the West, as well as in slowing down political mobilisation at home. But since the market remains the operating matrix, the process, as I have pointed out above, is not without deep contradictions.

Ideological justifications for the success of the markets in Asia, harping upon the Confucian values of authority, obedience and the salience of the family in economic affairs, are used not to establish the irrelevance of civil and political rights but their destructive qualities. Economic and social rights attempt to mediate between the market and the community, to soften the impact of market forces, to act as a safety net. Nothing in the present conjuncture enhances economic, social and cultural rights. On the contrary, the general acceptance of the market means that propertied and entrepreneurial classes have gained new salience, and that fresh restrictions on social and economic rights (including those of workers and in regard to the environment) are placed in the name of global competitiveness. Asian governments may have some justification to see the emphasis on workers rights and the environment as attempts by the West to reduce the competitiveness of Asian economies, but the restrictions nevertheless point to the shallowness of their commitment to economic rights. It is therefore unlikely that we shall get useful purchase on the question of economic and social versus political and civil rights by examining the stance of Asian governments.

If these inquires are unproductive, what then might be other approaches to the question? Here I must point to the negative consequences of the domination by lawyers of human rights questions. Armed with a number of international conventions, they have excessively juridified the debate, relying more on the text than the purpose of rights. Questions of justiciability have narrowed the range of rights that it is the responsibility of the State to protect. The focus on the State as the source of violations has tended to obscure the power (and the practice) of private groups to inflict massive denial of rights on individuals and communities, and to have led to a somewhat uncritical praise of civil society. Textual and legal analyses (which emphasise universalism) have also ignored the underlying social and economic circumstances which condition attitudes towards and the practice of human rights. I believe that it is in the examination of these circumstances that we can establish a link between political and economic rights.

Economic, social and cultural rights are particularly valuable in uncovering the rationale for human rights. Human rights were part of the post-war agenda of the United Nations which emphasised their close connection with peace, development and human dignity. Unlike the "negative" liberties of political rights, these other rights raise a different framework and pose larger questions—that of the purpose of society and State, of social responsibility and social justice, of equity, and the potential of the human person. They suggest that a person is born full of potentialities—potentialities which find fulfilment through civil and political rights, that of expression, association, and participation, but that these potentialities do not materialise without appropriate social and economic circumstances.[37] Undoubtedly poverty, as I have already argued, is the single most important cause of the violation of rights.

It is therefore necessary to move away from the polarities of civil and political rights on the one hand, and social and economic on the other. Each has a bundle of rights which vary in their impact on the State and citizens and not all are individually oriented (for example, the right of association serves political, economic and cultural functions). Their disaggregation and the purpose each

37 Fields and Narr, "Human Rights as a Holistic Concept" (1992) 14 *Human Rights Quarterly* 1.

serves may suggest different and more productive categorisations. The right of property is regarded as a civil right, yet it is pregnant with economic functions.

The better view is that rights are equal and indeed indivisible. Since one's perception of rights is governed by the state of one's belly, it could be argued that a certain level of literacy and economic security are essential for the exercise and enjoyment of civil and political rights. Equally, economic prosperity and high literacy without the freedom of expression or the right of association fail to develop the full potential of the human person, and the denial of these rights can be humiliating and degrading[38] (this position is increasingly being taken in recent international instruments on the rights of special groups—women, children and indigenous peoples, which have broken away from the bifurcation of the Covenants, being based on the understanding that real equality for women or indigenous people or the real protection of children's rights cannot be secured without major social transformations in their social and economic conditions).[39]

A variation of this position is to acknowledge that both sets of rights are important and even that they are indivisible, but to concede that it may not be possible to achieve them all at once (the reform of the legal system to ensure civil rights of fair and speedy trial, for example, can be as expensive as

---

38 The case of migrants provides an illustration. A large number of people migrate from the relatively democratic Philippines to work in States which are less protective of human rights, like Singapore, Malaysia and the Middle East, suggesting that they value economic advancement over rights. On the other hand, professionals from Singapore are emigrating to countries in the West where personal and artistic freedoms are more highly valued, suggesting that economic wellbeing is not sufficient for human happiness and fulfilment.

This example also illustrates another theme of my paper, that one's view of human rights is coloured by one's economic and social status.

39 For example, the Convention on the Elimination of All Forms of Discrimination Against Women (CEDAW) (1979) guarantees not only the traditional political and civil rights and the general entitlement to equality before the law, but sanctions affirmative action, and requires States parties to:

> take all appropriate measures (a) to modify the social and cultural patterns of conduct of men and women, with a view to achieving the elimination of prejudices and customary and other practices which are based on the idea of the inferiority or the superiority of either of the sexes or on the stereotyped roles for men and women; (b) to ensure that family education includes a proper understanding of maternity as a social function and the recognition of the common responsibility of men and women in the upbringing and development of their children...(article 5).

States have to take all steps to suppress all forms of traffic in women and exploitation of prostitution of women (article 6). Special responsibilities have been imposed on States in respect of rural women; in particular they are to ensure that rural women participate and benefit from rural development; participate in the elaboration and implementation of planning; have access to adequate health facilities, including information, counselling and services in family planning; obtain all types of training and education, formal and non-formal; access to agricultural credit and loans, and marketing facilities and appropriate technologies; and enjoy adequate living conditions, particularly in relation to housing, sanitation, electricity and water supply, transport and communications.

providing water supply to rural areas). This stance raises the question of the instrumentality and sequencing of rights. Professor Amaryta Sen has argued, for example, that a society that proclaims the urgency of basic needs, has first to have a democratic framework so that the society can decide what the basic needs are. He has also suggested that basic needs can probably not be met in a society which is not responsive to public pressures or public accountability.[40] One might add that the transformative potential of human rights (and that must be their role in many authoritarian and unequal societies in Asia) lies in the rights of association, speech and other trade union rights. One can turn to history for guidance on sequencing, but that might be another device to assert the priority of civil and political rights which may not be warranted in contemporary times. These issues are also raised in discussions on democratisation as it implies a process. They are therefore best explored in the section on governance below.

(c) Democratisation and governance

The context of this discussion is two-fold, one domestic and the other international. The domestic is the growing constitutionalisation of the political orders of several Asian countries—for example, Thailand, Taiwan, Pakistan, Cambodia, Bangladesh, the Philippines, South Korea, Hong Kong, Mongolia and Nepal. The international is the pressure for, or assistance towards, democratic and accountable political orders from Western donors and international economic institutions, particularly the World Bank (often expressed in the form of conditionalities). Sometimes domestic and international pressures coincide, but not always. Sometimes foreign pressures are towards marketisation (with the emphasis on clear legal regimes, transparency and level playing fields) as with the World Bank. At other times the stress is on democratisation as such.

The process towards better governance and democracy is extraordinarily complicated (even if governance and democracy had similar pre-conditions, which they may not), for it involves issues which, although they are often regarded as of a piece, have different dynamics and consequences—the development of civil rights, the rule of law and a liberal culture, democratic reforms through the extension of the franchise and other political rights, the securing of economic and social rights, and fair and transparent governance (to which in some instances we should add marketisation). One problem is that in contemporary constitutionalisation all these goals are being sought simultaneously. In any circumstances such a task would be daunting, but it becomes even more problematic because there may well, at least in the short

40 He illustrates his argument by a study of famines and shows that it was only when there was no freedom of expression or criticism that the governments were unable to anticipate shortages. He contrasts the relatively better position of immigrants in Britain, most of whom have the vote, with those in Germany, who do not. But he points to failures of democracy when preventing injuries or injustices in instances where it is not so easy to evoke human sympathy for them, unlike that in the case of major disasters. Sen, "Freedoms and Needs", *The New Republic* (10–17 January 1994), p 31.

run, be a conflict between them. In the 19th century, for example, the rule of law was considered to be under threat from democratisation. Many countries in the transition to democracy in this century have built in a deliberate "democracy deficit", in part to placate its former enemies, but also to create the capacity to absorb the social and political consequences of democratisation. It could be argued in historical terms that as democracy was preceded by civil rights and the rule of law, it was acceptable to the ruling group (because the economic and social rights of the bourgeoisie would be protected) and feasible (because of the importance attached to values and procedures which would moderate the consequences of popular demands), while democracy itself set the stage for economic and social rights. The relevance of this analysis in today's conditions may be questioned, although a plausible case can be made out that the fragility of democracy in many developing countries is due to the lack of traditions of civil liberties and the rule of law.

Democratic theory does not provide clear answers to a number of issues that require an instrumental solution—does economic liberalisation lead to political freedoms or vice versa (the Russia-China debate), is it more important to concentrate on the strengthening of civil society or the reform of State structures, can purely secular organisation of public power command legitimacy, what are the pre-conditions of democracy, what is the link between marketisation and human rights, and indeed the connection between different kinds of rights.

There is space only for some general comments. Let me first take the relationship between democracy and the market. The supporters of the market argue that it inevitably leads to democracy. The argument might be made on both logical and historical grounds. The market is a system of private economy, in which there is a massive decentralisation of decision-making and a wide scope for choice. Central to the market are private property, which ensures a measure of autonomy for individuals and groups, and the freedom of contract, which enhances choice and secures rights (and limits the powers of the State). Predictability and legal security, which are also essential to the market, lead to an expert and independent judiciary, and thus to the separation of powers. The market gives rise to or strengthens civil society, and provides a countervailing force to that of the State. In this analysis, the market is more dependent on rights than on democracy.

The historical case, however, is that the development of democracy in the West followed the rise of the market, and that parallel processes are underway in East Asia (in particular Taiwan and Korea). It would be argued that the market leads to certain forms of social formations which stimulate pressures for democracy. In particular it undermines traditional forms of economy and their corresponding forms of political authority, and frees labour from its previous constraints ("from status to contract"). It gives rise to a middle class with its specific interests, connected with rights and democracy, and the economic and political clout to protect them. It also facilitates the organisation of labour, leading to a competitive and pluralistic political order.

However, neither the logical or the historical evidence is conclusive. Drawing from a model of consumption, the former disregards the process of production (where economic coercion prevails and the mode of organisation is hierarchical). It also assumes a false dichotomy between the State and the market, ignoring their inter-penetration. The market favours a few and does not universalise rights, except perhaps at a formal level. The market oriented civil society substitutes economic pressures for direct political authority, but by that very fact removes accountability, and introduces a different mode of subordination. Similarly, the historical process may be no guide, since it was the market which shaped the State in the West, but it is the State which has shaped the market in Asia. Nor is the globalisation of capital and markets likely to be conducive to rights or democracy. Freed from a territorial nexus, capital may become even more irresponsible and less accountable—less responsive to public opinion and more accommodating of State restrictive practices in its pursuit of profit (as is demonstrated by the way in which both Murdoch and Turner have bent their communication empires to the censorship by China). The growing global dominance of the power of capital over political authority and structures diminishes rather than increases prospects of rights and democracy. The progress in rights and democracy has been achieved by the struggles of the workers and other disadvantaged communities, and not by the advocacy of capitalists.

Another problematic area is civil society, which has become something of a *deus ex machina* in the prescriptions for rights and democracy. The notions of civil society in contemporary discourse are hazy. Sometimes (as in Eastern Europe), it is used to refer to the marketisation of the economy—which I have argued is no reason for optimism. Other times it refers to non-State values and institutions outside the area of economy. But I have also tried to demonstrate that in most parts of Asia civil society so defined is responsible for great injustice and oppression, and is itself in much need of reform. Other times it is used to refer to civic organisations of professionals, workers, women and others, which not only lobby the State but also seek to humanise society. A particular species of them, the NGOs, have achieved much prominence in recent years, seen as champions of rights and democracy, and giving voice to the underprivileged. It is no time to enter into the debate on NGOs (whose positive contributions are numerous), except to sound a note of caution, as they proliferate under encouragement of or incentives from foreign donors, operate increasingly as consulting firms, and lose touch with, or accountability to, their local constituencies.

Let me finally explore some conflicts between human rights and democracy. (I do not refer to the older debates as to whether an entrenched bill of rights interpreted by non-elected judiciaries is compatible with democracy and whether it weakens the political process by its "legalisation" consequences, for it seems to me that the political process might be enriched, rather than impoverished, by rights in most developing countries and that the executive and the legislature have frequently few claims to democratic legitimacy). The formalisation and juridification of rights have thrust courts and tribunals at the centre of their definitions and enforcement and their discourse has become increasingly specialised. This detracts both from the responsibility and capacity of elected bodies for human rights. The globalisation of human rights detaches specific rights from the national context and relevance. The transformative consequences of economic and social rights (for example, the revolution in the position of women or the shift of power from one caste to another in rural Nepal) may be threatening to an infant democracy because of the interests of incumbent leaders and influential groups.

It is true that certain kinds of rights may be pre-requisites to democracy—franchise, expression, and association. It is also true that certain rights may be better protected in a democracy than in other political systems. But the logic of rights is different from the logic of democracy. The former are individual centred (even when they concern social rights), while democracy is majority-centred. The scope of rights is drawn from the nature of the human person, the scope of democracy from the general will. Rights serve to limit State power, while democracy justifies its expansion. Rights may be said to be "rational" and purposive, but democracy is frequently messy and manipulative.

When there are conflicts, rights are likely to give into democracy.[41] Although rights are now prescribed in considerable detail, and democracy is still nebulous (no international instrument defines or protects it), democracy seems to command greater legitimacy, at least in Asia. Rights are harder to enforce than democracy, in part because of the differing precision of definitions. It may also threaten existing power structures. For that reason, democracy may be used to suppress human rights. Politics are viewed largely as a formal business of professional politicians, as a kind of joust (to the finish) rather than as discourse, questioning the legitimacy of academics, journalists, and social workers, who wish to express opinions on policies (even in their areas of their own expertise). Democracy, seen largely as an electoral process, becomes plebiscitary. Democracy, seen as the access to State power, becomes manipulative and corrupting. Yet it is presented as the voice of the people, a talisman to ward off domestic and foreign pressures for rights and equity.[42] But for that very reason it increasingly relies on, and caters to, sectional interests.

In the South Asian context, ethnicity has frequently provided that sectional interest. Ethnicity, linked to the democratic or at least the electoral process, has had, for the most part, negative effect on governance and human rights. Political parties have aggregated and articulated ethnic demands, the majority community

41 The inability of the United States Government to maintain a consistent policy regarding human rights conditionalities, especially in relation to China, is itself the result of United States democracy, as the administration feels compelled, for electoral reasons, to take into account views of corporations and workers who benefit from investments in and trade with China.

42 Consider the following statement of Dr Mahathir, Prime Minister of Malaysia, in an attack on the power of judges to interpret and decide on the validity of laws, "If the people want the Government to be restricted so as not to be able to draft certain laws, the people will cause the downfall of the Government..." quoted in Hickling and Wishart, "Malaysia: Dr Mahathir's Thinking on Constitutional Issues" [1988–89] *Lawasia* 47 at 57.

has imposed its cultural forms on the State, and the rights of minorities have been trampled upon. The result has often been the militarisation of both the State and civil society and the application of oppressive legislation which has denied a whole array of political, civil, economic and social rights. And yet democracy of a sort has flourished and fed the process of the attrition of democratic values.

The time has come to forge and strengthen links between democracy and rights. Democracy, in all its dimensions, not merely electoral, has to be rehabilitated. The values of democracy provide the link to human rights. The strengthening of human rights would then mean strengthening democracy. But democracy, to validate and legitimise human rights, has to respond to the cultural and moral impulses of the society. Western forms of democracy (by which I mean the forms of former metropolitan powers) have not been appropriate for Asia (any more than for Africa). This may seem a route back to relativism. But it is the relativism of forms, not substance, and may be necessary for some sort of regime of universal values underpinning the dignity of women and men.

[13]

Human Rights in the Muslim World: Socio-Political Conditions and Scriptural Imperatives

A Preliminary Inquiry

Abdullahi Ahmed An-Na'im*

To hundreds of millions of Muslims, the historical formulations of Islamic law known as Shari'a determine the boundaries of legal and ethical conduct. In this Article, Professor An-Na'im explores the implications of Shari'a for Muslim observance of international human rights standards. Part I addresses the legitimacy of these standards in Muslim countries, focusing on the international legal principles of equality and nondiscrimination. Part II traces the development of Shari'a in Islamic history and its influence on Muslims. Professor An-Na'im discusses several conflicts between Shari'a and human rights standards, rejecting the contention that such inconsistencies do not exist. Part III explores the political and social forces associated with Islamization in Muslim countries. Professor An-Na'im argues that such pressures heighten the need to examine critically the effect of Shari'a on human rights violations. Part IV presents a case study on Shari'a and Muslim women's rights. Finally, in Part V, Professor An-Na'im offers a methodology for human rights advocates in the Muslim world: to reexamine the scriptural imperatives in the Qur'an to make the dictates of Shari'a consistent with international human rights norms.

INTRODUCTION

Historical formulations of Islamic religious law, commonly known as Shari'a,[1] include a universal system of law and ethics and purport

* I wrote this Article while holding the Ariel F. Sallows Chair in Human Rights at the College of Law, University of Saskatchewan, Canada. I am grateful for the research assistance of Charmaine Spencer and the editorial help and useful suggestions of Anne McGillivray.

1. In Islamic literature, the term Shari'a is used to refer to Divine Law based on the Qur'an and Sunna (traditions of the Prophet Muhammad), while the term *fiqh* (jurisprudence) refers to the opinions and commentaries of Muslim jurists. Some Muslim authors emphasize this distinction in order to suggest that they are criticizing merely *fiqh* and not Divine Law itself. *See, e.g.*, K. FARUKI, ISLAMIC JURISPRUDENCE 12–19 (1962); A. FYZEE, OUTLINES OF MUHAMMADAN LAW 14–24 (4th ed. 1974).

I use the term Shari'a because the aspects of Islamic law I discuss are directly based on the Qur'an and Sunna and not upon personal opinions and commentaries of jurists. As a Muslim, I am not challenging the divine nature of the Qur'an and Sunna. Rather, I am challenging the failure of contemporary Muslims to appreciate the impact of historical context upon the interpretation and application of those fundamental sources of Islam. I argue that given the historical to regulate every aspect of public and private life. The power of Shari'a to regulate the behavior of Muslims derives from its moral and religious authority as well as the formal enforcement of its legal norms. As such, Shari'a influences individual and collective behavior in Muslim countries through its role in the socialization processes of such nations regardless of its status in their formal legal systems. For example, the status and rights of women in the Muslim world have always been significantly influenced by Shari'a, regardless of the degree of Islamization in public life. Of course, Shari'a is not the sole determinant of human behavior nor the only formative force behind social and political institutions in Muslim countries.

In this Article, I explore the implications of Shari'a for the status of human rights[2] in the Muslim world.[3] After briefly discussing my methodological choice in Part I, in Part II I explain Shari'a and the human rights violations which result from the dominant interpretation of Shari'a. In Part III, I describe some of the political and social forces which translate this scriptural interpretation into action. In Part IV, I analyze in some detail the impact of Shari'a and Islamization on the status and rights of women in Muslim communities. And in Part V, I argue that human rights reform requires reinterpretation of Shari'a and I offer one possible reformulation.

---

contexts of both initial revelation and subsequent interpretations of the texts of the Qur'an and Sunna, some texts are no longer applicable while others need to be interpreted differently. I believe that divine revelation must be understood and applied in historical context because it addresses us in our human condition and circumstances which change over time.

2. This Article is not concerned with the origins and philosophical meaning of the term "human rights" and does not detail contemporary human rights standards. Rather, I take the International Bill of Human Rights as the source of international human rights standards. *See infra* note 7.

3. It is not possible in a work of this nature to offer extensive surveys and analyses of the situation in even a selected group of countries. I therefore focus on a number of broad human rights issues while illustrating my arguments with reference to conditions prevailing in representative Muslim countries. I have chosen Egypt, Indonesia, Iran, Morocco, Pakistan, and Saudi Arabia as reflecting varying degrees of secularization, fundamentalism, and traditionalism. The analysis is applicable to other Muslim countries provided, of course, that factors and conditions peculiar to each country are taken into account.

For the purpose of this Article, a "Muslim country" is one in which the majority of the population perceive themselves to be Muslims. Because I do not believe that it is within the realm of human discourse to agree on an objective conception of Islam, I must accept a people's self-perception. It should be borne in mind during the discussion that variation in the conception of Islam is inevitable.

As to the size of the Muslim majority which qualifies a country as a "Muslim country," 80% appears to be reasonable because such a majority normally would be large enough to significantly influence public policy and action. In other words, I assume that if 80% of the population is Muslim, then Islam is a significant factor in the life of that society regardless of whether the state is constituted as an "Islamic state" or whether Shari'a is the formal legal system of the land. All six countries selected for this discussion satisfy my criteria. *See, e.g.*, Muslim Peoples: An Ethnographic Survey 887, 891, 893, 900–902 (R. Weeks ed. 1984); D. Pipes, In the Path of God: Islam and Political Power 338–39 (1982).

I conclude that human rights advocates in the Muslim world must work within the framework of Islam to be effective. They need not be confined, however, to the particular historical interpretations of Islam known as Shari'a. Muslims are obliged, as a matter of faith, to conduct their private and public affairs in accordance with the dictates of Islam, but there is room for legitimate disagreement over the precise nature of these dictates in the modern context. Religious texts, like all other texts, are open to a variety of interpretations. Human rights advocates in the Muslim world should struggle to have their interpretations of the relevant texts adopted as the new Islamic scriptural imperatives for the contemporary world.

A. *Cultural Legitimacy for Human Rights*

The basic premise of my approach is that human rights violations reflect the lack or weakness of cultural legitimacy of international standards in a society. Insofar as these standards are perceived to be alien to or at variance with the values and institutions of a people, they are unlikely to elicit commitment or compliance. While cultural legitimacy may not be the sole or even primary determinant of compliance with human rights standards, it is, in my view, an extremely significant one. Thus, the underlying causes of any lack or weakness of legitimacy of human rights standards must be addressed in order to enhance the promotion and protection of human rights in that society.

Some commentators have focused on this lack of cultural legitimacy of international standards in the non-Western world to challenge the basic validity of international human rights standards. In fact, conduct which would amount to human rights violations under existing international standards has been justified precisely because these standards were perceived to be culturally illegitimate. This cultural illegitimacy, it is argued, derives from the historical conditions surrounding the creation of the particular human rights instruments. Most African and Asian countries did not participate in the formulation of the Universal Declaration of Human Rights[4] because, as victims of colonization, they were not members of the United Nations. When they did participate in the formulation of subsequent instruments, they did so on the basis of an established framework and philosophical assumptions adopted in their absence. For example, the preexisting framework and assumptions favored individual civil and political rights over collective solidarity rights, such as a right to development, an outcome which

4. *Universal Declaration of Human Rights*, G.A. Res. 217A (III), U.N. GAOR Res. 71, U.N. Doc. A/810 (1948) [hereinafter *Universal Declaration*].

remains problematic today. Some authors have gone so far as to argue that inherent differences exist between the Western notion of human rights as reflected in the international instruments and non-Western notions of human dignity.[5] In the Muslim world, for instance, there are obvious conflicts between Shari'a and certain human rights, especially of women and non-Muslims.[6]

Concern for the lack of universal participation in formulating international human rights instruments does not lead me to invalidate those existing instruments. On the contrary, for the purposes of this study, I take the International Bill of Human Rights as the source of these standards.[7] It is true that not all Muslim countries have endorsed or ratified these instruments, but neither have they publicly repudiated them.[8] The human rights idea is too powerful and popular now for any government to oppose openly. The governments of Muslim countries are no exception to this general rule. In this discussion, I focus on the principles of legal equality and nondiscrimination contained in many human rights instruments.[9] These principles relating to gender and religion are particularly problematic in the Muslim world.

---

5. *See, e.g.*, Donnelly, *Human Rights and Human Dignity: An Analytic Critique of non-Western Conceptions of Human Rights*, 76 AM. POL. SCI. REV. 303 (1982); Panikkar, *Is the Notion of Human Rights a Western Concept?* 120 DIOGENES 75 (1982).

6. *See infra* notes 101–137 and accompanying text.

7. The term "International Bill of Human Rights" refers to a collection of three United Nations instruments: *Universal Declaration*, *supra* note 4; *The International Covenant on Economic, Social and Cultural Rights*, G.A. Res. 2200 (XXI), 21 U.N. GAOR Supp. (No. 16) at 49, U.N. Doc. A/6316 (1966) (entered into force Jan. 3, 1976); and *International Covenant on Civil and Political Rights*, G.A. Res. 2200 (XXI), 21 U.N. GAOR Supp. (No. 16) at 52, U.N. Doc. A/6316 (1966) (entered into force Mar. 23, 1976).

8. During the first few years after the Iranian revolution, official representatives of the Islamic Republic of Iran expressed reservations toward international human rights standards, favoring what they believed to be Islamic standards. *See* E. MORTIMER, INDEX ON CENSORSHIP 5 (1983). Nevertheless, Iran remains a party to the International Covenant on Economic, Social and Cultural Rights and the International Covenant on Civil and Political Rights, *supra* note 7. *See* INTERNATIONAL HUMAN RIGHTS INSTRUMENTS 170.42, 180.18 (R. Lillich ed. rev. 1988).

9. Article 1 of the Universal Declaration states that "all human beings are born free and equal in dignity and rights." Article 2 specifies that "everyone is entitled to all the rights and freedoms set forth in this Declaration without distinction of any kind, such as race, colour, sex, language, religion, political or other opinion, national or social origin, property, birth or other status." *Universal Declaration*, *supra* note 4, at arts. 1, 2.

Article 2.2 of the International Covenant on Economic, Social and Cultural Rights obliges state parties to guarantee that the rights enunciated in the Covenant will be exercised without discrimination on grounds such as race, color, sex, language, and religion. Article 3 of the same Covenant creates the obligation to ensure the rights of men and women to the equal enjoyment of all economic, social, and cultural rights set forth in the Covenant. *See International Covenant on Economic, Social and Cultural Rights*, *supra* note 7, at arts. 2.2, 3.

Articles 2.2 and 3 of the International Covenant on Civil and Political Rights create similar obligations to ensure nondiscrimination and equality in relation to rights set forth in that Covenant. *See International Covenant on Civil and Political Rights*, *supra* note 7, at arts. 2.2, 3. The same principles underlie numerous specific rights set forth in both Covenants.

I realize that formal equality before the law and the implementation of nondiscrimination policies are necessary but insufficient conditions for the realization of substantive economic,

I adopt a constructive approach[10] to the problem of the cultural legitimacy of human rights norms. This approach posits that such problems can be overcome through a process of reinterpreting the fundamental sources of the Islamic tradition. The proposed new interpretation will have to be undertaken in a sensitive, legitimate manner, and time will be required for its acceptance and implementation by the population at large. The availability of such reinterpretation is a vital prelude to the political struggle which is integral to the whole process. The reformulation I offer in the final part of this Article is but a brief presentation of my arguments for a reinterpretive approach which I have explored in more detail elsewhere.[11] In the final part of this Article, I offer a brief presentation of the thesis and the prospects of its implementation in the Muslim world today.

II. ISLAM, SHARI'A AND HUMAN RIGHTS

In this part, I first discuss the formation of the Shari'a and address the impact which Shari'a has had upon the thinking and conduct of Muslims. I conclude with a discussion of recent mounting pressure in Muslim countries to adopt the Shari'a as their formal legal systems.

A. *The Development and Current Application of Shari'a*

To the over nine hundred million Muslims of the world, the Qur'an is the literal and final word of God and Muhammad is the final Prophet. During his mission, from 610 A.D. to his death in 632 A.D., the Prophet elaborated on the meaning of the Qur'an and supplemented its rulings through his statements and actions. This body of information came to be known as Sunna.[12] He also established the first Islamic state in Medina around 622 A.D. which emerged

---

political, and social equality. Questions remain of systemic discrimination and issues of affirmative action, as well as debates about equality of opportunity as opposed to equality of result. Nevertheless, these questions and issues must be discussed in the context of particular societies and mediated through the political and social processes of each society. An exploration of these questions and issues, even with respect to the countries selected, is outside the scope of this Article. With respect to India, see generally M. GALANTER, COMPETING EQUALITIES: LAW AND THE BACKWARD CLASSES IN INDIA (1984).

10. For a detailed discussion of this approach, see An-Na'im, *Problems of Universal Cultural Legitimacy for Human Rights*, in HUMAN RIGHTS IN AFRICA: CROSS-CULTURAL PERSPECTIVES (An-Na'im & Deng eds. forthcoming 1990); An-Na'im, *Religious Minorities under Islamic Law and the Limits of Cultural Relativism* 9 HUM. R. Q. 1 (1987).

11. A. AN-NA'IM, TOWARD AN ISLAMIC REFORMATION: CIVIL LIBERTIES, HUMAN RIGHTS AND INTERNATIONAL LAW (1990) [hereinafter TOWARD AN ISLAMIC REFORMATION]; An-Na'im, *The Rights of Women and International Law in the Muslim Context*, 9 WHITTIER L. REV. 491 (1987); An-Na'im, *Islamic Law, International Relations and Human Rights: Challenge and Response*, 20 CORNELL INT'L L. J. 17 (1987).

12. On these formative stages of Islam, see M. HODGSON, I THE VENTURE OF ISLAM, 146–230 (1974); I. LAPIDUS, A HISTORY OF ISLAMIC SOCIETIES, 21–80 (1988).

later as the ideal model of an Islamic state.[13] In addition, the practices of the first four caliphs, successors of the Prophet, are also binding or at least highly authoritative for the ninety percent of Muslims commonly known as Sunnis.[14] In contradistinction, the Shi'a minority insists that the fourth caliph Ali (the Prophet's cousin and son-in-law) and his descendants from Fatima, the Prophet's daughter, were the only rightful *imams*, leaders of the Muslim community.[15]

While the Qur'an was collected and recorded soon after the Prophet Muhammad's death, it took almost two centuries to collect, verify, and record the Sunna. Because it remained an oral tradition for a long time during a period of exceptional turmoil in Muslim history, some Sunna reports are still controversial in terms of both their authenticity and relationship to the Qur'an.[16]

Because Shari'a is derived from Sunna as well as the Qur'an, its development as a comprehensive legal and ethical system had to await the collection and authentication of Sunna. Shari'a was not developed until the second and third centuries of Islam.[17] The concept itself, in the sense of a unified body of law, was a relatively late development.[18] The first generation of Muslim legal scholars worked independently in various centers, discussing their views on the meaning of the Qur'an and Sunna and issuing individual opinions upon request.[19]

Shari'a, therefore, was constructed by Muslim jurists over a long period of time and did not become a comprehensive legal and ethical

13. For a detailed account and analysis of the Mecca and Medina phases of early Islam, see generally W. WATT, MUHAMMAD AT MECCA (1953); W. WATT, MUHAMMAD AT MEDINA (1956).

14. It should be noted, however, that those early caliphs enjoy authority among Muslims by virtue of their religious standing and not their political role. In fact, their political role is seen as a result of their religious learning and piety. Many other early companions of the Prophet share in those qualities and would therefore be accepted as authoritative jurisprudential and theological figures in Muslim history. *See* F. RAHMAN, ISLAM 79 (1979).

15. Upon the Prophet's death, the majority of Muslims accepted Abu Bakr as the first caliph, and they subsequently selected Umar and Uthman as the se ond and third caliphs before Ali became the fourth caliph. To a minority group, known at the time as *Shi'at* Ali, or the partisans of Ali, the first three caliphs were usurpers of the rightful position of the Prophet's cousin and son-in-law. This group eventually developed into a separate sect of Islam, following their line of "rightful" *imams* and developing their own schools of Islamic jurisprudence. At the present time, the main Shi'a groups are the Twelvers of Iran; the Isma'ilis of the Indian sub-continent, central Asia, Syria, and the Persian Gulf region; and the Zaydis of southern Arabia. *See* Fyzee, *Shi'i Legal Theories*, in LAW IN THE MIDDLE EAST 113 (Khadduri & Liebesny eds. 1955). For a theological account of these Shi'a sects see W. WATT, ISLAMIC PHILOSOPHY AND THEOLOGY, 122–28 (1985).

16. *See* Rahman, *supra* note 14, at 53–59; Vesey-Fitzgerald, *Nature and Sources of the Shari'a*, in LAW IN THE MIDDLE EAST 93 (Khadduri & Liebesny eds. 1955).

17. For explanations of this long and complicated process, see generally J. SCHACHT, AN INTRODUCTION TO ISLAMIC LAW 28–68 (1964); N. COULSON, A HISTORY OF ISLAMIC LAW 9–74 (1964).

18. *See* RAHMAN, *supra* note 14, at 101–09.

19. *See* A. HASAN, THE EARLY DEVELOPMENT OF ISLAMIC JURISPRUDENCE 20–21 (1970).

system until well into the third century of Islam. The jurists who founded the main schools of Islamic jurisprudence that are followed by the vast majority of modern Muslims did their founding work between the middle of the eighth century and the middle of the ninth century, one to two hundred years after the Prophet's death.[20] In fact, the techniques and methods for the derivation of general principles and specific rules of Shari'a, such as *ijma* (consensus) and *qiyas* (analogy), were not settled until the time of Shafi'i who died in 819.[21]

Shari'a is not a formally enacted legal code. It consists of a vast body of jurisprudence in which individual jurists express their views on the meaning of the Qur'an and Sunna and the legal implications of those views. Although most Muslims believe Shari'a to be a single logical whole, there is significant diversity of opinion not only among the various schools of thought, but also among the different jurists of a particular school.[22] The original founding jurists themselves were not attempting during the second and third centuries of Islam to establish permanent opinions of general application.

Furthermore, Muslim jurists were primarily concerned with the formulation of principles of Shari'a in terms of moral duties sanctioned by religious consequences rather than with legal obligations and rights and specific temporal remedies.[23] They categorized all fields of human activity as permissible or impermissible and recommended or reprehensible.[24] In other words, Shari'a addresses the conscience of the individual Muslim, whether in a private, or public and official, capacity, and not the institutions and corporate entities of society and the state.[25] Each Muslim is in theory entitled to follow whatever view

---

20. These were, for Sunni Muslims, Abu Hanifa, d. 767; Malik, d. 795; Shafi'i, d. 819; and Ibn Hanbal, d. 855. The majority of Shi'a Muslims follow the school attributed to Ja'far Al-Sadiq, d. 765.

21. For a detailed discussion and substantiation of this conclusion, see TOWARD AN ISLAMIC REFORMATION, *supra* note 11, at 14–27.

22. *See* N. COULSON, *supra* note 17, at 47–51; K. FARUKI, *supra* note 1, at 166–94 (1975).

23. *See* N. COULSON *supra* note 17, at 82–83.

24. *See id.* at 83–84; A. HASAN, *supra* note 19, at 34–39.

25. It is true that Muslims are required to constitute an Islamic society, *Umma*, and enforce the positive law aspects of Shari'a that entail the establishment of what might be called in modern terminology the executive and judicial organs of an Islamic state. But the relevant provisions of Shari'a are inherently matters of individual conscience. For example, the selection of the chief executive, caliph, is supposed to be based on subjective individual evaluation of his piety and religious knowledge as expressed through a religious oath of allegiance, *by'a*. Appointment to judicial office by the caliph or his representatives is also supposed to be based on similar subjective evaluation of piety and religious knowledge. Given its historical context, it is not surprising that Shari'a did not provide for an "institutionalized" executive and an independent judiciary. Such institutions may be developed today on the basis of some historical sources and practices, but they did not exist in Shari'a.

For detailed discussion of these issues and citation of sources, see TOWARD AN ISLAMIC REFORMATION, *supra* note 11, at 75–100.

is acceptable to his or her private conscience.[26] As a general rule, Muslims to the present day tend to identify themselves as observers of one or another of the established schools of thought.[27] One is entitled to choose not only from among the various views available within his or her school of thought, but also from those views available within other schools. In accordance with this principle, modern official legal reforms in the Muslim world have employed a technique known as *talfiq*: constructing a composite general principle or specific rule from a variety of sources regardless of whether they belong to the same school of thought.[28]

Shari'a, as a religious and moral body of principles and directives, has had and continues to have a significant impact on the thinking and behavior of Muslims. It forms an integral part of the socialization of every Muslim child and is one of the primary forces behind the institutions and customs of the vast majority of Muslim societies.

Whatever may have been the historical status of Shari'a as the legal system of Muslim countries, the scope of its application in the public domain has diminished significantly since the middle of the nineteenth century. Due to both internal factors and external influence, Shari'a principles had been replaced by European law governing commercial, criminal, and constitutional matters in almost all Muslim countries. Only family law and inheritance continued to be governed by Shari'a.[29] Even countries such as Saudi Arabia which claim always to have maintained Shari'a as their sole legal system have enacted numerous "regulations" based on European law and practice in the commercial and public administration fields.[30]

Recently, many Muslims have challenged the gradual weakening of Shari'a as the basis for their formal legal systems. Most Muslim countries have experienced mounting demands for the immediate application of Shari'a as the sole, or at least primary, legal system of the land. These movements have either succeeded in gaining complete control, as in Iran, or achieved significant success in having aspects of Shari'a introduced into the legal system, as in Pakistan and the Sudan. Governments of Muslim countries generally find it difficult to resist these demands out of fear of being condemned by their own populations as anti-Islamic. Therefore, it is likely that this so-called Islamic

---

26. *See* J. SCHACHT, *supra* note 17, at 68 n.1.

27. Most Sunni Muslims identify with the Hanafi, Maliki, Shafi'i, or Hanbali schools while the majority of Shi'a Muslims follow the Ja'fari school of thought.

28. *See* J. SCHACHT, *supra* note 17, at 106; N. COULSON, *supra* note 17, at 197–201.

29. *See generally* H. LIEBESNY, THE LAW OF THE NEAR AND MIDDLE EAST 46–76, 77–117, 118–25 (1975).

30. *See* Seaman, *Islamic Law and Modern Government: Saudi Arabia Supplements the Shari'a to Regulate Development*, 18 COLUM. J. TRANSNAT'L L. 413 (1980).

fundamentalism will achieve further successes in other Muslim countries.[31]

The possibility of further Islamization may convince more people of the urgency of understanding and discussing the relationship between Shari'a and human rights, because Shari'a would have a direct impact on a wider range of human rights issues if it became the formal legal system of any country.[32] To my mind, however, this need is urgent regardless of the official status of Shari'a. As a Muslim, I appreciate the extralegal power that Shari'a has on the minds and hearts of Muslims. Given this power, it is difficult to see how Muslim governments can honor their obligations to promote and protect human rights, even if they wish to do so, where those obligations are perceived to be contrary to Shari'a.

The above survey of the development and nature of Shari'a clearly indicates that Shari'a, as a unified body of moral and legal principles derived from both the Qur'an and Sunna, reflects specific historical interpretations of the scriptural imperatives of Islam. Other interpretations are possible and were in fact anticipated by the founding jurists of Shari'a themselves. Although modern Muslim reformers have expressed some support for this proposition, usually in more moderate terms, very little has been done to develop an adequate reform technique.[33] I believe that a modern version of Islamic law can and should be developed. Such a modern "Shari'a" could be, in my view, entirely consistent with current standards of human rights. These views, however, are appreciated by only a tiny minority of contemporary Muslims. To the overwhelming majority of Muslims today, Shari'a is the sole valid interpretation of Islam, and as such *ought* to prevail over any human law or policy.

---

31. *See generally* 10 THIRD WORLD QUARTERLY (1988) (a special issue on Islam and politics); Haddad, *Muslim Revivalist Thought in the Arab World: An Overview* 76 MUSLIM WORLD 143 - 66 (1986). *See also* sources cited *infra* note 53.

Some authors object to the use of the term "fundamentalism" in relation to the Muslim world. *See, e.g.*, Munson, Jr., *The Social Base of Islamic Militancy in Morocco*, 40 MIDDLE E. J. 267 (1986). Others find the term appropriate. Dessouki, for example, adopts the term "fundamentalism" to refer to "the affirmation, in radically changed environment, of traditional modes of understanding and behavior". Dessouki, *The Resurgence of Islamic Organizations in Egypt: An Interpretation*, in ISLAM AND POWER 107, 108 (Cudsi & Dessouki eds. 1981).

Whether one adopts the term "fundamentalism" or the term "Islamic activism" used in this study, the important thing is to be clear on the nature and context of the phenomenon under discussion. What are the world view and objectives of Islamic fundamentalists/activists? What are the likely consequences for Muslim countries? In particular, what is the probable impact on human rights? To the extent that the activists' objectives reflect a desire to expand and consolidate certain aspects of existing social realities, how do those realities affect human rights today?

32. This relationship has already been noted and discussed. *See, e.g.*, Note, *Human Rights Practices in the Arab States: The Modern Impact of Shari'a Values* 12 GA. J. INT'L & COMP. L. 55 (1982).

33. For a survey and critique of modern Islamic reforms, see TOWARD AN ISLAMIC REFORMATION, *supra* note 11, at 35–51.

B. Shari'a and Human Rights

In this part, I illustrate with specific examples how Shari'a conflicts with international human rights standards. Specifically, I will focus on discrimination against women and non-Muslims. Some contemporary Muslim authors have claimed that Shari'a is fully consistent with and has always protected human rights. Ali A. Wafi, for example, contends that "the most important human rights" can be classified into five principal rights relating to five kinds of liberty: "religious liberty; liberty of opinion and expression; liberty of work; liberty of instruction and culture; and civil liberty."[34] Wafi cites general Islamic sources in support of each liberty and concludes that "Islam" provided for that particular liberty.[35] I find this approach to be both simplistic and misleading. It is simplistic in its classification of human rights and failure to consider conceptual and structural aspects of the modern human rights movement. According to Wafi, civil liberty is the right to conclude contracts, shoulder civil obligations and to dispose freely of property.[36] This is hardly an adequate description of civil liberty as a human right even in the most formal and minimal sense. Wafi's approach is also misleading because it is highly selective and fails to mention other Islamic sources which contradict his contentions in relation to each of the five liberties. He fails to mention the ways in which jurists of Shari'a interpreted these sources and the manner in which Muslim states applied those interpretations through the ages.

The claim that Shari'a is fully consistent with and has always protected human rights is problematic both as a theoretical and a practical matter. As a theoretical matter, the concept of human rights as rights to which every human being is entitled by virtue of being human was unknown to Islamic jurisprudence or social philosophy until the last few decades and does not exist in Shari'a. Many rights are given under Shari'a in accordance with a strict classification based on faith and gender and are not given to human beings as such. As a practical matter, fundamental inconsistencies exist between Shari'a as practiced in Muslim countries and current standards of human rights. For example, many aspects of Shari'a discriminate against women and violate their fundamental human rights. I will discuss this further in Part IV. Three other specific examples of human rights violations can be cited here to illustrate the point.

Although slavery was formally abolished in all Muslim countries through secular law, the institution itself remains lawful under Shari'a

34. Wafi, *Human Rights in Islam*, 11 ISLAMIC Q. 64 (1967).
35. *See id.*
36. *See id.* at 69.

to the present day.[37] It is true that Islam originally discouraged slavery by restricting the "legitimate" sources of slaves and encouraging their emancipation, but it did not directly prohibit slavery and the institution of slavery has never been abolished under Shari'a. In fact, treatises on Shari'a discuss at length contractual and other arrangements relating to slaves.[38] In my view, the original intention of Islam was to eliminate slavery in due course, but that intention has never been realized through Shari'a.[39]

The second example is the Shari'a law of apostasy. According to Shari'a, a Muslim who repudiates his faith in Islam, whether directly or indirectly, is guilty of a capital offense punishable by death.[40] This aspect of Shari'a is in complete conflict with the fundamental human right of freedom of religion and conscience. The apostasy of a Muslim may be inferred by the court from the person's views or actions deemed by the court to contravene the basic tenets of Islam and therefore be tantamount to apostasy, regardless of the accused's personal belief that he or she is a Muslim.

The Shari'a law of apostasy can be used to restrict other human rights such as freedom of expression. A person may be liable to the death penalty for expressing views held by the authorities to contravene the official view of the tenets of Islam. Far from being an historical practice or a purely theoretical danger, this interpretation of the law of apostasy was applied in the Sudan as recently as 1985, when a Sudanese Muslim reformer was executed because the authorities deemed his views to be contrary to Islam.[41]

---

37. *See* S. TABANDEH, MUSLIM COMMENTARY ON THE UNIVERSAL DECLARATION OF HUMAN RIGHTS 27 (1970).

38. *See* N. COULSON, *supra* note 17, at 32–33, 44–46, 50; J. SCHACHT, *supra* note 17, at 127–30, 162, 166, 170, 174, 177–78, 186–87, 193.

39. *See* TOWARD AN ISLAMIC REFORMATION, *supra* note 11, at 172–75.

40. *See* M. EL-AWA, PUNISHMENT IN ISLAMIC LAW: A COMPARATIVE STUDY 43 (1982).

41. *See* An-Na'im, *The Islamic Law of Apostasy and its Modern Applicability: A Case from the Sudan*, 16 RELIGION 197 (1986).

The Salman Rushdie affair illustrates the serious negative implications of the law of apostasy to literary and artistic expression. Mr. Rushdie, a British national of Muslim background, published a novel entitled, *The Satanic Verses*, in which irreverent reference is made to the Prophet of Islam, his wives, and leading companions. Many Muslim governments banned the book because their populations found the author's style and connotations extremely offensive. The late Imam Khomeini of Iran sentenced Rushdie to death *in absentia* without charge or trial.

There are obvious procedural objections to that sentence from a Shari'a point of view, namely, that Mr. Rushdie was not subject to the jurisdiction of Iran and was not formally charged and allowed to defend himself. But beyond this formal objection remains the basic fundamental objection to the law of apostasy itself as a violation of freedoms of belief and expression. If Shari'a procedural requirements can be satisfied, an author can be sentenced to death under Shari'a for his views.

For a fuller discussion of this case and its implications, see TOWARD AN ISLAMIC REFORMATION, *supra* note 11, at 182–84.

A third and final example of conflict between Shari'a and human rights relates to the status and rights of non-Muslims. Shari'a classifies the subjects of an Islamic state in terms of their religious beliefs: Muslims, *ahl al-Kitab* or believers in a divinely revealed scripture (mainly Christian and Jews), and unbelievers.[42] In modern terms, Muslims are the only full citizens of an Islamic state, enjoying all the rights and freedoms granted by Shari'a and subject only to the limitations and restrictions imposed on women. *Ahl al-Kitab* are entitled to the status of *dhimma*, a special compact with the Muslim state which guarantees them security of persons and property and a degree of communal autonomy to practice their own religion and conduct their private affairs in accordance with their customs and laws. In exchange for these limited rights, *dhimmis* undertake to pay *jizya* or poll tax and submit to Muslim sovereignty and authority in all public affairs.[43] Unbelievers may be granted *aman* or safe conduct which secures their persons and property for the duration of the *aman* period.[44] Moreover, unbelievers that are permanent residents of an Islamic state may be recognized as *dhimmis*.

According to this scheme, non-Muslim subjects of an Islamic state can aspire only to the status of *dhimma*, under which they would suffer serious violations of their human rights. *Dhimmis* are not entitled to equality with Muslims. Their lives are evaluated as inferior in monetary terms as well: they are not entitled to the same amount of *diya* or financial compensation for homicide or bodily harm as Muslims.[45] The reputation of a *dhimmi* is not protected by Shari'a on equal terms with that of a Muslim since the *hadd* of *qadhf*, the special criminal penalty for an unproven accusation of fornication, does not apply unless the victim is a Muslim.[46] In the private law of Shari'a, discrimination against non-Muslims includes the rule that a Muslim man may marry a *dhimmi* woman but a *dhimmi* man may not marry a Muslim woman.[47]

Some of these restrictions against non-Muslims have not been enforced in most Muslim countries for some time, but they all remain

42. "Unbelievers," as defined by Shari'a, are those who do not believe in one of the recognized heavenly revelations. Originally, this category was taken to include all non-Muslims except Christians, Sabi'is, and Jews, but some jurists have argued that adherents of other religions such as Zoroastrians and Hindus should be included on the assumption that they have revealed scriptures. *See* SHORTER ENCYCLOPAEDIA OF ISLAM 16–17 (Gibb & Kramers eds. 1974); A. YUSUF, KITAB AL-KHARAJ 128–30 (1302 Hijri) (Arabic). Animists would not qualify as believers regardless of their own view of their belief in God.

43. *See* verse 9:29 of the HOLY QUR'AN. *See also* M. AL-SHAFI'I, 4 KITAB AL-UMM 172 *passim* (1961) (Arabic); M. KHADDURI, WAR AND PEACE IN THE LAW OF ISLAM 177, 195–99 (1955).

44. *See* M. KHADDURI, *supra* note 43, at 166–69.

45. See AL-SHAFI'I, 6 KITAB AL-UMM 105–6 (1961) (Arabic).

46. See I. RUSHD, 2 BIDAYAT AL-MUJTAHID WA NIHAYAT AL-MUQTASID 330 (Arabic); Safwat, *Offences and Penalties in Islamic Law*, 26 ISLAMIC Q. 149, 159 (1982).

47. *See* AL-SHAFI'I, 5 KITAB AL-UMM 6–9, 44, 50. (Arabic).

part of Shari'a, and consequent violations of the human rights of non-Muslims recently have occurred in some modern Muslim countries.[48] Not only are these human rights violations committed against those who identify themselves as non-Muslims, such as the Copts of Egypt,[49] but they are also committed against minority Muslim sects which are deemed by the majority to be apostates from Islam, such as the Ahmadis of Pakistan.[50] Members of these minorities are not only persecuted by governments, but are also frequently attacked and murdered by mobs unfettered by legal restrictions.[51]

The broader implications of the law of apostasy are also relevant to understanding the status and rights of other minority sects, such as the Shi'a of Pakistan and Saudi Arabia, who do not conform to orthodox Sunni beliefs dominant in those countries. Serious human rights violations are committed against these minorities by official and private actors.[52]

III. THE POLITICS AND SOCIOLOGY OF ISLAMIZATION

To appreciate the likely impact of Shari'a on human rights it is important to understand not only its historical formulations, but also the socio-political context of what has often been called the process of Islamization in various Muslim countries. Although there appears to be an obvious development toward greater Islamization in many Muslim countries, it is a process of fits and starts, backward and forward movements, reflecting general trends and the peculiar experience of

---

48. See, for example, the evaluation of Sudan's application of Shari'a since 1983 in TOWARD AN ISLAMIC REFORMATION, *supra* note 11, at 125–33.

49. *See generally* An-Na'im, *Religious Freedom in Egypt: Under the Shadow of the Dhimma System*, in RELIGIOUS LIBERTY AND HUMAN RIGHTS IN NATIONS AND RELIGIONS 43 (L. Swidler ed. 1986).

50. In Pakistan, the government of Z. Bhutto yielded to pressures to declare the Ahmadis a non-Muslim minority and as such exclude them from important official positions. J. ESPOSITO, ISLAM AND POLITICS 163 (rev. ed. 1987).

The Baha'is claim to be adherents of an independent religion and specifically state that they are not a sect of Islam. Iranian authorities reject this claim, because Islam does not accept the possibility of revelation after the Qur'an. The Baha'i faith cannot therefore qualify as an independent religion according to Shari'a. The Baha'is of Iran have been subjected to severe persecution since the founding of their faith during the nineteenth century. *See generally* G. NASH, IRAN'S SECRET POGROM (1982); D. MARTIN, THE PERSECUTION OF THE BAHA'IS OF IRAN, 1844-1984 (1984).

51. Government officials often instigate violence against members of these groups. Former President Zia ul-Haq of Pakistan, for example, said that "Ahmadis will not be tolerated. There is no place for infidels in Pakistan. If a man's honor is attacked he does not even hesitate from committing murder." Parker, *Pakistani sect's death sentence*, San Francisco Examiner, May 25, 1986, at A14 col. 4.

52. *See, e.g.*, Ziring, *From Islamic Republic to Islamic State in Pakistan*, 24 ASIAN SURV. 931 (1984); Ahmed, *The Shi'is of Pakistan*, in SHI'ISM, RESISTANCE AND REVOLUTION 275 (M. Kramer ed. 1987); Goldberg, *The Shi'i Minority in Saudi Arabia*, in SHI'ISM AND SOCIAL PROTEST 230 (Cole & Keddie eds. 1986).

each society.[53] Consequently, Shari'a-inspired impact on human rights varies significantly from Islamic nation to nation.[54] Governments facing mounting pressure to implement Islamic laws and policies, however, have tended to enunciate policies that have a differential impact upon the weaker segments of society. These governments adopt policies which restrict the rights of women and minorities, who have minimal influence and voice in society, rather than taking measures that challenge the status quo or effect vested interests.[55]

A. *Political Context and Developments*

The complexity of the politics of Islamization is illustrated by the recent history of almost any Muslim country. The dynamics of domestic politics and personalities, together with regional and international geopolitical factors, often render the whole process seemingly unpredictable and paradoxical. For example, the supposedly secular socialist regime of Zulfikar Ali Bhutto was the first to substantially advance the cause of Islamization in Pakistan's history. On the other hand, General Suharto in Indonesia, who came to power to counter a communist coup d'etat in 1965, has proven to be most resistant to Islamization in that country. Yet each situation has its own internal logic.

Bhutto was attempting to respond to a crisis in national identity caused by the secession of Bangladesh, to seek Muslim Arab financial support, and to dispel domestic charges of being un-Islamic.[56] This led him to implement policies that had drastic long-term human rights consequences, such as the persecution of the Ahmadi minority. Ironically his efforts to appease Islamic activists failed and opposition to his regime from Islamic groups eventually contributed to Zia ul-Haq's coup of July 1977. According to one author, Bhutto's introduction of Islamic measures and promise of more Shari'a law, rather than defusing the Islàmic revival movement "served to reinforce the Islamic character

53. The literature on this subject is extensive. *See generally* D. PIPES, IN THE PATH OF GOD: THE POLITICS OF ISLAMIC REASSERTION (M. Ayoob ed. 1981); RELIGION AND POLITICS IN THE MIDDLE EAST (M. Curtis ed. 1981); ISLAM IN THE POLITICAL PROCESS (J. Piscatori ed. 1983); VOICES OF RESURGENT ISLAM (J. Esposito ed. 1983); J. ESPOSITO, *supra* note 50.

54. This does not mean that a greater role for Islam in public life will necessarily lead to more violations of human rights. In fact, it may well be the case that resistance to such demands leads to more human rights violations where the government is willing and able to oppress Islamic activists.

55. The regime of General Zia ul-Haq in Pakistan, for example, was unwilling to heed demands by Islamic activists to lift martial law or conduct national elections, but was prepared to introduce a range of Islamic measures, including restrictions on women's rights. *See* J. ESPOSITO, *supra* note 50, at 167–70, 175; Faruki, *Pakistan: Islamic Government and Society*, in ISLAM IN ASIA 68–70 (J. Esposito ed. 1987).

56. *See* Richter, *The Political Dynamics of Islamic Resurgence in Pakistan*, 19 ASIA SURV. 547–57 (1979); Faruki, *supra* note 55, at 57–58.

of the conflict. Most importantly, a turning point had been reached. Islam and Pakistan's Islamic identity had re-emerged as the dominant theme in Pakistani politics in a manner and to a degree that had not been seen since Pakistan's establishment."[57]

Islam's dominance of Pakistani political discourse has been reinforced by more than ten years of Zia ul-Haq's rule. This dominance probably will continue unabated despite the return of democratic government and the election of Ali Bhutto's daughter, Benazir Bhutto, as Prime Minister. The paradox, however, continues: despite previously implemented Islamization measures, which included the drive to exclude women from public office in accordance with Shari'a provisions, a woman was elected as Prime Minister of Pakistan.

In contrast to Pakistan, Indonesia presents a different picture ot Islamization. One author has suggested that the restriction of Islam under the New Order of General Suharto

> reflects, on the one hand, the proclivities of state leaders influenced by both technocratic and pre-Islamic ideas and fearful of any institutions they do not control. It also, however, continues the experience of Indonesian Islam over a far longer time . . . . The ambiguity of Islam's political strength and role has been mirrored in the ambivalence of Indonesia's rulers towards it; by and large, while trying to use it as a source of legitimacy, they have held it at arm's length.[58]

While Islam currently plays a fairly minimal part in Indonesian politics, the situation is far from static. The present regime's policies on the role of Islam in Indonesian politics may change in the near future. Islamic activists may either achieve some moderate success with the present government by modifying their strategies or perhaps they will contribute to the regime's overthrow.[59]

The impact of the international Islamic dimension affects in different ways the internal politics of Islamization in Indonesia and other parts of south and southeast Asia.[60] While international Islam tends to affect the situation in Pakistan and Bangladesh by influencing government policies, it offers support for the Islamic opposition to

---

57. J. Esposito, *supra* note 50, at 166.

58. McVey, *Faith as the Outsider: Islam in Indonesian Politics*, in Islam in the Political Process 199, 201 (J. Piscatori ed. 1983).

59. *See* Liong, *Indonesian Muslims and the State: Accommodation or Revolt*, 10 Third World Q. 869 (1988); McVey, *supra* note 58, at 212–21.

60. *See* Gunn, *Radical Islam in Southeast Asia: Rhetoric and Reality in the Middle Eastern Connection*, 16 J. Contemp. Asia 30 (1986).

the government in Indonesia.[61] For example, the Iranian Revolution has had more than a purely inspirational impact on the politics of Islamization in Indonesia.[62]

Currently, the politics of Islamization in Indonesia are apparently producing human rights violations from official as well as private sources. The situation in Indonesia is a paradigmatic example of the demand for greater Islamization leading to gross violations of the human rights of Muslim activists at the hands of official authorities.[63] In the private arena as well, Islamic politics appear to be associated with some of the sectarian violence in Indonesia giving rise to many human rights violations.[64]

Other Muslim countries present their own surprising developments and peculiar politics of Islamization. In Iran, Muslim activists achieved their most spectacular success this century when one of the most secularized countries in the Muslim world was transformed into a totalitarian Islamic state in 1979. The stages and personalities of that "unexpected" development are well known and need not be described here.[65]

The Kingdom of Saudi Arabia may appear to most outsiders as the embodiment of Islam itself. In fact, the Saudi dynasty endeavors to cultivate this image and to manipulate Islam as the primary source of its legitimacy.[66] But, as dramatically evidenced by the seizure of the Great Mosque of Mecca in 1979, and by repeated Shi'a riots in eastern

61. *See* von der Mehden, *The Political and Social Challenge of the Islamic Revival in Malaysia and Indonesia*, 76 MUSLIM WORLD 219, 225, 231 (1986).

62. *See* Gunn, *supra* note 60, at 45–46.

63. *See id.* at 43–44. Of course, Islamic activists are not the only ones having to bear the brunt of the Indonesian government policies. The persecution of communists and other political activists of the 1960s is a continuing source of human rights violations in Indonesia. *See* Budiardjo, *The Abuse of Human Rights in Indonesia*, III CASE STUDIES ON HUMAN RIGHTS AND FUNDAMENTAL FREEDOMS: A WORLD SURVEY 211 (1976); AMNESTY INTERNATIONAL, INDONESIA: AN AMNESTY INTERNATIONAL REPORT 1 *passim* (AI PUB 77/00/77 1977) "Tens of thousands of political prisoners in Indonesia are held captive without trial, or used as servants by local military commanders, or exploited as forced labour, or subjected to an archaic policy of transportation to penal colonies." *Id.* at 9; *Indonesia in the 1980's*, 16 ASIAN AFFAIRS 125 (1985). Events in East Timor, which has been occupied by Indonesian troops since 1975, present another gruesome chapter of human rights violations unrelated to the politics of Islamization in that part of the world. *See generally* ASIA WATCH, HUMAN RIGHTS IN INDONESIA AND EAST TIMOR (1989).

64. McVey, *supra* note 58, at 202–3. Neither of the above-mentioned sources of human rights violations, however, are peculiar to Indonesia. Syria presents an example of an official source while recent events in Northern Nigeria illustrate the operation of a private source of human rights violations.

65. Literature on the subject is extensive. *See, e.g.*, R. RAMAZANI, REVOLUTIONARY IRAN: CHALLENGE AND RESPONSE IN THE MIDDLE EAST (1986); THE IRANIAN REVOLUTION AND THE ISLAMIC REPUBLIC (Keddie & Hooglund eds. 1986); A. HUSSAIN, ISLAMIC IRAN: REVOLUTION AND COUNTER-REVOLUTION (1985); S. IRFANI, REVOLUTIONARY ISLAM IN IRAN (1983).

66. J. Piscatori, *Ideological Politics in Sa'udi Arabia*, in ISLAM IN THE POLITICAL PROCESS 57–63 (J. Piscatori ed. 1983).

Saudi Arabia, Islam can also provide a significant source of challenge to the Saudi regime.[67]

As a result of rapid modernization in Muslim countries, a new technocratic middle class has emerged, which has, somewhat surprisingly, espoused Islamic fundamentalist positions rather than an enlightened Islamic interpretation or a secular ideology. It may appear paradoxical to speak of "modernized" segments of society adopting a fundamentalist posture; however, as indicated by studies in countries such as Egypt[68] and Morocco,[69] young, educated, urbanized Muslims often opt for Islamic fundamentalism. Moreover, the victimization of significant numbers of the population as a result of rapid modernization likely will cause the Saudi regime to confront challenges from both the left and right—"the secular radicals and the religious conservatives."[70] The dilemma facing the Saudi regime—which would trouble any ruling elite attempting to balance the push and pull of such conflicting forces—is that whatever measures it takes to satisfy one source of dissent will necessarily antagonize the other.

Accomodation may be particularly difficult for the Saudi regime given their Islamic ideology, namely the Hanbali school of Islamic jurisprudence as interpreted by Muhammad ibn Abd al-Wahab in the eighteenth century.[71] Western scholars differ in their evaluation of the central feature of Saudi ideology. Whereas most scholars perceive the Hanbali school as strict and rigid, others argue that it has proven to be particularly flexible, at least in Saudi hands. In espousing the latter view, Piscatori has argued that the former "misinterprets Hanbali conservatism: there must be faithful adherence to the Qur'an and the *hadiths* (the traditions of the Prophet), but when these have nothing to say on a subject, there are no rigid guidelines."[72]

I tend to agree with the first evaluation and disagree with that of Piscatori. The Hanbali school is generally the most strict of all Sunni schools in its interpretations of the Qur'an and Sunna, and the least likely to accept that these sources have nothing to say on a subject. The Hanbali school is therefore more likely to hold that the sources of Islam are explicit on a given subject—and more likely to adopt the stricter interpretation of these sources—than any of the other three

---

67. *See id.* at 66–67.

68. *See, e.g.*, Ibrahim, *Anatomy of Egypt's Militant Islamic Groups: Methodological Note and Preliminary Findings*, 12 INT'L J. MIDDLE E. STUD. 438, 439–40 (1980); Altman, *Islamic Movements in Egypt*, 10 JERUSALEM Q. 87, 96, 100 (1979).

69. *See* Munson, *The Social Base of Islamic Militancy in Morocco*, 40 MIDDLE E. J. 267, 269, 276, 278 (1986).

70. Piscatori, *supra* note 66, at 68.

71. *See* SHORTER ENCYCLOPEDIA OF ISLAM, *supra* note 42, at 20–21; H. WAHBA, JAZIRAT AL-'ARAB FI AL-QARN AL-'ISHRYN 324–31 (1961) (Arabic).

72. Piscatori, *supra* note 66, at 62.

schools of Sunni jurisprudence. In political terms, the severity of the Hanbali school, especially under Wahabi interpretations, probably will increase the tension between conflicting forces in Saudi Arabia today, making it harder for the Saudi dynasty to maintain the necessary balance between the conservative and modernized segments of its population.

Despite apparent differences from the Saudi case, and between themselves, Egypt and Morocco are open to similar analyses. Both the republican regime of Egypt and the Moroccan monarchy are trying to maintain Islamic legitimacy of their rule while containing the fundamentalist threat posed by Islamic activists.[73] The Moroccan government initially favored the growth of Islamic activism for the same reason Sadat initially supported similar movements in Egypt, namely, to curb Marxist and leftist groups. Both governments eventually realized that Islamic activism could pose a greater threat to their regimes.[74] The difficult balance these regimes are attempting to maintain is having negative consequences for human rights in both countries.[75]

B. *Sociological Considerations*

In this part, I consider the role of sociological factors in this analysis, which are important not only for their influence on political developments and impact on the accessibility and efficacy of legal remedies, but also because they underlay private or nonofficial human rights violations. This section puts forward some observations about who makes up the class of Islamic activists, how these activists influence social attitudes and behavior, what social forces counter their influence,

73. On Egypt see, *e.g.*, Hanafi, *The Relevance of the Islamic Alternative in Egypt*, 4 ARAB STUD. Q. 54 (1982); Ajami, *In the Pharaoh's Shadow: Religion and Authority in Egypt*, in ISLAM IN THE POLITICAL PROCESS, *supra* note 53, at 12. In relation to the situation in Morocco, see Munson, *Islamic Revivalism in Morocco and Tunisia*, 76 MUSLIM WORLD 203 (1986).

74. *See* Munson *id.* at 205.

75. These problems are extensively documented by human rights monitoring organizations, such as Amnesty International, Human Rights Internet, Middle East Watch, and the Arab Human Rights Organization. *See, e.g*, AMNESTY INTERNATIONAL, EGYPTIAN GOVERNMENT MUST ACT URGENTLY TO END TORTURE (Bulletin, MDE 12/03/88, 1988) ("Many reports of torture had followed the arrest of thousands of political suspects after the attempted assassinations in May and August last year of the former Interior Ministers . . . . The alleged victims [of torture] were mostly supporters of Islamic groups."); AMNESTY INTERNATIONAL, ARREST OF CHRISTIANS IN EGYPT (Bulletin, MDE 12/02/86, 1986) ("Amnesty International is concerned by reports it has received of the arrest of four converts from Islam to Christianity in Cairo in January 1986. The organisation believes that the detainees may be prisoners of conscience, detained for practising the Christian religion."); *see also* AMNESTY INTERNATIONAL, URGENT ACTION, UA 313/85 (1985) (Amnesty received reports that 37 people were arrested in Morocco for exercising freedoms of association and expression, held incommunicado, and ill-treated in prison.); MIDDLE EAST RESEARCH AND INFORMATION PROJECT (MERIP), HUMAN RIGHTS IN THE MIDDLE EAST (No. 149, Nov.-Dec. 1987).

and what arguments and methods are available to those who would counter the activists.

In Morocco, the overwhelming majority of Islamic activists are university and high school students. The movement also appeals to other segments of the "new middle class," as well as to some members of the traditional strata of society.[76] Studies of other Muslim societies generally confirm a similar composition of such Islamic fundamentalist movements.[77] Furthermore, the numbers of students and other youths who passively support the goals of Islamic activists are far greater than the numbers who become actively involved.[78] For example, while fewer than fifteen percent of Moroccan university students surveyed in a 1976 study were actively involved in protests and demands for reform, thirty-two percent favored the reestablishment of Islamic law (Shari'a), and thirty-eight percent saw a sincere return to Islamic values as the sole way for Morrocans to free themselves.[79] Despite their numerical insignificance, students in most Muslim countries tend to be much more politically active than the peasantry which constitutes the majority of the population.[80]

Another characteristic of student Islamic activists is that most of them come from the poorest strata,[81] which constitutes the vast majority of the population. They can therefore be presumed to be representative of the majority view or at least expected to receive its support.

The basic message of Islamic activists—a genuine return to Islam and outrage at moral and political decay and economic injustice—is deeply rooted in the Islamic tradition. The current cycle of Islamic activism draws on the long-established belief in the universality and centrality of Islam in the lives of Muslims, as the essential basis and focus of their identity and loyalty.[82] As explained by Smith, throughout the modern period, almost every Islamic movement has been, in some way, a variation on the double theme of protest against internal

---

76. Munson, *supra* note 69, at 267, 269, 276, 278 (1986). By the "new middle class" Munson refers to people who are neither extremely poor nor extremely rich and who have-had considerable exposure to Western culture, usually in basically secular public schools. *Id.* at 276.

77. *See, e.g.*, Ibrahim, *Anatomy of Egypt's Militant Islamic Groups: Methodological Note and Preliminary Findings*, 12 INT'L J. MIDDLE E. STUD. 438, at 439–40 (1980); Altman, *Islamic Movements in Egypt*, 10 JERUSALEM Q. 87, 96, 100 (1979).

78. *See* Munson, *supra* note 69, at 272–75.

79. *See* Munson, *supra* note 69, at 275 (reporting on a study for a doctoral thesis by Mohamed Tozy, *Champ et contre champ politico-religieux au Maroc* 248, 250–52. Université de Droit, d'Economie et de Sciences d'Aix-Marseille, 1984).

80. *See* Munson, *supra* note 69, at 271.

81. *See id.* at 275–76; Kupferschmidt, *Reformist and Militant Islam in Urban and Rural Egypt*, 23 MIDDLE E. STUD. 403 (1987).

82. *See* Lewis, *The Return to Islam*, in RELIGION AND POLITICS IN THE MIDDLE EAST, *supra* note 53, at 11.

deterioration and external encroachment.[83] Islamic activism can therefore be seen as a response to a protracted crisis of political, economic, and military dimensions, presenting Islam as "a practical political alternative as well as a secure spiritual niche and psychological anchor in a turbulent world."[84] Muslims are reminded of the Golden Age of the Islamic civilization, an age of political power, economic prosperity, and social justice as well as religious piety and spiritual well-being. Current political, economic, and social problems are attributed to a departure from Islam and the failure to implement Shari'a. The cure, obviously, is a return to Islam and the reestablishment of Shari'a.

In delivering this powerful message, Islamic activists enjoy two main advantages. First, they share with their audience a common belief, language, and history which enables them to draw on easily appreciated and highly effective symbols from the Islamic tradition. Second, they are delivering a message which their audience wants to accept, a single cause for all their problems and an apparently simple solution. Instead of looking for reasons or causes of Islamic activism, one should perhaps ask why it is not as successful as the power of its message and the nature of its methods would indicate.

One author has observed that the message of Islamic activists should be particularly appealing to the more traditional and less privileged strata of Muslim societies.[85] Yet, there is little evidence of widespread support for Islamic activists from these strata in Morocco and elsewhere in the Muslim world, notwithstanding the activism of Islamic students from these same strata.[86] Although many Islamic activists originate from among these less privileged sectors of society, they seem to have had little success in mobilizing the poor masses in support of their cause. The causes of this apparent lack of support can best be appreciated in the context of a particular society, but a few rather speculative general observations may be illustrative.

In the first place, the lack of evidence of support does not necessarily mean the support itself is lacking. The lack of evidence of popular support may be due to political factors, such as the suppression of freedom of expression or the lack of technological and other means of communication. There is usually little inclination and opportunity for conducting opinion polls in the Muslim world. Very few observers

---

83. *See* W. SMITH, ISLAM IN MODERN HISTORY 47 (1957).

84. Dekmejian, *The Anatomy of Islamic Revival: Legitimacy Crisis, Ethnic Conflict, and the Search for Islamic Alternatives*, in RELIGION AND POLITICS IN THE MIDDLE EAST, *supra* note 53, at 39. Many authors in the field offer similar analysis. *See, e.g.*, Dessouki, *supra* note 31, at 110–16; Esposito, *Introduction: Islam and Muslim Politics*, in VOICES OF RESURGENT ISLAM 11–13 (J. Esposito ed. 1983); Munson, *supra* note 69, at 215–18.

85. *See* Munson, *supra* note 69, at 279.

86. *See id.* at 279.

saw evidence of widespread support for Khomeini in 1979, yet Khomeini had enough support to overthrow a regime which was generally believed to be one of the most stable and durable in the Muslim World. As one author concluded in relation to Morocco, "it would be a mistake to assume that militant Islam will remain as politically impotent as it now appears to be."[87] I believe this conclusion is generally true of other Muslim countries as well.

Furthermore, the aspiration of Muslim peoples to establish an Islamic state has been dormant for so many centuries that it is no longer taken seriously as a realistic prospect by the lower, unsophisticated strata of society. Their hopes have been frustrated so many times and manipulated by their leaders for so long that ordinary Muslims have simply resigned themselves to postponing the idea indefinitely.

A related consideration is that the present rulers of the Muslim world are successful in claiming Islamic legitimacy. King Hassan II of Morocco, for example, is venerated by the majority of his subjects as a descendent of the Prophet and accepted as *Amir al-Mu'minin*, Commander of the Believers or the legitimate ruler of an Islamic state. In addition, the Saudi dynasty seems to have succeeded in cultivating the image of an Islamic state. Why should the people demand the establishment of an Islamic state, at considerable risk to their personal safety and well-being, if they are led to believe that they already have one?

My own hypothesis is that, despite their assumed or declared belief in the desirability of an Islamic state based on Shari'a, the majority of Muslims know instinctively that such a state is not really workable and may not be desirable in practice. I believe that it is this almost subconscious knowledge, more than colonialism and external influence, which caused the role of Shari'a in the public domain to diminish so drastically in modern times.

Nevertheless, I realize that Muslims find it extremely difficult to admit this fact even to themselves. So long as they are not forced to make an open decision on the matter, they will continue believing or pretending to believe in the myth of an Islamic state based on Shari'a. Consequently, they will probably remain passive to the demands of Islamic activists until they are forced to decide. Demographic, cultural, and other factors and forces may influence their decision. While these factors exist in all Muslim countries, the Indonesian case may provide better insights into the complexity and specificity of the issues.

The manner of the initial Islamization of Indonesia and the demographic composition of the country seem to be significant factors in the present status of Islamic activists there. It is generally accepted

87. *Id.* at 284.

that Islam was brought to that part of the world by Muslim merchants during the fourteenth and fifteenth centuries, or earlier.[88] Islam was consolidated on the main islands of Java and Sumatra and on other islands between the fifteenth and seventeenth centuries. Other developments followed which need not be detailed here. The point to emphasize is that the

> Muslim community in what is now Indonesia, then, is the heir to a variety of modalities by which Islam achieved a presence at particular points in Southeast Asia. In some, it remained simply a presence, in others, it disappeared and, in still others, it developed as the opportunities of time and place allowed.[89]

The interplay of local factors and external Dutch encroachment produced a complex mixture of Islamic and non-Islamic cultures in the region. For example, in Javanese society,

> [the term *santri*] denote the religiously observant orthodox Muslims as a group in society, in contradiction to the *abangan* (those who followed the old Javanese folk religion, intermingled with Islam) and the *priyayi* (the Javanese aristocrats and their descendants) who followed an Islam which had strong admixture of Hindu-Buddhist elements.[90]

Moreover, there are too many animist, regional, and ideological variations in perceptions of Islam to allow for unified or even vaguely allied action by Islamic activists.[91]

There has never been a real Muslim state in Indonesia in the sense experienced by Muslims in the Middle East, North Africa, and the Indian sub-continent.[92] This "has left a deep impact on Indonesian politics, particularly on the role of Muslim political as well as religious organizations."[93] The representatives of the Muslim community have consistently been assigned an outsider's role throughout Indonesian

88. Soebardi & Woodcroft-Lee, *Islam in Indonesia*, in THE CRESCENT IN THE EAST 180–82 (R. Israel ed. 1982).

89. Johns, *Modes of Islamization in Southeast Asia*, in RELIGIOUS CHANGE AND CULTURAL DOMINATION 61, 62 (1981).

90. Soebardi & Woodcraft-Lee, *supra* note 88, at 186. *See generally* C. GEERTZ, THE RELIGION OF JAVA (1960).

91. Johns, *Indonesia: Islam and Cultural Pluralism*, in ISLAM IN ASIA 202, 226 (J. Esposito ed. 1987).

92. Some states of the past, such as Acheh, could probably come close to full fledged Islamic states. *See* Johns, *supra* note 89, at 69.

93. Utrect, *Religion and Social Protest in Indonesia*, 25 SOC. COMPASS 395, 398 (1978).

history.[94] Therefore, ordinary Indonesian Muslims have difficulty relating to a total political Islamic experience or envisaging the application of Shari'a in the public domain, despite the intellectual efforts of elites to supplement this deficiency.

Another factor relevant to the status of Islamic activism in Indonesia today is the sheer distance between that country and the majority of Muslim countries. This inhibits communication between Indonesian and Middle Eastern Islamic activists and also reinforces the barriers of language and culture in general. Distance may not overly hamper elites in this age of jet travel and electronic communications, but it certainly diminishes the impact of religious and intellectual influences from the Middle East and North Africa on the majority of ordinary Indonesian Muslims.

Despite these factors, Islam does have a political role in Indonesia, although somewhat weak in comparison to its role in other Muslim countries. There is so much spiritual, intellectual, and organizational Islamic activism that some observers were led to suggest that Indonesia might be close to an Islamic revolution.[95] Paradoxically, although Islam was the banner of Indonesian nationalism during the struggle for independence, its political role declined after independence, especially during the last three decades.[96] The influence of Islam in that country is strongest, however, on human relations, especially in family law and inheritance.[97] The human rights implications of this aspect of Shari'a will be discussed later.[98]

The nature and rationale of factors and forces opposing the reestablishment of Shari'a are, in general, secular education and cross-cultural interaction. These forces have raised the consciousness and expectations of some segments of the population. Many women, for instance, have had the benefits of secular higher education and have travelled abroad or otherwise been exposed to external feminist influences. These women have also experienced some degree of equality and have had access to opportunities in public life through the somewhat secularized political regimes and legal systems of most Muslim countries. They have learned how to organize and lobby for their rights and how to establish networks with other women's rights groups. These women's organizations have engaged in some forms of resistance to Islamization

---

94. *See* Wertheim, *Islam in Indonesia: A House Divided*, in TEN YEARS' MILITARY TERROR IN INDONESIA 75 (M. Caldwell ed. 1975).

95. *See, e.g.*, G. JANSEN, MILITANT ISLAM (1979).

96. *See* Utrecht, *supra* note 93, at 408–11; Soebardi and Woodcroft-Lee, *supra* note 88, at 189–204; Johns, *supra* note 89, at 209–20. *See also* von der Mehden, *supra* note 61, at 222–25.

97. Utrecht, *supra* note 93, at 407.

98. *See infra* notes 102–38 and accompanying text.

in Pakistan and protested against measures which affected their status and rights during Zia ul-Haq's era.[99]

Although I appreciate the apprehensions of these groups about the strict application of Shari'a, I can see that they face a deep dilemma. Because what they are protesting is perceived by the Muslim populations of their countries to be the law of Islam, they can expect little sympathy and political support from those populations. These groups are therefore faced with a difficult choice: on the one hand, if they submit to the strict application of Shari'a they would be accepting the institutionalization of the violation of their human rights. Yet, resistance would lay them open to charges of being anti-Islamic, making it easy for the proponents of Islamization to mobilize public opinion against their cause. Moreover, to the extent that members of these vulnerable groups are Muslims themselves, they also face a strong psychological barrier against criticizing Shari'a, the embodiment and authoritative voice of their faith. Thus, the socio-political forces encouraging greater Islamization will exacerbate the difficulty of this dilemma faced by women in Muslim countries.

IV. A CASE STUDY: THE ISLAMIC DIMENSION OF THE STATUS OF WOMEN

Given the rising tide of Islamization in Muslim countries and its call for wider recognition of Shari'a as the primary legal basis of Muslim nations, concerns about Shari'a's conflict with human rights standards must be addressed. Such conflict and tension between historical formulations of Shari'a and modern standards of human rights is readily illustrated by the situation of women in Muslim countries today. The status and rights of women are a major human rights concern in all parts of the world: women are consistently oppressed, discriminated against, and denied their rightful equality with men. Although the situation has recently improved in some developed countries, I believe that it is by no means satisfactory anywhere in the world today. The present focus on Muslim violations of the human rights of women does not mean that these are peculiar to the Muslim world.[100] As a Muslim, however, I am particularly concerned with the

99. *See, e.g.*, 32 INT'L COMM'N OF JURISTS REV. 19, 19–21 (1984) (a brief survey on the activities of the Women's Action Forum).

100. It is difficult to distinguish between Islamic, or rather Shari'a, factors and extra-Shari'a factors affecting the status and rights of women. The fact that women's human rights are violated in all parts of the world suggests that there are universal social, economic, and political factors contributing to the persistence of this state of affairs. Nevertheless, the articulation and operation of these factors varies from one culture or context to the next. In particular, the rationalization of discrimination against and denial of equality for women is based on the values and customs of the particular society. In the Muslim world, these values and customs are supposed to be Islamic or at least consistent with the dictates of Islam. It is therefore useful to discuss the Islamic dimension of the status and rights of women.

situation in the Muslim world and wish to contribute to its improvement.

The following discussion is organized in terms of the status and rights of Muslim women in the private sphere, particularly within the family, and in public fora, in relation to access to work and participation in public affairs. This classification is recommended for the Muslim context because the personal law aspects of Shari'a, family law and inheritance, have been applied much more consistently than the public law doctrines.[101] The status and rights of women in private life have always been significantly influenced by Shari'a regardless of the extent of Islamization of the public debate.

A. *Shari'a and the Human Rights of Women*

This part begins with a brief survey of general principles and rules of Shari'a which are likely to have a negative impact on the status and rights of Muslim women.[102] This includes general principles which affect the socialization of both men and women and the orientation of society at large as well as legal rules in the formal sense. The most important general principle of Shari'a influencing the status and rights of women is the notion of *qawama*. *Qawama* has its origin in verse 4:34 of the Qur'an: "Men have *qawama* [guardianship and authority] over women because of the advantage they [men] have over them [women] and because they [men] spend their property in supporting them [women]."[103] According to Shari'a interpretations of this verse, men as a group are the guardians of and superior to women as a group, and the men of a particular family are the guardians of and superior to the women of that family.[104]

This notion of general and specific *qawama* has had far reaching consequences for the status and rights of women in both the private and public domains. For example, Shari'a provides that women are disqualified from holding general public office, which involves the exercise of authority over men, because, in keeping with the verse

---

101. The private/public dichotomy, however, is an artificial distinction. The two spheres of life overlap and interact. The socialization and treatment of both men and women at home affect their role in public life and vice versa. While this classification can be used for analysis in the Muslim context, its limitations should be noted. It is advisable to look for both the private and public dimensions of a given Shari'a principle or rule rather than assume that it has only private or public implications.

102. For a more detailed discussion of these issues, see generally An-Na'im, *The Rights of Women and International Law in the Muslim Context*, *supra* note 11.

103. HOLY QUR'AN 190–91 (A. Ali trans. & commentary).

104. I. KATHIYR, 1 MUKTHASAR TAFSIYR IBN KATHIYR 385 (M. Al-Sabuniy ed. 1400 a.h.) (Arabic).

4:34 of the Qur'an, men are entitled to exercise authority over women and not the reverse.[105]

Another general principle of Shari'a that has broad implications for the status and rights of Muslim women is the notion of *al-hijab*, the veil. This means more than requiring women to cover their bodies and faces in public. According to Shari'a interpretations of verses 24:31,[106] 33:33,[107] 33:53,[108] and 33:59[109] of the Qur'an, women are supposed to stay at home and not leave it except when required to by urgent necessity.[110] When they are permitted to venture beyond the home, they must do so with their bodies and faces covered. *Al-hijab* tends to reinforce women's inability to hold public office and restricts their access to public life. They are not supposed to participate in public life, because they must not mix with men even in public places.

In addition to these general limitations on the rights of women under Shari'a, there are a number of specific rules in private and public law that discriminate against women and highlight women's general inferiority and inequality.[111] In family law for example, men have the right to marry up to four wives and the power to exercise complete control over them during marriage, to the extent of punishing them

---

105. A. AL-QURTUBI, 5 AL-JAMI LI AHKAM AL-QUR'AN 169 (n.d.) (Arabic).

106. And say to the believing women that they should lower their gaze and guard their modesty; that they should not display their beauty and ornaments except what (must ordinarily) appear thereof; that they should draw their veil over their bosoms and not display their beauty except to their husbands, their fathers, their sons, their husband's sons, their brothers or their brother's sons, or their sister's sons or their women, or the slaves whom their right hand possess, or male servants free of physical needs, or small children who have no sense of shame of sex, and that they should not strike their feet in order to draw attention to their hidden ornaments. And O ye Believers! turn ye all together toward God, that ye may attain Bliss.

HOLY QUR'AN, *supra* note 103, at 904–5.

107. [O Consorts of the Prophet . . .] And stay quietly in your houses, and make not a dazzling display, like that of the former Times of Ignorance; and establish regular prayer, and give regular charity; and obey God and His Apostle. And God only wishes to remove all abomination from you, ye Members of the Family, and to make you pure and spotless.

Id. at 1115–16.

108. [O ye who believe . . .] And when ye ask (his ladies) [the Prophet's wives] for anything ye want, ask them from before [behind] a screen: that makes for greater purity for your hearts and for theirs.

Id. at 1124–25.

109. O Prophet! Tell thy wives and daughters, and the believing women, that they should cast their outer garments over their persons (when abroad): that is most convenient, that they should be known (as such) and not molested. And God is Oft-Forgiving, Most Merciful.

Id. at 1125–26.

110. Although some of these verses refer to the wives of the Prophet, they were taken to apply to all Muslim women.

111. For a general comparison between Shari'a and current standards of human rights in relation to the status and rights of women, see TABANDEH, *supra* note 37, at 35–67.

for disobedience if the men deem that to be necessary.[112] In contrast, the co-wives are supposed to submit to their husband's will and endure his punishments. While a husband is entitled to divorce any of his wives at will, a wife is not entitled to a divorce, except by judicial order on very specific and limited grounds.[113] Another private law feature of discrimination is found in the law of inheritance, where the general rule is that women are entitled to half the share of men.[114]

In addition to their general inferiority under the principle of *qawama* and lack of access to public life as a consequence of the notion of *al-hijab*, women are subjected to further specific limitations in the public domain. For instance, in the administration of justice, Shari'a holds women to be incompetent witnesses in serious criminal cases, regardless of their individual character and knowledge of the facts. In civil cases where a woman's testimony is accepted, it takes two women to make a single witness.[115] *Diya*, monetary compensation to be paid to victims of violent crimes or to their surviving kin, is less for female victims than it is for male victims.[116]

The private and public aspects of Shari'a overlap and interact.[117] The general principles of *qawama* and *al-hijab* operate at the public as well as the private levels. Public law discrimination against women emphasizes their inferiority at home. The inferior status and rights of women in private law justify discrimination against them in public life. These overlapping and interacting principles and rules play an extremely significant role in the socialization of both women and men. Notions of women's inferiority are deeply embedded in the character and attitudes of both women and men from early childhood.[118]

This does not mean that the whole of Shari'a has had a negative impact on the status and rights of women. Relatively early on, Shari'a granted women certain rights of equality which were not achieved by women in other legal systems until recently. For example, from the very beginning, Shari'a guaranteed a woman's independent legal per-

---

112. Polygamy is based on verse 4:3 of the Qur'an. The husband's power to chastise his wife to the extent of beating her is based on verse 4:34 of the Qur'an. *See* HOLY QUR'AN, *supra* note 103, at 179, 190–91.

113. *See talak* in SHORTER ENCYCLOPEDIA OF ISLAM, *supra* note 42, at 564–67.

114. Verses 4:11 and 4:176 of the Qur'an. *See* HOLY QUR'AN, *supra* note 103, at 181, 235–36.

115. This is based on verse 2:282 of the Qur'an. *See* HOLY QUR'AN, *supra* note 103, at 113–14.

116. A. AUDA, AL-TASHRI AL-JANA'IY AL-ISLAMIY paras. 155, 214 (n.d.) (Arabic).

117. *See supra* note 101.

118. *See, e.g.*, Vieille, *Iranian Women in Family Alliance and Sexual Politics*, in WOMEN IN THE MUSLIM WORLD 451 (Beck & Keddie eds. 1978) [hereinafter WOMEN IN THE MUSLIM WORLD]. *But cf.* Dwyer, *Women, Sufism, and Decision-Making in Moroccan Islam*, *id.* at 585 (suggesting that in the social reality of Sufi, Islamic mystic, traditions, women may have a stronger role than envisaged by Shari'a).

sonality to own and dispose of property in her own right on equal footing with men, and secured for women certain minimum rights in family law and inheritance long before other legal systems recognized similar rights.[119]

These theoretical rights under Shari'a, however, may not be realized in practice. Other Shari'a rules may hamper or inhibit women from exercising these rights in some societies. According to one author, "while legally recognized as 'economic persons' to whom property is transmitted, Muslim women are constrained from acting out economic roles because of other legal, as well as ideological, components of Muslim female status."[120] Customary practice in certain rural Muslim communities in Iran and Indonesia denies women their rightful inheritance under Shari'a.[121] While the strict application of Shari'a would improve the status and rights of women in comparison to customary practice in these situations, the position of women under Shari'a would nevertheless fall short of the standards set by international human rights instruments.[122]

This is Shari'a doctrine as it is understood by the vast majority of Muslims today. Significant possibilities exist for reform, but to undertake such reforms effectively, we must be clear on what Shari'a *is* rather than what it can or ought to be. Some Muslim feminists emphasize the positive aspects of Shari'a while overlooking the negative aspects. Others restrict their analysis to the Qur'an, and select only verses favoring the status of women while overlooking other parts and failing to take into account the ways in which the parts they select have been interpreted by the Shari'a jurists.[123] Neither approach is satisfactory. Shari'a is a complex and integrated whole and must be

---

119. *See generally* Smith, *Islam*, in WOMEN IN WORLD RELIGIONS 235 (A. Sharama ed. 1987).

120. Pastner, *The Status of Women and Property on a Baluchistan Oasis in Pakistan*, in WOMEN IN THE MUSLIM WORLD, *supra* note 118, at 434. Another author has noted that the financial activities of Saudi women take place behind the scenes, and often through the intermediary of hired male assistants. Furthermore, these activities were curtailed due to pressure to observe Shari'a more strictly after the seizure of the Grand Mosque of Mecca in 1979. *See* Ramazani, *Arab Women in the Gulf*, 39 MIDDLE E. J. 258, 260–61 (1985).

121. *See* Friedle, *State Ideology and Village Women*, in WOMEN AND REVOLUTION IN IRAN 217, 220 (G. Nashat ed. 1983) [hereinafter WOMEN AND REVOLUTION IN IRAN]; Cederroth, *Islam and Adat: Some Recent Changes in the Social Position of Women Among Sasak in Lombok*, in WOMEN IN ISLAMIC SOCIETIES 160, 164–66 (B. Utas ed. 1983).

122. Although these customary practices are inconsistent with the letter of Shari'a, they are reinforced by general notions of Shari'a that signify the inferiority of women and their subjection to men under the principle of *qawama*. Reform of these aspects of Shari'a through the reinterpretation of Qur'an and Sunna may therefore contribute to the eradication of those customary practices. The reformulation of Shari'a can then be used in specific educational programs and social policies designed to combat discriminatory practices in these Muslim communities.

123. For an example of this approach, see Hassan, *On Human Rights and the Qur'anic Perspectives*, 19 J. ECUMENICAL STUD. 52 (1982).

perceived as such. The status and rights of Muslim women are affected by the negative as well as the positive aspects of Shari'a. In fact, its negative aspects may receive greater emphasis than its positive aspects in some Muslim societies today. Moreover, Shari'a jurists have developed specific jurisprudential techniques which control and limit the prospects of reform within the framework of Shari'a. As will be explained in the final section on Islamic reform and human rights, modernist Muslims may need to challenge and change those techniques before they can implement significant reforms.

B. *Muslim Women at Home*

The human rights of Muslim women have been directly and continuously affected within the family by Shari'a, because its relevant aspects have remained in force under the legal systems of the vast majority of Muslim countries. This control which Shari'a exercises over the private realm of home and family is so entrenched, and its violation of human rights so clear, that it may explain in part why some Muslim countries refuse to ratify the relevant human rights instruments or at least entered reservations on their obligations under certain human rights treaties. For example, Egypt is one of the very few Muslim countries to have ratified the Convention on the Elimination of All Forms of Discrimination Against Women of 1979.[124] It entered, however, a reservation to Article 16[125] of the Convention which provides for the equality of men and women in all matters relating to marriage and family relations during the marriage and upon its dissolution. The Egyptian reservation specifically stated that since these matters were governed by Shari'a, Egypt had to derogate from its obligations under the Convention.[126]

The Shari'a personal law enforced in Iran is not significantly different from that prevailing in Sunni countries like Egypt except for the additional affront to the human dignity of women and the serious violation of their human rights caused by the institution of *mut'a*, or temporary marriage, peculiar to Shi'a jurisprudence.[127] According to this type of marriage, a man is entitled to take as many "temporary wives" as he can afford in addition to his four "permanent wives." In contrast to regular marriage which is contracted theoretically for life, *mut'a* marriage is contracted for a specific period of time, in terms of

124. Convention on the Elimination of All Forms of Discrimination Against Women, Dec. 18, 1979, G.A. Res. 34/180, 34 U.N. GAOR Supp. (No. 46) at 193, U.N. Doc. A/34/46 (1979).

125. *Id.* art. 16.

126. For the text of this Egyptian reservation, see INTERNATIONAL HUMAN RIGHTS INSTRUMENTS, *supra* note 8, at 220.13.

127. *See* SHORTER ENCYCLOPEDIA OF ISLAM, *supra* note 42, at 418–20.

years, months, days, or perhaps even hours. In addition to the discrimination and humiliation this type of "marriage" causes to the unfortunate temporary "wife," it demeans all women and degrades the institution of marriage itself. Despite these and many other extremely serious social and human rights implications of this type of "marriage," it is still practiced in Iran today.[128]

Some Muslim countries have introduced limited reforms in the family law field. These appear to be more likely to survive traditionalist and fundamentalist backlash than the Iranian ones discussed above, because of their modest nature. The 1979 amendments to the personal law of Egypt "were carefully formulated to forestall any unnecessary confrontation with conservative religious elements."[129] These amendments maintained the husband's rights of unilateral divorce and polygamy while seeking to balance those rights by some procedural and financial guarantees for the wife.[130] In Pakistan, the Muslim Family Laws Ordinance of 1961[131] introduced some reforms. Among other measures, it instituted a network of Arbitration Councils to deal with divorce, polygamy, and maintenance of wives. Now, the written permission of the Arbitration Council is required before a married man can take another wife.

These reforms are only small steps toward redressing human rights objections to the status and rights of women under Shari'a, and yet they are criticized by traditionalist and fundamentalist groups as un-Islamic. The repeal of the Iranian reforms and the threat of revision of the Egyptian and Pakistani reforms suggest to one author the need to use legitimate Islamic methodology in rendering such reforms.[132] I agree with this recommendation and add that the reforms must also go far enough to guarantee the full human rights of women in family and inheritance law.

---

128. Nashat, *Women in the Ideology of the Islamic Republic*, in WOMEN AND REVOLUTION IN IRAN, *supra* note 121, at 205–6.

The previous regime of the Shah introduced a number of limited improvements in the status and rights of women in Iran through the Family Protection Law of 1967 (amended in 1975). For example, the legislation required the consent of the first wife before a husband could take a second wife, and placed restrictions on the husband's right of unilateral divorce. For a discussion of these and other improvements see Bagley, *The Iranian Family Protection Law: A Milestone in the Advance of Women's Rights*, in IRAN AND ISLAM 47, 47–64 (C. Bosworth ed. 1971).

These limited gains have now been lost with the repeal of the Family Protection Law and the return of strict Shari'a provisions. *See generally* Higgins, *Women in the Islamic Republic of Iran: Legal, Social, and Ideological Changes*, 10 J. WOMEN IN CULTURE AND SOC'Y 477 (1985).

129. Hussein, *Recent Amendments to Egypt's Personal Status Law*, in WOMEN AND THE FAMILY IN THE MIDDLE EAST, 229 (E. Fernea ed. 1985) [hereinafter WOMEN AND THE FAMILY IN THE MIDDLE EAST].

130. *Id.* at 231–32.

131. PLD 1961, CS 209; CP Mar. 3, 161.

132. J. ESPOSITO, WOMEN IN MUSLIM FAMILY LAW 131 (1982).

C. Muslim Women in Public Life

A similar and perhaps more drastic conflict exists between reformist and conservative trends in relation to the status and rights of women in the public domain. Unlike personal law matters, where Shari'a was never displaced by secular law, in most Muslim countries, constitutional, criminal, and other public law matters have come to be based on secular, mainly Western, legal concepts and institutions. Consequently, the struggle over Islamization of public law has been concerned with the reestablishment of Shari'a where it has been absent for decades, or at least since the creation of the modern Muslim nation states in the first half of the twentieth century. In terms of women's rights, the struggle shall determine whether women can keep the degree of equality and rights in public life they have achieved under secular constitutions and laws.

In Pakistan, for example, the 1973 Constitution dealt with fundamental questions in relation to the role of Islam in constitutional and other public affairs.[133] However, such issues are rarely finally resolved by constitutional provisions. In fact, constitutional guarantees clearly did little to settle questions pertaining to the status and rights of women in Pakistan.

Article 25(2) of the 1973 Constitution prohibits discrimination based solely on gender.[134] Article 27(1) outlaws discrimination against qualified candidates for federal service solely on the basis of gender. Among the Principles of State Policy, Article 34 states that: "Steps shall be taken to ensure full participation of women in all spheres of national life."[135] The 1973 Constitution also provides for universal adult suffrage and reserves a certain number of seats for women in the National Assembly and regional assemblies in addition to their right to compete for non-reserved seats. Unfortunately these provisions have been contested and their practical value diminished in a variety of ways.[136]

The Council of Islamic Ideology was one of the institutional mechanisms that tended to diminish the value of constitutional protections for women's rights. According to Article 230(1)(c) of the 1973 Constitution, this Council is authorized to "make recommendations as to

---

133. For a brief survey of the debate at the time, see Rahman, *Islam and the New Constitution of Pakistan*, VIII J. ASIAN & AFR. STUD. 190 (1973).

134. For the text of the 1973 Constitution of Pakistan, see CONSTITUTIONS OF COUNTRIES OF THE WORLD: PAKISTAN (Blaustein & Flanz eds. 1986) [hereinafter CONSTITUTIONS OF COUNTRIES OF THE WORLD].

135. *Id.* art. 34.

136. *See generally* Carroll, *Nizam-I-Islam: Processes and Conflicts in Pakistan's Programme of Islamisation, with Special Reference to the Position of Women*, 20 J. COMMONWEALTH & COMP. POL. 57 (1982).

the measures for bringing existing laws into conformity with the Injunctions of Islam and the stages by which such measures should be brought into effect."[137] This mandate was taken seriously throughout the Zia ul-Haq period during which the Council played an active role in the implementation of policies of Islamization.[138]

One component of the New Education Policy adopted by Zia's regime in 1978 was the progressive segregation of men and women in higher education and the establishment of separate women's universities. As one observer commented:

> Such an eventuality could not but have disastrous repercussions on both women's higher education and their career opportunities. At a time when women were breaking ground in new fields—for instance, engineering, town planning, architecture, aeronautics—a women's university could not possibly offer these subjects to the few pioneers then undertaking them in a co-educational institution.[139]

Pakistani women have been concerned with the implications of the policy of Islamization for their careers and successfully have protested against encroachments on their role in public life. Zia ul-Haq's regime did show some sensitivity to protests and demands by women's organizations. He appointed the first female cabinet secretary in Pakistan's history, and later appointed a female minister of state.[140] In 1979 he established a Women's Division within his cabinet whose activities included cosponsorship of a conference which recommended the elimination of stereotyping of women in textbooks, the projection of a more responsible and positive image of women in national life, and greater representation of women in educational administration and policy-making. In response to protests by the All Pakistan Women's Association and seventeen other women's groups against instructions by the Minister of Information restricting the appearance of female models in commercial advertising, Zia's regime declared that it "had no intention whatsoever to debar them [women] from taking an active part in national affairs."[141]

With the election of Benazir Bhutto as the first female Prime Minister of Pakistan, one can expect more action in support of women's

137. CONSTITUTIONS OF COUNTRIES OF THE WORLD, *supra* note 134, art. 230(1)(c).

138. *See* Carroll, *supra* note 136, at 66.

139. *Id.* at 75. *See also* Hussain, *The Struggle of Women in the National Development of Pakistan*, in MUSLIM WOMEN 198, 210 - 11 (F. Hussain ed. 1984).

140. *See* Carroll, *supra* note 136, at 82.

141. *Id.* at 83–84; Hussain, *supra* note 139, at 213–14.

rights in public life. Nevertheless, one must not underestimate the power of the proponents of Shari'a in Pakistan or any other Muslim country. Neither women's organizations nor political parties and politicians can afford to disregard or downplay the Islamic factor.[142] Numerous studies show that a variety of economic and social factors contribute to the current status and rights of women in the Muslim world, and to their own perceptions of and reactions to their situation.[143] But these studies also emphasize, in one way or another, the Islamic dimensions of these same factors.

The Islamization slogan appears to have aroused considerable excitement and enthusiasm in Pakistan. Even the Pakistan People's Party, presently in power after the death of Zia ul-Haq, has declared its commitment to Islamization policy and continues to compete with the Islamic parties in this regard. But there are problems, as one observer noted:

> The matter, however, becomes complicated and contentious when an attempt is made to translate the slogan into actual policies. Not much imagination is required to realise that the vision of an Islamic social order entertained by the Ulema [Ulama, traditional religious scholars] differs radically from that envisaged by educated and articulate women. But even Sunni politicians of the religious-orientated parties are by no means unanimous in their conception of an Islamic state.[144]

This comment applies throughout the Muslim world, including Iran where differences exist among Shi'a politicians. Educated women and other modernist segments of society may not be able to articulate their vision of an Islamic state in terms of Shari'a, because aspects of

---

142. *See, e.g.*, the analysis and evaluation of the All Pakistan Women's Association in Chipp, *The Modern Pakistani Woman in a Muslim Society*, in ASIAN WOMEN IN TRANSITION 204 (Chipp & Green eds. 1980). For a similar analysis of a group of Indonesian women organizations see Douglas, *Women in Indonesian Politics: The Myth of Functional Interest*, *id.* at 152.

143. On Egypt and Morocco see, *e.g.*, Maher, *Women and Social Change in Morocco*, in WOMEN IN THE MUSLIM WORLD, *supra* note 118, at 100; Davis, *Working Women in a Moroccan Village*, *id.* at 416; El-Messiri, *Self-Images of Traditional Urban Women in Cairo*, *id.* at 522. *See also* Rugh, *Women and Work: Strategies and Choices in a Lower-Class Quarter of Cairo*, in WOMEN AND THE FAMILY IN THE MIDDLE EAST, *supra* note 129, at 272; Hatem, *Egypt's Middle Class in Crisis: The Sexual Division of Labor*, 42 MIDDLE E. J. 407 (1988).

In relation to Iran see Friedle, *supra* note 121; Nashat, *supra* note 128; Bauer, *Poor Women and Social Consciousness in Revolutionary Iran*, in WOMEN AND REVOLUTION IN IRAN, *supra* note 121, at 141.

On the situation in Saudi Arabia see Ramazani, *supra* note 120; Allaghi & Almana, *Survey of Research on Women in the Arab Gulf Region*, in UNESCO, SOCIAL SCIENCE RESEARCH AND WOMEN IN THE ARAB WORLD 14 (1984).

144. Carroll, *supra* note 136, at 85.

Shari'a are incompatible with certain concepts and institutions which these groups take for granted, including the protection of all human rights. To the extent that efforts for the protection and promotion of human rights in the Muslim world must take into account the Islamic dimension of the political and sociological situation in Muslim countries, a modernist conception of Islam is needed.

V. ISLAMIC REFORM AND HUMAN RIGHTS

I have referred several times in this Article to the need for Islamic reform to protect and promote human rights in the Muslim world. Such reform must be *sufficient* to resolve human rights problems with Shari'a while maintaining *legitimacy* from the Islamic point of view. On the one hand, reform efforts which fall short of resolving the serious human rights problems indicated earlier may not be worth pursuing. On the other hand, it is futile to advocate reforms which are unlikely to be acceptable to Muslims as satisfying the religious criteria of Islamic reform.

Islamic reform needs must be based on the Qur'an and Sunna, the primary sources of Islam. Although Muslims believe that the Qur'an is the literal and final word of God, and Sunna are the traditions of his final Prophet, they also appreciate that these sources have to be understood and applied through human interpretation and action. As I have pointed out above,[145] these sources have been interpreted by the founding jurists of Shari'a and applied throughout Muslim history. Because those interpretations were developed by Muslim jurists in the past, it should be possible for modern Muslim jurists to advance alternative interpretations of the Qur'an and Sunna.

A. *An Adequate Reform Methodology*

I have elsewhere argued extensively for this position and advanced a specific reform methodology which I believe would achieve the necessary degree of reform.[146] The basic premise of my position, based on the work of the late Sudanese Muslim reformer *Ustadh* Mahmoud Mohamed Taha,[147] is that the Shari'a reflects a historically-conditioned interpretation of Islamic scriptures in the sense that the founding jurists had to understand those sources in accordance with their own social, economic, and political circumstances. In relation to the status and rights of women, for example, equality between men and women

145. *See supra* notes 12–28 and accompanying text.

146. *See generally* TOWARD AN ISLAMIC REFORMATION, *supra* note 11.

147. *See generally* M. TAHA, THE SECOND MESSAGE OF ISLAM (A. An-Na'im trans. 1987).

in the eighth and ninth centuries in the Middle East, or anywhere else at the time, would have been inconceivable and impracticable. It was therefore natural and indeed inevitable that Muslim jurists would understand the relevant texts of the Qur'an and Sunna as confirming rather than repudiating the realities of the day.

In interpreting the primary sources of Islam in their historical context, the founding jurists of Shari'a tended not only to understand the Qur'an and Sunna as confirming existing social attitudes and institutions, but also to emphasize certain texts and "enact" them into Shari'a while de-emphasizing other texts or interpreting them in ways consistent with what they believed to be the intent and purpose of the sources. Working with the same primary sources, modern Muslim jurists might shift emphasis from one class of texts to the other, and interpret the previously enacted texts in ways consistent with a new understanding of what is believed to be the intent and purpose of the sources. This new understanding would be informed by contemporary social, economic, and political circumstances in the same way that the "old" understanding on which Shari'a jurists acted was informed by the then prevailing circumstances. The new understanding would qualify for Islamic legitimacy, in my view, if it is based on specific texts in opposing the application of other texts, and can be shown to be in accordance with the Qur'an and Sunna as a whole.

For example, the general principle of *qawama*, the guardianship and authority of men over women under Shari'a, is based on verse 4:34 of the Qur'an quoted earlier.[148] This verse presents *qawama* as a consequence of two conditions: men's advantage over and financial support of women. The fact that men are generally physically stronger than most women is not relevant in modern times where the rule of law prevails over physical might. Moreover, modern circumstances are making the economic independence of women from men more readily realized and appreciated. In other words, neither of the conditions—advantages of physical might or earning power—set by verse 4:34 as the justification for the *qawama* of men over women is tenable today.

The fundamental position of the modern human rights movement is that all human beings are equal in worth and dignity, regardless of gender, religion, or race. This position can be substantiated by the Qur'an and other Islamic sources, as understood under the radically transformed circumstances of today. For example, in numerous verses the Qur'an speaks of honor and dignity for "humankind" and "children of Adam," without distinction as to race, color, gender, or religion.[149]

---

148. *See supra* text following note 103.
149. For instance, verse 17:70 speaks of how God "honoured the children of Adam." Yusuf

By drawing on those sources and being willing to set aside archaic and dated interpretations of other sources, such as the one previously given to verse 4:34 of the Qur'an, we can provide Islamic legitimacy for the full range of human rights for women.

Similarly, numerous verses of the Qur'an provide for freedom of choice and non-compulsion in religious belief and conscience.[150] These verses have been either de-emphasized as having been "overruled" by other verses which were understood to legitimize coercion, or "interpreted" in ways which permitted such coercion. For example, verse 9:29[151] of the Qur'an was taken as the foundation of the whole system of *dhimma*, and its consequent discrimination against non-Muslims.[152] Relying on those verses which extoll freedom of religion rather than those that legitimize religious coercion, one can argue now that the *dhimma* system should no longer be part of Islamic law and that complete equality should be assured regardless of religion or belief. The same argument can be used to abolish all negative legal consequences of apostasy as inconsistent with the Islamic principle of freedom of religion.[153]

Reference has been made to the possible need to challenge some jurisprudential techniques of Shari'a in order to implement the necessary degree of reform.[154] One of the main mechanisms for development and reform within the framework of Shari'a is *ijtihad*—independent juristic reasoning to provide for new principles and rules of Shari'a in situations on which the Qur'an and Sunna were silent. By virtue of its rationale and textual support, *ijtihad* was not supposed to be exercised in any matter governed by clear and categorical texts of Qur'an and/or Sunna because that would amount to substituting jur-

---

Ali translates the Arabic term "*baniy* Adam" as "the sons of Adam," *see* HOLY QUR'AN, *supra* note 103, at 714, although the word "*baniy*" means "children," both male and female. Yusuf Ali may have intended the word "sons" to include both sexes, but it is important to use a gender neutral term in this context. Verse 49:13 of the Qur'an may be translated as follows:

> O, humankind, We [God] have created you into male and female, and made you into peoples and tribes so that you may be acquainted [and cooperate] with each other; the most favored by God among you are those who are righteous and pious.

150. See, for example, verse 2:256 of the Qur'an which provides: "Let there be no compulsion in religion: Truth stands out clear from error . . . ." In verse 18:29 God instructs the Prophet: "Say, the Truth is from your Lord. Let him who will, believe, and let him who will, reject (it) . . . ." HOLY QUR'AN, *supra* note 103, at 103, 738.

151.
> Fight those who believe not in God and the Last Day, nor hold that forbidden which hath been forbidden by God and His Apostle, nor acknowledge the Religion of Truth, [even if they are] of the People of the Book [*Ahl al-kitab*], until they pay *Jizya* with willing submission, and feel themselves subdued.

HOLY QUR'AN, *supra* note 103, at 447.

152. *See supra* notes 42–51 and accompanying text on the *dhimma* system and its human rights implications.

153. *See generally* A. RAHMAN, PUNISHMENT OF APOSTASY IN ISLAM (1972) (a strong argument for abolishing the death penalty for apostasy in Islamic law).

154. *See supra* text following note 123.

istic reasoning for the fundamental sources of Islam.[155] According to the prevailing view in Shari'a, *ijtihad* should not be exercised even in matters settled through *ijma*, consensus.[156]

Some of the problematic aspects of Shari'a identified in this Article, however, are based on clear and categorical texts of Qur'an and Sunna. To achieve the necessary degree of reform, I would therefore suggest that the scope of *ijtihad* be expanded to enable modern Muslim jurists not only to change rules settled through *ijma*, but also to substitute previously enacted texts with other, more general, texts of Qur'an and Sunna despite the categorical nature of the prior texts.[157] This proposal is not as radical as it may seem because the proposed new rule would also be based on the Qur'an or Sunna, albeit on a new interpretation of the text. For example, the above-mentioned categorical verse 9:29 regulating the status of non-Muslims would be superseded by the more general verses providing for freedom of religion and inherent dignity of all human beings without distinction as to faith or belief.

I believe that the choice of texts to be implemented as modern Islamic Shari'a is systematic and not arbitrary; it is based on the timing and circumstances of revelation as well as the relationship of the text to the themes and objectives of Islam as a whole. Moreover, I maintain that the proposed reinterpretation is consistent with normal Arabic usage and apparent sense of the text. It is neither contrived nor strained. The ultimate test of legitimacy and efficacy is, of course, acceptance and implementation by Muslims throughout the world.

B. *Prospects for Acceptance and Likely Impact of the Proposed Reform*

In addition to this methodology's own Islamic legitimacy and cohesion, at least two main factors are likely to affect the acceptance and implementation of this or any other reform. It must be timely, addressing urgent concerns and issues facing Muslim societies, and it must be disseminated and discussed in Muslim countries. I believe that my proposal will be acceptable to Muslim peoples if offered in an effective and organized manner. Paradoxical as it may seem, I suspect that the proposal may face difficulties of dissemination and discussion precisely because it is timely.

This proposal is timely because Muslims throughout the world are sensitive to charges that their religious law and cultural traditions permit and legitimize human rights violations; hence the efforts of

155. *See* D. MACDONALD, DEVELOPMENT OF MUSLIM THEOLOGY, JURISPRUDENCE AND CONSTITUTIONAL THEORY 86 (1903); Vesey-Fitzgerald, *supra* note 16, at 93.

156. N. COULSON, *supra* note 17, at 60.

157. For a full explanation and substantiation of this position, see TOWARD AN ISLAMIC REFORMATION, *supra* note 11, at 17–33, 53–68.

contemporary Muslim authors to dispel such allegations.[158] Governments of Muslim countries, like many other governments, formally subscribe to international human rights instruments because, in my view, they find the human rights idea an important legitimizing force both at home and abroad. Moreover, as explained earlier, many emerging women's organizations and modernist forces are now asserting and articulating their demands for justice and equality in terms of international human rights standards.

Nevertheless, the proposed reform will probably be resisted because it challenges the vested interests of powerful forces in the Muslim world and may upset male-dominated traditional political and social institutions. These forces probably will try to restrict opportunities for a genuine consideration of this reform methodology. It is equally likely that they will attempt to obstruct its acceptance and implementation in the name of Islamic orthodoxy. Proponents of Shari'a will also resist it because it challenges their view of the good Muslim society and the ideal Islamic state.

Consequently, the acceptance and implementation of this reform methodology will involve a political struggle within Muslim nations as part of a larger general struggle for human rights. I would recommend this proposal to participants in that struggle who champion the cause of justice and equality for women and non-Muslims, and freedom of belief and expression in the Muslim world. Given the extreme importance of Islamic legitimacy in Muslim societies, I urge human rights advocates to claim the Islamic platform and not concede it to the traditionalist and fundamentalist forces in their societies. I would also invite outside supporters of Muslim human rights advocates to express their support with due sensitivity and genuine concern for Islamic legitimacy in the Muslim world.

As I have tried to show throughout this Article, the problematic aspects of Shari'a are not the sole underlying causes of human rights violations in the Muslim world. Other extra-Islamic structural and socio-economic factors also contribute to human rights problems. But the primary objectives of this Article have been: (1) to address the extent to which Shari'a-related factors contribute to human rights violations in the Muslim world; and (2) to propose a way of overcoming that particular dimension of the status of human rights in the Muslim world.

VI. CONCLUSION

This Article began with the general premise that human rights violations reflect the lack or weakness of cultural legitimacy of inter-

158. *See, e.g.*, Wafi, *supra* note 34; Hassan, *supra* note 123; Ishaque, *Human Rights in Islamic Law*, 12 INT'L COMM'N OF JURISTS REV. 30 (1974); Al-Faruqi, *Islam and Human Rights*, 27 ISLAMIC Q. 12 (1983); A. ZAHIR, HUQUQ AL-INSAN (1988) (Arabic).

national standards in a particular society. In accordance with this premise, because Shari'a, as the accepted version of the law of Islam, is inconsistent with certain human rights, those rights probably will be violated in the Muslim world, regardless of formal participation in international human rights instruments. This is likely to occur even if Shari'a is not constituted as the formal legal system of the country in question. As a religious and ethical code, Shari'a has far-reaching political and social influence, irrespective of its official legal status in Muslim countries. The evidence reviewed above from case studies of several Muslim countries illustrates Shari'a's extensive influence under very different cultural and legal conditions.

Therefore, because Muslim countries are more likely to honor those human rights standards which have Islamic legitimacy, human rights advocates should struggle to have their interpretations of the scriptural imperatives of Islam accepted as valid and appropriate for application today. Authority for this reinterpretive activity comes from the fact that contemporary majority perspectives on Shari'a are not necessarily the only valid interpretations of the scriptural imperatives of Islam, a fact which has been recognized by some modernist Muslim reformers.[159] Unfortunately, little has been done so far to develop a comprehensive reform methodology. In terms of human rights concerns there has been little effort to reconcile Islamic law with fundamental human rights, especially in relation to women and non-Muslims. Reform efforts have so far been confined to the family law area, and even there they have tended to be inadequate and open to reversal. A much more comprehensive and effective reform methodology is required to provide genuine and lasting Islamic legitimacy for human rights in the Muslim world.

In the final part of this Article, I have explained briefly what I believe to be an adequate Islamic reform methodology aimed at achieving greater legitimacy for human rights in the Muslim world. As indicated in that section, however, this methodology does not offer an easy or quick solution to all human rights problems. In fact, strong resistance can be expected not only from those with vested interest in the status quo, but also from some of the beneficiaries of the proposed reforms. For example, some educated women are Islamic fundamentalists. Nor do I suggest that reformulating Shari'a alone will alleviate all human rights violations. Economic and other factors and forces must also be addressed. Yet, the extent of observance of human rights standards in any country is affected by prevailing attitudes and conceptions regarding who is a human being entitled to the full range of

159. *See, e.g.*, F. RAHMAN, ISLAM AND MODERNITY: TRANSFORMATION OF AN INTELLECTUAL TRADITION (1982); IN QUEST OF AN ISLAMIC HUMANISM: ARABIC AND ISLAMIC STUDIES IN MEMORY OF MOHAMED AL-NOWAIHI (A. Green ed. 1984).

human rights. In the Muslim context, these attitudes and conceptions are significantly influenced by commonly held views concerning what are the scriptural imperatives of Islam. Rethinking these scriptural imperatives is therefore one critical strategy for advancing human rights in Muslim countries. Human rights advocates have few allies in most parts of the world, including almost all Muslim countries. They need to enlist the support of powerful cultural and religious forces. Support will come if they look for it in an intelligent and sensitive manner.

[14]

What's Wrong with Chinese Rights?: Toward a Theory of Rights with Chinese Characteristics

R.P. PEERENBOOM*

The question "What's wrong with Chinese rights?" implies that there are Chinese rights. A quick glance at the constitution of the People's Republic of China suggests that a Chinese citizen shares the full complement of rights that members of modern, western liberal democracies have come to hold so dear: freedom of speech, press, association, religious belief and practice; inviolability of the person; protection from unlawful arrest and search of person, and so on.[1] Indeed, some claim that Chinese citizens enjoy rights unknown to their American counterparts: job placement and security, free access to medical care, and other "economic rights" are most often cited.[2]

Yet despite this seemingly rosy picture, the cry for human rights in China has grown steadily louder since the Tiananmen tragedy and the collapse of socialism in Eastern Europe and the former USSR. To be sure, qualifications are in order. The cry rises largely from foreigners and a coterie of Chinese dissidents and intellectuals, many now living abroad in exile.[3] As an on-site observer of the 1989 demonstrations, I was particularly struck by the low priority given to human rights by many of the protesters, reports of western journalists notwithstanding. While a few students and intellectuals called for human rights (and even fewer could state what that meant), the vast majority of the demonstrators seemed motivated primarily by economic concerns, with

---

* B.A., Philosophy, University of Wisconsin-Madison, 1980; M.A., Chinese Religions, University of Hawaii, 1987; Ph.D., Philosophy, University of Hawaii, 1990; J.D., Columbia Law School, 1993. An earlier version of this Article was presented at the Human Rights in China Conference sponsored by Asia Human Rights Watch and held at Columbia University in January 1991. The author thanks R. Randle Edwards for helpful comments on earlier drafts.

1. ZHONGGUO RENMIN GONGHEGUO XIANFA [Constitution of the People's Republic of China] arts. 33–40 (1982) [hereinafter PRC CONST.]. For a discussion of Chinese rights, see Louis Henkin, *The Human Rights Idea in Contemporary China: A Comparative Perspective*, *in* HUMAN RIGHTS IN CONTEMPORARY CHINA 25–26 (R. Randle Edwards et al. eds., 1986); Andrew J. Nathan, *Political Rights in the Chinese Constitutions*, *in id.* at 79–80.

2. *See* PRC CONST., *supra* note 1, arts. 42–46.

3. In the years since Tiananmen, the topic of human rights has been increasingly debated in China. For a useful overview of current issues and theories, *see* DANGDAI RENQUAN [CONTEMPORARY HUMAN RIGHTS] (The Legal Research Institute of the Chinese Academy of Social Sciences ed., 1992).

inflation and corruption heading the list.[4] Those rights that the demonstrators did seek—freedom of the press, greater voice in electing officials—were grounded in pragmatic concerns: a free, investigative press would keep tabs on and expose corrupt officials; elections would allow for the expulsion of those exposed.[5]

Further, the call for "human rights" in China tends to elide several issues. The rhetoric of human rights is often that of universal, inalienable, absolute rights—and indeed often that of so-called "natural" rights. But is that actually what Chinese need or want? As rhetoric, rights talk is glorious: all people are created equal, each individual possesses an inviolable right to life, liberty, and the pursuit of happiness.[6] But this is rhetoric—powerful, effective, socially significant rhetoric, but rhetoric nonetheless. As such, it has been criticized, at least in unqualified form, as nonsense on stilts.[7] More importantly, such a conception of human rights is at odds with reality in which intuitions about human dignity and individual rights are at odds with equally strong intuitions about utilitarian consequences, the overall social good, and duties to others.[8] The result is a compromise: one has a right to free speech, yet one cannot cry "fire" in a theater, to cite a familiar example.

---

4. Two of the more popular slogans were *dadao guandao* (smash profiteering) and *fandui fubai* (oppose corruption). A poll conducted in early May of 865 Beijing residents found that 71% believed corruption to be the main cause of instability in China. *See* Seth Faison, *Poll Shows Support for Demonstration*, S. CHINA MORNING POST, May 12, 1989, at 1. *See also* Nicholas Kristof, *China Erupts: The Reasons Why*, N.Y. TIMES MAGAZINE, June 4, 1989, at 26, 28 (noting that dissatisfaction stemmed not only from a desire for democracy, but also from economic frustration).

5. For a similar view, *see* Jane Macartney, *The Students: Heroes, Pawns, or Power-Brokers?*, *in* THE BROKEN MIRROR: CHINA AFTER TIANANMEN 3, 5, 12, 13 (George Hicks, ed., 1990). Andrew Nathan has noted that intellectuals attempted to limit the movement's agenda to issues of freedom of speech and dialogue with the government. Freedom of speech is, of course, particularly important to academics. *See* Andrew Nathan, *Tiananmen and the Cosmos*, NEW REPUBLIC, July 19, 1991, at 31, 32. *See also* Marsha L. Wagner, *The Strategies of the Student Democracy Movement in Beijing*, *in* TIANANMEN: CHINA'S STRUGGLE FOR DEMOCRACY 43, 59, 74–76 (Marsha L. Wagner & Winston L.Y. Yang eds., 1990) (students wanted a more honest government but continued to believe the Party and government officials could be reformed through moral suasion).

6. THE DECLARATION OF INDEPENDENCE (U.S. 1776). In Dworkinian terms, the rights of the individual trump the overall good of society; in Nozickian, "individuals have rights and there are things no person or group may do to them"; in Rawlsian, "each person possesses an inviolability founded on justice that even the welfare of society as a whole cannot override." *See* RONALD DWORKIN, TAKING RIGHTS SERIOUSLY (1977); ROBERT NOZICK, ANARCHY, STATE AND UTOPIA ix (1974); JOHN RAWLS, A THEORY OF JUSTICE 3 (1971).

7. Jeremy Bentham, *Anarchical Fallacies*, *in* 2 COLLECTED PAPERS (1843), *reprinted in* HUMAN RIGHTS 32 (A. I. Meldin ed., 1970).

8. In response to Kant's injunction against treating humans as things, Oliver Wendell Holmes candidly remarked, "If a man lives in society, he is liable to find himself so treated." OLIVER W. HOLMES, THE COMMON LAW 38 (Mark DeWolfe Howe, ed., Belknap Press of Harvard University 1963) (1881). Indeed, "No society has ever admitted that it could not sacrifice individual welfare to its own existence." *Id.* at 37.

Notwithstanding the stirring words of the Declaration of Independence and distinguished philosophers, all states impose limits on individual rights in the name of public interest. Indeed, the Universal Declaration of Human Rights explicitly provides:

> In the exercise of his rights and freedoms, everyone shall be subject only to such limitations as are determined by law solely for the purpose of securing due recognition and respect for the rights and freedoms of others and of meeting the *just requirements of morality, public order and the general welfare* in a democratic society.[9]

Rhetoric aside, we constantly perform a complex calculus by which the rights or protected interests of individuals are weighed against the good of the collective (and other rights). Reasonable people differ as to the proper balance to effect; that diverse cultures would reach different conclusions is only natural.[10]

Examining the criticisms China's human rights record raises three related questions. Are critics calling for a new kind Chinese right—absolute, inalienable, ahistorical, human cum natural rights—or simply a different calculus where the rights of individuals are not so readily traded off to promote the "collective good"?

Similarly, does the problem lie in the outcome of the calculus or in the manner in which the calculus is made? While the Tiananmen massacre shocks the conscience, the more basic problem may be *how* the tragic decisions that culminated in tanks rolling through the streets of Beijing were reached: that is, via an authoritarian one-party system rather than a democratic process.

Finally, it is not so much the *how* of the calculus but the *who*. Though some intellectuals call for democracy, one still encounters with alarming frequency the traditional paternalistic attitude that the "masses" are not sufficiently educated to shoulder the responsibilities

9. Universal Declaration of Human Rights, art. 29(2) U.N. GAOR, U.N. Doc. A/811 (1948) (emphasis added). The U.S. also limits rights in the name of the public good. Our system first distinguishes between rights. Some are classified as "fundamental" or "preferred"—for example, freedom of religion and speech. But even these fundamental rights are not absolute or inalienable; they may be overridden if on strict scrutiny the court finds a compelling state interest. Other rights, for example economic rights, may be infringed on finding nothing more than a minimally rational basis for the trumping legislation. Griswold v. Connecticut, 381 U.S. 479, 486 (1965) (Goldberg, J., concurring); Poe v. Ullman, 367 U.S. 497, 522 (1961) (Harlan, J., dissenting).

10. The point is not that China may justify or be excused for Tiananmen simply by waving a banner of cultural relativism. Some things—such as the torture of student activists—are clearly not acceptable, *by anyone's standards*, western or Chinese (be they Confucian or socialist). *See Activist Details Hunan Jail Abuse*, S. CHINA MORNING POST, June 1, 1992, at 10.

of democracy.[11] This suggests that in the eyes of many, what is needed is not an institutional change from dictatorship to democracy, but simply a change in dictators: just replace old guard conservatives with free-market reformers and all will be well.[12]

Whatever one's response to these questions, there can be little doubt that individuals in the PRC need some protection against the all-powerful state. There must be real constraints imposed on the government. If we were to impose these constraints through the vehicle of rights, then the PRC needs i) a stronger system of enforceable rights—rights in practice, not just name, and ii) a coherent theory of Chinese rights—a theory of rights justified on Chinese terms.

In Part I, I examine institutional obstacles to a workable system of rights in China. In Part II, I explore some of the philosophical assumptions that underwrite western rights theories. In Part III, I contrast these assumptions with the underlying premises of Confucianism. I do so because I believe Confucianism continues even today to be the basis of the Chinese world view, despite the attempts of the socialist government to eradicate such "feudal" thinking. Hence any workable theory of rights justifiable on Chinese terms will in all likelihood emerge out of and be consistent with the basic premises of Confucianism. Of course Confucianism is not the only intellectual influence. Thus I discuss socialism in Part IV. In Part V, I critique China's socialist regime not on the alien terms of western rights theories but from a Chinese perspective on rights. In Part VI, I sketch the contours of a Chinese rights theory and speculate as to the possibilities of its realization.[13]

I. INSTITUTIONAL OBSTACLES

A central obstacle to the protection of rights in China is the primacy of the Party over the rule of law. Party control eviscerates the rule of

11. *Cf.* Andrew Nathan, *Tiananmen and the Cosmos*, *supra* note 5, at 32, 35 (noting that intellectuals wanted democracy without the demos). Indeed, in a June 3, 1989 interview, the student leader Wuer Kaixi stated that "the Chinese people lack consciousness of democracy, and do not understand democracy." MING PAO, June 17, 1989; FOREIGN BROADCAST INFORMATION SERVICE, June 20, 1989, at 24–27 [hereinafter FBIS].

12. Witness the support for so-called new or neo-authoritarianism in the PRC modeled on the economically free-market and politically authoritarian approach of Taiwan, Singapore, and South Korea. *See* XIN QUANWEIZHUYI [NEW AUTHORITARIANISM] (Liu Jun & Li Lin eds., 1989); *see also* Michel Oksenberg et al. eds., BEIJING SPRING, 1989: CONFRONTATION & CONFLICT 123–49 (1990).

13. The claim is not that Chinese intellectual traditions alone will determine the nature and course of human rights in China. No doubt Chinese rights are and will continue to be influenced by a host of other factors, including domestic and foreign political and economic realities. *But see infra* notes 113–115 and accompanying text. Nor do I claim that Chinese intellectual traditions "lock in" a particular form of rights—or that, for instance, the Chinese cannot escape from the walls of Confucian political philosophy. The thesis is simply that these intellectual traditions, particularly Confucianism, will most likely exert considerable influence on Chinese human rights.

law, prevents the development of a genuinely independent judiciary, and renders meaningless the concept of constitutional review. According to the constitution, the Party is to follow the law,[14] yet in practice, the Party remains the law.[15] This is to be expected, given the basic premises of socialism. Mao once described law and courts as "instruments with which one class oppresses another. As far as the hostile classes are concerned these are instruments of oppression. They are violent and certainly not 'benevolent things.'"[16] As a tool of socialism, the law must serve the Party rather than individuals. That such ideas retain their currency despite repeated calls for a rule of law independent of Party control is scarcely surprising. What is perhaps somewhat surprising is the articulation of such views by the most senior members of the judiciary. For example, a major newspaper recently quoted Justice Minister Cai Cheng as declaring: "Chinese law must be at the service of class struggle . . . [T]here can be no question of 'the law being supreme' . . . . China must jettison the concept of 'the supremacy of the law' because the judicial code and system must be at the service of the proletariat class."[17]

There will be no way to protect the rights and interests of individuals if political might makes right—as the history of many other countries demonstrates. If rights are to become meaningful in China, limitations on Party power are essential.

To justify state abuse of individual rights, the Party can turn to article 51 of the constitution, itself a major impediment to practicable rights: "The exercise of citizens of the PRC of their freedoms and rights may not infringe upon the interests of the state, of society, and of the collective, or upon the lawful freedoms and rights of other citizens."[18] This manifestly asserts the hierarchy of state over individual, undermining the *raison d'être* of rights as a guarantee that "each person possesses an inviolability founded on justice that even the welfare of society as a whole cannot override."[19]

---

14. PRC CONST., *supra* note 1, art. 5; *see also Human Rights in China*, 34 BEIJING REV., Nov. 4–10, 1991 at 8, 14 [hereinafter WHITE PAPER]. (This is Beijing's official statement on human rights.)

15. *See* Nathan, *supra* note 1, at 101–02, 108–12; *see also* Andrew Nathan, *Sources of Chinese Rights Thinking*, in HUMAN RIGHTS IN CONTEMPORARY CHINA, *supra* note 1, at 125, 132–37; SHAO-CHUAN LENG & HUNGDAH CHIU, CRIMINAL JUSTICE IN POST-MAO CHINA 98–104 (1985); Li Maoguan, *Why "Laws Go Unenforced,"* 32 BEIJING REV. 17–18 (1980). While in theory the 1982 Constitution limits Party authority, the ultimate authority of the Party is explicit in the 1975 and 1978 constitutions. Further, during all periods since 1949, the Party has in practice dominated the People's Congresses, courts and other organs of state. For continuing problems in the establishment of a truly independent judiciary, *see* REPORT OF THE AUSTRALIAN HUMAN RIGHTS DELEGATION TO CHINA 14–26, 27–29 (1991).

16. MAO ZEDONG, ON PEOPLE'S DEMOCRATIC DICTATORSHIP 16–17 (1951).

17. Willy Wo-lap Lam, *Justice Minister Rejects "Supremacy of the Law"*, S. CHINA MORNING POST, Nov. 12, 1991, at 12.

18. PRC CONST., *supra* note 1, art. 51.

19. RAWLS, *supra* note 6. Whether state interest may trump individual interest, and if so,

Another institutional impediment, related to but distinct from the issue of an independent judiciary and rule of law, is the lack of constitutional review. In the United States, the judiciary has emerged as the body that reviews governmental actions for conformity with the Constitution, but other arrangements are possible.[20] What matters is not so much the particular method, but that some agency other than the one that created the law be given the power of review. The 1982 PRC constitution gives the power to interpret and enforce the constitution not to the judiciary or an independent constitutional review body but to the standing committee of the supreme legislature, the National People's Congress. Because it is the National People's Congress that drafts and adopts laws in the first place, "[i]t seems unlikely that the standing committee would interpret any statute or amendment as inconsistent with the constitution or the basic principles of the statutes (such as Criminal Law)."[21]

Constitutional review is one element of what some scholars have termed "constitutionalism." Although constitutionalism has not been definitively defined, the lack of it is generally considered fatal to human rights. Noting that variations are possible and no authoritative definition exists, Louis Henkin, a prominent champion of this new *ism*, offers several core elements: government according to the constitution; separation of powers; popular sovereignty and democratic government; constitutional review; independent judiciary; civilian control of the military; individual rights; and limitations on suspension, derogation, or amendment of the constitution by political organs.[22] Obviously China fails several, if not all, of these threshold tests. For example, the government has not only suspended the constitution but regularly promulgated new ones.[23] More importantly, by all accounts the government has disregarded all of its constitutions at one time or another.[24] In addition, separation of powers is nonexistent. As noted, the Party dominates all aspects of government, including the military.

---

under what conditions, are discussed *infra*. As noted in *supra* notes 6–7 and accompanying text, all states impose limits on individual rights in the name of the public good.

20. *See* Louis Favoreu, *Constitutional Review in Europe*, *in* CONSTITUTIONALISM AND RIGHTS 38, 47–54 (Louis Henkin & Albert Rosenthal eds., 1990).

21. LENG & CHIU *supra* note 15, at 43; PRC CONST., *supra* note 1, at 43. *See also* Nathan, *supra* note 1, at 120.

22. Louis Henkin, Constitutions and the Elements of Constitutionalism, paper prepared for the American Council of Learned Societies Conference on Constitutionalism and the Transition to Democracy in Eastern Europe, Pecs, Hungary (June 18–20, 1990) (on file at Chinese Legal Studies Center, Columbia University), *passim*.

23. China has had four constitutions since 1949. The first was promulgated in 1954, followed by new ones in 1975, 1978, and 1982. For a comparison, see Nathan, *supra* note 1, at 80–81.

24. For abuses of the constitution and the criminal process arising out of the Tiananmen "incident" see Jerome Cohen, *Tiananmen and the Rule of Law*, *in* THE BROKEN MIRROR, *supra*

Taken collectively, wholesale violation of these elements is perhaps a good indicator of the absence of a strong commitment to individual rights.[25] More debatable is whether possessing any single element or combination of elements is either necessary or sufficient to ensure human rights. England, for instance, does not even have a written constitution, and many states allow suspension of the constitution during times of crisis.[26] Conversely, the PRC at least nominally provides for separation of powers and functions.[27] How can England, a country without a written constitution, succeed in providing human rights while the PRC, constitution in hand, fails? "In the end," concludes Henkin, "constitutionalism depends on political, social and economic stability and a political culture that is committed to constitutionalism."[28] Perhaps most importantly, for human rights to be respected, there must be rights consciousness, a culture of rights, an attitude among the people that the government cannot do to them as it wishes.[29] The people must learn to stand up to the government and insist on their rights. They must demand that the judiciary and the body responsible for constitutional review perform their designated functions in the face of opposition from political powers. This attitude is sorely lacking in China.[30]

---

note 5, at 325–26. Ironically, one important motivation behind the return to a rule of law called for by Deng and other leaders in the late 1970's was personal experience of widespread legal abuse during the Cultural Revolution. *See* LENG & CHIU, *supra* note 15, at 35–37 (noting also the importance of rule of law to the "four modernizations" and economic reform).

25. Simply as an analytical matter, wholesale rejection of constitutionalism necessarily entails rejection of rights because one element of constitutionalism *is* individual rights. Indeed, to the extent that a commitment to rights is a necessary condition of constitutionalism, the argument is circular: constitutionalism is necessary for rights, and rights are necessary for constitutionalism. If individual rights are not a necessary element, one can avoid the apparent circularity by defining constitutionalism without reference to rights for the purpose of the discussion.

26. Even the *International Covenant on Civil and Political Rights*, U.N. GAOR, 21st Sess., Annex, 1496th plen. mtg. at art. 4 (1966), provides that "[i]n time of public emergency which threatens the life of the nation," States may "take measures derogating from their obligations under the present Covenant to the extent strictly required by the exigencies of the situation."

27. *See, e.g.*, PRC CONST., *supra* note 1, art. 126 (providing for an independent judiciary).

28. Henkin, *supra* note 1, at 19.

29. As Peter Lin notes, even a consciousness of rights is not sufficient. In addition,

> there must be a widespread, entrenched, and "self-sacrificial" commitment by the elites to act consistently with the values and standard of rationality generally accepted by the people. Such a commitment involves "self-sacrifice" because the governing elites have to forgo the advantage they could otherwise gain by abusing their power, in exchange for a system from which all will benefit.

Peter Lin, *Between Theory and Practice: The Possibility of a Right to Free Speech in the People's Republic of China*, 4 J. CHINESE L. 257, 268 (1990).

30. To be sure, some have stood up and continue to stand up to the government. One need only recall the unforgettable image of the sole demonstrator standing resolutely in front of a row of tanks. Similarly, the existence of underground newspapers and dissidents both in China and living abroad in exile demonstrates that some Chinese are prepared to oppose the government. Even more direct evidence is the recent phenomenon of politically motivated lawsuits against

Many in the United States turn to the judiciary when they feel their rights have been violated. However for historical reasons, many Chinese continue to shy away from and fear the courts.[31] Chinese tradition frowned on judicial resolution of conflicts.[32]

Conflicts were to be resolved through informal, extrajudicial means such as mediation spearheaded by a local elder.[33] To end up in court was shameful and risky. The pitfalls of even successful litigation are enshrined in the Chinese proverb: "Win your lawsuit but lose your money."[34] Traditional distrust of and reluctance to rely on the formal legal system remain an impediment to the development of a rights attitude and culture in China.[35]

Even assuming that these obstacles could be overcome—the influence of the Party diminished, article 51 rewritten (or limited by interpretation), constitutional review established, and the deep-rooted fear of the courts overcome—it is unlikely that a strong theory of individual rights would emerge in China. To understand this, one must examine the philosophical assumptions that lie at heart of the Chinese world view. Perhaps the best way to do this is to begin with a brief overview of the underpinnings of western rights theories.

II. UNDERPINNINGS OF HUMAN RIGHTS THEORIES

Western theories of human or natural rights have as a whole been foundational and universal in character.[36] They tend to be written as

---

the government. *See* Sheryl WuDunn, *Chinese Bite Back at Beijing with Lawsuits*, N.Y. TIMES, Sept. 13, 1992, at 9 (noting that the government is unlikely to lose a politically sensitive lawsuit).

Nevertheless, such pockets of resistance remain the exception and not the rule. The few people willing to challenge the political authority of the government directly fall far short of the kind of broad-based social support that Henkin sees as necessary to constitutionalism.

31. *See* Li Maoguan, *supra* note 15, at 18–19.

32. "In hearing litigation," remarked Confucius, "I am no different from any other man. But if you insist on a difference, it is, perhaps, that I try to get the parties not to resort to litigation in the first place." CONFUCIUS, LUN YÜ [ANALECTS] 12:13 [hereinafter ANALECTS]. For an English translation, see D.C. LAU, CONFUCIUS: THE ANALECTS (1979). Citations to the Analects follow the numbering of Lau.

33. For informal or "extralegal" methods of conflict resolution in contemporary China, see VICTOR H. LI, LAW WITHOUT LAWYERS 14–16, 44–65 (1978); JEROME A. COHEN, THE CRIMINAL PROCESS IN THE PEOPLE'S REPUBLIC OF CHINA 1949–1963 97–199 (1968).

34. SYBILLE VAN DER SPRENKEL, LEGAL INSTITUTIONS IN MANCHU CHINA 135 (1966). For an excellent "insider's view" of the Chinese legal system of the Qing, see HUANG LIU-HONG, A COMPLETE BOOK CONCERNING HAPPINESS AND BENEVOLENCE (Djang Chu trans. & ed., 1984). Huang describes frankly the corruption plaguing every level of the judicial system.

35. There is some evidence that the historical stereotypes are losing their validity. In 1989, Chinese brought 1.85 million civil cases. This represented a 24% increase over 1988 and a sevenfold jump over 1978. Edward Epstein, *China's Legal Reforms*, *in* CHINA REVIEW 9.33 (Kuan Hsin-Chi & Maurice Brosseau eds., 1991) (citing RENMIN ERBAO [PEOPLE'S DAILY], Apr. 10, 1990, at 2). Nevertheless, traditional attitudes continue to exert an influence, as noted by Li Maoguan, *supra* note 15.

36. More accurately, civil and political rights are understood as universal, abstract, and

if equally applicable to contemporary Asia as to seventeenth-century Europe or twentieth-century United States. For instance, one popular form of expression is that human rights are "self-evident."[37] As Henry Rosemont has noted, "it is a bedrock presupposition of our moral, social, and political thinking that human beings have rights, solely by virtue of being human . . . [T]he concept of human beings as right-bearers is not itself in serious question in contemporary Western moral, social and political philosophy."[38] This, like so many other self-evident axioms of western social and political philosophy, is far from obvious in a Chinese context. The oft-noted late arrival of the concept "right" to China, along with classical Confucianism's emphasis on rites[39] rather than rights, suggests that within a Chinese cultural and philosophical milieu, it is far from self-evident that everyone enjoys rights that even the good of society as a whole cannot override.

A second source of human rights is God. So-called natural rights are often said to be God-given. Many today dismiss such a suggestion as preposterous, truly nonsense on stilts. Rights, they argue, do not rain down from heaven: they are political creations. In any case, the Chinese can hardly be expected to ground a rights theory upon Judeo-Christian religious conceptions.

A third scenario is the Hobbesian/Lockean fable of the ascent of humans from a brutal and savage state of nature to the civilized wonder

---

natural whereas social, economic, and collective rights are understood as contingent, non-universal, and decidedly secondary. *See* Ann Kent, *Waiting for Rights: China's Human Rights and China's Constitutions, 1949–1989*, 13 HUM. RTS. Q. 170, 174 (1991). I do not mean to imply that all rights theories, even political rights theories, are universal natural rights theories. Nevertheless, I consider such theories in this section for several reasons. First, the rhetoric of rights theories is often that of universal, natural rights. The claim that China needs human rights is often the claim that China needs universal human rights. Second, such theories have been and remain extremely influential in the western tradition. Third, understanding how assumptions underlying such theories are at odds with Chinese political tradition helps explain why China is more likely to adopt the kind of contingent, communitarian rights theory described in part VI. Of course, westerners may also favor similar theories. Indeed, communitarian theories are currently in vogue. I do not claim that such theories must be unique to China or that no western thinkers have advanced similar views.

37. The poverty of this "justification" is itself evident from Alasdair MacIntyre's observation that:

> there is no expression in any ancient or medieval language correctly translated by our expression "a right" until near the close of the middle ages: the concept lacks any means of expression in Hebrew, Greek, Latin or Arabic, classical or medieval, before 1400, let alone in Old English, or in Japanese even as late as the mid-nineteenth century.

ALASDAIR MACINTYRE, AFTER VIRTUE 69 (1984).

38. Henry Rosemont, *Why Take Rights Seriously? A Confucian Critique*, *in* HUMAN RIGHTS AND THE WORLD'S RELIGIONS 167 (Leroy Rouner ed., 1988). Some western thinkers have begun to challenge the notion that humans possess rights simply by virtue of birth.

39. *Li*, conventionally translated as rites, refers to the full range of social customs, ethical norms, and political principles that inform interpersonal relations, social institutions, and normative discourse in China.

of a social life where each person's autonomy and dignity is safeguarded by a strong theory of rights. The story begins with atomistic, rational individuals free from any duty to others, who realize the gains in safety and self-protection from cooperation and consent to limit individual freedom. By signing a mythical social compact, one limits one's liberty in exchange for certain rights. Just what these rights are varies from thinker to thinker. The same basic story-line underwrites the minimalist libertarian state of Locke and Nozick;[40] the autocratic, sovereign-dominated Leviathan of Hobbes;[41] the majoritarianism of Rousseau;[42] and, in a slightly altered version, the contemporary liberal democracy of Rawls.[43]

If one allows that society is an arena in which self-interested individuals compete for scarce resources and goods, some set of principles, rules, or laws may be needed to protect the rightful claims of individuals to goods or liberties from invasion by others. By contrast, Confucianism rejects both the atomistic individual and inevitable competition assumptions. But before turning to Confucianism, one further point merits comment. Contemporary rights thinking revolves around the distinction between Kantian deontic principles and utilitarian consequences or social policy.[44] Those who take rights seriously side with Dworkin in privileging principle over policy.[45] Those more concerned with the distributive effects of legal and political decisions give primacy to policy. A third, more pragmatic faction refuses to privilege either side, insisting instead on a situational analysis where one effects justice by balancing the rights of individuals to pursue their own ideals against the social consequences of individual choice.[46]

Confucianism, however, rejects both the atomistic individual and inevitable competition assumptions. Part of my project shall be to argue that the situational character of Confucian ethics and the pragmatism of Chinese leaders make unlikely the pressing concern with

---

40. JOHN LOCKE, TWO TREATISES OF GOVERNMENT bk. II, chs. VIII–XV, 361–99 (Peter Laslett ed., 1960) (3d ed. 1698); NOZICK, *supra* note 6, at 10–25.

41. THOMAS HOBBES, LEVIATHAN P. I, chs. 13–15, 17–19, P. II, ch. 26, 183–217, 223–39, 313 (Crawford B. Macpherson ed., 1951) (1651).

42. JEAN JACQUES ROUSSEAU, ON SOCIAL CONTRACT bk. IV, ch. 2, *in* THE ESSENTIAL ROUSSEAU 88 (Lowell Bair tr., 1974) (1762).

43. RAWLS, *supra* note 6, at 11–17. The Rawlsian variant adds a twist or two: rational agents in the "original position" now make life-choices from behind a veil of ignorance. *Id.* at 17–22, 136–41. However, the key assumptions remain the same. One is still in a world of atomistic individuals in competition for scarce goods, a world where individual rights and liberties precede obligations to the state and to each other.

44. *See* Philip Soper, *Dworkin's Domain*, 100 HARV. L. REV. 1166, 1180–81 (1987).

45. DWORKIN, *supra* note 6, at 219–24.

46. *See* R. Kent Greenwalt, *Law's Empire*, 84 J. PHIL. 284, 290 (1987) (book review); *see also* R.P. Peerenboom, *A Coup D'Etat in Law's Empire: Dworkin's Hercules Meets Atlas*, 9 LAW & PHIL. 95, 108–11 (1990).

deontic principles necessary to underwrite a strong theory of individual rights. Indeed, the context-specificity of Confucian ethics militates against any attempt to pass off historically and culturally contingent political policies and theories as universal, ahistorical absolutes.[47]

III. CONFUCIANISM

In asking how individuals become obligated to the state (and each other), Hobbes achieved the equivalent of a Copernican revolution in social and political thought. Previously the assumption was that the individual was born a member of a state. A human being, in the words of Aristotle, was a political animal, part and parcel of a polis.[48] Few doubted that the interests of the state naturally preceded those of the individual. The question in Plato's Republic was "How can one best serve the state," not "What can the state do for me."[49]

Chinese thinking to this day is dominated by this pre-Hobbesian world view. State interests override the interests and rights of any given individual. The apparent one-sidedness of this relationship is diminished to some extent, however, by a second basic assumption in Chinese thought: that the interests of the state and individual are in, or at least can be brought into, harmony.

One of the primary concerns of Tocqueville and Mill was that individuals and minorities would be overwhelmed by the more pow-

---

47. Of course, not all western ethical theories are foundational and universalist in character. For instance, situational ethics and the normative views of American pragmatists such as Dewey share much in common with Confucianism. *See* RANDALL P. PEERENBOOM, LAW AND MORALITY IN ANCIENT CHINA: THE SILK MANUSCRIPTS OF HUANG-LAO, ch. IV (1993). Similarly, many writers now accept that normative theories and systems are contingent. Indeed, even Rawls has conceded that his arguments for justice as fairness are framed to apply to the "'basic structure' of a modern constitutional democracy." John Rawls, *Justice as Fairness: Political not Metaphysical*, 14 PHIL. & PUB. AFFS. 223, 224 (1985). *See also* John Rawls, *Kantian Constructivism in Moral Theory*, 77 J. PHIL. 515, 518 (1980); John Rawls, *The Idea of an Overlapping Consensus*, 7 OXFORD J. LEGAL STUDIES 1 (1987) ("[T]he aims of political philosophy depend on the society it addresses"). He then proceeds to list seven features of modern constitutional democracies, including "the fact that the political culture of a society with a democratic tradition implicitly contains certain fundamental intuitive ideas from which it is possible to work up a political conception of justice suitable for a constitutional regime." *Id.* at 4–5.

48. ARISTOTLE, POLITICS, *in* THE COMPLETE WORKS OF ARISTOTLE, bk. I, ch. 2, at 1987 (Jonathan Barnes ed., 1984) ("[M]an is by nature a political animal"). He adds, "[H]e who is unable to live in society, or who has no need because he is sufficient for himself, must be either a beast or a god." *Id.* at 1988. For a similar view, see CONFUCIUS, ANALECTS, *supra* note 32, at 18:7 ("One cannot associate with birds and beasts. Am I not a member of this human race? Who, then, is there for me to associate with?"). For the Confucian view of the self as a nexus of relations—social, political, cultural, religious, and so forth—see *infra* notes 57–61, 74 and accompanying text.

49. PLATO, THE REPUBLIC, *in* PLATO: THE COLLECTED DIALOGUES 575–844 (Edith Hamilton & Huntington Cairns eds., 1961).

erful majority and state.[50] In contrast, early rights advocates in China saw no contradiction between individual rights and the goals of the state.[51] On the contrary, the belief was that unleashing individual initiative would further the interests of the state. Convinced of the fundamental harmony of state and individual, Chinese leaders and intellectuals never developed a strong theory of rights to protect the individual against the dominant interests of the majority and state.

In fact, Chinese leaders tended to view rights as derivative from the state. As R. Randle Edwards explains, "China's leaders today, like the imperial and bureaucratic rulers of the past, hold that rights flow from the state in the form of a gratuitous grant that can be subjected to conditions or abrogation by the unilateral decision of the state."[52] In contrast, most western theorists maintain that the state is designed to protect rights which derive from one's status as a human being. To override these rights, the state must meet stringent political and legal standards and demonstrate compelling state interests.[53]

By drawing a distinction between human beings *qua* members of a biological species and humans *qua* social beings, classical Confucianism rejects the assumption that individuals are entitled to certain inalienable rights from birth. The well-publicized and much debated distinction between masses (*min*) and persons (*ren*) as well as that between the small person (*xiao ren*) and the exemplary person (*jun zi*)[54] suggests that one must earn rights by achieving some minimal level of person-

50. Their worries were in part a response to the autocratic, all-powerful sovereign of Hobbes and the majoritarian universal will of Rousseau. *See* ALEXIS DE TOCQUEVILLE, DEMOCRACY IN AMERICA, ch. 15, *in* ALEXIS DE TOCQUEVILLE: DEMOCRACY, REVOLUTION AND SOCIETY, 99–101 (John Stone & Stephen Mennell eds., 1980) (1835) (warning against the "tyranny of the majority"). *See also* JOHN STUART MILL, ON LIBERTY, ch. 4, 141–62 (Gertrude Himmelfarb ed., 1982) (1859).

51. ANDREW NATHAN, CHINESE DEMOCRACY 50–51 (1985).

52. R. Randle Edwards, *Civil and Social Rights: Theory and Practice in Chinese Law Today*, in HUMAN RIGHTS IN CONTEMPORARY CHINA, *supra* note 1, at 44–45.

53. The compelling interest standard applies to "fundamental" or "preferred" rights. Nonfundamental rights are measured by a mere minimum rationality test: the legislature must have had some intelligible reason for enacting the rights limiting legislation. *See supra* note 9 and accompanying text. Of course, this points to one of the major conceptual equivocations underlying rights talk. Not all rights are created equal. One must distinguish between explicit constitutional rights, implicit constitutional rights, legislative rights, legal rights, and nonlegal rights (social rights or rights in theory—philosophical rights—and so forth).

54. Linguistic distinctions continue to be important. Ann Kent notes that despite the restrictive nature of the 1982 constitution, Chinese citizens experienced in practice an expansion of civil and political rights during the early to mid-1980s. Consonant with greater liberties was a shift from collective to individual consciousness, as symbolized by the increasing use of *gongmin* (citizen) as opposed to the previously dominant *qunzhong* (masses). Kent, *supra* note 36, at 188.

During the 1989 protests, some of the working class demonstrators referred to themselves as *shimin* (urbanites or civilians). Significantly, intellectuals continued to refer to these demonstrators as *qunzhong* (masses) or *laobaixing* (common people), reinforcing the appearance, if not the reality, of anti-democratic elitism. Nathan, *supra* note 5, at 32.

hood, of humanity.[55] That is, entitlement to the privileges and benefits offered by society requires demonstration of credentials as a participating member of society. As David Hall and Roger Ames remark:

> A person is not entitled to political participation because he is born into an exclusive *jen* [human being] class. Rather, he becomes *jen* as a consequence of that personal cultivation and socialization that renders him particular. Being a person is something one does, not something one is; it is an achievement rather than a given.[56]

The achievement, it should be emphasized, is a social one. For Confucius, one *becomes* a human being, a humane person, by virtue of participation in society. Personhood and humanity are functions of socialization. At birth, before the process of enculturation, of becoming humane, we are not different than the other beasts.[57] It is this joining with others, overcoming one's natural conditionality (*ming*) in creating a different and better society, which is distinctive about humans. If one cannot overcome the passions, instincts and desires that human beings share with beasts, then one fails to achieve humanity, to become the kind of person society has an interest in protecting and granting even minimal rights.[58]

The Confucian (and socialist) challenge then is to inspire in members of society the desire to achieve a humane society and to encourage them to direct their energies toward the attainment of a harmonious social order where the interests of individuals and of the state are reconciled. This requires a willingness to participate in collective

---

55. Mary Anne Warren was one of the first in the contemporary western literature to draw a similar distinction between "genetic humans" and "persons." *See* Mary Anne Warren, *On the Moral and Legal Status of Abortion*, 57 MONIST 43–61 (1973).

56. DAVID L. HALL & ROGER T. AMES, THINKING THROUGH CONFUCIUS 139 (1987).

57. *See* ANALECTS, *supra* note 32, at 18:6, 10:17. Humans, of course, have the potential to differentiate themselves from animals. This may provide a justification for extending some degree of moral consideration to children, though it does little for the severely impaired. The relatively high degree of infanticide, the almost non-existence of opposition to abortion, and the fact that in traditional Chinese law children were provided little protection against their parents, suggest that children were not full-fledged members of society and that one's right to consideration was indeed linked to social achievement. In the Qin, for example, the father was permitted to kill or mutilate his son as long as he first petitioned for approval. A.F.P. HULSEWE, REMNANTS OF HAN LAW 8 (1985). If the child was born deformed, infanticide was permitted. *Id.* at 139. Harsh treatment of one's offspring was also permitted in other dynasties. *See* GU TANG LU SHUYI [THE TANG CODE AND COMMENTARIES], arts. 253, 256; for an English translation, see WALLACE JOHNSON, THE TANG CODE 21, 31–32 (1979).

58. The view that some members of society have no claim right on society even to life is not completely alien to the American mind: presumably some such notion underlies the popular appeal of capital punishment in the United States. The difference is that in China one must first earn one's rights whereas in the United States one starts with rights but can forfeit them through socially inappropriate behavior.

living, to search for a cooperative solution, to become humane (*ren*). It is in this sense that humanity is not something that can be conferred by law or by right of birth.

Confucianism would consider it a failure for society to aim at securing a minimum level of basic rights for alienated individuals unable or unwilling to participate cooperatively in collective living. If one accepts that there is no way to overcome the self-interested passions and desires of the animal world, then there is no hope for a humane society. Confucius realized that laws cannot force people to be humane.[59] For society to achieve collective humanity, the people that *constitute* it must be willing to put aside narrow self-interest and see their interests as inextricably tied to societal interests.

The ethical focus, therefore, cannot be on determining and implementing a universal system of laws that establishes a minimum standard of basic rights for individuals alienated from each other and society. Rather, the ethical orientation must be directed to the achievement of the highest quality of life made possible by the joint efforts of humans cooperating in collective living.[60] The call is for realization of excellence in interpersonal relations (*ren*).[61]

Rights may serve well to provide a minimum level of protection for the individual. But rights, particularly as conceived and enforced in the United States, are no panacea: such rights are negative, not positive rights.[62] They are rights against the state, providing freedom *from* state intervention, but they generally do not entitle one *to* sub-

---

59. "Lead the people by edicts, keep them in line with penal law, and they will avoid punishments but have no sense of shame. Lead them with virtue, keep them in line with the rites, and they will not only have a sense of shame but will order themselves harmoniously." ANALECTS, *supra* note 32, at 2:3.

60. In a Confucian world, ethical standards—of which rights are one species—serve not so much as aspirational norms as inspirational themes. *See* A.S. Cua, DIMENSIONS IN MORAL CREATIVITY 124 (1978). That is, one is not simply to conform to a particular rule or standard. Rather one is to embody and give expression to the underlying ideal in one's own way, in light of one's own circumstances. To act appropriately in a given circumstance, one must "appropriate" the ethical value—one must make that value one's own. As a consequence, one has a great deal of discretion in how one translates an ethical rule or norm into practice.

The inspirational character of Confucian ethics explains in part an observation of Andrew Nathan, namely, that rights in Chinese constitutions are programmatic—"that is, they are presented as goals to be realized." *See* Nathan, *supra* note 1, at 121. What are minimal ethical and political restraints imposed on the government in the West become in Confucian China ethical ideals through which social beings can realize a humane society. These ideals must be translated into practice and given expression in light of the particular circumstances. Thus, in seeking harmony, one begins but does not end with rights.

61. Thus, one is transformed from a human being *qua* animal to a social person entitled to deference and respect. As A.S. Cua observes, "concept of ren is the concept of an ideal of moral excellence . . . . The focus is on man himself and what he can morally accomplish in relation to others." CUA, *supra* note 60, at 68.

62. *See* David Currie, *Positive and Negative Constitutional Rights*, 53 U. CHI. L. REV. 864 (1986).

stantive benefits.[63] For instance, one has no legal claim to the economic rights enumerated in the Universal Declaration of Human Rights.[64]

Furthermore, rights are but half of the picture—the other half is duties. One indication of the different orientation of Confucian China and the United States is the contrasting conceptions of the relation between, and relative importance of, rights and duties. In the United States, much is made of rights, but duties, if discussed at all, are considered merely as corollaries to rights: in Hohfeldian terms, if one has a claim right, then others, including the state, have a duty not to interfere with that right.[65] There is generally no legal duty to the state or to fellow citizens. There is, for instance, no constitutional obligation to render aid to another;[66] indeed, in all but two states, one need not throw a life-jacket to a drowning person even though the inconvenience would be trivial.[67]

Emphasizing duties rather than rights, Chinese tradition turns Hohfeld on his head: rights are corollaries to duties.[68] For instance, a child has a duty of piety to his parents; as a result, parents have a "claim

---

63. *See, e.g.*, DeShaney v. Winnebago County Dep't of Social Servs., 489 U.S. 189, 196 (1989):

> [The Due Process Clause's] purpose was to protect the people from the State, not to ensure that the State protected them from each other . . . . Consistent with these principles, our cases have recognized that the Due Process Clauses generally confer no affirmative right to governmental aid, even where such aid may be necessary to secure life, liberty, or property . . . .

64. Universal Declaration of Human Rights, *supra* note 9, arts. 22–25 (right to work, social security, and an adequate standard of living, including food, clothing, housing, and medical care).

65. *See* Westley Newcomb Hohfeld, *Fundamental Legal Conceptions as Applied in Judicial Reasoning*, 23 YALE L.J. 16, 31–32 (1913).

66. U.S. tort law does impose specific duties on some individuals in certain circumstances based on a "special relationship" between the parties. For instance, innkeepers have certain duties toward their guests, as do jailors to their prisoners, and hosts to guests invited onto the premises. *See* RESTATEMENT (SECOND) OF TORTS § 314A (1965). Similarly, one who attempts to aid another but leaves that person worse off or who intentionally prevents a third party from coming to the aid of someone injured may be held liable. *Id.* at §§ 322, 323, 324A, 326, 327. Further, a small number of states have enacted good samaritan laws. *See infra* note 67. Nevertheless, in the vast majority of states, the general rule is that in the absence of a special relation, "the fact that the actor realized or should realize that action on his part is necessary for another's aid or protection does not of itself impose upon him a duty to take such action." RESTATEMENT at § 314.

67. *See* VT. STAT. ANN. tit. 12, sec. 519 (1973); MINN. STAT. sec. 604.05 (1984). More than a dozen European states have good samaritan laws that impose criminal sanctions for failing to provide aid to one in peril. For good samaritan laws in Europe, see Rudzinski, *The Duty to Rescue: A Comparative Analysis*, *in* THE GOOD SAMARITAN AND THE LAW 91 (J. Ratcliffe ed., 1966).

68. Of course, this is largely a matter of rhetorical emphasis. On the Hohfeldian view, claim rights and duties are but two sides of the same coin. Nevertheless, the rhetorical difference is illuminating. *See* Wang Jiafu et al., *Lun Fazhi Gaige* [*On Reform of the Legal System*], 2 FAXUE YANJIU 1, 8 (1989) (arguing that while rights entail duties and duties entail rights, rights should nonetheless occupy the leading position).

right" to support. Not surprisingly, the current constitution requires children to support their parents.[69] Individuals have legal duties not only to their parents but also to each other and the state.[70]

More broadly, the Confucian concept of *ren* is a duty to act appropriately in relation to others. At first blush, Confucianism appears to promote not natural rights but natural duties. Human beings, born into a family, a society, a state, owe duties to other members by virtue of birth. Some Confucians have even attempted to ground the hierarchial five primary social relations in a hierarchical natural order: just as heaven is above earth and yang superior to yin, so is the ruler above the official, the husband superior to the wife,[71] and so on.[72]

Yet at the heart of a duty lies not simply the natural relation but also deference. One becomes an authority, a person to whom others will defer, in part by age and natural relation but, more importantly, by earning the respect of others. To do so, one must show cultural and moral achievement and demonstrate to others that they are better off following one's advice than had they set out on their own.[73] In times of conflict, people turn to the authoritative person (*jun zi*) as the one best able to envision a solution and thereby restore harmony.

In the Confucian world, there are no ahistorical or abstract rational beings. Confucianism concurs in this regard with Edmund Pincoffs, who maintains that "individualism makes sense only against a background of social organization. There is no human situation that consists of an aggregate of unrelated individuals . . . . We come into a world that is already organized; . . . we understand ourselves through our reflection in the perceptions of others . . . ."[74]

The historicized, relational character of the Chinese self/person makes it difficult to isolate the basic ethical unit, the individual, to

---

69. PRC CONST., *supra* note 1, art. 49 (also providing that parents have a duty to rear and educate their minor children).

70. *Id.* arts. 42, 46, 49, 54–56.

71. The issue of Confucianism's role in the historical subordination of women in China is a difficult one. No doubt the traditional hierarchical status relationships of Confucianism contributed to discrimination against women in practice. Nevertheless, Confucian theory does not mandate such a result. As a contextual ethical system, it is able to pay greater heed to women's interests, in keeping with their changed circumstances and status in contemporary society. That said, women's issues will most likely remain a concern.

72. The five primary relations are ruler/official, husband/wife, parent/child, older brother/younger brother, friend/friend. Only the last is not hierarchical. One of the first to ground the five relations in the natural order was Dong Zhongshu. *See* WING-TSIT CHAN, A SOURCEBOOK IN CHINESE PHILOSOPHY 277–78 (1963).

73. Thus, one condition for deference is that the authority, the person in the superior position, respect the interests of the deferring party. Obviously the leaders in Beijing did not meet this condition in dealing with the students and workers in 1989. Indeed, the failure of creativity resulting in the excessive and unnecessary use of force by the *authoritarian* regime reveals their bankruptcy as *authoritative* Confucian rulers.

74. EDMUND PINCOFFS, QUANDARIES AND VIRTUES 8 (1986).

whom ahistorical, universal rights would attach. Identity constantly changes, varying with the context; duties and, correspondingly, rights/rites are also constantly being redefined as other actors change. A son owes deference and filial piety to his father; the father owes deference and piety to his son. Confucianism requires sensitivity to the particular person and the web of relations that define the person. Whereas Kantian rights are based on the fundamental dignity and equality of every human being, Confucian rites give full play to the relational differences that distinguish each person. Thus, ethical duties radiate out in concentric circles—at the center, oneself, then one's parents, the rest of the nuclear family, relatives, friends, neighbors, state, nation, world—the larger the circle, the lesser the duty. The notion that generic rights or duties attach to individuals *simpliciter* is alien to the more graded and finely tuned rites-oriented mind.

Of central importance to the historically rich Confucian world view and its non-rights based method of conflict resolution are the *li*. The *li*—conventionally translated as rites—may be understood more broadly to include the full range of social customs, ethical norms, and political principles embodied in the complex relations, organizations, and institutions of society. They are culture-specific norms, the contingent, ever-changing values of a particular society. But the *li* are important not merely as the amassed wisdom of the ages, but also because they are the communally-owned repository of shared meaning and value on which people can draw in times of conflict. However different people may be, there are still deep chords of affinity which bind them together as a result of a shared past. By tapping the areas of commonality, one may be able to find the ground upon which to build consensus, to forge new harmony.

Placing the burden of achieving or failing to achieve a humane society on the members of society fosters an environment in which compromise and innovative solutions can occur. The absence of any fixed, external, or privileged standards deprives one of a foundation on which to ground a dogmatic position.

There is then little room for the privileging of deontological principles that underwrite contemporary liberal rights theory. To the pragmatic Chinese mind, to ignore social consequences is sheer folly. Indeed, it is not at all clear that deontic principles make much sense in a Chinese context; to paraphrase Cardozo, rights (or duties) in the air are no rights (or duties) at all:[75] rights and duties can only arise out of a particular context. Consequently, one must approach afresh

75. Palsgraf v. Long Island Railroad Co., 162 N.E. 99 (N.Y. 1928) (citing FREDERICK POLLOCK, TORTS 455 (1891)) ("Proof of negligence in the air, so to speak, will not do.").

each new conflict between principle and policy, between rights and consequences.[76]

To insist on one's rights in a Chinese context is a cultural *faux pas*—one must be willing to negotiate, to compromise. Even when the legal system is invoked, the emphasis most often remains on compromise. Most contractual disputes are resolved through mediation or arbitration, in which "the court's judgment is not phrased in terms of a holding or a directive. Rather, after mediation by the court, the record indicates that the parties agreed to the particular resolution."[77] To be sure, court mediation in China may often be considerably less than voluntary.[78] Significantly, however, it seems the court wants to at least maintain the appearance that the parties themselves have come to a harmonious resolution on mutually agreeable terms (just as our courts strive to keep alive the myth of impartial, apolitical justice).[79]

The emphasis placed on compromise, mutual agreement, and harmony even in the legal context suggests that substantive justice tends to take precedence over formal justice. When a mutually acceptable solution cannot be reached, or the interests of the individual and the state cannot be reconciled, then the lack of procedural rights is particularly worrisome, as in the trials of the 1989 student demonstrators.[80]

---

76. Lest anyone believe that socialist China has succeeded in eradicating Confucian values, consider the government's official statement on human rights:

> China is in favor of strengthening international cooperation in the realm of human rights on the basis of mutual understanding and seeking a common ground while reserving differences. However, no country in its effort to realize and protect human rights can take a route that is divorced from its history and its economic, political and cultural realities . . . . It is also noted in the resolution of the 46th conference on human rights that no single mode of development is applicable to all cultures and peoples. It is neither proper nor feasible for any country to judge other countries by the yardstick of its own mode or to impose its own mode on others . . . . Consideration should be given to the differing views on human rights held by countries with different political, economic and social systems, as well as different historical, religious and cultural backgrounds. International human rights activities should be carried on in the spirit of seeking common ground while reserving differences, mutual respect, and the promotion of understanding and cooperation.

WHITE PAPER, *supra* note 14, at 8. Present are many of the key features of Confucianism: rejection of abstract, universal dogmas and ethical principles; attention to the particular historical context of the parties; attempt to find and build on common ground in order to realize a solution amenable to all parties; belief in multiple possible resolutions to social and political conflicts; focus on persuasion and rejection of force. Indeed, if one had to summarize Confucian teaching in a single sentence, one would be hard pressed to do better than Beijing's twice repeated slogan: seek common ground while reserving differences, maintain mutual respect, and promote understanding and cooperation. Again, by their own self-selected standards, the leaders in Beijing failed utterly in violently oppressing the 1989 demonstrators.

77. Roderick Macneil, *Contract in China: Law, Practice, and Dispute Resolution*, 38 STAN. L. REV. 303, 333 (1986).

78. *See* Donald Clarke, *Dispute Resolution in China*, 5 J. CHINESE L. 245, 245–46 (1991).

79. Macneil, *supra* note 77, at 342. *See also* Economic Contract Law of the People's Republic of China, art. 32 (adopted Dec. 13, 1981) (if both parties have "committed mistakes," they should "share responsibility" according to "actual circumstances").

80. *See infra* note 102.

Indeed, one may object to this picture of a harmonious Confucian society on several fronts. First, extralegal methods of resolving conflict such as informal mediation may not fully respect legal rights and interests. In the absence of formal oversight, abuse and corruption are possible. One side may be able to take advantage of personal connections (*guan xi*) to influence the mediator. Even if the process is not corrupt, the social pressure from neighbors and colleagues to accept a solution that compromises legal rights and interests may be overwhelming.

Second, a key assumption of mediation and the Confucian approach to conflict resolution more generally is that harmony is possible and interests reconcilable. But perhaps Mill was right in posing private and public, individual interest and state interest as fundamental antinomies.[81] Third, even if harmony is theoretically possible, in practice, people must be willing to seek a solution amenable to all. This attitude seems sorely lacking in the present-day China. Today, the number of encounters between strangers is ever increasing; perhaps an inevitable consequence is a breakdown in the kind of cooperative behavior and attitudes required by Confucianism. Fourth, even assuming sufficient altruism and a willingness to compromise, there must be sufficient common ground on which to build a solution acceptable to all. Such common ground may not exist in many instances in China.

A fifth problem is that Confucius' ethical gaze was so trained on the lofty heights attainable by humankind that he neglected to provide for even a minimal level of institutional protection for the individual against the state and others. The emphasis on duty, rather than on rights, leaves the individual vulnerable to the whims of the state. A related objection is that the Confucian system encourages authoritarianism. In the absence of external ethical or internal political constraints, the authoritative Confucian leader all too readily becomes an authoritarian despot. The Confucian system confers great discretionary power on the ruler, relying on the moral character of the ruler and internal monitoring by officials to ensure that the state serves the people. Far from being politically benign, the rhetoric of harmony is easily manipulable in the service of dictators.

IV. SOCIALISM

Socialism may take many forms, some of which are more rights-friendly than others, but Marxism, at least Marx's Marxism, is not an ideology hospitable to rights. Marx viewed rights as an illusion, crumbs thrown to the alienated worker to dupe her or him into

81. *See* MILL, *supra* note 50.

accepting the legitimacy of the state and the current economic order. Rights play no role in the ideal communist society, for the state withers away and with it the need for rights as protections from the state. Nor would rights be needed to protect against others, because self-interested individuals coveting the property of others would no longer exist. Once one does away with private property, which leads to class conflict and "the struggle of the isolated individual against the relationship of dominance,"[82] a new socialist human being is created, more other-regarding than the self-interested capitalist ancestor. Similarly, because everyone would be provided for, positive rights would be unnecessary. The result for Marx—as for Confucius—is that harmony would prevail. Each person would achieve full potential in a self-regulating society. Order would emerge from the bottom up, out of the particular historical conditions, rather than being imposed from above in accordance with allegedly universal or natural principles that in fact only represent the interests of the ruling class.[83]

For the present, rights and law may be useful tools to serve socialism's ends. Beyond doubt, law has served as an important tool in the factional power struggles of socialist China.[84] Official attitudes toward the judiciary and law have swung radically. Even so, rights have never been taken seriously in any period. Emphasis on "formal" law has resulted in harsher penalties in practice, with the Party exerting control over the legal process in order to realize its political objectives.[85] On the other hand, the less formal approaches have often been equally detrimental to individual rights.

At one end of the informal spectrum lay mediation, with disputes resolved outside the courts, either with a village elder's assistance or under the guidance of local Party officials, neighborhood committees, or the police.[86] Other informal sanctions during the Maoist years varied from private criticism and education to public criticism, censure, and struggle.[87] There were in fact different forms of struggle. The lesser exposed one to "intense vituperation from those in attendance, amid

---

82. KARL MARX, THE GERMAN IDEOLOGY, *quoted in* COHEN, *supra* note 33, at 75.

83. Unlike Marx, Mao rejected the utopian "theory of no clashes." Instead, he called for permanent revolution to ensure that the bureaucracy remained faithful to the needs of the masses and to prevent the emergence of class conflicts. *See* Mao Tsetung, *The Vision of the Great Leap*, *in* THE PEOPLE'S REPUBLIC OF CHINA: A DOCUMENTARY HISTORY OF REVOLUTIONARY CHANGE 381, 385–87 (Mark Selden ed., 1979).

84. For an overview of law in Maoist China, see Alice E.-S. Tay, *The Struggle for Law in China*, 21 U. BRIT. COLUM. L. REV. 561 (1987).

85. *See* Note, *Concepts of Law in the Chinese Anti-Crime Campaign*, 98 HARV. L. REV. 1890 (1985).

86. As noted earlier, legal rights are often compromised in the mediation process. *See supra* note 78 and accompanying text.

87. *See* COHEN, *supra* note 33, at 20.

shaking fists, shouts, and accusing fingers";[88] the more severe forms often resulted in physical violence.

Political status determined treatment, for Mao distinguished contradictions between the people and the enemy from contradictions among the people.[89] Conflicts among the people were to be handled through "democratic" means—education and persuasion—with formal legal punishment meted out only to those resistant to persuasion and rehabilitation. But severe sanctions and dictatorial methods were to be employed in dealing with enemies such as "reactionaries, exploiters, counterrevolutionaries, landlords, bureaucrat-capitalists, robbers . . . and other scoundrels who disrupt social order."[90] Thus the more serious forms of informal sanction, such as struggle, were reserved for those with bad political backgrounds or guilty of political crimes. The scope of "political" crime, however, could be extraordinarily broad.

In any event, none of these various "informal" means of social control focused particularly on individual rights. To the contrary, insisting upon one's rights would only have subjected a person to greater abuse for maintaining incorrect political views.

On a more theoretical level, throughout the socialist period, rights have been seen as political expedients, granted by the state as needed and revoked when necessary. Furthermore, duties coexist with rights: for example, the duty as well as the right to work and receive education.[91] More ominously, one has the duty to safeguard the security, honor, and interests of the motherland.[92] Indeed, duties are owed primarily to the state rather than to other individuals.[93] Commentators have criticized the tendency in the PRC to emphasize duties at the expense of rights.[94] But the existence of duties *per se* does not account so much for the detriment to the individual as the fact that duties are owed to the *state* and the demands upon the individual in the name of socialism are essentially unlimited, defined primarily by the transitory dictates of the Party.

One positive aspect of socialism, however, is the importance invested in economic and social rights. The PRC constitution provides not only the right to a job, education, and vocational training, but to rest, medical care, and material support for the elderly, ill, or

88. *Id.*

89. MAO TSETUNG, *On the Correct Handling of Contradictions Among the People*, *in* 5 SELECTED WORKS OF MAO TSETUNG 391 (1977).

90. *Id.* at 393.

91. PRC CONST., *supra* note 1, arts. 42, 46.

92. *Id.* art. 54; *see also* art. 33 ("Every citizen enjoys the rights and at the same time must perform the duties prescribed by the Constitution and the law.").

93. *See id.* arts. 42, 46, 52, 54–56. *But see* art. 49 (duty of parents to rear and educate children and duty of children to support parents).

94. *See, e.g.*, Wang et al., *supra* note 68, at 8.

disabled.[95] Indeed, one of Beijing's major complaints has been that international rights organizations have focused myopically on political rights, ignoring China's commitment to economic rights and actual improvements in the basic material living conditions of many citizens. There is some truth to that assertion, but it is far from the whole story.

V. A CRITIQUE, ON CHINESE TERMS

Discussion of China's record on human rights all too often ends up with both sides talking past rather than to each other.[96] Westerners, particularly the United States and its representatives, denounce China for abuse of political freedoms and rights. Chinese retort that the foremost human right is the right to subsistence.[97] By all accounts, China has made remarkable economic progress, given its huge population and history of imperialist exploitation and decades of war with rights-conscious western nations. Indeed, the Chinese may well wonder at the authenticity of western protestations given the severe mistreatment of Chinese citizens by the imperial powers.[98] Even today, states far wealthier than China fail to provide the economic rights mandated by the Universal Declaration and arguably achieved to some extent in the PRC.

Despite the rhetoric of universal human rights, the reality is that different states have different conceptions and practices with respect to rights, reflecting their own cultural, philosophical, political, ethical, and economic traditions. Thus a more productive approach than simply attempting to impose one's own particular rights ideology on another sovereign state is to engage the other on its own terms. To do so is not to endorse an anything-goes cultural relativism or to deny the legitimacy of judging another culture. At minimum, a country must stand up to scrutiny on its own terms: it must be able to withstand criticism of both its theory (or underlying philosophies) and empirical practice. More importantly, many terms are shared terms.

95. PRC CONST., *supra* note 1, arts. 43–45.

96. If indeed they talk to each other at all. Recently, Britain's Home Office refused to see a human rights delegation from China, fearing that the Chinese group was planning to criticize Britain's human rights record, particularly with respect to Northern Ireland. Under pressure from the Foreign Office, the Home Office relented. Refusal to see the delegation might have jeopardized Prime Minister Major's request to send Britain's own human rights delegation to China. Geoffrey Crothall, *U.K. Averts Incident by Agreeing to See China Team*, S. CHINA MORNING POST, Feb. 14, 1992, at 1.

97. WHITE PAPER, *supra* note 14, at 9.

98. For an account of these atrocities and human rights abuses inflicted on Chinese citizens, see *id.* at 10.

One need not be an ethical absolutist to decry the massacre of unarmed students and citizens in and around Tiananmen Square.[99]

To begin with the positive, China may be praised for the progress it has made in its efforts to secure economic rights for citizens. There is, of course, room for improvement. Citizens have a right to a job, but it may not be a job to which they are inclined or suited. In practice, the duty to work means that people are assigned jobs, at times in cities far from their spouse's place of work. In addition, medical care could be improved and a more comprehensive welfare system implemented. But these are to a large measure social policy choices; how one society directs resources will differ from another.[100]

China's most noticeable failure is in the area of political rights. Beijing's assertions that "the people are the real masters of the country with the right to run the country's economic and social affairs"[101] is of course absurd. Nor can one take seriously the government's attempt to portray the current system as one of free elections with politically independent multiple parties, or its claim that "the Party conducts its activities within the framework of the Constitution and the law."[102] The assertion that there is no censorship in China and that the government upholds the principle of "letting a hundred flowers blossom and a hundred schools of thought contend" is patently false.[103] To

---

99. The theoretically interesting metaethical issue is whether one may legitimately judge another individual or culture according to values *not* shared by that individual or culture. Because I rely on shared and indigenous Chinese values, I need not address the issue. For a defense of "evaluative universalism," where one judges another culture according to the values one believes in, see Andrew Nathan, *The Place of Values in Cross-Cultural Studies: The Example of Democracy in China*, *in* IDEAS ACROSS CULTURES 293–314 (Paul A. Cohen & Merle Goldman eds., 1990). Little is to be gained from judging another culture according to exogenous values if the other side refuses to engage in dialogue on those terms or believes its own values to be superior. That such coercive methods would succeed with Beijing is unlikely. *See infra* notes 113–115 and accompanying text.

100. Ann Kent argues that notwithstanding previous achievements, China in the 1980s experienced several setbacks in the actual realization of economic rights. For instance, the right to work was increasingly out of step with the realities of the fledgling commodity or market economy spawned by reform policies. Further negative developments included: "(1) the commodification of social welfare; (2) the increase of the rural-urban gap in the provision of social services; (3) the devolution of responsibility for social welfare and social security; and (4) the lack of a comprehensive unemployment insurance system." *See* Kent, *supra* note 36, at 193–99.

101. WHITE PAPER, *supra* note 14, at 13.

102. *Id.* at 14–15. For an account of Beijing's abuse of PRC criminal procedure laws in the treatment of 1989 demonstrators, see Asia Watch, *Rough Justice in Beijing: Punishing the "Black Hands" of Tiananmen Square*, *in* NEWS FROM ASIA WATCH, Jan. 27, 1991, at 4–7.

103. WHITE PAPER, *supra* note 14, at 15–16, 19. Witness the treatment of Zhang Yimou's films. *See* Lynn Pan, *A Chinese Master*, N.Y. TIMES MAGAZINE, Mar. 1, 1992, at 30. Foreign reporters are also subject to restrictions. For a discussion of post-Tiananmen suppression of freedom of expression, see Asia Watch, *Punishment Season: Human Rights in China After Martial Law*, *in* THE BROKEN MIRROR, *supra* note 5, at 383–86; for limits on the press, see International League for Human Rights & the Ad Hoc Study Group on Human Rights in China, *Winter in Beijing: Continuing Repression Since the Beijing Massacre*, Feb. 18, 1990, at 20–22.

declare that there are no political prisoners in China (only "counter-revolutionaries") is insulting not only to the courageous demonstrators of 1989 but to those around the world who witnessed the events on television.[104]

Although the constitution and other laws nominally provide various rights, many are not legally enforceable in practice. For instance, while the recently promulgated Administrative Law allows citizens to sue the government,[105] the government has never lost a politically sensitive case.[106] Thus, another reason why citizens often do not pursue their legal rights is their belief that to do so is futile.

Beijing's issuance of a lengthy statement on human rights denying this familiar catalogue of complaints demonstrates that it is aware of a problem. In many instances, the PRC baldly lied rather than attempt to justify human rights abuses, which indicates a failure according not to alien western principles but to China's own standards. The Chinese Constitution provides for these rights—they are the self-selected goals and commitments of the government itself. Failure to realize them is a failure of the current regime to make good on its own promises.

With rights violations so widespread, Beijing cannot simply attempt to explain away particular instances. One government justification argues that China is a poor country, and economic stability must therefore take priority over all else, including political rights.[107] Though there may be a kernel of truth to this argument, it cannot justify the many specific instances of censorship, suppression of political speech, imprisonment of political activists, and so on. Not every attempt to exercise a political right threatens economic progress, but such attempts threaten the continued rulership of the current regime, and socialism itself.

The problem, therefore, is systemic. As noted, socialism is hostile to genuine political rights. Thus one can scarcely be surprised at the host of institutional impediments to rights discussed previously: Party domination of both the legislature and judiciary (despite constitutional provisions of independence); elevation of the interests of the state over the rights of the individual as sanctioned in article 51; use of the language of duty to override rights, and so on. Enjoyment of genuine rights apparently is incompatible with the continued existence of

---

104. White Paper, *supra* note 14, at 24. One report based on Chinese documents estimated that, as of 1991, as many as 100,000 people were imprisoned for opposing the government. *See* Charles Lane, *The Last Gulag*, Newsweek, Sept. 23, 1991, at 26.

105. *See* Zhonghua Renmin Gongheguo Xingzheng Susong Fa (Administrative Litigation Law of the PRC) (promulgated April 4, 1989), Renmin Ribao, Apr. 10, 1989, at 2, *trans. in* China Law and Practice, June 5, 1989, at 37–57.

106. *See supra* note 30.

107. *Cf.* White Paper, *supra* note 14, at 11–12.

statist socialism in China. Beijing's only possible remaining justification is that the future benefits of socialism outweigh the present costs of exploiting, lying to, and abusing the people. But the collapse of socialism around the world and the bankruptcy of Communism as a practicable ideal cut against any such justification.

In any event, even if the current regime, or a post-socialist China, decides to take rights seriously, these rights will be rights with Chinese characteristics. That a Chinese rights culture will share western philosophical conceptions is highly doubtful. Many of the basic elements of traditional Chinese thought and practice militate against a strong theory of rights: the historical conception of person where one is born into a family, community, and state rather than the Hobbesian view of rights-bearing individuals preceding the state; the notion that rights are grants from the state rather than manna from heaven; the rejection of deontological and universal principles in favor of contingent, culture-sensitive ethics; the lack of foundational external restraints on authoritarian political rulers; the preference for informal mediation rather than appeal to the courts for enforcement of rights.

What then will rights with a Chinese face look like? Will such a theory provide rights that genuinely protect the individual in practice? Although one cannot be sure, certain guesses may be ventured.

VI. A CHINESE THEORY OF RIGHTS

Given the pragmatic, anti-foundational character of much of Chinese philosophy, and of Confucianism in particular, any rights theory justifiable on Chinese terms will almost assuredly be a contingent one. There will be no attempt to pass off Chinese rights as universal rights—rights in China will be viewed as a product of Chinese culture, traditions, and historical and economic conditions.[108] As such, they may or may not be appropriate for other countries.[109] Further, rights will differ not only between China and other states but within China from one period to the next. This of course is the reality everywhere in the world. What will differ is that in China jurisprudential rhetoric may match reality.[110]

---

108. In this respect, Marxism's emphasis on historical materialism coincides with Confucianism's sensitivity to the particular conditions of society, reinforcing the view of rights as contingent. Even some scholars who argue for an expansive theory of human rights based on the commonality (*gongtongxing*) of all people reflect the influence of Marxism in maintaining that rights are a product of the particular historical, economic, and material conditions of a society. *See, e.g.*, Li Buyun, *Lun renquan de sanzhong cunzai xingtai* [*On Three Forms of Existence of Human Rights*], 65 FAXUE YANJIU [STUDIES IN LAW] 11, 13 (1992).

109. It is true that all state *may* share some similar rights. Such rights, however, would be contingent on political, cultural, and economic factors.

110. As Nathan points out, a prominent feature of Chinese rights is that they have varied from one constitution to the next. He attributes this to the belief of authors of the Chinese

Second, Chinese rights will be more communitarian in theory and in practice. The traditional emphasis on social harmony and duties will be manifested in a theory that imposes duties as well as confers rights. Rights will provide a minimum level of protection for the individual against others and the state; duties will point to social solidarity and possibilities for human achievement. One will owe duties to fellow citizens as well as to the state, although not as in statist socialism to the *socialist* state as such. In contrast to PRC practice today, duties will not be used to limit rights in the name of the socialist cause but rather to supplement rights as ethical standards and guideposts.

Third, rights will continue to be looked upon as inspirational ethical themes to be realized in light of the particular situation by individuals seeking a harmonious solution to problems rather than simply as minimalist protections against the state and others.[111] Thus, rights will be one resource, a starting point, for resolving conflicts. The goal will still be to move beyond strident insistence on rights to the detriment of others to creative solutions acceptable to all. Of course, in some cases, such solutions may not be possible. This may be because those involved are unwilling to put aside narrow self-interest—in which case there may yet be hope for persuasion—or it may be because there simply are not sufficient resources to satisfy everyone, or because some issues do not lend themselves to compromise. In such instances, where the ideal of harmony cannot be attained and the best solution is a more modest one, rights will play an important role in ensuring that certain individual interests are afforded at least special consideration and perhaps some minimum level of protection.

Fourth, given the historicized conception of the self in which a person is born into a complex social matrix, one would expect a relational theory of rights. One's rights (and duties) will vary depending on the relation of the parties. Not all rights and duties will be created equal; there will be greater duties to (and claim greater rights from) one's family than fellow citizens. Indeed, there will be greater duties to some citizens than others: for instance, the duty to neighbors or colleagues may be more stringent than those to strangers.

One constraint on the full realization of a highly articulated relational model of rights is the limited capacity of the formal legal system to take into account the particulars of the parties. Thus, a fifth aspect of Chinese rights culture will be the continued reliance on informal

---

Constitutions that rights are grants from the state, and hence may be added or subtracted at the will of the state. Nathan, *supra* note 1, at 121. The conception of social order as historically contingent and evolving may also explain this phenomenon: as the society changes, so must rights.

111. *See supra* note 60 and accompanying text.

means for conflict resolution. Although far from perfect, traditional methods such as mediation offer many advantages. Both parties save face, fully participate in the proceeding, and shape the ultimate solution. The process, usually faster and cheaper than more formal methods, allows for a more particularized justice and for the restoration of social harmony, with both sides feeling they have received their due.

A sixth characteristic of Chinese rights and one positive result of socialism will be the continued prominence given to economic rights. Citizens have come to expect certain economic and material benefits from the state. Any regime that assumes power would be hard pressed to justify the elimination of medical care, for instance. The provision of a minimum level of material support is also consistent with the ideals, if not the historical reality, of Chinese traditions. Now that the people have actually observed that it is possible for the state to provide a minimum standard of living for all, they will not accept the old excuse that China is simply too poor.

A seventh characteristic is that rights will continue to be instrumental, construed as political and ethical tools for achieving the ultimate goal of harmony. The extreme deontological position that an individual possesses an inviolability that even the good of society as a whole cannot override is out of step with Chinese ethical traditions.

An eighth characteristic and a corollary of the rejection of the extreme deontological rights position is that the balance between the rights of the individual and the interests of the collective will probably be more inclined toward the latter than in the United States, though to what extent is difficult to predict.

As for whether Chinese rights will continue to be considered grants from the state, that too is uncertain. The idea that humans are born into this world with a full complement of rights as well as duties might take hold in the popular mind—as may the idea that the state is to serve the people rather than the rulers. Surely, greater contact with the world outside China will tend to reinforce such notions. If assimilated, such beliefs will make more likely the development of a viable rights culture in China.[112]

The seeds of a rights culture have already been planted in China, at least to the extent that the litany of rights provided in the constitution is not simply empty rhetoric. International pressure and a desire to enjoy the benefits of membership in the community of civilized

112. There is no inherent contradiction between an instrumental, harmony-based theory of rights and the view that such rights attach to human beings *qua* human beings. One could believe that one is born with certain rights that protect one against certain intrusions by the state and others and yet do not trump all social consequences.

nations may push China marginally further in the direction of a more rights-oriented public policy. Arguably, international pressure has already produced results. One can point not only to the government White Paper on rights but also to the release of prisoners tied to visits of foreign diplomats or to congressional votes on key issues such as most-favored nation status.[113]

However, the government will do what is necessary to maintain power—most importantly, maintaining economic progress and a higher standard of living. For this it needs foreign assistance.[114] Thus, in dealing with foreigners, Beijing must play high stakes poker. Whenever possible, the government goes on the attack, citing past imperialist abuses and contemporary rights failures within foreigners' own countries, or it stonewalls, simply denying that there are political prisoners or human rights abuses in China. Only when the potential economic gains are high and the international pressure unrelenting does Beijing make concessions to the international community, releasing a few prisoners here, making a conciliatory statement there. Ultimately, little changes within the Great Wall, as indicated by the recent statements of Justice Minister Cai Cheng rejecting the rule of law for the supremacy of the Party.[115]

Even if post-socialist China implements a contingent, communitarian rights program like the one outlined, the question remains whether it will be of much use. When push comes to shove, will the rights promulgated in the future constitution be worth the paper they are written on? When the interests of the individual conflict with those of the state, will the latter inevitably prevail, as they have throughout much of Chinese history?

The danger of an avowedly contingent theory of rights is that once one allows rights to be compromised to secure other normative considerations, the Pandora's box is open. Powerful political parties may abuse this window of discretionary opportunity to inappropriately override legitimate individual rights. Since absolute power in the hands of the foolhardy—or self-interested—is a real and ominous possibility, there should be many and stringent institutional safe-

---

113. However, the extent to which the international community can exercise influence over China is limited. Having suffered through 100 years of imperialist oppression, China is highly sensitive to foreign criticism and intrusions in sovereign affairs. One need only reflect on Tiananmen to appreciate Beijing's disdain for world opinion. More importantly, the leaders of the PRC are fully aware that foreign commitment to human rights is not deep. When economic goals conflict with concern for human rights abuse, economics wins out all too often. In light of such short-term self-interest and transitory commitment, the PRC need but stay the course.

114. It bears noting that even in the immediate days following Tiananmen, Beijing insisted that its open-door policies would continue unabated. *See, e.g.*, Deng Xiaoping's remarks on June 9, 1989, BEIJING REV., June 12–25, 1989, at 4.

115. *See supra* note 17 and accompanying text.

guards. Decisions as to when state interests are sufficiently compelling to override constitutional rights granted to individuals should not be in the hands of a single branch of government, much less a single person. Constitutional review and a truly independent judiciary seem imperative. Whether these institutional adjustments alone or in combination with other changes are sufficient is difficult to predict. At a minimum, a rights culture with a heightened rights consciousness on the part of the people also seems essential. If the people do not stand up for their rights, the courts surely will not.

CONCLUSION

Not all rights theories are theories of natural rights. Nor does taking human rights seriously necessarily entail that rights be considered absolute and inalienable, a trump against any and all interests of the state, or as invariably of greater moral weight than matters of policy or social consequences. Indeed, no system takes human rights that seriously in practice.

There can be little doubt that the calculus as to the proper balance of individual autonomy versus social good will differ between the United States and China, as it does between the United States and every other country in the world. Although the ultimate ability of a contingent, communitarian rights theory to protect Chinese citizens against their government is uncertain, one thing is clear: the rhetoric of absolute, ahistorical, universal rights is at odds with China's philosophical and cultural traditions. The hope that China will adopt wholesale American rights ideology is misplaced. China may adopt a more rights-oriented public policy, but even then, rights in China will remain rights with Chinese characteristics.

[15]

Female Subjects of Public International Law: Human Rights and the Exotic Other Female*

Karen Engle**

Mary Joe Frug greatly influenced my thinking about the categories discussed in this essay. She did so through her own work and through specific comments and inquiries about a related project, both of which have pushed me to clarify many of the assumptions and distinctions I present here. Mary Joe's enthusiasm and her engagement with issues of gender identity made doing this type of work exciting, challenging and fun. While she endeavored to open space for more "play" in our thinking and acting about gender, Mary Joe never lost sight of the very serious impact that these issues have on women's lives. More than anyone I have encountered, Mary Joe devoted her energy to understanding all types of people, attempting to learn what made them tick. This essay is for Mary Joe, with her enthusiasm and engagement in mind.

For centuries, several societies—primarily located in Muslim Africa—have engaged in a practice that is often, perhaps euphemistically, referred to as female circumcision.[1] Some call it genital mutilation. Others use more specific and technical language to describe the partic-

** Associate Professor of Law, University of Utah.

For their helpful comments and suggestions on earlier drafts of this essay, I am grateful to Abe Chayes, Dan Danielsen, Marcella David, Rainer Forst, David Kennedy, Duncan Kennedy, Martha Minow and Ileana Porras. Thanks also to participants of the Legal Theory Circle at the University of Helsinki Faculty of Law and the Dutch/American Critical Legal Studies Summer Camp for reacting to this work in its early stages. An earlier version of this essay is published in Finnish as *Nainen kansainvalisen oikeuden subjektina: Esimerkkina klitorodektomia*, 3 OIKEUS 214 (1991).

1. Although this procedure is today most commonly performed in parts of Africa that are predominantly Muslim, it is neither exclusively performed in those areas nor done in all countries of the region. History of the practice in the Sudan indicates that the operation antedates both the arrival of Islam and of Christianity. Janice Boddy, *Body Politics: Continuing the Anticircumcision Crusade*, 5 MED. ANTHROPOLOGY Q. 15, 15 (1991). While Muslim clerics generally insist that clitoridectomy in any of its various forms is not an Islamic religious custom, "most rural Sudanese believe some form of pharaonic circumcision is to be required on religious grounds." *Id.*

ular form the practice takes, such as clitoridectomy or infibulation.[2]

The subjects (some would say objects) of this procedure are young girls ranging in age from several days just prior to marriage, depending on the particular cultural practices of the region involved. Clitoridectomy serves largely as a prerequisite, if not a direct rite of passage, to a girl's adulthood, or womanhood. A woman who has not participated in the ritual is likely to be denied the possibility of marriage and is thereby foreclosed access to certain privileges of her society. The procedure is almost universally performed by women, either trained or lay. It often proves to be dangerous, sometimes fatal, because it is not always done in hygienic circumstances.

As might be expected, many feminists have attacked this custom, and pointed to it as one more, yet quite extreme, example of misogyny and (male) societal control over female bodies. Many Western feminists have reacted with outrage, calling for an abrupt end to the practice. Their outrage has been fueled, or at least justified, by the condemnation of the practice by some women within societies that engage in it, such as Egyptian Nawal El Saadawi.[3] Some African women who oppose the practice encourage Western women to condemn it, in the belief that Western women have more clout to pressure governments to put an end to it.

For others, including other feminists, clitoridectomy poses a more complex set of issues. The complexity arises in part from the fact that women perform the operation on other females and that girls, if old enough to consider it, often claim to desire the procedure. That the

---

2. For (varied) descriptions of the practice, see Halima Warzazi, *Report of the Working Group on Traditional Practices Affecting the Health of Women and Children*, U.N. ESCOR, Commission on Human Rights, 42d Sess., Prov. Agenda item 19, U.N. Doc. E/CN.4/1986/42 (1986) [hereinafter *U.N. Report on Traditional Practices*]; OLAYINKA KOSO-THOMAS, THE CIRCUMCISION OF WOMEN: A STRATEGY FOR ERADICATION 16-17 (1987); Alison Slack, *Female Circumcision: A Critical Appraisal*, 10 HUM. RTS. Q. 437, 440-42 (1988). The different types of practice often account for variations in the language used to describe it. Other language differences stem from a wide range of, and often opposing, views about the practice.

I generally use the term clitoridectomy because of its anatomical specificity, its particular reference to the clitoris. I also use it because of its technicality, as a way of avoiding the sometimes rhetorical extremes of "circumcision" and "mutilation." In applying the term, however, I realize that I am failing to accurately portray many of the procedures, both those that are more akin to male circumcision in that they excise only a small portion of the clitoris and those that remove and operate on much more than the clitoris, such as infibulation. The former is often performed in Egypt while the latter is most common in the Sudan. For a more thorough description of practices in those countries, see Daniel Gordon, *Female Circumcision and Genital Operations in Egypt and the Sudan: A Dilemma for Medical Anthropology*, 5 MED. ANTHROPOLOGY Q. 3 (1991).

3. *See generally* NAWAL EL SAADAWI, THE HIDDEN FACE OF EVE: WOMEN IN THE ARAB WORLD (Sherif Hetata ed. & trans., 1980); NAWAL EL SAADAWI, WOMAN AT POINT ZERO (Sherif Hetata trans., 1983).

practice is deeply rooted in culture also poses difficulties. One Western feminist has suggested that Western women ought not be so shocked by the practice, given our own forms of bodily self mutilation, through, for example, plastic surgery, incessant dieting, or wearing shoes that are too small.[4] In a similar vein, Gayatri Spivak has discussed what she calls "symbolic clitoridectomy," which "has always been the 'normal' accession to womanhood and the unacknowledged name of motherhood."[5]

As the practice has become more widely known throughout the world, many have begun to talk about it as an international human rights violation. The last decade has paved the way for this kind of analysis, as public international law has expanded—at least formally—to include issues specifically pertaining to women.

With this expansion, a body of literature has developed that advocates women's rights as international human rights. Three broad approaches have emerged within that literature which I have labeled doctrinalist, institutionalist and external critique. The three approaches represent different feminist attitudes toward law, ranging from liberal to radical, as well as different approaches to rights discourse in general and to human rights law in particular.[6]

In this essay, I explore some of the ways that these different approaches confront, or would confront, clitoridectomy. I do so with an eye toward the various notions of women's subjectivity the approaches display. Specifically, as Western women's rights advocates attempt to use universal international human rights law, institutions, and discourse as means for eradicating clitoridectomy,[7] I am interested in the ways and extent to which the advocates recognize and respond to differences among women. I focus particularly on their assumptions about and reactions to what might be considered the Exotic Other Female.

---

4. *See* Rhoda E. Howard, *Health and the Social Degradation of Dishonored Groups*, paper presented at Conference on Human Rights in the 21st Century, in Banff, Alberta, Canada (Oct. 24, 1990) (on file with the *New England Law Review*); *see also* Ruth Rosen, *Perspective on Women's Health: Draw the Line at the Knife*, L.A. TIMES, Nov. 17, 1991, at M5 (describing breast implant surgery as "barbaric" and similar to other "mutilations" that are considered violations of human rights, such as foot-binding, dowry deaths, and clitoridectomies).

5. Gayatri C. Spivak, *French Feminism in an International Frame*, *in* IN OTHER WORLDS: ESSAYS IN CULTURAL POLITICS 134, 151 (1987).

6. I have set forth and defined these approaches in detail in Karen Engle, *International Human Rights and Feminism: When Discourses Meet*, 13 MICH. J. INT'L L. 517 (1992).

7. While many women's rights advocates are not from the "West," those I discuss or allude to in this essay live, as far as I know, in North America or Europe. I believe that the positions they take, however, are due more to the fact that they rely on universal international human rights law and discourse than that they are Western. But I am not certain.

I use Exotic Other Female here to signify collectively those women within a culture that practices clitoridectomy, who through their action (or inaction) condone the practice. Implicit in this label is the assumption that the Exotic Other Female, or at least her needs and desires, are not totally accessible to someone outside her culture.

I name and discuss the Exotic Other Female in an attempt to introduce her overtly into the discourse about women's human rights. Even though women's human rights advocates usually fail to acknowledge openly—much less engage—the Exotic Other Female, I argue that they nevertheless imagine her and in doing so make many assumptions about her. The existence of the Exotic Other Female (as something "out there") seems to guide much of their analysis.

In discussing the Exotic Other Female, I do not mean to essentialize her; she is only that when she is merely imagined and not engaged. Once engaged, *she* will become *they*—many and complex—which might be one reason many have for not engaging her (and for not allowing her to engage them). One of the questions I hope to begin to address in this essay is how it would be possible to move beyond merely imagining this Other.[8]

Exploring the various ways that women's human rights advocates imagine the Exotic Other Female as they approach the issue of clitoridectomy yields some surprising and paradoxical results. It might seem, for example, due to the universalizing nature of international human rights doctrine, that liberal feminists, who are most committed to using legal doctrine to eradicate clitoridectomy, would be least likely to acknowledge differences among women. In fact, doctrinal advocates turn out to be the most overt in taking account of the Exotic Other Female. That they take account of her, however, does not mean that they engage her; rather, they attempt to change her mind about the practice by choosing a doctrinal position with which she might agree.

A similar paradox unfolds through exploration of the radical feminist positions taken by women's human rights advocates. It might seem that those advocates most critical of what they see as the "maleness" of the international human rights framework would be most able to take into account women's differences, since they would not be tied to formal universal norms as embodied in "male" international human rights doctrine. It happens, though, that the radical feminists are much less likely than the liberal feminists to confront the fact that some women defend and practice clitoridectomy. Indeed, the radical feminists do not generally even acknowledge the existence of the Exotic Other Female. The failure to acknowledge her is due largely, I believe, to their radical focus on a male/female dichotomy that they identify in human

8. For a provocative discussion of a similar question in the context of sati in India, see Gayatri C. Spivak, *Can the Subaltern Speak? Speculations on Widow-Sacrifice*, 7/8 WEDGE 120 (1985).

rights discourse, which they see as the primary obstacle to achieving women's human rights.

I. The Doctrinalist Approach

Doctrinalists generally approach international human rights law by focussing on one practice that they believe violates a particular right, here the practice of "female circumcision" (as they label it).[9] They then attempt to demonstrate doctrinally how the practice ought to be eradicated on the basis of rights derived from international law. Because no legal provisions specifically mention clitoridectomy or female circumcision, those who advocate its end go through one human rights instrument after another to show that the practice is prohibited by the existence of rights such as "rights of the child,"[10] "the right to sexual and corporal integrity,"[11] and the "right to health."[12]

In attempting to assimilate a particular woman's right to the dominant human rights framework, doctrinalists tend to make liberal feminist assumptions. That is, they do not indicate that bringing women into the human rights structure would radically change or disrupt the structure; indeed, their arguments assume that the positive law already includes women by providing, if indirectly, the right they advocate.

Although doctrinalists basically rely on the assimilation of women's rights to positive human rights law, they recognize that international human rights law is difficult to enforce. Enforcement seems particularly tough in the case of women's human rights, since those claims are plagued by a counter-claim of cultural relativism. So strong is the counter-claim that Alison Slack frames the purpose of her article as determining "at what point the 'tradition' [of] female circumcision becomes a human rights violation justifying pressure from foreign cultures to end this 'tradition.' "[13]

While those who take other approaches to women's human rights do not openly confront this counter-claim of cultural relativism, doctrinalists often do. Although in the end they reject a cultural relativist perspective as they argue for "universal" human rights, they are nevertheless acutely aware that disagreements about the scope and shape of women's rights exist, particularly in the case of clitoridectomy. These disagreements are not just between men and women or between cultures; they actually exist between women. The acknowledgement of

---

9. In describing this approach to clitoridectomy, I rely primarily on articles by Kay Boulware-Miller and Alison Slack. *See* Kay Boulware-Miller, *Female Circumcision: Challenges to the Practice as a Human Rights Violation*, 8 HARV. WOMEN'S L.J. 155 (1985); Slack, *supra* note 2.

10. *See* Boulware-Miller, *supra* note 9, at 165-69.

11. *See id.* at 169-72.

12. *See id.* at 172-76; Slack, *supra* note 2, at 485-86.

13. Slack, *supra* note 2, at 439.

disagreements among women is, in my mind, a strength of the doctrinalists' feminist approaches. It allows them to engage women's differences to a greater extent than those who take the other approaches, which tend to assume, albeit to different degrees, a monolithic or essential "woman."

Although doctrinalists acknowledge these differences among women's attitudes, they eventually attempt to work around them. They seem to imagine the existence of the Exotic Other Female, the one who opposes abolition of the practice she might even help perpetuate, as something that must be reckoned with. For the doctrinalists, this imagined Other is a reminder that the right, no matter how enshrined in public international law, is not universally accepted. Rather than denying the existence of the Exotic Other Female, doctrinalists propose strategies for changing her mind and thus for removing an obstacle to universal recognition of the right. In choosing among strategies, they express sensitivity to cultural differences.

At this stage, doctrinalists engage in what I call strategic positivism. Although a number of rights exist in positive law that would seemingly prohibit clitoridectomy (right to corporal and sexual integrity, rights of children, right to health), those who oppose the practice do not stress them all. Instead, they make a strategic decision about which right to pursue, depending on which rights rubric governments and the Exotic Other Female (as victim, and often as victimizer) are most likely to accept. Alison Slack and Kay Boulware-Miller agree that governments are most likely to accept a right to health argument, since, as Boulware-Miller puts it, they "are more concerned with basic health and economic problems than with the arguably more elitist rights they associate with Western countries, such as political rights and fundamental freedoms."[14] Boulware-Miller believes women, too, will be most likely to accept an end to the practice based on a health argument, because, unlike the other potential rights arguments, it avoids an "imposing and judgmental approach."[15]

Doctrinalists, therefore, deal with the tension between cultures by acknowledging the tension and then working around it. While a

14. Boulware-Miller, *supra* note 9, at 173; *see also* Slack, *supra* note 2, at 486.

15. Boulware-Miller, *supra* note 9, at 166-67, 171-72. Health arguments have been the most common means of attempting to eradicate clitoridectomy, both by intergovernmental and nongovernmental actors. *See, e.g.*, Halima Warzazi, *Study on Traditional Practices Affecting the Health of Women and Children*, U.N. ESCOR, Commission on Human Rights, 43d Sess., Prov. Agenda item 4, U.N. Doc. E/CN.4/Sub.2/1991/6 (1991); *U.N. Report on Traditional Practices*, *supra* note 2; Koso-Thomas, *supra* note 2. Even those who have taken a more radical approach to clitoridectomy, calling it "genital mutilation" for example, have responded favorably to the health approach. *See, e.g.*, *Progress Report: WIN News Grass Roots Campaign to Eradicate GM [Genital Mutilation]*, 18 Women's Int'l Network News 38-39 (1992).

strength of their approach is that they recognize and even take account of differences among women, they neither engage those women that practice clitoridectomy nor confront the practice itself. Rather than finding out why women defend the practice, they try to convince them to change their minds, by phrasing the issue as one of health. They do so despite the United Nations own research on "traditional practices affecting the health of women and children," which indicates that women who oppose clitoridectomy within those cultures where it is practiced rarely cite health as a reason.[16]

By approaching the issue as one of health, doctrinalists seem to have avoided taking any overtly "political" stance on the issue of clitoridectomy. For them, international human rights law, by guaranteeing a right to health, demands an end to the practice. Approaching clitoridectomy as a health issue raises another concern. If the practice could be done without negative health consequences, international law might actually become complicit in the practice, obligating states to ensure that it is performed under better health conditions. This possibility is one the doctrinalists do not address.[17]

II. The Institutionalist Approach

The institutionalist approach to women's human rights concentrates on the institutions that have been created by international law to enforce human rights.[18] Those who take this approach do not generally advocate particular rights, and they are not concerned with which international instruments guarantee which rights. They believe that if posi-

16. *See U.N. Report on Traditional Practices*, *supra* note 2, at 15 (discussing reasons women give for opposing the practice as "violation of fundamental human rights," "violation of women's image," "social complications," and "cultural conformism"); *see also id.* at 14 (Of the "sample of persons opposed to female circumcision," only 12.72 per cent gave "illnesses and accidents" as a reason, as opposed to 43.63 per cent who said the practice is pointless and 32.72 per cent who listed "diminution of sensitivity" for the reason.).

17. The possibility is not as remote as it might seem. Gordon reports that in urban parts of the Sudan, there is already an official policy of using the health care system to perform the procedures in order to reduce complications and health risks. Moreover, trained medical personnel with drugs and equipment have been disseminated and used to perform clitoridectomies and other genital operations. *See* Gordon, *supra* note 2, at 12 (citing Asma El Dareer, Women, Why Do You Weep? (1982); Fran P. Hosken, The Hosken Report: Genital and Social Mutilation of Females 47, 287 (1982)).

18. I primarily base my description of this approach on Margaret E. Galey, *International Enforcement of Women's Rights*, 6 Hum. Rts. Q. 463 (1984) and Laura Reanda, *Human Rights and Women's Rights: The United Nations Approach*, 3 Hum. Rts. Q. 11 (1981). More recent literature takes very similar approaches. *See, e.g.*, Theodor Meron, *Editorial Comments: Enhancing the Effectiveness of the Prohibition of Discrimination Against Women*, 84 Am. J. Int'l L. 213 (1990); Andrew C. Byrnes, *The "Other" Human Rights Treaty Body: The Work of the Committee on the Elimination of Discrimination Against Women*, 14 Yale J. Int'l L. 1 (1989).

tive law or doctrine guaranteeing women's rights is to be meaningful, institutions must transform that law or doctrine into action, through pragmatic, meaningful enforcement mechanisms. To the extent that transformation has not occurred, they largely hold responsible the (primarily male) actors that deploy human rights discourse through international institutions. Institutionalists do not attack the international institutional framework per se. Instead, they argue either that mainstream institutions—those institutions that see themselves as enforcing all human rights, not differentiating between women and men—need to rearrange their priorities to include issues of women, or that specialized women's institutions—meant specifically to enforce women's rights and generally comprised of women—must be given power equal to mainstream ones.

Because of their reliance on existing institutional structures to assimilate women's rights, I also consider these advocates liberal feminists. Their approaches, however, could be understood as more radical than those of the doctrinalists, as the institutionalists are critical of the present (male) deployment of the system. The difficulties the institutionalists point to are more directly attributed to a male dominated structure than those identified by the doctrinalists. These advocates provide useful insights into the power plays within the institutional framework that keep men in control and women's rights at the periphery.

Although institutionalists do not generally focus on particular human rights violations, we can imagine a way that they might approach clitoridectomy. They would likely start by taking for granted that the practice is in violation of international human rights law (although a brief discussion with a doctrinalist might be required to convince them). Their task would then be to see international institutions enforce the rights the doctrinalists derive.

As they make proposals for greater enforcement of women's rights, institutionalists—unlike doctrinalists—are not concerned with the possibility that women might disagree about particular rights. Rather, they focus on what they see as male/female disagreements, which manifest themselves in the bureaucratic structures of international institutions, both mainstream and specialized. In this context, institutionalists often act as if international institutional actors are largely free from the cultures from which they hail (except that male actors are obvious products of patriarchy). The Exotic Other Female never enters into the sterile institutional framework because within that framework there is nothing to be other to but the male actors who have power to deploy and control international institutions.

Applying their analysis to clitoridectomy, institutionalists would argue that international institutions could in theory, and partly within their present structure, address the issue. For the institutional framework to be effective in combatting the practice, however, they would contend that either mainstream institutions must expand their (presently male) focus or specialized women's institutions must be granted power equal to the mainstream ones. Institutionalists would generally pursue the second possibility, implying that were the specialized institutions given sufficient power, clitoridectomy could be brought to an end. Hence, although the Commission on Human Rights, through its Sub-commission on the Protection of Minorities, has investigated clitoridectomy as a practice affecting women's health, institutionalists might argue that the issue could be addressed more effectively and directly by a specialized institution, such as the Commission on the Status of Women. But, they would point out, the Commission on the Status of Women could only even potentially do so if it were granted investigatory powers equal to the Commission on Human Rights.

Within the institutionalists' discussions and proposals, however, lies the very real possibility that even if women's institutions were given the power needed to pursue their agendas, women comprising those institutions might reject that power. Margaret Galey, for example, has discussed a meeting of the Commission on the Status of Women where some members were reluctant to accept responsibility for investigating individual cases, a power she sees as essential to enforcing women's rights, because they "recognized that this would involve investigation of allegations, a politically sensitive matter, and a considerable expense, which the Commission's membership was unlikely to support."[19] Although the Commission eventually passed the resolution, its members have continued to debate whether to increase their capacity to receive communications.[20] They have also rejected possibilities for greater power in other areas.[21]

The reality that women, even within specialized women's institutions might disagree about "what they want," poses a very real, although largely unacknowledged, obstacle to actualizing the solutions these advocates propose. Hence, while those who pursue women's rights institutionally offer a powerful analysis of the workings and priorities of the international institutional framework, as well as of the

19. Galey, *supra* note 18, at 469.

20. Even as recently as the 1991 meeting of the Commission, members were unable to agree on a resolution that purported to grant greater power to receive or investigate complaints. Indeed, a draft resolution on "Communications concerning the status of women," *Monitoring the Implementation of the Nairobi Forward-Looking Strategies for the Advancement of Women*, U.N. ESCOR, Commission on the Status of Women, 35th Sess., Agenda item 4, U.N. Doc. E/CN.6/1991/L.14 (1991), did not even make it to the floor.

21. In 1988, for example, the Commission chose not to request an increase in the length of its meetings, even though the General Assembly encouraged it to do so. Sandra Colliver, *United Nations Machineries on Women's Rights: How Might They Better Help Women Whose Rights are Being Violated*, *in* NEW DIRECTIONS IN HUMAN RIGHTS 25, 29 (Ellen L. Lutz et al. eds., 1989).

often gendered nature of presumably neutral bureaucratic structures, they are prevented from fully exploring the changes they seek by only focussing on, and in turn reinforcing, male/female differences.

III. External Critiques

Other women's human rights advocates begin by situating themselves outside the human rights system looking in at the discourse. From their (initial) external perches, they raise questions about whether human rights discourse can really assimilate women's issues/demands/rights.

In this section, I identify and discuss three external critiques, each of which suggests a different level of belief in the ability of international rights discourse and the human rights framework to address issues of women. Unlike the doctrinalists and institutionalists, who believe that the human rights framework can assimilate women's rights, the external critics believe structural changes—whether in human rights theory, doctrine, institutions or language—are needed to accommodate women's concerns.

For the most part, I consider those who take these approaches to be radical feminists because they critique the human rights system for the ways it perpetuates women's subordination.[22] To a certain extent, they also approach women's human rights as if all women were essentially the same.

The radical feminist positions of these critics do not, I believe, make them incapable of accepting that women disagree, even about clitoridectomy. Rather, they focus so much on the subordination of women by men that they tend to generalize the extent to which all women have an interest in overcoming men's power, the assumption here being that "genital mutilation" (as they call the practice) is a clear exercise of male power. This near exclusive focus on subordination, I maintain, is largely responsible for the failure of radical feminists to engage the Exotic Other Female. Were the external critics to confront the fact that females disagree about clitoridectomy, they would likely assign "false consciousness" to those whom they consider do not recognize their own oppression.

A. *Integration*

The integrationist approach to international human rights challenges human rights advocates to accept a coherent or integrated theory of *human* rights—one that represents the rights of both women and men—and to realize "human rights which are genuinely human."[23]

22. *See* Alison M. Jaggar, Feminist Politics and Human Nature 83-85 (1983).
23. Fran P. Hosken, *Toward a Definition of Women's Human Rights*, 3 Hum. Rts. Q. 1, 10 (1981).

Those who take this approach often refer to the rights of "half of humanity."[24] For them it is because women are human, not just women, that their human rights should be protected. That they are not protected is not directly due to women's differences from men (or from each other) but to the failure of the human rights system to pay attention to women's (human) situation.

Although this approach might sound similar to the doctrinalist approach, since it suggests an underlying belief in a human rights framework that can incorporate women's rights, it differs in an important respect. While the doctrinalists assume that the framework already assimilates women, the integrationists argue that the human rights system must change its focus to accommodate women's rights. And even though the integrationists do not stress women's differences from men—hoping that both male and female can be dealt with under the human rubric—they do have some sense of a gender struggle. The problem with human rights practice, they argue, is that it has focussed on men's rights.

Integrationists begin their critique of the international human rights system by noting rampant violations of what they assume to be women's human rights. One example of such violations is "genital mutilations of women which still kill, maim, and blight the physical and psychological health of millions of women and little children every year."[25] They then argue that the international human rights system is disingenuous because it does not declare clitoridectomy a human rights violation and aim to end the practice.

To the extent that those who take this approach confront the issue of cultural relativism, they see the relativist claim as false and inconsistent, made by those who simply want to exclude practices such as clitoridectomy from human rights analysis. Riane Eisler, for example, abruptly dismisses the argument that "the enactments and enforcement of laws prohibiting genital mutilation would be improper interference with ethnic traditions, constituting merely one more form of 'Western cultural imperialism' "[26] with the following response: "All institutionalized behavior, including cannibalism and slavery, are cultural traditions. And surely no human rights advocate . . . would today dare to justify cannibalism or slavery . . . on cultural or traditional grounds."[27] Implicit in this rejection of the claim is that clitoridectomy is analogous to cannibalism and slavery. Referring to the practice as mutilation makes this analogy more likely; no one would *choose* to be eaten, enslaved, or mutilated.

---

24. *See, e.g.*, Riane Eisler, *Human Rights: Toward an Integrated Theory of Action*, 9 HUM. RTS. Q. 287, 287, 289 (1987).

25. *Id.* at 295.

26. *Id.*

27. *Id.* at 296.

Integrationists believe that the difficulty in bringing women's rights into the human rights arena lies not with international human rights discourse per se, but rather with its presently exclusive male focus. That focus, which is not only not endemic to human rights theory but in opposition to it, must be changed if the practice of clitoridectomy is to be brought to an end.

Integrationists provide important insights into the often inconsistent claims that keep women's rights at the periphery of international human rights law and discourse.[28] The refusal of the integrationists to see human rights theory as preventing the protection of women's rights allows them to pursue possibilities for using international rights as a site for struggling for the improvement of women's condition. The question they do not explore, however, is what it means to improve women's condition. For them, ending "genital mutilation" is only a matter of changing the focus of the international human rights system. These advocates do not confront the possibility that "culture" might really be an obstacle to achieving change. In particular, they do not consider that resistance to ending the practice, and even to labeling it "mutilation," might come from (some) women themselves. For integrationists, the Exotic Other Female is not to be engaged.

B. *Reconceptualization/Redefinition*

Human rights critics who take this approach do not have as much faith as the integrationists in the ability of human rights theory to merely expand its focus to accommodate women's rights. For them, international human rights theory is seriously flawed because it is centered on a "male" definition of human rights. Hence, to accommodate women's rights, the theory would require reconceptualizing and redefining. Specifically, women would have to define their own rights.

This approach differs from the integrationist approach, then, in a subtle way. Avoiding the possibility that women might need any special rights, the integrationists aim to normalize or universalize women's rights, making them an essential part of human rights (hence the discussion of the *human* rights of women). Those who call for reconceptualization, on the other hand, embrace women's differences from men, through their call upon women to define their own rights.[29]

28. The integrationists' undermining of the public/private distinction is perhaps a better example of the inconsistency of the claims than their response to cultural relativism. *See infra* note 30.

29. *See, e.g.*, Noreen Burrows, *International Law and Human Rights: The Case of Women's Rights*, *in* HUMAN RIGHTS: FROM RHETORIC TO REALITY 80, 89-96 (Tom Campbell et al. eds., 1986). In describing this approach, I rely largely on this article by Noreen Burrows and a lecture by Felice Gaer. *See* Felice Gaer, Address at 1988 Harvard Human Rights Program Symposium on Women's Rights and Human Rights: Possibilities and Contradictions (Apr. 16, 1988) (videotape on file with the *New England Law Review*).

If they were to talk about "genital mutilation," reconceptualists might argue that the human rights system has not begun to deal with the issue because women have not defined the rights necessary to end the practice. Without such definition, human rights law regarding women, with its present focus on discrimination, is bound to respond insufficiently to the issue.

For these advocates, once women define their rights, it will become clear that human rights must be reconceptualized. Essential to this reconceptualization is the entry of human rights law into the traditional private sphere. The reconceptualist position assumes a distinction between public and private realms and takes for granted that international human rights, as presently theorized, excludes from its purview the private sphere.[30] From that perspective, clitoridectomy—because it is a "private" (not officially state conducted) practice—cannot be seen as a violation of international human rights until the human rights field has been reconceptualized to include the private.

By calling for women to define their rights, the reconceptualist position, unlike that of the integrationists, in principle opens itself up to the possibility of listening to a multiplicity of women's voices and even to engaging the Exotic Other Female. Yet, one of the central assumptions of this position seems to be that women will agree about what are or should be their rights. The goal of the reconceptualist is, if not to shift from the male vision of human rights, at least to supplement that vision with a female one. Male and female are, for these purposes, static notions.

The reconceptualist position is not, however, unaware of claims of cultural relativism. Noreen Burrows, for example, sees cultural differences as posing difficulties to the process of achieving recognition of women's rights: "Given the diversity in the forms of interpersonal relations and cultural variations which exist, say in the structure of the family, it may prove difficult to specify with sufficient precision those rights which the international community would recognize as being the rights of women."[31] Even as Burrows expresses this concern, however, she never suggests that women themselves might disagree about which rights they have; rather, her concern is that the "international community" might have trouble accepting or properly interpreting the rights because of its apparent sympathy with cultural variations. That women might be a part of that conflictual international community is not an issue she addresses.

---

30. This approach to the public/private distinction is also a significant departure from the integrationist approach, which argues that the claim that human rights does not enter the private sphere is as irrational and politically determined as the cultural relativism claim. *See, e.g.*, Eisler, *supra* note 24, at 293.

31. Burrows, *supra* note 29, at 85.

C. *Linguistic Critique*

Whether through integration or reconceptualization, those who pose the first two external critiques assume that the international human rights framework can be made to accommodate women's concerns. The problems integrationists and reconceptualists identify with human rights theory turn in large part on the view that it has addressed itself, perhaps exclusively, to the concerns of men. They disagree primarily about whether that focus is endemic to the theory. Another external critique poses what I call a linguistic challenge to human rights discourse. Those who aim this critique at international rights discourse generally explicitly situate themselves outside it; identifying with a particular cause or discipline (for example, feminism or biology) to examine the biases reflected in the discourse. For them, human rights discourse is not just male focussed, controlled or deployed; it is "male."

Here I focus on only one strand of this critique, which poses what it considers to be the feminist critique of rights. Although the critique borrows from communitarianism and early Marxism, and resonates with many of the critiques of rights by critical legal theorists, it does so with a strong cultural feminist perspective. That is, it assumes that there are certain essential values that are female and that cannot be realized through traditional rights discourse.

For these critics, "the concept of 'rights' is masculinist and patriarchal, a concept that came into its own with the rise of capitalism."[32] Adding an essentialist feminist twist to other critiques of rights, they suggest that "in our assertion of rights we [feminists] play a masculinist game."[33] Moreover:

> "[r]ights" language seems to assume . . . that society is a collection of atomic particles in which any given individual's happiness . . . is viewed as mutually disinterested from another's, that communities or love relationships are not ethically relevant in deciding what action ought to be taken. Rights language is fundamentally adversarial and negative . . . . Feminists seek a framework that emphasizes positive values such as helping, cooperating and acting out of love, friendship or relatedness, as well as fairness.[34]

Other problems these advocates identify with rights discourse are that it "fails to resolve moral disputes cohesively" and that it is "static and does not challenge the social structures."[35]

Even after setting forth this harsh critique, these advocates (as with many rights critics) return to rights language. They claim to do so,

32. Helen B. Holmes & Susan R. Petersen, *Rights Over One's Own Body: A Woman-Affirming Health Care Policy*, 3 Hum. Rts. Q. 71, 73 (1981).

33. *Id.*

34. *Id.*

35. *Id.*

however, "in a nonabsolutist fashion . . . affirm[ing] other moral criteria than rights—such as duty, loyalty, friendship, responsibility, goodness, and justice—as the basis of moral action."[36] In the end, then, they accept rights language by adding to their use of it what they consider to be essential women's values.

Although these advocates raise a number of important issues about the lack of neutrality of language and the role(s) that language plays in social struggles, their critique eventually relies on a deeply entrenched male/female dichotomy. Even though all the other advocates, save the doctrinalists, also rely to some extent on this dichotomy, this one is most based on essential, and thereby presumably unchangeable, differences between men and women. Along with their notion that men and women fundamentally differ comes a strong sense that all women are the same. Hence, in their assumption and even promotion of an essential woman's culture, the linguistic critics come the closest of any women's rights advocates to erasing the experiences/beliefs/desires of the Exotic Other Female. Their theory cannot accommodate any recognition of disagreements among women; it would disrupt their totalizing scheme.

* * *

All the authors who challenge human rights discourse from the outside—never assuming that it was meant to protect or assimilate their feminist demands—eventually defend the discourse in some form. Their greatest strength, I believe, is their self-conscious approach and insightful understanding of the nuances of language and of power. With all the potential obstacles to achieving women's human rights these advocates identify, however, they fail to consider seriously the possibility that women are not all the same and that legitimate differences might exist among them, particularly regarding issues such as clitoridectomy. The extent to which that failure problematizes their position differs with the various approaches.

IV. Conclusion: Beyond Imagination

At first glance, it would appear that approaching the practice of clitoridectomy as a violation of human rights would prohibit any discussion of cultural relativism. It seems that universal and international human rights implicitly represent a denial of the validity of any cultural difference that might stand in opposition to the declared universal norm. If this were the case, one might expect the debate about clitoridectomy in the international rights context to differ significantly from the debate among feminists described at the beginning of this essay.

It turns out, though, that as with the debate about clitoridectomy in other contexts, some women's rights advocates are sensitive to the de-

36. *Id.* at 74.

sire of the Exotic Other Female to maintain and participate in the practice of her culture, while other women's rights advocates refuse to engage the Other's "desires," presumably because they are mere products of false consciousness. Hence, the possibility or impossibility of taking account of "real" cultural differences and beliefs informs much of how women's rights advocates approach clitoridectomy.

Another puzzle has emerged. Just as it seems that a universal human rights approach would prohibit discussion of cultural relativism, it also would seem that those advocates most committed to formal international legal doctrine would be less sensitive to discussion of cultural difference than those advocates who appear to have a sophisticated understanding of the nuances of legal doctrine. I maintain, however, that at least in the context of women's human rights advocacy, the opposite happens. The more doctrinally oriented the advocate is, the more open she is to recognizing differences among women. And the more she moves outside the formal legal structures, the more she assumes an essential woman's voice.

This puzzle is due in part, I believe, to the differing attitudes that women's rights advocates display toward rights. While the doctrinalists stake their universal claims in liberal positive rights agreed to by sovereigns, those who apply an external critique often rely on some inherent moral basis, generally rights, for their claims. Positive law seems to free up the doctrinalists, allowing them to choose any doctrinally derived right they believe to be effective in persuading the Exotic Other Female. Those who claim moral rights do not experience the same type of liberty; a right is a right regardless of whether those they entitle want to claim it.

The puzzle is also related to the different feminist postures assumed by the advocates. While the most formalist advocates tend to be liberal (tolerant) feminists, those most external to the formal structures tend to be radical (in this case often essentialist) feminists. To the extent that liberal feminists are concerned with increasing women's choices and radical feminists are concerned with increasing women's power,[37] it makes sense that the liberals would be more open to a variety of women's views and desires. The radicals, by concentrating on women's power (versus men's power), are invested in making women one cohesive group.

As advocates move from the more liberal to the more radical positions, they become progressively more concerned about changing the power dynamics, and they move further outside the formal legal structures to try to achieve that change. Hence, institutionalists play the perfect middle-ground, assuming the institutional structures can eventually assimilate their feminist demands but nevertheless recognizing

37. *See* Robin L. West, *The Difference in Women's Hedonic Lives: A Phenomenological Critique of Feminist Legal Theory*, 3 WIS. WOMEN'S L.J. 81, 87 (1987).

that the male domination of the structure makes the assimilation difficult. The further they move outside doctrine, the more advocates work within a dichotomous male/female framework. That dichotomy seems to keep women's differences, or different women, at bay.

Whether they work inside or outside the doctrinal and institutional frameworks, most women's rights advocates recognize at some level that women have been marginalized, consciously or not, from those frameworks. But they do not generally recognize that their own pursuit of women's rights is also marginalizing. Just as human rights advocates might keep women at the periphery, if not exclude them altogether, women's rights advocates keep the Exotic Other Female at the margins. The Exotic Other Female, however, apparently present or not, affects women's rights advocacy. Whether or not advocates openly acknowledge or engage her needs and desires, she is always just below the surface or around the corner, even as a potential disruption to their critiques and proposals. Perhaps it is to avoid that potential disruption, increased exponentially and possibly infinitely, that she is kept at bay.

I do not mean to suggest in this essay that the "male" side of the male/female split is unproblematic. I believe that it is largely because so many of the women's rights advocates readily accept a stereotypical and essentialist view of men that they are unable to problematize the female side. Being caught in the male/female dichotomy prevents further exploration of either "male" or "female."

Doctrinalists seem to have avoided this trap by assuming that women can assimilate to the (gender-neutral) human rights doctrine. They are able to take account of the existence of the Exotic Other Female through their attempts at persuading her (which requires using doctrine strategically). But through their concentrated effort at bringing all females into the realm of human rights doctrine, they fail to recognize the very biases reflected in that doctrine, as well as in human rights institutions and discourse, that might keep women outside its scope.

It appears, then, that even though each approach provides some valuable insights into the workings of the international human rights framework, none actively engages the Exotic Other Female. Either the advocates maternalistically try to change her mind or they seem to ignore or not believe her desires, often dissipating her by attributing to her false consciousness. Either way, advocates' imagined constructs of her guide their strategies for gaining recognition of women's rights.

Gayatri Spivak has said that "[b]etween patriarchy and imperialism, subject-constitution and object-formation, the figure of the woman disappears, not into pristine nothingness, but into a violent shuttling which is the displaced figuration of the 'Third World Woman' caught between tradition and modernization."[38] The failure of advocates to engage the Exotic Other Female does not erase her; she is not absent. The task ahead for women's human rights advocates is to acknowledge the presence of the Exotic Other Female, even in her sometimes apparent absence, and to use some of those insights already provided by their varied approaches to begin to move from imagination to engagement.

38. Spivak, *supra* note 8, at 128.

Part III
Political Participation, Democracy and Human Rights

[16]

Ratio Juris. Vol. 7 No. 1 March 1994 (1–13)

Human Rights and Popular Sovereignty: The Liberal and Republican Versions*

JÜRGEN HABERMAS

Abstract. Popular sovereignty and human rights are the modern pillars of legal legitimacy and political power. Liberal and republican thought, however, tend to interpret the two notions from different perspectives: either as moral principles, emphasizing the self-legislation and autonomy of individuals, or as ethical values, stressing the self-realization of the political community. Adhering to his theory of communicative action, the author brings the two principles together in a non-competitive relation. Here the connection between popular sovereignty and human rights is given by the procedures of a discursive process of opinion- and will-formation. Theoretically, the institutionalization of this process through law leads to a normative model of contemporary democracy, which is based on the substance of human rights as a formal condition for deliberative politics.**

The two ideas of popular sovereignty and human rights have shaped the normative self-understanding of constitutional states up to the present day. With the first idea we postulate that members of a democratic community are governed by themselves collectively; with the second, that they are governed by law and not by men. This is no less true for the United States than for any modern constitutional regime. Let me start with this quote from Frank Michelman:

> I take American constitutionalism—as manifest in academic constitutional theory, in the professional praxis of lawyers and judges, and in the ordinary political self-understanding of Americans at large—to rest on two premises regarding political freedom: first, that the American people are politically free insomuch as they are governed by themselves collectively, and, second, that the American people are politically free insomuch as they are governed by law and not by men. I take it that no

* This is the text of a lecture given at the Philosophy Department of North-Western-University, Evanston held on September 23, 1992.

** Abstract by Francesco Belvisi.

earnest, non-disruptive participant in American constitutional debate is quite free to reject either of those two professions of belief. (Michelman 1988, 1499f.)

However, the meaning and the problematic relationship of these contested concepts has been endlessly debated for more than two hundred years. I would like to raise and discuss two questions: (I) Why do we not look at these debates, after all, as simply a closed chapter in the history of political ideas? We have to explain why these rather imaginary pillars of constitutional construction still stand upright in the face of all the disavowals of a contradicting social and political reality. Therefore, I will take up (II) the question of whether these two premises can be made compatible without giving priority to either human rights or popular sovereignty. The two main strands of political thought, labelled as "liberal" and as "republican," tend to subordinate either popular sovereignty to human rights or vice versa. Neither of these two responses satisfies our normative intuition that human rights and popular sovereignty are not only interwoven, but of equal importance and even of the same origin: The two are, on a conceptual level, co-original. In the last part of the paper (III), I will briefly analyze Rousseau's concept of autonomy. This analysis is intended to explain in what sense human rights and popular sovereignty mutually presuppose each other.

I.

Turning to the first of my questions, I am going to argue that the two ideas of human rights and popular sovereignty somehow inevitably result from reflection on what might justify, under conditions of postmetaphysical thought, the validity of positive, that is enacted, law. Since modern law rests on the changeable decisions of a political legislator, the tension between this positivity of law and the legitimacy it claims can neither be trivialized nor simply be ignored. Nor may members of a modern society any longer assume that they could resolve the tension by making recourse to doctrines rooted in just one comprehensive worldview shared by all and everybody. This traditional mode of legitimation is incompatible with the fact of pluralism. The postmetaphysical legitimation of positive law must instead draw on peculiarly modern ideas—such as autonomy and self-realization—which grew out of the very same process that destroyed the pool of premodern legitimations.

The classical, primarily Aristotelian, doctrine of natural law, whose influence extended well into the nineteenth century, as well as its remodelled Christian versions, still presumed an encompassing societal ethos that extended through all social classes of the population and clamped the different social orders together. In the vertical dimension of the components of the lifeworld, this ethos was supposed to ensure that cultural value-patterns and institutions sufficiently overlapped with the value-orientations and motives embodied in personality structures. At the horizontal level of legitimate orders, this ethos supposedly linked together the normative limbs of ethical life, politics, and law. In the train of developments, which I interpret as the "rationalization of the lifeworld," this clamp is sprung open. In the first place, cultural traditions and processes of socialization came under the pressure of reflection, so that they gradually moved from a background, taken for granted, into a topic of discussion. At the same time, traditional and prereflective practices and patterns of interpretation of an ethical life boiled down to mere conventions and were differentiated from those practical decisions that henceforth had to pass through the filter of reflection and independent judgement. During this process, the use of practical reason arrived at that level of differentiation with which I am concerned in the present context.

The modern ideas of *self-realization* and *autonomy* signal not only different themes but two different kinds of discourse tailored to the logics of *ethical* and *moral* issues. Briefly, *ethical issues* are those that come up when we are concerned with questions of my or our own plan of life, questions of the good life, while *moral issues* are at stake when we wish to solve interpersonal conflicts in concordance with the interests of everybody involved and affected. The respective logics peculiar to these two issues became manifest in philosophical developments that only began in the late eighteenth century.

What had been considered "ethics" since the time of Aristotle now, during the nineteenth century, assumed a new, subjectivistic sense. This holds equally for individual life histories and for intersubjectively shared traditions and forms of life.

In connection with a growing autobiographical literature of personal confessions and self-examinations—running from Rousseau through Kierkegaard to Sartre—a kind of reflection developed that altered attitudes toward one's own life. To put it in a nutshell, in place of exemplary instructions on the virtuous life and instead of typical models of an appropriate or happy life recommended for imitation, one finds, in increasing strength, an abstract demand for a conscious and self-critical appropriation, a responsible taking-possession-of one's own individual, irreplaceable and contingent life history. Radicalized interiority is burdened with the task of achieving a self-understanding in which scrutinized self-knowledge and existential choice interpenetrate. Heidegger used the formulation "thrown project" to express the expectation of this probing apprehension of factually given but identity-moulding possibilities (Heidegger 1962). The incursion of reflection into one's own life-project generates a new kind of tension between the consciousness of contingency, self-reflection, and liability for one's own existence. To the extent that this constellation broadens into social influence through prevailing patterns of socialization, *ethical-existential* or *clinical discourses* become not only possible but in a certain sense unavoidable: If conflicts springing from such a constellation are not resolved consciously and deliberately, they make themselves felt in painful symptoms. To lead one's own life self-consciously appears as the task of self-realization.

In addition to the personal conduct of life, the transmission of cultural values was increasingly adapted to discourses in which the public and communities carry on debates on their collective self-understanding. In connection with the rise of the historical sciences, in the nineteenth century, the appropriation of our own intersubjectively shared traditions was rendered even more problematic. Significant for this development is the type of hermeneutic reflection that developed from Schleiermacher through Droysen and Dilthey up to Gadamer. In place of religious or metaphysical self-interpretations, history now became the medium in which cultures and peoples found their self-assurance. Although philosophical hermeneutics sprung from methodological questions of the humanities, it also responded to an insecurity at large, an insecurity released by the spirit of historicism; it responded to a reflexive refraction in the mode of public appropriation of traditions performed in the first person plural. During the nineteenth century a posttraditional collective identity first took on a definite shape under the banner of an unhappy marriage between historicism and nationalism. But this form of identity was nourished on idolatrous national histories, the dogmatism of which had meanwhile been in a process of disintegration. Pluralism in the ways of reading one's own ambivalent traditions has again and again occasioned discussions which make it clear that the disputing parties are expected to consciously choose the continuities they want to live out of, and to decide which traditions they want to break off or continue. To the extent that collective identities can only develop in the fragile, dynamic, and fuzzy shape of such a decentered public consciousness, *ethical-political* discourses become both possible and unavoidable.

So the incursion of reflection into personal life histories and shared cultural traditions fostered the *idea of self-realization* in individual life projects and a *pluralism* of collective forms of life. Simultaneously, however, social norms, regulating interpersonal behavior and conflict, also became reflexive; on this road universalistic value orientations gained ascendancy.

An altered normative consciousness is reflected in the relevant philosophical theories since the end of the eighteenth century. One no longer legitimated maxims, action strategies, and rules of action simply by calling attention to the authority of tradition, that is to the contexts in which they were handed down. The new distinction between autonomous and heteronomous actions indeed revolutionized the general moral consciousness. Thereby there grew a need for justification, which under the conditions of postmetaphysical thinking could only be met by *moral discourse* aiming at the impartial regulation of action conflicts. In contrast to ethical deliberations, which are oriented to the telos of my own or our shared good (at least not misspent) life, moral deliberations required a perspective freed of the egocentrism or ethnocentrism of a first person point of view. Under the moral viewpoint of equal respect for each person and of equal consideration for the interests of all, the henceforth sharply focused normative claims of legitimately regulated interpersonal relationships were sucked into a whirlpool of problematization. At the posttraditional level of justification, the individual develops a principled moral consciousness and orients her action by the idea of *self-determination*. And what self-legislation or moral autonomy is in the sphere of personal life conduct corresponds, in the political sphere, to the contractualist ideas of freedom and justice in terms of the democratic *self-legislation* of free and equal citizens.

So, to the extent that cultural traditions and processes of socialization became reflexive, there was a growing awareness of the different logics of ethical and moral questions. Without the guidance of religious or metaphysical worldviews immune to criticism, practical orientations can, in the final analysis, only be obtained from argumentation among those involved, i.e., from the reflexive forms of communicative action itself. The rationalization of a lifeworld is measured by the extent to which the rationality potentials, built into communicative action and released in discourse, penetrate the lifeworld and set them aflow. Once the *logic of ethical* and *moral questions* has been articulated, alternatives to the prevailing normative ideas of self-realization and autonomy can no longer be justified in the long run. The conscious life conduct of the individual person finds its standards in the expressivist ideal of self-realization on the one hand, in the deontological ideal of autonomy on the other. Corresponding to the ideal of self-realization, the normative substance of collective forms of life takes its standards from utopias of nonalienated, integrated forms of life in the horizon of traditions that have been self-consciously appropriated and critically passed on. On the other hand, models of a just society emerge, whose institutions are so constituted as to regulate behavior expectations and conflicts in the equal interest of all, and thus conform to the self-legislation of their citizens.

One result of these rather sketchy considerations is of particular interest in the present context: To the extent that "culture" and "personality structures" are, so to speak, idealistically charged in this fashion, and oriented towards self-realization and autonomy, a law robbed of its sacred foundation also comes under pressure. Let me remind you that the third component of the lifeworld, "society" as the totality of legitimate orders, concentrates itself more intensely in the legal system, the more the latter is burdened with the functional imperative of integrating society as a whole. The changes just sketched in culture and personality can explain why modern legal orders must find their legitimation, to an increasing degree, in sources that do not bring the law into conflict with the posttraditional life ideals and the ideas of freedom and justice that have become more and more authoritative for both personal life and culture. The propositions that legitimate legal orders express must, on pain of cognitive dissonance, harmonize with the moral principles of autonomy and justice as well as with these ethical principles of self-realization and a consciously "projected" life conduct for which subjects themselves, at both the individual and collective levels, take responsibility.

So it is no accident that human rights and the principle of popular sovereignty constitute *the* ideas in the light of which alone positive law can still be legitimated. For these two ideas represented the residue left behind, so to speak, once the normative substance of an ethos anchored in religious and metaphysical traditions has been forced through the filter of post-traditional reflection and justification procedures. To the extent that moral and ethical questions have been differentiated from one another, the normative substance of traditional worldviews is transformed through the channels of moral and ethical discourses that correspond to the dimensions of autonomy and self-realization. However, one cannot simply align these two dimensions in a linear fashion with human rights and the sovereignty of the people. Still, there exist affinities between these two pairs of concepts, affinities that can be emphasized to a greater or lesser degree. If I may use these labels, "liberal" or Lockean political traditions conceive human rights as the embodiment of moral autonomy and take them to be prior to popular sovereignty, while "republican" traditions conceive popular sovereignty as the expression of ethical self-realization of a people and give it priority over human rights. In both views human rights and popular sovereignty do not so much mutually presuppose and supplement each other as compete with each other.

II.

I will first explain these competitive views, before I deal with the integrative views of Kant and Rousseau. So far we have two pairs of concepts: autonomy vs. self-realization on the one hand, human rights vs. popular sovereignty on the other. In order to link autonomy with human rights in the moral dimension and self-realization with popular sovereignty in the ethical dimension, one must give quite specific readings to both of the political concepts. These correspondences are far from obvious; I will explain them in terms of the liberal and republican traditions, both of which inspired the Founding Fathers' understanding of American democracy. In this context the republican tradition is connected with the work of James Harrington, an opponent of Hobbes, who presented civic humanism as an alternative to Lockean liberalism (see Kahn 1989).

While the concepts of Roman law serve in modernity to define the *negative liberties* of legal subjects in order to secure the property and commercial traffic of private persons against the interventions of an administratively exercised political power from which those persons were excluded, the language of ethics and rhetoric retains the picture of a political practice in which the *positive liberties* of equally entitled, participating citizens can be realized. The republican concept of "politics" refers not to the subjective rights of private citizens to life, liberty, and property, but preeminently to the praxis of self-legislation on the part of citizens who are oriented to the common good, who understand themselves as free and equal members of a cooperative self-governing community. Laws are secondary to the particular *ethical* life context of a community in which the virtue of active participation in public affairs can develop and stabilize. Only in this civic praxis can the human being realize the telos of his species. Following Frank Michelman, I will present to you a shorthand description of the liberal and the republican paradigms of politics as they still form the background of contemporary discussions.

The decisive difference consists in the understanding of the role of the democratic process. According to the "liberal" or Lockean view, the democratic process accomplishes the task of programming the government in the interest of society, where the government is represented as an apparatus of public administration, society as a market-structured network of interactions among private persons. Here politics (in the sense of the citizens' political will-formation) has the function of bundling together and pushing private interests over against a government apparatus specialized for the administrative employment of political power for collective goals. On the "republican" view, however, politics involves more than this mediating function; it is rather constitutive for the processes of society as a whole. "Politics" is conceived as the reflective form of substantial ethical life, namely as the medium in which the members of somehow integrated communities become aware of their dependence on one another and, acting with full deliberation as citizens, further shape and develop existing relations of reciprocal recognition into an association of free and equal consociates under law. With this development, the liberal architectonic of government and society undergoes an important change: In addition to the hierarchical regulations of the state and the decentralized regulations of the market, that is, besides administrative power and individual personal interests, *solidarity* and orientation to the common good appear as a *third source* of social integration. In fact, this horizontal political will-formation aimed at mutual understanding or communicatively achieved consensus is even supposed to enjoy priority, both in a genetic and a normative sense. An autonomous basis in civil society, a basis independent of public administration and market-mediated private commerce, is assumed for the praxis of civic self-determination. This basis prevents political communication from being swallowed up by the government apparatus or assimilated to market structures. In the republican conception, the political public sphere acquires, along with its base in civil society, a strategic significance. These competing approaches yield to contrasting images of the citizen.

According to the liberal view, the citizens' status is primarily determined by negative rights they have *vis-à-vis* the state and other citizens. As bearers of these rights they enjoy the protection of government, so long as they pursue their private interests within the boundaries drawn by the law—and this includes protection against government intervention. Political rights, such as voting rights and free speech, have not only the same structure but also a similar meaning as civil rights that provide a space within which legal subjects are released from external compulsions. They give citizens the possibility of asserting their private interests in such a way that through elections, the composition of parliamentary bodies, and the formation of a government, these interests finally aggregrate into a political will that makes an impact on the administration.

According to the republican view, the status of citizens is not determined by the model of negative liberties to which they can lay claim *as* private persons. Rather, political rights—preeminently rights of political participation and communication—are positive liberties. They guarantee not freedom from external compulsion but the possibility of participation in a common praxis, through the exercise of which citizens can first make themselves into what they want to be—politically autonomous authors of a community of free and equal persons. To this extent, the political process does not just serve to keep government activity under the surveillance of citizens who have already acquired a prior social autonomy in the exercise of their private rights and pre-political liberties. Just as little does it act as a hinge between state and society, for administrative authority is not at all an autochthonous authority. It is not something given. Rather, this authority emerges from the citizens' power produced communicatively in the praxis of self-legislation, and it finds its legitimation in the fact that it protects this praxis by institutionalizing public liberty. So the state's *raison d'être* does not lie primarily in the protection of equal private rights, but in the guarantee of an inclusive opinion- and will-formation in which free and equal citizens reach an understanding as to which goals and norms lie in the equal interest of all.

The polemic against the classical concept of the legal person as bearer of private rights reveals a controversy about the *concept of law* itself. While in the liberal view the point of a legal order is to make it possible to determine in each case which individuals are entitled to which rights, in the republican view these "subjective" rights owe their existence to an "objective" legal order that both enables and guarantees the integrity of an autonomous life in common based on mutual respect. For republicans, rights ultimately are nothing but determinations of the prevailing political will, while for liberals some rights are always grounded in a higher law of reason.

Finally, the different ways of conceptualizing the roles of citizen and of law express a deeper disagreement about the *nature of the political process*. In the liberal view, the political process of opinion- and will-formation in the public sphere and in parliament is determined by the competition of collectivities acting strategically to maintain or acquire positions of power. Success is measured by the citizen's approval, quantified in votes, of persons and programs. In their choices at the polls, voters give expression to their preferences. Their voting decisions have the same structure as the acts of choice made by participants in a market. They license access to the positives of power that political parties fight over in the same success-oriented attitude.

In the republican view, the political opinion- and will-formation occurring in the public sphere and in parliament obeys not the structures of market processes but the abstinent structures of a public communication oriented to mutual understanding. For politics, in the sense of a praxis of civic self-legislation, the paradigm is not the market but dialogue. This dialogic conception imagines politics as contestation over questions of value and not simply questions of preference.

Hence the conflict of opinions carried out in the political arena has legitimating force not just in the sense of authorizing access to positions of administrative power; rather, ongoing political discourse also has binding force for the ways in which and purposes for which administrative power is used. Administrative power should only be employed on the basis of policies, and within the boundaries of laws, that issue from democratic processes.

These contrasting images should be sufficient to make it plausible why liberals favor the impersonal rule of laws founded on human rights, particularly those that secure negative liberties, whereas republicans stress the priority of a spontaneous self-organization of the community so that the deeper aspirations of their constitutive traditions find their expression in the legal order. Both draw on the legitimating ideals of moral autonomy and expressivist self-realization in quite different ways.

In the liberal view the ideal of self-realization is given a secondary status and is only applied to private legal subjects who are entitled to pursue their different life plans within the limits of their civil rights. What is of primary importance is the equal distribution of negative liberties according to general laws. The moral ideals of autonomy and justice are constitutionally embodied in impersonal civil rights and protected by the fair administration of law. This conception retains, however, from the strong notion of autonomy, only the element of the impartiality of universal laws expressing generalizable interests, while it neglects the element of self-determination, which demands that we should only obey those laws which we have given to ourselves. Liberals invoke the danger of a "tyranny of the majority" and postulate the priority of human rights, so that these can guarantee the pre-political liberties of the individual and constrain the sovereign will of the political legislator. Republicans, on the other hand, emphasize the intrinsic value of civic self-organization; they stress the public exercise of political autonomy as an ongoing process and the pursuit of a common enterprise.

This does not mean, however, that the two elements of the same notion of autonomy would be accepted and merely rearranged in reverse order. The republican notion of self-legislation is not at all a moral notion. It is, instead, assimilated to an ethical notion. Republicans conceive the exercise of political autonomy as the conscious self-realization of the collective will of a particular community. Human rights can gain a binding character for citizens of such a community only as elements of their own consciously appropriated traditions. Whereas in the liberal view human rights impose themselves on political will-formation as something anchored in a fictive state of nature, in the republican view, the ethical-political will of a self-realizing collectivity is forbidden to recognize anything that does not fit into the people's own authentic form and project of life.

Both paradigms engage modern ethical ideals and moral concepts for an obviously selective reading of human rights and popular sovereignty. The liberal paradigm does not exhaust the full-fledged meaning of the autonomy of a sovereign citizenry, because it introduces human rights as antecedent or external constraints on the democratic process, whereas the republican paradigm cannot account for the universalistic meaning of human rights, because it ties the democratic process to the prior bond and shared self-understanding of some particular ethical community.

III.

By contrast, Rousseau and Kant explained autonomy (*Selbstgesetzgebung*) as unifying practical reason and sovereign will in such a way that the idea of human rights and the principle of popular sovereignty would mutually interpret each other. An autonomous will follows just those norms which it chooses on the basis of moral insight. And laws count as legitimate only if their *addressees* can jointly regard themselves as their *authors*. Nevertheless, the two authors who invented the modern idea of autonomy did not quite succeed in interlocking the two concepts in a fully symmetric way. On the whole Kant suggests more of a liberal reading of political autonomy, Rousseau a republican reading.

I leave aside Kant's legal philosophy and focus on Rousseau's *Social Contract*. While Kant first introduces natural rights of a moral nature, which then inform the political will of the democratic legislator, Rousseau starts immediately with the constitution of civic autonomy and produces an internal connection between popular sovereignty and human rights. The basic argument is simply this: Since the sovereign will of the people can express itself only in the language of universal and abstract laws, it is directly *inscribed* with the very right to equal liberties that Kant conceived as a morally grounded human right and, thus, *put ahead of* political will-formation. Thus, in Rousseau the exercise of political autonomy is no longer subject to the proviso of innate rights. The normative content of the idea of human rights rather enters into the very *mode* of carrying out popular sovereignty. The united will of citizens is bound, through the medium of universal and abstract laws, to a democratic legislative *procedure,* which excludes *per se* all non-generalizable interests and only admits regulations that guarantee equal liberties for all and everybody. According to this idea, the procedurally correct exercise of popular sovereignty simultaneously secures the liberal principle of legal equality (which grants everybody equal liberties according to general laws).

But Rousseau does not consistently carry through this plausible idea. He owes a greater debt to the republican tradition than does Kant. He gives the idea of self-legislation more an ethical than a moral interpretation, conceiving autonomy as the realization of the consciously apprehended form of life of a particular people. As is well known, Rousseau imagines the constitution of popular sovereignty through the social contract as a kind of existential act of primary socialization through which isolated and success-oriented individuals *transform themselves* into citizens oriented to the common good of an ethical community. As members of a collective body they fuse together into the macrosubject of a legislative praxis—the author of laws, who has broken with the particular interests of private persons who, as addressees, are merely subjected to laws. Rousseau takes the strong ethical demands of a transpicuous, more or less homogeneous community integrated through common cultural traditions. The only alternative would be coercion executed by state agencies.

However, if the practice of self-legislation must live off the ethical substance of people's *agreement in advance* on their value orientations, then Rousseau cannot explain how the required ethical orientation of the citizens toward the common good can be reconciled with the different and partly contradictory interest-positions of private persons and collective actors. He cannot explain how the normatively construed common will can, without repression, be mediated by the free choice of individuals. This would require a genuinely moral standpoint that would allow one to look beyond what is good *for us* and examine what lies equally in the interest of each. In the final analysis, the ethical version of the concept of popular sovereignty must lose sight of the universalistic meaning of the principle of right—and of the necessity to admit fairly regulated bargaining-processes.

The normative content of human rights cannot be fully captured by the grammar of general and abstract laws alone, as Rousseau assumed (even if we leave aside the fact that the regulatory state can no longer formulate its policies solely in terms of these conditional programs, that is, that the materialized law no longer fits the pattern of general and abstract laws). Rousseau rightly took as central to modern law's claim to legitimacy equality in the content of law, which allows for equal protection and grants that equal things are treated equally; this kind of equality cannot be satisfactorily explained, as Rousseau falsely supposed, by the *semantic* properties of general laws. The semantic form of universal precepts says nothing about their legitimacy. Rather, the claim that a norm lies equally in the interest of all has the sense of rational acceptability—all those possibly affected would have to be able to accept the norm on the basis of good reasons. But this can be proved only under the *pragmatic conditions of discourses* in which the only thing that counts is the compelling force of the better argument based on relevant information. Rousseau looks for the normative content of the principle of rights in the semantic properties of *what* is willed, a content he could in fact only read off from those pragmatic conditions that establish *how* the legislative will is formed. It is not the grammar of legal propositions which is decisive, but the discursive mode and the procedural setting in which they are explained and justified. The sought-for internal connection between popular sovereignty and human rights lies only in the normative content of a mode of exercising political autonomy. This is the explanation of Rousseau's fruitful intuition. That mode is not secured merely through the form of general laws, but only through the procedures for a discursive process of opinion- and will-formation.

This connection remained hidden from Kant and Rousseau alike. They succeeded in bringing reason and will together in a concept of autonomy, but only within the limits of a philosophy of the subject. Under these premises they had to ascribe the capacity for self-determination to a subject, be it to the intelligible ego of the *Critique of Practical Reason* or to the people of the *Social Contract*. If the rational will can constitute itself only in the individual subject, then the individual's moral autonomy must reach through the political autonomy of the united will of all, in order to secure via natural law the private autonomy of each in advance. If the rational will can constitute itself only in the macrosubject of a people or nation, then political autonomy must be understood as the self-conscious realization of the ethical substance of a concrete community; and private autonomy can be protected from the overpowering force of political autonomy only by the non-discriminating form of general laws. Both conceptions miss the legitimating force of a discursive process of opinion- and will-formation, in which the illocutionary and bonding forces of a communicative and argumentative use of language serve to bring reason and will together—and to arrive at convincing positions to which all as individuals can agree without coercion.

Networks of moral, ethical and pragmatic discourses (and, we should add, of fair negotiations) represent the place where a more or less rational political will can constitute itself. Then the legitimacy of law ultimately depends on a *communicative arrangement*: As participants in more or less rational discourses, in more or less fair negotiations, consociates under law must be able to examine whether a contested norm meets with, or could meet with, the agreement of all those possibly affected. The internal connection between popular sovereignty and human rights that we are looking for consists in the fact that human rights state precisely the conditions under which the various forms of communication necessary for politically autonomous law-making can be legally institutionalized. These conditions are no longer constraints, but *enabling* conditions for the exercise of popular sovereignty. The system of rights can be reduced neither to a moral reading of human rights nor to an ethical reading of popular sovereignty, because the private autonomy of citizens must neither be set above nor made subordinate to their political autonomy. The normative intuitions we associate with human rights and popular sovereignty only achieve their *full* articulation in the system of negative and private rights if we assume that negative liberties and private autonomy may neither be imposed as a moral right in a way that constrains political legislation, nor instrumentalized just as a functional requisite for the democratic process. Private and public autonomy are co-original and of equal weight. The substance of human rights then resides in the formal conditions for the legal institutionalization of those discursive processes of opinion- and will-formation through which the sovereignty of the people can be exercised.

I have focused on a comparison between the liberal and republican versions of democracy. From the analysis of the complementary deficits of these views we can develop a perspective for a procedural notion of deliberative politics that yields a fuller understanding of how human rights and popular sovereignty mutually presuppose each other. Of course, this procedural interpretation of a constitutional regime again only provides a *normative* model of democracy, which is still in need of a sober confrontation with the structures and mechanisms of the complex societies in which we live.

Johann Wolfgang Goethe-University
Faculty of Philosophy
Dantestraße 4–6
D-6000 Frankfurt a. M. 11
Germany

References

Heidegger, Martin. 1962. *Being and Time*. Trans. J. MacQuarrie and E. Robinson. New York: Harper.
Kahn, Paul W. 1989. Reason and Will in the Origins of American Constitutionalism. *Yale Law Journal* 98: 449–517.
Michelman, Frank. 1988. Law's Republic. *Yale Law Journal* 97: 1493–537.

Ratio Juris. Vol. 7 No. 1 March 1994 (14–40)

Positivism and Communitarianism: Between Human Rights and Democracy*

CARLOS SANTIAGO NINO

Abstract. The author deals with theoretical connections between legal positivism and communitarianism. Such connections prove to be relevant not only for a better understanding of these two trends of thought but also in order to throw light on important philosophical issues like human rights and democracy. Deep links are traced and recognized between the so-called positivism "in action," and especially its ideological thesis, and communitarianism.

Legal positivism is, obviously, a doctrine about law, while communitarianism is a conception of morality. Legal positivism is defended by scholars who tend to be liberal in politics and they fear that some liberal values like tolerance and the free pursuit of truth would be hampered if the tenets of positivism—whatever they are—are rejected. On the other hand, communitarianism was developed precisely as a doctrine which controverts central liberal stands, and it is held by some scholars who seem to be friends of natural law rather than of positivism. Despite this somewhat pragmatical tension, there could logically be positivists about law who are either liberal or communitarian about political morality, as well as non-positivists who are of one or the other persuasion, which is a good indication that the two doctrines operate at different, unrelated, levels.

Therefore, the possibility of significantly connecting these two movements seemed at first hopeless to me. However, when I began to probe more

* I must confess that, when Professor Massimo La Torre invited me to speak at the European University Institute about positivism *and* communitarianism, I felt at first both flattered and puzzled. Flattered because I have written quite extensively about the two subjects and it is always good for an author that there remains some interest in discussing further what one has dealt with. Puzzled because I never dealt with the two topics *together*, and, at first sight, they seemed to me to be so far apart from each other that I envisaged the risk of treating them in a merely juxtaposed way. But the invitation of Professor La Torre to relate both issues proved, after all, to be very wise indeed. This lecture was given at the E.U.I. in Florence on 22 April 1993.

carefully into possible connections, I discovered that there are indeed such relevant connections, and, moreover, that they throw light on different issues concerning the treatment of human rights and democracy.

I.

Let us begin with legal positivism *in action*. I underscore this "in action" because, as we shall see soon, "legal positivism" is quite a proteic label and perhaps the best way to detect what it centrally covers is to see what an undoubtedly positivist thinker defending an undoubtedly positivist position has to say about some concrete issue of controversy. I propose to direct our attention to Norberto Bobbio and his stand concerning the foundation of human rights.

Bobbio has dealt with this subject in a very provocative essay (Bobbio 1990). There he says that the search for an absolute foundation for human rights is the search for a power which should be irresistible to the mind. However, he thinks that this search is an illusion since it is hampered by obstacles which in fact are quite similar to those which led Hans Kelsen to think that that of justice was an "irrational ideal" (Kelsen 1975). The first obstacle is that "human rights" is too vague an expression, being filled up in quite contrasting ways according to the ideology of the interpreter. Second, the class of human rights is extremely variable throughout history —comprising for instance either an absolute right of property or quite a limited one—which reflects the plurality and relativity of political conceptions which is what in fact grounds some rights like that of freedom of expression or of religion. Furthermore, the class of human rights is, in the third place, extremely heterogeneous, since some of them seem to be unlimited and valid for all persons in all circumstances, while some others, though fundamental, admit restrictions for the sake of other rights or for variations according to social circumstances. Fourth, even rights which may be invoked by the same individuals are sometimes antinomic, like the classic liberties which require abstentions from the state and the new social rights or powers which necessitate positive action which often involves restricting the former liberties.

Bobbio thinks that these four problems obstruct any possibility of finding a common foundation for human rights. But he goes further in thinking that the search itself is a waste of time and energy since it is a myth to think that the hypothetical discovery of an absolute ground for human rights will ensure their materialization: Precisely when scholars thought that they had grasped that foundation human rights were generally ignored, and now that there is growing skepticism about that foundation there has been important progress in their recognition through various seminal international conventions. Bobbio concludes with his quite famous statement that now that human rights have been the object of very definite international compacts and declarations, "[. . .] the substantial problem is not so much that of *justifying* them but that of *protecting* them. It is not a philosophical problem but a political one."

Before evaluating this thesis in the light of the communitarian offensive, let us see how it is related to the basic tenets of legal positivism, which Bobbio has defended in some other works. As he himself has contributed much to perceive, the label "legal positivism" refers to quite different positions. Relying heavily on his own contribution, on that of Alf Ross (1958) and on that of Genaro Carrio (1970), I generally find it useful to distinguish between four theses which are generally associated with legal positivism: The first thesis is that of *ethical skepticism*, that is, the idea that there is no rational and intersubjective way to ground basic principles of justice and social morality. The second thesis is that of *legal formalism*, that is, the view that the law is constituted by standards deliberately enacted—i.e., legislation—, and that these standards are complete, consistent and precise, so that they may be applied by judges and others to particular cases without need to resort to their own ideas of justice and morality. The third thesis is the one that Bobbio deems *ideological positivism* and Ross *pseudo-positivism* and which asserts that the law identified exclusively on the basis of some social facts provides ultimate reasons for justifying actions and decisions, reasons which are independent of moral or political considerations. The last thesis is *conceptual positivism*, that is, the stand which sustains that as legal system may be identified and described without the need to evaluate its coincidence or not with ideals of justice and social morality.

It is useful to contrast these theses with those which it is fair to ascribe to the main rival of positivism, that is natural law theory. There are also a variety of natural law views but unlike positivist ones they are not so variegated up to the point of sometimes even being inconsistent with each other, but they belong in a continuum of greater or lesser metaphysical commitment. I shall only mention here what I generally call "minimal natural law"—which is accepted by all the other varieties which add to it further theses. It distinguishes itself by holding two theses: The first one is that principles of justice or social morality may indeed be grounded in an intersubjective manner; the second one is that a set of positive norms which does not accord with these principles cannot be conceived of as a legal system. It is easy to see that this minimal natural law does not oppose all the varieties of positivism, but only those which defend theses one and four, that is, ethical skepticism and conceptual positivism.

Now, if we revise which theses are explicitly defended in common by the main protagonists of the legal positivist movement in different times and places—that is, thinkers like John Austin, Jeremy Bentham, Hans Kelsen, Alf Ross, Norberto Bobbio, Genaro Carrio, Carlos Alchourrón and Eugenio Bulygin—we will find, I believe, that the only one which all of them share is thesis number four. There are, of course, many positivists who are ethical skeptics—like Kelsen, Ross and Alchourrón and Bulygin—but there are others who are not—like Austin, Bentham and possibly Hart and Carrio. There are positivists who are legal formalists—like in some sense Kelsen when he rejects the existence of gaps and contradictions in a legal system (though he admits other indeterminacies)—but most of them emphasize the existence of different sources of legal norms and insist on the existence of indeterminacies of different kinds which call for judges and others making evaluative judgements in the application of the legal system. Almost no important positivist thinker—and certainly none of those mentioned above—subscribes in the context of the discussion about the nature of law to the ideological positivist thesis that a legal system which is factually identified and described may by itself provide reasons for justifying actions and decisions. Though most positivists have not dealt much with this subject, when they develop their general theories of law they make scattered remarks to the effect that the fact of identifying a system as legal does not mean that one is justifying applying it for adopting decisions or course of actions. Whether this is so or not may well depend on other sorts of considerations like moral ones.

Kelsen seems to be an exception because of his doctrine of the "basic norm": As is known, this norm is an epistemic hypothesis which may be predicated of any system of efficacious positive rules, and once predicated of them it has the implication of granting them validity or binding force. Thus, it seems—and so Kelsen has often been interpreted—that through the expedient of presupposing a basic norm for it we can conclude that any system backed by coercion is binding upon its subjects and, therefore, that their decisions based on it are justified. But this interpretation simply misses the elementary point that the adoption of the basic norm in legal reasoning in order to conceive of as normative propositions—e.g., *whoever commits murder should be punished with prison*—what otherwise would be mere facts—e.g., the fact that somebody with power issued the words "whoever commits murder [. . .]"—is *hypothetical*, that it gets into legal reasoning after not being categorically asserted but being just presupposed in the same way as axioms are by geometers in order to infer some theorems. That hypothetical character of the basic norm transmits itself of course to the ascription of validity to positive legal norms. And that means that those norms so conceived to be valid cannot serve as reasons for justifying decisions since hypothetical reasons cannot ground actual decisions. This accords perfectly well with the fact that Kelsen seems always to have in mind scholarly legal thinking when formulating his idea of the basic norm. He does not focus on the judicial task, since judges cannot adopt decisions on the basis of mere presuppositions. They must categorically assume the validity of the norms on the basis of which they justify their decisions and this requires something other than the hypothetical basic norm (something else which Kelsen eludes characterizing). Following the analogy, judges should be for Kelsen like physicists or, better, engineers facing the axioms of the geometers: They should categorically assume their truth in order to act on their basis.

Whatever their positions with regard to these three theses, all the important legal positivist thinkers adhere to the thesis of conceptual positivism: That is to say that the legal system of a society can be identified and described on the basis of certain factual circumstances and without any need to evaluate its coincidence or not with principles of justice and social morality. This means that they think that the concept of law is purely descriptive: Its use in propositions does not commit the user to certain values and the meaning of those propositions can be exhausted by pointing out to space-temporal circumstances. Of course, if this thesis is distinguished from that of ideological positivism the identification of a legal rule does not imply at all that somebody is justified in acting on the basis of that rule. What is the use, therefore, of this descriptive concept of law? According to positivists, it reflects the distinction between the *law that is* and the *law that ought to be,* it makes possible a value-free knowledge of the law and of its connection with other social phenomena, and it even helps evaluation by allowing us to distinguish whether the values which we adopt are materialized in current systems.

However, I have alleged elsewhere (Nino 1985; 1989) that these arguments are either circular or are only valid for some kinds of discourses about law and not necessarily for others. But the most important thing is that these arguments presuppose that there is *only one* concept of law in the manner of a conceptual essentialism that most positivists are so intent on rejecting. If we reject essentialism about concepts—that is, the idea that concepts are true or false according to whether they reflect or not underlying structures of reality—and if we conceive of them, in the conventionalist manner, as tools for classifying phenomena taking into account analogies or differences, there is no reason whatsoever for not accepting that there may be *a plurality of concepts of law*. Many of these concepts may be purely descriptive and many may be normative or evaluative, and there may even be mixed concepts of law. Some of them may be useful in one context of discourse and some others useful in some other discursive contexts, or in none at all. There are underlying conditions which have to do with the goals of each type of discourse in which the concept of law is used—the practical discourse of judges and lawyers, the normative discourse of legal scholars, the descriptive discourse of legal sociologists, anthropologists, and historians—which may make useful one or other concept of law.

If this is so, the whole dispute between natural lawyers and legal positivists—centered in the second thesis of natural law and the fourth thesis of legal positivism—becomes vacuous and spurious once conceptual essentialism is rejected. This is not perceived by authors like Dworkin who assumes wrongly that positivists adopt a normative concept of law—not as those standards which are in fact accepted by bodies like the courts but as those standards which the courts *should* accept—and proceeds automatically to reduce positivism to the ideological stand—which results from the combination of identifying law on the basis of some facts and assuming that law provides reasons for justifying actions.

This is I think a fair account of what is the status of the controversy around legal positivism when the work of its spokesmen remains in the domain of that rather *inert* discipline which is the so-called "general theory of law" (later on I shall have a word or two to say about this discipline). But when legal positivists concern themselves, as Bobbio has done in so many valuable works, with normative issues—be they about the law or under the law—their positivism generally acquires a quite different configuration. This is the natural consequence of the inoffensiveness of legal positivism when it is defended as a conceptual position: It may only be relevant within a context of discourse which deals with definitions which are themselves neutral to descriptive or normative stands. When the discourse deals with more substantive and controverted matters and a participant in it takes what is understood to be a legal positivist position, this must mean that he is being positivist in some of the other senses, that is, some of the senses which refer to positions which are not shared by all legal positivists.

That legal positivism acquires in these more substantive contexts of discourse a more "meaty" embodiment is shown clearly in the work of Bobbio just cited: Ethical skepticism comes quite clearly to the surface in his references to the vagueness, ambiguity, *et cetera* of the concept of human rights which makes it impossible to look for an absolute foundation of what it denotes and to the lack of relevance that anyway such a foundation would have. Moreover, the *factum* of law becomes directly relevant for justifying actions and decisions, as ideological positivism propounds, in the allusion to the recognition of human rights in positive conventions as making unnecessary the task of giving reasons for them.

Thus, the ethical skepticism and the ideological positivism which cannot be necessarily associated with legal positivism when it is defended in the context of discussion about the nature of law often emerge when positivism is put "in action" in order to argue about more substantial theoretical or practical issues. This occurs despite the fact that when positivists are shown some of the implications of grounding decisions not on values but on mere spatio-temporal facts, they often retreat to a more comfortable merely conceptual stand.

However, what drives positivists like Bobbio to adopt these less generally shared theses when confronted with substantial problems is understandable and quite compelling. The invocation of absolute values recalls religious fanaticism or political absolutism which lead to intolerance. On the other hand, if decisions were conceived as radically ungroundable once the former alternative is rejected, the phantom of arbitrariness and naked power would haunt us. Once tolerance and a scientific view of the world lead us to reject objective ideals as the source of arrangements like those involved in the recognition of human rights, it seems that we need to rely on something like the factum of their positive acceptance as a way of putting an end to deliberation about whether they should or should not be respected. Skepticism about objective values seems to lead, at least pragmatically, to something like the ideological positivist stand of conceiving of positive law as generating reasons for action and decision.

II.

What I would like to focus on here, however, is the confrontation between this sort of positivism "in action" and some implications of communitarianism. I think that to analyze this confrontation would also draw attention to some weakness of even the more inert varieties of legal positivism.

I wish to call your attention to how a thesis like that of Bobbio fares when it is confronted with some theoretical developments which emphasize the relativization of human rights to historical or cultural contexts. For instance Abdullahi Ahmed An-Na'im defends the need for a cross-cultural approach in defining the international standards of human rights which takes into account the fact of cultural and religious variations like that of Islamic peoples who do not consider that following the Qur'an in cutting off the hand of a thief, under certain circumstances, constitutes cruel, inhuman or degrading punishment as defined in international conventions (An-Na'im 1992).

As another example of an even more relativist view of human rights, we may mention Rhoda E. Howard's position expressed in assertions like the following: "[. . .] Human rights is, to repeat, one particular conception of human dignity and social justice. It is not synonymous, despite their joining in the Universal Declaration of Human Rights, with human dignity. All societies and all social and political philosophies have conceptions of human dignity. Some of these—especially those rooted in the view that nation, "people," community, or family must take precedence over the individual—are radically at odds with the idea of human rights. The recent tendency to substitute collective rights for human rights in international debate, or to assume that the two types of rights can exist compatibly, fails to note this crucial difference" (Howard 1992).

These are statements by jurists and anthropologists who resist being completely silenced in their different interpretation or even denial of human rights by the factum of their recognition by international conventions. But these statements are being supported by an increasingly popular philosophical conception, which re-enacts old qualms about the liberal conception of rights. I refer, of course, to communitarianism.

In recent years, the liberal conception of rights has been put into question by philosophers who exhibit an acute intellectual sophistication: Charles Taylor (1985), Alasdair MacIntyre (1981), Michael Sandel (1982), and in part Michael Walzer (1983), Bernard Williams (1985), Stuart Hampshire (1983) and Susan Wolf (1982). The influence of Hegel is noticeable in many of these philosophers—through their insistence on the social character of humans and on the connection between morality and the customs of each society. But behind Hegel also looms the figure of Aristotle, since many of these communitarian philosophers also defend a conception of the good related to a teleological vision of human nature and reflected in a set of virtues.

One of the contributions of the communitarian trend consists in giving a picture of liberalism which is sometimes clearer than that provided by liberals themselves. In this way, MacIntyre, for instance, puts forward the following distinguishing features of liberalism, mainly in the Kantian variant. First, the idea that morality is mainly composed of rules which would be accepted by any rational individual under ideal circumstances. Second, the requirement that these rules should be neutral with regard to the interests of individuals. Third, the demand that moral rules should be also neutral with regard to conceptions of the good individuals may hold. Finally, the requirement that moral rules should be applied equally to all individual human beings regardless of their social context.

Communitarianism objects to each one of these assumptions of liberalism and it does so after proposing a diagnosis of the common source of so many philosophical mistakes. Charles Taylor, for instance, locates that source in an "atomist" conception of individuals according to which they are self-sufficient regardless of their social environment. Sandel expands the argument maintaining that Kantian liberalism assumes an outlook of moral agents as constant along time, disconnected thus from their own varying desires and interests, free from the causal flux which affects those desires and interests, mutually separated, and isolated from the social context. MacIntyre in his turn maintains that the abandonment of a teleological conception of human nature seriously disrupted moral discourse, since it now lacks the element which constituted the bridge between factual propositions about actual human behavior and moral rules which have a normative character.

These authors maintain that only an impoverished conception of the moral person, such as that referred to above, allows liberalism to sustain its distinctive thesis about the independence of justice and human rights from a conception of what is good in life. Liberal neutrality about the ideals of virtue or of human excellence is achieved at the expense of adhering to a view of human agents as noumenal entities which not only lack a distinctive telos, but also possess an identity which is not dependent on their own desires, on their relationship with other individuals, and on their insertion in a specific social environment.

Therefore, liberals are being accused of endorsing a social morality centered on human rights without realizing that they require a conception of the good, as is shown in cases like conflicts of rights which can only be solved by resorting to such a conception. Alternatively, liberals are also being accused of smuggling in a hidden conception of the good despite their pretense of neutrality. The conception of the good which liberals are said to endorse implicitly is the same as that of utilitarianism in the prevailing version: The satisfaction of desires or preferences of individuals whatever their content. This conception of the good is, in its turn, put into question by communitarians: They say that its apparent plausibility derives from a confusion between the satisfaction of desires and pleasure (which, despite being a good, cannot be the only one). The object of some desires and preferences may be to obtain pleasure and sometimes the satisfaction of desires causes pleasure; but not all desires have as their object the achievement of pleasure and not every satisfaction of desires is pleasurable. If we disconnect in this way desires and preferences from pleasure, the idea that a satisfaction of a preference regardless of its content is something valuable in itself loses plausibility. If each one of us desires something only in so far as we believe it to be valuable—in some or other sense—, it does not appear reasonable to assign objective value to the satisfaction of desires regardless of the value of that which is desired.

Charles Taylor intends to show, in almost syllogistic fashion, how liberal thinking contradicts itself when it assumes there is a set of individual rights which have primacy over other normative relations (these relations which are subaltern to rights include even the duty of being loyal to a society or state, since for liberalism this should be based on consent given within the framework of those rights). Taylor's reasoning runs as follows: (1) The ascription of rights depends on the recognition of certain capacities, like expressing opinions, developing a spiritual life, feeling pleasure and pain, etc. The liberal may want to block this move putting forth the case of children and the comatose, but they would have to desist as soon they are asked why rights are not also ascribed to trees or clouds; then they must admit that in the case of children the potential capacity is relevant, and in the case of the comatose either rights are relevant or are ascribed for special reasons; (2) It is not enough for ascribing rights to recognize certain capacities. These should be considered *valuable* so as to be differentiated from others which are not the grounds of rights; (3) If something is valuable there is a duty to preserve and to expand it, materializing the conditions on which that materialization or expansion depends; (4) The majority if not all the capacities on which the ascription of rights depends are conditioned to membership in a society; they require tools like language, conceptual schemes and institutions which are inherently social. Liberalism may pretend to block this move also either through the limitation of the relevant capacities to that of feeling pleasure or pain, or through the limitation of associative relationships to those based on consent, like the family. But the capacity of sentience seems to be insufficient to ground a broad set of rights, which in any case can only be reduced to an ample capacity to choose plans of life, and the consensual associations do not seem to be sufficient for developing the relevant capacities.

The conclusion of this reasoning is, of course, that the ascription of the rights presupposes the duty to preserve the links of community which make possible the development of the valuable capacities which underlie rights. Liberalism would contradict itself when it gives to rights primacy over the duties related to the preservation of society which makes the former possible.

MacIntyre arrives at the same conclusion with light variations in the premises: The rules which ascribe rights are justified on the basis of certain goods; these goods are internal to changing social practices. Thus, moral evaluation is subject to the traditions and practices of each society. This author recognized that this may be dangerous, since it restricts the capacity of criticism of social institutions and practices; but he contends that the dissociation between morality and social practices which underlies liberalism is also dangerous since it neutralizes all motivation to be moral.

This allows us to distinguish the following aspects of the communitarian program: In the first place, the derivation of the principles of justice and rights from a certain conception of the good. Second, a conception of the good in which the social dimension is central and even dominant. Third, a relativization of the rights and duties of individuals to their particular attachments to other individuals and to the particular features and traditions of their society. Finally, a dependency of moral *criticism* on moral *practice* as it is manifested in the traditions, conventions and institutions of each society. Even when we cannot proceed further here in order to see how different thinkers link together these aspects of the communitarian conception of rights (see Nino 1991b), I think that what I said is enough to perceive that the pivotal element is the thesis that conceptions of the good prevail over principles of rights and that plausible conceptions both include as central membership in society and other smaller groups and are developed through the practice carried out within the society and those groups.

Of course, this communitarian vision of rights fully backs the more concrete concerns about the impact of social context on rights, and therefore about their cultural conditionality, voiced moderately, as we saw before, by authors like An-Na'im and in a more radical way by scholars like Howard.

III.

When a positivist in action like Bobbio confronts positions like those of the authors just cited, An-Na'im and Howard, of course he must be troubled. They do not think that the question of the recognition and extent of human rights is settled just because they are part of international conventions. They either would like those conventions to be modified or interpreted in ways which perhaps Bobbio might dispute. Moreover, they do not think that the question of justification is behind us and we should face only the question of protection. They would argue that the question of whether to protect the thief whose hand is going to be cut off depends on the question of whether it is justifiable to ban such punishment as degrading, inhuman or cruel. Of course, if they rely on philosophical communitarianism as that of Taylor or MacIntyre they would back their statements in the way we saw in the last section. And that will go to the heart of the question of justification, i.e., they would offer a justification of human rights such that their recognition and scope would depend on conceptions of the good embedded in social practices.

Therefore, communitarianism seems to confront positivism in action. But what is the nature of this confrontation? Is it due to the fact that positivism has an underlying connection—as many have thought—with liberalism and it is merely getting the blows that communitarianism directs to the latter position? I do not think so. The nature of the confrontation seems to be more superficial and contingent. Positivism in action seems a position which wants to foreclose a certain quest and communitarianism is an answer to that quest, which presupposes of course the need of it.

The quest that the ideological positivism which emerges when substantial issues are discussed wants to foreclose is the quest for reasons beyond positive legal norms: Those positive legal norms *are* the reasons we need for decisions and it is both unnecessary and impossible to look for further reasons beyond law, that is, in morality. Communitarianism aims, instead, to provide those further reasons through a certain view of morality.

If positivism in action clashes with communitarianism in the particular field of the international recognition of human rights, it is just because the relevant positive laws have a liberal inspiration. Thus, positivists conclude that they provide reasons for action not because of the liberal morality behind these laws but because of their positivity, whereas communitarians may well doubt the justificatory force of those conventions since they think that their positivity does not preclude the weakness of the putative reasons generated by the liberal moral principles behind them. If the international conventions were to absorb the communitarian offensive and provide major leeways in the balance and scope of human rights according to social context, the dispute would be between the positivist in action and the liberal, and not the communitarian.

Moreover, I think that positivism in action has many things in common with communitarianism. There is a superficial way of making them converge. This consists in observing that authors like Bobbio end up by adopting a conventionalist meta-ethical stand which seems to be part also of the communitarian movement. In effect, in other work on the subject on the foundation of human rights, Bobbio defends the idea that rather than seeking absolute grounds for those rights we must conform ourselves with the wide consensus that their international recognition shows that exists around them in the world of today. But I prefer not to rely on this addition of Bobbio to the legal positivist thesis that the positive enactment of human rights makes the task of justifying them superfluous. This is for several reasons: First, because, the moral conventionalist thesis seems to be incompatible with the last statement about the superfluousness of justification (the former thesis provides a justification which is independent of the positivity of the recognition of human rights, since there can be positive recognition without consensus and vice versa). Second, because this moral conventionalism seems to be idiosyncratic of Bobbio and not shared by other positivists when dealing with substantial issues. Third, because that moral conventionalism is rather weak in the crude way presented by Bobbio, and it is vulnerable to the emergence of dissenters like the communitarian ones. Even when the dissenters did not emerge, the possibility that they do throws doubt about any moral view based on crude consensus.

Therefore, what I want is to trace deeper links between positivism in action, and especially its ideological thesis, and communitarianism. The links must thus be established between the latter view of morality and the thesis that positive law by itself—whether backed or not by moral consensus—provides reasons for justifying actions and decisions. If we could trace such links perhaps we may throw doubts about the supposed association between positivism and liberalism which float in the air of so many analyses.

IV.

The first association which I want to establish between the two positions is that, though the cases which I alluded to in order to exemplify them—Bobbio's view of human rights, on the one hand, and An-Na'im and Howard's view of the same subject and the general philosophical conception of philosophers like Taylor, Sandel, or MacIntyre, on the other, present quite amiable faces, both positivism in action which acquires ideological undertones and communitarianism may also show us quite frightful countenances.

In the case of ideological positivism, all of us know how the doctrine that whoever has the coercive power to make a social group obey certain prescriptions acquires legitimacy to issue them and is the recipient of the corresponding duty to abide by them of the people was used to justify extreme authoritarian regimes, like the Nazi or Fascist ones. This resulted in an endorsement of might and force and a glorification of success. As Alf Ross says (1958), this doctine may be influenced by Hegel's dictum that whatever is real is rational and vice versa. Of course, this does not mean that only ideological positivism is used to legitimize authoritarian regimes like Nazism. Different varieties of natural law theory—like those based on the "nature of things"—have been used for the same ignoble purpose. But it is clear that the doctrine that positive law whatever its content provides reasons for justifying actions and decisions constitutes the most direct and easy way conceivable to justify an authoritarian regime while it is in force. Even Bobbio's way of defending highly valuable covenants on human rights may be used straightforwardly for abhorrent purposes if those covenants were replaced by others which established obnoxious arrangements (imagine the international covenants which would have ensued if Hitler had succeeded in conquering Europe and what results the application of Bobbio's arguments to them would have had).

But in order not to look for remote or hypothetical examples, let me illustrate the grim face of ideological positivism with the case of Argentina. Since 1865, and especially since 1930 on until 1984, each time that there was a *coup d'état* in Argentina the Supreme Court recognized the power of the *de facto* regime to issue valid laws and the obligation of the population and officials to obey and to apply them on the basis that that regime had acquired the control of the coercive power of the State and was able to impose order on society. This recognition of legitimacy was at the beginning quite restricted, mostly to issuing executive decrees, but with time the power to enact legislation and even to modify and to suspend the Constitution was recognized on the mere basis of the *factum* of positive law. Genaro Carrio noted the logical oddity that we shall comment on later involved in the passage from physical to normative power incurred in these judicial decisions (Carrio 1973). In 1984, the Argentine Supreme Court changed its doctrine on the basis that the validity of the law was a normative predicate which could only be applied to those enacted democratically, so that only when the *de facto* laws were explicitly or implicitly ratified or not rejected by democratic bodies could they acquire validity. But the Supreme Court expanded by President Menem went back in 1990 to its old doctrine of clearly positivist inspiration (it said that whatever are our "affective or ideological attitudes" concerning military regimes we must recognize as a fact that they are able to enact valid laws; see Nino 1985, 1992).

Communitarianism may also develop in a quite unattractive way, even though none of the authors mentioned promotes that development. Despite the appeal of its realist vision of man, of the value of family and social links as grounds for special rights and duties, of the connection between values and social practices, each one of the distinguishing marks of communitarianism may generate, when it is developed in all its implications, a different aspect of a totalitarian vision of society.

The primacy of the good over individual rights allows for the justification of perfectionist policies which intends to impose ideals of excellence or personal virtue, even when individuals do not perceive them and thus do not subscribe to them. In effect, if rights are the only means to satisfy a certain conception of the good, why not prescind from them when that conception of the good may be more efficaciously materialized through other routes? Here it is also possible to allude to the example of Argentina, where military governments, backed by conservative sectors of the Catholic Church, had the invariable policy of coercing citizens into supposed ideals of virtue even with regard to private life. Thus, films and publications were censored even for adult exhibitions, deviant sexual behavior was persecuted, and even the ways in which people dressed or had their hair cut were overseen.

The idea that the social dimension is dominant in the conception of the good may lead one to justify sacrifices of individuals for the sake of promoting the well-being of society or the State conceived of in holistic terms. The glorification of particular links with social groups, like the family or the Nation, may serve as ground for collectivist, tribalist or nationalist attitudes which underlie many of the conflicts that humanity must endure, and which have come lately to the surface in Eastern and Western Europe. Here it is also useful to allude to the example of Argentina during military regimes: The so-called "dirty war against subversion," which led to the disappearance, death and torture of thousands of people, often unrelated to left-wing subversion, was carried out under the "doctrine of national security," which is a holistic conception based on the good of the "national being," the interests of whom were held to prevail over those of individuals, and were interpreted in a privileged way by certain groups like the armed forces or the Church. In a more circumscribed dimension, the idea that the primary good is that of associations like the family, to whom the rights of individuals must cede, was resorted to at that time by the Argentine Supreme Court in order to allow a kidney transplant from a girl to her brother, notwithstanding that because being a minor it was doubtful whether she had validly consented to it.

Lastly, the dependence of criticism on moral practice which is also one of the main aspects of communitarianism may lead to a conservative relativism that, on the one hand, is inept for solving conflicts among those who appeal to different traditions or conventions, and, on the other hand, does not permit the evaluations of those traditions and conventions in the context of a society, since the evaluation would presuppose social practices without counting with independent principles to discriminate between them. To give an extreme example again taken from the last dictatorship in Argentina: The military authorities of the Province of Cordoba prohibited the teaching of modern mathematics in schools, under the idea that it would train students in a degree of abstraction which could later on be expanded in other fields of thought, and thus, when applied to the political and moral realm, would create the risk of making people prone to criticize the traditions and conventions which define the national being (I am sorry for these rather truculent examples, but I think that it is important for those who nurture the germ of these outlooks in the midst of safe, liberal, havens to be aware of what sort of fire it is they are playing with).

Consequently, these two ugly faces which ideological positivism and communitarianism may present, instead of the noble faces of Bobbio or An-Na'im, may combine together to legitimize abhorrent regimes: Ideological positivism may justify their authoritarian origin, and communitarianism their totalitarian content.

V.

The second connection between the two positions which I want to mention is rather like the other side of the coin with regard to the former one: It has to do with some coincidence between vague but legitimate preoccupations which make plausible both legal positivism and communitarianism in their best versions. I mentioned earlier what are those preoccupations of positivism: The subjectivity and arbitrariness of decisions which affect social relationships if the factum of positive law were not held to bind those decisions and if they were thought to be either unavoidably radically groundless or grounded on non-graspable moral invocations. The terror of ideological positivists materializes in the image of a judge who leaves aside a clear text of the law and takes a decision which cannot be derived from a reasonable interpretation of it, either alleging that a decision against the law is as good as one according to it or invoking *his* moral values to disqualify the law and to decide directly according to those values. This is the terror of moralism.

If one digs deep into the concerns of many communitarians, I think that *some* of them (of course, not others which have to do with their perception that liberalism does not take into account ideals like patriotism, fraternity, personal commitments, etc.) are of a similar tenor. They think that liberalism, mainly in its Kantian variety, lends itself to subjective and arbitrary moral conclusions. This is so, first, because the accusation of Hegel against Kant that formal structures of practical reasoning are not enough for determining substantive moral conclusions still stands, and any pretension to derive those results must imply arbitrary logical jumps. Constraints like universability cannot avoid adopting opposite principles as long as we are committed to apply them universally, and the conception of noumenal beings which are abstracted from particular interests, conceptions of the good held by them and social circumstances are "too slender a basis" (to use

Rawls' own expression that communitarians would like to use not only against Kant but also against himself) to derive univocal moral principles. But, secondly and more important, liberalism seems to imply an individualist moral epistemology in which some "enlightened" individuals may come to the conclusion of what morality requires on the basis of assumptions of practical reasoning, even when those requirements apply to faraway people in time, space and customs, without regard to the collective practices of the people concerned themselves which result from their own experiences and struggles.

Thus, one strand of communitarianism is distinctively worried about the epistemic elitism which it perceives in liberalism. For instance, Michael Walzer (1981) inveighs against the new " philosopher-kings" who try to influence mainly judges and mainly in the exercise of judicial review about what is the true set of rights enshrined in the Constitution whatever the experience of the people in their political practices. This concern about elitism is not necessarily shared by ideological legal positivism. But elitism presupposes the wider phenomenon of subjectivism and arbitrariness and here is where the minds of one and the others meet. Therefore, when a typical morally inspired judge of the North American Supreme Court nullifies a statute on the basis that it violates the right of privacy—as in "Griswold"—the positivist and the communitarian may both complain in chorus: The positivist because she does not see that right consecrated within the four corners of the Constitution, the communitarians because they do not see that right to emerge as derived from a conception of the good embedded in the social practice of the relevant community. But they coincide not only in their complaints but in the fear that Justices are imposing arbitrarily their own subjective views of social morality on the rest of the community. I would conjoin the object of their respective fears under the label "liberal moralism."

What I would like to argue next is that, though this concern of both ideological positivists and communitarians about the subjectivity and arbitrariness involved in liberal moralism is quite justified, they give to it two different wrong solutions because of another feature they have in common. This time what they share is a serious philosophical misconception which explains why these positions may degenerate into obnoxious moral and political stands.

VI.

Let us begin with how ideological positivism, as manifested by positivism in action, incurs the philosophical misconception which I am imputing to both views.

There is an easy way to begin the diagnosis of what is wrong with ideological positivism: It just commits the so-called "naturalistic fallacy," that is, the fallacy of trying to derive norms of values from mere factual circumstances, or, perhaps more precisely, to try to justify decisions on the basis of facts which are compatible with either them or the opposite ones. Ideological positivism just believes that it is possible to justify a decision like "Peter should go to jail for having committed murder" by citing a description of a certain fact like "Legislator L has prescribed that those who commit murder should go to jail." But it is possible to assert sincerely the latter proposition and to adopt a contrary decision concerning Peter, the murderer, without incurring a logical or pragmatical contradiction. That shows that the descriptive proposition in question does not express a sufficient reason for the decision, that is, it is not irrational to accept it and not to decide to send Peter the murderer to jail when one could have done that.

The same holds for much that we expound on the descriptive content of the concept of legislator. For instance if we assume a further premise to the effect that a legislator is whoever may in fact issue prescriptions and be generally obeyed by the members of the group of addressees, perhaps because there is a social practice of obeying him or a class of persons with certain features to which he belongs, or perhaps because he has the actual capacity of putting in action a coercive apparatus to sanction non-compliers. All this may be added, and still it is not irrational to accept this description of the situation and to decide nevertheless not to comply with the prescription of the legislator by not punishing Peter.

Things are different if in the concept of legislator a normative or evaluative feature were included, as the feature that he is a legitimate authority, or somebody who should be obeyed, or somebody whose prescriptions have binding or obligatory force, or are valid in that sense. This difference will of course be spurious if all these properties were in the end reduced to spatio-temporal facts of the sort mentioned in the above paragraph. In this case, again the addition of these assumptions would not make the description to express a sufficient reason to act in a certain way. But if the properties in question were given by norms or value-judgements which were not accepted because of certain spatio-temporal facts and the conditions of their truth or existence were not reducible to those facts, now it would seem that there is some sort of inconsistency, at least under the clause that other things are equal, if one accepted that legislator L has prescribed p, that legislator L ought to be obeyed and that, nevertheless, p ought not to be done.

Therefore, ideological positivism commits some sort of logical error when assuming that a description of the issuing and observance of prescriptions, the conditions of existence of which are exhausted by some spatio-temporal facts constitutes by itself a sufficient reason for justifying decisions.

But this is still a quite superficial account of the mistake the ideological positivist commits. This is so because I think that the naturalist fallacy is not a proper fallacy in a logical sense. The impression that it is comes, I think, from the assumption that when it is said that a norm is derived from a factual description sometimes by norm is understood a prescription, that is, the *act* of formulating a normative-judgement with the intention that the formulation is taken as part of the reason to act on the part of the addressee (see my "Razones y prescripciones" in Nino 1985). It is clear that a prescription so conceived cannot derive from a descriptive proposition just because it is an act which cannot derive from any proposition whatsoever! But the content or the justification of a decision is not a prescription in this sense. It is a normative proposition which differs from others simply because it resorts to deontic predicates for qualifying action. Therefore, there is nothing *a priori* which would prevent them from deriving from purely descriptions of spatio-temporal facts.

In fact, I believe that the naturalistic fallacy is no more than a simple *non sequitur* given by the fact that there is no relevant connection between the predicates of the premises and those of the conclusion (like in "1.—All men are mortal. 2.—Socrates is a man. 3.—Therefore, Socrates is a philosopher").

This means that once the charge of logical fallacy is left aside, a deeper explanation is needed of why there is no relevant connection between the facts of issuing prescriptions by those in charge of power in a society and the bindingness of those prescriptions, given the fact that many sensible people have thought that there is indeed such connection.

I think that that explanation is provided by pointing out that ideological positivism misconceives the nature of legal discourse. It conceives of that discourse as an *insular* one, when in fact it is only part of a wider and integrated practical discourse which aims at determining moral reasons, that is, reasons which are accepted autonomously and that have other features like universability, generality, finality, *et cetera*. For me, it is crucial that we get right the nature of justificatory discourse, since all the ultimate intersubjective reasons we have for acting or deciding one way or the other in matters which may affect other people are those which we can infer from the assumptions of our social practice of giving reasons to each other (Nino 1991b, ch. 3; Nino 1989).

If ideological positivism were right, as perhaps it is right with regard to different cultures with quite diverse modalities of justificatory discourse, to say that some prescriptions have been enacted by those who have control of the coercive apparatus of society would put an end to all possible discussion and it would be irrational to accept that fact and to deny that one should act consequently. But this is not so, as we already saw. In legal discourse to say that some standard is *legal* is itself a reason, and not merely a description of a neutral fact, for accepting it and acting as it prescribes. This is what I think that Dworkin (1986) implies by his observation that disputes about what the law provides cannot be merely semantic or factual. But the reason for acting and deciding which consists in ascribing legal character to a certain standard cannot, ultimately, be in and of itself a legal reason. It must be an extra-legal reason, a reason which does not rely on authority and which thus, given some specificity of content, amounts to a moral reason.

The same can be shown if we ask ourselves how we can detect what standards operate as legal ones in practical reasoning. The plausible answers do not rely, as Kelsen proposed, on their content, but on the fact that they are accepted because they have been enacted by certain distinctive authorities. That is to say, the reasons why they are accepted in certain tokens of practical reasoning is what distinguishes legal standards from other standards accepted also in practical reasoning. But those reasons of acceptance of legal standards have a distinctive structure: They cannot consist in the mere description that they have been prescribed by certain authorities since this, as we saw, is compatible with not accepting the standards and, therefore, does not constitute a reason at all. Such a reason must consist in the description of the fact that somebody prescribed something plus a proposition to the effect that that body is legitimate in the manner that we saw previously. Given the fact that the latter proposition cannot be a description of a further fact of prescription, but should be a norm autonomously accepted, a moral norm, in the identification of legal norms, moral norms intervene. We identify legal norms in practical reasons for the fact that they are being derived in that reasoning from moral norms.

The dependence of legal discourse on wider moral discourse manifests itself in many ways. Mainly it emerges in critical cases in which the authority of the issuer of a legal prescription is put in question, like, for instance, in the case of usurpation of who was normally taken to be the ultimate authority, or when there is a conflict between different basic sources, or when a conflict between international and domestic law ensues, or when there are problems of interpretations which cannot be settled by legal standards since they are themselves affected by problems of interpretation. There are concepts, like that of *validity*, which serve as bridges between legal discourse and the wider justificatory discourse: To say that a law is valid is to say that it passes the tests of that wider discourse and that thus there are moral reasons for observing it. I have argued elsewhere that the effort of legal theorists to define these concepts in a way which they are made to operate without connection with the wider moral discourse led these theorists to many puzzles about problems like the contradiction of laws of different levels or the problem of reforming the very law which establishes how other laws and itself should be reforming. This is so because it becomes impossible to absorb in the reconstructed concept the features that they have when they are spontaneously used in order to connect legal discourse with the wider moral one.

It is here where there is a relevant connection between conceptual and ideological positivisms, as distinguished in the first section: Conceptual positivism defines the basic legal concepts without taking into account the immersion of legal discourse within the wider moral one: This happens, as we saw at the beginning with the very concept of law and here we saw that it occurs with the concept of validity. Even when conceptual positivism does not assert or presuppose with this that legal discourse is insular, it is hard to see what would be the use of those concepts in justificatory contexts if it were not in the attempt to develop an autonomous legal discourse. Therefore, while conceptual positivism is in itself inert and innocuous, it provides the tools for positivism in action, which turns itself ideological.

To summarize, ideological positivism misconceives legal discourse, because it sees it as autonomous and insular, when in fact it is dependent on and it is part of a wider moral discourse. In this misconception of legal discourse, ideological positivism views it as substituting moral discourse. The attempted substitution ascribes to the supposed "legal reasons" some of the features of moral ones, like finality, but not others, like generality and universability. Of course, the attempt of substitution fails since basic discourses are not transformed and replaced at will but are the most fundamental aspect of whole cultures, if not of all cultures. Curiously enough, positivism which seems to be so respectful of the *facta* behind some norms ignores the very basic fact of how normative discourse is constituted in our culture.

VII.

I believe that communitarianism incurs in essentially the same mistake as ideological positivism of misapprehending the nature of our justificatory discourse, for much of that misapprehension has here some other particularities.

One of the aspects of our social practice of moral discussion is that it allows us to criticize any social institution or practice, including, of course, itself— as is done by the very communitarian authors. This is because, as we saw before, arguments of authority religious, legal or *conventional* are never final and conclusive within our practice of giving reasons to each other. All authority should be justified on the basis of principles which are not themselves accepted on the basis of authority. This, of course, applies to traditions and conventions. Therefore, communitarians are wrong in thinking that some social traditions or conventions may be exempted from moral criticism, as may be shown immediately as soon as they point out to any real example of a convention or tradition which would be so immunized from critical appraisal.

Secondly, it is not true that the post-Enlightenment practice of moral discussion, the assumptions of which we all, including communitarians, share, pretends to allow for the derivation of rights without a previous conception of the good. As I tried to show elsewhere (Nino 1991b, ch. 5), the practice of giving reasons to each other presupposes the value of acting on the basis of reasons freely accepted and this constitutes the value of autonomy, in the Kantian sense. From this general value of moral autonomy, which refers to the value of acting on the basis of any moral principle freely accepted, may be inferred the more specific and unrestrained value of personal autonomy, which refers to the value of acting on the basis of self-referential moral principles and ideals (acting which unlike that based on interpersonal moral principles cannot be restricted for the sake of preserving the autonomy of others). Therefore, the liberalism implicit in our practice of moral discussion is not entirely neutral towards conceptions of the good, as communitarians object, but it presupposes the good of autonomy. Now, it is true that autonomy is a special kind of good: It involves the permission to each person to search freely for other goods, even some which may be antagonistic to the very good of autonomy (which is nevertheless realized when that other "good" has been achieved freely by the very person concerned). Communitarians are wrong in asserting that liberals who rely on assumptions of our practice of moral discussion intend to derive rights out of the blue without any conception of the good, and are doubly wrong when they introduce, contravening those assumptions, supposed goods which preclude that of autonomy. Of course, autonomy requires some pre-conditions which allow people to choose and materialize their own conception of the good and personal ideals; among those pre-conditions there is, of course, the membership of social groups: But if that membership is valued just because it is an instrument of autonomy, it should be made as voluntary as possible in order not to frustrate the good which it serves.

Of course, our practice of moral discourse does not only assume the value of autonomy, which is not fully acknowledged by communitarians. It also assumes the requirement of impartiality which qualifies the former value. When we discuss with each other we try to determine which is the principle which an ideal arbiter would accept in order to solve the conflict. This includes the requirements of generality and universability, since we do not think that impartial principles may make differences on the basis of circumstances identified by proper names or definite descriptions or those which are applied differently to cases which do not differ in properties taken into account by those very principles. This is what commits us to apply the same principles we apply to ourselves to faraway peoples in time and space, at least if it is not shown that they differ in circumstances which those principles make relevant. Contrary to what Rhonda Howard asserts in the passage quoted earlier, we do not think that the mere fact of living in Africa, for instance, gives somebody a different moral status, though some circumstances like starvation, ignorance, illness, etc. may make a difference to the implications of general and universal principles. Communitarians are never clear about what are the principles of their traditions that they refuse to apply to others and why. In a less philosophical context, An-Na'im alleges, as we saw, that the punishment prescribed by the Qu'ran should not be applied to non-Muslims, but the general principle cannot surely be that everybody should be treated according to the principles in which she believes (when these are intersubjective principles), since in that case somebody who did not believe in property could not be punished for theft at all!

Of course, the assumptions of autonomy and impartiality implicit in the social practice of moral discourse lead to a certain conception of the person, according to which the identity of a person does not depend on the ends she chooses or the wishes she happens to have, the identity of each person is separable from that of each other, and that identity is not affected by her membership of one or other social group. It is no use for communitarians to make fun of this conception as unrealistic considering all we know of actual people, since this conception is not anthropological but normative: It is just an abstraction of the normative requirements of autonomy and impartiality and determines what sort of reasons we can give to others are valid and what are not. For instance, the idea of separation of persons involved in this conception does not deny that persons are deeply attached to each other and the good of others may be central for the interests of each of us; it only implies that we cannot give as sole reason for harming the autonomy of somebody that this serves to grant greater autonomy to others.

In sum, like ideological positivists, communitarians contradict their own main tenet: In this case, that main tenet is to take into account social practices in the derivation of moral principles. But they do not consider the assumptions of the very practice of moral discussion that we all share. It is not logically possible both to criticize our culture for features of its practice of moral discussion—like autonomy and universal impartiality—, and to advocate taking into account cultural specificity. It just happens that the specificity of our culture is not to take into account cultural specificities in making basic moral judgements!

Of course, this way of shooting communitarianism with its own weapon does not involve adopting that weapon ourselves. The argument in favor of extending human rights universally is that the fact of being Muslim or of living in Iran is not a relevant property for distinguishing people with regard to the enjoyment of those rights; it is not the fact that justificatory discourse of our culture relies on universal impartiality. This means that somebody like An-Na'im could not retort that, as the assumptions of the discourse of *his* culture admits that cultural diversity makes a moral difference, he is justified in concluding that some penalties are not degrading when applied to Muslims and they are when applied to other people. What he would be saying would not be intelligible to us, since that would be something different from the perfectly reasonable description that Muslims consider those penalties not to be degrading; he would be saying that they *are not* degrading for the mere fact that the person to whom they are applied happens to be Muslim. Still this might make sense to us if what is implied is that everybody should be treated according to his own moral or religious ideas; however, as we saw, this cannot be what it is meant, besides the fact that this judgement itself does not seem to be relative to some religious or moral affiliation. Perhaps, the statement that basic moral judgements should vary with cultural specificity may be intelligible to those with a different conceptual apparatus from that involved in our culture; but perhaps it is intelligible to no-one since it infringes on some non-variable requirement of practical thinking.

Though communitarianism incurs the same mistake as ideological positivism of misconceiving the nature of justificatory discourse, the misconception runs this time in the opposite direction to that of the former case: I said that ideological positivism treats legal discourse as if it were the whole of moral discourse, and not a mere specialized part of it. Well, communitarianism treats the whole of moral discourse as if it were its legal province: It conceives of it as one in which one may conclude that what is permitted or prohibited may vary according to borders which are given by social conventions and traditions.

VIII.

What about the legitimate preoccupation of both positivists and communitarians that liberal moralism leads to the subjectivity, arbitrariness, and elitism of some people—scholars, judges, leaders of powerful countries, heads of international agencies—who would impose universally and uniformly their "moral inspiration" about the proper extent, balance and application of human rights, without taking into account the experiences, wishes, and practices of the very peoples concerned?

I think that what is being raised here is not an ontological but an epistemic concern and that it should be tackled in its own terms. That is, the legitimate preoccupation put forth is not about whether human rights are universal but how we know what human rights are there, what is the proper balance between them when they are in conflict, which are the duties which correspond to them, what acts in what circumstances infringe on those duties, *et cetera*.

My own view is that the exercise of the very practice of moral discussion by the people concerned with a conflict or controversy and the consensus which is reached as a result of that exercise have epistemic power for indicating what is the right solution for intersubjective moral problems as those mentioned about the extent of human rights. I believe that if all the people involved in a conflict about the scope of different rights and about which acts violate them deliberate and reach a certain agreement about the conflict there is a strong likelihood that his would be the solution that an impartial arbitrator would have reached.

Elsewhere (Nino 1991a), I have argued that this epistemic value extends, though in a diminished way, to a democratic process which substitutes the original practice of moral discussion, unanimous consensus by majority rule, when a time for adopting a certain solution must be settled and there is a need for not giving veto power to a minority in favor of the status quo. This epistemic value of the democratic process—the basis of which I cannot explain here—does not involve infallibility but only more confiability than any other method for taking collective decisions, it is relative to the satisfaction of certain conditions and to the degree of its satisfaction, and it applies in general to the overall results of the democratic process and not to each one of its decisions (so that there is a reason to accept each one, even when one is sure that a specific one of them is wrong, if the likelihood of having right solutions is to be maximized).

I think that this resort to democracy about the extent, balance, and modes of violations of human rights is what prevents the elitism, subjectivism and arbitrariness which positivists like Bobbio and communitarians perceive behind liberal moralism. In the national sphere, except when the preconditions for the value of the democratic process, which constitute a kind of *a priori* rights, are in danger, the determination of the scope and weight of rights should be left to the democratic practice of the people and should not be tampered with *dicta* from an aristocratic bench. In the international sphere, external pressures may be much needed for reaching acceptable degrees of respect of human dignity, but those pressures, when possible, should be rather directed to make sure that the people concerned discuss and negotiate among themselves about which duties are to be fulfilled in support of human rights and which acts infringe on it, rather than intervening directly to impose standards of behavior. I think that the model of external humanitarian intervention is more the one going on in South Africa rather than what was done in the Gulf war.

This public deliberation about the extent of human rights and the range of their violations is probably what An-Na'im has in mind when referring in his works to internal and external exchanges, quite apart from the relativist way in which he puts it. In fact his example of cruel, degrading and inhuman punishment illustrates so perfectly well my point that it is worth dwelling briefly on it before ending this paper.

I have problems with the example of the penalty of cutting off the hands of thieves because in other works (see, e.g., Nino 1983) I advanced a theory of punishment which does not seem to exclude it. That theory is based on the requirements that punishment should be a rational means of social protection (which requires that it should be an efficacious and economic way of preventing less harms than those involved in it) and that it should be consented to by the individual on whom it is imposed (which requires that the individual commits voluntarily an act knowing that the liability to punishment is a necessary normative consequence of that act, however much he might hope that it would not be actually imposed). I have excluded the possibility of justifying capital punishment, not only because the requisites of efficacy and economy are hardly met in this case according to empirical accounts, but mainly because the consent of the individual cannot justify excluding him from the community of public deliberation which is the source of all justification. But this rationale does not apply to mutilations like those ordered by the Qu'ran. So how can I deal satisfactorily with this punishment, that many, including me, find abhorrent?

The first thing to notice is that our feeling of abhorrency towards these mutilations may well be matched by possible similar feelings of other people towards our usual punishments: We cannot discard that people from faraway tribes, accustomed to more direct chastisements, may have the same chilling feelings when observing our prison system, with all its grimness, discipline, and bureaucratic coldness. How can this be explained without falling in relativism about the principles for justifying punishment.

I think that principles that the ones that I have defended leave enough leeway as to allow for different solutions adopting through the democratic practice of the people concerned. First, the requirement of prudential protection of society depends on the preferences and feelings of people in different ways. If in one society most people feel much more aggrieved and humiliated by some sort of deprivation than by another, the harm involved in the former may be uneconomical, in the sense that the same beneficial results may perhaps be achieved with the lesser harm, while in another society the calculus may be the opposite because of the different feelings of people. Besides, if people in a certain society prefer mutilation to jail, when in another society the general preference goes the other way, this also affects the calculus of the efficaciousness of punishment. Second, there is a non-moral feeling of abhorrency which varies from society to society and laws imposing punishment, as any other laws, should respect this: If in a certain society people abhor eating dogs or rats, while in other social groups this is taken as a treat, this should be taken into account in legal measures. The idea of officially mutilating or flogging a human being may provoke in a society this sort of non-moral feelings of abhorrency, the same as in another society may be provoked by the idea of people being locked in state cells; these varying social feelings should be respected according to non-varying principles for justifying punishment. These varying preference and feelings which affect the justification of imposing specific penalities, even accepting invariable requirements for that justification, are best processed in a participatory deliberation in which all the people concerned may express them (as well as to estimate whether there are typical situations in which the consent of the individuals to liability to punishment is vitiated because they are subject to unequal social conditioning).

This may give some satisfaction to An-Na'im's concern about the variability of the idea of degrading, cruel or inhuman punishment. However, the satisfaction should be quite limited, since in the particular example he gives the support of the penalty by the democratic process is rather dubious: First, most countries in which this kind of punishment is applied are not precisely models of democracy. Second, even if they were, they are theocratic countries in which collective decisions—like those imposing those punishments—are taken on the basis of ideals of personal excellence, infringing on personal autonomy. Third, laws about what punishments to impose cannot be based on those ideals of excellence of religious inspiration not only because that infringes on personal autonomy but also because democracy has only epistemic value with regard to intersubjective ideals, the validity of which is based on impartiality and not on other authority, like a religious one. It is quite probable that, if the societies in which hand-cutting is now seen as acceptable punishment became, as they should, more democratic and secular, their attitude towards this kind of punishment would change (as occurred in other predominantly Muslim countries which underwent the process of democratization and secularization).

At any rate, I think that this combination between an objective interpersonal morality, as the provider of ultimate reasons for action, based on the assumptions of the practice of moral deliberation, and the epistemic value which accrues to the varying results of the democratic process absorbs what is legitimate of the concerns of positivists and communitarians, avoiding their implications which may lead to endorsing totalitarian schemes. As ideological positivists aspire, some legal enactments provide reasons for action, though this applies only to the democratic ones and the reasons they provide are rather reasons to believe that there are reasons to act. As communitarians emphasize the scope, balance, patterns of violation of rights are determined by social practice, though not any practice would do: It must be a practice of collective deliberation, complying with pre-conditions—some of which constitute *a priori* rights—and aiming at discovering the extent of universal moral principles involved in justification.

University of Buenos Aires
Faculty of Law and Social Sciences
Avenida Figueroa
1007 Buenos Aires
Argentina

References

An-Na'im, Abdullahi A. 1992. Toward a Cross-Cultural Approach to Defining International Standards of Human Rights. In *Human Rights in Cross Cultural Pespectives. A Quest for Consensus*. Ed. Abdullahi A. An-Na'im. Philadelphia: University of Pennsylvania Press.

Bobbio, Norberto. 1990. Sul fondamento dei diritti dell'uomo. In Norberto Bobbio, *L'età dei diritti*. Turin: Einaudi (first ed. 1965: *Rivista internazionale di filosofia del diritto*: 301–9).

Carrio, Genaro R. 1970. *Principios jurídicos y positivismo jurídico*. Buenos Aires: Abeledo-Perot.

———. 1973. *Sobre los limites del lenguaje normativo*. Buenos Aires: Astrea.

Dworkin, Ronald D. 1986. *Law's Empire*. Cambridge, Mass.: Belknap Press.
Hampshire, Stuart. 1983. *Morality and Conflict*. Oxford: Blackwell.
Howard, Rhoda E. 1992. Dignity, Community and Human Rights. In *Human Rights in Cross Cultural Perspectives. A Quest for Consensus*. Ed. Abdullahi A. An-Na'im. Philadelphia: University of Pennsylvania Press.
Kelsen, Hans. 1975. *What is Justice? Justice, Law and Politics in the Mirror of Science*. Berkeley: University of California Press.
MacIntyre, Alasdair C. 1981. *After Virtue*. Notre Dame, Ind.: University of Notre Dame Press.
Nino, Carlos S. 1983. A Consensual Theory of Punishment. *Philosophy & Public Affairs* 3.
———. 1985. *La validez del derecho*. Buenos Aires: Astrea.
———. 1989. *El constructivismo ético*. Madrid: Centro de Estudios Constitucionales.
———. 1991a. The Epistemic Value of Democracy. *Ratio Juris* 1: 36–51.
———. 1991b. *The Ethics of Human Rights*. Oxford: Clarendon.
———. 1992. *Fundamentos de derecho constitucional*. Buenos Aires: Astrea.
Ross, Alf. 1958. *On Law and Justice*. London: Stevens.
Sandel, Michael. 1982. *Liberalism and the Limits of Justice*. Cambridge: University Press.
Taylor, Charles. 1985. *Philosophical Papers*. 2 vols. Cambridge: University Press.
Walzer, Michael. 1981. Philosophy and Democracy. *Political Theory* 3: 379–99.
———. 1983. *Spheres of Justice. A Defence of Pluralism and Equality*. New York: Basic Books.
Williams, Bernard. 1985. *Ethics and the Limits of Philosophy*. Cambridge, Mass.: Harvard University Press.
Wolf, Susan. 1982. Moral Saints. *The Journal of Philosophy* 8.

[18]

Political Participation as a Human Right

Henry J. Steiner*

In the postwar construction of human rights law, the concept of political participation has been an indispensable building block. The right to such participation figures prominently in the full range of international instruments: declarations, resolutions, regional and universal treaties. Countries with markedly different political systems have termed political participation the vital human right. In its absence, it is said, all others fall to a perilous existence.[1] Governments invoke it to justify their own political systems and to delegitimate those of their opponents. National groups struggling for political participation draw broad international support. No one doubts that success in their struggles would open avenues to basic change.

For a right regarded as foundational, political participation suffers from serious infirmities. The norms defining it are either vague or, when explicit, bear sharply disputed meanings. Within the framework of human rights law, the right expresses less a vital concept meant to universalize certain practices than a bundle of concepts, sometimes complementary but sometimes antagonistic. On occasion this human right serves as a universal rallying cry against a friendless outlaw nation. But more often it becomes another weapon of rhetorical battle, a convenient, even authoritative concept through which each of the world's ideological blocs, infusing the right with its own understandings, attacks the others for violating those understandings.

I intend to explore this controversy over the character of the right, both its reasons and consequences. My central concern is whether this right of political participation, in the light of its vagueness and the plural meanings attributed to it, expresses *any* shared ideal, or serves any useful purpose in the developing international law of human rights. Such questions suggest a broader issue. Although distinctive in some respects, the right of political participation forms part of a complex of related rights set forth in the international instruments. It shares with them an essential characteristic of the new human rights norms—the claim to a universal validity, if not quite efficacy. That

* Professor of Law and Director of Human Rights Program, Harvard Law School. I owe special thanks to Lewis Sargentich for his criticism. I benefited from his comments, and from those of Harold Berman and Detlev Vagts, on a draft of this article.

1. In Wesberry v. Sanders, 376 U.S. 1, 17 (1964), a decision finding malapportionment in Congressional districts in violation of the Constitution, the Court stated: "No right is more precious in a free country than that of having a voice in the election of those who make the laws under which, as good citizens, we must live. Other rights, even the most basic, are illusory if the right to vote is undermined."

claim is frequently disputed, and a study of the right of political participation illustrates the larger debate about human rights norms' absolute or relative character.

The article examines the diverse understandings of this international-law norm as such, rather than the postwar experience of participation among the liberal democracies, communist states and third-world states which have agreed to observe it, or which in any event view themselves as meeting its requirements. My discussion therefore stresses the theories and ideologies about political participation which have shaped those understandings. Although attentive to ways of institutionalizing those ideologies, it says little about the actual practices of states—practices which may faithfully reflect or flagrantly contradict an official theory of participation. The discussion bypasses such historical and empirical issues as the influence of class on political participation, the effects of heightened participation on a country's political stabilty or economic development, or the role of participation in legitimating a regime.

The article first locates the right to political participation within the conceptual framework of human rights instruments. It then examines the norms expressing this right that are included in two principal international instruments of universal scope: the Universal Declaration of Human Rights, and the International Covenant on Civil and Political Rights.[2] Those norms grant citizens the right to take part, directly or through representatives, in the conduct of public affairs and government, and to vote at genuine periodic elections based on universal suffrage and the secret ballot. My discussion emphasizes these two different ways in which the international norms express citizens' right to political participation: the relatively vague and abstract right to take part in the conduct of public affairs or government, and the relatively specific right to vote in elections. It builds upon that distinction to explore different modes of political participation. The nature of and relationship between the two components of the international norms constitute the integrating theme for the article as a whole.

After examining the basic norms and some issues raised during their drafting periods, I describe relevant themes in the contemporary debate within the liberal democracies about the nature of political participation, in order to indicate ways in which the international human rights norms absorb, or reflect, the distinct theories about participation and ideologies about government which figure in that debate. My description contrasts so-called thin, protective and representation theories of democratic participation with strong, developmental and par-

2. For the relevant texts of these two instruments, see *infra* at Sec. IIA.

ticipation theories. Discussion follows of the human rights norms relationship to the radically different theories of political participation within the Communist-Party states. Rather than attempting to embrace the many variations within the communist world, that discussion concentrates illustratively on the Soviet Union.

My method is to portray and compare these theories—and, to some extent, related practices—in the liberal democracies and communist states within the conceptual framework suggested by the human rights norms. Both description and analysis are organized in terms of the distinction between the "take part" and "elections" clauses in those norms. A concluding section speculates about the role of universal norms of political participation in so fractious a world.

I. POLITICAL PARTICIPATION IN THE CONTEXT OF OTHER RIGHTS

As background for an examination of the right to political participation, the article here situates that right within the doctrinal and conceptual framework of human rights instruments. My emphasis will be on instruments of universal scope. It then suffices to draw upon the two most significant: the Universal Declaration of Human Rights of 1948 ("Universal Declaration"),[3] spiritual parent of and inspiration for many human rights treaties,[4] and the International Covenant on Civil and Political Rights ("International Covenant"),[5] effective in 1976. The International Covenant has eighty-six state parties representing all the world's regions and ideological blocs.[6] Each party

3. G.A. Res. 217A (III), U.N. Doc. A/810 (1948) [hereinafter the *Universal Declaration*].

4. The Universal Declaration was unanimously approved by the General Assembly. Together with the International Covenant on Civil and Political Rights, *infra* note 5, and the International Covenant on Economic, Social, and Cultural Rights, *infra* note 32, it forms what has come to be known as the "international bill of rights." *See generally* THE INTERNATIONAL BILL OF RIGHTS: THE COVENANT ON CIVIL AND POLITICAL RIGHTS (L. Henkin ed. 1981) [hereinafter THE INTERNATIONAL BILL OF RIGHTS]. Approved as a statement of principle that was not meant to bind states legally, the Universal Declaration is acquiring a more ambiguous status as an instrument that is formally relevant to the international law of human rights. Several arguments have contributed to this change in status, including: (1) The Universal Declaration should be understood as a clarification of the requirements of Articles 55 and 56 of the United Nations Charter. Article 55(c) enjoins the UN to promote "universal respect for, and observance of, human rights" and members pledge in Article 56 to take action to achieve the purposes of Article 55; (2) The inclusion of many of the Universal Declaration's provisions in several broadly accepted human rights treaties, together with the practice of invoking it in argument among states, give the Universal Declaration the status of customary international law.

5. G.A. Res. 2200, 21 U.N. GAOR Supp. (No. 16) 52, U.N. Doc. A/6316 (1966) [hereinafter the *International Covenant*].

6. The number is accurate as of September 1, 1987. The parties include Argentina, Chile, Mexico, Nicaragua; Australia, Canada; Federal Republic of Germany, France, Spain, United Kingdom; Czechoslovakia, German Democratic Republic, Poland, U.S.S.R.; Gabon, Kenya, Zaire, Zambia; Egypt, Iran, Iraq, Jordan; India, Japan, Sri Lanka. CENTRE FOR HUMAN RIGHTS, UNITED NATIONS, HUMAN RIGHTS: STATUS OF INTERNATIONAL INSTRUMENTS 12 (Supp.

"undertakes to . . . ensure to all individuals within its territory . . . the rights recognized" in it.[7]

From the diverse perspectives of the International Covenant's parties, the defined rights may be understood to be rooted in natural law or positive enactment. They may be justified by liberal postulates or by the imperative of socialist construction. These different beliefs about the rights' origins and justifications are not, however, central to my discussion. For this article's purposes, it will be more useful to group the rights declared in the International Covenant in five categories placed on a spectrum.[8] On one end are those rights over which a near-universal consensus exists, at least a formal, verbal consensus about the content of such rights. States charged with violating these rights do not seek to justify their conduct as consistent with human rights norms.

At the other end of the spectrum are those rights whose meanings and purposes are disputed, and whose content will consequently vary with the forum in which they are invoked. States accused of violating such rights may deny the accusation by advancing their different understanding of the relevant norm. Such disputes about meaning evidence the fundamental significance of these rights for the different political orders to which they are relevant.

At every point in the spectrum differences may arise over the meaning of a treaty provision. The right to life,[9] broadly understood to bar extrajudicial killings, would characteristically be placed on the "consensus" side of the spectrum. But it is also interpreted by some to condemn abortion, or to impose obligations on governments to assure their populations of the minimum of welfare which makes life human.[10] No state formally dissents from the bar on torture and "cruel,

---

1987) [hereinafter STATUS OF INTERNATIONAL INSTRUMENTS]. In 1978, President Carter transmitted the International Covenant to the Senate for its advice and consent to ratification. For a summary of the President's transmittal letter and the reasons for seeking certain reservations, prepared by the Office of the Legal Adviser, United States Department of State, see 72 AM. J. INT'L L. 620 (1978). None of these proposed reservations involved the International Covenant's clause on political participation. The consent of the Senate was not obtained during that session of Congress and has not subsequently been sought by the Reagan Administration.

7. *International Covenant*, *supra* note 5, art. 2(1).

8. The rights divided among these five categories do not cover all those declared by the International Covenant. Some of the excluded articles treat issues of nationality such as free movement and expulsion of aliens (Articles 12–13), matters involving the family and children (Articles 23–24), rights of members of minorities to enjoy their own culture (Article 27), and most problematic and contentious of all, the right of "peoples" to self-determination (Article 1). *See International Covenant*, *supra* note 5.

9. *International Covenant*, *supra* note 5, art. 6(1) ("Every human being has the inherent right to life.").

10. With respect to abortion, see generally M.A. GLENDON, ABORTION AND DIVORCE IN WESTERN LAW 10–62 (1987). With respect to welfare rights, compare the remarks of Bhagwati, J., in Francis Coralie v. Union Territory of Delhi, A.I.R. (S.C.) 746, 752–53 (1981), referring

inhuman or degrading treatment,"[11] but the boundaries of that prohibition—whether certain governmental conduct is degrading—have no certain location.[12]

My five categories cannot then effectively distinguish rights enjoying unbroken agreement over meanings from rights bearing several interpretations. Rather, the categories move along the spectrum from relative consensus to a divergence over meanings which has systemic and structural implications for a society. That divergence does not bear simply on the scope of a particular right, such as the extent of protection against torture, or on a relatively discrete aspect of social life, such as abortion. It cuts to the core of a society's political order.

The first category consists of the traditional hands-off or negative rights which lie at the heart of the liberal tradition's commitment to individual autonomy and choice, and hence to limited and controllable government. Countries rejecting liberal democracy's stress on individual rights, pluralism and limited government also profess adherence to these rights.[13] Many negative rights in the International Covenant stress the individual's physical integrity: rights not to be arbitrarily deprived of life, or not to be subjected to torture, slavery, arbitrary arrest or detention.[14] Other rights assure spiritual autonomy and intellectual integrity by protecting freedom of thought and conscience.[15] Although the International Covenant permits states, under extreme conditions and after a proclamation of public emergency, to derogate in carefully limited ways from many rights, most of those in the first category are excepted and treated as non-derogable.[16]

National political systems vary greatly in the adequacy or even availability of remedies for victims of violations of such rights. International remedial paths remain fragile, often illusory.[17] In these cir-

---

to the "right to life enshrined in Article 21" of the Indian Constitution. He asks "whether the right to life is limited only to protection of limb or faculty . . . . We think that [it] includes the right to life with human dignity and all that goes along with it, namely, the bare necessaries of life such as adequate nutrition, clothing and shelter . . . ."

11. *International Covenant*, *supra* note 5, art. 7.

12. *See* Committee on Int'l Human Rights, *Convention against Torture and other Cruel, Inhuman or Degrading Treatment or Punishment*, 42 THE RECORD 235, 238–41 (1987) (publication of the Association of the Bar of the City of New York) (discussing definitions of vital terms such as "torture" or "degrading").

13. *See, e.g.*, CONSTITUTION OF THE USSR arts. 54–58, *reprinted in* BASIC DOCUMENTS ON THE SOVIET LEGAL SYSTEM 3 (W.E. Butler ed. and trans. 1983) [hereinafter BASIC DOCUMENTS].

14. *International Covenant*, *supra* note 5, arts. 6–9. *See* C. FRIED, RIGHT AND WRONG 108–14 (1978) (discussing negative and positive rights).

15. *International Covenant*, *supra* note 5, art. 18.

16. *Id.* art. 4. The public emergency must be one which "threatens the life of the nation," and the measures in derogation are permitted only "to the extent strictly required by the exigencies of the situation." Articles 6–8 and Article 18 are among those from which a state cannot derogate. *Id.*

17. *See* GUIDE TO INTERNATIONAL HUMAN RIGHTS PRACTICE (H. Hannum ed. 1984);

cumstances, consensus over the content of a norm hardly assures broad observance. Indeed, systematic violations of rights to personal security, rights so basic that they are recognized as part of customary international law,[18] have provided the postwar world with the vilest examples of inhumane conduct. In countries like Cambodia and Uganda, governments committed mass slaughter, whereas in others like Argentina or Chile, they brutalized targeted groups to protect their rule.

Nonetheless, such governments do not advance legal justifications for their murders and torture, as they might to defend against certain charges of group discrimination or censorship. Rather they try to shield their conduct from the public eye, or accuse their critics of distortion, or attribute responsibility to nongovernmental terrorists, or simply bear the label of outlaw as they ignore foreign censure.[19] Even if governments claim moral justification for such conduct because of temporary exigent circumstances, they do not dispute what a full realization of the right would entail.

A second group of rights, also enjoying a formal consensus about their cross-cultural validity, assure procedural fairness when a government curtails individual liberty. The International Covenant regulates the means of detention, requires humane treatment for the accused and their access to courts, spells out procedural protections for defendants in criminal trials, and provides that arrests and convictions shall be in accordance with existing laws.[20] Again, nations violating these requirements do not justify their conduct by interpreting the pertinent norms to permit, say, coerced confessions or staged trials.

The third category involves anti-discrimination norms. Although expressed in terms of individual rights, it implicitly addresses groups. The individual is entitled to nondiscriminatory treatment notwithstanding identification with a group that is defined in racial, gender, religious or political terms.[21] Such norms respond to liberal ideology's stress on individuals' civil and political equality and on the state's

---

Robertson, *The Implementation System: International Measures*, in THE INTERNATIONAL BILL OF RIGHTS, *supra* note 4, at 332; Sohn, *Human Rights: Their Implementation and Supervision by the United Nations*, in 2 HUMAN RIGHTS IN INTERNATIONAL LAW 369 (T. Meron ed. 1984).

18. *See* Filartiga v. Pena-Irala, 630 F.2d 876, 880–85 (2d Cir. 1980); 1 RESTATEMENT OF FOREIGN RELATIONS LAW OF THE UNITED STATES (REV.) § 702 (Tent. Draft No. 6, 1985).

19. *See* AMNESTY INTERNATIONAL, TORTURE IN THE EIGHTIES (1984). This report contains accounts of torture from 98 countries. "While governments universally and collectively condemn torture, more than a third of the world's governments have used or tolerated torture or ill-treatment of prisoners in the 1980s. . . . No state legalizes torture in its constitution or penal code . . . ." *Id.* at 2, 4.

20. *International Covenant*, *supra* note 5, arts. 9–10, 14–15.

21. *Id.* arts. 2(1), 3, 14(1), 24(1), 25. For a description of United Nations actions aimed at the elimination of discrimination, including descriptions of conventions addressing specifically racial and gender discrimination, see UNITED NATIONS, UNITED NATIONS ACTION IN THE FIELD OF HUMAN RIGHTS 39–124 (1983).

neutrality. They also figure prominently in the ideology of communist states.[22]

Equal-protection norms have been employed to censure a range of legally instituted practices among the International Covenant's parties. Apartheid draws near universal indictment.[23] But moral judgments about systemic discriminations based on, say, gender or religion differ among cultures. Imbedded in long tradition and viewed as natural attributes of a state's culture, such practices may be justified in terms of premises and values rejected by most of the international community.[24] Here one encounters not simply divergent practices but explicit disagreement over the content and reach of the international norm itself.

In the fourth category of expressive rights, dispute sharpens about the reach and purpose of norms. The International Covenant recognizes the problematic character of these rights to free speech, assembly and association by qualifying them in broad, open-textured ways. Beyond permitting derogation from them during periods of public emergency,[25] the Covenant cautions that the right to freedom of expression "carries with it special duties and responsibilities," and hence may be subjected to restrictions that "are necessary . . . [f]or the protection of national security or of public order (*ordre public*), or of public health or morals."[26] Similarly, restrictions on freedoms of assembly and association are permitted if "necessary in a democratic society in the interests of national security or public safety, public order (*ordre public*), the protection of public health or morals or the protection of the rights and freedoms of others."[27]

---

22. *See, e.g.*, CONSTITUTION OF THE USSR, *supra* note 13, preamble, ch. 1, arts. 1–9.

23. The International Convention on the Suppression and Punishment of the Crime of *Apartheid*, Nov. 30, 1973, 1015 U.N.T.S. 244 (effective in 1976), had 86 state parties as of September 1, 1987. STATUS OF INTERNATIONAL INSTRUMENTS, *supra* note 6, at 12.

24. The status of women in Arab countries illustrates such problems. Despite significant changes in several countries under Western influence and the pressures of modernization, deep institutionalized differences in treatment of men and women remain in place. A 1985 decision of Kuwait's highest religious lawmaking authority illustrates such differences in an extreme way, implicating other human rights in the same measure, by decreeing that Moslem women be denied the vote and candidacy for parliament. "The nature of election processes befits men, who are endowed with ability and expertise . . . . Islam does not permit women to forfeit their basic commitments" of bearing and rearing children. Arab Times, July 23, 1985, at 1 (English language version), *reprinted in* JOINT PUBLICATIONS RESEARCH SERVICE, Aug. 15, 1985, at 57. The characteristic examples of discrimination between men and women in the contemporary world involve family law. *See generally* MINORITY RIGHTS GROUP, ARAB WOMEN, Report No. 27 (rev. ed. 1983). In addition to the provisions of the International Covenant, the broadly accepted *Convention on the Elimination of All Forms of Discrimination Against Women*, G.A. Res.34/180, U.N. Doc. A/RES/34/180 (1980) (effective Sept. 3, 1981) forbids such discrimination.

25. *See supra* note 16.

26. *International Covenant*, *supra* note 5, art. 19(3).

27. *Id.* arts. 21, 22(2).

Because of their level of generality, such qualifications of expressive rights do not necessarily offend liberal democracies, all of which limit these rights in ways consistent with the noted criteria. Differences of viewpoint concern less the need for such qualifications than the ways in which they are understood and applied. Conceptions as malleable as national security or public order lend themselves to extreme applications.[28] But given the differences in political systems among the International Covenant's parties, and the direct bearing of expressive freedoms on political participation, disagreements inevitably become explicit. Typical of many communist states, the Soviet Constitution guarantees citizens the rights of free speech, press and assembly "[i]n accordance with the interests of the working people and with a view to strengthening the socialist system . . . ."[29] Citizens have the right to form associations to further political initiatives and satisfy their interests "[i]n accordance with the aims of communist construction . . . ."[30] On their face, such restraints reach well beyond a liberal understanding of the qualifications in the International Covenant.[31]

My final category,[32] at the extreme end of contention, treats the right to political participation itself. The discordant understandings of this right were made explicit during the periods of drafting of the Universal Declaration and International Covenant. They stem from the incompatible political theories and practices which inform the right. The disagreements are as basic as whether the right requires political pluralism or can be fully satisfied in a one-party state.[33] In comparison with disputes over other of the Covenant's provisions, these disagreements reveal more clearly the effects of human rights norms on the distribution and exercise of political power.

Of course, many rights other than the right to participation implicate the basic political structure of a society. The negative rights, benefiting from a formal consensus about their meaning and hence at

---

28. *See infra* note 57 (comments by a Romanian representative on the relation between restrictions permitted under the International Covenant and provisions of Romanian law restricting speech hostile to the Communist Party or to the struggle of the working people).

29. CONSTITUTION OF THE USSR, *supra* note 13, art. 50.

30. *Id.* art. 51.

31. *See infra* text accompanying notes 125–26; *see also infra* note 129.

32. In view of the purpose of this article and hence of the typology of rights developed in the text, I exclude from consideration economic and social rights such as those to food, education or health care. Distinctive in many respects, such rights are not readily located within the typology. Some among them appear in the *Universal Declaration*, *supra* note 3, arts. 22–27. The full range of these rights is set forth in the *International Covenant on Economic, Social and Political Rights*, G.A. Res. 2200, 21 U.N. GAOR Supp. (No. 16) 49, U.N. Doc. A/6316 (1966). That covenant, effective in 1976, figures in later discussion. *See infra* text accompanying note 176. My discussion also excludes so-called third-generation rights (to peace, to development), discussed in Alston, *Making Space for New Human Rights: The Case of the Right to Development*, 1 HARV. HUM. RTS. Y.B. (1988), *supra*.

33. *See infra* text accompanying notes 45–53.

the opposite side of my spectrum, clearly affect that structure. Torture, disappearances, arbitrary detentions, rigged trials—such phenomena often constitute not discrete and episodic violations that are open to early correction, but the price of dissent, the systematic means employed by a government to retain command.[34] Like discriminatory practices or denial of political participation, violation of such rights may have causes and consequences cutting to the core of a society's political and economic structure.

Nonetheless a vital difference remains between violations of negative rights and of the right to participate. Criticism of a state for practicing torture or for arbitrary detentions can be met by termination of the practice. The termination may have little effect on the exercise of political or economic power. Other practices, as well as inertia or tradition or fear of resumption of the challenged practice, may effectively suppress dissent. However beneficial to prospective victims, the termination may in this sense appear cosmetic, unlikely to affect the quality of life or distribution of power.

Criticism that a given mode of political participation is so restrictive as to violate a human rights norm cannot be so readily met. A state cannot "terminate" a given practice of political participation without instituting another. Particularly if it moves toward broader debate and heightened participation, the new practice may be fatal to those in power.

II. THE TEXTS: THEIR MAKING AND INTERPRETATION

I here compare the provisions for political participation in a few human rights instruments, and draw from debates during their drafting periods to illustrate the ways in which the issues explored in this article were dealt with, or avoided. My discussion, fragmentary as were the debates, anticipates the more systematic inquiries which follow. It reveals the greater attention given during the drafting periods to the "elections" clause than to the "take part" clause. What is indeed striking is less the sharp disputes among states' representatives about the import of the "elections" clause than the absence of a serious effort to explore or elaborate the "take part" clause.

What emerged from the periods of drafting and debates were norms that expressed an important ideal of political participation. But they gave little indication of the different ways of institutionalizing that ideal. It cannot have been by chance that their language was suffi-

34. *See* AMNESTY INTERNATIONAL, *supra* note 19, at 4 (examining motivations for torture and stating that torture "is usually part of the state-controlled machinery to suppress dissent. . . . [It] is most often used as an integral part of a government's security strategy." Its rationale may be "the intimidation of targeted social sectors.").

ciently confined—with respect to the "elections" clause—and sufficiently abstract and porous—with respect to the "take part" clause—to permit democratic and nondemocratic states to assert that they satisfied the norms' demands. More specific norms would have put at risk the goal of achieving broad support for the human rights instruments as a whole.

A. *The Two Basic Provisions*

Article 25 of the International Covenant, the principal treaty declaring a right to political participation, states:

> Every citizen shall have the right and the opportunity, without . . . unreasonable restrictions:
>
> (a) To take part in the conduct of public affairs, directly or through freely chosen representatives;
>
> (b) To vote and to be elected at genuine periodic elections which shall be by universal and equal suffrage and shall be held by secret ballot, guaranteeing the free expression of the will of the electors. . . .

Alone among the International Covenant's provisions, this article restricts a right to citizens. It distinguishes between direct and representative participation, but validates both. The article does not indicate how citizens are to "take part in the conduct of public affairs," other than by identifying periodic and "genuine" elections as an ingredient of the right to participate.

Article 25 indicates that citizens shall exercise the stated rights without "unreasonable restrictions," a phrase covering a multitude of possible issues such as age, residency or registration requirements for voters. In its clause (c), omitted from the text set forth above, the article grants citizens the right to have "access, on general terms of equality, to public service." That clause bars discriminatory exclusion from the civil service or other types of governmental administration. Another omitted provision generally bars discrimination among citizens in the exercise of the defined rights on such grounds as race, gender or political belief. Although of central importance to the right of political participation, all these protections of the right are distant from my concerns in this article. Hence I confine my discussion to the "take part" and "elections" clauses.

The provisions of Article 25 are unusual among human rights norms in that they do more than declare a right. They articulate a political ideal inspiring that right. Though not invoking a particular political tradition such as democracy, Article 25 affirms that the popular vote is meant to guarantee "the free expression of the will of the electors."

The Universal Declaration, an inspiration and important model for the International Covenant and similar in content to it, contains the analogous provision in its Article 21:

> (1) Everyone has the right to take part in the government of his country, directly or through freely chosen representatives. . . .
>
> (3) The will of the people shall be the basis of the authority of government; this will shall be expressed in periodic and genuine elections which shall be by universal and equal suffrage and shall be held by secret vote or by equivalent free voting procedures.

This earlier instrument, influenced to a greater degree than the International Covenant by the tradition of liberal democracy, gives more emphasis to the role of the "will of the people" as the "basis of the authority of government." But like the International Covenant, Article 21 neither employs the term "democracy," nor makes explicit whether plural political parties and contested elections must be permitted.

The influence of the Universal Declaration on the International Covenant extends to the internal structure of Article 25. It too begins with, and thereby gives an apparent priority and emphasis to, the "take part" clause, and continues with the "elections" clause. The first clause appears to be of general scope, an all-embracing provision which by itself would be understood by liberal democracies to require elections open to contest. The second clause can then be understood as one realization or institutionalization of citizens' right to take part in public affairs and government—the only one specified in either Article 21 or 25. Generally I shall use the two clauses to refer, respectively, to non-electoral and electoral (voting) participation in political processes.

Let us concentrate upon the International Covenant. It is striking how its preamble recalls the liberal natural rights tradition, through its references to people's "inherent dignity" and "equal and inalienable rights." But neither through the preamble nor through its enumeration of rights does the Covenant invoke a single political tradition to the necessary exclusion of others. Despite its numerous provisions condemning practices associated with overtly repressive regimes of the historical right or left—arbitrary detention, torture, severe censorship, refusal to hold elections—the Covenant does not by its terms distinguish among such political systems as liberal democracy, democratic socialism, corporatism, or communism.

Thus a scholar examining the International Covenant's development during almost two decades of drafting and debates in several United Nations organs, including the Human Rights Commission, observes: "Nothing in the records suggests that the Commission ever felt the need of a uniform theory, let alone ideology, of human rights." Rather than seek a consensus over a unified conception of the relationship between the individual and the state, the Commission sought "to reach a set of agreements that might be justified even on highly divergent doctrinal grounds."[35]

Notwithstanding its mixed ancestry and ambiguities, the Covenant gives some internal guidance for an understanding of Article 25. In view of their essential role in most political activities, the expressive rights to free speech, press, assembly and association must in some way inform any theory of participation. Their prominence in the International Covenant reminds us that Article 25 should not be approached as an isolated provision, detached from the larger structure of rights in the Covenant. That larger structure here suggests that the "take part" and "elections" clauses assume some degree of public political debate and of citizens' participation in political groups expressing their beliefs or interests.

In one special context, the International Covenant and the Universal Declaration do specifically invoke the democratic tradition. Article 29(2) of the Universal Declaration states that the exercise of rights defined by it remains subject to law-determined limitations for the purpose of "meeting the just requirements of morality, public order and the general welfare in a democratic society." The International Covenant's articles on rights to peaceful assembly and association allow restriction of those rights "as necessary in a democratic society" in the

---

35. Pechota, *The Development of the Covenant on Civil and Political Rights*, in THE INTERNATIONAL BILL OF RIGHTS, *supra* note 4, at 32, 36; *cf.* Henkin, *The Human Rights Idea in Contemporary China: A Comparative Perspective*, in R. EDWARDS, L. HENKIN & A. NATHAN, HUMAN RIGHTS IN CONTEMPORARY CHINA 6, 29 (1986) ("International human rights instruments reflect no commitment to any particular conception of rights, or to any particular political or economic system."). *But see* Garibaldi, *On the Ideological Content of Human Rights Instruments: The Clause "In a Democratic Society,"* in CONTEMPORARY ISSUES IN INTERNATIONAL LAW: ESSAYS IN HONOR OF LOUIS B. SOHN 23 (T. Buergenthal ed. 1984). Although emphasizing the meaning of the quoted clause, Garibaldi states generally that "the whole purpose of a human rights instrument is to convey a particular political ideology in a comprehensive and systematic way. . . . Thus, each human rights instrument is essentially a codification, in the language of rights, of a particular ideological view on the proper functions and limits of governmental power." *Id.* at 23–24. The Universal Declaration and International Covenant show "a clear ideological commitment: rejection of communism and incorporation by reference, for limited but important purposes, of the political ideologies of the West." *Id.* at 68.

interests of national security, public order or morals, and protection of others' rights.[36]

Neither instrument uses the expression "democratic society" to elucidate a declared right, such as political speech or participation. Instead both employ it to control the reasons for which declared rights may be limited. In the International Covenant, that control strengthens the rights of assembly and association by requiring that restrictions on them conform not only with criteria like national security or public order, but also with a contextual test: whether a particular kind of society would view them as necessary. Particularly in view of its origin in the Universal Declaration, a document drafted when the hegemony in the United Nations of the liberal democracies was unquestioned, the expression "democratic society" invites comparison with restrictions on assembly and association in those democracies rather than, for example, with the practices of communist countries.[37]

But the International Covenant was born into a world where the term "democracy," like the rhetoric of right, had become the common property of political systems with little in common beyond that term and rhetoric. Liberal democracies stood beside socialist and people's democracies. As part of a title for states, "democratic" lost in descriptive power what it gained in popularity.[38] In view of the special function of the references to "democratic society" in the limitations clauses of a few articles of the Covenant and its absence from Article 25, the expression appears to be only tangentially relevant to the task of expounding the right to political participation.

B. *Debates during the Drafting Periods*

1. The Two Universal Instruments

In this section I explore some themes in the drafting sessions for the International Covenant and Universal Declaration. The drafting phase in United Nations organs for the International Covenant lasted from the fifth to tenth sessions of the General Assembly, 1949–1954.

36. *International Covenant*, *supra* note 5, arts. 21–22. The expression "democratic society" also appears in Article 14(1) with respect to permitted reasons for excluding the press from a trial.

37. *See* Garibaldi, *supra* note 35, at 23. The author draws on the drafting history of the Universal Declaration and the International Covenant to support his argument that the expression "democratic society" referred to Western concepts of democracy rather than "socialist democracy." *Id.* at 50–65. *See also* Partsch, *Freedom of Conscience and Expression, and Political Freedoms*, in THE INTERNATIONAL BILL OF RIGHTS, *supra* note 4, at 209, 232 (commenting that this expression was meant to guard against arbitrary restrictions, but "whether this provision will prove effective is open to doubt in view of the diverging concepts of 'democracy.'").

38. Illustrations today of the diverse uses of this designation include the German Democratic Republic, Democratic Kampuchea, and the Democratic People's Republic of Korea.

When completed, the draft of the Covenant reflected views of members of the Human Rights Commission, as well as comments by the Economic and Social Committee and the General Assembly. It included present Article 25 in a form close to final. No substantive changes in that article were made thereafter when the General Assembly's Third Committee deliberated on the draft.[39]

Over this period of almost two decades, the membership of the United Nations changed dramatically through the addition of the new African and Asian states. Debates about the International Covenant, and its unanimous adoption in 1966 by the General Assembly preceding the opening of the Covenant for ratification, took place within a more ideologically diverse group.

Much discussion during the drafting period addressed elections. Broad agreement developed that the International Covenant could not impose upon its parties one or another of the different electoral systems current among liberal democracies. For example, neither single-member constituencies nor proportional voting could be preferred. No choice could be made between presidential or parliamentary systems.

The United Kingdom delegate to the Human Rights Commission stressed "how hard it would be to devise a general text on the right of suffrage which would take into account all the variation in national practice and would not require changes in existing institutions."[40] The French delegate argued against any principle that all votes had the same weight, for such a principle would condemn territorial constituencies and point toward proportional representation.[41] It was unrealistic to expect a convention of great detail, or "rules so uniform that the covenant would be foredoomed to failure."[42]

The Ukranian delegate to the Commission similarly argued that the International Covenant should not enter into details, at least with respect to electoral systems. Its function was to "lay down fundamental principles, leaving each country to devise within the framework of its national system its own method of applying them."[43] The point, said a Chilean member of the Third Committee, was that the Covenant should not be viewed as license for some regions to impose their views

39. *See* Pechota, *supra* note 35, at 59.

40. 9 U.N. ESCOR (365th mtg.), Commission on Human Rights, at 5, U.N. Doc. E/CN.4/SR.365 (1953). A number of UN documents cited in this and later footnotes are summary records of proceedings, as indicated by the designation "SR" in the UN document number. Quotations in text of the remarks of delegates taken from such documents are therefore quotations of summaries rather than direct quotations.

41. 9 U.N. ESCOR (364th mtg.), Commission on Human Rights, at 8, U.N. Doc. E/CN.4/SR.364 (1953).

42. *Id.* at 9.

43. *Id.* at 4.

on all. Rather it made allowance for the coexistence of various types of democracy.[44]

Rarely did debate turn to the question whether Article 25 should require freedom for opposition parties. More extensive discussions of the relationship between a participatory norm and political pluralism had taken place years before during the debates of the Third Committee on the proposed Article 21 of the Universal Declaration. A number of delegates from European and Latin American countries had then argued for an explicit statement that the right to political participation included the right to oppose a government and to seek to replace it by legal means. Otherwise there would be "no real democracy."[45]

This earlier debate had considered an amendment to the draft Universal Declaration that was proposed by the Belgian delegate to the Third Committee. He argued that the "very essence of the democratic system was the electoral competition between different political parties." Absent a guarantee of competition, "the whole democratic character of free, equal, [periodic] and secret elections might be distorted."[46]

The Soviet delegate had protested, claiming that the Belgian amendment was "absolutely irreconcilable with the social structure of certain Member States."[47] It would place the Universal Declaration "in contradiction with the electoral procedures" of the Soviet Union, to the point of constituting an intervention into the domestic affairs of his country.[48] No justification for a pluralist party system could be found in Soviet society, since the class antagonisms which such a system reflected, in particular the bourgeois class, had ceased to exist. The Soviet delegate urged that it would be sufficient for Article 21 to indicate the necessity for free elections under universal suffrage. The Belgian delegate later withdrew his amendment "as a conciliatory gesture."[49]

Discussions of drafts of the International Covenant yielded occasional remarks about, but no explicit resolution of, this issue. The Greek delegate to the Third Committee observed: "Without the most basic of all human rights—the right to free elections, involving a choice between at least two parties, the right to organize a political

44. 16 U.N. GAOR Third Comm. (1096th mtg.) at 179, U.N. Doc. A/C.3/SR.1059–1134 (1961).

45. 3 U.N. GAOR Third Comm. (132d mtg.) at 5, U.N. Doc. A/C.3/SR. 132 (1948). *See generally id.* (discussion at that meeting); 3 U.N. GAOR Third Comm. (133d mtg.), U.N. Doc. A/C.3/SR. 133 (1948).

46. 3 U.N. GAOR Third Comm. (133rd mtg.) at 11, U.N. Doc. A/C.3/SR.133 (1948).

47. 3 U.N. GAOR Third Comm. (134th mtg.) at 6, U.N. Doc. A/C.3/SR.134 (1948).

48. *Id.* at 4.

49. *Id.* at 7.

opposition . . .—the building which the United Nations was attempting to erect in the field of human rights would lack a keystone . . . ."[50] An Italian delegate to that Committee noted that the value of electoral procedures like equal suffrage and the secret ballot depended upon freedom of choice between candidates.[51] But these and a few similar statements—for example, an observation about the importance of the related freedoms of information and assembly[52]—did not produce sustained debate about the issue.[53]

Analysis of the phrase "genuine . . . elections" in Article 25 addressed only indirectly the issue of single or plural parties. For example, a Chilean delegate to the Third Committee asserted that the term "genuine" guaranteed elections that faithfully reflected the opinions of the population.[54] Debate involving this term was predominantly formal. Delegates questioned which of the adjectives "genuine" or "honest" were preferable, or considered the appropriate position of the adjective in Article 25.[55]

Uncertainty about the import of the "elections" clause for single-party or contested elections, and failure to elaborate the "take part" clause, continued after the International Covenant became effective in 1976. Discussions about Article 25 in the United Nations Commission on Human Rights, and in the Human Rights Committee created as a treaty organ by the International Covenant, did not illuminate either issue. On a few occasions, proceedings of the Human Rights Committee, considering the periodic reports which parties to the International Covenant are required to submit to it,[56] have ventilated the issue of opposition parties.[57] The reports themselves have tended to

---

50. 5 U.N. GAOR Third Comm. (298th mtg.) at 179, U.N. Doc. A/C.3/SR.298 (1950).

51. 16 U.N. GAOR Third Comm. (1097th mtg.) at 186, U.N. Doc. A/C.3/SR.1097 (1961).

52. *Id.* at 179.

53. *See* Partsch, *supra* note 37, at 240 (commenting on the failure of Article 25 to refer to the right to form an opposition party, and speculating that "perhaps it was sought to make it possible for single-party states to adhere to the Covenant.").

54. 16 U.N. GAOR Third Comm. (1096th mtg.), *supra* note 44, at 180.

55. *See* 10 U.N. GAOR, *Annotation Prepared by the Secretary-General* at 173, U.N. Doc. A/2929 (1955); 16 U.N. GAOR, *Report of the Third Comm. on Draft International Covenants on Human Rights* at 29, U.N. Doc. A/5000 (1961).

56. *See International Covenant*, *supra* note 5, art. 40 (obligating parties to submit reports "on the measures they have adopted which give effect to the rights recognized herein and on the progress made in the enjoyment of those rights.").

57. *See* 28 Human Rights Comm. (688th mtg.) at 5, 7, U.N. Doc. CCPR/C/SR.688 (1986) (consideration of report submitted by Hungary); 31 Human Rights Comm. (776th mtg.) at 10–11, U.N. Doc. CCPR/C/SR.776 (1987) (consideration of report submitted by Zambia). The discussion of the report submitted by Romania is instructive. Committee members (described in the *International Covenant*, *supra* note 5, art. 28 as persons of "recognized competence" in the field of human rights who are elected and serve "in their personal capacity" rather than as representatives of their governments) referred to provisions of Romanian law describing the correct role of the press in fostering love for the Romanian Communist Party and for the

be formal, sometimes no more than paraphrases of legal texts. Essentially exchanges between the representative of a state submitting a report and a Committee member, the discussions have not been able to probe this issue in a systematic way. In any event, they carry no authoritative consequence.

Disputes between an individual and a party to the International Covenant involving alleged violations of Article 25 have several times come before the Human Rights Committee for its views.[58] These opinions of the Committee have treated such relatively discrete matters as denial of the vote to a number of a government's principal political opponents.[59] Of course, such provisions may have important systemic implications for elections and political power. But they touch upon conventional issues of discrimination in voting rights that are peripheral to this article's concern with modes of participation.

The International Covenant does not, then, offer the explicit guidance for the interpretation of Article 25 that a reference to Western pluralist theory would have provided. Its provision for elections fails to resolve some basic issues. Countries of radically different political systems which included *some* form of electoral process ratified it, without considering themselves to be in instant violation of Article 25 and without expressing their willingness to conform to any one political tradition's prescription of basic political processes.[60] Signifi-

---

traditions of the working-class struggle, and warning that failure to act correctly could involve loss of credentials. They wondered whether any criticism of the existing political system would amount to a breach of law, and whether all such provisions accorded with Article 19 of the International Covenant. *See supra* text accompanying note 26. 30 Human Rights Comm. (743d mtg.) at 2–3, U.N. Doc. CCPR/C/SR.743 (1987).

The Romanian representative defending the report argued that press limitations reflected the concerns for protection of national security and public order which were recognized in Article 19 as valid, and that under the Romanian Constitution, related freedoms of association "could not be exercised for purposes hostile to the socialist system or to the interests of the workers." *Id.* at 4–5. He added tersely: "The question of political parties does not arise since Romania is a single-party state." Nonetheless, millions of people "participated in political opinion-forming bodies" such as organs of the Communist Party, trade unions and women's committees. *Id.* at 6.

58. Under Article 1 of an *Optional Protocol to the International Covenant on Civil and Political Rights*, G.A.Res. 2200, 21 U.N. GAOR Supp. (No. 16) 59, U.N. Doc. A/6316 (1966), 99 U.N.T.S. 171, state parties to the Covenant may recognize the competence of the Human Rights Committee to consider "communications from individuals subject to [the state's] jurisdiction who claim to be victims of a violation by that [state] of any of the rights set forth in the Covenant." The Committee is to receive written information from the individual and state, hold closed meetings and after consideration "forward its views to the [state] concerned and to the individual." *Id.* art. 5. As of September 1, 1987, 38 parties to the International Covenant were also parties to the Optional Protocol. STATUS OF INTERNATIONAL INSTRUMENTS, *supra* note 6, at 12.

59. Communication No. 28/1978 (Weinberger v. Uruguay), Human Rights Comm., *Selected Decisions under the Optional Protocol* at 57, U.N. Doc. CCPR/C/OP/1 (1978).

60. Given the ambiguities and central importance of Article 25, it is significant that few of the state parties to the International Covenant made reservations with respect to that article.

cantly, Article 25 is silent, and the debates during the drafting period are not illuminating, about other ways to realize or institutionalize citizens' right to "take part" in public affairs.

2. Comparison with a Regional Instrument: The European Convention

It is instructive to compare the drafting of the International Covenant with some episodes in the drafting of the most effective of the human rights treaties of regional scope, the 1950 European Convention on Human Rights and Fundamental Freedoms ("European Convention").[61] In a debate by a Committee of Experts over a draft of the European Convention, the British expert advised against including undertakings of parties about the "machinery of elections and the right of political opposition." Such matters of a "constitutional and political character" were "not appropriate" because of their numerous practical difficulties, including the "impossibility of reaching agreement on what precisely are the fundamental principles of democracy . . . ." Moreover, criteria such as universal suffrage and the secret ballot "cannot always and of necessity ensure that governmental action and legislation [are] an expression of the will of the people." A provision stressing such criteria would be a "rather misleading over-simplification."[62]

In any event, some argued, political rights stood outside the traditional limits of human rights, and hence outside the proper scope of the European Convention.[63] Other experts held different views, believing "that even if universal suffrage and secret ballot [were] not an absolute guarantee of democracy, [they] nevertheless constituted an important guarantee which merited protection by the Convention."[64]

Despite strong arguments in the Consultative Assembly (one of the institutions involved in the drafting) for a clause on political partici-

The rare reservation was not substantial. For example, Mexico made a reservation as to Article 25(b), to allow for a provision of the Mexican constitution which prohibited ministers of religion from voting. *See* UNITED NATIONS, MULTILATERAL TREATIES DEPOSITED WITH THE SECRETARY GENERAL 59 (1986).

61. 213 U.N.T.S. 221, Europ. T.S. No. 5 [hereinafter European Convention]. Twenty-one countries were parties to this Convention as of December 31, 1985. MULTILATERAL TREATIES: INDEX AND CURRENT STATUS 163 (M. Bowman & D. Harris eds. 1984 & Supp. 1986) [hereinafter MULTILATERAL TREATIES].

62. 3 COUNCIL OF EUROPE, COLLECTED EDITION OF THE "TRAVAUX PRÉPARATOIRES" OF THE EUROPEAN CONVENTION ON HUMAN RIGHTS 182 (1976) (the amendment cited here was proposed on Feb. 2, 1950).

63. *See, e.g.*, 4 COUNCIL OF EUROPE, COLLECTED EDITION OF THE "TRAVAUX PRÉPARATOIRES" OF THE EUROPEAN CONVENTION ON HUMAN RIGHTS 140 (1976).

64. 3 COUNCIL OF EUROPE, *supra* note 62, at 264.

pation,[65] the European Convention did not include one. But two years later Article 3 of the First Protocol to the Convention[66] required parties to hold "free elections" at reasonable intervals under conditions ensuring "the free expression of the opinion of the people in the choice of legislature." That provision makes explicit what appears to be assumed in the other human rights instruments: the right to participation requires popular elections only for a legislature, not for principal executive officials as well.

The telling distinction between the European Convention and the International Covenant lies in the former's regional character and in the relative homogeneity of its members' political systems and traditions. Nonetheless, on its face, the European Convention's provision for political participation is no more specific and exacting than those in the universal instruments. It is, however, clear from context and from the drafting period that Article 3 of the First Protocol resolves issues that were left vague by the International Covenant. It refers to elections within the framework of West European rather than geographically diverse political systems, including multi-party rather than one-party states. It is grounded in Western conceptions of contested elections under democratic governments.

For example, the terms "democracy" and "democratic" appear in the European Convention more frequently than in the International Covenant.[67] A Belgian member of the Consultative Assembly observed that "the pride of this organization of ours is to group together democratic States for whom the scrupulous practice of democracy is the primary condition of all the other freedoms . . . based upon respect for the human person."[68] A French member of the Consultative Assembly cited cases of denials of political rights "in the so-called 'peoples' democracies,'" and emphasized the European Convention's aim "to prevent the establishment of a totalitarian regime in any country whatsoever."[69]

---

65. 6 COUNCIL OF EUROPE, COLLECTED EDITION OF THE "TRAVAUX PRÉPARATOIRES" OF THE EUROPEAN CONVENTION ON HUMAN RIGHTS 124, 126 (1976); 7 COUNCIL OF EUROPE, COLLECTED EDITION OF THE "TRAVAUX PRÉPARATOIRES" OF THE EUROPEAN CONVENTION ON HUMAN RIGHTS 158 (1976).

66. Protocol of March 20, 1952, 213 U.N.T.S. 262, Europ. T.S. No. 9. Eighteen states were parties to this protocol as of December 31, 1985. MULTILATERAL TREATIES, *supra* note 61, at 176. The European Convention itself includes rights closely related to political participation, such as those to free speech and association. *See* European Convention, *supra* note 61, arts. 9–11.

67. The expression "in a democratic society" appears in the European Convention, *supra* note 61, arts. 6(1), 8(2), 9(2), 10(2), 11(2).

68. 6 COUNCIL OF EUROPE, *supra* note 65, at 126.

69. 7 COUNCIL OF EUROPE, *supra* note 65, at 158; *see* J.E.S. FAWCETT, THE APPLICATION OF THE EUROPEAN CONVENTION ON HUMAN RIGHTS 417 (1987) (noting that Article 3 of the First Protocol uses the term "free" to qualify the necessary elections, and observing that "an

Decisions of the European Commission of Human Rights, a treaty organ created by the European Convention, have wrestled with Article 3's implications for the design of an electoral system. While asserting, for example, that the phrase "choice of legislature" in Article 3 requires that different political parties be guaranteed a reasonable opportunity to present their candidates,[70] the Commission has stressed that this article does not impose upon states a particular kind of electoral system—majority voting in single-member constituencies, or proportional voting. "Both these forms of elections may be considered as a part of the common heritage of political traditions to which reference can be found in the Convention's Preamble."[71]

The European Convention goes, then, beyond the International Covenant with respect to the clarity of prescription of an "elections clause." But the First Protocol, while bringing the problem of political participation into the Convention, speaks only to the requirement of elections. It says nothing about non-electoral participation, for it includes no equivalent to the general "take part" clause of Article 25 of the International Covenant. On its face, the European Convention suggests that the tradition of liberal democracy from which it developed insists firmly but solely upon a government's commitment to an open political process culminating in periodic contested elections.

III. TREATY PROVISIONS IN RELATION TO CONTEMPORARY DEBATE ABOUT PARTICIPATION IN THE LIBERAL DEMOCRACIES

An attempt to formulate a universal norm about political participation confronts mutually antagonistic theories and practices among the liberal democracies, communist states, military dictatorships and a range of third world governments. Consensus over a norm limited to West European, North American and Commonwealth democracies should then be easier to achieve. Basic obstacles to agreement about reasonably specific provisions fall away when, for example, none of the proposed signatories is a one-party state or imposes strict censorship.

---

election could be said not to be . . . a free expression of opinion, if there was only one candidate, or, possibly, only one party . . . .").

70. *See* X v. the United Kingdom, 7 EUROPEAN COMMISSION OF HUMAN RIGHTS, DECISIONS AND REPORTS 95, 96 (1977) [hereinafter X v. the United Kingdom]. Commentators have emphasized the use of the word "choice" in Article 3, and stated that a "one-party system imposed by the State therefore must be considered contrary to Article 3." P. VAN DIJK & G.J.H. VAN HOOF, THEORY AND PRACTICE OF THE EUROPEAN CONVENTION ON HUMAN RIGHTS 356 (1984).

71. X v. the United Kingdom, *supra* note 70, at 97.

Even among the democracies, however, a norm about political participation must leave significant matters open. To gain adoption, a regional norm embracing West European and North American countries would have to be understood as consistent with distinct theories of participation informing these countries' political systems. It would have to accommodate important variations in forms of government and in related practices institutionalizing political participation.

In this section, I sketch the theories about democratic participation that are debated in the writings of contemporary American and European scholars, and indicate their relevance to an understanding of the international norms. My reason for so doing is not to explore the different bodies of theory as such, in order to analyze their premises and structure. My more modest goal is to trace their implications for different modes of political participation, for the variety of ways in which participation can be institutionalized. Article 25 of the International Covenant suggests such a view of the relevance of theory to its provisions. It is concerned not with the foundations of participatory practices in one or another political theory, but with those practices themselves.

The writings here examined revise or build on, invoke critically or admiringly, themes in the traditions of political thought stemming from Locke, Bentham, Mill and Rousseau. My discussion does not treat these classical theorists directly. Rather it describes the arguments about the nature of political participation which have been made by theorists during the same decades in which the postwar law of international human rights developed. At the same time, it indicates the consequences of those arguments for different practices and institutions. I then briefly discuss the human rights instruments' requirement of elections, to show how little agreement exists among Western democracies about even so traditional a liberal injunction. The section concludes with thoughts about why liberal democratic theory has treated elections as the paramount form of participation.

A. *Political Participation in the Large: Competing Conceptions*

All regimes, including over time the most repressive, permit or encourage or even require some institutionalized modes of political participation.[72] Reasons additional to the need to be informed of

72. *See* S. Verba, N. Nie & J. Kim, Participation and Political Equality: A Seven Nation Comparison 53–60 (1978) (identifying four basic modes of contemporary political participation: voting, campaign activity, communal activity outside the electoral process, and particularized (individual) contacts). *See also* S. Huntington & J. Nelson, No Easy Choice: Political Participation in Developing Countries 1 (1976). The authors refer to "broadening political participation" as a "hallmark" of political modernization. They correlate higher participation with socio-economic development in both democratic and totalitarian societies. *Id.*

popular discontent argue for a government's inviting political participation. The government may thereby enlist popular support and gain international as well as domestic legitimacy. It may reduce the risks accompanying efforts to rule exclusively by force.

In nondemocratic societies, such participation will reach beyond the ruling elite, however defined, to include broader elements of the population. It may stop shy even of controlled elections, and involve no more than informal consultations or legally approved ways to express grievances. It may be relatively self-generated *or* mobilized and manipulated, relatively genuine and effectual *or* ceremonial and insubstantial. Like the forms of popular political participation in all societies, it will represent some combination of institutionalized ideals, practical functions, public ritual, and legitimating myth.

Liberal democracies, then, are not distinctive in institutionalizing modes of political participation, but the modes which they stress are. The traditional negative rights and expressive rights of liberalism protect the environment of political pluralism. Political processes culminating in a popular and contested election are meant to yield a representative legislature, and a chief executive or government elected directly (presidential system) or elected indirectly by such legislature (parliamentary system).

Elections serve a variety of purposes for both the voters and the polity. So do the less common forms of citizens' political activities in liberal societies. No one ideal of political participation succeeds in rationalizing these diverse purposes. Therefore, no single scale can measure political participation comparatively, even among several liberal democracies without consideration of Communist-Party states. Scales calibrated to different values would weigh different phenomena, or give varying weights to phenomena like elections.[73] It is not then sufficient for a believer in political participation simply to urge "more," an urge indeed not felt by all theorists of democracy.[74] Rather, an

at 159. They define political participation as "activity by private citizens designed to influence governmental decision-making." *Id.* at 3.

73. *See* T.H. FRIEDGUT, POLITICAL PARTICIPATION IN THE USSR 13–20 (1979) (comparing the different meanings of political participation in the United States and the Soviet Union and noting how these differences hamper effective comparative inquiry); *see also* HUNTINGTON & NELSON, *supra* note 72, at 171 (observing that "[t]he forms and patterns assumed by expanding political participation are malleable; they can be molded and formed into a wide range of systems, differing so sharply that what is viewed as participatory in one society is not even recognized by that label in another."); Nelson, *Political Participation*, in M. WEINER & S. HUNTINGTON, UNDERSTANDING POLITICAL DEVELOPMENT 103–16, 123–25 (1987) (commenting on the shift in conceptions of political participation in Western scholarship from the early 1960s to the 1980s). The earlier image "conceives of participation almost entirely in democratic contexts." *Id.* at 104. The newer image grows out of an effort to encompass more of the world intellectually by examining aspects of participation in all political contexts, including authoritarian systems. *See id.*

74. *See* C. PATEMAN, PARTICIPATION AND DEMOCRATIC THEORY 1–16 (1970) (discussing

advocate must address underlying questions: what type of participation, by which groups or classes or interests, through what institutional arrangements, for what individual or collective purposes, with what likely consequences?

I draw some responses to these questions from the ongoing debates among political theorists in the Western democracies. These theorists, both influencing and reacting to public political debate, employ terms to capture their insights about political participation which are often paired to express contrasting ideals or practices. They write, for example, about thin and strong democracy,[75] representation theories and participation theories,[76] protective and developmental democracy,[77] or negative and positive liberty.[78] Broadly speaking, the first term of each of these pairs can be associated with classical figures like Hobbes, Bentham and James Mill, while the second term can be associated with the traditions of Rousseau or J.S. Mill.[79]

For our purposes, it is useful to concentrate on the divide between theories in which elections constitute a near-sufficient form of political

---

the revival of the concept of participation in the 1960s, noting the growing concern in some strands of democratic theory about excessive participation as destabilizing, and referring to the companion growth of elite representative-institutional theories of democracy); *see infra* text accompanying note 84; *see also* B. BARBER, STRONG DEMOCRACY: PARTICIPATORY POLITICS FOR A NEW AGE 7–8 (1984) (emphasizing some contradictions between liberal theory and (strong) democratic theory, such as the liberal aim not that citizens be part of community but that they contain governmental power and community, and the liberal distrust of too much democracy or participation).

75. *See* B. BARBER, *supra* note 74, for a development of this distinction. Barber associates the "thin" side with emphasis on individual ends and protection by the state against abuse, and absence of theories of citizenship, participation and civic virtue. *See id.* at 4. The program of strong democracy emphasizes the ideal of self-governing citizens, educated to a sense of civic virtue, capable of common purpose, bound up with each other in participatory institutions. *See id.* at 117.

76. *See* C. PATEMAN, *supra* note 74, at 22–44 (associating the tradition of representative democracy with Bentham and James Mill, and that of participatory democracy with Rousseau, J.S. Mill and G.D.H. Cole). For an analogous distinction, see C.B. MACPHERSON, THE LIFE AND TIMES OF LIBERAL DEMOCRACY 93–115 (1977) [hereinafter C.B. MACPHERSON, LIFE AND TIMES] (describing a model of participatory democracy).

77. *See* C.B. MACPHERSON, LIFE AND TIMES, *supra* note 76, at 23–76; Keim, *Participation in Contemporary Democratic Theories*, in PARTICIPATION IN POLITICS 1–7 (J. Pennock & J. Chapman eds. 1975).

78. *See generally* I. BERLIN, *Two Concepts of Liberty*, in FOUR ESSAYS ON LIBERTY 118 (1969); C.B. MACPHERSON, *Berlin's Division of Liberty*, in DEMOCRATIC THEORY: ESSAYS IN RETRIEVAL 95 (1973) [hereinafter C.B. MACPHERSON, DEMOCRATIC THEORY].

79. My discussion does not draw on the contemporary scholarly debate about the civic republican tradition of political thought. That tradition, much disputed as to its underlying character and import, bears a complex relationship to themes in this article. Broadly speaking, some aspects of republican thought are associated with themes of writers propounding theories of strong, direct or participatory democracy. But the associations are subtle, and such concepts in the republican tradition as civic virtue or the common or public good require independent discussion. For a description and analysis of the contemporary debate about civic republicanism, see Michelman, *Foreword: Traces of Self-Government*, 100 HARV. L. REV. 4, 17–55 (1986). For a number of articles on republicanism in United States history, see 37 AM. Q. 461–598 (1985).

participation for the great majority of the people, and theories urging more. Within this article's framework, that divide could be expressed in terms of the "elections" clause and "take part" clause of the international norms. While recognizing that elections are indispensable, the more demanding theories argue for a continuing rather than episodic experience of participation, for a broad conception of a right to "take part" in the conduct of public affairs. They involve varied and flexible modes of non-electoral participation that supplement rather than substitute for voting. This dispute about the sufficiency of electoral democracy reflects deeper disagreement over the ends of participation. It is to such disagreement that the discussion now turns.

Permeating these writings is a distinction between notions of participation as an instrumental and as an inherent good. This distinction serves to organize my discussion.[80] Like most such contrasts, it wrenches apart elements in the psychology and practice of political participation that may usefully complement each other and comfortably coexist for most citizens. But understanding one or the other as a dominant justification for political participation helps to elucidate some underlying themes.

Emphasis on participation's instrumental character suggests that the function of political participation must be to influence public policy, to gain governmental recognition of individual or group interests. The value of participation lies in its instrumental efficacy. It is a means toward a goal rather than an end in itself. Elections are the paramount means for influencing governmental action.[81] They give the electorate some degree of control over and thereby impose some degree of responsibility on those exercising power.[82] Of all modes of political participation, elections enlist the largest number of citizens, including the largest number of those toward the bottom of the socio-economic ladder.

Other more demanding political activities, engaged in by relatively small percentages of the population, are oriented toward and culminate in elections: active membership in a political party, raising campaign

---

80. *See* S. Verba & N. Nie, Participation in America: Political Democracy and Social Equality 5 (1972) (drawing on the writings of J.S. Mill for views of participation as an end in itself).

81. *Cf.* J. Schumpeter, Capitalism, Socialism and Democracy 271 (3d ed. 1950). Schumpeter analogizes political to economic competition. He describes democracy as a method by which the competitive struggle for the people's vote is conducted, and observes that "the electoral method is practically the only one available for communities of any size." *Id.*

82. *See* R. Dahl, A Preface to Democratic Theory 3 (1956) [hereinafter R. Dahl, Democratic Theory] (noting the difficulty in clearly defining "democracy"). "[A]t a minimum, it seems to me, democratic theory is concerned with processes by which ordinary citizens exert a relatively high degree of control over leaders." Elections are the critical technique for assuring "that governmental leaders will be relatively responsive to non-leaders." *Id.* at 125. For related views of Dahl in his later writing, see *infra* note 94.

funds, soliciting votes for a candidate. They form part of a complex electoral process which is itself part of the larger political process. Some activities which continue between election campaigns require greater devotion from their participants and longer-run planning—for example, the work of the interest groups which have become endemic to liberal societies. Lobbying and other strategies of those groups supplement the electoral process.

Within this prevalent justification for political participation—influencing public policy and governmental action—citizens' votes play a role as vital as it is confined. Theorists emphasize that, in modern mass society, elections cannot convey with any clarity to elected officials the preferences of citizens which they are meant to take into account. Populations are fragmented in many ways, and issues are often national rather than local.[83] Although the prevalent ideology of democratic participation stresses the exertion of influence from bottom to top, in reality the ruling elites must formulate general policies or concrete programs and put them to the people for their electoral decisions. The people, then, do not determine policy. Rather they react to the policies set by competing political parties. Contested elections mean that the people have a choice, but political elites rather than the people decide what that choice is between.[84]

The popular vote influences or constrains government only indirectly. In modern democracies, these theorists argue, no other arrangement is viable. The people cannot directly govern by participating in the setting of a political agenda or the making of governmental decisions. The New England town meeting cannot be writ large to embrace the nation. Nor will occasional resort to techniques like recalls or referenda, or a use of specific mandates, significantly change the role of the electorate. The underlying constraints on direct participation remain. Elected officals must govern not under specific injunctions, but as general representatives of the electorate, with a broad sense of the mandate, subject to the knowledge that they will be accountable for their actions at an approaching election.

Despite the indirect and limited control that it exercises, electoral participation does establish boundaries for governmental action. It

---

83. Dahl stresses that "in no large nation-state can elections tell us much about the preferences of majorities and minorities beyond the bare fact that among those who went to the polls a majority, plurality or minority indicated their first choices for some particular candidate or group of candidates." R. DAHL, DEMOCRATIC THEORY, *supra* note 82, at 129.

84. *See generally* J. SCHUMPETER, *supra* note 81, at 269–83 (3d ed. 1950). "Party and machine politicians are simply the response to the fact that the electoral mass is incapable of action other than a stampede, and they constitute an attempt to regulate political competition exactly similar to the corresponding practices of a trade association." *Id.* at 283. *See* C. PATEMAN, *supra* note 74, at 3–21 (discussing the relationship drawn between Schumpeter's views and those of Bentham and James Mill); C.B. MACPHERSON, LIFE AND TIMES, *supra* note 76, at 77–82.

rules out policies that meet wide opposition, at least if groups with a political voice are among that opposition. Elections thereby serve a vital protective function, one also served by courts in societies where judicial review vindicates constitutional norms. By periodically subjecting elected officials to the approval of the electorate, they help to arrest governmental violations of widely valued rights, or to counter threats to the interests of sufficiently important groups among the electorate.[85] Such indirect participation in the making of public policy thereby becomes one important path toward realizing liberalism's traditional goal of guarding the individual against abusive state action and assuring "negative liberty."[86]

Other theorists, faulting a solely functional approach to political participation, hold that participation constitutes an inherent as well as an instrumental good. They do not claim that influencing governmental policies and checking governmental abuses are mythical or trivial consequences of the vote. Rather, they argue that elections and political activities closely related to the electoral process are indispensable, but themselves insufficient to realize the democratic ideal of the citizenry's continuing involvement in public life. Within the framework of the international norms on participation, these theorists could be said to elaborate the "take part" clause.

Such theorists criticize exclusively instrumental views of participation because of their tendency to value only liberal premises of individualism, of the hegemony of private rights, and of limited government whose primary function is to honor those rights. A nearly exclusive reliance on elections heightens the sense of powerlessness of the many to act other than passively by reacting to choices formulated by others. Most citizens, at least those who even choose to vote,[87]

---

85. *See* C. Pateman, *supra* note 74, at 9–10; C.B. Macpherson, Life and Times, *supra* note 76, at 34–36 (1977); M. Walzer, Radical Principles 37 (1980) (pointing out that "the electoral process has gradually taken on the character of an outer limit, a form of ultimate popular defense rather than of popular self-government . . . ."); H. Pitkin, The Concept of Representation 234 (1975) ("Our concern with . . . whether elections are free and genuine, results from our conviction that [they are] necessary to assure systematic responsiveness.").

86. Berlin associates negative liberty with "liberty from" or the absence of restraints upon some inviolable core of the individual. I. Berlin, *supra* note 78, at 126; *cf.* the discussion of negative rights *supra* text accompanying note 13. Berlin observes that there is no necessary incompatibility between the protection of negative liberty and non-democratic government, say a benevolent despot. By the same token, a democratic majority may invade the area of private autonomy. "Self-government may, on the whole, provide a better guarantee of the preservation of civil liberties than other regimes . . . [b]ut there is no necessary connexion between individual liberty and democratic rule." *Id.* at 130. Berlin builds on that observation to develop his contrast between negative and positive liberty, the latter responding to a participatory and communitarian vision of democracy but constituting a potential threat to negative liberty. *See* C.B. Macpherson, Democratic Theory *supra* note 78, at 109 (observing that, as Berlin points out, historically democracies rather than other regimes have protected negative liberty, and that extensive participation may even be a prerequisite for extensive negative liberty).

87. *See* M. Walzer, *supra* note 85, at 64–65 (stating that electoral participation in the

treat that act as meeting their full responsibility for participating in public affairs.[88] Voting satisfies that responsibility in an undemanding and individualistic way without need for collegial discussion or group action.[89] Reducing the participation of most citizens to the periodic vote denies them the benefits of a continuing experience of involvement in public life, of "taking part" in the conduct of public affairs.

Recognizing the impossibility of extensive participation in the central government of modern states, theorists of direct or strong or participatory democracy emphasize other contexts. Inevitably they advocate decentralization of authority, and direct attention toward local governments of a size and functions more conducive to continuing and active public involvement. That participation can, and in many states now does, take various forms: citizen representation on governmental boards, public meetings and discussions, formally structured relationships between the managers of public enterprises and their consumers or the general citizenry, more extensive functions of city government responsive to citizens' needs.[90]

In effect, these theorists urge the further development of established trends in the legislation of many liberal democracies increasing citizen participation in local government units, ranging from school or zoning boards and consumer protection agencies to environmental agencies. The character of the participation becomes vital. Active involvement in a neighborhood group addressing local concerns would be favored over a passive dues-paying membership in a political party or interest group.

United States, high in the nineteenth century, has declined as a percentage of the voting populace to roughly half of what it was in the 1890s); Allison & Smith, *A Democracy with Ever Fewer Voters?*, N.Y. Times, Mar. 11, 1988, at A35, col. 2 (pointing out that the percentage of Americans voting in presidential elections has steadily declined since a postwar apex of 62.8 percent, reaching 53 percent in the 1984 elections).

88. *See* S. Verba & N. Nie, *supra* note 80, at 26–27 (1972) (pointing out that in the United States, voting is the sole political experience for most citizens, and that surveys show "a picture of low levels of citizen participation and the concentration of political activity in the hands of a small portion of the citizens.").

89. As Barber explains:

> Voting—which is already the least significant act of citizenship in a democracy—has in America been stripped of almost all pomp and ritual, largely in the name of the kind of efficiency symbolized by the voting machines and the kind of privatism represented by the secret ballot. . . . Because our vote is secret—'private'—we do not need to explain or justify it to others (or, indeed, to ourselves) in a fashion that would require us to think publicly or politically.

B. Barber, *supra* note 74, at 187–88.

90. *See* Frug, *The City as a Legal Concept*, 93 Harv. L. Rev. 1057, 1120–49 (1980); M. Walzer, *supra* note 85, at 36 (pointing out that political parties in the United States never developed as membership organizations with grass roots activities competitive with the family and work). Walzer identifies the most likely areas of democratic politics within the welfare state as local units of work, schools, churches, union locals, political clubs, or neighborhood associations. *Id.* at 47. See the discussion of legislative reforms facilitating such heightened participation, *infra* text accompanying notes 110–12.

Such proposals reach beyond the involvement of citizens in local government. They urge active participation in the formulation of policies of nongovernmental institutions like churches or clubs. That is, they challenge the traditional distinction between public and private in the organization of social life.[91] All institutions which exert significant social influence are in that sense political and public. The conception of political participation therefore expands to embrace activities in a broad range of institutional settings. Active participation of citizens in formulating goals and strategies moves the affected institutions in the direction of self-governance. It also heightens the incentive and skills of citizens for engagement in political processes intended to influence government.

Theorists of direct and strong democracy apply these arguments with particular force to greater participation of workers in union government and in decision-making in the workplace.[92] The proposals reach well beyond the traditional domain of collective bargaining between labor and management over wages and conditions of employment.[93] They reflect and build upon developments in many countries toward greater worker responsiblity for job definitions, worker supervision of production units, and new forms of participation by workers in decision-making by management. The supporters of such reforms argue that many citizens experience social power and life most intensely within the workplace, and therefore should have a role in the construction and reconstruction of that life. Whether conventionally associated with the public or private sphere, business managers exercise substantial power over the lives of workers. Through the developing institutional processes and frameworks, workers are able to expand their influence over the way that power is exercised.[94]

---

91. Thus a proponent of "strong" rather than "thin" democracy suggests that the strong form can be institutionalized in a variety of contexts. In traditional terms, those contexts would have been divided between public and private activities, the latter group being thought of as unrelated to participation in public affairs. But that classical division confuses more than clarifies the issues of active citizen participation. Barber refers to neighborhood associations, community boards, zoning and school boards, public interest groups to deal with neighborhood problems, and the workplace. *See* B. BARBER, *supra* note 74, at 261–311.

92. *See* C. PATEMAN, *supra* note 74, at 45–102; *cf.* S. VERBA, N. NIE & J. KIM, PARTICIPATION AND POLITICAL EQUALITY: A SEVEN NATION SURVEY 216–19 (1978) (noting the distinctive routes to participation in Yugoslavia). Despite absence of competitive elections Verba, Nie and Kim find a range of "quite meaningful self-government institutions in local communities, the workplace, residential units, and elsewhere, that represent significant channels of participation." *Id.* at 216. They observe that "[m]any students of democracy see a possible solution to the problems of participation in the establishment of direct participatory channels in decentralized socioeconomic and political institutions similar to those found in Yugoslavia . . . ." *Id.* at 219.

93. *See* Klare, *Judicial Deradicalization of the Wagner Act and the Origins of Modern Legal Consciousness, 1937-1941*, 62 MINN. L. REV. 265 (1978). For Germpn legislation on worker codetermination, see *infra* note 112.

94. *See* R. DAHL, A PREFACE TO ECONOMIC DEMOCRACY 115 (1985) [hereinafter R. DAHL,

The purposes of this extensive popular involvement in an enlarged domain of public life are at once greater self-government and self-realization. The two are interrelated. By taking responsibility for public life and committing their personal resources to it, citizens experience differently their relationship to society. Through increased participation in the institutions affecting their lives, they develop a sense of their worth and significance. That is, the benefits of participation are at once material and psychological. More citizens will feel empowered to act rather than only react. This heightened sense of responsibility and competence strengthens an ethic of civic virtue which points toward participation for reasons additional to the advancement of self-interest.[95] The inherent good of political participation stems from this possibility of self-realization through development of the social self as a member of the polity.[96]

B. *Electoral Systems: Their Range and Effects*

Elections, meant in the language of Article 25 of the International Covenant to "[guarantee] the free expression of the will of the electors," may fall far short of that ideal. They take place through electoral processes designed and administered by the state. Those processes, and the larger political systems on which they depend, may facilitate or frustrate access of the people to political activity and institutions. Moreover, the very "technology" of electoral systems, the electoral structure selected for choosing a legislature, will significantly influence the degree of representation and power of many groups in a society.

Elections may offer relatively accessible or relatively closed avenues, real or sham avenues, toward the people's participation in governance.[97] The factors determining which of these avenues is opened by

---

ECONOMIC DEMOCRACY]. Dahl, arguing for enterprise democracy through greater worker participation, states that if democracy is justified for the state, then so should it be for the workplace. He draws an analogy between the firm and a political system with respect to relations between the governors and governed.

95. *See* M. WALZER, *supra* note 85, at 64 (describing active participation in political life as an aspect of citizenship, observing that "any stable commitment has to be based . . . on some notion of the public good" and asserting that voting constitutes "the minimal form of virtuous conduct . . . ."); *see also supra* note 79 (referring to the civic republican tradition of political thought).

96. *See* R. DAHL, ECONOMIC DEMOCRACY, *supra* note 94, at 94–101. Although Dahl concludes that the evidence on effects of workplace democracy is mixed so far, so that the results are uncertain, he argues that through democratic participation workers would cultivate important virtues such as moral responsibility for their actions. *See id.*

97. *See* Parker, *The Past of Constitutional Theory—And its Future*, 42 OHIO ST. L.J. 223 (1981), for an attack on the "articles of faith" about political life which inform the work of some scholars. One such "article of faith" is that adequate functioning of representative democracy is assured when a government is responsible to the people in periodic elections, for it will take majority interests into account, and majorities are shifting coalitions formed by competition among many "minority" interests. Parker points to the inequalities in power, wealth and status which prevent

a given country's electoral system largely escape consideration or regulation by the international norms. The present discussion bears out this observation by concentrating on the structure or architecture of electoral systems. The following section raises broader questions about the effect on electoral participation of the political and socio-economic context in which elections are held.

Article 25 of the International Covenant and Article 21 of the Universal Declaration require periodic and genuine elections. The contrast with the indeterminate "take part" clause is striking. Here at least these international norms appear to speak unambiguously about a specific embodiment of the ideal of political participation. But the appearance is deceptive. Even apart from questions about one-party elections and about barring certain political groups from electoral competition,[98] the international norms leave to the states decisions which carry important consequences for the quality of participation and the distribution of political power.

Consider the alternative systems for election of a legislature: proportional representation ("PR" system), under which the legislature is divided among parties according to the percentage vote received by each party list in the popular election; and single-member constituencies, in which the winner in an electoral district, the first past the post, takes all ("district" system). A choice between these systems or among their many variations will not be determined by the logic of a broadly shared theory of representation, participation or democracy. No such choice will be detached from practical politics.[99]

---

many people from recognizing and asserting their interests, and to correlations between political participation and socio-economic status which indicate that access of some minorities to the political process may be very problematic. *Id.* at 241–46. The important consequence for elections, related to the modest rate of electoral participation in countries like the United States, is the undue influence upon them of effective minorities. *Cf.* R. DAHL, ECONOMIC DEMOCRACY, *supra* note 94, at 52–55 (on various sources of political inequality, including the control of economic enterprises).

98. For reasons deemed urgent, a number of political democracies bar from electoral participation parties with platforms or ideologies viewed as extreme and as threatening to those societies' deep premises. *See, e.g.*, THE BASIC LAW OF THE FEDERAL REPUBLIC OF GERMANY art. 21(2), *reprinted in* 6 CONSTITUTIONS OF THE COUNTRIES OF THE WORLD 43, 50 (A. Blaustein & G. Flanz eds. 1985) (making unconstitutional parties which "seek to impair or abolish the free democratic basic order or to endanger the existence" of the state); BASIC LAW: THE KNESSET § 7(a), *amended in* BASIC LAW: THE KNESSET AMEND. NO. 9, 1155 Sefer Hahukim [S.H.] 196 (1985) (barring participation in elections to the Israeli legislature of parties which deny the existence of the State of Israel as the state of the Jewish nation, deny the democratic character of the state, or incite to racism.).

99. *See* Duverger, *Which is the Best Electoral System?*, in CHOOSING AN ELECTORAL SYSTEM: ISSUES AND ALTERNATIVES (A. Lijphart & B. Grofman eds. 1984) [hereinafter CHOOSING AN ELECTORAL SYSTEM]. Duverger argues that neither a PR nor a district system can be said to be truer to "public opinion," which can be captured and interpreted in many ways. Those systems are simply different ways of organizing public opinion, and indeed the chosen electoral system will as much determine as reflect what public opinion consists of. *Id.* at 34.

In a given context, it will generally be clear which groups will benefit from a proposed change in an electoral system.[100] It is not, for example, surprising that suggestions in the United Kingdom for a form of PR come from the smaller parties that have been underrepresented by the district system.[101] On the other hand, PR's structural problems, namely the party fragmentation often caused by PR and the related politics of coalition governments that may give disproportionate strength to small parties, have led to proposals in countries like Israel for significant modifications.[102]

Electoral systems, including the nominating or selection processes through which parties' candidates are chosen,[103] thus both reflect and mold political power. Each system will favor some interests at the expense of others by defining the avenues and strategies through which political power must be gained.[104] Electoral participation can then be arranged consistently with human rights norms to yield many different arrangements of power.

Variations among electoral systems thereby resemble other variations in the governmental structures of liberal democracies which are both consistent with the requirements of the "elections" clause of Article 25 and exert markedly different influences on the distribution of political power. Consider the problem of access of an ethnic minority to political processes. It is obvious that PR and district systems may have radically different implications for political access.[105] In a given

---

100. *See, e.g.*, Oberst, *Proportional Representation and Electoral System Change in Sri Lanka*, in SRI LANKA IN CHANGE AND CRISIS 118 (J. Manor ed. 1984).

101. *See* Lakeman, *The Case for Proportional Representation*, in CHOOSING AN ELECTORAL SYSTEM, *supra* note 99, at 41–42.

102. *See* A. ARIAN, POLITICS IN ISRAEL: THE SECOND GENERATION 124 (1985) (stating that debate over electoral reform has become "a regular feature of Israeli political life. . . . Reform is championed as the way of changing the nature of the political system, making the member of the Knesset more responsible and responsive to voters and altering the very moral climate of the country."). In 1987 a group of professors at Tel Aviv University Law School prepared a much discussed proposal for a written constitution for Israel. Article 51 of that proposal provides that 60 of the 120 members of the Knesset are to be elected "on a personal candidature basis" in district elections in 60 electoral constituencies, while the remaining members of the Knesset are to be chosen in proportional national elections. Constitution of the State of Israel (unpublished manuscript) (1987) (on file at *Harvard Human Rights Yearbook*).

103. State primaries and caucuses in the 1988 campaign in the United States for nomination as the Democratic or Republican candidate for president demonstrated the significance of the choice between electoral systems. In most states, Democrats used a PR system for allocating the state delegates to the national nominating convention, whereas Republicans more frequently used a winner-take-all method. It therefore was more difficult for a Democrat to win a majority of the delegates prior to the nominating convention. N.Y. Times, Mar. 10, 1988, at A1, col. 8.

104. *See* D. RAE, THE POLITICAL CONSEQUENCES OF ELECTORAL LAWS 134 (rev. ed. 1971) ("If a single pattern emerges from this study . . . it is the persistent bias of electoral laws in favor of strong parties as against their weaker competitors . . . .").

105. See D. HOROWITZ, ETHNIC GROUPS IN CONFLICT 601–52 (1985), for an examination of structural techniques, including design of electoral systems, to reduce ethnic conflict. "The

context, one may blot out and the other may heighten the minority's political power. As dramatic consequences for the electoral power of a minority group may flow from the choice between a unitary or federal system of government, or in a unitary system from the choice between centralizing authority or devolving self-governing powers to regions.

The "elections" clause of Article 25 holds forth the promise of extensive popular participation in an open political process. The quality of that participation is strongly affected by the ways in which elections are institutionalized. Nonetheless, human rights law offers no guidelines for the selection of an electoral system in a given political and socio-economic context, no theory of broad or fair electoral participation or access which might influence the contextual choice by a state among the many possibilities.[106] By its terms and in view of the debates during its drafting period, the "elections" clause remains neutral about these choices.[107]

C. *Elections as the Paramount Mode of Political Participation in Liberal Democracies*

The debates over the drafting of the international norms on political participation concentrated on the "elections" clause. References to the "take part" clause were sparse and undeveloped. No party to those debates expressed doubt that elections were essential. Even the states with one-party electoral systems questioned the import of the "elections" clause rather than the need for its inclusion in Article 25 of the International Covenant. For many in the West, choosing among candidates or parties *is* democracy, so much so that contested elections

---

delimitation of constituencies, the electoral principle . . . the number of members per constituency, and the structure of the ballot all have a potential impact on ethnic alignments, ethnic electoral appeals, multi-ethnic coalitions, the growth of extremist parties, and policy outcomes." *Id.* at 628. See V. VAN DYKE, HUMAN RIGHTS, ETHNICITY, AND DISCRIMINATION 120–21, 137–47, 217 (1985), for a discussion of the effects of electoral systems on minorities in Africa, Asia and the United States.

106. Of course, in given contexts an electoral system may be judged to violate other human rights norms, particularly nondiscrimination norms. Electoral systems as a whole, or concrete applications such as the design of electoral districts, are open to challenge as unfairly or unconstitutionally disadvantaging particular groups and barring fair access to electoral processes and political power. See the discussion of problems of gerrymandering and multimember districts in the United States in L. TRIBE, AMERICAN CONSTITUTIONAL LAW 1074–84 (2d ed. 1988); *see also* Reynolds v. Sims, 377 U.S. 533 (1964) (related problem of malapportionment). Nondiscrimination norms have indeed been a powerful force for expansion of the suffrage in the liberal democracies which, like the United States, have no constitutional norm declaring a right of political participation as such. Tribe states in the preface to his discussion of rights of political participation in the United States that "most of the law in this area is . . . part of equal protection doctrine . . . ." L. TRIBE, *supra*, at 1062.

107. *See supra* text accompanying notes 40–41.

stand as the salient distinction between democratic and authoritarian systems.[108]

The question here considered is not then *why* Article 25 of the International Covenant specifies elections, but why it specifies *only* elections and leaves the "take part" clause suggestive and unelaborated. An answer to that question lies in part in the conceptual structure of the human rights instruments and in ideological premises to liberal society. Those instruments impose on governments, not on individuals or nongovernmental instituitions, most of the duties that correspond to the individual rights which they declare. Their requirements address principally state action: respect by government for individuals' integrity, governmental protection of individuals against lawless behavior, provision of fair trials, equal protection in the making and enforcement of law. This observation holds for the right to political participation as well. A government's correlative duty requires it to permit, foster or arrange for such participation.

In liberal democracies, most political participation stems from the initiatives of individuals or of institutions that are not formally part of government. Consider, for example, the International Covenant's declaration of rights to free speech and association, rights related to the electoral process.[109] Under the traditional understandings of liberal democratic theory, the correlative duties of government do not obligate it to create the institutional frameworks for political debate and action, or to assure all groups of equal ability to propagate their views. Rather, those traditional understandings require governments to protect citizens in their political organizations and activities: forming political parties, mobilizing interest groups, soliciting campaign funds, petitioning and demonstrating, campaigning for votes, establishing associations to monitor local government, lobbying.

Such governmental duties of tolerance and equal protection for all political activities could be viewed as a minimum, essential elaboration of the "take part" clause. They respond to the liberal commitment to guarantee citizens their political and legal equality. Assured of that equality, citizens will decide for themselves where to assign their resources and energy. Government makes many paths possible, but it is for citizens to open and pursue them. Political participation is one such path. Choices about types and degrees of participation may

108. *See* R. DAHL, DEMOCRATIC THEORY, *supra* note 82, at 131–32. Commenting on his demonstration of the inadequacy of elections as a way of indicating majority preferences, Dahl states that nonetheless "the election process is one of two fundamental methods of social control which, operating together, make governmental leaders responsive to non-leaders so that the distinction between democracy and dictatorship still makes sense." The other method requires continuous political competition among individuals and parties. *Id.*

109. *See supra* text accompanying note 25.

depend on citizens' economic resources and social status. But it is not government's responsibility to alleviate that dependence, to open paths to political participation which lack of funds or education or status would otherwise block.

Emphasis upon a right to vote, without elaboration of companion rights to other ways of taking part in public affairs, therefore fits traditional liberal conceptions of public and private spheres of competence. Unlike other participatory activities such as the formation of interest groups, elections do not happen merely with the benefit of the state's permission and protection. Governments must design and administer an electoral process. Limiting governmental duty to what only governments can do, the construction of an electoral system, leaves the rest of the participatory framework to private initiative. Although Article 25 imposes no such limitation on governmental action, neither does it impose specific obligations other than the conduct of elections.

These understandings do not, however, constitute the whole of the tradition of liberal democracy. Changing ideologies and practices—those associated with the classical and contemporary theorists of direct, strong and participatory democracy—have blurred older lines between private and public spheres. Many states no longer treat the establishment of electoral machinery and the protection of citizens' political speech and association as the outer boundary of a government's duty to honor citizens' right to participate. Governmental functions in liberal democracies have expanded in ways that heighten popular participation. Legislative reforms overcome socio-economic barriers to participation, and open new ways for citizens to "take part in the conduct of public affairs."

Political parties themselves occupy an ambiguous position, in some respects independent and "nongovernmental," in other respects integrally part of a framework of governance. Laws common to many countries regulate their activities in ways that assure nondiscriminatory access to their processes,[110] define campaign periods, put limits on the sources or amounts of campaign contributions and restrict spending by candidates, provide for public funding of campaigns, or assure equal access to media. Other laws relax qualifying tests for voters. In brief, regulation of the entire electoral process, with a view to heightening electoral competition and expanding electoral participation, has become commonplace.

Legislation has reached beyond the traditional participatory activities within an electoral process. States have devolved power to regional

110. United States constitutional law has dealt with issues of state action in the activities of political parties, as in the White Primary Cases, discussed in L. TRIBE, *supra* note 106, at 1118–21.

or local government for reasons including the facilitation of broader citizen participation. Citizens' groups—concerned with issues as varied as the environment, human rights, education, welfare institutions, consumer protection and disarmament—have been brought into formal consultative arrangements with relevant governmental bodies.[111] Statutory schemes affecting town planning or health care mandate citizen participation. This wealth of statutory invention bearing on popular participation has extended beyond governmental bodies to affect the workplace as well. Legislation has required new forms of participation for workers that include their election of representatives to the supervisory boards of large corporate employers and provision for elected work councils with certain codetermination rights at the plant level.[112]

Such developing involvement of government in the institutionalization of political participation within and outside electoral processes stems from a theory which my prior discussion of liberal democracy has characterized as participatory and strong rather than representative and thin. That theory understands participation as both an instrumental and inherent good. It takes increasing account of barriers to electoral and other forms of political participation, and invests government with an obligation to lower those barriers. It has become a part of liberal ideology.

That theory is, however, more complex and contentious than one which aims only at justifying elections. Difficulties lie not only in its formulation but also in assessing compliance with an international norm embodying it. Suppose, for example, that such theory were understood to inform the "take part" clause of Article 25, and thereby to give coherent direction to its elaboration. Problems would arise in reaching a judgment whether a government had satisfied its duty to enact legislation extending opportunities for citizens—for all citizens, powerful and powerless—to "take part in the conduct of public affairs."

As generally understood, the "elections" clause poses no comparable difficulty. A government's violation of that clause, like torture or mock trials, is relatively easy to determine. Elections either take place or they don't; they are or are not contested; fact finders can make judgments about the integrity of the casting and counting of ballots; those elected do or do not take and hold office.[113] The expression

111. Laws in The Netherlands have set up consultative bodies to give decision-makers advice. For example, representatives of the women's movement, environmentalists and human rights organizations advise different governmental bodies. *See* 40 U.N. ESCOR, Commission on Human Rights, (Prov. Agenda item 8) Annex at 3, 5, U.N. Doc. No. E/CN.4/1984/12 (1984).

112. For a discussion of legislation in the Federal Republic of Germany, see Wiedemann, *Codetermination by Workers in German Enterprises*, 28 AM. J. COMP. L. 79 (1980). For critical analysis of the direction which American labor law has followed and proposals for heightened self-governance in the workplace, see Klare, *supra* note 93.

113. *See* Farer, *Human Rights and Human Wrongs: Is the Liberal Model Sufficient?*, 7 HUM. RTS.

"genuine elections" in the human rights instruments is generally understood to cover these formal, even measurable criteria.[114] By meeting those criteria, elections are understood to comply with the human rights norms.[115]

One can imagine the use of a more complex criterion than procedural correctness to determine whether an election satisfies Article 25—for example, the criterion whether it constitutes, in the article's language, the "free expression of the will of the electors." That phrase, if interpreted to require more than a non-coerced and secret ballot, could make relevant those considerations which a concentration on the formal integrity of an electoral process enables one to ignore: the distribution of political and economic power, its effect on differential access of classes and ethnic groups to the electoral process and political power, the obstacles to greater access, the power of elected officials relative

Q. 189 (1985). Farer, a former Chairman of the Inter-American Commission on Human Rights, comments on a report of the Commission on Colombia, prepared during his tenure. He criticizes the Commission for not attempting "to peer behind the form of party competition to determine whether . . . the right to participate in government was inhibited" by such factors as limited access to the media by left-wing parties, and an agreement between leaders of the two major parties "to keep certain potentially popular programs off the political agenda." *Id.* at 199.

Farer observes that nothing in the text of the governing convention (the American Convention on Human Rights) "compels [or] precludes deep analysis of the political process as a condition for assessing compliance with the right to participate." He points to the deep liberal assumption informing such inquiries of human rights groups "that in a state where associational rights are reasonably well protected, the right of political participation is realized in all cases where formal political power coincides with electoral achievement. As long as the franchise is not arbitrarily restricted and the ballots are accurately counted, traditional liberal criteria are satisfied." *Id.*

114. Despite procedurally correct conduct on election day, a government may have violated other human rights norms relevant to the broad electoral process, but not incorporated as such within Article 25 of the International Covenant. For example, its restrictions on speech and association may have impaired the electoral campaign of an opposing party. For such provisions of the International Covenant, see *infra* text accompanying note 25.

115. The problem of determining whether elections meet requirements of international norms takes center stage before world opinion when elections are instituted or, after a long suspension, revived in states with sorry human rights records that have been under dictatorial government. Other states, and nongovernmental human rights organizations, have sent representatives to monitor the proceedings of election day. Their reported observations have tended to fasten on the events of the election itself—whether there was intimidation of voters, violence, fraudulent voting or counting—and on whether the victor in a "genuine" election took office.

See The International Human Rights Law Group, Guidelines for International Election Observing, at i (noting that the relevant provisions of human rights instruments for assessing electoral processes are "vague"). The International Human Rights Law Group advocates a broader approach. It urges that missions evaluating elections consider related rights such as those to expression and association. *See id.* at 6. But missions of national governments, intergovernmental organizations, or nongovernmental human rights groups "have as a prime focus an assessment of the fairness of the election process." *Id.* at 1. Matters relevant to a free and fair election include a franchise without unreasonable limitations, rights to organize and advocate, a secret ballot, honest voting and counting, and absence of intimidation of voters. *See id.* at 34–36. The "basic thesis" of the project of election observing, as described by Dr. Griesgraber, speaker at a conference on the subject, "is that procedurally correct elections are a necessary but not sufficient ingredient for democracy." *Id.* at 72.

to other centers of power in the society.[116] What escapes analysis in the contemporary understanding of international norms on political participation is the quality and significance of electoral participation itself.

IV. COMMUNIST STATES AND POLITICAL PARTICIPATION

This article cannot address the broad range of alternatives to theories of participation in the liberal democracies: the ideologies and practices of corporative states and military dictatorships, of theocracies and monarchies, of distinctive countries like Mexico or Japan. Instead it considers the most significant alternative in the contemporary world to the liberal democracies, Communist-Party states.

Even that ambition must be sharply qualified. The world of communist states is far from monolithic with respect to either the ideology or practice of political participation. The Soviet Union and the People's Republic of China, Yugoslavia and Poland, offer important contrasts as well as similarities. The differences appear not only among countries but over time within the same country: the China of the Cultural Revolution and of Deng Xiaoping, the Soviet Union of Stalin's terror and of Gorbachev's *glasnost*. Generally the exclusive political party and the hegemonic political force, the Communist Party has at times been neither. Some communist countries have permitted other, acceptable parties of subordinate power. During periods of some countries' history, institutions such as the military, secret police or church have exercised power competitively with the Party.

In view of this diversity, the article concentrates illustratively on one communist country, the Soviet Union. To some degree, the contrasts here drawn with the ideologies and practices of the liberal democracies apply to all Communist-Party states. The discussion first describes post-Stalin trends in official ideology about political and popular participation. It then turns to different views about the types of institutionalization of these theories in Soviet life, and makes comparisons with liberal democracies.

---

116. *See* H. PITKIN, *supra* note 85, at 230. Pitkin suggests that although inquiry into the representative character of a government must start with the question whether rulers are elected, other considerations soon become relevant: "We want to know how genuine the elections are, who has the right to vote, whether the elected officials have the real governmenmental power, and how much opposition is permitted." *Id. See also* J. PAINTER, GUATEMALA: FALSE HOPE, FALSE FREEDOM (1987). Painter comments on the favorable international evaluation of the 1986 election of Vinicio Cerezo; it was judged to be free of fraud and overt military control. "In a characteristically bold equation of elections and democracy, the U.S. State Department triumphantly described the elections as the 'final step in the reestablishment of democracy.'" *Id.* at xiv. He argues, however, that the election, a "ritual of the ballot box," could hardly be viewed as a return to freedom for most Guatemalans. *Id.* at 79. The civilian winner could do no more than exercise a formal power on behalf of those with economic and political control.

My purpose remains the same. I shall not examine theory abstractly in terms of its premises and structure. Nor shall I attempt to portray the reality of participatory institutions or the actual experience of participants. Rather, my discussion traces the implications of Soviet theory for the practices and institutions of political participation. Again I shall employ Article 25 of the International Covenant to organize my observations and to facilitate comparison between theories and types of participation in the contexts of democratic and communist societies. My discussion emphasizes the priority given by the Soviet Union to the "take part" clause, to forms of popular participation distinct from the electoral processes which continue to form the core of liberal democratic theory and practice.

A. *The Stated Theories of Mass Participation*

The right to political participation has become an element of rituals of accusation between the West and a country like the Soviet Union. Liberal democracies typically denigrate concepts of political participation in nondemocratic states. They charge that the uncontested elections in one-party states are by definition sham and ceremonial; that the non-electoral modes of widespread participation are imposed and manipulated to serve interests of the regime rather than to express those of the people; and that the government in communist states, however elected, must defer to the leadership of the Communist Party.[117] The characteristic counter-charges contend that electors' choice in liberal democracies is generally illusory because of the similarity among the powerful political parties;[118] that effective partici-

117. The turbulent decades from the October Revolution to the period of Stalin's terror witnessed similar criticisms from figures like Rosa Luxemburg and Trotsky. Soon after the October Revolution, Luxemburg attacked Leninist conceptions of the state and party, charging that the soviets established by Lenin and Trotsky had displaced "representative bodies created by general, popular elections . . . ." What remained to control government was not a dictatorship of the proletariat but of a "handful of politicians, that is a dictatorship in the bourgeois sense . . . ." R. LUXEMBURG, THE RUSSIAN REVOLUTION AND LENINISM OR MARXISM? 71–72 (1961). In 1937, the embittered, exiled Trotsky censured Stalinism as a betrayal of the revolution through the usurpation of workers' power by the bureaucracy. "Politics is thus once for all declared the monopoly of an uncontrolled bureaucracy," although the heterogeneous Soviet society "can furnish adequate nourishing soil for several parties." L. TROTSKY, THE REVOLUTION BETRAYED: WHAT IS THE SOVIET UNION AND WHERE IS IT GOING? 266, 268 (M. Eastman trans. 1972).

118. *See The Civil War in France*, in THE MARX-ENGELS READER 618 (R. Tucker ed. 1972) (Marx praising the Paris Commune, consisting principally of working men elected by universal suffrage in wards throughout Paris). "Instead of deciding once in three or six years which member of the ruling class was to misrepresent the people in Parliament," universal suffrage here served the people, "constituted in the Communes." *Id.* at 633. *See also* A. NATHAN, CHINESE DEMOCRACY 38 (1985) (describing the view of many Chinese commentators that a competitive

pation in political processes is denied to populous groups lacking the status or resources to compete;[119] and that mass political participation stops with the vote, an episodic act which exhausts most citizens' sense of obligation to their fellow citizens and to the state.

Since the Stalinist period, the official ideology of the Soviet Union—the speeches and writings of political leaders, spokespersons and highly placed scholars—has given heightened prominence to the ideal of popular participation. In this respect, the current Constitution of 1977 goes considerably beyond Stalin's 1934 constitution. It describes a "society of genuine democracy, whose political system ensures . . . the more active participation of the working people in state life."[120] Not only are there periodic elections to the soviets, under universal suffrage and by secret ballot, but the "most important questions of state life" may be submitted to the entire people for discussion by popular referenda.[121] Numerous provisions assure "more extensive participation of citizens" in the administration of social affairs.[122] Article 48 formally grants citizens

> the right to participate in the administration of state and social affairs and in the discussion and adoption of laws and decisions of general state and local significance. This right shall be ensured by the opportunity to elect and to be elected to soviets of people's deputies and other elective state agencies, take part in all-people's discussions and voting, people's control, the work of state agencies, social organizations, and public initiative agencies, and in meetings of labor collectives and at their place of residence.

---

party system and a free press in the United States disguise the class dictatorship of the bourgeoisie—a one party system masquerading as a multi-party system).

Comments about the limited choice given the electorate in liberal democracies are not of course restricted to observers from communist states. *See* R. DAHL, DEMOCRATIC THEORY, *supra* note 82, at 127 (noting that often "a great many voters do not really perceive a choice between candidate A and candidate B; for many people the only perceived alternatives are to vote for one of the candidates or not to vote at all.").

119. *See The State and Revolution*, in THE LENIN ANTHOLOGY 311, 373 (R. Tucker ed. 1975) (Lenin's contrasting of Marx's description of the Paris Commune with the capitalist democracies, where one sees "restriction after restriction upon democracy [which] in their sum total . . . exclude and squeeze out the poor from politics, from active participation in democracy."). In a discussion in the Human Rights Committee of a report of the Soviet Union under Article 40 of the International Covenant (*see supra* note 56 and accompanying text), a member from West Germany inquired whether the Soviet Union understood itself to be in compliance with the Covenant and international law in view of the monopoly of power given the Communist Party. 23 Human Rights Comm. (565th mtg.) at 8, U.N. Doc. CCPR/C/SR.565 (1984). Another member from East Germany promptly observed: "Equal participation in public life was in no sense guaranteed in countries where individuals could spend millions to promote political parties while workers were unemployed and had no real choice as to how to cast their vote." *Id.*

120. CONSTITUTION OF THE USSR, *supra* note 13, preamble.

121. *Id.* art. 5.

122. *See, e.g.*, *id.* art. 9.

Such assurances and declarations of rights are accompanied by a reaffirmation of the Communist Party's role. "Having fulfilled the tasks of the dictatorship of the proletariat the Soviet state has become an all-people's state. The leading role of the Communist Party, vanguard of the whole people, has grown."[123] The Party, based upon "rigorous observance" of Leninist norms of party life, builds its work on "the all-round development of intra-party democracy."[124]

Burlatsky, a prominent Soviet writer on constitutional matters, responded to Western criticism that rights to political participation and expression were hollow since they could not be employed to challenge the socialist system.[125] He argued that the conceptions of human rights developed in the United States had to be rejected as a model for the Soviet Union. Its people had chosen socialism as a system responsive to their needs for progress and social equality, "and that choice is final." Subject to that constraint, there existed a "wide range of alternative ideas, proposals and judgements current in the political life of the country."[126] Citizens could find many ways under the 1977 Constitution to participate in the management of state and public affairs.

Western scepticism about Soviet claims of extensive socialist self-government and of a tolerated pluralism of political ideas stems principally from the leading role of the Party—a party, it has been said, that rules but doesn't govern.[127] In his 1977 report on the new Constitution, Brezhnev described the Party as

> inseparable from the people as a whole. The Party has no interests except the interests of the people. To try to counterpose the Party to the people, to talk of the "dictatorship of the Party," is tantamount to trying to counterpose, let us say, the heart to the rest of the human body.[128]

Subject to the postulate that Marxist-Leninist ideology must be defended, and to related prohibitions on speech or association which is

123. *Id.* at preamble.

124. Rules of the Communist Party of the Soviet Union, Preamble, in BASIC DOCUMENTS, *supra* note 13, at 33. Claims that the Party is moving toward an open process in debate and elections are much disputed. *See* O. IOFFE, SOVIET LAW AND SOVIET REALITY 60 (Law in Eastern Europe No. 30, 1985) (contending that elections to Party agencies "are no less fictitious than elections of soviets' deputies predetermined as they are by appointments.").

125. Burlatsky, *Fixed in Law*, in F. BURLATSKY, V. DAVIDOV, A. LEBEDEV & A. MOVCHAN, THE RIGHTS OF THE INDIVIDUAL IN SOCIALIST SOCIETY 93 (1982).

126. *Id.* at 101.

127. W.E. BUTLER, SOVIET LAW 152 (1983).

128. Report by L.I. Brezhnev at Session of USSR Supreme Soviet, *On the Draft Constitution of the Unions of SSR and the Results of its Nationwide Discussion*, 29 CURRENT DIGEST OF SOVIET PRESS No. 39, at 1, 7 (Oct. 26, 1977) [hereinafter Report by Brezhnev].

hostile to the building of socialism and the people's interests,[129] the Party fosters debate. That debate, Burlatsky explains, "continues as long as the decision is being worked out. . . ." Then, however, the principle of democratic centralism obtains. Once a decision is adopted, discussion ends and it "has to be carried out jointly by everybody concerned."[130]

Soviet political theorists and leaders stress two domains of mass participation in public affairs. They describe elections of deputies to the soviets and the efforts to achieve closer relationships between voters and their deputies.[131] But unlike their Western counterparts in liberal-capitalist countries, they have given increased emphasis to types of non-electoral participation, such as the active role of the people in the implementation of official policies, including the administration of the economy. Of course these two domains can be associated with the "elections" clause and "take part" clause of Article 25 of the International Covenant.

Let us start with electoral participation. Representatives to the Soviets of People's Deputies are elected periodically through universal and equal suffrage, and by secret ballot. The right to nominate candidates for election rests with organizations of the Communist Party, trade unions and other public organizations. Although no law restricts the number of candidates nominated for a post, uncontested elections are the almost invariable rule.[132]

Brezhnev drew attention in his 1977 Report to innovations in the new Constitution bearing on relations between the people and the

---

129. For relevant excerpts from Article 50 and 51 of the Constitution, see *supra* text accompanying notes 29–30. See INSTITUTE OF STATE AND LAW OF THE USSR ACADEMY OF SCIENCES, INTERNATIONAL COVENANTS ON HUMAN RIGHTS AND SOVIET LEGISLATION (1986), which justifies Soviet restrictions on expression or association simply by noting that the Constitution explicitly guarantees political rights only to realize the aims set forth in its preamble. Hence it is "impossible" to guarantee freedoms used to oppose those aims. *Id.* at 35. The Institute asserts without argument that these restrictions conform with Articles 19 and 20 of the International Covenant. *See supra* text accompanying note 25.

Prohibitions on political activity viewed as hostile to stated ends of the state or to the regime have been rigorously enforced against persons exercising or advocating national, religious and human rights. *See, e.g.*, L. ALEXEYEVA, SOVIET DISSENT 449 (1985) (concluding particularly with respect to human rights movements: "The history of dissent in the USSR is a tragic one. It is an endless chain of crippled and ruined fates. The movement never became a mass movement and the immediate demands of dissidents were almost wholly frustrated."); *see also* M. GILBERT, THE JEWS OF HOPE (1985); J. RUBENSTEIN, SOVIET DISSIDENTS: THEIR STRUGGLE FOR HUMAN RIGHTS (rev. ed. 1985).

130. Burlatsky, *supra* note 125, at 118.

131. "Election of his representatives by the citizen has emerged as an almost universal form of participation in the modern world." T.H. FRIEDGUT, *supra* note 73, at 71. Rare are states with no level of elected officials, "no matter how authoritarian their political systems may be." *Id.*

132. W.E. BUTLER, *supra* note 127, at 146 (referring to the "accepted practice" that only one candidate appears on the ballot for each position to be elected).

soviets. For example, provision for voters' mandates to deputies would guarantee that the soviets took account of concrete interests of working people. This "fulfillment of mandates is an important part of the work of the Soviets," and "a real manifestation of socialist democracy."[133]

In his 1986 report to the Twenty-seventh Congress of the Communist Party, Gorbachev proposed further decentralization of power to the local soviets and other bodies of power.[134] Two years later, in a talk to the party's Central Committee, he announced that the "Politburo considers the perfection of the Soviet electoral system to be one of the main avenues in democratizing our life . . . ."[135] He stressed current proposals that voters, in election meetings as well as work collectives, discuss several candidacies. Such an innovation, coupled with larger multi-member districts, "will enable party and local government bodies to get to know better the sentiments and will of the population." Nothing in these comments suggests, however, that the several candidates for, say, the post of deputy to a soviet would not all be chosen or approved by the Party.[136] Gorbachev's comments also addressed the need for "further democratizing" Party structures themselves, through having more than one candidate for a post. He added that it would seem "logical to democratize the elections of leading bodies in other public organizations as well."[137]

Soviet leaders repeatedly emphasize the direct character of mass participation. They note as an example the broad participation in nationwide discussions of major legal events, such as preparation of the 1977 Constitution. The point is often made statistically. Over 140,000,000 people, Brezhnev pointed out, took part in discussions of the draft constitution, at about 1,500,000 meetings at enterprises, farms, trade unions or residences, and at over 450,000 open party meetings.[138] He commented on the "unending flow" of letters from the people to drafting groups. The Constitutional Commission reported that such nationwide discussion made possible large improvements in the draft constitution. It recommended changes in 110 articles in view of 400,000 proposals for amendments. "Never before has our country known public activeness on such a scale."

---

133. Report by Brezhnev, *supra* note 128, at 3.

134. Gorbachev, *The Political Report of the CPSU Central Committee to the 27th Congress of the Communist Party of the of Soviet Union*, 38 CURRENT DIGEST OF SOVIET PRESS No. 8, at 4, 23–26 (Mar. 6, 1986).

135. N.Y. Times, Jan. 28, 1988, at A8, col. 6.

136. *Cf.* Dominguez, *Revolutionary Politics: The New Demands for Orderliness*, in CUBA: INTERNAL AND INTERNATIONAL AFFAIRS 19 (J. Dominguez ed. 1982). The author describes Cuban reforms in the mid-1970s which provided for direct election to the municipal assemblies and for two candidates per post. The Party, however, controlled nomination procedures. There was no freedom to campaign or to associate with other candidates. *See id.* at 40–41.

137. N.Y. Times, *supra* note 135.

138. Report by Brezhnev, *supra* note 128, at 1.

Given the Party's control of periodic elections to the soviets, it is understandable that Soviet theorists and leaders give prominence to a broad range of non-electoral activities that fit within the "take part" clause of Article 25. Mass political participation in processes of decision-making for political and economic matters has become a major theme. Burlatsky observes that the "main emphasis is placed on everyday participation"—for example, activities of work collectives at plants or farms, heightened worker participation in managing production, programs of the Communist Party or Young Communist League members or the work of trade unions.[139] Much attention is given to the direct democracy of the workplace even with respect to general political issues. Workers "take an active part in managing the affairs of the state," through mass discussions of bills, debates over accounts to the people of the elected deputies to the local soviets and proposals to administrative bodies.[140]

Brezhnev summarizes these trends in the development of Soviet society in his 1977 Report. More citizens, Brezhenv writes,

> are participating more and more actively in the work of the bodies of power and people's control, in the management of production and distribution, in social and cultural policy and in the administration of justice. In short, as socialist democracy develops our statehood is gradually being transformed into communist socialist self-government.[141]

This theme of mass participation of citizens figured in portions of Gorbachev's 1986 report to the Twenty-seventh Congress of the Communist Party. Socialism will have developed successfully "only when the people themselves actually manage their affairs, when millions of people participate in political life," enriching the principle of democratic centralism.[142] To overcome bureaucratic rigidity, citizens must have "a real opportunity to influence the working out of managerial decisions . . . ."[143] Gorbachev emphasized the "direct" character of such participation of the masses in the "elaboration, adoption, and fulfillment" of governmental and other decisions. These proposals bridge the fields of political and economic decision-making. Through the labor collectives, workers must become involved in management

139. Burlatsky, *supra* note 125, at 102.
140. *Id.* at 126.
141. Report by Brezhnev, *supra* note 128, at 7.
142. Gorbachev, *supra* note 134, at 24.
143. *Id.*

and gain "the feeling that they are full-fledged masters of production."[144]

B. Views about Elections and Mass Non-electoral Participation

The eventful years of Gorbachev's leadership complicate any effort at evaluation of Soviet ideology and programs to institutionalize political participation. The change in both rhetoric and in the degree of public debate and dissent from, say, the dark period of Stalin's rule must be viewed as dramatic. But the rhetoric has far exceeded achievement. The Soviet Union has yet to institutionalize reforms protecting competing factions or organized dissent. It has not opened elections to the soviets or to Party positions to unregulated contest.

The entrenched obstacles to institutionalization of such changes are evident. Inertia, fear of political disintegration and resistance to loss of privilege will all play their role. But the recent trend in ideology and public debate would have been viewed by many observers of the Soviet Union as implausible as little as a decade ago. Given the obvious inability to predict the durability or long-run implications of the policy of *glasnost*, further incremental change or sharp reversal both remain possible. Despite the inevitable uncertainty, one should not dismiss the trend in official ideology as irrelevant to the possible development of a norm like Article 25 of the International Covenant. Less influential than institutionalized practices, aspirations expressed in ideologies can nonetheless provoke debate and experiments in different societies and thereby contribute to the evolving understanding of international norms.

Surely with respect to the Supreme Soviet of the Soviet Union and generally with respect to the local soviets as well, elections cannot be understood as choices between competing candidates and policies. Uncontested, with candidates selected by the Party or in any event subject to its approval, they serve ceremonial functions of support and affirmation.[145] Through the ninety-nine percent approval generally given candidates, elections are meant to express solidarity between people and government. Citizens can vote against the single candidate, but a remarkably small percentage of nominees fails to receive the majority of all votes cast.[146]

---

144. *Id.* at 25.

145. *See* H. BERMAN, JUSTICE IN THE U.S.S.R.: AN INTERPRETATION OF SOVIET LAW 374 (rev. ed. 1963).

146. Single candidates failing to win over 50 percent of the votes cast amounted to about one in 7,200 in 1961 and one in 30,000 in 1975. Most defeats were at the village level. T.H. FRIEDGUT, *supra* note 73, at 130.

Perhaps the key importance of popular elections in the Soviet Union lies not in the voting or its known consequences, but in the pre-election activities of the Party. Campaigns preceding elections become periods of intense political mobilization of the people, recruitment into the Party, and communication to the Party of popular grievances through the techniques of large meetings and agit-prop (agitation-propaganda)—that is, myriad consultations of voters, often in their residences.[147]

The recent intimations of heightened competition for election to the soviets have uncertain significance. The two or more candidates who may compete for a given post will still be chosen or approved by the Party.[148] Traditional restraints on public debate or association that challenge the commitment to Marxism-Leninism remain in place. Control of policy on matters of high importance stays with the Party, whose decisions are implemented, generally by unanimous vote, by the Supreme Soviet and whose members compose a majority of deputies in the higher legislative bodies.[149]

Intra-party debate and contest could to some extent substitute for the arranged character of elections to the soviets.[150] The possibility of election of party officials at the lower levels has entered public discussion. But a major political transformation would be necessary to displace the current system of uncontested nominations for high Party posts. Moreover, intra-party politics excludes most citizens. However unlikely unconstrained debate or even a tolerance of the formation of political factions would be, such development would still involve only

---

147. Friedgut states that elections are not presented "as a possible redistribution of power, but as an affirmation of the existing power. The nominations, the campaigning, and the voting serve as an intensified period of recruitment into participation." "Agitators," who are generally Party members, visit many homes to discuss issues and see what people's complaints are. *Id.* at 95.

148. "The Party will continue to see to it that the most worthy people, capable of conducting state affairs at a high level, are elected Deputies . . . ." Gorbachev, *supra* note 134, at 24.

149. *See* H. BERMAN, *supra* note 145, at 374 (describing the Supreme Soviet as essentially an honorary society with little genuine debate and unanimous enactments).

150. Butler notes that the election procedures within the Party are obscure, but that the general rule for elections to the Central Committee of the Party appears to be a consensus slate. W.E. BUTLER, *supra* note 127, at 155. *See also* Huntington, *Social and Institutional Dynamics of One-Party States*, in AUTHORITARIAN POLITICS IN MODERN SOCIETY 3 (S. Huntington & C. Moore eds. 1970). Huntington observes that as one-party states consolidate their authority after periods of revolution or rapid adaptation, elements of electoral competition may appear. If domestic enemies are destroyed, why not permit popular choice between candidates "all of whom share the same fundamental commitment to the party and the system?" *Id.* at 38. But the threat to the bureaucratic position of party officials remains. "Consequently, electoral competition is more likely initially to develop for governmental than for party positions." *Id.* at 39. Opening the party to competition, the author notes, runs the large risk of leading to organized blocs or factions, of turning the system into a multi-party one in all but name. *Id.* *See infra* note 175 for observations on one-party African states.

about 20,000,000 Party members or one fourteenth of the total Soviet population.[151]

In the second major domain of Soviet political participation, it is clear that ongoing, institutionally based and mass participation has far greater significance in Soviet than in democratic theory.[152] Here the Soviet leaders emphasize their duty and achievements in enabling citizens—to use the language of Article 25—to "take part in the conduct of public affairs." In a socialized economy where productive resources are state owned and in a political system where the Communist Party monopolizes power, such participation will inevitably be planned and implemented, or approved and monitored, by the government and Party. What emerges in Soviet society is not the self-governance emphasized by Western theories of strong or participatory democracy, but rather forms of participation that are consistent with the Party's central control and that advance its programs. Soviet ideology and society point toward a different realization, in a radically different political context, of the "take part" clause.

Mass participation occurs dominantly at the local levels of life. Participation at that level in organized activities, which in some sense are all governmental activities, implicates a broader and more important range of issues than would, say, the involvement of citizens' groups with local governments in liberal democracies.

The functions of mass participation extend from degrees of management reponsibilities of workers in industrial or farm enterprises, to the expression of complaints or recommendations to local authorities through official channels of communication. Such participation in processes of political and economic decision-making often bear on the bureaucratic implementation of legislation or general government policy.[153] For example, local associations monitor the government bureaucracies, provide some check on their tendencies toward corruption or lethargy, and make proposals for more efficient ways to achieve official goals. Such types of mass participation thereby build contacts between an affected citizenry—workers, lodgers, the environmentally conscious and so on—and the relevant bureaucracies.

Systems of mass participation in communist and third world countries, with their abundance of local organizations and activities, serve multiple functions which make them susceptible to radically different

151. O. IOFFE, *supra* note 124, at 60.

152. *See* J. HOUGH & M. FAINSOD, HOW THE SOVIET UNION IS GOVERNED 317 (1979) [hereinafter HOUGH & FAINSOD].

153. *See* W.E. BUTLER, *supra* note 127, at 122–23 (describing the growth of people's control commissions from a volunteer membership in 1963 of about 2 million to over 10 million in 1982).

evaluations. Empirically based judgments about their effects, or knowledge of how they are experienced by the participants, are hard to come by. Foreign scholars have only limited ability to explore local organizations, and to question or poll groups of citizens.[154]

From one perspective, these local institutions can be said to achieve ongoing involvement in public life that advances citizens' as well as the polity's interests. Complaints and proposals are heard, influence is exerted on policy, bureaucratic implementation of laws is monitored to correct inefficiencies. Workers feel respected and empowered as they are given a role in planning and supervising production.[155] Social discontent is allayed as citizens are educated about the aims of the political system through a myriad of institutions, and encouraged to express grievances through officially designated channels.

From a different perspective, such mass participation constitutes a vehicle for the imposition of government policy and for socialization of the population into a controlled political system. The Party mobilizes and directs people to draw them into the administration by government bureaucracies of policies which are determined on high. The people continue without voice in the policies' formulation. Feedback of popular grievances to the government and Party serves less to make government responsive to the popular will than to improve its strategies for imposing the Party's will.[156]

One perspective emphasizes influence from bottom to top, the other from top to bottom. What is required is not a choice between these polar understandings of developing Soviet theory and practice, both of which have some validity, but an assessment recognizing these contradictory implications of mass participation in a one-party state.[157] Surely some participatory institutions, such as those monitoring bureaucratic performance or encouraging expression of grievances, send

154. *See* T.H. FRIEDGUT, *supra* note 73, at 74–75; HOUGH & FAINSOD, *supra* note 152, at 315–18.

155. *See* T.H. FRIEDGUT, *supra* note 73, at 5 (speculating that competence and influence at local levels of life may give citizens a sense of total political involvement and blunt the effect of their exclusion from higher levels of policy making and control).

156. For a description of five functions of mass political participation in Marxist-Leninist countries, see B. Roth, Taking "People's Democracy" Seriously: Marxism-Leninism and the Right to Political Participation 47–63 (Spring 1987) (unpublished paper available at Harvard Law School Library). These functions are ratification of party rule; political education; performance of revolutionary tasks; policing of bureaucratic performance; and "in a limited respect, contribution to the formulation of the general will." *Id.* at 61.

157. Friedgut concludes an extended discussion of the electoral system by stating: "Faced once more with the problem of trying to distinguish truth from fiction in any given Soviet setting, the reader must be painfully aware that we are dealing with extremely complex and sometimes contradictory processes taking place within an evolving political culture that is subject to a multitude of pressures." T.H. FRIEDGUT, *supra* note 73, at 153.

ideas upward in the Soviet hierarchy. Surely mass participation will be employed to reinforce control from the top, by educating citizens to revolutionary tasks or mobilizing support for given policies.[158]

Some scholars reach harsh judgments about Soviet claims for these local mechanisms.[159] Instruments of mobilization and socialization, they are meant to create a sense among the people—an illusory sense, to be sure—of their power in a political system from which, at its higher and more important levels, they are effectively barred. The programs of mass involvement in the formulation and implementation of policy can themselves become intrusive strategies for keeping check on a population. They can become coercive and deeply abusive, as during China's Cultural Revolution. The primary function of much of this directed local participation remains the legitimation of a regime which, despite its apparent recourse to the people's views, continues to repress independent political groups or organized dissent.[160]

Other Western scholars, while recognizing the force of such views and the Party's control over participatory activities, reach qualified but more affirmative judgments.[161] They find in these institutions potential ways of protesting and influencing policies of local impact. Citizens may thereby play a role in the administration of government which bears so heavily on their everyday lives. Citizens' participation in resolving such issues of importance in their lives may be genuine and effective.

C. *Comparison with Liberal Democracies*

I turn to some general comparisons with theories and practices in the Western states. Opposite to liberal democracies, the Soviet system couples strong central control through the Party's hold on political power with local mass participation. In common with one-party systems in and outside the communist world, it severs the theory and practice of political participation from democratic control of govern-

---

158. The functions of participatory institutions become more complex, and the problems of evaluation more acute, during revolutions or the period of their consolidation. Assuring national security may become a major task of such institutions. The new, mass organizations in a number of revolutionary societies have performed that task. *See, e.g.*, J. DOMINGUEZ, CUBA: ORDER AND REVOLUTION 261 (1978); G. RUCHWARGER, PEOPLE IN POWER: FORGING A GRASSROOTS DEMOCRACY IN NICARAGUA 74–95 (1987).

159. See the description of views of critics in HOUGH & FAINSOD, *supra* note 152, at 319. *See generally* Tay, *Marxism, Socialism and Human Rights*, in HUMAN RIGHTS 104 (E. Kamenka & A. Tay eds. 1978); O. IOFFE, *supra* note 124. One can only speculate whether the views expressed by observers of the Soviet Union, whatever their conclusions, would have been modified in some ways in the light of the policies of the Gorbachev administration.

160. *See generally* L. ALEXEYEVA, *supra* note 129; O. IOFFE, *supra* note 124.

161. *See, e.g.*, HOUGH & FAINSOD, *supra* note 152, at 277–319. Compare Nelson, *infra* note 167 (comparing mobilized and autonomous participation).

ment by the people. Severance appears essential, given the state's formal commitment to the building of a socialist-communist society. This goal is to be realized through the leadership of a Communist Party which derives its legitimacy not from periodic electoral expressions of the will of the people, but from deep premises of Marxist-Leninist theory including identification of the Party with the people and with objective laws of history.[162] Such a goal and commitment to Party leadership distance the state from the neutrality about the good to which liberal states are formally committed.

An open political system including party pluralism and genuinely contested elections would frontally contradict such characteristics of the Soviet system. It might modify or even abandon the commitment to the goal of communist construction and to Party leadership. A fixed end cannot tolerate an open process. Nor, from a more practical perspective, can a hegemonic party with its operational core of bureaucratically entrenched, full-time, salaried officials readily relinquish space for others.[163]

Such a political system must then assign a subsidiary role to the popular vote. Soviet elections have little in common with the emphasis in democratic theory on elections' protective purpose: controlling government through periodic popular choice between competing parties and policies. Postulating harmony between government and people and the guiding role of the Party, Soviet theory could acknowledge no need for an electoral control intended to secure the individual against governmental abuse.[164] Electoral participation serves more to advance goals assumed to be shared—particularly the goal of Party leadership of the people to communism—than to permit groups to vote instrumentally to advance either their distinctive interests or their independent view of social or political goals.

From a Western perspective, it is impossible to reconcile Soviet elections with the provision in Article 25 of the International Covenant for "genuine" elections "guaranteeing the free expression of the will of the electors . . . ." Even assuming that "genuine" were understood to refer to no more than the procedural integrity of the electoral process,[165] and that "free" were understood to imply no more than the

162. Writing about Cuba, Dominguez states: "Legitimation and decision-making do not depend on votes; the bottom does not control the top, nor can it vote it out of office. . . . The revolution claims to rule because it is right . . . ." J. DOMINGUEZ, *supra* note 158, at 305.

163. *See* Huntington, *supra* note 150, at 39.

164. Limiting state power "has been a minor and extremely belated consideration for Soviet constitutional draftsmen." Their purpose was not to limit the state but rather to use it "optimally" to reach the constitutionally stated ends. W.E. BUTLER, *supra* note 127, at 135.

165. Dr. Griesgraber, a speaker at a conference on election observing, referred to a third person's observation that "the cleanest elections, where everyone votes in secret, ballots are

right of the electorate to vote "against" a single candidate, a reconciliation would require a commitment to the deepest claims of Soviet ideology: that the Party constitutes the people's "vanguard" and "most advanced segment," objectively represents the people's higher interests and "has no interests except the interests of the people."[166]

On the other hand, the Soviet stress on mass participation in local administration invites comparisons with Western theories of strong, direct and participatory democracy. Those theories, to be sure, urge forms of participation that supplement voting in elections open to contest within democratic societies. They aim at maximum possible self-governance by civic-minded citizens, whereas the Soviet institutions are organized and supervised by the government and Party.

Comparisons between the Soviet experience of mass participation and Western theories of strong or participatory democracy should underscore a further difference between them. The Soviet experience is carefully limited to the important area of life that is of local importance. Participatory groups do not debate the military budget, propose a shift in foreign policy, urge the domestic implementation of human rights norms or advocate the recognition of demands of the Soviet Union's different nationalities for greater autonomy. Nor are participatory organizations of national scope permitted to address such issues. To the contrary, the Western theories of participatory democracy, while designating local government and contexts like the workplace as fertile fields for citizens' involvement, also embrace activities that seek to influence national policy at the highest level.

Nonetheless, Soviet institutions may nourish a sense of participation as an inherent as well as an instrumental good, as a way of fostering individual responsibility for the goals and methods of the larger polity. What starts as mobilized activity held to local concerns may over time become more independent and self generated.[167] From such points of view, mass local participation in a controlled society like the Soviet Union can be understood as a partial but potentially important realization of the right articulated in Article 25 of the International Covenant, to "take part in the conduct of public affairs, directly or through freely chosen representatives."

---

tallied, and winners take office, occur in the Soviet Union and Eastern Europe." THE INTERNATIONAL HUMAN RIGHTS LAW GROUP, *supra* note 115, at 72.

166. *See supra* text accompanying note 128.

167. *See* Nelson, *supra* note 73, at 103, 149 (1987). The author argues that scholars must rethink the distinction between mobilized and autonomous participation, for much participatory activity reflects both elements, and what starts dominantly as one may move toward the other. She adds that, in principle, all organizations "are potentially two-way streets: communication, pressure, and influence may flow up or down, in varying proportions, and those proportions may change over time." *Id.* at 151.

It is now possible to describe within the framework of Article 25 some basic relationships among the three bodies of theory treating the practices of political participation which have figured in my discussion. Thin, protective, representation theories of liberal democracy concentrate (in effect) on the "elections" clause. They have little to say about more ample realization within electoral democracies of the "take part" clause. Strong, direct, participation theories of democracy also view the "elections" clause as indispensable. But those theories reach further to insist on governments' duty to aid in the progressive development of participatory institutions and activities within the spirit of the "take part" clause. Contemporary Soviet theory about institutionalizing participation downplays the "elections" clause, separates the character and purposes of popular participation from control of government by the people, and points to distinctive programs for institutionalizing the "take part" clause in states with a single controlling party.

D. *Other Illustrations*

It should be clear that communist and other one-party states have not had monolithic experiences with political participation. Moves toward political democracy through the formation of interest or protest groups at the national level, and related demands for modification of the Communist Party's dominant role, have met firm repression. The fate of the Solidarity movement in Poland is a prime illustration.[168] Within such limits,[169] socialist states in general appear in flux. They hold to tenets like the hegemonic role of the Party, yet within those constraints sometimes devise experimental forms of popular participation that soften an earlier sharp contrast between, say, liberal democracies and Stalin's state.

For example, countries such as Hungary have made room for more play of political as well as economic forces and for plural viewpoints.[170]

---

168. *See* Bielasiak, *The Party: Permanent Crisis*, in POLAND: GENESIS OF A REVOLUTION 10 (A. Brumberg ed. 1983).

169. *Cf.* A. NATHAN, *supra* note 118, at 101 (quoting Deng Xiaoping's statement in 1980):

> But our party became the ruling party and the core force uniting the whole country, bringing to end the countless splits and little kingdoms . . . . China is led by the CCP and China's cause of socialist modernization is carried out under the leadership of the CCP. This principle cannot be shaken. If it is, China will regress into divisons and confusion, and will then be unable to accomplish modernization.

Together with the PRC Constitution, Deng has emphasized the "four basic principles:" the socialist road, dictatorship of the proletariat, Communist Party leadership, and Marxism-Leninism-Mao Zedong Thought. He has referred to Party leadership as the core of these principles. *Id.* at 36.

170. *See* 38 Human Rights Comm., *Consideration of Reports Submitted by States Parties under Article 40 of the Covenant*, U.N. Doc. CCPR/C/37/Add.1 (1985). As a part of a periodic report submitted to the Human Rights Committee under the International Covenant, Hungary described its recent legislation bearing on political participation. "[T]he building of a socialist

A great instability of policies about popular participation, decentralization of authority and permitted forms of protest has characterized the period in China subsequent to the Cultural Revolution.[171] Invention has been richest and most striking at the local level of mass participation. Yugoslavia, for example, has gone well beyond the Soviet Union in its decentralization of authority and delegation of self-management powers to workers in economic enterprises.[172] Yugoslavian theory points toward workers' participation in decision making, implementation of policies and distribution of benefits.

The Yugoslavian example has been important to a broader movement of so-called popular participation as an ingredient of economic and social development.[173] The movement, particularly strong among some third world countries, assumes that such participation will aid the processes of economic growth. Official programs, it is hoped, would gain in efficiency if the people affected by them could participate in their formulation and be charged with monitoring their implementation.

The prominence of this instrumental justification distinguishes the movement from the liberal democracies' stress on participation as a

---

society has made it necessary to improve democratism. . . . These requirements include . . . simplifying the preparation and conduct of elections." *Id.* at 13. The new laws required "mandatory nomination of two or more candidates for membership of the National Assembly" to "increase the political significance of elections and the activism of electors" as well as to "stimulate the efforts of elected members of the National Assembly . . . ." *Id. See also* U.S. HELSINKI WATCH COMMITTEE, VIOLATIONS OF THE HELSINKI ACCORDS: HUNGARY 29 (Report for the Helsinki Review Conference, 1986) (pointing out the strict limitations to these electoral changes). All candidates were required to sign a pledge to uphold the Party's program. Nonetheless, unofficial candidates were able to defeat between 20 and 30 of the candidates favored by the Party. "This was the first time that a Warsaw Pact nation has made competition compulsory for any political office." *Id.*

171. See at the formal normative level the description of political rights in the three Chinese constitutions of 1975, 1978 and 1982, in Nathan, *Political Rights in Chinese Constitutions*, in R. EDWARDS, L. HENKIN & A. NATHAN, HUMAN RIGHTS IN CONTEMPORARY CHINA 77 (1986). For an account of the ebb and flow of public dissent and forceful repression, of centralization and decentralization, see generally A. NATHAN, *supra* note 118.

172. For a statement of principles of worker participation, see the comments submitted by Yugoslavia to a United Nations study on the right to popular participation, in *Commission on Human Rights, Preliminary Report by the Secretary General*, 40 U.N. ESCOR (Prov. Agenda Item 8) Annex at 7, U.N. Doc. E/CN.4/1984/12. *See generally* E. COMISSO, WORKERS' CONTROL UNDER PLAN AND MARKET: IMPLICATIONS OF YUGOSLAV SELF-MANAGEMENT (1979).

173. A series of United Nations documents, including Reports of the Secretary-General, debates in the Third Committee and in the Commission on Human Rights, and reports of governments, have explored the theme of popular participation. *See, e.g., Report of Secretary-General, International Seminar on Popular Participation*, 37 U.N. GAOR (Prov. Agenda Item 78), U.N. Doc. A/37/442 (1982); *Report of the Secretary-General on Popular Participation in its Various Forms as an Important Factor in Development and in the Realization of Human Rights*, 38 U.N. GAOR (Prov. Agenda Item 85), U.N. Doc. A/38/338/Add.1 (1983); *Commission on Human Rights, Study by the Secretary General on Popular Participation in its Various Forms as an Important Factor in Development and in the Full Realization of Human Rights*, 41 U.N. ESCOR (Prov. Agenda Item 8(c)), U.N. Doc. E/CN.4/1985/10 (1985).

means of influencing government and of protection against governmental abuse. It is not then surprising that debates about popular participation give relatively sparse attention to what Western democracies stress, elections.[174] Indeed, many states developing the conception of popular participation have one-party systems.[175] The conception is susceptible to the familiar divergent understandings: a strategy to mobilize human resources for the government's purposes, or a recognition of the human need to participate and of the fairness of giving citizens both voice and power.

V. POLITICAL PARTICIPATION AS A PROGRAMMATIC RIGHT

The international norms expressing the ideal of political participation share the character of much of the newly created human rights law. For many centuries, international law deferred to another ideal, that of state sovereignty, by barely addressing a state's treatment of its own citizens. The developments of recent decades are less modest. International law has shed its deferential posture. By supporting declarations and agreeing to treaties, states have subjected their treatment of their own citizens to international norms and scrutiny. International law has thereby gained critical power. By the same token, relative to the older international law of lesser ambition, these human rights

174. *See* Fagen, *The Politics of Transition*, in TRANSITION AND DEVELOPMENT: PROBLEMS IN THIRD WORLD SOCIALISM 249 (R. Fagen, C. Deere & J. Coraggio eds. 1986). The author notes the frequently antidemocratic answers given to the question of an appropriate political system by leaders of third world countries in process of rapid change. For many, the logic of quick development points toward centralized decision-making within a one-party state, coupled with the use of mass organizations to implement state policies. *See id.* at 258–61.

175. An international seminar convened by the International Commission of Jurists in 1976 explored the status of human rights in African countries with one-party states. Several speakers argued that effective participation was possible in such states if the single party were, for example, of mass rather than exclusive membership and permitted internal dissent, if there were elections for party leaders and indeed power in the people to change party leaders, and if the single party allowed several candidates of different political positions to run for governmental office. *See* INTERNATIONAL COMMISSION OF JURISTS, HUMAN RIGHTS IN A ONE-PARTY STATE 27–28, 45, 51 (1978). Such prescriptions, whatever the likelihood of their political realization, seem tantamount to installation of an effective multi-party system in the guise of a single party.

Discussions in the Human Rights Committee of reports required to be filed by parties to the International Covenant have considered the question of participation in one-party states. *See* 31 Human Rights Comm. (776th mtg), U.N. Doc. CCPR/C/SR.776 (1984). Responding to questions from Committee members about Zambia's report, the Zambian representative argued that a one-party system was not incompatible with the enjoyment of civil and political rights. Abuses of power could occur as readily in multi-party systems. One-party rule had brought Zambians peace and stability. Moreover, "the political system in Zambia was based on free choice. . . . A reading of the . . . Constitution would show that the Party was open to criticism and change by decision of the majority." *Id.* at 11. A Committee member asserted that whatever Zambia's difficult circumstances, the one-party system "should be taken as transitory. It was not that the Committee preferred a certain structure for a State but that the structure offered guarantees for implementing the Covenant." *Id.*

norms cause a larger gap between normative order and political order. Ideals are more distanced from behavior. Compared with its traditional content, today's international law seeks more but achieves less of what it seeks.

Bearing these considerations in mind, I return to questions earlier posed. Do the human rights norms about participation express any ideal common to diverse nations? Are they more than indeterminate prescriptions which, in a fractious world, were fated or even meant to be understood in dramatically different ways? Do they serve any useful purpose?

The answers which I propose turn on the suggestion that the right to political participation be viewed as a programmatic right, one responsive to a shared ideal but to be realized progressively over time in different ways in different contexts through invention and planning that will often have a programmatic character. That suggestion makes relevant the contrast frequently drawn between the civil and political rights which this article has examined, and economic and social rights such as those to employment, lodging or health care—the so-called welfare or distributive rights. In developing this contrast, I put to the side the poverty of the remedial system and assume that internationally recognized rights are readily enforced.

The first category of rights—to freedom of conscience, to a fair trial, to free speech—are viewed as fully effective from the time of their recognition as part of customary international law or of their acceptance by parties to a convention. As a formal matter under international law, such rights can be promptly invoked in appropriate fora by those claiming to be victims of their violations and seeking relief.

This seems clear on the face of things. States of emergency aside, no article of the International Covenant postpones the effectiveness of the designated rights by establishing a schedule for their implementation or justifying states' delays in recognizing and protecting them. Governments cannot, for example, legally practice torture for another decade, and thereafter honor progressively stricter constraints until their practice terminates in, say, twenty-five years. To the contrary, Article 2 of the International Covenant requires its parties to "undertake to . . . ensure to all individuals . . . the rights recognized" therein. Nothing qualifies their present obligation to take the "legislative or other measures" necessary to give effect to such rights.

Economic and social rights differ, even apart from the different fora and modes of enforcement that are appropriate to them. Rights to food or health care are not "fully" effective upon a nation's ratification of the International Covenant on Economic, Social, and Cultural

Rights.[176] A party to that covenant "undertakes to take steps . . . to the maximum of its available resources, with a view to achieving progressively the full realization of the rights recognized" in it.[177] Specific provisions such as the right to work underscore the distinctive pace of this convenant, one of gradual movement toward fulfillment.[178] Time, resources and an administrative infrastructure are necessary for governments to fulfill their duties corresponding to these rights. Frequently governmental programs must be constituted to develop the policies to be implemented and the institutions for that implementation. Moreover, the rights themselves must be open to elaboration and redefinition over time. As a country's resources grow, as ideas evolve about the content of a minimum standard of living that comports with human dignity, so may a country's duties expand.[179]

Civil and political rights share some of these characteristics. Governments, for example, must protect and vindicate such rights by providing institutions like the police and courts. Planning and resources are essential; programs will again be implicated. Moreover, some civil rights must be open to developing understandings—the implications of the "inherent right to life," the meaning of "inhuman and degrading treatment." Despite such similarities, the conventional contrast between these categories of rights illuminates important differences. International normative order assumes that the torture victim now has a valid legal claim against the offending government. The homeless family's claim against a party to the covenant on economic rights is, at the least, problematic.

At first look, political participation falls within the first, immediately effective, category of international human rights. It figures in the International Covenant as a right so fundamental that the realization of many others depends upon it. Nothing in Article 25 or in other text of the Covenant justifies a distinction between the clarity or immediacy of a state's duties under that article and, say, its duty to refrain from torture. Citizens of a party to the Covenant would have a valid claim under international law if their government had seized power and abolished elections.

176. *See International Covenant on Economic, Social, and Cultural Rights*, *supra* note 32.

177. *Id.* art. 2(1).

178. Article 6(2) provides that steps to be taken by a state fully to realize the right to work include technical and vocational programs and strategies and policies to achieve steady economic development and productive employment. *Id.*

179. For analyses of the character of economic rights, including their developing character over time, see Alston, *International Law and the Human Right to Food*, in THE RIGHT TO FOOD 9 (P. Alston & K. Tomasevski eds. 1984); Trubek, *Economic, Social, and Cultural Rights in the Third World: Human Rights Law and Human Needs Programs*, in 1 HUMAN RIGHTS IN INTERNATIONAL LAW, *supra* note 16, at 205–71; Van Hoof, *The Legal Nature of Economic, Social and Cultural Rights: A Rebuttal of Some Traditional Views*, in THE RIGHT TO FOOD, *supra*, at 97.

Nonetheless, I argue that the right to political participation can be better understood as sharing the programmatic character of many economic and social rights. So understood, it nourishes a vital ideal and serves important purposes. I mean, to be sure, a programmatic right of a distinct character from the typical economic rights.[180] Moreover, my characterization applies to the "take part" clause of the international norms rather than to the "elections" clause. To be sure, the latter clause is understood differently in the liberal democracies and in communist states. But neither group of countries views the requirement of elections as in some sense a *tabula rasa*, as open to fresh experimental definition. In democratic states, the structure of an electoral process may change. Legislation may expand competition and participation in that process. In the communist states, there may be trends toward some degree of electoral contest. But the disputes over the import of the clause are well known, and the evolution of liberal and communist societies is unlikely to introduce significant changes in understanding.

The "take part" clause differs. My characterization of that clause as declaring a programmatic right stems from several related observations. One cannot identify broadly shared and stable views of its import, or even crystallized disputes about appropriate forms of institutionalization or about the types of governmental duties that it imposes. Recent decades have witnessed in both liberal democracies and communist states some development in theories and some innovative governmental policies which may influence the degree and types of citizens' non-electoral participation in the conduct of public affairs.

As societies change—through industrialization or urbanization, evolving relations between public and private sectors, reorganization of political and economic life, ideological shifts—the content of the right must be open to experimental reformulation. The notion of what it requires of governments will change significantly with ongoing national experiences. New needs and possibilities will emerge.

The clearer if still open-textured character of the "elections" clause, together with the programmatic character of the "take part" clause, nourish the argument that Article 25 now expresses some "positive law," but also contains an aspirational or hortatory element which

---

180. *See* Trubek, *supra* note 179, at 206–07 (using the expression "programmatic obligation" to describe the trend in international law "towards the creation of obligations which bind states to undertake programs" to guarantee minimum welfare standards). "The language of progressive realization [in Article 2 of the Covenant] indicates that the rights must be implemented, if only over time, by a program of activities." *Id.* at 214; for reference to Article 2 of the International Covenant, see *supra* text accompanying note 177. The term "programmatic" is congenial to my ideas in the distinct context of this article, although I connect it with citizens' "rights" rather than states' "obligations" to emphasize its relationship to ideal aspiration.

distinguishes it from most provisions of the International Covenant. The aspirations that it expresses are of course shaped by the different strands of political theory and the different national practices with which the world is familiar. But this rich historical deposit of ideas and practices cannot exhaust the ways of understanding or institutionalizing an ideal of political participation.

There is no shortage of types of and experiments about political participation among the liberal democracies, Communist-Party states and post colonial third world states. Many of these ideologies of participation were developed during the same decades which saw the creation of the major human rights instruments. I do not suggest that they directly responded to a perceived aspiration or ideal in the human rights instruments. But neither was that ideal irrelevant. Its authoritative expression in universal instruments, its evocation in the debates within international organizations, even its analysis by scholars make the norm known to political elites and, in many societies, to large portions of the population. Whatever the hypocrisy involved, the right is now proclaimed in many national constitutions as well. It has entered public political debate, legal and moral discourse, in many new countries of the postwar world, as well as in older societies to whose political elites the notion of popular participation in the selection of leaders and shaping of policy had been both alien and repugnant.

Although the practice of participation may be severely suppressed in a given state, the norm stands as an invitation to the disenfranchised or repressed to draw on the example of other societies where it is better appreciated. Its recognition in national and universal instruments legitimates inquiry and may spur protest. Dormant or imprisoned within a hostile environment—as lay dormant for many decades the ideal of equality expressed in the Equal Protection Clause of the Fourteenth Amendment of the United States Constitution—the norm retains its subversive potential.

What is now often a polemical discourse of accusation among conflicting groups of states could become a common inquiry through which states recognize aspects of other states' systems which appear to respond to an ideal element in the norm. One-party states, in pursuit of such interests as efficient implementation of laws, economic development, or legitimation of a regime, might enlarge public debate over policies and introduce greater electoral choice. The routes could be many, from a willingness of the party to nominate competing candidates with different political programs, to the growth of intra-party democracy which could bring aspects of pluralism into the Party structure. Innovations in one-party states that achieve significant, ongoing citizen participation in governmental and economic administration through local institutions may stimulate further legislative experiments in countries where elections have traditionally set a boundary to most governments' duty.

In such ways, a norm like Article 25 of the International Covenant may contribute to ongoing realizations of the spacious ideal of political participation. Unlike norms expressing negative rights, such as the norm enjoining torture, it could never be fully realized. Fresh understandings and different institutionalizations of the right in different cultural and political contexts may reveal what an increasing number of states believe to be a necessary minimum of political participation for all states. That minimum should never require less of a government than provision for meaningful exercise of choice by citizens in some form of electoral process permitting active debate on a broad if not unlimited range of issues. But it could require much more.

[19]

THE EMERGING RIGHT TO DEMOCRATIC GOVERNANCE

*By Thomas M. Franck**

> Legitimacy in 1991 flows not from the barrel of a gun but from the will of the people.
>
> *U.S. Secretary of State James A. Baker III*

> I know what real democracy is, what democracy is worth.
>
> *A thirty-seven-year-old Soviet lieutenant colonel who early on sided with anticoup forces*[†]

I. Introduction: The Power of Democratic Legitimacy

More than two centuries have elapsed since the signatories of the U.S. Declaration of Independence sought to manifest two radical propositions. The first is that governments, instituted to secure the "unalienable rights" of their citizens, derive "their just powers from the consent of the governed." We may call this the "democratic entitlement." The second proposition, perhaps less noted by commentators, is that a nation earns "separate and equal station" in the community of states by demonstrating "a decent respect to the opinions of mankind." The authors of the Declaration apparently believed that the legitimacy of the new Confederation of American States was not made evident solely by the transfer of power from Britain but also needed to be acknowledged by "mankind." This we may perceive as a prescient glimpse of the legitimating power of the community of nations.

For two hundred years, these two notions have remained a radical vision. The purpose of this essay is to demonstrate that the radical vision, while not yet fully word made law, is rapidly becoming, in our time, a normative rule of the international system. In the process, the two notions have merged. Increasingly, governments recognize that their legitimacy depends on meeting a normative expectation of the community of states. This recognition has led to the emergence of a community expectation: that those who seek the validation of their empowerment patently govern with the consent of the governed. Democracy, thus, is on the way to becoming a global entitlement, one that increasingly will be promoted and protected by collective international processes.

II. The Validation of Governance

Two recent events underscore this trend. The failure of the August coup in the Soviet Union, an event of inestimable human, political and historic import, demonstrates—for those sensitive to trends—that democracy is beginning to be seen as the *sine qua non* for validating governance. While President Boris Yeltsin of the Russian Republic and many Soviet citizens deserve primary credit for this

* Editor in Chief. The author wishes to express warm appreciation to many members of the Board of Editors for their helpful comments, as well as Paul Szasz, Robert Crouse, Gregory Fox, Dennis Sughrue, and the members of my honors seminar at the NYU Center for International Studies. Special thanks are due to the Filomen D'Agostino and Max E. Greenberg Research Fund of New York University School of Law.

† N.Y. Times, Aug. 22, 1991, at A15, col. 6; and *id.*, Aug. 21, 1991, at A9, col. 1.

triumph, it also derived considerable impetus from the new global climate, as evidenced by the vigor with which leaders of other democracies around the world aligned themselves against the coup's leaders. Equally significant is the reaction of governments in the Organization of American States and the United Nations General Assembly to the overthrow, in September 1991, of the elected President of Haiti, Jean-Bertrand Aristide, by a military coup. On October 11, the Assembly unanimously, without vote, approved a ground-breaking resolution demanding the return of Aristide to office, full application of the Haitian Constitution and full observance of human rights in Haiti.[1] The OAS, a week earlier, had unanimously recommended that its member states take "action to bring about the diplomatic isolation of those who hold power illegally in Haiti" and "suspend their economic, financial, and commercial ties" with the country until constitutional rule is restored.[2]

In both the Soviet and the Haitian cases, the leaders of states constituting the international community vigorously asserted that *only* democracy validates governance. This dramatic statement attains even more potency if, as in the Haitian case, it is transposed from political philosophy, where it is "mere" moral prescription, to law, where a newly recognized "democratic entitlement" was used in both the OAS and the UN General Assembly to impose new and important legal obligations on states. The OAS resolution, for one, stated that "the solidarity of the American states and the high aims which are sought through it require the political organization of those states on the basis of the effective exercise of representative democracy."[3] Undeniably, a new legal entitlement is being created, based in part on custom and in part on the collective interpretation of treaties.

This newly emerging "law"—which requires democracy to validate governance—is not merely the law of a particular state that, like the United States under its Constitution, has imposed such a precondition on national governance. It is also becoming a requirement of international law, applicable to all and implemented through global standards, with the help of regional and international organizations.

The transformation of the democratic entitlement from moral prescription to international legal obligation has evolved gradually. In the past decade, however, the tendency has accelerated. Most remarkable is the extent to which an international law-based entitlement is now urged by governments themselves. This is a cosmic, but unmysterious, change. For nations surfacing from long, tragic submergence beneath bogus "people's democracy" or outright dictatorship, the legitimation of power is a basic, but elusive, move in the direction of reform. As of late 1991, there are more than 110 governments, almost all represented in the United Nations, that are legally committed to permitting open, multiparty, secret-ballot elections with a universal franchise. Most joined the trend in the past five years.[4] While a few, arguably, are democracies more in form than in substance,

[1] UN Doc. A/46/L.8/Rev.1 (1991).

[2] Support to the Democratic Government of Haiti, OEA/Ser.F/V.1/MRE/RES.1/91, corr.1, paras. 5, 6 (1991).

[3] *Id.*, preamble.

[4] This enumeration was compiled by reference to reports in the *New York Times* and the *Country Reports on Human Rights Practices for 1990, infra* note 10, submitted by the Department of State to the appropriate committees of Congress. States that currently make legal provision for determining their governments by recourse to multiparty, secret-ballot elections are: Albania, Angola, Antigua and Barbuda, Argentina, Australia, Austria, the Bahamas, Bangladesh, Barbados, Belgium, Belize, Benin, Byelorussia, Bolivia, Botswana, Brazil, Bulgaria, Canada, Cape Verde, Chile, Colombia, the Comoros,

most are, or are becoming, genuinely open to meaningful political choice. Many of these new regimes want, indeed need, to be validated by being seen to comply with global standards for free and open elections.

That governments themselves now argue for the entitlement merely indicates their long-overdue recognition of an immutable fact of life: government cannot govern by force alone. To be effective, pace Austin,[5] law needs to secure the habitual, *voluntary* compliance of its subjects; it cannot rely entirely, or even primarily, upon the commanding power of a sovereign to compel obedience. Consequently, governments no longer blinded by the totalitarian miasma seek to validate themselves in such a way as to secure a high degree of voluntary public acquiescence in the governing process. Consent benefits the governing as much as the governed: that sociological truism is at last becoming a political axiom. In western industrialized nations, at least since the middle of the nineteenth century, such validation has increasingly been sought and achieved by governments. This is the hard-won tradition most of the world now seeks to emulate.

Since the beginning of the twentieth century, however, there has also been a countertendency. The notion of democracy as validation has been challenged, quite powerfully, first, by the notion of the "dictatorship of the proletariat" and, more recently, by a related theory of forced-march "modernization."

The doctrine of the dictatorship of the proletariat argued, with considerable force, that governing, especially in an industrial society, should not be an art but a science. It postulated, at least in theory, a dictatorship of trained and doctrinally correct economists, administrators, sociologists and political scientists capable of implementing correct policies. The complexities of governance were thought to be too great to be left to amateurs selected by the vagaries of popular passion.[6]

Congo, the Cook Islands, Costa Rica, the Côte d'Ivoire, Cyprus, Czechoslovakia, Denmark, Dominica, the Dominican Republic, Ecuador, Egypt, El Salvador, Estonia, Finland, France, Gabon, Gambia, Germany, Greece, Grenada, Guatemala, Guyana, Hungary, Honduras, Iceland, India, Ireland, Israel, Italy, Jamaica, Japan, Kiribati, Korea (Republic of), Latvia, Liberia, Liechtenstein, Lithuania, Luxembourg, Madagascar, Malaysia, Mali, Malta, the Marshall Islands, Mauritius, Mexico, the Micronesian Federation, Mongolia, Morocco, Mozambique, Namibia, Nauru, Nepal, the Netherlands, New Zealand, Nicaragua, Niger, Norway, Pakistan, Panama, Papua New Guinea, Paraguay, Peru, the Philippines, Poland, Portugal, Romania, São Tomé, Senegal, Singapore, the Solomon Islands, the Soviet Union, Spain, Sri Lanka, St. Kitts, St. Lucia, St. Vincent, Sweden, Switzerland, Tonga, Trinidad, Tunisia, Turkey, the Ukraine, the United Kingdom, Uruguay, Vanuatu, Venezuela, Western Samoa, Zambia and Zimbabwe. Several more states, such as Nigeria and Ethiopia, are committed to free, multiparty elections but have not yet enacted the necessary constitutional or legislative fiat. It must also be conceded that there are borderline cases, such as Morocco (included) and Jordan (not included), in which the elections are not necessarily decisive, depending on various factors, including the disposition of a monarch with substantial residual powers. In the large majority of cases, however, the decision to include or exclude is not seriously in doubt—though it should be recalled that the test for inclusion is whether the legal system establishes free and secret elections. Whether these are conducted fairly is another question.

[5] Austin defined law as the enforced command of a sovereign to a subject. J. AUSTIN, THE PROVINCE OF JURISPRUDENCE DETERMINED 201 (I. Berlin, S. Hampshire & R. Wollheim eds. 1954) (1832).

[6] *See, e.g.*, Theses on the Role of the Communist Party in the Proletarian Revolution Adopted by the Second Congress, in 1 THE COMMUNIST INTERNATIONAL: 1919–1943 DOCUMENTS 127 (J. Degras ed. 1971).

In 1920 Trotsky offered this response to a suggestion that the dictatorship of the Communist Party and the dictatorship of the proletariat were not identical:

> Today we received peace proposals from the Polish Government. Who decides this question? We have the Council of People's Commissars, but that too must be subject to a certain control. Whose

The contemporary theory of "modernization," which originated in the European fascist-charterist dictatorships of the 1930s, found new respectability among leaders of postcolonial Latin America, Africa and Asia, as well as some western friends of the Third World.[7] In the Third World, it was argued, the task of modern nation building—melding disparate tribes and clans to create new economies of scale—was said to warrant suspending imported bourgeois democratic values which, at any rate, were virtually meaningless in a largely rural, communal and illiterate society. The model was not a pompous Mussolini making Italian trains run punctually but Oliver Cromwell dismissing Parliament and getting Britain organized. In a few countries—Singapore, South Korea and Taiwan—the model seemed to work for a time, in the sense that much social and economic progress was achieved. In most instances, however, the implied promise was not kept.

Since the middle of the 1980s, both the "dictatorship of the proletariat" and the theory of "modernization" have collapsed under the weight of their evident failure. Throughout socialist Eastern Europe and in most of the dictatorships of Africa and Asia, the people have rejected both theories, together with the espousing governments, beginning with the televised popular revolution against Ferdinand Marcos in the Philippines. Instead, people almost everywhere now demand that government be validated by western-style parliamentary, multiparty democratic process. Only a few, usually military or theocratic, regimes still resist the trend. Very few argue that parliamentary democracy is a western illusion and a neocolonialist trap for unwary Third World peoples.

This almost-complete triumph of the democratic notions of Hume, Locke, Jefferson and Madison—in Latin America, Africa, Eastern Europe and, to a lesser extent, Asia—may well prove to be the most profound event of the twentieth century and, in all likelihood, the fulcrum on which the future development of global society will turn. It is the unanswerable response to those who have said that free, open, multiparty, electoral parliamentary democracy is neither desired nor desirable outside a small enclave of western industrial states.

The question is not whether democracy has swept the boards, but whether global society is ready for an era in which *only* democracy and the rule of law will be capable of validating governance. This may be a venerable philosophical issue known to Plato,[8] but it is also a functional question that can be, and now is being, stated in global legal terms. Are we witnessing the evolution of an international rule system that defines the minimal requisites of a democratic process capable of validating the exercise of power? What norms will such a rule system encompass? Is the international community capable of developing, consensually, an institutional and normative framework for monitoring compliance with those requisites? Is the community of nations able to define and manage appropriate consequences of noncompliance?

> control? That of the working class as a formless, chaotic mass? No. So we convened the central committee of the party to discuss the proposal and decide on the answer. . . . The same is true of the agrarian question, the food question, and all other questions.

Id. at 127–28.

[7] *Cf.* D. APTER, THE POLITICS OF MODERNIZATION (1965).

[8] Plato's effort, in the *Statesman*, the *Laws* and the *Republic*, to define the extent to which a ruler's legitimacy is validated by wisdom, on the one hand, and by his subordination to the laws, on the other, is analyzed in G. SABINE, A HISTORY OF POLITICAL THEORY 67–105 (rev. ed. 1953).

III. Legitimacy and the International System of Rules

These questions, in turn, raise two separate issues of legitimacy that are related but should not be confused: first, the legitimacy of national governments and, second, the legitimacy of the emerging international rules and processes by which the governance of nations is increasingly being monitored and validated. The latter issue is of primary interest to the international lawyer, but its importance is due to its manifest connection with the former. We are witnessing a sea change in international law, as a result of which the legitimacy of each government someday will be measured definitively by international rules and processes. We are not quite there, but we can see the outlines of this new world in which the citizens of each state will look to international law and organization to guarantee their democratic entitlement. For some states, that process will merely embellish rights already protected by their existing domestic constitutional order. For others, it could be the realization of a cherished dream.

Citizens, however, will not be the only beneficiaries. We have observed that the engine pulling the democratic entitlement is the craving of governments for validation. Without validation, the task of governance becomes fraught with difficulty. Regimes prize validation, then, as evidence of their legitimacy. Legitimacy, in turn, is the quality of a rule, or a system of rules, or a process for making or interpreting rules that pulls both the rule makers and those addressed by the rules toward voluntary compliance.

Western democracies have achieved legitimacy largely by subjecting the political process to rules, often immutably entrenched in an intrepid constitution. These lucky few nations have succeeded in evolving their own legitimate means of validating the process by which the people choose those they entrust with the exercise of power. To achieve such a system of autochthonous validation (and thus to facilitate governing), those who hold or seek political power have made a far-sighted bargain comparable to John Locke's social compact;[9] they have surrendered control over the nation's validation process to various others: national electoral commissions, judges, an inquisitive press and, above all, the citizenry acting at the ballot box. This collectivity decides whether the standards of the democratic entitlement have been met by those who claim the right to govern. In return, the legitimacy bestowed by that process gives back far more power to those who govern than they surrendered.

In many nations, unfortunately, no such bargain was struck. Those who claim to govern cannot demonstrate that they have fulfilled the requirements of the democratic entitlement, even if they purport to recognize that entitlement. Senegal, for example, is a multiparty state with universal franchise and a secret ballot, but the results of the 1988 national elections were rejected as fraudulent both by opposition parties and by other social institutions. The other parties subsequently boycotted the 1990 local elections and refused to accept the Government's legitimacy.[10] Increasingly, as will be demonstrated later in this essay, governments whose legitimacy is questioned are turning to the international system for that

[9] *See* J. Locke, Two Treatises of Government 119–20, 164–66 (W. Carpenter ed. 1955) (1690).

[10] U.S. Department of State, 102d Cong., 1st Sess., Country Reports on Human Rights Practices for 1990: Report submitted to the Committee on Foreign Relations, U.S. Senate and the Committee on Foreign Affairs, House of Representatives 322–23 (Comm. Print 1991).

validation which their national *polis* is as yet unable to give. They do so to avoid the alternative—persistent challenge to authority by coups, countercoups, instability and stasis—and to enable themselves to govern with essential societal acquiescence. What they seek is legitimation by a global standard monitored by processes of the international system.

The capacity of the international community to extend legitimacy to national governments, however, depends not only on its capacity to monitor an election or to recognize the credentials of a regime's delegates to the UN General Assembly, but also on the extent to which such international activity has evolved from the ad hoc to the normative: that is, the degree to which the process of legitimation itself has become legitimate.

In any rule system, national or international, legitimacy has its own modalities. It is to the latter that the international lawyer's creative perspective must turn. Do the global requisites for democratic validation of governments now include, or are they evolving into, rules and procedures that are perceived as legitimate by those to whom they are addressed? In the international context,[11] legitimacy is achieved if—or to the extent that—those addressed by a rule, or by a rule-making institution, perceive the rule or institution to have come into being and to be operating in accordance with generally accepted principles of right process.[12]

Empirically, legitimacy can be demonstrated by observing rules, and the decisions of rule-making or rule-applying institutions. Some are habitually obeyed, without recourse to police enforcement, while others are largely ignored. Different rules exhibit varying degrees of compliance pull, which is the measure of a rule's legitimacy. However, the degree of a rule's pull to compliance cannot be measured solely by observing actual compliance. A more sensitive measure would have to take into account, additionally, the degree to which a violator exhibits deference to a rule even while violating it: for example, by lying about, or covering up, the violation or the circumstances in which the violation occurred.

Purely deductive research on rule legitimacy—pulse taking in the form of large-scale empirical investigation of compliance pull—is difficult to structure. Abstract/inductive reasoning about the nature of legitimacy is more feasible. Thus, one may postulate four indicators: *pedigree, determinacy, coherence* and *adherence*.[13] The content of these four indicators of legitimacy will be defined in ensuing sections of this essay. For this general overview, it is sufficient to summarize as follows: pedigree refers to the depth of the rule's roots in a historical process; determinacy refers to the rule's ability to communicate content; coherence refers to the rule's internal consistency and lateral connectedness to the principles underlying other rules; and adherence refers to the rule's vertical connectedness to a normative hierarchy, culminating in an ultimate rule of recognition, which embodies the principled purposes and values that define the community of states. A hypothesis may now be ventured: the degree to which a rule, or a rule-making process, exhibits these four qualities will determine the degree to which the rule or the process has matured and is perceived to be legitimate.

Those indicators provide a conceptual map with which to approach the previously posed questions. They afford a convenient way of sorting through the welter

[11] Legitimacy, in this as in all other contexts, is a matter of degree. Some rules and institutions enjoy more legitimacy than others.

[12] T. Franck, The Power of Legitimacy Among Nations 19 (1990).

[13] *Id.* at 50–194.

of data to reach some estimate as to whether the global system is evolving legitimate rules and institutions capable of validating national governance. That estimate, in turn, will help us understand and react appropriately to the inevitable counterindicative challenges: recidivist tendencies and totalitarian holdouts.

In seeking to assess whether an international democratic order is emerging, data will be marshaled from three related generations of rule making and implementation. The oldest and most highly developed is that subset of democratic norms which emerged under the heading of "self-determination." The second subset—freedom of expression—developed as part of the exponential growth of human rights since the mid-1950s and focuses on maintaining an open marketplace of ideas. The third and newest subset seeks to establish, define and monitor a right to free and open elections.

These three subsets somewhat overlap, both chronologically and normatively. Collectively, they do not necessarily penetrate every nook and cranny of democratic theory. For example, the three subsets do not yet address normatively the thorny issue of the right of a disaffected portion of an independent state to secede; nor, as we shall see, is it conceptually or strategically helpful—at least at this stage of its evolution—to treat the democratic entitlement as inextricably linked to the claim of minorities to secession. Still, these three increasingly normative subsets are large building stones, gradually reinforcing each other and assuming the shape of a coherent normative edifice. Moreover, regional subsets are adding some supernumerary buttresses, cornices and lintels to the new structure that dovetail with, and enrich, the emerging global architecture. Some examples of these will be included in our inventory.

IV. Pedigree: The Case of Self-Determination

Self-determination is the historic root from which the democratic entitlement grew. Its deep-rootedness continues to confer important elements of legitimacy on self-determination, as well as on the entitlement's two newer branches, freedom of expression and the electoral right.

Symbolic validation and pedigree provide legitimacy's cultural and anthropological dimension.[14] As with any rule, the capacity of the democratic entitlement to pull toward voluntary compliance depends, in part, on the strength of what W. Michael Reisman refers to as "the authority signal."[15] Specifically, the legitimacy of a rule reflects the durability, as well as the consistency, of its acknowledgment and application in practice.

Since self-determination is the oldest aspect of the democratic entitlement, its pedigree is the best established. Self-determination postulates the right of a people organized in an established territory to determine its collective political destiny in a democratic fashion and is therefore at the core of the democratic entitlement. Symbolically, it is signified by a long-evolving tradition of maintaining observers, on behalf of international and regional organizations, at elections in colonies and trust territories. Early observer missions developed operational procedures. They sent reports to their sponsoring international agency or committee, which helped the community's political organs and individual member governments make deductions about the legitimacy of the decolonization process. Gradually, with many variations, the observer missions' methods became the standard operating proce-

[14] *Id.* at 91.

[15] Reisman, *International Lawmaking: A Process of Communication*, 75 ASIL Proc. 101, 110 (1981).

dure for validating an exercise of self-determination. Later in this essay, we will recapitulate these rules and procedures. Here, however, we are concerned with the pedigree, the time frame within which those processes took root and matured.

The aspiration that underpins the principle of self-determination is of an antiquity traceable, in the West, at least to the Hebrews' exodus from Egypt,[16] estimated to have been approximately in 1000 B.C.[17] Its modern rise to the status of universal entitlement began when the Versailles Peace Conference[18] undid, or brought into line with late nineteenth-century European nationalist sensibilities, the work of the Congress of Vienna, which had utterly disregarded ethnic sensibilities in redrawing the map of post-Napoleonic Europe. Embarking on another redesign of Europe after the First World War, President Woodrow Wilson made self-determination his lodestar. To this end, firmly overriding the doubts of Secretary of State Robert Lansing,[19] he reinforced the U.S. team of negotiators with an unusual contingent of historians, geographers and ethnologists,[20] the more effectively to argue for the norm's supremacy over power politics and strategic or economic considerations. Consequently, the American delegation summoned up extensive data on demographics and evidence of ethnicity in advocating free choice by "peoples."[21]

Thus prodded, the conference authorized twenty-six on-site consultations with different European groups seeking self-determination.[22] The Danes of Schleswig, annexed to Prussia in 1864, were able to secure agreement that "the frontier between Germany and Denmark shall be fixed in conformity with the wishes of the population."[23] Wilson also prevailed in the view "that all branches of the Slav race" in what was to become Czechoslovakia "should be completely freed from German and Austrian rule"[24] in full consultation with Slavic representatives.[25] He resisted efforts by France's Premier Clemenceau to establish an independent Rhenish buffer state consisting of unwilling Germans.[26] Although the Versailles settlement also brought self-determination to Poland,[27] as regards the Upper Silesian and Czech boundary settlements, as well as Fiume, Wilson reluctantly came to concede that sometimes one had to consider "other principles"—strategic, economic and logistic—that could "clash with the requirements of self-determination."[28]

[16] *Exodus* 1:2.

[17] The author is indebted to Fr. Robert Crouse, Professor of Classics at Dalhousie University and King's College, for this approximation, one carefully hedged with caveats appropriate to so risky an enterprise.

[18] *See* H. HANNUM, AUTONOMY, SOVEREIGNTY, AND SELF-DETERMINATION 20–31 (1990). The use of self-determination at Versailles and subsequently is also discussed more fully in Franck, *Legitimacy in the International System*, 82 AJIL 705, 743–48 (1988).

[19] "[T]he phrase [self-determination] is simply loaded with dynamite. It will raise hopes which can never be realized." R. LANSING, THE PEACE NEGOTIATIONS, A PERSONAL NARRATIVE 97 (1921). *See* Brilmayer, *Secession and Self-Determination: A Territorial Interpretation*, 16 YALE J. INT'L L. 177 (1991).

[20] 1 R. S. BAKER, WOODROW WILSON AND WORLD SETTLEMENT 109 (1922).

[21] 1 S. WAMBAUGH, PLEBISCITES SINCE THE WORLD WAR 13 (1933).

[22] 1 R. S. BAKER, *supra* note 20, at 188.

[23] 2 A HISTORY OF THE PEACE CONFERENCE OF PARIS 203 (H. W. V. Temperley ed. 1920).

[24] 4 *id.* at 261.

[25] *Id.* at 262.

[26] 4 THE INTIMATE PAPERS OF COLONEL HOUSE 334–35, 345 (C. Seymour ed. 1928).

[27] 1 S. WAMBAUGH, *supra* note 21, at 16.

[28] M. POMERANCE, SELF-DETERMINATION IN LAW AND PRACTICE 4 (1982); D. FLEMING, THE UNITED STATES AND WORLD ORGANIZATION 152–55 (1938). For example, Czechoslovakia ended up with defensible boundaries only by denying self-determination to a large Sudeten-German minority.

Nevertheless, the principle of self-determination, as championed by Wilson and the minorities released from the embrace of the German, Russian and Austro-Hungarian Empires, was applied vigorously, if sometimes imperfectly, to the vanquished lands of postwar Europe. In the rest of Europe, however, it was applied only in Ireland. In denying self-determination to the Aaland Islands—which sought to join Sweden by breaking away from Finland, itself newly emancipated from Russia—a Versailles-created international commission of jurists observed that the Covenant of the League of Nations did not even mention the principle and that it had not yet attained the status of a positive rule of law.[29] More important, self-determination played little part in the disposition of the vast overseas lands and peoples of the former German Empire, which were doled out to Australia, Belgium, Britain, France, Japan, New Zealand and South Africa. It was applied badly, if at all, to the former Turkish dependencies in Asia. The League's mandate system evinced only muted concern for the wishes of those territories' inhabitants.

Remarkably, after the Second World War the principle of self-determination became the most dynamic concept in international relations. Former German, Japanese and Italian colonies were placed under the trusteeship of the victors (and, in one case, the vanquished), with the clear obligation "to promote . . . progressive development towards self-government or independence" in accordance with "the freely expressed wishes of the peoples concerned."[30] Conceptual evolution, however, did not stop there. Soon not only was self-determination recognized as a writ for obtaining decolonization but, by the terms of the very first article of the UN Charter, it achieved the status of a fundamental right of all "peoples" as a necessary prerequisite to the development of "friendly relations among nations." At least potentially, the concept was thus both universalized and internationalized, for it could now be said to portend a duty owed by all governments to their peoples and by each government to all members of the international community.

This was no random theoretical happenstance. In the postwar world of rising nationalisms, denials of self-determination were palpably no mere domestic matter. Repression tended to generate friction with neighboring states where liberation movements habitually sought sanctuary and succor. As in Bangladesh, Eritrea and the Southern Sudan, self-determination, denied, precipitated the flight of hordes of refugees, placing onerous economic, social and political strains on the neighboring states of refuge. Thus was self-determination firmly linked in theory and fact to the main UN task of preventing conflict among nations, a link that carries far-reaching, but ambiguous, implications for its future normative development (as this essay later seeks to demonstrate).

In the thirty-five years following the surrender of the Axis powers, self-determination transformed the world's political landscape. At this stage, the norm had clear, though limited, secessionist overtones, in the sense that it legitimated the secession of colonies from empires. Concurrently, the norm also evolved in a way that did not legitimate self-determination of minorities *within* a colony. The General Assembly warned against efforts to compromise a colony's "territorial integrity" by those—like Nigeria's Ibos—seeking to secede.[31] Beginning with India,

[29] L. Buchheit, Secession: The Legitimacy of Self-Determination 71 (1978).

[30] UN Charter Art. 76(b).

[31] Note, however, the decision of the political leaders of imperial India to partition the country, in effect permitting Pakistan to secede. On "territorial integrity," see Declaration on the Granting of

Burma and West Africa's Gold Coast, Britain acted in compliance with the norm's evolving requirements; it was followed, with more or less enthusiasm, by France, the Netherlands, Belgium, Spain, Portugal and South Africa. Imperial powers complained about the General Assembly's use of Charter Article 73(c) to monitor political developments in their colonies, but the resistance gradually abated. As a result of the impetus of decolonization, UN membership almost tripled. That this remarkable devolution could have been accomplished, for the most part, without recourse to war or revolution is a tribute to the normative legitimacy and primacy accorded self-determination by the consistent practice—despite lapses—of the community of states.[32] As we shall see, the growth of this process was facilitated by UN reporting requirements, the Organization's close scrutiny of the work of colonial administrations and the active involvement of the United Nations in monitoring elections and plebiscites in territories advancing toward independence. Self-determination was seen to require democratic consultation with colonial peoples, legitimated by an international presence at elections immediately preceding the creative moment of independence.

Today, the process of decolonization is nearly complete. Nevertheless, the principle of self-determination retains vigor, manifestly having contributed to the decision by the leaders of the Soviet Union, beginning in 1989, to withdraw their military forces and political suzerainty from Eastern Europe and, more recently, from the Baltic States. Its pull prompted South Africa's decision to give independence to Namibia and Morocco's *volte-face* regarding Western Sahara. When another vestige of imperfect decolonization, the Angolan civil war, ended in 1991, it was on the basis of an agreement to hold free, internationally observed elections, which, *nunc pro tunc,* would give Angola the legitimate regime it had failed to acquire at the chaotic moment of its independence.[33] Another UN-supervised process of popular consultation was created by the Paris agreement ending the civil war in Cambodia.[34] As we shall discuss in detail, the idea of self-determination has evolved into a more general notion of internationally validated political consultation, one that is beginning to be applied even to independent (postcolonial) states like Nicaragua and Angola, albeit without implying the community's right to validate secessionist movements within sovereign states.

The story of self-determination, as the first building block in the creation of a democratic entitlement, may thus be seen as a remarkable saga that tells of a rule that gradually augments its compliance pull, overcomes resistance and ultimately brings about an incontestable, historic transformation. Rules that acquire this

---

Independence to Colonial Countries and Peoples, GA Res. 1514, 15 UN GAOR Supp. (No. 16) at 66, UN Doc. A/4684 (1960); and Declaration on Principles of International Law concerning Friendly Relations and Co-operation among States in accordance with the Charter of the United Nations, Annex to GA Res. 2625, 25 UN GAOR Supp. (No. 28) at 121, UN Doc. A/8028 (1970), *reprinted in* 9 ILM 1292 (1970) [hereinafter Friendly Relations Declaration]. Note also GA Res. 1654 of 1961, in which, without dissent, the Assembly expressed itself as "[d]eeply concerned that, contrary to the provisions of paragraph 6 of the Declaration, acts aimed at the partial or total disruption of national unity and territorial integrity are still being carried out in certain countries in the process of decolonization." 16 UN GAOR Supp. (No. 17) at 65, UN Doc. A/5100 (1961).

[32] *See* Franck, *The Stealing of the Sahara*, 70 AJIL 694 (1976).

[33] As part of the cease-fire package, UNAVEM, the UN observer mission in Angola, oversaw the withdrawal of Cuban troops. The mission will culminate in the observance of elections in 1992. *See* N.Y. Times, May 26, 1991, §1, at 9, col. 1; and *id.*, June 1, 1991, at A1, col. 3.

[34] Final Act of the Paris Conference on Cambodia, UN Doc. A/46/608–S/23177, Annex (1991).

kind of pedigree have a unique claim to legitimacy. Moreover, the deeply embedded roots of self-determination also anchor the legitimacy claims of other, more recent, components of the democratic entitlement.

V. Determinacy: Its Function in Bestowing Legitimacy

Thus we see that the democratic entitlement has roots in the conduct of states dating back at least to 1918. From this beginning, practice has proliferated. But practice is not enough to legitimate new norms. The dots of practice must be connected by lines of enunciated principle—conceptualized reasons for acting—if the shapes of legitimate rules are to emerge. The production of legitimate norms depends on a combination of persistent practice and enunciated concepts. In addition, to legitimate a rule, the underlying principles must be enunciated in a way that makes their content determinate. In this section, then, we will look at the determinacy of those principles that stake out the democratic entitlement. Just as an enunciated principle needs to be implemented in common practice before achieving recognition as a binding rule, so a common practice, to be accepted as establishing a norm, needs principled enunciation.

By determinacy we mean the literary property of a rule: that which makes its message clear.[55] The determinacy of a rule directly affects its legitimacy because it increases the rule's transparency and thus its capacity to pull members of the international community toward voluntary compliance. It is true that all written communications, including rule texts, suffer from some degree of elasticity of meaning. It is also true that "moderate indeterminacy does not undermine the law's legitimacy."[56] Nevertheless, the more opaque and elastic the rule text, the less compliance pull it is likely to exert. Obviously, a rule that cannot be understood is unlikely to be obeyed. A rule that is vague opens itself to creative misconstruction by those whose conduct it is intended to regulate. Perhaps most important, the indeterminacy of a rule undermines its compliance pull by reducing the contingent expectation of reciprocity that helps pull states toward compliance. States, like persons, often obey rules even when it is to their short-run advantage not to do so, in the expectation that by denying themselves the gain that would accrue from noncompliance they will reinforce the power of the rule to pull others toward compliance, to the states' future benefit. This deferred-gratification rationale for rule compliance falls away, however, when the rule text is so indeterminate as not to support a reasonable expectation that compliance in one instance will reinforce the pull toward compliance in future contingent situations. Reciprocity affords little inducement to voluntary rule compliance if the rule is so fuzzy that its applicability to future cases will be easy to dispute and hard to demonstrate.

While the determinacy of a rule may initially be judged by examining the clarity of its text, even a quite elastic text may be rendered more determinate if it is subjected regularly to case-by-case interpretation, utilizing administrative or adjudicatory procedures accepted as legitimate in the community to which the rule is addressed. For example, the International Court of Justice, in interpreting Article 83(1) of the Convention negotiated by the Third United Nations Conference on the Law of the Sea, has taken a highly indeterminate text—one that calls for "an equitable solution" in apportioning an undersea coastal shelf among neighboring

[55] T. Franck, *supra* note 12, at 52–55.

[56] Kress, *Legal Indeterminacy*, 77 Cal. L. Rev. 283 (1989).

states—and has rendered it increasingly determinate.[37] So, too, as a result of litigation between Finland and Denmark currently before the Court, will we "discover" whether a tall, self-propelled oil rig constitutes a "vessel" under the right of unimpeded passage through straits as established by the Law of the Sea Convention.[38] The determinacy of a rule may therefore depend not only on its text, but also on the work of legitimate institutions charged with reducing textual indeterminacy in specific disputes.

Thus understood, how fares the determinacy of a normative entitlement to democracy? Are there rule texts that convey principles that are specific, or capable of being rendered so, by persuasive case-by-case interpretation and application? We shall now examine the determinacy of existing and emerging rules that bear on the previously identified main historic components of the democratic entitlement: self-determination, freedom of expression and electoral rights.

Determinacy and Self-Determination

As noted, self-determination is legitimated by its long pedigree. Despite lacunae, it also has a large and precise textual canon, refined by a growing "jurisprudence" of interpretation. In addition to the role of self-determination among the purposes of the UN Charter and in the UN trusteeship system, under Article 73, members responsible for administering non-self-governing territories pledged to "develop self-government, to take due account of the political aspirations of the peoples, and to assist them in the progressive development of their free political institutions." These provisions not only were implemented zealously by the UN system, but also were augmented by additional normative texts that concerned two issues essential to the determinacy of self-determination: *to whom* does it apply and *how* is it to be implemented? If rule texts establishing rights do not provide answers to these basic questions, they lack determinacy and the rule's legitimacy is diminished.

To whom does self-determination apply? The first serious effort to enunciate the applicable principles was undertaken by the fifteenth General Assembly in the annex to Resolution 1541 of December 15, 1960. It attempts to stipulate the test for determining whether a territory is non-self-governing within the meaning of Article 73(e) of the Charter. Under Principle IV of the resolution, non-self-governing status exists *prima facie* "in respect of a territory which is geographically separate and is distinct ethnically and/or culturally from the country administering it." Once that test has been met, Principle V states, "other elements may then be brought into consideration," including those "of an administrative, political, juridical, economic or historical nature. If they affect the relationship between the metropolitan State and the territory concerned in a manner which arbitrarily places the latter in a position or status of subordination, they support the presumption" that the territory is non-self-governing.[39]

[37] United Nations Convention on the Law of the Sea, *opened for signature* Dec. 10, 1982, UN Doc. A/CONF.62/122, *reprinted in* UNITED NATIONS, OFFICIAL TEXT OF THE UNITED NATIONS CONVENTION ON THE LAW OF THE SEA WITH ANNEXES AND INDEX, UN Sales No. E.83.V.5 (1983), 21 ILM 1261 (1982). For the Court's interpretation of Article 83(1), see Continental Shelf (Tunisia/Libyan Arab Jamahiriya), 1982 ICJ REP. 18 (Judgment of Feb. 24); Continental Shelf (Libyan Arab Jamahiriya/Malta), 1985 ICJ REP. 13 (Judgment of June 3).

[38] *See* Passage through the Great Belt, 1991 ICJ REP. 12 (Order of July 29).

[39] GA Res. 1541, 15 UN GAOR Supp. (No. 16), *supra* note 31, at 29.

The 1970 Declaration on Friendly Relations elaborated the Charter "principle of equal rights and self-determination of peoples" by reiterating the duty to end colonialism and to permit each colonial territory to assume a "political status freely determined by" the inhabitants. More broadly, the declaration attributes to "all peoples"—not merely the inhabitants of colonies—"the right freely to determine, without external interference, their political status."[40]

This broader concept of a *universal* right of self-determination is further enunciated in Article 1 of the International Covenant on Civil and Political Rights.[41] This treaty, ratified or acceded to by 113 states as of November 1991, but probably binding on other states as customary law,[42] states categorically: "All peoples have the right of self-determination. By virtue of that right they freely determine their political status and freely pursue their economic, social and cultural development." This provision has been called the "most controversial" in a document created and steeped in considerable controversy.[43] Western powers, in particular, at first argued that the right was only a political principle, that it was ill-defined and unsuited to a treaty enumerating individual—as opposed to collective—rights and thus inappropriate to the unique quasi-judicial enforcement machinery envisaged by the Covenant. Nevertheless, its proponents insisted that the norm of self-determination was fundamental, and a precondition, to the enjoyment of all other enumerated individual rights and freedoms. As a result, "the tide of political opinion in favour of including a right of self-determination proved irresistible"[44] and the principle was given pride of place among the designated entitlements. More significantly for the long term, the majority—including states that had opposed inclusion of the right—utterly rejected the notion that the entitlement applied only to colonial "peoples," declaring, rather, that if included, it must apply to peoples anywhere, whether in a politically independent state or a dependent territory.[45]

The Covenant clearly intends to make the right of self-determination applicable to the citizens of all nations, entitling them to determine their collective political status through democratic means. It also makes an important distinction between that right of each nation's collective *polis* and the rights of minorities within each state, which the Covenant elucidates in Article 27. Under Article 27, "ethnic, religious or linguistic minorities . . . shall not be denied the right, in community with the other members of their group, to enjoy their own culture, to profess and practice their own religion, or to use their own language."

Notably, not included among the enumerated rights of these minorities as defined in Article 27 is any entitlement to secede.[46] When the Covenant came into force, the right of self-determination entered its third phase of enunciation: it ceased to be a rule applicable only to specific territories (at first, the defeated European powers; later, the overseas trust territories and colonies) and became a

[40] Annex to GA Res. 2625, *supra* note 31, principle 4.

[41] International Covenant on Civil and Political Rights, Dec. 16, 1966, 999 UNTS 171, *reprinted in* 6 ILM 368 (1967) (entered into force Mar. 23, 1976) [hereinafter ICCPR]. The same provision is stated as Article 1 of the International Covenant on Economic, Social and Cultural Rights, Dec. 16, 1966, 993 UNTS 3, *reprinted in* 6 ILM 360 (1967) (entered into force Jan. 3, 1976).

[42] T. MERON, HUMAN RIGHTS AND HUMANITARIAN NORMS AS CUSTOMARY LAW 80–81 (1989); Sohn, *Generally Accepted International Rules*, 61 WASH. L. REV. 1073, 1077–78 (1986); Schachter, *International Law Implications of U.S. Human Rights Policies*, 24 N.Y.L. SCH. L. REV. 63, 68 (1978).

[43] D. MCGOLDRICK, THE HUMAN RIGHTS COMMITTEE 14 (1991).

[44] *Id.*

[45] *Id.* at 15.

[46] For a different view as to the legal status of the right to secede, see Brilmayer, *supra* note 19.

right of everyone. It also, at least for now, stopped being a principle of exclusion (secession) and became one of inclusion: the right to participate. The right now entitles peoples in all states to free, fair and open participation in the democratic process of governance freely chosen by each state. When such participation is denied, when a people that, in the terms of the aforementioned 1960 General Assembly resolution, "is geographically separate and is distinct ethnically and/or culturally" has been placed "in a position or status of subordination,"[47] perhaps a secession option may reemerge as an international legal entitlement. That aspect of self-determination, however, is far less clear at present than the entitlement to democratic participation in governance.

How is self-determination to be implemented? Gradually, answers to this question have also emerged. During the first forty years of the United Nations, members responsible for trust territories and colonies were charged with making periodic reports on their progress; these reports were subjected to increasing scrutiny by various UN bodies. Since the coming into force of the Covenant, reporting and scrutiny have been formalized, depoliticized to an extent, and welded to the process of case-by-case norm application. This development will help shape the postcolonial concept of self-determination and give it more determinacy. The Covenant thus foresees a continuing, growing body of law made by means of the interpretation and application of its provisions by an expert, independent, quasi-judicial body.

As usual, this process begins with a form of monitoring. The 113 states parties to the Covenant are legally obliged to "undertake to submit reports on the measures they have adopted which give effect to the rights recognized herein and on the progress made in the enjoyment of those rights."[48] These reports are scrutinized by a Human Rights Committee of eighteen members elected by states parties to the Covenant, who serve in their personal capacities[49] for a term of four years.[50] While the Committee is not a court, it does have the right to question the reports submitted by members. It transmits its reviews and such general comments as it thinks appropriate to the states parties to the Covenant and to the UN Economic and Social Council.[51] Under an optional procedure, parties may also agree to permit other parties to allege violations in a formal complaint.[52] An Optional Protocol permits individuals to lodge complaints against accepting states.[53] As of November 1991, sixty-three of the parties to the Covenant had agreed to give the Committee the competence to consider petitions. A recent study concluded that the Committee members have succeeded in establishing a high degree of independence and judiciousness.[54]

Formally, all petitions brought under the Optional Protocol are drawn to the Committee's attention by the UN Secretary-General.[55] More than a hundred such

[47] GA Res. 1541, *supra* note 39.

[48] ICCPR, *supra* note 41, Art. 40(1).

[49] *Id.*, Arts. 28, 30.

[50] *Id.*, Art. 32.

[51] For a discussion of this procedure, see D. McGoldrick, *supra* note 43, at 62–119.

[52] ICCPR, *supra* note 41, Art. 41. For a discussion of this procedure, see D. McGoldrick, *supra* note 43, at 120–246.

[53] ICCPR, *supra* note 41, Optional Protocol, *opened for signature* Dec. 19, 1966, Art. 1, 999 UNTS 302; *see also* D. McGoldrick, *supra* note 43, at 127.

[54] D. McGoldrick, *supra* note 43, at 45.

[55] Human Rights Committee, Provisional Rules of Procedure, Rule 78(1), UN Doc. CCPR/C/3/Rev.2 (1989). *See* Report of the Human Rights Committee, 44 UN GAOR Supp. (No. 40) at 179–82, UN Doc. A/44/40 (1989).

"cases" have been taken up and fewer than twenty were dismissed for lack of evidence of a violation. Some 150 more petitions are pending.[56] Although the Covenant envisages the possibility of voting, the Committee's decisions to date have been taken by consensus.[57]

The Committee, so far, has not had much occasion to explain the content of the right of self-determination. Only one petition-based case has been heard. While it rejected as inadmissible a claim by a Grand Captain of the Mikmaq tribal society that Canada was denying his people their right of self-determination, the Committee based its rejection on the applicant's inability to demonstrate that he was authorized to represent the tribe or that he, personally, had been deprived of a right protected by the Covenant.[58] As noted, the Covenant validates free and equal political participation as well as the cultural rights of minorities, but not necessarily secession. The Committee's finding leaves open the possibility that another individual might succeed in bringing a comparable petition if he or she can demonstrate having the *bona fides* to act in a representative capacity and alleges a denial of cultural autonomy or free and equal political participation.

The Committee does not merely consider reports and complaints. Periodically, it also makes more general findings on the state of civil and political rights and prepares summaries of the developing normative expectations arising from the Covenant. In its general commentary on Article 1, the Committee has been rather cautious, merely reiterating the primacy of self-determination among the human rights enumerated in the Covenant. "In accordance with the purposes and principles of the Charter of the United Nations," the Committee has written, "article 1 . . . recognizes that all peoples have the right of self-determination. The right . . . is of particular importance because its realization is an essential condition for the effective guarantee and observance of individual human rights and for the promotion and strengthening of those rights."[59]

The right to self-determination, in sum, may be said to be poised to move toward still greater determinacy. Its general normative content already has been spelled out in General Assembly resolutions to which a large majority of the international community has assented, and in several widely ratified treaties, beginning with the UN Charter and culminating in the Covenant. Equally important to the determinacy of the right of self-determination is the institutional potential for applying and clarifying the emerging rules; while the Committee's accomplishments have been modest, a systemic basis has been laid for more solid results. Now that the inhibitions of Cold War politics have been lifted and the liberal democratic sensibility is widely shared by the membership, what began as review by politicized, anticolonial committees of the General Assembly and by the Trusteeship Council may be expected to become a judicious process of principled rule interpretation by independent experts.

[56] D. McGoldrick, *supra* note 43, at 127. [57] *Id.* at 48.

[58] A.D. v. Canada, Report of the Human Rights Committee, 39 UN GAOR Supp. (No. 40) at 200, UN Doc. A/39/40 (1984). *See also* Ominayak and Lubicon Lake Band v. Canada, Report of the Human Rights Committee, 45 UN GAOR Supp. (No. 40), vol. 2, App. A, UN Doc. A/45/40 (1990). See discussion in D. McGoldrick, *supra* note 43, at 254–56; and McGoldrick, *Canadian Indians, Cultural Rights and the Human Rights Committee*, 40 Int'l & Comp. L.Q. 658 (1991).

[59] General Comments of the Human Rights Committee, UN Doc. CCPR/C/21/Rev.1, at 10–11 (1989). *See also* D. McGoldrick, *supra* note 43, at 247–48.

Determinacy and Free Expression

The second building block in constructing a normative entitlement to democracy is the right of free political expression. This right originated conceptually in the antitotalitarianism born of World War II and was first enunciated normatively in the Universal Declaration of Human Rights, adopted by the General Assembly on December 10, 1948.[60] As a mere resolution, the Universal Declaration does not have the force of a treaty; yet it was passed with such overwhelming support, and such prestige has accrued to it in succeeding years, that it may be said to have become a customary rule of state obligation. More to the point, its text manifests considerable determinacy, specifically recognizing a universal right to freedom of opinion and expression (Article 19), as well as to peaceful assembly and association (Article 20).

These entitlements reappear with even greater specificity in the legally binding Covenant on Civil and Political Rights.[61] Spelled out in that treaty are specific rights to freedom of thought (Article 18) and freedom of association (Article 22). Article 19(2) is an especially important component of the democratic entitlement. It states: "Everyone shall have the right to freedom of expression; this right shall include freedom to seek, receive and impart information and ideas of all kinds, regardless of frontiers, either orally, in writing or in print, in the form of art, or through any other media of his choice." While Article 19(2) is subject to restriction by law where "necessary . . . [f]or the protection of . . . public order . . . , or of public health or morals,"[62] these restrictions, like the rule itself, are subject to case-by-case review and application by the Human Rights Committee.[63]

Rights to opinion, expression and association contained in Articles 18, 19 and 22 look both backward and forward. They are a refinement of an aspect of the older right of self-determination; they also constitute the essential preconditions for an open electoral process, which is the newest component of the democratic entitlement. First mooted in the Universal Declaration, they became explicit treaty-based entitlements by incorporation into the Covenant and are likely to be made even more explicitly determinate by the review and monitoring of required national reports on compliance and specific petitions by complainants. The Human Rights Committee, for example, has been critical, albeit in a circumspect manner, of the compliance of Uganda and Zanzibar under Tanzanian control.[64] The Committee has also posed searching questions to representatives of Mali[65] and Jamaica[66] regarding the openness of their marketplaces of ideas. Professor Dominic McGoldrick has commended

> the close, detailed and critical analysis undertaken by members under the reporting process. The dialogue between the [Committee] and the States parties, in so far as it has developed, has been both direct and constructive. [Committee] members have in a diplomatic but forthright way criticized or expressed strong doubts concerning the compatibility with article 19 of specific ideological conceptions of and wide restrictions on freedom of expression.[67]

[60] GA Res. 217A (III), UN Doc. A/810, at 71 (1948).

[61] ICCPR, *supra* note 41.

[62] *Id.*, Art. 19(3).

[63] *See* D. McGoldrick, *supra* note 43, at 461.

[64] Report of the Human Rights Committee, 36 UN GAOR Supp. (No. 40) at 42–43, UN Doc. A/36/40 (1981) [hereinafter 1981 Report].

[65] *Id.* at 50–51.

[66] *Id.* at 56–57.

[67] D. McGoldrick, *supra* note 43, at 469–70.

In their tough questioning of the representatives of reporting states, the Committee's members are now aided regularly, behind the scenes, by a network of nongovernmental organizations.

While most of these critiques have occurred under the aegis of the general reporting requirement, a few case-by-case reviews have taken place under the Optional Protocol. The Committee found Uruguay's military regime in violation of Article 19(2) of the Covenant when it denied a petitioner the right freely to engage in political and trade union activities.[68] In *Perdoma and DeLanza v. Uruguay*,[69] the complainants alleged that they had been detained on account of "subversive association" based on their political views and connections. The Committee concluded that there was no evidence to substantiate the authorities' charge and that the arrest, detention and trial of the petitioners had not been justified on any of the grounds permitted in Article 19(3).[70]

When rules are impartially applied, whether by judges, administrators or experts, the determinacy of those rules increases and so, also, their legitimacy. Thus far, the Human Rights Committee's review of complaints regarding restrictions on expressive rights has just begun to have an impact, but in view of the end of the Cold War, the prognosis is much better. Moreover, other avenues for international protection of these rights are opening up, as evidenced by the requests of the intergovernmental Human Rights Commission to the UN Secretary-General that he appoint special representatives to report on alleged gross violations by various governments. In this respect, a significant new role for the Secretary-General was recently agreed upon by both the Government and insurgents in El Salvador. Under UN auspices, the parties consented to the establishment of ONUSAL, the UN Observer Group in El Salvador, which is to be controlled by the Secretary-General and is to supervise, and thereby seek to ensure citizens' rights to, free expression and association as part of a plan to create the circumstances for civil peace.[71]

In addition to such activity at the global level, parallel and reinforcing norm building and defining is under way at the regional level. The European Convention for the Protection of Human Rights and Fundamental Freedoms, the best-established regional normative system, provides in Article 10, paragraph 1: "Everyone has the right to freedom of expression. This right shall include freedom to hold opinions and to receive and impart information and ideas without interference by public authority and regardless of frontiers."[72]

Paragraph 2 of Article 10 does permit derogation in the form of

> restrictions . . . necessary in a democratic society, in the interests of national security, territorial integrity or public safety, for the prevention of disorder or crime, for the protection of health or morals, for the protection of the

[68] Alba Pietroroia v. Uruguay, Communication R.10/44, 1981 Report, *supra* note 64, at 153–59.

[69] Report of the Human Rights Committee, 35 UN GAOR Supp. (No. 40) at 111, UN Doc. A/35/40 (1980) [hereinafter 1980 Report].

[70] *Id. See also* Grille Motta v. Uruguay, Communication R.2/11, 1980 Report, *supra* note 69, at 132; Weinberg Weisz v. Uruguay, Communication R.7/28, 1981 Report, *supra* note 64, at 114; Hertzberg v. Finland, Communication R.14/61, Report of the Human Rights Committee, 37 UN GAOR Supp. (No. 40) at 161, UN Doc. A/37/40 (1982).

[71] Central America: Efforts Towards Peace: Report of the Secretary-General, UN Doc. S/22494 and Corr.1 (1991); *see also* N.Y. Times, Aug. 13, 1991, at A8, col. 3.

[72] European Convention for the Protection of Human Rights and Fundamental Freedoms, Nov. 4, 1950, 213 UNTS 221, Europ. TS No. 5 (entered into force Sept. 3, 1953) [hereinafter European Convention].

> reputation or rights of others, for preventing the disclosure of information received in confidence, or for maintaining the authority and impartiality of the judiciary.

The application of both the rule and its exceptions, however, is subject to review by a commission of experts and a European Human Rights Court.[73] These bodies have augmented the determinacy of the system. As in a mature regime, the European Commission and Court of Human Rights have made key decisions balancing the rights of individuals against specific exceptions. The Court has weighed freedom of the press against a defendant's right to an impartial trial.[74] It has drawn boundaries between free expression and obscenity[75] and sought a balance between a free press and the laws of libel and slander.[76] In so doing, it has made far more specific—hence legitimate—the Council of Europe's system of norms pertaining to expressive rights, just when it is rapidly expanding to include the newly freed nations of Eastern Europe.

Comparable progress is being made by the more recently established inter-American regional system. The 1969 American Convention on Human Rights[77] provides an elaborate textual basis for freedom of thought and expression (Article 13), the right of assembly (Article 15) and freedom of association (Article 16). Monitoring and enforcement is performed by two institutions created by the OAS Charter: the Inter-American Commission on Human Rights (Articles 34 and 64(1)) and the Inter-American Court of Human Rights (Articles 33, 62 and 64). The Court consists of seven judges elected by the states adhering to the Convention, who serve for a term of six years. As of May 1990, ten states—not including the United States—had accepted its jurisdiction.[78]

Determinacy and Electoral Rights

The third and newest building block in constructing the entitlement to democracy is the emerging normative requirement of a participatory *electoral* process. Despite its infancy, it, too, is rapidly evolving toward that determinacy which is essential to being perceived as legitimate. As early as 1948, the Universal Declaration of Human Rights, in Article 21, clearly enunciated the right of all persons to take part in government, as well as in "periodic and genuine elections which shall be by universal and equal suffrage and shall be held by secret vote or by equivalent free voting procedures." At the time, only UN members outside the socialist, Arab and Latin American blocs took this as a restatement of conditions already prevailing in their *polis*. With rapid decolonization, the proportion of UN members actually practicing free and open electoral democracy began to shrink further under the aegis of one-party modernizing authoritarianism in Africa and

[73] *Id.*, Art. 19, establishing the European Commission on Human Rights and the European Court of Human Rights. *See also* Arts. 20–55.

[74] The Sunday Times Case, 30 Eur. Ct. H.R. (ser. A) (1978).

[75] Handyside Case, 24 Eur. Ct. H.R. (ser. A) (1976); Case of Muller and Others, 133 Eur. Ct. H.R. (ser. A) (1988).

[76] Lingens Case, 103 Eur. Ct. H.R. (ser. A) (1986).

[77] American Convention on Human Rights, Nov. 22, 1969, OEA/Ser.K/XVI.1.1, doc. 70, rev.1, corr.1 (1970), *reprinted in* 1 THE INTER-AMERICAN SYSTEM, pt. II at 51 (F. V. García-Amador ed. 1983), 9 ILM 673 (1970) (entered into force July 18, 1978) [hereinafter American Convention].

[78] Argentina, Colombia, Costa Rica, Ecuador, Guatemala, Honduras, Peru, Suriname, Uruguay and Venezuela. *See* Current State of Conventions and Protocols on Human Rights, Annual Report of the Inter-American Commission on Human Rights, OEA/Ser.L/V.II.79, doc. 12, rev.1, Ann. A (1991).

Asia. Nevertheless, even in that relatively hostile atmosphere, few states were willing openly to block the textual evolution of a specific electoral entitlement, however many mental reservations their regimes may have harbored. Thus, two decades later, the Civil and Political Covenant was opened for signature,[79] entering into force in 1976 as a set of legal obligations now binding on more than two-thirds of all states. With the balance now heavily tilting toward the substantial new majority of states actually practicing a reasonably credible version of electoral democracy, the treaty-based legal entitlement also begins to approximate prevailing practice and thus may be said to be stating what is becoming a customary legal norm applicable to all.

Article 25 extends to every citizen the right:

> (*a*) To take part in the conduct of public affairs, directly or through freely chosen representatives;
>
> (*b*) To vote and to be elected at genuine periodic elections which shall be by universal and equal suffrage and shall be held by secret ballot, guaranteeing the free expression of the will of the electors.

Admirable as it is, this standard still needs greater specificity. Textual determinacy, once again, is gradually being augmented by process determinacy under the auspices of the Human Rights Committee, which is authorized to monitor compliance. That body has discussed the implications of Article 25 in connection with its review of national reports on implementation and a small number of petitions lodged under the Optional Protocol. In reviewing two citizens' complaints against the military regime of Uruguay, the Committee concluded that the complainants had been arbitrarily deprived of protected rights by decrees banning their political party and by being barred from running for office.[80]

During the Cold War, it was difficult to utilize the Human Rights Committee to hone the rule outlined in Article 25. Now the Committee is likely to perform that function more effectively as the members' ideological divisions narrow and citizens become more willing to risk submitting complaints. This evolution would be accelerated if, as seems likely, the United States ratified the Covenant. If, as seems *less* likely, the United States also ratified the Protocol permitting individual complaints,[81] the determinacy of the entitlement would be further legitimized, which, surely, must accord with our nation's interest and ethos.

The new climate has also permeated the General Assembly. At its forty-fifth session, that body adopted a resolution entitled Enhancing the effectiveness of the principle of periodic and genuine elections.[82] This nonbinding, yet important, document reaffirms and further specifies the electoral entitlement first outlined in the Universal Declaration of Human Rights and later embodied in Article 25 of the Covenant. It "stresses" the member nations'

> conviction that periodic and genuine elections are a necessary and indispensable element of sustained efforts to protect the rights and interests of the governed and that, as a matter of practical experience, the right of everyone to take part in the government of his or her country is a crucial factor in the effective enjoyment by all of a wide range of other human rights and fundamental freedoms, embracing political, economic, social and cultural rights.[83]

[79] ICCPR, *supra* note 41.

[80] Case 34/1979, 1981 Report, *supra* note 64, at 130; Case 44/1979, *id.*, Ann. XVI, at 153.

[81] *Supra* note 53.

[82] GA Res. 45/150 (Feb. 21, 1991).

[83] *Id.*, para. 2.

The resolution also declares "that determining the will of the people requires an electoral process that provides an equal opportunity for all citizens to become candidates and put forward their political views, individually and in co-operation with others, as provided in national constitutions and laws."[84] It commends "the value of the electoral assistance" the United Nations has provided member states at their request,[85] and asks the Secretary-General to seek the views of members and others on how the Organization can best respond to further such requests and to report his findings to the next Assembly, together with "an account of United Nations experience in election monitoring."[86]

At its next session the Assembly, with only four dissents, passed Resolution 46/137 of December 17, 1991, which declared that "periodic and genuine elections" are a "necessary and indispensable element" and a "crucial factor in the effective enjoyment . . . of a wide range of other human rights." The resolution established a procedure for authorizing the monitoring of national elections and endorsed the Secretary-General's decision to create an office, headed by a senior official, "to act as a focal point . . . in order to ensure consistency in the handling of requests of Member States organizing elections."

Parallel and reinforcing norm-generating activity occurring in regional frameworks has accelerated this evolution. The Charter of the Organization of American States, in Article 5, establishes the duty of members to promote "the effective exercise of representative democracy." The OAS Ministers of Foreign Affairs and the Organization's Permanent Council have issued a series of resolutions affirming this regional entitlement while censuring those committing apparent violations. For example, in June 1979, the Ministers demanded the "immediate and definitive replacement of the Somoza regime" in Nicaragua and the installation of a "democratic government" with the "holding of free elections as soon as possible."[87] Similarly, in December 1987, the Permanent Council took note of the "deplorable acts of violence and disorder" that had taken place in Haiti during that year's failed elections, expressed its "conviction that it is necessary to resume the democratic process" and urged the "Government of Haiti to adopt all necessary measures so that the people of Haiti may express their will through free elections."[88] In May 1989, the Ministers decided that "General Manuel Antonio Noriega . . . [had] abridged the right of the Panamanian people to freely elect their legitimate authorities" and thus had "seriously jeopardize[d]" an "essential purpose" of the OAS, which "is to promote and consolidate representative democracy." They further called for a "transfer of power in the shortest possible time" by means of "democratic mechanisms."[89]

On June 5, 1991, the Ministers adopted a crucial resolution on representative democracy. Its preamble states that the principles of the OAS Charter "require the political representation of [member] states to be based on effective exercise of representative democracy" and, in its operative sections, the resolution decides that the Secretary General shall

> call for the immediate convocation of a meeting of the Permanent Council in the event of any occurrences giving rise to the sudden or irregular interruption of the democratic political institutional process or of the legitimate exer-

[84] *Id.*, para. 3.

[85] *Id.*, para. 8.

[86] *Id.*, paras. 10, 11. The Secretary-General's report to the Assembly is UN Doc. A/46/609 (1991).

[87] OEA/Ser.F/II.17, doc. 40, rev.2 (1979).

[88] OEA/Ser.G/CP/RES.489, doc. 720 (1987).

[89] OEA/Ser.F/II.21, doc. 8, rev.2 (1989); *see also* OEA/Ser.F/II.21, doc. 45 (1989).

> cise of power by the democratically elected government in any of the Organization's member states.[90]

Within ten days, the Ministers of Foreign Affairs or the OAS General Assembly must convene so as to "look into the events collectively and adopt any decisions deemed appropriate."[91] It was this procedure that was invoked to bring about sanctions against the regime established by the military coup in Haiti in September 1991.[92]

Alongside these quasi-legislative developments, a regional quasi jurisprudence is germinating. In 1990, the Inter-American Commission on Human Rights, in considering a complaint of electoral fraud and other impropriety against Mexico, began to spell out in some detail the right of access, under general conditions of equality, to a nation's public functions.[93]

Even more dramatic are recent efforts by the nations of Europe to make the electoral entitlement explicit and specific. Article 3 of Protocol 1 to the European Human Rights Convention obliges the parties to "undertake to hold free elections at reasonable intervals by secret ballot, under conditions which will ensure the free expression of the opinion of the people in the choice of the legislature."[94] Finding the Greek colonels' regime in violation, the European Court of Human Rights interpreted this Protocol to require "the existence of a representative legislature, elected at reasonable intervals."[95] The European Commission, meanwhile, has rejected the purist argument that the Protocol requires states to adopt a system of proportional representation.[96]

As members of the Conference on Security and Co-operation in Europe,[97] the same nations, augmented by Canada, the United States and the nations of Eastern Europe, recently joined unanimously in spelling out the contents of the new right to participate in free and open elections. At a meeting in Copenhagen in June 1990, they affirmed that "democracy is an inherent element of the rule of law" and recognized "the importance of pluralism with regard to political organizations."[98] Among the "inalienable rights of all human beings," they decided, is the democratic entitlement, including "free elections that will be held at reasonable intervals by secret ballot or by equivalent free voting procedure, under conditions which ensure in practice the free expression of the opinion of the electors in the choice of their representatives"; a government "representative in character, in which the executive is accountable to the elected legislature or the electorate"; and political parties that are clearly separate from the state.[99] The thirty-five

[90] Representative Democracy, OEA/Ser.P/AG/RES.1080 (XXI-0/91), para. 1.

[91] *Id.*, para. 2.

[92] Support to the Democratic Government of Haiti, *supra* note 2.

[93] Annual Report of the Inter-American Commission on Human Rights, OEA/Ser.L/V/II.77, doc. 7, rev.1, at 97 (1990) (Mexico Report).

[94] Protocol 1 to the European Convention, *supra* note 72, Mar. 20, 1952, 213 UNTS 262, entered into force May 18, 1954, and, as of June 1991, had been ratified by all but one party to the Convention (Liechtenstein).

[95] The Greek Case, 12 Y.B. EUR. CONV. ON HUM. RTS. 179 (1969); *see also* Case of Mathieu-Mohin, 113 Eur. Ct. H.R. (ser. A) at 22 (1987).

[96] Application 7140/75, 7 Eur. Comm'n H.R. 95, 97 (1977).

[97] Conference on Security and Co-operation in Europe, Final Act, Aug. 1, 1975, 73 DEP'T ST. BULL. 323 (1975), *reprinted in* 14 ILM 1292 (1975).

[98] Conference on Security and Co-operation in Europe, Document of the Copenhagen Meeting of the Conference on the Human Dimension, June 29, 1990, *reprinted in* 29 ILM 1305, 1308, para. 3 (1990) [hereinafter Copenhagen Document].

[99] *Id.*, para. 5.

CSCE participants also linked recognition of the democratic entitlement by governments to the validation of their right to govern: "the will of the people, freely and fairly expressed through periodic and genuine elections, is the basis of the authority and legitimacy of all government,"[100] they declared, implying the illegitimacy of regimes that deny their citizens basic democratic rights.

According to Professor Theodor Meron, one of the public members of the U.S. delegation, the "language of Copenhagen goes far beyond any existing human rights instruments."[101] The document is detailed to an unprecedented degree, establishing a standard that the UN General Assembly might profitably emulate in a resolution. Citizens have the right to expect "free elections at reasonable intervals, as established by law"; a national legislature in which at least one chamber's membership is "freely contested in a popular vote"; a system of universal and equal adult suffrage; a secret ballot or its equivalent; free, nondiscriminatory candidature for office; freedom to form political parties that compete "on a basis of equal treatment before the law and by the authorities"; fair and free campaigning; "no legal or administrative obstacle" to media access, which must be available "on a non-discriminatory basis for all political groupings and individuals wishing to participate in the electoral process"; and a guarantee that the "candidates who obtain the necessary number of votes required by law are duly installed in office and are permitted to remain in office until their term expires or is otherwise" terminated in accordance with law.[102]

This unprecedented North Atlantic and Europe-wide initiative to endorse and define a popular right of electoral democracy[103] went on to commend the growing practice of involving foreign observers in national elections. The participating states invited "observers from any other CSCE participating States and any appropriate private institutions and organizations who may wish to do so to observe the course of their national election proceedings, to the extent permitted by law," and pledged to "endeavour to facilitate similar access for election proceedings held below the national level."[104]

Later in 1990, the leaders of the thirty-four CSCE states joined in Paris to declare "a new era of democracy, peace and unity."[105] Unanimously, they endorsed an extraordinary Charter, which commits them "to build, consolidate and strengthen democracy as the only system of government of our nations."[106] The Charter restates the older entitlement to free expression but adds the right of every individual, without discrimination, "to participate in free and fair elections,"[107] backed by the leaders' pledge to "co-operate and support each other with the aim of making democratic gains irreversible."[108] Although the Charter is not a treaty, its language is weighted with the terminology of *opinio juris.* It is deliberately norm creating. In particular, the Charter builds on the assumption

[100] *Id.* at 1309, para. 6.

[101] Meron, *Democracy and the Rule of Law,* 153 WORLD AFF. 23, 24 (1990). *See also* Steiner, *Political Participation as a Human Right,* 1 HARV. HUM. RTS. Y.B. 77 (1988).

[102] Copenhagen Document, *supra* note 98, at 1310, para. 7.

[103] Buergenthal, *The Copenhagen CSCE Meeting: A New Public Order for Europe,* 11 HUM. RTS. L.J. 217, 221–22 (1990).

[104] Copenhagen Document, *supra* note 98, at 1310, para. 8.

[105] Conference on Security and Co-operation in Europe, Charter of Paris for a New Europe and Supplementary Document to Give Effect to Certain Provisions of the Charter, Nov. 21, 1990, Preamble, *reprinted in* 30 ILM 190, 193 (1991) [hereinafter Paris Charter].

[106] Paris Charter, *supra* note 105, at 193.

[107] *Id.* at 194.

[108] *Id.* at 195.

that electoral democracy is owed not only by each government to its own people, but also by each CSCE state to all the others. According to Judge Thomas Buergenthal, another U.S. participant in the Copenhagen meeting, today

> no domestic institution or norm, in theory, is beyond the jurisdictional reach of the CSCE. Here the traditional domestic jurisdiction doctrine, which has tended to shield the oppressive state practices and institutions from international scrutiny, has for all practical purposes lost its meaning. And this notwithstanding the fact that non-intervention in the domestic affairs of a state is a basic CSCE principle. Once the rule of law, human rights and democratic pluralism are made the subject of international commitments, there is little left in terms of governmental institutions that is domestic.[109]

In this connection, one should note that the United States *is* a party to this normative evolution of the CSCE process.

To safeguard the rights concerned, the Paris Charter establishes an institutionalized process for monitoring compliance with the electoral duties of states. It gives the CSCE several organs, including a secretariat at Prague[110] and an Office for Free Elections at Warsaw. The latter is to "facilitate contacts and the exchange of information on elections within participating States."[111] The Charter also envisages the eventual creation, after further consultations, of a "CSCE parliamentary assembly, involving members of parliaments from all participating States," to achieve "greater parliamentary involvement in the CSCE."[112]

The new Office for Free Elections and its functions are described in the "supplementary document" appended to the Charter.[113] The office is to "foster the implementation" of the provisions of the Copenhagen Document pertaining to electoral democracy and, to this end, is authorized to "compile information," including, but not limited to, reports by governments on elections and the electoral process in participating states, "as well as reports of election observations." It is also to "serve to facilitate contact among governments, parliaments or private organizations wishing to observe elections and competent authorities of the States in which elections are to take place."[114]

Most recently, in September to October 1991, these nations' representatives unanimously endorsed the Document of the Moscow Meeting of the Conference on the Human Dimension of the CSCE. It reaffirms "that issues relating to human rights, fundamental freedoms, democracy and the rule of law are of international concern, as respect for these rights and freedoms constitutes one of the foundations of the international order." The participating states "categorically and irrevocably declare[d] that the commitments undertaken in the field of the human dimension of the CSCE are matters of direct and legitimate concern to all participating States and do not belong exclusively to the internal affairs of the State concerned."[115] More important yet is the mechanism and procedure established in paragraphs 3–16, which envisages a "resource" of experts, up to three of whom may be named by a state requesting good offices or mediation services in connec-

[109] Buergenthal, *CSCE Human Dimension: The Birth of a System*, 1 COLLECTED COURSES OF THE ACADEMY OF EUROPEAN LAW, No. 2, at 3, 42–43 (forthcoming).

[110] Paris Charter, *supra* note 105, at 206.

[111] *Id.* at 207.

[112] *Id.*

[113] *Id.* at 214–15.

[114] *Id.* at 214.

[115] Conference on Security and Co-operation in Europe, Document of the Moscow Meeting of the Conference on the Human Dimension of the CSCE, Oct. 3, 1991, Preamble, at 2 (unofficial text of the U.S. delegation), *reprinted in* 30 ILM 1670 (1991). [hereinafter Moscow Document].

tion with any domestic dispute arising under the "human dimension." If a CSCE state poses a human dimension question to another member and that member does not itself invite such a mission of inquiry, the requesting state and five others may invoke the process, with one expert of the three-person panel to be selected from the "resource" list by the requesting state, one by the requested state, and the third by agreement between the other two or by the ranking official of the CSCE designated by its Council. These "rapporteurs" are to establish the facts and report on them, and they may give advice on possible solutions to the problems raised. Most important of all is part II of the Moscow Document, in which the members pledge that they

> will support vigorously, in accordance with the Charter of the United Nations, in case of overthrow or attempted overthrow of a legitimately elected government of a participating State by undemocratic means, the legitimate organs of that State upholding human rights, democracy and the rule of law, recognizing their common commitment to countering any attempt to curb these basic values.[116]

The evolution of textual determinacy with respect to the electoral entitlement is a relatively recent development. In practice, however, the monitoring component of the entitlement has a long history. The long record of UN election monitoring both in the former trusteeship territories and in some colonies immediately before they attained independence was already mentioned as instrumental in establishing pedigree. But that practice also honed the normative content of the entitlement. As early as May 1956, the Trusteeship Council sent monitors to the plebiscite in which the people of British Togoland chose to join Ghana.[117] Its monitors were involved in conducting the preindependence plebiscites in the British Cameroons in November 1959 and February 1961.[118] Similarly, following the November 1959 violence between the Hutu and Tutsi tribes in what was then Belgian-administered Ruanda-Urundi, the United Nations supervised a preindependence election and referendum that determined the separation of the linked indigenous kingdoms and the future of the monarchy.[119]

In 1961 the United Nations assisted New Zealand, the administering authority, in conducting a plebiscite in Western Samoa that endorsed a draft constitution and a form of association with the former trustee.[120] On June 17, 1975, the

[116] Moscow Document, *supra* note 115, para. 17, at 9.

[117] Report of the United Nations Plebiscite Commissioner for the Trust Territory of Togoland under British Administration, UN Doc. T/1258 and Add.1 (1956).

[118] *See* GA Res. 1350, 13 UN GAOR Supp. (No. 18A) at 2, UN Doc. A/4090/Add.1 (1959) (whether the Northern Cameroons wished "to be part of the Northern Region of Nigeria when the Federation of Nigeria becomes independent"); GA Res. 1352, 14 UN GAOR Supp. (No. 16) at 26, UN Doc. A/4354 (1959) (whether the Southern Cameroons wished to achieve independence by "joining the independent Federation of Nigeria [or] the independent Republic of Cameroons"); GA Res. 1473, *id.* at 38 (putting the questions posed in the GA Res. 1352 plebiscite before the Northern Cameroons); *see also* Report of United Nations Commissioner for the Supervision of the Plebiscites in the Southern and Northern Parts of the Trust Territory of the Cameroons under United Kingdom Administration, UN Doc. T/1556 and app. (1961).

[119] GA Res. 1579, 15 UN GAOR Supp. (No. 16), *supra* note 31, at 34 (elections); GA Res. 1605, 15 UN GAOR Supp. (No. 16A) at 8, UN Doc. A/4684/Add.1 (1961) (referendum).

[120] GA Res. 1569, 15 UN GAOR Supp. (No. 16), *supra* note 31, at 33 (whether the inhabitants of the territory accepted "the Constitution adopted by the Constitutional Convention on 28 October 1960" and endorsed "that on 1 January 1962 Western Samoa should become an independent State on the basis of that Constitution"); *see also* Report of United Nations Commissioner for the Supervision of the Plebiscite in Western Samoa, UN Doc. T/1564 and Add.1 (1961).

United Nations observed the vote in which residents of the Northern Mariana Islands endorsed a loose form of political confederation with the United States;[121] and, at various times in the 1980s, it supervised plebiscites in the rest of the U.S. Pacific Islands Trust that determined the future status of those several archipelagoes.[122]

The monitoring of political progress in trust territories led to the case-by-case enunciation of principles applicable to the democratic entitlement. Throughout the 1950s and 1960s, the Trusteeship Council and the General Assembly, on the basis of reports made by visiting missions, made recommendations to the states administering trust territories. These frequently specified the steps necessary to effect democratic participation by the inhabitants in choosing their political future. For example, in its 1959 report on Belgian administration of the Ruanda-Urundi Trust, the Council urged that the representation of inhabitants in the legislative body be increased and that it be given greater power. The Council also called for direct universal suffrage and an increase in the responsibilities of elected local authorities.[123] Such advice was influential both in determining the rate and direction of a territory's emancipation and in crystallizing a broadly shared expectation about the requirements of the democratic entitlement.

Although the United Nations had a specific legal ground for intervening in, and validating, the democratic process within trust territories, it also found bases for supervising colonial elections and referendums just prior to independence and this role gradually came to be an accepted element in legitimizing those crucial transitions. Thus, UN observers oversaw the referendum establishing a new constitution for the Cook Islands in 1965[124] and the preindependence referendum and elections in Spanish Equatorial Guinea in 1968.[125] The United Nations undertook similar monitoring of the referendum on the future status of West New Guinea (West Irian) from July 14 to August 2, 1969,[126] as well as of the November 1980 elections conducted in the New Hebrides under French and British administration, which led to the creation of independent Vanuatu.[127]

As the colonial era drew to a close, the significance of the UN election-monitoring role, instead of declining, appears to have increased, partly because the last

[121] Report of the United Nations Visiting Mission to Observe the Plebiscite in the Northern Mariana Islands, Trust Territory of the Pacific Islands, 43 UN TCOR Supp. (No. 2) at 24, UN Doc. T/1771 (1976).

[122] *See* Report of the United Nations Visiting Mission to Observe the Plebiscite in the Federated States of Micronesia, Trust Territory of the Pacific Islands, 51 UN TCOR Supp. (No. 1) at 14, UN Doc. T/1860 (1984) (June 21, 1983 plebiscite for the islands of Truk, Yap, Kosrae and Ponape); Report of the United Nations Visiting Mission to Observe the Plebiscite in the Marshall Islands, Trust Territory of the Pacific Islands, *id.* (No. 2) at 12–13, UN Doc. T/1865 (1984) (Sept. 7, 1983 plebiscite); Report of the United Nations Visiting Mission to Observe the Plebiscite in Palau, Trust Territory of the Pacific Islands, 53 UN TCOR Supp. (No. 2) at 14, UN Doc. T/1885 (1986) (Feb. 21, 1986 plebiscite).

[123] 24 UN TCOR Annex 1 (Agenda Item 3) at 21, UN Doc. T/L.928 (1959).

[124] GA Res. 2005, 19 UN GAOR Supp. (No. 15) at 7, UN Doc. A/5815 (1965); Report of the United Nations Representatives for the Supervision of the Elections in the Cook Islands, UN Doc. A/5962 and Corr.1 (1965).

[125] GA Res. 2355, 22 UN GAOR Supp. (No. 16) at 54, UN Doc. A/6716 (1967); United Nations Mission for the Supervision of the Referendum and the Elections in Equatorial Guinea, UN Doc. A/7200/Add.4, Anns. V, VI (1968). Independence was formally achieved on October 12, 1968.

[126] GA Res. 1752, 17 UN GAOR Supp. (No. 17) at 70, UN Doc. A/5217 (1962); Report of the Secretary-General regarding the Act of Self-determination in West Irian, UN Doc. A/7641 (1969).

[127] GA Res. 34/10, 34 UN GAOR Supp. (No. 46) at 199, UN Doc. A/34/46 (1979); Report of the United Nations Mission to Observe the Elections in the New Hebrides, UN Doc. A/34/852 (1979).

cases of decolonization were among the most difficult. In these, a UN "honest broker" role proved indispensable. A remarkable example is UNTAG, the UN transitional administration that acted as midwife in the birth of independent Namibia. Under South African administration since Germany's defeat in World War I, the territory was set on the road to independence first by the General Assembly's termination of South Africa's mandate in 1966, followed by a landmark advisory opinion by the International Court of Justice in 1971,[128] and by a decision of the Security Council in 1978 establishing the parameters for the territory's political development and democratic entitlement.[129] It took another decade, however, for the political climate in South Africa to change sufficiently to permit international implementation of self-determination through a UN-supervised vote. By that time, tribal and racial cleavages had become potential obstacles to a peaceful transition. Created by the Security Council precisely to prevent a preindependence civil conflict, UNTAG monitored the final months of South African administration and supervised the elections immediately prior to independence. But UNTAG did not merely monitor a vote. It took responsibility for maintaining peace, overseeing the South African military withdrawal and assisting in the drafting of a new constitution. It helped achieve the rapid repeal of discriminatory legislation, implementation of an amnesty and the return of political refugees; and it was instrumental in keeping the election peaceful and productive. Deploying more than seven thousand military and civilian personnel at a cost of $373 million, it prepared the November 1989 elections and conducted them so successfully that a risk-filled situation became, instead, a model of political transformation.[130]

The Security Council authorized a similarly complex role for the United Nations in a resolution of April 29, 1991, that established a United Nations Mission for the Referendum in the Western Sahara.[131] Under the plan negotiated by the Secretary-General with the Government of Morocco and the POLISARIO liberation movement, electoral monitoring is to be but one component of a project that gives the Organization predominant responsibility for governance of the territory in the period leading up to, and during, the crucial plebiscite. After almost two decades of war for control of the territory, the United Nations is to ensure security, facilitate large-scale repatriation of refugees, oversee the withdrawal of rival militias, and supervise the delicate process of determining who is eligible to vote.[132]

Even more remarkable than its monitoring in trust territories and colonies is the recent supervision by the United Nations of crucial votes in independent member states. In the first of these, the 1990 election in Nicaragua, UN monitoring was the culmination of the Secretary-General's far more extensive "good offices" negotiations, in cooperation with the OAS, aimed at ending the Central American regional conflict. This effort led, in August 1987, to the Esquipulas II agreement

[128] Legal Consequences for States of the Continued Presence of South Africa in Namibia (South West Africa) notwithstanding Security Council Resolution 276 (1970), 1971 ICJ REP. 16 (Advisory Opinion of June 21).

[129] SC Res. 435, 33 UN SCOR (Res. & Dec.) at 13, UN Doc. S/INF/34 (1978). It did not authorize the sending of UNTAG until 1989. SC Res. 628, 44 UN SCOR (Res. & Dec.) at 2, UN Doc. S/INF/45 (1989); SC Res. 629, *id.*

[130] *Namibia, Independence at Last,* UN CHRON., June 1990, at 4. Namibia formally achieved independence on March 21, 1990. *Id.*

[131] SC Res. 690 (Apr. 29, 1991).

[132] The Situation Concerning Western Sahara: Report by the Secretary-General, UN Doc. S/22464 (1991).

between five Central American Presidents, which established a blueprint for restoring peace and ensuring legitimacy in Nicaragua. In response to its call for free, internationally monitored elections, on March 3, 1989, the Nicaraguan Foreign Minister requested that the Secretary-General establish an observer mission.[133] The General Assembly had already authorized the Secretary-General to assist the Esquipulas process in appropriate ways,[134] but that resolution had made no mention of election monitoring. Nevertheless, the Secretary-General thought he had a "sufficient legislative basis" to comply with Nicaragua's request.[135] As a result, he established ONUVEN on July 6, 1989,[136] an initiative approved by the Security Council three weeks later.[137]

The active, far-reaching role of the UN observers in Nicaragua clearly illustrates how much the ground rules for international election monitoring had evolved in practice from the days of the missions to British Togoland and Ruanda-Urundi. The observers sent by the Secretary-General monitored the activities of the Supreme Electoral Council in drafting and implementing new laws applicable to nominating, campaigning and related activities. They were deployed throughout the electoral campaign and mediated disputes between candidates concerning access to funding, the media and even the streets. They oversaw the rights of political parties to organize and campaign, verified the campaigners' right of access to radio, television and newspapers, and investigated numerous charges of abuses and irregularities that might have undermined the legitimacy of the outcome.[138] At the final stage, ONUVEN observed the voting and established its own projection of the results.[139] Commenting on these varied functions, the head of ONUVEN, Elliot Richardson, noted that his group had decided early in its career "that responsibility for verification of the electoral process demanded more than merely recording the process, more than monitoring, and could not stop short of actively seeking to get corrected whatever substantial defects had been discovered."[140]

Creating a UN mandate for ONUVEH, the mission established on October 10, 1990, to oversee Haitian elections, was more controversial. The Haitian case—greeted by many but feared by others—was seen as a potential precedent for international monitoring in any independent state. While the same might have been said of ONUVEN, Nicaragua's long civil war could have been seen as sufficiently threatening to the peace to justify, exceptionally, a UN role in validating those national elections. In Haiti's case, however, there was no obvious threat to international peace and the elections did not constitute part of a regional program for internationally supervised postwar reconciliation. In fact, the UN monitoring role there resulted solely from a request in a letter to the Secretary-General from the Haitian Transitional Government.[141] In normative terms, Haiti may be understood as the first instance in which the United Nations, acting at the request of

[133] *See* The Situation in Central America: Threats to International Peace and Security and Peace Initiatives, UN Doc. A/44/642, at 2 (1989) [hereinafter First Nicaragua Report].

[134] GA Res. 43/24, 43 UN GAOR Supp. (No. 49) at 27, UN Doc. A/43/49 (1988).

[135] UN Doc. A/44/304, at 2 (1989). [136] UN Doc. A/44/375 (1989).

[137] SC Res. 637, 44 UN SCOR, *supra* note 129, at 19.

[138] *See, e.g.*, The Situation in Central America: Threat to International Peace and Security and Peace Initiatives, UN Doc. A/44/927 (1990) [hereinafter Fifth Nicaragua Report]. *See also* First Nicaragua Report, *supra* note 133; UN Doc. A/44/834 (1990) (Second Report); UN Doc. A/44/917 (1990) (Third Report); UN Doc. A/44/921 (1990) (Fourth Report).

[139] Fifth Nicaragua Report, *supra* note 138. [140] *Id.* at 3.

[141] UN Doc. A/44/965 (1990).

a national government, intervened in the electoral process solely to validate the legitimacy of the outcome.

Despite misgivings, ONUVEH secured the imprimatur of the General Assembly.[142] Once again, the monitors were authorized to do far more than oversee the ballot count. Their first report noted the lack of democratic traditions in Haiti and its long history of totalitarianism and violence, much of it government inspired and some of it quite recent.[143] In preemptive response to this problem, the Assembly had authorized the recruiting of observers "with solid experience in the public order field."[144] As ONUVEH soon discovered, the

> first task . . . was to help create a psychological climate conducive to the holding of democratic elections. . . . In this they were assisted by a radio and television campaign conducted by an ONUVEH information team. . . .
>
> . . . [They] inquired into difficulties encountered by the registration and polling stations in registering voters and into irregularities reported to them. They attended political meetings . . . and monitored radio and television broadcasts to make sure that all candidates had equal access to the mass media.[145]

Although the Secretary-General, in his final report on ONUVEH, expressed satisfaction with the fairness of the electoral process and the role played by the United Nations, he also noted the formidable obstacles that lay ahead for Haitian democracy and called for "launching a civil education campaign on the importance of the parliament and local authorities."[146] The Secretary-General rightly warned that, if electoral democracy is to be more than a one-time event in the history of a state with little experience in such matters, a far more sustained effort will have to be made under the auspices of the community of nations. This warning suggests the need for a long-term, preemptive assistance program. More, it at least implies the need for a longer-term international effort to create the grass roots elements of democratic political institutions and processes—a particularly challenging form of technical assistance—in nations without that tradition. This need, in turn, suggests an important future role for the nongovernmental, citizen-to-citizen organizations—at present, an underused, but invaluable, component of the UN system.

The military coup that ousted Haiti's elected Government on September 30, 1991, verified the Secretary-General's warning that elections are not necessarily a cure-all. The General Assembly responded less than two weeks later, passing by consensus a resolution that "[s]trongly condemns both the attempted illegal replacement of the constitutional President of Haiti and the use of violence, military coercion and the violation of human rights in that country" and "demands the immediate restoration of the legitimate Government." It also "[a]ppeals to the . . . Members" to "take measures in support" of action by the OAS to isolate Haiti diplomatically and economically.[147] By these provisions, the Assembly made clear its intention henceforth to regard the overthrow of a democratically elected

[142] GA Res. 45/2 (Oct. 12, 1990).

[143] First Report of the United Nations Observer Group for the Verification of the Elections in Haiti, UN Doc. A/45/870, at 9–10 (1990).

[144] GA Res. 45/2, *supra* note 142, para. 1(*d*).

[145] United Nations Electoral Assistance to Haiti, UN Doc. DPI/1120 (1991).

[146] Electoral Assistance to Haiti: Note by the Secretary-General, UN Doc. A/45/870/Add.1, at 23 (1991).

[147] GA Res. A/46/L.8/Rev.1, paras. 1, 2, 4 (Oct. 11, 1991) (italics omitted).

regime as an appropriate subject for censure and even for recommending collective measures.[148]

The Organization of American States has also engaged in election monitoring. Its members authorized the dispatch of a 435-person commission to Nicaragua in 1990 to observe 70 percent of the polling sites.[149] In addition, the OAS maintained a major presence during the Haitian elections,[150] not only to watch the polls, but also to assist in drafting the electoral law and organizing voter registration.[151] Over the past two years, OAS monitors have observed elections in Suriname, El Salvador, Paraguay and Panama as well.[152] As a result, in part, of such collective efforts,[153] the thirty-four OAS member states—with the lamentable exception of Haiti—all have governments chosen in accordance with the democratic entitlement.[154]

Monitoring by governmental and nongovernmental observers also became an important ad hoc part of the post-1989 transition from Communist to democratic regimes in Eastern Europe. These events foreshadowed the textual declarations regarding election standards and procedures in the Copenhagen and Paris documents. Once again, practice preceded the drafting of new principles. The United States sent an official mission to monitor Bulgaria's 1990 election, as did several other CSCE governments.[155] Several members of Congress observed the electoral campaigns in Bulgaria[156] and Czechoslovakia,[157] as did their counterparts from some Western European parliaments.

At the unofficial level, additional election monitoring has taken place in recent years. Emissaries of the Council of Freely Elected Heads of Government of the Carter Center observed the 1990 Nicaraguan and 1991 Zambian elections.[158] The (U.S.) National Democratic Institute for International Affairs has monitored elections in twelve countries since 1986.[159] At least half a dozen teams of foreign observers, including experts from the United States, the Philippines, Japan and the British Commonwealth, monitored parliamentary elections in Bangladesh on February 27, 1991.[160] International observers from Canada, France, Germany and the United States verified the propriety of elections held in Benin in March 1991.[161] Perhaps most remarkable was the authorized presence of sixty-five inter-

[148] The "secondary" role of the General Assembly in recommending collective measures by the members has been controversial, but was found to be justified by Article 17, paragraph 2 of the Charter. *See* Certain expenses of the United Nations (Article 17, paragraph 2, of the Charter), 1962 ICJ Rep. 151, 163 (Advisory Opinion of July 20).

[149] N.Y. Times, Feb. 23, 1990, at A3, col. 4.

[150] OEA/Ser.G/CP/RES.537, doc. 805 (1990).

[151] Report of the Secretary General on the Assistance the Organization Is Giving to the Provisional Government of Haiti in its Electoral Process, OEA/Ser.G/CP/doc.2108/90, at 1.

[152] N.Y. Times, June 9, 1991, §4, at 2, col. 1.

[153] See, e.g., the OAS condemnation of General Manuel Noriega's usurpation of democratic electoral process in Panama's election of May 7, 1989, *supra* note 89. *See also* N.Y. Times, May 18, 1989, at A8, col. 3; *id.*, Aug. 16, 1989, at A9, col. 1.

[154] N.Y. Times, June 9, 1991, §4, at 2, col. 1. Cuba is not a member.

[155] N.Y. Times, June 6, 1990, at A10, col. 3.

[156] *See* Kahn, *Bulgaria's Different Pathway,* Christian Sci. Monitor, June 22, 1990, at 18. Helsinki Watch also sent monitors. N.Y. Times, June 11, 1990, at A1, col. 1.

[157] N.Y. Times, June 10, 1990, §1, at 31, col. 1.

[158] N.Y. Times, Aug. 9, 1989, at A13, col. 1; N.Y. Times, Nov. 1, 1991, at A3, col. 1.

[159] National Democratic Institute for International Affairs, Response to United Nations General Assembly Resolution 45/150: Developing a United Nations Elections Assistance Capability 2 (1991) (memorandum submitted to the Secretary-General).

[160] N.Y. Times, Feb. 28, 1991, at A5, col. 4.

[161] N.Y. Times, Mar. 12, 1991, at A11, col. 1.

national observers at the referendum on independence conducted in Latvia on March 3, 1991.[162]

Elliot Richardson, as head of the UN observers in Nicaragua, predicted that "the United Nations is likely in the future to be called upon for similar assignments in other countries."[163] "The results of such elections," as Professor Reisman recently observed, "serve as evidence of popular sovereignty and become the basis for international endorsement of the elected government."[164] Appropriately, President George Bush, in addressing the forty-fifth General Assembly, proposed the establishment of a standing UN electoral commission to assist nations, at their request, in guaranteeing that their elections will be free and fair.[165] A year later, as noted, the Assembly implemented that proposal.

Requesting international electoral monitoring thus will likely become an increasingly routine part of national practice, particularly useful whenever the democratic legitimacy of a regime is in question. Of course, there are still hard-core holdouts, such as the totalitarian governments of Myanmar, North Korea and China. Their number, however, is diminishing. The Government formed in Ethiopia in May 1991, after the end of the civil war, has undertaken to conduct "free, democratic and internationally monitored elections" within a year.[166] The insurgents who took power in Eritrea have committed themselves not to secede from Ethiopia until after a UN-monitored plebiscite, to be held within two years.[167]

A recent study by the UN Secretariat, noting the rising demand for monitoring, made a start at setting out the juridical, institutional, administrative and fiscal parameters of an expanded UN electoral monitoring service.[168] The OAS was authorized to prepare a similar study.[169] These begin the conceptually difficult task of sifting through the increasing body of practice to clarify the meaning of the normative concept signaled by the phrase "democratic entitlement." These data make it strikingly apparent that international election monitoring cannot be limited to guaranteeing citizens' right to vote, but rather must also ensure a far broader panoply of democratic rights of the sort enunciated in the Civil and Political Rights Covenant and the Charter of Paris. In case-by-case implementation and the distillation of that experience, greater determinacy will be achieved.

A study that seeks to connect the dots of practice with lines of enunciated principle must also look at the several instances when election monitoring was denied. For example, in 1990 the Secretary-General refused to monitor the Romanian elections on the ground that his participation had not been authorized by the General Assembly or Security Council. He added, perhaps even more persuasively, that he had not been invited to participate early enough in establishing the rules and methods to be used in conducting the election campaign.[170] In

[162] Fin. Times (London), Mar. 4, 1991, at 14.

[163] Fifth Nicaragua Report, *supra* note 138, at 3.

[164] Reisman, *Sovereignty and Human Rights in Contemporary International Law*, 84 AJIL 866, 868–69 (1990).

[165] N.Y. Times, Oct. 2, 1990, at A12, col. 1.

[166] N.Y. Times, May 29, 1991, at A6, col. 5.

[167] N.Y. Times, June 22, 1991, at 3, col. 1.

[168] Principles for United Nations Observance of Elections, Confidential Memorandum (June 6, 1989) (in the possession of the author).

[169] OEA/Ser.G/CP/RES.421, doc. 606 (1985).

[170] *See U.N. Says It Won't Monitor Romanian Elections* (NEXIS, CURRNT Library, Reuters, Jan. 25, 1990).

1991 the Office of the Secretary-General rejected requests for election monitoring made by Lesotho and Zambia, again on the ground that he felt he was unauthorized, in the absence of special circumstances, to monitor elections in sovereign states. The political organs of the United Nations may have been too cautious, so far, in giving the Secretary-General authority to respond favorably to a bona fide request by a member. On the other hand, the office of the Secretary-General may have been too cautious in denying requests for monitoring without even presenting them for approval to the Security Council or the General Assembly.

There is reason, nonetheless, for some caution. Commentators have rightly warned that the bare monitoring of the act of voting may place observers in the position of seeming to legitimate an electoral victory that was not fairly achieved. This reservation need not implicate fraud or repression but, more likely, concerns the effect on free choice of the normal operation of entrenched social and political institutions. In the words of a recent report to the General Assembly by the Secretary-General:

> [R]equests should pertain primarily to situations with a clear international dimension; the monitoring of an election or referendum should cover the entire electoral process in order to secure conditions of fairness and impartiality; . . . there must be broad public support in the State for the United Nations assuming such a role; and, finally, there should be approval by the competent organ of the United Nations.[171]

In future, in keeping with Assembly Resolution 46/137 of December 17, 1991, all requests for monitoring will be considered by the Council or Assembly, which will have the task of evolving standards for accepting or refusing.

While no observation process can reach back far enough into a nation's history to extirpate the impacted roots of social and cultural inequalities, observers can do—and already have done—more than simply watch tellers count ballots. To make citizens' rights to free and open elections a legitimate entitlement, its parameters need to be made clear and specific. To that end, a robust repertory of practice, a canon of enunciated principles and an institutional framework for implementation are developing that are capable of giving the entitlement increasing determinacy.

As the entitlement becomes an accepted norm, a drawn-out debate in international law will draw to a close. Do governments validate international law or does international law validate governments? It is becoming apparent that each legitimates the other.

The capacity of the international system to validate governments in this fashion is rapidly being accepted as an appropriate role of the United Nations, the regional systems and, supplementarily, the NGOs. A recent study conducted by the Netherlands Minister of Foreign Affairs gives expression to the new normative expectation. It asked: what can reasonably be expected of a European state seeking to join the European Communities and the Council of Europe? The study finds that applicant states "must be plural democracies; they must regularly hold free elections by secret ballot; they must respect the rule of law; [and] they must have signed the European Convention on Human Rights and Fundamental Free-

[171] Enhancing the Effectiveness of the Principle of Periodic and Genuine Elections, Report of the Secretary-General, UN Doc. A/46/609, para. 79, at 25 (1991). *See also* Gelb, *The Free Elections Trap*, N.Y. Times, May 29, 1991, at A23, col. 1.

doms."[172] Such a test for validation of governance and entry into a society of nations would have been unthinkable even a decade ago; it is considered unexceptionable in the new Europe. Some comparable rule in future should, and undoubtedly will, become the standard for participation in the multinational institutions of the global community.

As a step in this direction, the UN General Assembly might adopt and adapt the guidelines in the CSCE's Copenhagen Document and Paris Charter and declare these applicable to Article 25 of the Civil and Political Covenant. Such a resolution, among other things, would guide and assist the Human Rights Committee in more efficaciously carrying out its monitoring of compliance by the large majority of states parties to that global instrument. It would also help to make more determinate the content of the evolving customary law applicable to national political practices. Bringing the evolution of UN practice approximately into line with that of the CSCE would endow the emerging democratic entitlement with greater specificity and coherence.

VI. Coherence of the Democratic Entitlement

Pedigree and determinacy, as we have seen, give a rule the pull to compliance that we have identified as evidence of its perceived legitimacy. So also coherence. Coherence is that quality of a rule which permits it to be seen holistically: that is, as part of a rule context in which the parts gather compliance pull from the purpose and meaning of a larger whole. A rule that can plausibly lay claim to being part of such a skein exercises a greater compliance pull than one that cannot.[173]

Another way of understanding coherence is to examine the extent to which the compliance pull of a rule, invoked in one case, is augmented by evidence that it has connections that lead beyond the specifics of that dispute. Such augmentation may appear in several forms. First, it may become apparent that the rule being tested is so intimately connected with a larger regulatory scheme—for example, as one clause of an entire treaty—as to bring into play the weight and purpose of the larger whole. Second, the rule being tested may evince an important principle—English common law abounds in such "maxims": *nemo dat quod non habet,* for example—on which many distinct rules depend. Third, the issues in one instance may resemble those in others, creating a form of imperative to treat likes alike by applying the same rule.

How coherent, thus understood, is the normative canon of the democratic entitlement? Our examination of global and regional texts and processes will reveal that the rules pertaining to self-determination, freedom of expression and the right to participate in free and open elections are closely interwoven strands of a single fabric. These three generations of democratic entitlement, reinforced by regional systems, not only share many of the same or similar norms, but also have developed common or comparable kinds of institutions, procedures and customs. Each thread reinforces, and is reinforced by, the weave of the cloth.

When it comes to shared underlying principles, however, the connections are less straightforward. The democratic entitlement, after all, rests on the still-radi-

[172] Letter from the Minister for Foreign Affairs (H. van den Broek) to the Advisory Committee on Human Rights and Foreign Policy (June 20, 1990), *reprinted in* NETHERLANDS ADVISORY COMMITTEE ON HUMAN RIGHTS AND FOREIGN POLICY, DEMOCRACY AND HUMAN RIGHTS IN EASTERN EUROPE 30–31 (1990).

[173] *See* T. FRANCK, *supra* note 12, at 150–82.

cal principle that the community of states is empowered to compose and apply codes governing the comportment of governments toward their own citizens. No doubt, some such assumption long ago justified "enlightened" colonialism; its relic is still on view in Article 38(1)(c) of the International Court's Statute, which authorizes the judges to consult "general principles of law recognized by *civilized* nations" (italics mine). The term "civilized" may still be tainted by association with Cecil Rhodes, but the notion that governments can be graded for deportment is not. The Charter limits UN membership to states that are "peace-loving" (Article 4(1)) and enjoins governments to respect the "equal rights and self-determination of [their own] peoples" (Article 1(2)). The Genocide[174] and Racism Conventions[175] certainly do qualify as rules of deportment imposed on all states by the community of nations. Having become customary as well as treaty law—if not also rules of *jus cogens*—these Conventions may be said to exemplify the principle that states collectively have the authority to determine minimum standards of conduct from which none may long deviate without eventually endangering their membership in the club.

Nevertheless, the notion that the community can impose such standards, on which the democratic entitlement is based, has always been challenged by reference to another, embodied in Article 2(7) of the Charter. It provides, as formal recognition of the centuries-old principle of state sovereignty, that the Organization shall not interfere in matters "essentially within the domestic jurisdiction of states." While, as noted above, this conflict may have been resolved within the regional context of the CSCE with the recognition by the Copenhagen Document and the Paris Charter of the paramountcy of the democratic entitlement, the clear-cut supremacy of that entitlement is not yet apparent in the global context. Of course, state sovereignty, by operation of technological advances as much as of heightened humanistic sensitivity, is not what it used to be. Even those who defend the continued vitality of the principle would probably concede that genocide does not fall "essentially" within the ambit of protected "domestic" government activity. Nor, certainly, do egregious racism and, at least since the 1960s, denials of self-determination. Since the coming into force of the Civil and Political Rights Covenant, aggravated denials of the right to free speech and to free and open elections also have become generally acknowledged exceptions to the principle of noninterference in states' domestic jurisdiction. Nevertheless, a residual conflict of principles still troubles many states.

The problem is not so apparent in general theory as in application. To proclaim a general right to free elections is less intrusive than monitoring any particular election in an independent state. Effective monitoring is even more intrusive than the mere observation of balloting. And collective action to compel states to adhere to a standard is the most intrusive of all. Thus, the conflict of principles needs to be recognized, made explicit, and reconciled to the general satisfaction of the large preponderance of states before the democratic entitlement's global legitimacy is demonstrated by real, as opposed to formulaic, coherence. That will require action to meet the practical concerns of states that still regard the nonintervention principle as of overriding importance to their national well-being.

[174] Convention on the Prevention and Punishment of the Crime of Genocide, Dec. 9, 1948, 78 UNTS 277 (entered into force Jan. 12, 1951).

[175] International Convention on the Elimination of All Forms of Racial Discrimination, *opened for signature* Mar. 7, 1966, 660 UNTS 195, *reprinted in* 5 ILM 352 (1966) (entered into force Jan. 4, 1969) [hereinafter Racial Convention].

Also unclear is the extent to which the various parts of the democratic entitlement can yet claim the legitimacy that derives from "treating like cases alike." Are virtually all states, for example, ready to have their elections monitored by a credible global process? This and other issues need to be examined in detail before the democratic entitlement can be said to have achieved universal coherence.

Significance of the Human Rights Connection

A bright line links the three components of the democratic entitlement. The rules, and the processes for realizing self-determination, freedom of expression and electoral rights, have much in common and evidently aim at achieving a coherent purpose: creating the opportunity for all persons to assume responsibility for shaping the kind of civil society in which they live and work. There is a large normative canon for promoting that objective: the UN Charter, the Universal Declaration of Human Rights,[176] the International Covenant on Civil and Political Rights,[177] the International Convention on the Elimination of All Forms of Racial Discrimination,[178] the International Convention on the Suppression and Punishment of the Crime of *Apartheid*,[179] the Declaration on the Elimination of All Forms of Intolerance and of Discrimination Based on Religion or Belief,[180] and the Convention on the Elimination of All Forms of Discrimination against Women.[181] These universally based rights are supplemented by regional instruments such as the European Convention for the Protection of Human Rights and Fundamental Freedoms,[182] the American Convention on Human Rights,[183] the African Charter on Human and Peoples' Rights,[184] the Copenhagen Document[185] and the Paris Charter.[186]

Each of these instruments recognizes related specific entitlements as accruing to individual citizens. These constitute internationally mandated restraints on governments. As we have seen, they embody rights of free and equal participation in governance, a cluster within which electoral rights are a consistent and probably necessary segment. The result is a net of participatory entitlements. The various texts speak of similar goals and deploy, for the most part, a similar range of processes for monitoring compliance, several of which have already become common usage in connection with the democratic entitlement. One can convincingly argue that states which deny their citizens the right to free and open elections are violating a rule that is fast becoming an integral part of the elaborately woven human rights fabric. Thus, the democratic entitlement has acquired a degree of legitimacy by its association with a far broader panoply of laws pertaining to the rights of persons vis-à-vis their governments.

[176] GA Res. 217A (III), *supra* note 60. [177] ICCPR, *supra* note 41.

[178] Racial Convention, *supra* note 175.

[179] GA Res. 3068, 28 UN GAOR Supp. (No. 30) at 75, UN Doc. A/9030 (1973), *reprinted in* 13 ILM 56 (1974) (entered into force July 18, 1976) [hereinafter Apartheid Convention].

[180] GA Res. 36/55, 36 UN GAOR Supp. (No. 51) at 171, UN Doc. A/36/51 (1981), *reprinted in* 21 ILM 205 (1982).

[181] GA Res. 34/180, 34 UN GAOR Supp. (No. 46) at 193, UN Doc. A/34/46 (1979), *reprinted in* 19 ILM 33 (1980) (entered into force Sept. 3, 1981).

[182] European Convention, *supra* note 72. [183] American Convention, *supra* note 77.

[184] African Charter on Human and Peoples' Rights, *adopted* June 27, 1981, OAU Doc. CAB/LEG/67/3/Rev.5, *reprinted in* 21 ILM 58 (1982) [hereinafter Banjul Charter].

[185] Copenhagen Document, *supra* note 98. [186] Paris Charter, *supra* note 105.

Nevertheless, while we may well be moving in this direction, we may not have arrived. When, in November 1989, the UN Secretary-General was asked by the Nicaraguan Sandinista Government to monitor national elections, he felt compelled to link his acceptance not to the human rights framework but to older, perhaps better-established, norms of the international system. Indeed, he went out of his way to reassure the General Assembly that, while the United Nations had frequently supervised elections in the context of decolonization, "it has not been the practice to do so in respect of independent States." He even noted with pride that, "on a number of occasions over the years, we have declined invitations from Member States to that effect." Nevertheless, the Nicaraguan case could be distinguished because the request was not from "a single Member State, but one which has the support of the Presidents of Costa Rica, El Salvador, Guatemala, Honduras and Nicaragua," and thus "clearly belongs in the context of the Central American peace efforts."[187] The same effort to link the democratic entitlement and peacemaking is evident in the 1990 agreement negotiated by the Secretary-General between the Government of El Salvador and the insurgent Frente Farabundo Martí para la Liberación Nacional (FMLN).[188] It links the dispatch of UN monitors (ONUSAL) to observe human rights and the process leading up to Salvadoran elections with their larger role in ending the civil war.[189] Clearly, the content and scope of the democratic entitlement, in practice, will be shaped by whether it is connected to, and legitimized by, the relatively narrow *peacemaking*, or the much more expansive *human rights*, canon.

Coherence of Underlying Principles

So far, the Secretary-General's choice of the peacemaking linkage strategy has avoided a head-on conflict between proponents and opponents of election monitoring as a general normative democratic entitlement. Sooner or later, however, an unresolved conflict of deep-seated principles—the emerging right to free and fair elections and nonintervention in domestic affairs—is likely to generate a clash of political wills in the global and regional communities unless these dissonant principles are reconciled.

The very idea of general international monitoring of elections in sovereign states still arouses the most passionate ire, not only of the increasingly isolated residue of totalitarian regimes, but also of nations with long memories of humiliating interventions by states bent on "civilizing" missions. While they will accept occasional monitoring of elections to end a civil war or regional conflict, they consider it a necessary exception, not a normal manifestation of a universal democratic entitlement.

[187] UN Doc. A/44/210, at 2 (1989).

[188] Central America: Efforts Towards Peace, *supra* note 71.

[189] ONUSAL, the United Nations Observer Mission in El Salvador, will monitor the "release of individuals who have been imprisoned for political reasons . . . , the right of all persons to associate freely with others for ideological . . . political . . . or other purposes . . . , freedom of expression and of the press" and "freedom of movement." Agreement on Human Rights, Annex to Note verbale dated 14 August 1990 from the Charge d'affaires of the Permanent Mission of El Salvador to the United Nations addressed to the Secretary-General, UN Doc. A/44/971–S/21541, ann. at 4–5 (1990). For the March 1991 elections in El Salvador, however, the United Nations declined to mount an observer operation, dedicating its strained resources to other aspects of the peacemaking and monitoring process while letting the OAS take the lead, supported by nongovernmental organizations, in observing those elections. National Democratic Institute for International Affairs, *supra* note 159, at 14.

Conflict was clearly foreshadowed in 1990 when the General Assembly weighed the proposal to establish ONUVEH, the aforementioned observer group to monitor Haiti's elections. Since linkage between election monitoring and peace was much harder to demonstrate in the absence of armed hostilities, the creation of ONUVEH encountered significant opposition, notably from China, Cuba and Colombia.[190] The long specter of U.S. hemispheric interventions was invoked in the Assembly's corridors. Several months elapsed before suspicions could be assuaged by diplomatic assurances that the Haitian case, too, would set no general precedent. Cuba, in the debate prior to the vote authorizing ONUVEH, spoke emphatically against "any attempt to use this United Nations resolution or activity as a pretext for interfering in the internal affairs of Haiti"[191] and stressed that elections "can never be regarded as affecting international peace and security."[192] Mexico also went on record as denying any precedential value to the authorization of ONUVEH.[193] These states contended that UN election monitoring in an independent nation is unlawful *per se*, in the absence of exceptional peacemaking exigencies.

The International Court of Justice rebuffed this view indirectly in its 1986 *Nicaragua* decision. The majority stated, in connection with commitments binding a nation to electoral standards, that it could not

> discover, within the range of subjects open to international agreement, any obstacle or provision to hinder a State from making a commitment of this kind. A State, which is free to decide upon the principle and methods of popular consultation within its domestic order, is sovereign for the purpose of accepting a limitation of its sovereignty in this field. This is a conceivable situation for a State which is bound by institutional links to a confederation of States, or indeed to an international organization.[194]

There are thus no legal impediments to institutionalizing voluntary international election monitoring as one way to give effect to the emerging right of all peoples to free and open electoral democracy, but this is not to say that states as yet have a *duty* to submit their elections to international validation. Although the CSCE, in Europe, seems poised to pioneer a generalized duty to be monitored, even it has not made the duty mandatory for all. In the international community, while there may be a duty under Article 25 of the Civil and Political Rights Covenant and its regional and customary law analogues to permit free and open elections and review of national compliance by the Human Rights Committee, there is as yet no obligation to permit actual election monitoring by international or regional organizations. Indeed, one should expect resistance to any effort to transform an election-monitoring option, exercisable at the discretion of each government, into an obligation owed by each government to its own people and to the other states of the global community. Admittedly, however, a "rule" that only applies self-selectively has far less legitimacy than one of general application.

[190] The Security Council failed to reach consensus on the issue, with China threatening to veto. In the General Assembly, Cuba and Colombia argued that election monitoring in an independent state, unrelated to a threat to the peace, constituted a violation of Article 2(7) of the Charter. *See* UN Doc. A/45/PV.29 (1990).

[191] *Id.* at 62.

[192] *Id.* at 59–60.

[193] *Id.* at 64–65.

[194] Military and Paramilitary Activities in and against Nicaragua (Nicar. v. U.S.), 1986 ICJ Rep. 14, 131 (Judgment of June 27) [hereinafter *Nicaragua* opinion].

This deficiency was demonstrated by the General Assembly's incoherent tiptoeing around the democratic entitlement at its session in the fall of 1990. The members passed two seemingly incongruent resolutions on monitoring, which reflect the concern of Third World states as they contemplate the seemingly inexorable evolution of an entitlement to democracy, including free elections and resultant international supervision. We have already noted the first of these resolutions, in which the democratic entitlement was restated by the Assembly and election monitoring commended as one way to ensure its implementation.[195] Almost in the same breath, however—and over the opposition of only twenty-nine states, mostly European, but also including Australia, Canada, Israel, New Zealand, Turkey and the United States—the second resolution affirmed "that it is the concern solely of peoples [of each state] to determine methods and to establish institutions regarding the electoral process, as well as to determine the ways for its implementation according to their constitutional and national legislation";[196] and it urged all states "to respect the principle of non-interference in the internal affairs of States."[197] The vast preponderance of states voting for this resolution did not do so out of concern to protect dictatorships. Rather, they were worried about the underlying principle.

When underlying principles are coherent, the rules manifesting them assume increased legitimacy. When rules exemplify principles in collision, those rules are perceived as of low legitimacy. The principle underlying a universal democratic entitlement is that the participatory rights of persons in shaping their civil society may not be abridged arbitrarily by governments. This principle has powered the rights of self-determination and freedom of expression and, now, energizes the move to provide international protection for electoral rights.

There was a time when international efforts to implement the right of self-determination were vigorously opposed as trenching upon the right of governments, under Article 2(7) of the UN Charter, to administer their colonies without outside interference. That opposition gradually abated, as the principle of self-determination gained in determinacy. Efforts to monitor compliance with the right to freedom of expression have encountered similar expressions of outraged *amour-propre* by states called to task for arbitrarily silencing their own citizens. It is not surprising that passionate resentments should also arise in some quarters at the prospect of seeing the international community insinuate itself into the intimate political process by which governments are empowered by the citizenry.

The opponents are mostly motivated by fear that monitoring will be used to reimpose a form of neocolonialism under the banner of establishing democracy. That fear must be addressed, but it must also be put in perspective. History has warned, repeatedly, that the natural right of all people to liberty and democracy is too precious, and too vulnerable, to be entrusted entirely to those who govern. John Stuart Mill once observed that the moral fiber of a nation is weakened if the intervention of outsiders spares its people the trouble of liberating themselves.[198] In view of the technological edge dictators nowadays enjoy over their people, this proposition is no longer wholly defensible. The opposite case was stated by Uganda's President Godfrey L. Binaisa, who, after the overthrow of Idi Amin's

[195] See *supra* text at and notes 82–86.

[196] GA Res. 45/151, para. 2 (Dec. 18, 1990).

[197] *Id.*, para. 4.

[198] 3 J. S. MILL, DISSERTATIONS AND DISCUSSIONS: POLITICAL, PHILOSOPHICAL AND HISTORICAL 238–63 (1873).

bloody junta, went before the General Assembly to chide its delegates for their indifference to his people's plight. "In the light of the clear commitment set out in . . . provisions of the Charter," he said, "our people naturally looked to the United Nations for solidarity and support in their struggle against the Fascist dictatorship. For eight years they cried out in the wilderness for help; unfortunately, their cries seemed to have fallen on deaf ears." Acerbically, Binaisa observed that, "somehow, it is thought to be in bad taste or contrary to diplomatic etiquette to raise matters of violations of human rights by Member States within the forums of the United Nations."[199]

Where dictators can only be confronted effectively with the active support of the international community, inhibitions about interference in the "domestic jurisdiction" of states seem less compelling than they used to be. "We are arriving at the conclusion," then Soviet Foreign Minister Boris D. Pankin observed recently, "that national guarantees [of human rights] are not sufficient. So we have to review the principle of noninterference in affairs of other governments."[200] To this end, the Declaration of Human Rights and Freedoms, adopted by the Soviet Congress of People's Deputies on September 5, 1991, after the coup, states that "[e]very person possesses natural, inalienable and inviolable rights and freedoms. They are sealed in laws that must correspond to the universal declaration of human rights, the international covenants on human rights and other international norms and this declaration."[201] The OAS Foreign Ministers' 1991 resolution to the same effect has already been noted,[202] as have the CSCE heads' Paris Charter[203] and Moscow Document.[204]

It thus appears that support is increasing even—perhaps *particularly*—among former totalitarian states for the proposition that the democratic entitlement, enhanced by linkage with other basic human rights and the accompanying international monitoring of compliance, has trumped the principle of noninterference. Even the 1991 resolution of the General Assembly warning about outside "interference" in the electoral process[205] seemed to acknowledge this development, for it added an otherwise incongruous caveat,

> that only the total eradication of *apartheid* and the establishment of a non-racial, democratic society based on majority rule, through the full and free exercise of adult suffrage by all the people in a united and non-fragmented South Africa, can lead to a just and lasting solution to the explosive situation in South Africa.[206]

Surely, this assertion demonstrates not the supremacy of nonintervention but, rather, its opposite: that undemocratic electoral processes imposed upon a people by their government are now almost universally regarded as counternormative and not beyond the purview of the international community. In 1991 the UN Human Rights Commission further affirmed this view by voting unanimously to condemn the military Government of Myanmar for having failed to carry out its promise to return that country to democratic, civilian rule.[207] The junta's refusal to allow the elected legislature to meet and its arrest of many parliamentary

[199] UN Doc. A/34/PV.14, at 4–6 (1979).
[200] N.Y. Times, Sept. 10, 1991, at A13, col. 5.
[201] N.Y. Times, Sept. 7, 1991, at 5, col. 3.
[202] Resolution on Representative Democracy, *supra* note 90.
[203] Paris Charter, *supra* note 105.
[204] Moscow Document, *supra* note 116.
[205] *See supra* text at and notes 196–97.
[206] GA Res. 45/151, *supra* note 196, para. 7.
[207] N.Y. Times, Mar. 7, 1991, at A14, col. 1.

leaders were perceived as an international—not merely a domestic—issue, warranting a response from the community of nations.

Nevertheless, steps should be taken to meet the fear of some smaller states that election monitoring will lead to more Panama-style unilateral military interventions by the powerful, perhaps even for reasons less convincing than those which provoked the 1989 U.S. military strike against the Noriega dictatorship. That a new rule might authorize actions to enforce democracy still conjures up just such chilling images to weaker states, which see themselves as the potential objects of enforcement of dubious democratic norms under circumstances of doubtful probity. Of course, to give coherence to a general norm requiring free and open elections does not necessarily implicate military enforcement action.

If there is to be monitoring, some consequences could reasonably be expected to ensue for those who "fail the test." And if monitoring evolves into a systemwide obligation, perhaps some consequences will attach even to a refusal to be monitored. As Judge Buergenthal has observed about the effect of the Copenhagen Document and the Paris Charter, there is bound to evolve a "linkage of human rights to other questions (trade, security, environment, etc.). . . . Linkage permits the participating States . . . to condition their bilateral and multilateral relations in general upon progress in the human dimension sphere."[208] While perhaps true, today, only regarding the CSCE, this effect is likely to point the way toward the enforcement of the democratic entitlement in the global community, as well.

This prospect evokes hope, but also justified fears that must be abated. The coherence of the democratic entitlement ultimately will depend on whether most states, most of the time, freely agree to be monitored: whether, in short, the process is perceived as legitimate. To achieve this normative coherence, monitoring will have to be uncoupled, in the clearest fashion, from a long history of unilateral enforcement of a tainted, colonialist "civilizing" mission. If the duty to be monitored is to develop as customary law, it must be reconciled in the minds of governments with their residual sovereignty. This requires that all states unambiguously renounce the use of unilateral, or even regional, *military* force to compel compliance with the democratic entitlement in the absence of prior Security Council authorization under chapter VII of the Charter; such authorization, except for *regional* action under Article 53, would require a finding that the violation had risen to the level of a threat to the peace.[209] Such a pledge would merely reiterate the existing normative structure of the Charter, Articles 2(4), 51 and 53 in particular. Yet this reiteration is necessary, in view of the history of unilateral interventionism which has undermined that self-denying ordinance. Specifically, states must acknowledge that the evolution of a democratic entitlement cannot entitle a state or group of states to enforce the right by military action under the pretext of invoking Articles 51 or 53. *Ça va sans dire* is no answer to those demanding that assurance in the light of recent Soviet and U.S.-led unilateral or pseudoregional actions alleged to promote "democracy" in neighboring states and justified as "collective self-defense."

[208] Buergenthal, *supra* note 109, at 43.

[209] The General Assembly, in the case of the 1991 Haitian military coup, appears to have concluded that it is empowered to recommend action of an economic and diplomatic kind to its members. In approving regional military action under Article 53, the Security Council appears not to be limited to cases in which international peace has been threatened or breached.

A specific renunciation of unilateralism would obviously not obviate every possibility that some negative consequences might ensue for governments unwilling to be monitored or to hold free elections; nor should it. The international community long has asserted, in the case of South Africa, a right of all states to take hortatory, economic and—in extreme cases—even military action to enforce aspects of the democratic entitlement,[210] but only when duly authorized by the United Nations in accordance with its Charter. Article 2(7), in barring UN intervention "in matters which are essentially within the domestic jurisdiction of any state," stipulates that "this principle shall not prejudice the application of enforcement measures under Chapter VII." Rhodesia's Unilateral Declaration of Independence provoked a UN resolution permitting Britain to use military force.[211] It is no longer arguable that the United Nations cannot exert pressure against governments that oppress their own peoples by egregious racism, denials of self-determination and suppression of freedom of expression. That litany is being augmented by new sins: refusals to permit demonstrably free elections or to implement their results. However, if the sin is committed, the international community may only invoke collective enforcement measures such as sanctions, blockade or military intervention in limited circumstances—as when the Security Council finds that a threat or breach of the peace has occurred—or if it collectively determines that it is not engaging in enforcement *against* a member but is acting at the request of a legitimate government against a usurper. These prerequisite determinations, however, must be made by the appropriate collective machinery of the community and not by individual members.

This procedure is both legally required and politically essential. To obtain the general consent necessary to render the denial of democracy a cognizable violation of an international community standard, it must be understood that whatever countermeasures are taken must first be authorized collectively by the appropriate UN institutions. Collective action—so the tremulous must understand and the powerful aver—is not a substitute for, but the opposite of, unilateral enforcement. In this respect, as in many others, the principal enemy of the evolution of a new rule is fear of its vigilante enforcement.[212] For that reason, the entitlement to democracy can only be expected to flourish if it is coupled with a reiterated prohibition on such unilateral initiatives. Only then will the rule enjoy the degree of principled coherence necessary to the widespread perception of its legitimacy.

Treating Like Cases Alike

If voluntary acceptance of monitoring becomes the general practice of states, it will gradually evolve from an optional to a customary and, ultimately, mandatory means of satisfying the democratic entitlement. This transformation, surely, is to be encouraged, but it is unlikely to occur as a consequence of a global treaty. Too many states, especially smaller ones, still fear that it will erode the rule of nonintervention. It may occur, however, through gradual, incremental steps that make

[210] *See* Apartheid Convention, *supra* note 179. *See also* R. BISSELL, APARTHEID AND INTERNATIONAL ORGANIZATIONS 156–59 (1977).

[211] SC Res. 253, 23 UN SCOR (Res. & Dec.) at 5, UN Doc. S/INF/23/Rev.1 (1968).

[212] *See* Arend, *International Law and the Recourse to Force: A Shift in Paradigms*, 27 STAN. J. INT'L L. 1, 40–45 (1991).

voluntary submission an attractive option for most governments.[213] If the United Nations' concern to restore democracy in Haiti is grounded, in part, on the ousted government's having been legitimated by a monitored election, that constitutes a palpable inducement to governments to take up the option. When that option is generally taken, the international monitoring of an election will cease to be a special case and will have become normative, a rule that treats like cases alike.

We have already noted that the right of self-determination, as first enunciated and practiced at Versailles, lacked coherence because it applied only to the European territories of the former German, Austro-Hungarian and Turkish Empires. After the Second World War, the UN Charter, in Article 1(2), made "the principle of equal rights and self-determination of peoples" universally applicable. Nevertheless, for forty years thereafter, the right of self-determination was implemented only selectively, primarily in colonies and trusteeship territories. There may have been a reason it was applied to India but not to Hungary or Czechoslovakia, but, if so, no persuasive, principled distinction was advanced.[214]

Undoubtedly, this incoherence undermined its legitimacy. More recently, we have seen the right at last becoming—in theory and increasingly in practice—one of universal application as it merges with newer aspects of the democratic entitlement. Thus, we may conclude that self-determination is evolving from incoherence to coherence, which reinforces its legitimacy.

The same may be said of the right of free expression. We have already observed the work of the Human Rights Committee in implementing Article 19 of the Civil and Political Covenant and protecting citizens' expressive rights. In giving effect to the general reporting requirement, the Committee has begun to impart principled coherence to the textual provisions, in the sense of filling in the interstices and fitting the parts to the purposes of the whole.[215] With the end of the Cold War, the remnants of the "double standard" in applying expressive rights through international monitoring institutions will mostly wither away.

Coherence is being aided by parallel regional initiatives. These tend to monitor and implement the rules equally, regardless of "whose ox is gored." Notable in this respect is the aforementioned work of the European Court of Human Rights and the Inter-American Court of Human Rights, as well as the as-yet inchoate potential of the new African Human Rights Commission.[216] Equal application of the expressive entitlement is reinforced by the textual convergence regarding

[213] While it is true that General Assembly resolutions, state practice or even a subsequent treaty cannot vitiate a specific rule of the UN Charter, all three can affect a Charter rule's interpretation. *See* Czaplinski & Danilenko, *Conflicts of Norms in International Law*, 21 NETH. Y.B. INT'L L. 3, 35–41 (1990).

[214] *See* T. FRANCK, NATION AGAINST NATION 224–45 (1985).

[215] D. MCGOLDRICK, *supra* note 43, at 459–79. Under the procedure for review of country reports, the Committee has sought to

> examine, comment, and request clarification in respect of the different aspects of freedom of expression revealed in the State reports. This has involved, for example, such matters as general and specific banning or censorship, registration or notification requirements, governmental control and direction in its various forms, limitations applicable to particular groups, for example, armed forces, civil servants, prior restraints or subsequent penal responsibility for publications, rights of reply or correction, the applicable limitations embodied in the criminal law or penal codes for offences such as blasphemy or blasphemous libel, sedition, subversive propaganda, anti-State or anti-ideological propaganda, and the effective remedies demanded by . . . an individual who claims that his rights under article 19 have been violated.

Id. at 461.

[216] The Commission is established by part II of the Banjul Charter, *supra* note 184.

freedom of expression of the European Convention on Human Rights,[217] the American Convention on Human Rights,[218] and the African Charter on Human and Peoples' Rights.[219] The too-long failure of the United States to ratify the Civil and Political Rights Covenant and the American Convention nevertheless has detracted from this convergence and is only in part mitigated by the fact that the U.S. Constitution, as implemented by the courts and Congress, puts the United States essentially, if not wholly, in compliance with the international and regional standards.

So far, less uniformity of application, and thus less global coherence, can be ascribed to the emerging rule on citizens' right to participate in free and open elections. As we have observed, on-site monitoring remains voluntary and exceptional. If it is to become a more general obligation, likes must be treated alike, which means that the new majority of democratic states must submit to it. They, who have the least to fear and the most to gain, should want to participate in universalizing the practice, if only to help legitimize it. Few states are likely to volunteer as long as participation in international monitoring is tantamount to a government's admission that it does not have credibility with its own people. To induce a pull toward compliance in deviant and recalcitrant regimes—those that most need it—on-site monitoring must also be practiced by the states that least need it. It must become an unremarkable universal habit.

VII. Adherence and the Democratic Entitlement

Adherence refers to the vertical connection between a specific rule of obligation and other "higher" principles that define the objectives of the rule system or set out its normative standards. A particular rule ("cross on the green, stop on the red") is more likely to pull toward voluntary compliance if it is seen to be within the framework of a community's normative hierarchy than if it is a mere ad hoc arrangement.[220] The democratic entitlement also is more likely to be perceived as a legitimate rule if it can be seen as a necessary part of a normative hierarchy. As it happens, the right to democracy can readily be shown to be an important subsidiary of the community's most important norm: the right to peace.

With the exception of the principle *pacta sunt servanda,* no principle of international law has been more firmly established—first by the Kellogg-Briand Pact and, particularly since 1945, by the UN Charter—than that states "shall refrain in their international relations from the threat or use of force against the territorial integrity or political independence of any state."[221] Not only has this peace principle been featured in treaty law, but it has been resoundingly echoed in the jurisprudence of the International Court of Justice[222] and in *opinio juris* expressed in key UN resolutions.[223]

[217] European Convention, *supra* note 72, Arts. 9, 10, 11.

[218] American Convention, *supra* note 77, Arts. 13, 14, 15, 16.

[219] Banjul Charter, *supra* note 184, Arts. 8, 9, 10, 11.

[220] T. Franck, *supra* note 12, at 184.

[221] UN Charter, Art. 2(4). *See also* Treaty Providing for the Renunciation of War as an Instrument of National Policy, Aug. 27, 1928, Art. 1, 46 Stat. 2343, TS No. 796, 94 LNTS 57 (Kellogg-Briand Pact).

[222] *See Nicaragua* opinion, 1986 ICJ Rep. 14.

[223] The customary law is well summarized in the Court's *Nicaragua* opinion, *id.* at 98–105. *See, especially,* Friendly Relations Declaration, *supra* note 31; Definition of Aggression, GA Res. 3314, 29 UN GAOR Supp. (No. 31) at 142, UN Doc. A/9631 (1974), *reprinted in* 13 ILM 710 (1974).

Most recently, the Security Council, in its resolutions[224] and actions to reverse Iraq's attack on Kuwait, reiterated the primacy of the entitlement to peace and protection against aggression. More than thirty nations joined in liberating Kuwait because, at last, aggression against one has begun to be seen as a contingent violation of the common peace. Stopping aggression and maintaining the peace has become the central concern of a newly cohesive international community.

If that principle indeed stands at the apex of the global normative system, the democratic governance of states must be recognized as a necessary, although certainly not a sufficient, means to that end. Peace is the consequence of many circumstances: economic well-being, security, and the unimpeded movement of persons, ideas and goods. States' nonaggressiveness, however, depends fundamentally on domestic democracy. Although the argument is not entirely conclusive, historians have emphasized that, in the past 150 years, "no liberal democracies have ever fought against each other."[225] It has been argued persuasively that "a democratic society operating under a market economy has a strong predisposition towards peace."[226] This stands to reason: a society that makes its decisions democratically and openly will be reluctant to engage its members' lives and treasure in causes espoused by leaders deluded by fantasies of grievance or grandeur.

No one has stated this position more eloquently than the eighteenth-century German philosopher Immanuel Kant. He examined the correlation between democratic governance and nonaggressiveness in his essay *Perpetual Peace*.[227] There, he argued that democracy, leading to a "pacific union" among liberal states, would counteract the aggressive tendencies of absolutist monarchies by making government accountable to the majority. In contrast, a state of perpetual war would likely prevail between democracies and totalitarian states.[228] Moreover, Kant discerned a three-way linkage among democracy, peace and human rights.[229]

Neither Kant nor his modern interpreters make the argument that democracies will not fight: only that they are not disposed to fight each other. The historical record bears this out.[230] Consequently, one way to promote universal and perpetual nonaggression—probably the best and, perhaps, the only way—is to make democracy an entitlement of all peoples. This conclusion was eloquently and unanimously accepted as axiomatic by the CSCE representatives at their aforementioned 1990 Copenhagen meeting. Unanimously, they proclaimed "their conviction that . . . pluralistic democracy" is a prerequisite "for progress in setting up the lasting order of peace, security, justice and co-operation that they seek to establish in Europe."[231]

[224] SC Res. 660 (Aug. 2, 1990), *reprinted in* 29 ILM 1325 (1990), and subsequent resolutions. *See* Schachter, *United Nations Law in the Gulf Conflict*, 85 AJIL 452 (1991).

[225] Mearsheimer, *Why We Will Soon Miss the Cold War*, ATLANTIC MONTHLY, August 1990, at 35, 46.

[226] T. Smith, *Democracy Resurgent*, in SEA CHANGES 152, 157 (N. Rizopoulos ed. 1990).

[227] I. KANT, PERPETUAL PEACE 107–39 (T. Humphrey rev. ed. 1983) (1795).

[228] *See* Doyle, *Liberalism and World Politics*, 80 AM. POL. SCI. REV. 1151 (1986).

[229] Note, however, that the notion of human rights operates to limit not only totalitarian, but also democratic, excess. Thomas Jefferson underscored this with his oft-quoted observation that "an *elective despotism* was not the government we fought for." T. JEFFERSON, NOTES ON THE STATE OF VIRGINIA 120 (W. Peden ed. 1954).

[230] The point is well developed by Doyle, *An International Liberal Community*, in RETHINKING AMERICA'S SECURITY (G. Allison ed., forthcoming).

[231] Copenhagen Document, *supra* note 98, Preamble, at 1307.

The symbiotic linkage among democracy, human rights and peace is now widely recognized. Already in 1968, Security Council Resolution 253 invoked chapter VII of the Charter to impose military sanctions on Rhodesia. It expressly proceeded on the theory that gross denials of both human rights and the democratic entitlement can constitute "a threat to international peace and security."[232] At the regional level, the OAS Ministers of Foreign Affairs, in demanding the replacement of Nicaragua's Somoza dictatorship with a government chosen through free elections, declared in 1979 that democracy was the necessary precondition to "peace, freedom and justice." The dictatorship was characterized as "disrupting the peace of the Hemisphere."[233] A decade later, in condemning the fraudulent Panamanian elections staged by General Noriega, the OAS Ministers stated that this crisis of governmental legitimacy "involves internal and external factors . . . and could seriously endanger international peace and security."[234]

This understanding of the three-way linkage among democracy, human rights and peace is further illustrated by the recent cease-fire agreement negotiated by the UN Secretary-General between the Government of El Salvador and the FMLN.[235] As noted, it obliges the Government and the insurgents to work with yet another UN observer mission (ONUSAL), which is authorized to monitor and verify compliance with the basic human rights guaranteed by the signatories. The parties specifically recognized that compliance with human rights is a *sine qua non* to ending the war. They also accepted that the democratic entitlement must be guaranteed—and monitored by international observers—if peace is to be established.

Thus, it appears with increasing clarity, in normative text and practice, that compliance with the norms prohibiting war making is inextricably linked to observance of human rights and the democratic entitlement. The achievement of none of these basic objectives of the international community is possible, in any lasting sense, without the realization of them all. This interdependence suggests that the legitimacy of the democratic entitlement is augmented by its hierarchic relation to the peremptory norm of global peaceability.

A distinction needs to be noted here. As we have observed, some governments have argued that the international community's jurisdiction to intervene in the domestic affairs of states to secure compliance with the democratic entitlement is (or should be) limited to cases where its violation has given rise to breaches of the peace. Others have disagreed, claiming that the jurisdiction to intervene is also based on broader human rights law, which authorizes various intrusive forms of monitoring and even envisages sanctions against gross violators. One can prefer this latter view, while still agreeing that the democratic entitlement does have a connection to the United Nations' "peace" role, that the *legitimacy* of any collective international intervention to support a democratic entitlement is augmented by the entitlement's intimate link to peace. The substance of that link, however, is not merely the role of democracy in *making* or *restoring* peace after conflict has arisen but also—indeed preeminently—its role in *maintaining* peace and *preventing* conflict.

The World Court observed in the *Bernadotte* case that established rights and duties implicitly validate a penumbra of unenunciated, yet legitimate, means nec-

[232] SC Res. 253, *supra* note 211.

[233] OEA/Ser.F/II.17, doc. 40/79, rev.2.

[234] OEA/Ser.F/II.21, doc. 8/89, rev.2.

[235] Central America: Efforts Toward Peace, *supra* note 71.

essary to give them effect.[236] If the "end" of global peace demands the "means" of global democracy, a Charter-based system established to ensure peace must also be presumed to be authorized to ensure universal adherence to democratic political rights.

VIII. The Emergence of Democracy as a Global Normative Entitlement

The entitlement to democracy in international law has gone through both a normative and a customary evolution. It has evolved both as a system of rules and in the practice of states and organizations. This evolution has occurred in three phases. First came the normative entitlement to self-determination. Then came the normative entitlement to free expression as a human right. Now we see the emergence of a normative entitlement to a participatory electoral process.

The democratic entitlement, despite its newness, already enjoys a high degree of legitimacy, derived both from various texts and from the practice of global and regional organizations, supplemented by that of a significant number of nongovernmental organizations. These texts and practices have attained a surprising degree of specificity, given the newness of the entitlement and especially of its requirement for free and open elections.

It is easy to deconstruct this now commonly used set of textual formulations and the accompanying practice. The terms (e.g., elections, free, fair) inevitably convey different meanings in various political cultures but, remarkably, evoke an amply demonstrable degree of convergent expectations. They crisscross sociocultural and political boundaries. The entitlement now aborning is widely enough understood to be almost universally celebrated. It is welcomed from Malagache to Mongolia, in the streets, the universities and the legislatures, not only because it portends a new, global political culture supported by common rules and communitarian implementing institutions, but also because it opens the stagnant political economies of states to economic, social and cultural, as well as political, development. As the heads of European Community states and governments pointed out in the group's conclusions of June 1991, "suppression of individual freedoms impede[s] an individual from participating in and contributing" to "the process of development."[237] Economic development, as even the Chinese leadership must be discovering, is linked inextricably with political freedom. An economic free market cannot long flourish without creating pressure for a free market of ideas. At the same time, the problems of underdevelopment can only be addressed successfully in a world of stable, peaceable nations, which, in turn, also presupposes a world of open democracies.

The democratic entitlement's newness and recent rapid evolution make it understandable that important problems remain. We have considered these primarily under the rubric of coherence, indicating that this entitlement is not yet entirely coherent. The key to solving these residual problems is: (1) that the older democracies should be among the first to volunteer to be monitored in the hope that this will lead the way to near-universal voluntary compliance, thus gradually transforming a sovereign option into a customary legal obligation; (2) that a credible international monitoring service should be established with clearly defined

[236] Reparations for injuries suffered in the service of the United Nations, 1949 ICJ Rep. 174, 179–80 (Advisory Opinion of Apr. 11).

[237] European Council, Presidency Conclusions, Doc. SN 151/2/91 (Ann. V) at 27 (1991).

parameters and procedures covering all aspects of voting, from the time an election is called until the newly elected take office; (3) that each nation's duty to be monitored should be linked to a commensurate right to nonintervention by states acting unilaterally; and (4) that legitimate governments should be assured of protection from overthrow by totalitarian forces through concerted systemic action after—and *only* after—the community has recognized that such an exigency has arisen. In the longer term, compliance with the democratic entitlement should also be linked to a right of representation in international organs, to international fiscal, trade and development benefits, and to the protection of UN and regional collective security measures.[238]

Both textually and in practice, the international system is moving toward a clearly designated democratic entitlement, with national governance validated by international standards and systematic monitoring of compliance. The task is to perfect what has been so wondrously begun.

[238] To limit collective security measures to cases of attack against democratic states is a change in the system's rules that is unlikely to come about in the near future. Yet it is worth contemplating. Would it help Kuwait to establish a democratic internal order if its future protection by UN-authorized collective measures depended upon such a transformation?

[20]

*Benedict Kingsbury**

Claims by Non-State Groups in International Law

I. Objectives and Structure of this Article

The capacity of international society[1] to deal with the challenges posed by the claims of non-state groups[2] is a matter of pressing concern. The adequacy of existing international structures is highly questionable. Fundamental conflicts exist between values of justice and the hitherto dominant values of order. While many of the issues are not primarily legal, public international law is necessarily involved. This article examines the norms developed in the international legal system to address issues arising in relations between states and non-state groups. This article argues that in international political debates, and in much (but by no means all) of the principal legal material, three distinct general domains of discourse have been employed to express and address claims by non-state groups.[3] The separate structure of each of these domains has obscured the overlap (if not the identity) of underlying justificatory purposes among these different domains.

Certain fundamental problems in the application of international legal norms to relations between states and non-state groups might be

* University Lecturer in Law, Oxford University; Visiting Professor of Law, Cornell Law School (Fall 1991); Visiting Professor of Law, Duke Law School. The author would like to thank Don Horowitz and Lisa Pirozzolo for comments, and the Cornell International Law Journal for the kind invitation to present this preliminary study for a larger work at the 25th anniversary symposium.

1. Hedley Bull's definition of a society of states, modified to include a wider range of actors, suggests that an international society exists where a group of actors, "conscious of certain common interests and common values, form a society in the sense that they conceive themselves to be bound by a common set of rules in their relations with one another, and share in the working of common institutions." HEDLEY BULL, THE ANARCHICAL SOCIETY: A STUDY OF ORDER IN WORLD POLITICS 13 (1977).

2. The term "non-state groups" is used here in a non-technical way to denote encompassing groups important to the identity of individual members in which individual membership, while not necessarily resting on ascriptive identity, is not simply a matter of readily-reversed voluntary choice. It thus includes, but is not limited to, ethnic groups. The existence or absence of formal legal personality for the group under municipal or international law is not directly material.

3. The three general domains of discourse are: claims to self-determination, minority rights claims, and human rights claims. *See infra* text accompanying note 4.

avoided by focusing attention on the commonality of justificatory purpose. In particular, such a unified analysis would help in resolving some of the problems of commensurability or reconciliation where the different domains appear to conflict, and ought to open the way to better balancing of competing rights and interests. More generally, this article argues that the international community has not done enough to develop either the normative framework, or the systems of monitoring and enforcement necessary to make the norms effective. The result is that in relations between states and non-state groups there is often no consensus among parties or non-parties concerning the nature or application of relevant norms. The response of the international community to particular conflicts or crises has often been ad hoc rather than a straightforward and predictable application of clear rules. Such a response diminishes the authority and effectiveness of international community action when it is finally attempted.

Many areas of international law, including state succession, state responsibility, the law of treaties, the law relating to title to territory, recognition, and the law of international organizations, are relevant to the legal analysis of claims by non-state groups. However, claims by non-state groups are characteristically expressed at the international level in five principal domains of discourse. Three of these are general: claims to self-determination; minority rights claims; and human rights claims, including those relying on principles of equality or non-discrimination.[4] The other two, while important, by their nature have value only in a more limited and specialized range of circumstances. These are claims to sovereignty legitimized by historical arguments or other special circumstances, and claims to special rights by virtue of prior occupation.

Each of these five domains of discourse has its own bounded structure of legitimacy and justification, and thus shapes claims and responses made within it. It is common for claims by the same group, or arising out of the same situation, to be articulated simultaneously within different domains. The domain of discourse in which the claim is articulated and assessed will affect its political and legal nature, perceptions of its justification and merits, and the form of its legal expression and resolution, for both claimants and respondents.[5] There are both overlaps

4. The claims of the Korean minority in Japan appear to have been expressed and addressed primarily in this latter domain of discourse. *See* Onuma Yasuaki, *Interplay Between Human Rights Activities and Legal Standards of Human Rights: A Case Study on the Korean Minority in Japan*, 25 CORNELL INT'L L.J. 515 (1992).

5. For instance, there may well be political and legal differences depending on whether a particular indigenous land rights claim is: a claim to reassert an anterior sovereignty; a claim to special measures justified on grounds of the special historical circumstances of an indigenous people; a means of attaining a degree of self-determination; a general minority rights claim which should also be open to other minorities; simply a substantive equality claim. *Cf.* the issues relating to the Pitjantjatjara Land Rights Act (1981) (South Australia) (a state act providing for the vesting of title to a large area of land in the northwest of South Australia in the Pitjantjatjara people), and the decision on the validity of sections of this act by the High Court of Australia

and conflicts between the different domains. The conflicts come sharply into focus where particular competing programs are in contention, as where conflicts appear between programs of group autonomy and gender equality.[6] Often the rights and interests of one group are articulated and protected under one program, but this program does not itself take adequate account of the rights and interests of other groups or of affected individuals.[7] An important part of the international normative agenda is to address such conflicts between programs, to avoid the structure of irreconcilable clashes between competing universal norms.

Why is the development of a general international normative framework an objective worth pursuing? Law in this area has many functions, including that of mandating or guiding behavior of parties and non-parties, structuring coordinated responses, providing procedures for dispute or conflict resolution, and establishing the basis for an authoritative, perhaps even dispositive, decision. Particularly important for present purposes is the compliance-pull exerted by legal norms. One useful account of compliance-pull in international law is Franck's discussion of legitimacy.[8] In his terminology: "Legitimacy is a property of a rule or rule-making institution which itself exerts a pull toward compliance on those addressed normatively because those addressed believe that the rule or institution has come into being and operates in accordance with generally accepted principles of right process."[9] Expressed this way, legitimacy is a function of the norm-creating process and of fairness and efficacy in implementation. This interpretation of legitimacy resembles Fuller's inner morality of law in the emphasis on propriety of sources and of operation.[10] Certainly this form of procedural

---

in Gerhardy v. Brown, 57 A.L.R. 472 (High Court of Australia 1985) (per curiam) (upholding Section 19 of the state act, which had been challenged as contrary to the Racial Discrimination Act 1975, a commonwealth act).

6. *See, e.g.*, Santa Clara Pueblo v. Martinez, 436 U.S. 49 (1978) (discrimination suit against tribe barred under the Indian Civil Rights Act of 1968); Attorney-General of Canada v. Lavell, 1974 S.C.R. 1349 (Sup. Ct. Can.) (provisions of the Indian Act excluding women of Indian birth who marry non-Indians from the tribe are not rendered inoperative by the Canadian Bill of Rights); Lovelace v. Canada, 68 I.L.R. 17 (1981) (U.N. Hum. Rts. Comm.) (denying female Indian who married a non-Indian the right to live on a reservation violates international covenant on civil and political rights).

7. Some well-known examples of problems of this type are summarized in Douglas Sanders, *Collective Rights*, 13 Hum. Rts. Q. 368, 378-86 (1991). This theme is developed by Ian Brownlie, *The Rights of Peoples in Modern International Law*, *in* The Rights of Peoples 1 (James Crawford ed., 1988).

8. Thomas M. Franck, The Power of Legitimacy Among Nations 24 (1990). Franck seeks to advance the voluntarist thesis that nations (coterminous with states in this usage) obey rules "[b]ecause they perceive the rule and its institutional penumbra to have a high degree of legitimacy." *Id.* at 25.

9. *Id.* at 25.

10. *Cf.* Lon L. Fuller, The Morality of Law 33-94 (rev. ed. 1969). Franck's correlates of rule legitimacy include pedigree (meaning "the depth of the rule's roots in a historical process"), determinacy ("the rule's ability to communicate content"), coherence ("the rule's internal consistency and lateral connectedness to the principles underlying other rules"), and adherence ("the rule's vertical connectedness to a

justice is important to international compliance-pull. Indeed, one of the concerns about international responses to the emergence of new states in the territory of Yugoslavia and the Soviet Union was that norms of minority protection, in particular, were being invented in the heat of the moment, applied on a case-by-case basis to new states by existing states which were not domestically committed to their internal application, and propounded without adequate systems of international monitoring and enforcement.

Franck, however, takes the further step of avoiding making legitimacy contingent on substantive justice, arguing that the secular international community must be distinguished from the moral community, and that in view of divergent perceptions of justice it is imperative for the global secular rule community to focus instead on legitimacy.[11] He adheres to this view notwithstanding that "a legitimate rule may pull less powerfully toward compliance when it is seen to be unjust."[12] In relation to non-state claims which, to the state directly involved, have an acutely internal character, the compliance-pull arising from international legitimacy may well be insufficient to influence the behavior of the state unless there is also some perception that vindication of the claim does not involve profound injustice for the state and its major constituencies. The same is true, *mutatis mutandis*, to the extent that the behavior of non-state groups is directly affected by the compliance-pull of international norms: the more so because the direct involvement of these groups in the rule-making and supervision process has typically been very limited.

Does "legitimacy" have a definite meaning, and do the components of legitimacy have a significant impact on the effectiveness of international law? Koskenniemi argues that as used by Franck, " '[l]egitimacy' is an intermediate concept whose very imprecision makes it available to avoid the attacks routinely mounted against the formal (but too abstract) idea of legal validity and the substantive (but too controversial) notion of justness."[13] The "imprecision" referred to by Koskenniemi is a function of intermediacy between these poles: the concept of legitimacy is not itself incapable of concrete application. Doubtless the principal use of the concept of legitimacy as here articulated is by neo-liberal advocates of international cooperation in positing explanations of international behavior which go beyond those of classic realism. Nevertheless, the concept has a wider attraction, and does not involve discarding the insights of realism. Some variant of legitimacy is part of the explanation for rule-governed behavior, but the configurations of power and interest

normative hierarchy, culminating in an ultimate rule of recognition, which embodies the principled purposes and values that define the community of states"). Thomas M. Franck, *The Emerging Right to Democratic Governance*, 86 AM. J. INT'L L. 46, 51 (1992).

11. FRANCK, *supra* note 8, at 236.

12. *Id.* at 242.

13. Martti Koskenniemi, Book Review, 86 AM. J. INT'L L. 175 (1992) (reviewing THOMAS M. FRANCK, THE POWER OF LEGITIMACY AMONG NATIONS (1990)).

also remain central to any understanding of relations between states and non-state groups.

The configurations of power and interest have limited the effectiveness, and hence the scope of claims by non-state groups since 1945. New states emerging in Europe have accepted commitments to protect minority rights through their domestic legal orders, and to tolerate international supervision through such mechanisms as those established by the Conference on Security and Cooperation in Europe (CSCE). This is undoubtedly both a response to international pressure and a reflection of the overwhelming interest of the new states in providing any undertakings necessary to secure recognition of their statehood. However, acknowledgement that the acceptance and honoring by states of such commitments is influenced by perceptions of their interests does not itself call into question the significance of legitimacy as an independent variable. External forces encouraging and even coercing compliance with legitimate norms and institutions are themselves, in part, a product of the collective interest in maintaining legitimacy. In addition to the pressures from these external forces, the other factors of compliance-pull identified by Franck have played, and continue to play, a significant role.

The remainder of this article will be structured as follows. Section II will examine the five domains of discourse within which claims by non-state groups are typically expressed in international law. Section III will discuss the presently unsolved problem of how the principle of self-determination can be reconciled with the concern of states to maintain their territorial integrity and with the concern of the international community not to risk unlimited fragmentation of existing states. Section IV will use a recent case study relating to the three general domains of discourse to illustrate the difficulties of developing ad hoc responses to acute issues raised by non-state claims where no adequate normative or procedural framework has been established in advance. This case study is of the views of the Arbitration Commission, established by the Conference on Yugoslavia, on questions as to whether and on what terms the European Community should recognize the new states which had formerly been republics of Yugoslavia. Faced with the imperative to accede to demands for recognition of self-determination by some units, the EC was not able to establish effective minority rights and human rights guarantees that might (conceivably) have limited the pressure for revisionist forms of self-determination. It will be argued that the compliance-pull or legitimacy of the norms and procedures prescribed ad hoc was thus, almost inevitably, very limited. Section V will examine some of the implications for the normative development of international law of recent experience relating to claims by non-state groups, and will discuss problems arising from the separation of, and limitations of, the existing domains of discourse.

II. Five Domains of Discourse for Claims by Non-State Groups

Each of the five international domains of discourse in which claims by non-state groups are expressed is of considerable contemporary importance. Three are very general in their range of potential application. The other two domains of discourse themselves incorporate conditions of eligibility which, however open-ended, limit the range of situations in which they may effectively be invoked, and they will be mentioned only briefly.

A. Self-Determination Claims

The charismatic principle of self-determination, and the nationalism to which it gives operational expression, has had a powerful normative appeal for more than a century. The political principle of nationalities had a significant pedigree before giving way to the more sweeping doctrines of self-determination espoused by Lenin and Wilson. In the United Nations period the principal normative formulations have been the principle of "equal rights and self-determination of peoples,"[14] contained in the UN Charter and elaborated in various subsequent non-treaty instruments, and the right of all peoples to self-determination, which is expressed in common Article 1 of the 1966 Covenants: "All peoples have the right of self-determination. By virtue of that right they freely determine their political status and freely pursue their economic, social and cultural development."[15]

Self-determination and its socio-political analog, nationalism, are often associated, particularly in United States thinking, with liberalism. This tradition links self-determination with democratic choice, and especially with "free elections."[16] Historically, however, nationalism has been variously associated with liberty and with the suppression of freedom, with democratization and with inequality for non-members of the nation. As Acton (who thought the theory of nationality retrogressive) wrote in 1862, nationalism "was appealed to in the name of the most contradictory principles of government, and served all parties in succession, because it was one in which all could unite."[17] Self-determination is not simply an end result or a legal process of choice: as Minogue points out, nationalism is "a spirit or style of politics."[18]

The rhetoric of self-determination is universal, and the range of possible claimants (peoples) supported by the rhetoric is very wide. The

14. U.N. CHARTER, art. 1, ¶ 2.

15. International Covenant on Economic, Social and Cultural Rights, 993 U.N.T.S. 3, art. 1, ¶ 1 (1966).

16. *Cf.* the material discussed in Franck, *The Emerging Right to Democratic Governance*, *supra* note 10.

17. John Emerich Edward Dalberg-Acton, *Nationality*, *in* ESSAYS ON FREEDOM AND POWER 166, 181 (Gertrude Himmelfarb ed., 1948).

18. KENNETH R. MINOGUE, NATIONALISM 135 (1968). He adds his assessment, based mainly on nineteenth century European examples, that as a style of politics nationalism is aimed at radical transformation, and "is hostile to long-established institutions and connections." *Id.* at 135.

reality of international practice has been that self-determination has been available only to a limited range of units, each of which is, in principle, eligible for separate statehood if that is the choice of the unit. Having been interpreted as a right to form separate states, the international community has endeavored to limit the right to self-determination to a very narrow range of rightholders.

Not surprisingly, the practical response of existing states to claims to separate statehood by new entities has been favorable only in a limited range of cases, which may be broken down into five principal categories:[19]

(i) Mandated territories, trust territories, and territories treated as non-self-governing under Chapter XI of the UN Charter;
(ii) Distinct political-geographical entities subject to carence de souveraineté (the only entity to have achieved statehood in accordance with this criterion thus far is Bangladesh, and even this case is not easy to interpret);[20]
(iii) Other territories in respect of which self-determination is applied by the parties, as where a plebiscite it held to determine the fate of a territory;
(iv) Highest level constituent units of a federal state which has been (or is in the process of being) dissolved by agreement among all (or, in the case of Yugoslavia, most) of the constituent units; and possibly
(v) Formerly independent entities reasserting their independence with at least the tacit consent of the established state where incorporation into the other state was illegal or of dubious legality.[21]

Thus most secessionist entities, such as the Turkish Republic of Northern Cyprus, have received minimal international recognition.[22] Irredentist claims on the basis of nationality, such as that espoused by Somalia before the civil war which began in 1991, have also received very little support. The general argument against accepting these claims has been that of territorial integrity and stability of frontiers. Where transitions have occurred, as in the case of decolonization, these principles are reinforced by the doctrine of *uti possidetis juris*.[23] The doctrine of *uti possidetis*

19. The first three categories are discussed in JAMES CRAWFORD, THE CREATION OF STATES IN INTERNATIONAL LAW 84-102 (1979).

20. For a recent non-legal analysis of this category, see Alexis Heraclides, *Secession, Self-Determination and Non-Intervention: In Quest of a Normative Symbiosis*, 45 J. INT'L AFF. 399-420 (1992).

21. It is arguable that the principal candidates for category (v), the recognition of the three Baltic republics, particularly by states such as Spain and the Netherlands which had recognized their incorporation de jure into the USSR (*see Recognition of States* (A. V. Lowe & Colin Warbrick eds.), 41 INT'L & COMP. L.Q. 473, 474 (1992)), and the prospect of the gradual recognition of Eritrea, could properly be accommodated within category (iii).

22. The question of a "right to secede" raises different issues from the right to self-determination, and is not addressed in this article. For a recent discussion of some of the questions of political philosophy relating to a "right to secede," see ALLEN BUCHANAN, SECESSION: THE MORALITY OF POLITICAL DIVORCE FROM FORT SUMTER TO LITHUANIA AND QUEBEC (1991).

23. This doctrine states that parties should retain possession of that which they have acquired.

juris has been invoked to limit the fragmentation of dissolved or disintegrated federations in the cases of the USSR and Yugoslavia, in what will represent, if generally accepted,[24] a significant extension of the doctrine. Whereas in decolonization the boundaries set by one or more colonial powers are inherited by the new states without regard to ethnic or other considerations, here the internal boundaries of federal states were treated as establishing the international boundaries unless modified by agreement. In the case of Yugoslavia, this was treated by the EC as entailing that units within Republics, such as Kosovo, were not entitled to separate statehood. The Federal Constitution, under which Republics were the federating units and were alone entitled to secede, was cited as establishing the legal framework in respect of which the principle of *uti possidetis juris* would apply. While this is readily intelligible as an attempt to prevent virtually unlimited fragmentation, the logic of accepting statehood for Republics while denying any right to statehood to sub-Republic entities which enjoyed a considerable degree of autonomy within the federal state, and the exact status of which depended on particular political configurations and internal legal practices, is not itself compelling. Some of the difficulties with this approach are presently being confronted in the former Soviet Union. Within the 15 Union Republics of the USSR there were 20 Autonomous Republics, 8 Autonomous Regions (*oblast'*), 10 Autonomous Areas (*okrug*), and many lower-level units, as well as numerous groups now seeking autonomy rights.[25]

B. Minority Rights Claims

There is a sharp contrast between the sweeping entitlements associated in standard international practice with the right to self-determination and the very limited provisions applicable expressly to minorities since 1945. Minority protection provisions have long been included in bilateral treaties or in multilateral treaties involving particular territories or areas,[26] and there were several 19th century examples of diplomatic

24. As this article goes to press Bosnia-Herzegovina, Croatia, Moldova, Georgia, and other former highest-level republics are divided de facto, although there is, as yet, no indication that the international community has reached the point of formally endorsing non-peaceful (or at least non-negotiated) divisions in any of these cases.

25. *See* 1977 U.S.S.R. Constitution, arts. 82-88, *reprinted in* John N. Hazard, *The Union of Soviet Socialist Republics*, *in* 18 CONSTITUTIONS OF THE COUNTRIES OF THE WORLD (Albert P. Blaustein & Gisbert H. Flanz eds., 1990); *see generally* BOHDAN NAHAYLO & VICTOR SWOBODA, SOVIET DISUNION: A HISTORY OF THE NATIONALITIES PROBLEM IN THE USSR 360-61 (1990).

26. *See, e.g.*, Treaty of Utrecht, April 12, 1713, Eng.-Fr., art. 15; Jay Treaty, 1794, Eng.-U.S., art. 3; Third Additional Article to the 1822 Treaty between Great Britain and Muscat on the Prohibition of the Slave Trade (added in 1839); Treaty of Guadalupe-Hidalgo, 1848, U.S.-Mex., art. 11; and Berlin Conference, Feb. 26, 1885, final act. Concerning the Balkans, see, *e.g.*, the 1830 Treaty on the Independence of Greece; the Protocol of the Conference of Constantinople (1856); the Treaty of San Stefano, Mar. 3, 1878; Treaty of Berlin, July 13, 1878; and Treaty of Constantinople, Sept. 29, 1913.

representations or military intervention in response to oppression of minorities.[27] A more general (although far from universal) institutional system of minority protection, involving the League of Nations and the Permanent Court of International Justice, was a particular feature of the public order of Europe, 1919-39. This model fell into disfavor during and after the Second World War. The focus shifted away from minority rights to universalization of individual human rights, although several local minority protection arrangements were adopted on a case-by-case basis,[28] and the UN was required to face a number of contentious minority questions.[29] Minority concerns are partially addressed through equality and non-discrimination provisions, and other human rights norms. However, the cautiously-worded Article 27 of the International Covenant on Civil and Political Rights (I.C.C.P.R.) remains for the time being the only express and legally binding minority rights provision of general application.[30] Article 27 provides:

> In those States in which ethnic, religious or linguistic minorities exist, persons belonging to such minorities shall not be denied the right, in community with the other members of their group, to enjoy their own culture, to profess and practice their own religion, or to use their own language.

This provision is narrow in scope, and does not adequately address the range of minorities issues with which the international community is again being confronted.[31]

---

27. *See, e.g.*, Antoine Rougier, *La theorie de l'intervention d'humanité*, 17 REVUE GÉNÉRALE DE DROIT INTERNATIONAL PUBLIC 468 (1910); G. Rolin-Jaecquemyns, *Note sur la theorie du droit d'intervention*, 8 REVUE DE DROIT INTERNATIONAL ET LEGISLATION COMPARÉE 673 (1876); President Harrison's message to the U.S. Congress in 1891, quoted in 83 BRIT. & FOREIGN STATE PAPERS 427, 436-37 (1897); and RAYMOND PEARSON, NATIONAL MINORITIES IN EASTERN EUROPE 1848-1945 (1983).

28. *See, e.g.*, Special Statute for the Free City of Trieste, Memorandum of Understanding 1954, Italy-U.K.-USA-Yugoslavia, 538 U.N.T.S. 99, providing in detail for the "unhampered cultural development" of the minorities in each zone; the guarantees for the Slovene and Croat minorities in the Austrian State Treaty, 1955, arts. 7 & 26, 217 U.N.T.S. 223; the Treaty of Guarantee, 1960, U.K.-Greece-Turkey-Cyprus, 382 U.N.T.S. 3, recognizing the state of affairs established by the Basic Articles of the 1960 Cyprus Constitution (now essentially inoperative as regards the rights and powers accorded to each community—*cf.*, G.A. Res. 37/253, U.N. GAOR, 37th Sess., calling for "a mutually acceptable agreement based on the fundamental and legitimate rights of the two communities"); and the Treaty of Osimo, 1975, Italy-Aus., providing for an autonomy regime for Bolzano-Bozen. Francisco Capotorti, *Study on the Rights of Persons Belonging to Ethnic, Religious and Linguistic Minorities*, Special Rapporteur of the Sub-Commission on Prevention of Discrimination and Protection of Minorities, at 30, U.N. Doc. E/CN.4/Sub.2/384/Rev.1 (1977).

29. *See, e.g.*, G.A. Res. 44(I) concerning the treatment of Indians in South Africa, U.N. Doc. A/Res./44/1; and S.C. Res. 47 (1948) asking that India ensure that "minorities in all parts of the State [Jammu and Kashmir] are accorded adequate protection."

30. The wording of Article 27 was adopted *mutatis mutandis* in the U.N. Convention on the Rights of the Child, art. 30 (1989), with the exception that members of indigenous peoples were there referred to separately from members of minorities.

31. Probably the most influential current definition of "minority" is Capotorti's:

The subject of minorities is extremely sensitive for many states. Such concerns have been reflected to some extent in the Human Rights Committee, which has been divided over numerous issues concerning the application of Article 27, and has been unable even to adopt a General Comment on the article.[32]

Article 27 is a limited provision. Several of the leading cases on it have in fact been brought by individual members of minority communities seeking what was in effect protection from policies of the minority community itself. As to the scope for protection of the interests of minority communities under Article 27, questions remain regarding the extent to which it places states under a duty to take positive measures, whether the right to enjoy "culture" extends to land and resource rights, and whether it effectively establishes rights for human groups as such. The case of *Ominayak v. Canada*[33] was one of the most expansive decisions of the Human Rights Committee on the two latter questions. The case involved a claim brought by a group of Canadian indigenous people who had never received an adequate area of land and had suffered disastrous problems as a probable result. The Committee found that:

> Historical inequities, to which the State party refers, and certain more recent developments threaten the way of life and culture of the Lubicon Lake Band, and constitute a violation of Article 27 so long as they continue. The State party proposes to rectify the situation by a remedy that the Committee deems appropriate within the meaning of Article 2 of the Covenant.[34]

This implies that the right of members of a group to enjoy their culture may be violated where they are not allocated the land and control of resource development necessary to pursue economic activities of central importance to their culture, such as hunting or trapping. The right to enjoyment of culture also seems to extend to maintenance of the group's cohesiveness through, for instance, possession of a land base and pursuit of important cultural activities of an economic nature.[35]

> A group numerically inferior to the rest of the population of a State, in a non-dominant position, whose members - being nationals of the State - possess ethnic, religious or linguistic characteristics differing from those of the rest of the population and show, if only implicitly, a sense of solidarity, directed toward preserving their culture, traditions, religion or language.

Capotorti Report, *supra* note 28, p. 96, para. 568. *See also* Jules Deschênes, *Proposal Concerning A Definition of the Term "Minority"*, at 30, para. 181, U.N. Doc. E/CN.4/Sub.2/1985/31 (1985); and the discussion of Deschênes' report in the Sub-Commission, U.N. Doc. E/CN.4/Sub.2/1985/SR.13-16. *See further* PATRICK THORNBERRY, INTERNATIONAL LAW AND THE RIGHTS OF MINORITIES 1-21 (1991).

32. U.N. Doc. CCPR/C/SR.625 and SR.633 (1985).

33. Final Views, March 26, 1990, U.N. Doc. CCPR/C/38/D/167/1984 (1990).

34. *Id.* at 29.

35. *See also* Kitok v. Sweden, *Report of the Human Rights Committee*, at 221, U.N. Doc. A/43/40 (1988), where the Committee implies that the right of an individual Sami to engage in reindeer husbandry as a member of a Sami community is protected by Article 27.

While longstanding or "traditional" economic activities are more likely to fall within the ambit of "culture," this is a matter of appreciation; no such limitation is inherent in Article 27.

The dispositif in *Ominayak* is very brief and is not easy to interpret. Nevertheless, the finding that historical inequities which continued were a major component of the violation is potentially very significant. In *Ominayak*, historical inequities resulted especially from the failure of Canada (including, for responsibility purposes, the Province of Alberta) to honor the terms of a treaty with indigenous people (Treaty 8), and possibly also the terms of certain legislation, by ensuring reasonable land rights for the Lubicon Lake Band. In particular, they were never allocated a suitable reservation despite a morally (and perhaps legally) compelling claim to one. The recent developments included rapid energy and other developments in the Band's traditional area from the early 1970s onward, with serious repercussions for the Band's hunting and trapping activities as well as for the life of the community. Thus Canada was responsible under the Covenant for the failure to rectify a continuing inequity, notwithstanding that the initial injustices predated the entry into force of the Covenant by many years.

It is also of interest that the Human Rights Committee's views in *Ominayak* address the position of the Band rather than the rights of Chief Ominayak, although he was the only individual author. This is an illustration of how Article 27 is likely to be regarded increasingly as a vehicle for direct recognition of collective rights.

It is clear that if some very serious conflicts are to be adequately addressed, more comprehensive and more detailed provisions for minority protection are needed, and that such provisions will only function effectively with adequate and dependable international supervision, monitoring, and national and international enforcement mechanisms. Two approaches to normative development are presently being pursued: particularized country-specific obligations, and general normative instruments.

1. Particularized Obligations

The first possible approach is to endeavor to secure the acceptance by specific states of particularized obligations with respect to minorities. Particularized obligations are naturally favored by representatives of non-target states, who are reluctant to assume potentially intrusive international obligations in this sensitive area. Policymakers from countries where potential ethnic fissures have not developed likewise do not wish to encourage latent tendencies to ethnic division within their own countries through promulgation of sweeping minority rights norms of general application, although there is debate about the risks and benefits of general normative commitments in such situations. A particularized approach was proposed by the EC in the November 1991 Draft

Convention on Yugoslavia,[36] but even if the obstacles are overcome and such an instrument is eventually adopted by the states of former Yugoslavia, it is unlikely that many other states will be induced to undertake such customized obligations in the absence of general agreement. There are also serious problems of supervision and of enforcement with respect to such instruments.

The experience of the League of Nations is an important reminder of the difficulties facing such a particularized approach. In total, some 25 treaties dealing with minorities in Europe were concluded and entered into force between 1919 and 1934.[37] The minorities treaties established that minority issues were, in certain circumstances, appropriate matters for international concern. Individuals and groups were provided with a forum of moderate effectiveness to which to address complaints,[38] but they did not have direct rights to a hearing or a remedy.[39] Some cases were settled effectively, but non-state petitioners had no formal standing or right to representation, little access to information on the progress of their petition, no power to expedite it or to appeal against an adverse finding, and no certainty of their individual grievances being rectified. This was especially so if they lacked the backing of an influential state. The obligations concerning minorities were imposed on new states, defeated states, or states struggling to attain full international sovereignty. They did not apply to established victor states, and did relatively little in practice to protect any minorities outside Europe. They did not apply to any of the Great Powers except

36. Treaty Provisions for the Convention (1991) (text issued by the EC Commission).

37. These provisions have been treated, in general, as having ceased to have effect on account of the fundamental change of circumstances wrought by the Second World War and the ensuing reordering of the international system. *See generally* U.N. Secretariat, *Study on the Legal Validity of the Undertakings Concerning Minorities*, U.N. Doc. E/CN.4/367/Add.1 (1950). It is possible that certain of the instruments may nevertheless retain legal significance for specific and limited purposes—*see, e.g.*, LOUIS B. SOHN & THOMAS M. BUERGENTHAL, INTERNATIONAL PROTECTION OF HUMAN RIGHTS 304-5 (1973), concerning Greece and Turkey. A number were clearly superseded by post-1944 instruments, including peace treaties and, possibly, the Helsinki Final Act. New questions may conceivably arise, however, as old states reemerge.

38. Approximately 300 petitions (excluding those concerning Upper Silesia) were received in the period 1921-29, of which some 150 were declared unreceivable. More precise statistics concerning petitions were published from 1930: 204 petitions were received in 1931, 101 in 1932, and between 45 and 70 in 1930, 1933, 1934 and 1935. After 1935 the numbers plummeted, and the Minorities Section was dissolved in 1939. *See* U.N. Doc. E/CN.4/Sub.2/6 (1947); and JACOB ROBINSON ET AL., WERE THE MINORITIES TREATIES A FAILURE? 124-34 (1943).

39. In League practice a procedure evolved whereby petitions received from any non-anonymous source alleging violations of minorities treaties were first considered by the Minorities Section of the Secretariat which determined (subject to appeal by states) whether they were receivable, solicited responses from the governments concerned, and played an important intermediary role. Receivable complaints were considered by committees of the League Council, which could drop the case, refer it to the Council, or initiate "informal and benevolent negotiations." For assessment of the procedure, see, for example, PABLO DE AZCÁRATE, LEAGUE OF NATIONS AND NATIONAL MINORITIES: AN EXPERIMENT (Eileen E. Brooke trans., 1945).

Germany, and then only in respect of Upper Silesia. The States bound by minorities obligations not unnaturally tended to resent the discrimination inherent in this selective minority protection, and compliance and supervision problems became increasingly acute throughout the latter part of the 1930s. Proposals for a general international treaty on minorities were made frequently, but once the particularized obligations were established it was not surprising that other states showed little interest in a universal instrument under which they would also assume obligations. This difficulty also confronts contemporary particularist efforts.

2. *Development of General Norms on Rights of Minorities*

Urgent efforts are now being directed to implementing the second approach: developing additional and more detailed normative standards, together with more effective and systematic procedures for implementation and enforcement. A Working Group of the United Nations Commission on Human Rights has, after many years of slow progress, been able to elaborate a draft Declaration on the Rights of Persons Belonging to National or Ethnic, Religious and Linguistic Minorities for consideration by the UN General Assembly.[40] The Council of Europe is considering a European Charter for Regional or Minority Languages, and the European Commission for Democracy Through Law (the Venice Commission) in 1991 proposed that the Council of Europe adopt a European Convention for the Protection of Minorities, implementation of which would be supervised by a European Committee for the Protection of Minorities.[41] The CSCE included a cautious provision on minorities in the Helsinki Final Act of 1975, to the effect that:

> The Participating States on whose territory national minorities exist will respect the right of persons belonging to such minorities to equality before the law, will afford them the full opportunity for the actual enjoyment of human rights and fundamental freedoms and will, in this manner, protect their legitimate interests in this sphere.[42]

The Document of the Copenhagen Meeting on the Human Dimension (1990) contains much more elaborate provisions, which have been reiterated and elaborated in subsequent CSCE documents.[43] The CSCE has also begun to contribute significantly to monitoring and supervision.

---

40. It is ironic that the Commission on Human Rights finally reached agreement on a modest draft Declaration in the shadow of the human misery accompanying the disintegration of Yugoslavia; the diplomatic impetus for such a Declaration was for many years provided by Yugoslavia, and a Yugoslav representative chaired the Working Group.

41. For text of the proposed Convention, see 12 HUM. RTS. L.J. 269 (1991). Other proposals for Council of Europe action have also been mooted, including a Protocol on minority rights to the European Convention on Human Rights.

42. Declaration on Principles Guiding Relations Between Participating States, section VII, *reprinted in* 14 I.L.M. 1292, 1295 (1975).

43. *See, e.g.*, Report to the CSCE Council from the CSCE Seminar of Experts on Democratic Institutions (1991), 31 I.L.M. 375 (1992).

The Vienna Mechanism for monitoring of state compliance with CSCE commitments, and other Mechanisms in place or being developed, may help promote compliance in certain limited classes of situations where other states take a particular interest in the target state's treatment of minorities. The provision in the 1992 CSCE Helsinki Document for appointment of a High Commissioner on National Minorities with power to monitor national minority issues and to provide early warning to the Committee of Senior Officials is a step toward more general independent monitoring and supervision, although the effectiveness of this step will depend on the stature and resources of the High Commissioner as well as further supervision and sanctions initiatives. The High Commissioner's mandate relates to groups: the High Commissioner is expressly barred from considering "violations of CSCE commitments with regard to an individual person belonging to a national minority."[44]

C. Human Rights Claims

The principles of human rights are a major source of legitimation for claims by non-state groups.[45] Such human rights claims have the greatest purchase when articulated as claims by aggregates of individuals who are seeking vindication only of the same rights as those enjoyed or espoused by other members of the ambient society. More difficult problems arise with this domain of discourse where the claim of the group is couched as something more than simply an aggregate of individual rights claims, or where the rights sought are not demonstrably identical with those enjoyed by the ambient population. In these and other situations the discourse of human rights and equality may lose its purchase for non-state groups, and they may find that their claims are opposed by others on human rights grounds. Equality rights, like other human rights, inure for the benefit of everyone, and may thus provide grounds for upholding or for rejecting a particular group claim.

The paucity of provisions for express minority rights has meant that many of the claims of non-dominant groups have been assessed only in the standard universalist discourse of human rights. Turpel[46] rightly draws attention to the very cautious approach of the Human Rights Committee in its interpretation of the right to participate in public affairs (Article 25 of the I.C.C.P.R.) in the case brought by Mikmaq leaders with respect to the refusal of the Canadian Government to accept direct Mikmaq Grand Council participation in the First Ministers Conferences on matters concerning aboriginal peoples.[47] The general right to political participation in constitutional deliberations was treated as

44. *The Challenges of Change*, CSCE Helsinki Document 1992, Helsinki Decisions, Chapter II (on file with author).

45. *Cf.* Onuma, *supra* note 4.

46. Mary Ellen Turpel, *Indigenous Peoples' Rights of Political Participation and Self-Determination: Recent International Legal Developments and the Continuing Struggle for Recognition*, 25 CORNELL INT'L L.J. 579 (1992).

47. *Human Rights Committee Final Views* (Communication No. 205/1986) *Mikmaq Tribal Society v. Canada*, U.N. Doc. CCPR/C/43/D/205/1986 (1991).

being satisfied by the national system of representative government. The Human Rights Committee did not regard Article 25 as necessitating specific representation of particular groups, no matter that the agenda item may be of particular importance to them, and no matter that they may not be satisfied with their "representation" in the representative system. The concern of the Human Rights Committee to maintain a universalist interpretation of the Covenant, and thus not to set standards for political participation in one polity which it might feel unable to apply in another, is evident in the case law. The Committee's reticence is compounded by its unwillingness to adopt the concept of a margin of appreciation, so that its findings of no violation appear not simply as refusals to substitute its judgment for that of the state, but as legitimations of state policy. While the Committee has good reasons not to take an overly expansive view of its own role too quickly, and to emphasize universality, it has not done enough to elaborate the meaning of participation and representation in plural societies.

While the scope of existing norms is sometimes underestimated, there is a need for further normative development to deal with difficult problems in relating claims by non-state groups to human rights and equality norms. Non-state groups typically emphasize the need for greater sensitivity in accommodating their concerns within a human rights framework. It is also important that effective means be devised to hold non-state groups accountable, in appropriate circumstances, for their own violations of human rights. More generally, norms and procedures to resolve conflicts between group claims and rights of individual members of the group require further refinement, particularly where state power or other third party interests are involved.

D. Claims by Indigenous Peoples

Claims based on prior occupation or "indigeneity," which are discussed extensively in the articles by Lam and Turpel in this issue,[48] have the politically important characteristic of distinguishing and narrowing the range of potential claimants. Claims based on the special status of indigenous peoples are made by non-state groups in most parts of the world, and are aired internationally in the UN's Working Group on Indigenous Populations and many other fora.[49] The term "indigenous people" is not yet well defined,[50] and the label "indigenous" has without doubt been arrogated on occasion to legitimize chauvinist assertions contrary to the human rights of others.[51] Nevertheless, the category of "indigenous peoples" is a circumscribed one; it may well come to influ-

48. Maivân Clech Lâm, *Making Room for Peoples at the United Nations: Thoughts Provoked by Indigenous Claims to Self-Determination*, 25 Cornell Int'l L.J. 603 (1992); Turpel, *supra* note 46.

49. *See generally* Lâm, *supra* note 48.

50. *See generally* Benedict Kingsbury, *"Indigenous Peoples" as an International Legal Concept*, *in* Indigenous Peoples in Asia (R.H. Barnes et al. eds., forthcoming).

51. *Compare* the argument made by Ved P. Nanda, *Ethnic Conflict in Fiji and International Human Rights Law*, 25 Cornell Int'l L.J. 565 (1992).

ence discourse in the other three categories, but this process is only just beginning. At present indigenous peoples also utilize other domains of discourse in pursuing their claims. Cree in Quebec, for example, have argued that if the province proceeded to exercise the right to self-determination, the Cree would have a separate international legal right to self-determination; that historically Cree sovereignty was not surrendered to Quebec and could properly be (re)asserted; and that, international norms specifically applicable to indigenous peoples would also apply.[52]

E. Historical Sovereignty Claims

Historically-based claims to sovereignty typically involve an assertion of territorial exclusivity. Although historical assertions are an important element in many claims to sovereignty (including some by "indigenous peoples"), claims of major international political significance directed toward a change of international sovereignty, in which historical revendication was the chief domain of discourse, had until recently largely been limited to: claims to retrocession of small colonial territories, such as Hong Kong, the Falklands/Malvinas, or Gibraltar; irredentist claims pursued without much immediate success, such as that of Venezuela in respect of part of Guyana and that of Guatemala in respect of Belize;[53] certain boundary disputes; and possibly a small range of special situations where such historical assertions either accompanied or contradicted claims couched in terms of self-determination or rights of indigenous peoples. More recently, however, such assertions of historical sovereignty have been important in the dissolution or disintegration of federal states, and were crucial in legitimizing the claims to independence of Lithuania, Latvia and Estonia at a time when it seemed highly possible that decisionmakers in the Soviet Union would consider trying to use military force to prevent these claims from succeeding.

F. Impact of Legal Structure on Formulation of Claims

The structure of the law has had a strong shaping effect on international discourse; thus an inordinate amount of attention has been focused on the refusal of some states to describe indigenous groups internationally as indigenous peoples (even though these states use the term peoples freely in domestic political discourse). The equally fervent strategy on the part of some indigenous peoples is to secure recognition interna-

52. *See* Grand Council of the Crees (of Quebec), *Status and Rights of the James Bay Crees in the Context of Quebec's Secession from Canada*, Submission to UN Commission on Human Rights, February 1992 (United Nations files, Geneva).

53. To clarify the terms in this article, "secession" refers to attempts by a group within a state to withdraw from state control part of the territory and population of the state. "Irredentism" refers to attempts to alter state borders so as to combine groups presently separated by one or more borders, the groups to be combined either in an existing state or in a new state. *See generally* Donald Horowitz, *Irredentas and Secessions: Adjacent Phenomena, Neglected Connections*, *in* IRREDENTISM AND INTERNATIONAL POLITICS 9-22 (Naomi Chazan ed., 1991).

tionally as "peoples" so that they will win much of the battle with respect to all other claims. Legal structure—the preoccupation with "peoples" or "minorities"—interacts with social science and media classification to artificially reduce a great many claims and conflicts to single categories. In particular, there is a clear preoccupation with "ethnic" claims and "ethnic" conflicts (taking ethnicity to include religious and linguistic elements). These classifications are often simplistic, and miss important parts of identities,[54] and of the structure of claims and conflicts, including their territorial,[55] historical, resource, and class aspects. The power of the lexicon shapes the way in which claims are formulated and groups define themselves: thus, for instance, the scramble to be considered one of the "backward classes" in India,[56] or the rapid adoption among many non-state groups in Asia of the self-description "indigenous people" as it has become an empowering term internationally, even where the very same group may still have origin myths which recount their migration and subordination of another group still living in the same territory. Where a conflict may be largely about access to resources or about social stratification, the temptation for outsiders, and for participants, is often to define it as ethnic, thus clouding analysis and perhaps eventually altering its structure.[57]

Persuasive arguments are made that in some situations attention ought to focus on the inadequacies of a system that does not secure fair access to positions in the civil administration and the military, rather than on ethnic tensions associated with marginalization. Powerful voices argue that normative acceptance of extensive claims couched in terms of ethnicity or other group identity provides a strong incentive for claims to be formulated this way, leads politics to become irretrievably dominated by ethnic demands and divisions, and impels the society and eventually the polity toward fracture.[58] Many states deny that ethnic differences exist. Others assert that the differences that exist are not (and ought not to be) of any significance for the law, and in some states various peaceful forms of ethnic self-assertion are prohibited as threats to national unity. While some such denials and prohibitions are abusive, chauvinist ethnic claims have undoubtedly contributed to terrible ethnic conflicts, and there are proper concerns about deepening or causing divisions, and about fanning conflict.

---

54. *See, e.g.*, FREDRIK BARTH, ETHNIC GROUPS AND BOUNDARIES (1970).

55. *See, e.g.*, Lea Brilmayer, *Secession and Self-Determination: A Territorial Interpretation*, 16 YALE J. INT'L L. 177 (1991).

56. *See, e.g.*, MARC GALANTER, COMPETING EQUALITIES: LAW AND THE BACKWARD CLASSES IN INDIA (1984).

57. In a similar vein, Minogue correctly warns about overestimating the centrality of nationalism: "It is the business of the ideologist of nationalism to persuade us that history culminates in nationalism. . . . Ideologists, like egoists, see little else but their own reflection, and it is part of their strength that they should do so." KENNETH MINOGUE, NATIONALISM 25 (1967).

58. *See, e.g.*, ELIE KEDOURIE, NATIONALISM (1960); and Solomon F. Bloom, *The Peoples of My Home Town: Before Nationalism Crushed Rumania's Design For Living*, COMMENTARY 329-35 (1947).

Not every claim by a non-state group has equal (nor necessarily any) moral merit. Blanket moral relativism about such claims attracts a strong charge of moral irresponsibility. The International Covenant on Civil and Political Rights (ICCPR) addresses one aspect of this issue in providing that nothing in the Covenant "may be interpreted as implying for any State, group or person any right to engage in any activity or perform any act aimed at the destruction of any of the rights and freedoms recognized herein or at their limitation to a greater extent than is provided for. . . ."[59] The further question of whether it is possible or desirable to prescribe general substantive norms in these areas is highly problematic. The circumspection of international tribunals in this area is to be noted: indeed, the scope for most non-state groups to bring claims remains very limited. On the other hand, it is clear that the claims of non-state groups, and the related problems of structuring relationships between states and non-state groups, are of central and enduring concern in contemporary international society. While they ought not to obscure other important questions from view, the dangers associated with abusive claims and demagoguery must be kept firmly in mind. The strategy of ignoring questions concerning the relations between states and non-state groups is neither viable nor internationally supported.

Having outlined the structure of the existing domains of discourse and pointed to the general need for further normative development, the next section will indicate a specific strategy for future development of the law concerning self-determination in a manner that both enhances the ability of the international community to respond to current problems and better reconciles the three general domains of discourse.

III. Self-Determination

The appeal of the principle of self-determination has long rested (in part) on its generalizability, indeed its ostensible universality. At no stage have justifications of a general principle of self-determination successfully escaped the conundrum presented by the fact that legitimization of the claims of any one group has implications for the interests and claims of many other groups. The principal strategies intended to make it possible both to invoke and to limit self-determination have been either to call upon countervailing principles, such as territorial integrity, or to try to formulate claims to self-determination as rights claims with a limited category of rightholders, described as "peoples." A more promising strategy, insufficiently pursued, is to argue that the right to self-determination is a generalized right but that its realization does not always entail the option of separate statehood, and that its application in specific circumstances depends on those same circumstances. This strategy entails recognizing a degree of unity of justificatory principle

59. International Covenant on Civil and Political Rights, 999 U.N.T.S. 171, art. 5, para. 1 (1966).

between self-determination, autonomy, rights to language, culture, and participation, equality and non-discrimination, and general human rights in plural societies.[60] A major attraction of such a unified approach is that it allows for the rights and interests of non-members of the group—or even dissentient members—to be weighed on the same scale as the claim to self-determination. This aids in ensuring that the rights of all are effectively protected during the immediate self-determination process and after any ensuing transition. This is of particular importance where a territory is shared by more than one group. Such considerations suggest that it may be desirable to reexamine self-determination at the theoretical normative level. What follows is a tentative pointer toward one possible strategy—and it is not itself free from problems—for reconceptualizing self-determination.[61] It is not intended as an examination of lex lata or even lex ferenda.

A. Defining Rightholders

The phrase "all peoples have the right to self-determination," found inter alia in Article 1 of the International Covenant on Civil and Political Rights, has for three decades been reified as the governing normative stipulation. The accompanying description of what the right entails ("By virtue of that right they freely determine their political status and freely pursue their economic, social and cultural development"), and the other rights or powers conferred on "[a]ll peoples" in e.g., Article 1(2) of the 1966 Covenants, have been read back as indicators that the category of rightholders ("peoples") must in fact be narrow. So narrow, indeed, according to most states, that the expression "peoples" has been stripped of its ordinary meaning and reconstructed as something quite different. This attempt to contain the category of rightholders within very narrow bounds is showing some signs of breaking down. Historically there have been opposing tendencies in the rhetoric (and indeed in practice) of self-determination, toward, on the one hand, universalizing, and, on the other hand, containing, the principle. The substantive tendency to universalization, while to some extent in eclipse again from the decolonization debates until the late 1980s, has not been permanently subdued. Rhetorically, the use of the phrase "all peoples"

60. Recognition of the difficulties of drawing principled distinctions which would tightly control the number of new entities eligible for statehood, and of the value of "minority rights" as a means of avoiding demands for statehood, is evident in the UN Secretary-General's report "An Agenda For Peace."

> The United Nations has not closed its door. Yet if every ethnic, religious or linguistic group claimed statehood, there would be no limit to fragmentation, and peace, security and economic well-being for all would become ever more difficult . . . . One requirement for solutions to these problems lies in commitment to human rights with a special sensitivity to those of minorities, whether ethnic, religious, social or linguistic.

At 5, U.N. Doc A/47/277 (1992).

61. Much of the following discussion is based on a more specific argument made in Benedict Kingsbury, *Self-Determination and "Indigenous Peoples,"* 86 PROCEEDINGS OF THE AM. SOC'Y OF INT'L LAW (forthcoming 1992).

to designate the category of rightholders has provided an opening which many non-state groups have been energetic in exploiting.

According to the strategy discussed here, what is needed is to get beyond the arid assumption that, in the field of self-determination, the act of classification by reference to one or other of the socio-referential labels used to identify rightholders is itself determinative of virtually all questions as to the precise rights involved and their concrete application. Thus, for instance, the bifurcation in the Gros Espiell report[62] and in some Human Rights Committee practices under the Civil and Political Rights Covenant: "peoples" have the right to self-determination but "minorities" do not. In fact, it is increasingly evident that the right to self-determination must be more complex, and that its vindication in any particular situation depends upon the complex matrix of factual and legal considerations, rather than on the simple assignment of labels.

B. The Meaning of the Right to Self-Determination

The question of what is entailed by "self-determination" is fundamental. The logic of the principle of self-determination extends beyond the question of independent statehood, to political and cultural options exercisable within the established state.[63] This point is reinforced by the increasing emphasis on rights of political participation, on political structures providing for some degree of genuine representation and accountability, on a semblance of democratic process in the choice of government/representatives, and even on the choice of constitutional order after an upheaval.

When lobbying in the UN about general normative formulations, groups seeking "self-determination" have tended to maintain that in all cases self-determination includes the possibility of separate statehood. On the other hand, many are aware of the strength of the opposition this elicits among other states and acknowledge that in a large number of cases (perhaps the majority) separate statehood would not be sought or would be a most unlikely outcome.[64]

The notion of a widespread option to form separate states is, to some, intrinsically destabilizing, whether or not the options are ever exercised. Many fear cataclysmic division and conflict if any such general right is countenanced. A more abstract issue concerns competing visions of future international order. United Nations membership has now passed 175, including such "microstates" as Liechtenstein and San Marino whose suitability for membership had earlier been in doubt. A multifarious world, with many small states enjoying various relations with larger neighbors and regional bodies, is no longer far-fetched as a

62. Héctor Gros Espiell, The Right to Self-Determination: Implementation of United Nations Resolutions (1980).

63. *See, e.g.*, Brownlie, *supra* note 7, at 6; Hurst Hannum, Autonomy, Sovereignty and Self-Determination 473-77 (1989); and Turpel, *supra* note 46.

64. *See generally* Independent Commission on International Humanitarian Issues, Indigenous Peoples: A Global Quest for Justice 36-40 (1987).

vision of the international system, and if attained probably need not of itself raise disastrous systemic instability problems. On the other hand, such a proliferation of small states would have significant practical (and perhaps eventually legal) effects on the nature of statehood, with the potential for further erosion of assumptions about the essential incidents of state sovereignty. This will be seen by some as an advance toward an effective international society, and by others as a step toward the abyss. A possible third perspective, however, held by some members of non-state groups, is that this threatens to debase the currency they are striving to secure. In this respect, the non-state group may share the perspectives of a good many citizens of decolonized states—with, however, a potential difference in cases where self-determination follows ethnic boundaries more closely and where allegiance to the state is thus slightly less central as a basis of unity.

There is understandable reluctance on the part of representatives of non-state groups to concede as a normative matter that the right to self-determination could *ever* be vindicated where the state(s) dealing with an ethnic minority dominant in a severable territory refuses to countenance even the option of separate statehood. Not only does such a concession appear to risk breaking ranks with, and indeed selling out, groups seeking separate statehood, it also moves away from, and thus risks losing some of the authority of, the U.N. practice on decolonization. In U.N. practice (with some glaring exceptions), separate statehood for colonial units was the presumptive option. In fact, the Special Committee on Decolonization was deeply suspicious whenever it appeared that another option might be exercised.

Several observations may be made with respect to this strategic view that self-determination must always entail the option of separate statehood. First, self-determination must be understood, not simply in terms of end result, but also in terms of process and of political legitimation; early commitment to the process, and to the legitimacy of the values associated with self-determination, may in some cases avert separation or violence. Arrangements for some degree of autonomy within a federal state structure have in many cases staved off or eclipsed demands for self-determination that might otherwise have tended toward secession. A federal structure may also establish units that, should the union disintegrate or secessionist pressures rise, are better equipped to move to independent statehood and to take advantage of the stabilizing principle of *uti possidetis juris*.[65] On the other hand, autonomy arrangements do leave important powers de facto or de jure in the hands of the central authorities; autonomous regions may be vulnerable to resource exploitation or demographic alteration.

Second, when concrete cases are addressed, there is an element of reductionism in treating "statehood" as a single outcome, as if this

65. This fact does, of course, contribute to the reticence of powerful forces in unitary states about assuming a more federal character.

juridical form utterly transcends the specific features of spatial, economic, and political organization, of culture, environment, conflict, and militarization, which in fact loom large when individuals and groups come to make any determination for themselves. Inquiries by theorists into the "archaeology of the state," the "parcelization of sovereignty," the localism which has resisted the so-called upward displacement of power associated with modernization, and even the "ethnography of the state," all ought to remind us that the simplifications—and the sense of ultimate—sometimes found in discourses about statehood, may miss many important human dimensions with which human rights and self-determination are inevitably and properly bound up.

Third, there is the prudential caution that some of the groups making claims now may find themselves resisting them in the not-so-distant future.

There is nevertheless a deeply entrenched assumption in international practice and discourse that what self-determination is about is the right to determine, under certain conditions, whether a group or unit wishes to form a separate state or choose some other option. The question whether the character of self-determination applies also to situations where on the facts separate statehood is not a required option raises the fundamental issue of what justifies the right to self-determination.

One approach begins with the group, and with the proposition that the interests of the group itself are sufficient to establish a right. This is not the basis on which human rights analysis proceeds, although reference to it is a reminder that self-determination claims are not always premised on human rights considerations.[66] If self-determination is to be understood, as international instruments suggest, as a human right, the starting point must be the value to the interests of individuals of membership and participation in a particular kind of group. Following Raz and others,[67] the well-being of a group is related to, but different from, the aggregation of the interests of individuals.[68] In some circumstances the group's well-being can be secured only where it is self-governing (or has the option of being self-governing). Self-government is thus justified instrumentally; the case for an intrinsic justification is much harder to make. The idea of self-government is broad: it "speaks of groups determining the character of their social and economic environment, their fortunes, the course of their development, and the for-

66. Arguments of this sort have generated a longstanding mistrust about nationalism and national self-determination within the tradition of liberalism. As MacCormick notes: "From Hitler to Ceaucescu, there has been no shortage of illustrative evils showing how the pursuit of national liberty and national values can lead to denigration, servility, torture and death for those outwith the charmed national circle, and even for many within it." Neil MacCormick, *Is Nationalism Philosophically Credible?*, *in* ISSUES OF SELF-DETERMINATION 10-11 (William Twining ed., 1991).

67. *See* Avishai Margalit & Joseph Raz, *National Self-Determination*, 87 J. PHILOS. 439-61 (1990); and *generally* JOSEPH RAZ, THE MORALITY OF FREEDOM 207-13 (1986).

68. This involves a rejection of methodological individualism.

tunes of their members by [the groups'] own actions . . ."[69] Self-determination in the sense of a choice among options that include separate statehood is a means of attaining self-government. Given the breadth covered by "self-government" in a range of different situations, however, it appears that self-determination in this narrow sense by no means exhausts the means of securing it. Other means of securing the objectives of (instrumentally-justified) self-government ought thus to be regarded as sharing the instrumental purposes of the narrow version of self-determination. While the existing formulations of the right to self-determination in international instruments do not so extend, provisions as to other human rights do bear on wider aspects of self-government. The point to be emphasized is that in their grounds or justifications self-determination and other rights are not sharply distinct, and depending on the facts of the particular case, the realization of other rights ought to be regarded as realizing purposes underlying self-determination. This being so, at least two possibilities are open. One possibility is to regard self-determination as the end of a continuum on which other rights beneficial to the group and the purposes it serves are also located. The other is to reformulate the right of self-determination so that it opens the way to a wider range of different relations between an ethnic group styling itself as a distinct "people" and an existing state, dependent not simply on the choice of the group but also on more precise criteria tied to the underlying justificatory purposes served by the right.

The first of these approaches has the advantages of being more consistent with established and evolving international law, and of being somewhat more realistic. A disadvantage of this approach for non-state "peoples" is that many of the sought rights may emerge only slowly and with heavy qualifications in general international human rights practice, and may never have the legitimating force of the general commitment to self-determination. The second approach could open the way to forms of functional self-determination for groups that cannot expect to form separate states because of, for instance, insufficient size or lack of preponderance in any significant territory. It could also eventually focus attention on the achievement of the underlying justificatory purposes for which the right to self-determination is at present a rather blunt, unnuanced, and underinclusive instrument.

C. Operation of the Right

A statement that a right exists and that it is held by a particular category of rightholders by no means disposes of all the relevant issues. In practice, as in legal philosophy, it is quite possible that, while the right must ground some duties for some other actor(s), these duties will not correlate perfectly with the scope of the right. Furthermore, consideration of the operation of any right must also entail consideration of its consequences. For instance, a right to self-determination may affect persons

69. Margalit & Raz, *supra* note 67, at 440.

living in a particular territory who are not members of the group seeking self-determination, or who are dissentient members not well served by the group, or who also belong to other welfare- or interest- or autonomy-serving groups (with different boundaries) that would be threatened or fissured by the proposed self-determination, or who simply belong to some such alternative group and seek self-determination for it. A typical result of weighing all these factors is that separate statehood would not be the optimal outcome, or that it would serve human rights purposes only where hedged by conditions.

These points reinforce the oft-made point that, while rights might be trumps, they are not absolute. The discourse of proponents of the right to self-determination has often had an absolutist overtone. This has been associated with a tendency to treat self-determination as a one-shot right, vindicated and exhausted by liberation from alien domination. A focus on the grounds or justifications of the right reaffirms that the performance of the group must be continually judged by reference to the wellbeing of individual members and, in a different way, non-members. The instrumental justifications of self-government are not served at all times by every form and means of government. Where a particular governmental arrangement is grossly failing to serve the purposes on which its instrumental justification rests, it is likely that rights resting on the same instrumental justification will be invoked in favor of change. In view of its justification, it would be surprising indeed if the operational right to self-determination were construed as never extending to such situations; recent practice strongly supports this view.

Finally, although much of the contemporary discussion about self-determination relates to outcomes, it is well to recall that much of the international practice concerning the right to self-determination relates to issues of process—not simply to who decides or to what the choices are, but to how the decision is to be made and with what supervision, accountability and guarantees. In this area, practice has been somewhat ad hoc; existing international law, including the law and practice of institutions, is not sufficiently developed, and future international efforts to set standards must address these issues systematically.

A recent illustration of the limitations of the prevailing domains of discourse, as presently structured, is the attempts by the European Community to respond to events in Yugoslavia. These attempts will be examined as a case study of some of the problems with the present normative framework.

IV. A Recent Case Study: The European Community and Yugoslavia

The international community has had particular difficulty in responding to post-cold war claims by new entities, especially those established on the territories of the former Soviet Union and the former Yugoslavia.[70] Here, considerations arising from the traditional law and practice of recognition of new states and governments have combined with political concerns about the nature and stability of new entities, and about controlling the rate and extent of state disintegration. European Community practice with regard to Yugoslavia exhibits an amalgam of often contradictory and unreconciled considerations about existing law, order, and justice. One of the Community's responses to issues arising in Yugoslavia was to establish the Conference on Yugoslavia.[71] In addition to promoting European Political Cooperation, the EC hoped to use the Conference to control and condition the pace and nature of transition in Yugoslavia.

In two Declarations on December 16, 1991, the European Community and its member states set forth general guidelines concerning the recognition of new states in Eastern Europe and the Soviet Union. These declarations also set forth a policy and procedure whereby the Conference on Yugoslavia, with the advice of the Arbitration Commission,[72] would consider requests for recognition from Republics that had formed part of Yugoslavia. The stated general policy was that new states would be recognized only if they were democratic, had accepted the relevant international obligations, and committed themselves to proceed peacefully and by negotiation in good faith. More precisely, new states were required to respect the provisions of the UN Charter, the Helsinki Final Act, and the CSCE Charter of Paris for a New Europe, particularly concerning the rule of law, democracy, and human rights. They were expected to guarantee the rights of ethnic and national groups and of minorities, in conformity with engagements undertaken within the framework of the CSCE.

This formulation itself is revealing. Outside the declarations of the CSCE, which are not legally binding, there were no international treaties that set forth in detail the meaning of—let alone the means of realizing and ensuring—the rule of law, democracy, or rights of ethnic groups, national groups, or minorities. Indeed, these latter categories have not

70. The bifurcation of Czechoslovakia, if it does come to pass, may raise comparable issues, although many major questions are likely to remain unresolved for some time.

71. The Community established a Conference on Yugoslavia, chaired by Lord Carrington, comprising the EC, its member states, the Yugoslav federal government, and such Republics of the former Yugoslavia as wished to participate. This Conference began to function in September 1991. It was supplanted in August 1992 by a broader conference also involving the UN; the plenum was chaired jointly by UN Secretary-General Boutros Boutros Ghali and British Prime Minister John Major, the United Kingdom then holding the Presidency of the EC. Carrington resigned as EC special envoy just before this conference.

72. The Arbitration Commission, established by the EC alongside the Conference on Yugoslavia, comprised presiding judges from constitutional courts of EC member states under the Presidency of Robert Badinter, President of the French Conseil Constitutionnel. The Commission was not in fact empowered to arbitrate claims, but was expected to respond to requests for advice from the Conference.

been fully defined. Furthermore, CSCE member states took very different views as to the meaning of relevant CSCE commitments when applied to themselves, such as the French position on the non-existence of minorities within the French Republic. In the case of Yugoslavia, these problems were partially addressed by the stopgap expedient of conditioning recognition on compliance with a draft Convention then under consideration by the Conference on Yugoslavia.[73] The other general requirements propounded by the EC related more closely to traditional interests of other states, although serious questions existed as to how even these requirements could be implemented. These requirements included respect for inviolability of frontiers and for the principle that frontiers can be changed only by peaceful means and on the basis of free agreement; respect for relevant commitments concerning disarmament, nuclear non-proliferation, security, and regional stability; and commitment to settle regional disputes and questions about state succession by agreement or, if necessary, by arbitration.[74]

The opinions issued by the Arbitration Commission on November 29, 1991 and January 11, 1992, are an interesting blend of traditional and innovative international law. They are propositions that would not be generally accepted by international lawyers but clearly appealed to constitutional law judges seeking to address unusual and difficult situations.[75] The Commission declared on November 29, 1991, that the existence of a federal state, combining entities endowed with a degree of autonomy and with political power in relation to the federal institutions, implied that the Federal organs must represent the component units and must be effective; that, four of the six republics having made declarations of independence or sovereignty, the essential organs of the Federation no longer satisfied the requirements of participation and representativity; and that Yugoslavia ought thus to be regarded as a federation in the process of disintegration, rather than as a rump state from which certain units had seceded. Thus the rump state would not automatically succeed to the rights of Yugoslavia; questions of succession would have to be agreed upon by the Republics themselves, in conformity with international law. This view is broadly tenable under established international law, although some questions arise as to whether it is consistent with the treatment of state succession in relation to the former USSR.

73. This draft was not transformed into an agreed treaty in the November 1991 negotiations, primarily because the adherence of the Milosevic regime in Belgrade could not be obtained. It continued to be discussed as a possible basis for future arrangements in the new phase of the peace process inaugurated in August 1992 by the enlarged London conference.

74. Additional undertakings not to make territorial claims or engage in propaganda against a member of the Community were included to assuage Greek concerns about Macedonia.

75. Opinions 1, 2 and 3 have been published in 92 Revue Générale de Droit International Public 264-69 (1992). The comments which follow are based on the original French texts of the Commission's opinions; official English translations were not available to the author at the time of writing.

The Commission also emphasized principles of order in response to a question, raised by Serbia, as to whether the internal boundaries between Serbia and Croatia, and Serbia and Bosnia-Herzegovina, were to be regarded as frontiers in international law.[76] The Commission stated that the external borders of Yugoslavia must be respected; that the internal boundaries of Yugoslavia could only be modified by free agreement; that in the absence of such agreement the internal boundaries would take on the character of frontiers protected by international law by virtue of the general international legal principle of uti possidetis juris; and that any purported modification of external frontiers or internal boundaries effected by force would have no juridical effects. The last of these propositions was supported by reference to the U.N. General Assembly's 1970 Declaration on Friendly Relations, the Helsinki Final Act, and the draft Convention on Yugoslavia. Although the principle as to borders between independent states is well established,[77] it is interesting that none of the texts cited by the Commission is directly binding, and indeed the Commission's position as to modification of internal boundaries, an activity not infrequently attempted by various colonial powers, is not fully consistent with practice.

As to self-determination and minority rights, the Commission found more difficulty in simply basing itself on established international law. Serbia had posed the question whether the ethnic Serbs of Croatia and Bosnia-Herzegovina had the right to self-determination. The Commission asserted that the principle of uti possidetis juris trumped irredentist claims based on the right to self-determination, holding that borders existing at the moment of independence were not subject to alteration to satisfy the requirements of self-determination except where the states involved so agreed. The Commission further held that in the present state of international law, not all the consequences of the right to self-determination are specified. The Commission pointedly refrained from saying that the ethnic Serbs in the two other Republics did not have the right to self-determination. Indeed, the Commission stated that Article 1 of the 1966 Covenants established that the right to self-determination was a principle protecting human rights, and that by virtue of this right each human being could properly claim to belong to the ethnic, religious or linguistic community of her or his choice.[78] The Commission drew from the principle of self-determination the operational conse-

76. Opinion No. 3, January 11, 1992.

77. This was reaffirmed by the Security Council following Iraq's purported annexation of Kuwait. *See, e.g.*, U.N. SCOR Res. 661 (1990).

78. The assertion that Article 1 establishes an operational right to self-determination for individuals seems to be inconsistent with assumptions made by the UN Human Rights Committee in its case law denying that individuals are ever entitled to bring Optional Protocol claims in respect of Article 1. *See* Communication No. 167/1984 Ominayak v. Canada (Final Views of March 26, 1990), discussed above; Communication No. 413/1990 A.B. et al. v. Italy (inadmissibility decision of November 2, 1990); Communication No. 358/1989 R.L. et al. v. Canada (inadmissibility decision of 5 November 1991); and Communication No. 205/1986 Mikmaq Tribal Society v. Canada (Final Views published December 3, 1991).

quence that, if the Republics so agreed, members of the Serbian communities in Bosnia-Herzegovina and Croatia could have the nationality of their choice, with all the rights and obligations following from that. Although the Commission is not explicit, it is presumed that choice of Serbian nationality would not entail loss of the right of residence in whichever state the individual lived. The Commission further found that imperative norms of international law (*i.e.*, jus cogens) oblige states to ensure respect for minorities' rights. The Commission applied these obligations to the Republics in respect of all minorities within their territories. The Republics had to recognize the identity of ethnic, linguistic or religious communities. Beyond this, however, the Commission did not state what other rights international law conferred upon minorities, although it referred in general terms to international treaties in force, and to chapter II of the draft Convention on Yugoslavia of November 4, 1991.[79] The Commission, however, in its unpublished Opinions concerning application for recognition by particular Republics, had necessarily to consider in detail the adequacy of particular legal provisions concerning use of minority languages, education, political representation or authority of minority communities, etc.[80]

V. Implications for the Development of International Law

Earlier sections pointed to the urgent need for development of more general international law principles, rules and structures suitable for dealing effectively with claims by non-state groups. The inability—or the failure—of the international community to develop sufficiently comprehensive and effective normative and procedural provisions for addressing claims by non-state groups has resulted in ad hoc attempts to develop these provisions in response to recent crises. These ad hoc provisions have come too late to effectively shape behavior, and they have lacked the legitimacy necessary to avoid or mitigate conflict. The lack of a generalized normative and procedural framework has also reinforced inevitable tendencies of major states to react in different ways to different claims, not for principled universal reasons but for particularist reasons reflecting the special interests of major states and decisionmakers.[81]

79. Opinion No. 3, *supra* note 75.

80. Thus it is understood that in its unpublished Opinion concerning the request for recognition by Macedonia, the Commission noted in some detail provisions of the new Macedonian Constitution concerning rights of minorities to identity, cultural expression, establishment of private schools, education in their own language, etc. It is understood that the Commission took the view that education for members of minorities should also be provided in the Macedonian language, and that more detailed laws are needed to make these various constitutional guarantees operational. Somewhat similar material is understood to be contained in the unpublished Opinion concerning the request for recognition by Slovenia.

81. The fragmentary response of the major actors in the international community to events in Somalia in 1991-92, and the difference in promptitude (and at least initially in scale) between these attempts and the contemporaneous undertakings in

There are many explanations for the inadequate development of the norms of international law with respect to claims by non-state groups. In some respects this underdevelopment was deliberate; thus anxiety about the potentially harmful implications for state interests—and for individual rights—of conferring rights on non-state groups was a constant factor for most of the period from 1945 until about 1990. Normative development has also been impeded by well-known political obstacles, especially East-West and West-South divisions, associated with the structure of the post-1945 legal order. The absence of a focus on non-state groups was also an incidental byproduct of the preoccupation since 1945 with the development of norms and institutions for the protection of individual human rights, and with developing legal structures to facilitate specific and foreseen developments such as decolonization.

The political climate for normative development has become somewhat more propitious, although major differences continue. Perhaps equally important are the gradual changes in the structure of international order, including changes in the nature of state sovereignty. The changes in the nature of sovereignty are complex and uneven, but have been influenced by the proliferation of transnational non-state interactions; the transmission of ideas about such things as governance, markets, human rights, information, and environment; and increasing international accountability. The heightened level of self-assertion among national and other groups, and the increased willingness of the international community to consider some accommodation of the claims pressed by such groups, is sharpening the international focus on the nature of the state and of state sovereignty. An important report, issued by the United Nations Secretary-General in June 1992 and entitled "An Agenda For Peace," is evidence of changing views on state sovereignty, even within an inter-state organization. The Report examines the pressing need to enhance preventive diplomacy, peacemaking, peacekeeping, rebuilding peace after civil and international war, and amelioration of economic despair, social injustice, and political oppression, but adds:

> The foundation-stone of this work is and must remain the State. Respect for its fundamental sovereignty and integrity are crucial to any common international progress. The time of absolute and exclusive sovereignty, however, has passed; its theory was never matched by reality. It is the task of leaders of States today to understand this and to find a balance between the needs of good internal governance and the requirements of an ever more interdependent world. Commerce, communications and environmental matters transcend administrative borders; but inside these borders is where individuals carry out the first order of their economic, political and social lives.[82]

Bosnia-Herzegovina and Croatia, illustrates this point. There were, without doubt, serious obstacles to effective action in each case.

82. At 5, para. 17, U.N. Doc. A/47/277 (1992).

A major obstacle to further normative development is that posed by the real problems in formulating and agreeing upon norms of general application with sufficient specificity, and with the necessary hierarchical ordering and coherence, to be useful at the operational level. The universal substantive normative formulations in the field of self-determination are very broad and have in practice been hedged with exceptions and limitations. Furthermore, they are part of the same legal system as other potentially conflicting general normative propositions of apparently equal value. It has proved difficult to secure the level of agreement and acceptance necessary to adopt sweeping substantive prescriptions dealing specifically with minority rights. Detailed and workable norms of general application have been adopted in the field of human rights,[83] and this area may provide the best starting point for a substantive effort to unify the three general domains of discourse by reference to the underlying justificatory purposes of each. The ICCPR indeed, despite its limitations, provides a modest textual basis for such an enterprise, in that it does not itself formally separate the three general domains of discourse. It recognizes that self-determination is indispensable to the realization of other human rights, and interpreted literally it treats minority rights as essentially the same as human rights. In practice, however, the domains have been divided. Self-determination has been permitted to operate largely in a separate plane, and the efforts of the international community to relate self-determination to protection of minorities and human rights have been patchy and enjoyed only modest practical success. The powerful discourse of individual human rights has not been extended with sufficient sensitivity to particular problems relating to non-state groups. The regime of minority rights has been severely limited, in part because inadequate normative development in the three domains left room for anxiety that it might impair individual rights on the one hand, or shade threateningly into overdrawn self-determination claims on the other.

Agreement is more easily secured on procedural rules. With respect to claims by non-state groups, however, procedural rules are not as well developed. Some of the procedural limitations are a result of the historically inter-state character of the international legal system. More effective procedural norms are beginning to appear, due to both the changing nature of the state and the increasing transnationalization of the international legal system. Nevertheless, with the monumental exception of decolonization, international bodies remain cautious when handling major claims by non-state groups. One reason for caution is the tendency of these bodies to maintain a universalist view of their practice, and thus to avoid setting workable precedents in one context which might, from their viewpoint, have disastrous political ramifica-

83. There continue to be important challenges to the validity of fundamental human rights norms, including challenges to the norms of equality and non-discrimination; the major general challenge, that posed by the international law principle of non-interference in domestic affairs, has gradually been eclipsed.

tions in another context.[84] The most ambitious practice is often particularist, frequently undertaken in ways designed to minimize precedential implications. The response of various countries to the claims and interests of Kurds in Northern Iraq in 1991 is one illustration.[85]

The concentration on process, and the substantive neutrality of what Franck describes as the secular international rule community,[86] has important implications. It suggests that as a practical matter all eligible claims must be regarded as equally worthy. This is a politically impossible and morally uneasy position. A common response of international bodies has been to sidestep the problem by remaining circumspect. The normative response has been to try to restrict eligibility by narrow circumscription of the categories of rightholders. As this article has pointed out, however, definition of rightholders is only one aspect of the analysis of self-determination, minority rights, and equality provisions. The further questions of the meaning of the right, the justification of the right, and the consequences of the right, are at least as important.

Even if it is possible to articulate worthwhile general norms and to devise effective systems of international supervision, what is the proper role of the international community in relation to claims by non-state groups? Liberal internationalism tends to assume a moral obligation on the part of the international community to become involved, at least where basic rights are threatened or justice claims are denied.[87] Foreign states and decisionmakers have generally been more circumspect, supporting significant involvement only where international security or other external interests are directly jeopardized, or in some extreme humanitarian emergencies, especially where domestic political circumstances are favorable to involvement. In the wake of the question, "who ought to act?" comes the question, "who ought to pay?" Public international law has been concerned with these questions mainly with regard to international organizations. More fundamentally, however, they are moral and political questions. There is a continuing tension between the universalism of liberal ethics, in which proximity and connection are irrelevant to moral worth, and the ordinary human instinct to attach

84. This explains the frustration exemplified in Turpel's conclusion that in terms both of norms and supervisory or political pressure "the United Nations and the Human Rights Committee have been of virtually no assistance in indigenous struggles [in Canada]." Turpel, *supra* note 46, at 602.

85. Note also, for example, the express provision in the 1992 CSCE Helsinki Document whereby the participating States reaffirm "the need to develop appropriate programmes addressing problems of their respective nationals belonging to Roma and other groups traditionally identified as Gypsies and to create conditions for them to have equal opportunities to participate fully in the life of the society." *The Challenges of Change*, CSCE Helsinki Document 1992, Helsinki Decisions, Chapter VI, para. 35 (on file with author).

86. Franck, *supra* note 8.

87. This does not mean, of course, that international involvement will always be adverse to the target state. The purposes served by rights are thwarted, and justice effectively denied, by non-state groups, by states, and by conflict for which responsibility is mixed or unattributable.

greater importance to family, to community, and to what one is intimate or at least familiar with. Indeed, one of the ethical arguments for nationalism is precisely that it is instrumental in realizing these particularist individual goods.[88]

Would the existence of comprehensive and precise international normative provisions and supervisory machinery have made any difference to events in Yugoslavia, or Somalia, or anywhere else? Certainly the factors which caused states and other actors to be unwilling to engage in norm-creating and institution-building endeavors would also have militated against the effectiveness of any such norms or institutions, and little is to be gained from a counterfactual exercise in which normative and institutional issues are isolated from the political and ideological background. For present purposes it is more useful to address the further skeptical claim that even if developed in the future, international legal provisions and machinery are still unlikely to be effective. This claim fits poorly with the vigorous efforts of states and other international actors to develop such provisions and machinery with uncharacteristic speed. While a skeptic may discern traces of delusion, illusion, or even hypocrisy, the rapid innovations in the CSCE, for example, seem to manifest a strong belief that the normative provisions matter, although the provisions are formally political rather than "legal," and that the institutional mechanisms will work.[89] More generally, reference may be made to studies of the effectiveness of various legal and other regimes.[90] While these studies provide some grounds for optimism about the potential effectiveness of international norms and institutions, few of them address human rights regimes, and fewer still address regimes dealing with claims by non-state groups.[91] Problems of methodology, perspective, and data collection in these areas are formi-

88. *See* David Miller, *The Ethical Significance of Nationality*, 98 ETHICS 647 (1988); and Brian Barry, *Self-Government Revisited*, *in* THE NATURE OF POLITICAL THEORY 121-54 (David Miller and Larry Siedentop eds., 1983).

89. Formal records as to the use of the various CSCE Mechanisms have not generally been kept hitherto. Unofficial records compiled by the Netherlands Helsinki Committee show that between adoption of the Vienna Mechanism in 1989 and October 1990 the first phase of that Mechanism was invoked 103 times (7 against western states, 4 against neutral and non-aligned states, and 92 against eastern European states). The other three phases were also used on several occasions. *See* Arie Bloed & Pieter van Dijk, *Supervisory Mechanism for the Human Dimension of the CSCE*, *in* THE HUMAN DIMENSION OF THE HELSINKI PROCESS 73, 79 (Arie Bloed & Pieter van Dijk eds., 1991).

90. A few of many examples of such studies are Jack Donnelly, *International Human Rights: A Regime Analysis*, 40 INT'L ORG. 599 (1986); ORAN R. YOUNG, INTERNATIONAL COOPERATION: BUILDING REGIMES FOR NATURAL RESOURCES AND THE ENVIRONMENT (1989); INTERNATIONAL REGIMES IN EAST-WEST POLITICS (Volker Rittberger ed. 1990); Ethan A. Nadelmann, *Global Prohibition Regimes: The Evolution of Norms in International Society*, 44 INT'L ORG. 479 (1990); Martin List & Volker Rittberger, *Regime Theory and International Environmental Management*, *in* THE INTERNATIONAL POLITICS OF THE ENVIRONMENT 85-109 (Andrew Hurrell & Benedict Kingsbury eds., 1992).

91. Studies have been undertaken of the relative success of the international legal and institutional regime for dealing with decolonization, and of international contributions to transitions to democracy.

dable. Experience in other issue areas suggests that future regimes for relations between state and non-state groups might be workable, effective, and preferable to the alternatives. The importance of further work in this area has been widely recognized; the UN Sub-Commission on Prevention of Discrimination and Protection of Minorities has appointed a Special Rapporteur on "possible ways and means of facilitating the peaceful and constructive solution of problems involving minorities,"[92] and the CSCE has resolved to convene a seminar in 1993 on "Case Studies of National Minorities Issues: Positive Results."

Established international law principles, doctrines, and institutions for supervision and implementation may contribute significantly to the adjustment of relations between states and non-state groups. Even when the best possible interpretation is given to existing legal materials, however, it is clear that further normative and institutional development is urgently needed if adequate frameworks are to be established. It is also clear that part of the normative development involves more sophisticated reconciliation of the existing domains of discourse. The adequacy and effectiveness of such frameworks depends in part on their legitimacy, which itself has an impact on the willingness of those with the necessary power to apply or ignore them. In so far as legitimacy is the compliance-pull felt by established states or entities emerging in accordance with well-established legal standards, legitimacy is likely to attach to principles of order, including principles for managed transition where necessary. In so far as legitimacy is influenced by the perceptions of non-state groups with revisionist demands, it will depend both on the actual efficacy of the rules and on the extent to which they are consistent with claims of substantive and procedural justice. Given existing distributions of power, and the instrumental value of stability, considerations of order are likely to remain central to the international normative structure.

92. The Special Rapporteur is Mr. Asbjorn Eide. For his preliminary report, see U.N. Doc. E/CN.4/Sub.2/1991/43 (1991).

[21]

THE RIGHT TO REBEL[1]

TONY HONORÉ*

There is a dilemma concerning the relation between human rights and criminal responsibility. Unless in certain conditions we have the right to rebel, much talk of human rights can be dismissed as empty rhetoric. But if there is such a right, we are at times entitled to use violence against our fellow citizens as if we were at war with them. We may properly commit what are by ordinary standards the gravest of crimes. Either conclusion—that talk of human rights is empty or that we are sometimes entitled to kill and maim certain of our fellow citizens—is hard to stomach. I expound a conceptual framework for thinking about the dilemma, and suggest certain conclusions, but with no great confidence that they will command general assent.

One sense of the phrase 'human rights' is that which refers to the rights which citizens or members of a community possess against states and other political entities. An example, taken from the *Universal Declaration of Human Rights (UDHR)*,[2] is the right to freedom from arbitrary arrest, detention or exile.[3] Despite its listing in *UDHR*, in many countries people are in practice exposed to arbitrary arrest, detention and exile. It would be rash to assert that more people have a remedy should they be the victims of arbitrary arrest etc than have not. That being so, can we plausibly affirm that a citizen has a right against his state and its rulers not to be subjected to arbitrary arrest, detention or exile? Or is the truth that, whereas we can give reasons, perhaps cogent, for the view that states *should* recognize that right and provide remedies for its violation, the claim to be free from arbitrary arrest is in many countries no more than an aspiration? Perhaps a well-supported aspiration, but not a right.

An intelligible answer will have to begin by specifying the conception of a right on which it is based. The conception from which I start builds on that of Raz:[4] that for a right to exist the potential rightholder must have an interest weighty enough to provide a sufficient[5] reason for holding some other person to

*Regius Professor of Civil Law, University of Oxford.

1 Paper given at a conference on Criminal Justice and Human Rights, Buenos Aires, 14–16 April 1987.

2 General Assembly of the United Nations, 10 December 1948.

3 *UDHR*, art 9.

4 'Legal Rights', 4 *Oxford J Legal Stud* (1984) 1, 5.

5 Raz says 'sufficient', which in the context means, I think, sufficient as a matter of policy or of moral justification. This leaves open whether conditions other than the weight of the interest to be protected must be satisfied before we conclude that a person not merely ought to have a right but actually has one.

have a duty towards him. On this view the substantive debate about a given right will be concerned with what counts for this purpose as a sufficient reason and whether such a reason exists in the case of the interest which the right is meant to protect. At this first stage of the argument, however, I concentrate not on the substantive reasons for asserting the existence of a right but rather on what may be termed its scaffolding. In this regard we should, I believe, add to the criteria mentioned by Raz. In order to keep firm the distinction, so telling in practice, between rights and aspirations, two further related items are needed to prevent the structure of a right from collapse: *recognition* and *remedy*. First, the right must be recognized, generally by the society within which it is asserted, but sometimes only by members of a wider society. Secondly, if the right is violated, there must be a remedy for that violation. *Ubi ius, ibi remedium* is more than a legal tag. If there were (primary) rights without remedies the rightholder would in the last resort be a mere critic: he could properly condemn the violation of his interests but no more. Unless pressure can be brought to bear on violators, so-called rights are naked and unprotected; and an unprotected right is no more a right than is an unprotected fortress a fortress. The same is true, *mutatis mutandis*, of the corresponding duties.

These two elements, recognition and remedy, the latter of which presupposes the former, serve to distinguish a right from even a justified aspiration. This does not entail, however, that a right requires to be *officially* recognized or endowed with a *formal* remedy. True, if the state affirms the existence of the alleged right and provides legal remedies for its breach, it thereby does one of two things. It either creates a new right which is from the beginning formal or turns an existing informal right into a formal one. But, short of formal recognition, there can be informal, non-institutional rights, which may be purely moral, social or political. They too, according to the conception here adopted, require to be recognized and backed by a remedy; but the recognition and remedy, like the right, can be informal. For example private convention may attest the existence of a moral right and informal social pressure serve to support it. The same is true *mutatis mutandis* of political rights which rest on the political culture of a society, its public conventions and modes of argument.

I. WHAT SORT OF RIGHT IS THE RIGHT TO REBEL, IF IT EXISTS?

So much, in brief, for rights in general. The subject of this article is a specific right, the alleged right of subjects, given certain conditions, to rebel against their rulers.[6] The right to rebel has not been much discussed by recent writers, though it was a familiar enough topic in earlier centuries. For this and other reasons it may be well to define it at the outset. But as the definition incorporates

6 The term 'subject' here includes both citizens and non-citizens such as aliens and slaves.

the main justifying aims of a rebellion, it presupposes a certain structure of theory.

I mean then by the right to rebel *the right of an individual or group to resort to violence, if necessary on a large scale, in order either*

(a) to secure on behalf of individuals or groups conceived as exploited or oppressed a change in the government, structure or policies of the society to which they belong (radical rebellion), or

(b) to resist on behalf of individuals or groups who are attached to their way of life a change in the government, structure or policies of their society which the rulers of the society intend to bring about (conservative rebellion), or

(c) to secure on behalf of a group conceived as distinct the right to independence from the society to which it at present belongs (rebellion in aid of self-determination).

Some preliminary remarks about the character of this right will be in order. If it exists—and for purposes of exposition I assume that it does—it is of a special sort. For it is a right to commit acts which are almost certainly unlawful and probably criminal by the standards of the state against which the rebellion is directed.[7] These unlawful acts will sometimes be acts, for example shooting people or planting bombs, which by some moral theories are in all circumstances forbidden. Is it even worth discussing the possible existence of a right which gets off to so dubious a start?[8] Is the topic interesting only psychologically rather than from a legal or moral point of view? Ought we rather to be asking what motives impel people to rebel? What role rebellion can play in the emancipation of an individual? Is there not something absurd in solemnly assessing from the safety of an armchair or computer screen the predicament of one impelled by passionate commitment to defy the state at the risk of his life? Even if his situation is a proper subject of evaluation, can it be assessed from any point of view other than that of its likely consequences? Does it make sense to speak of a *right* to rebel, to which will presumably correspond a duty on the part of the state not to resist the rebellion, and on third parties to help the rebels, or at least not to obstruct them?

There are reasons to think that it does. Potential rebels often put to themselves the question whether they have a right, or even duty, to rebel; and some find the search for the answer intractable and even agonizing. True, other rebels are concerned only to calculate whether the likely benefits of their action outweigh the dangers. Others again are moved to take the plunge by the prospect of an exciting or liberating experience. Yet others are swept up in a gust of Mazzinian enthusiasm. But to many those issues and motives are

7 The term 'state' here includes provinces and other subdivisions of sovereign states and such political entities as international agencies.

8 E.g. Georges Sorel, *Reflections on Violence* (ed Collier 1961), 59, 'I am not at all concerned to justify the perpetrators of violence, but to inquire into the function of violence of the working class in contemporary socialism'.

subsidiary. To them the crucial question is whether it is ever right to make war on certain of one's fellow citizens. To some it would seem obvious that the answer must be 'No'. But on reflection it is arguable that, given certain conditions, there is indeed a right to rebel, a right which has some claim to a recognized place in international law and political morality. It possesses a plausible theoretical basis in peremptory notions of human dignity, autonomy and co-operative morality. Its claims are worth examining.

A second point about the right to rebel as defined above is that it covers a wide range of acts of political violence. It can inhere either in an individual or a group, since either an individual or a group can have an interest which justifies the imposition of a duty on others. If it pertains to an individual it can therefore inhere in him either as such or as a member of a group. Thus, take a society in which smallholders are exploited. The right to rebel on the ground of exploitation may inhere in an individual exploited smallholder as such, given that the exploitation is a grave violation of his interests, or in a smallholder who is not exploited but who is a member of the class which, taken as a whole, is exploited. On the other hand the right to rebel on the ground of self-determination, though it too can inhere in an individual, can do so only by virtue of his membership of a group which constitutes a unit of self-determination. An individual cannot by himself have a right to self-determination, but he may have a right to rebel by virtue of his membership of a group (e.g. Palestinians) which has such a right.

In contrast a collective or group right to rebel can be of two sorts. It may be the sum of individual rights, for example those of a number of oppressed people, such as foreign workers, who possess similar interests. In that case an individual foreign worker may have a right to rebel even though it would be unwise, perhaps even wrong,[9] for him to exercise that right unless many others were ready to join him and there were some prospect of success. Alternatively the collective right can, like the right of self-determination, be a right which inheres exclusively in a large number of people.

Again, the right to rebel can be *exercised* in a proper case by an individual either on his own behalf or on behalf of a group, and in the latter case either at its behest or not. Thus in some conditions an isolated individual may be entitled to use force against the state, for example by killing a tyrant. It is arguable that anyone would have been justified in killing Hitler; and it may even be said that those who had the opportunity and failed to take it showed a want of courage. That isolated act would have counted on my definition as an act of rebellion. Indeed even the exercise of a collective right to rebel need not demand mass action, though it may need mass support. Urban guerilla warfare, for example, which can be conducted by a few individuals or small groups on behalf of a mass movement, falls within the conception of rebellion here presented.

9 It can sometimes be wrong to exercise a right; that notion underlies the doctrine of abuse of right.

Thirdly, a rebellion can on the definition set out have one of three justifying aims. The aim may be the radical one of changing or the conservative one of preventing change in an existing society. Alternatively the goal may be to break away from an existing society and create a new one. Of this more later. A fourth point is that on my definition revolution counts as a species of rebellion. Leaving aside the possibility of a peaceful revolution, the word normally designates a rebellion which results in drastic social or political change. Hence a revolutionary aim may require a stronger justification than a conservative or less radical aim. Forms of upheaval which are likely to involve widespread violence and disruption, and which in the event often change things for the worse, are to be contemplated only in extreme cases. But rebels can cause a revolution without aiming at one. For example at the inception of the French revolution virtually no reformer wanted to abolish the monarchy, still less to introduce a system of terror or a programme of conquest. Whatever is to be said about the right to rebel must take account of the fact that rebels are often in no position accurately to forecast the outcome of their actions.

So much for the definition. How does the right to rebel, so defined, fit the structure of rights previously outlined? That structure was designed to explain primary rights, which are antecedent to and independent of the commission of a wrong by another. The right to rebel, however, must be a secondary rather than a primary right. It exists only when a wrong has been committed. Its point is to provide a remedy in the event of the violation on a large scale of primary rights like the right to freedom from arbitrary arrest. The sustained denial of those rights may arguably amount to such oppression or exploitation as justifies rebellion. If, therefore, subjects have in certain conditions a right to rebel, the existence of that right can be used to support the view that, as *UDHR* asserts, they really possess rights such as the right to freedom from arbitrary arrest, detention and exile. Their claim to them does more than express a justified aspiration.

This will be true even if there is no one-to-one correlation between, say, wrongful arrest and the right to rebel. For in regard to informal rights, it need not be the case that there is a simple correlation such as exists between a breach of contract and an action for damages viz that when a party to a contract commits a breach of it which results in loss, he is *ipso facto* liable to an action for damages. The right to rebel could instead provide the steady 'background radiation' that is needed to shore up the whole range of human rights against the state, of which the right to freedom from arbitrary arrest is one. This could be the case even though it is not true that, whenever the state breaches a particular human right, the injured party has a consequent right to rebel. Hence, if there is a right to rebel, freedom from arbitrary arrest can be accounted a right even though neither the state which makes a practice of arbitrary arrest nor the international order of which that state is a member formally provides a remedy for the victims of such arrests.

In sum, given that there is a right in certain conditions to rebel, the citizen's right to freedom from arbitrary arrest fits the conception of a right already stated. He has

(i) an interest in freedom from arbitrary arrest which (we will assume) justifies the imposition on sovereign states of an obligation to refrain from it. That interest is

(ii) recognized by member states of the UN and subscribers to *UDHR* as imposing on them a duty to respect and give effect to that right. It is true that *UDHR*, though it serves as an aid to the interpretation of the UN charter, is not technically part of international law. But that merely shows that the right in question is not a formal right. Freedom from arbitrary arrest is a formal right in some systems of municipal law but not in all. Neither is it a formal right in international law. But for the victim to have a right, albeit informal, recognition by the political morality of the international community is an important asset. For

(iii) given that recognition, the right to rebel supplies the missing element in the structure of the right to freedom from arbitrary arrest and detention and of other human rights. It supplies a potential remedy for the violation of that primary right, even if resort to the remedy is not always justified, and will in any event often have to be rejected as imprudent or impracticable. That is after all often the case with legal, moral and political remedies for the violation of rights. There are many reasons why a customer should decide not to sue a supplier for breach of contract, even when he has the right to do so. But it is crucial to the protection to his interests that, if driven to it, he *could* sue. In like manner, pending a suitable occasion for the exercise of the right to rebel, should it prove necessary, it is of great importance to the rightholder that he has a *potential* remedy in the form of rebellion. In the meantime he can remind his state, its rulers and those officials who violate this and other rights that if they continue on their present course they run the risk of justifying the rebellion they are likely in the long run to provoke.

The question whether in certain conditions there is a right to rebel is important from another point of view. Rebellion cuts near the bone. People who combine courage with sensibility can face a dilemma of the following sort. Are they in certain conditions entitled and even bound to join a movement dedicated to the violent overthrow of the state (say the ANC, PLO or IRA), the violent defence of the status quo (say a militant Protestant organization in Northern Ireland or a similar Afrikaner group in South Africa) or the violent assertion of a right of self-determination (say the Tamil Eelams in Sri Lanka)? Is it sometimes their right or duty to plant bombs? If it is, no doubt they must observe the same restraints as in a war between states; but even so some of those killed or maimed will inevitably be innocent, unless bare membership of an obnoxious class, religion or race is to count as guilt. If on the other hand citizens do not in any circumstances have the right to rebel there is ultimately no way in which they can vindicate for themselves and others those items which are listed as human rights in documents such as *UDHR*. In that case would it not be better frankly to concede that there are no human rights? Or at any rate no rights of this sort, viz rights against states as opposed to rights against the world-wide human community, supposing that there is one,[10] and against human beings as members of that community? We will then be driven to confess that in the late twentieth century citizens remain in the limbo to which Kant consigned them when he asserted that it was the duty of the people to bear any abuse of the supreme power, even though it should be considered to be intolerable.[11]

II. DOES IT EXIST?

In the seventeenth and eighteenth centuries the problem of the right to rebel was widely discussed. In recent years it has been a little neglected. The exceptions include a masterpiece. In *L'homme revolté* (1951), Camus meditates on 'crimes of logic', premeditated killings in the cause of revolt or revolution for which a systematic philosophical justification is adduced. Can the love of humanity justify massacres? Are the innocent, the moment they decide to act, committed to violence? Camus rejects systematic justifications, such as those advanced by certain Marxists; and though he treats revolt as a demonstration that human existence is not absurd, he eschews the self-indulgent view which would justify rebellion as a means of becoming truly human. He appeals in the end to a moral rule, grounded in human nature, which requires those who are conscious that their situation is intolerable, and so have already escaped from despair, to act according to that perception.[12] In a lesser key Ted Honderich's *Three Essays on Political Violence* (1976) bravely attempt to spell out when if ever in a democratic state political violence can be justified. He concludes that in certain conditions only acts of political violence can effectively serve the ends of approximate equality and uncoerced influence on decision making which he sees as essential to democracy. Some bombs are like votes, but votes which kill and maim. Honderich's argument is directed more towards the use of violence to draw attention to injustices than as an instrument of rebellion; and the aims which he regards as sufficient to justify violence in a democratic society seem to me insufficient to justify rebellion. There is, however, a part of his argument which corresponds to mine. Suppose there are good reasons to believe that that certain political aims are of compelling value. Given that assurance, what may in the last resort justify violence or rebellion is that only the use of force gives hope

10 On which see my *Making Law Bind* (1987), ch 11.

11 Kant, *Metaphysische Anfangsgründe der Rechtslehre* (2nd ed 1798), 206. The note on 207–9 implicitly modifies this harsh view. Rebels who bring pressure on a monarch to abdicate can rely on the defence of necessity, provided they do not use violence against his person, but have no right to punish the former monarch for his oppressive rule.

12 Op cit, 310–14.

of achieving those aims within a reasonable span of time. Like Camus, Honderich seems to be making an important point. But, penetrating as are their contributions, these authors are exceptions. Most theorists, no doubt dismayed by the tempestuous landscape of violence, opt for the pacific pastures of the nearly just society.

In what follows I heed Honderich's stricture that 'just about all political philosophy of the recommending kind is factless and presumptuous'.[13] Value judgments, which to some will smack of presumption, are inevitable. But the discussion can remain close to experience if we sprinkle it with examples, historical and contemporary.

Do subjects, then, have the right to rebel against their states, their rulers and their fellow-citizens? If so, in what circumstances? The hypothetical right to rebel presents complications from the point of view of all three elements which were taken to be necessary to the existence of a right: (a) Can the interest of citizens in achieving their aims justify recourse to violence on their part? If so, does it follow that the authorities against whom the rebellion is directed are disentitled to defend themselves?[14] Do outsiders have a duty to aid, or at least not to obstruct, the rebellion? (b) Is the right recognized and, if so, by whom? (c) Can there be a remedy for the violation of the right to rebel, or would such a remedy lead to a regress?

It is convenient to deal with these points in reverse order. The last question (c) can be shortly answered. There is no *remedy* for violation of the right to rebel, unless perhaps a later rebellion succeeds where the first one failed. Rebellion is the ultimate sanction for the violation of other rights, but to rebel is to play the last card. If the rebel fails, he may argue that he was justified in doing so. He may appeal for sympathy in his predicament. But there is no further remedial right to which he can appeal. The right to rebel differs from other rights in that it is ultimate and so peculiarly dangerous to exercise. It is no use rebels demanding a receipt in advance, as the peasants did of Kropotkin when he wanted them to ferry him across a half-frozen river.[15] 'What sort of receipt do you want?' 'Well, you write on a paper "I, the undersigned hereby testify that I was drowned by the will of God, and through no fault of the peasants", and you sign this paper, "With pleasure", on the other side.'

Some may conclude that, because of its uncertainty and the lack of further recourse, the right to rebel cannot count as a right. It depends on the point of view we adopt. Viewed from within a scheme of rights, some right for which there is no remedy has to function as the ultimate sanction, and the right to rebel fulfils this role. Viewed from outside, sociologically, rebellion is simply a danger

13 *Three Essays On Political Violence* (1976), 1.

14 The point could arise in the following way. I am punished for a justified but unsuccessful attempt to rebel. A later rebellion overthrows the oppressive regime. Can I now properly claim to be compensated for the earlier violation of my right to rebel?

15 P. Kropotkin, *Memoirs of a Revolutionist* (1899).

of which states should take account. The conclusion must be that the right to rebel is a right, but not in the same sense as are other rights. Rebellion is both the last resort and the ultimate gamble.

It is different as regards (b) *recognition*. Sovereign states can hardly be expected as a matter of course to grant their subjects a right to secede or rebel. Still, they sometimes do so. The *Declaration of American Independence*—a formal statement of a political point of view, it is true, rather than a state document—asserts that, whenever a form of government is destructive of the ends for which government is instituted, 'it is the right of the people to alter or abolish it'. Formal provisions of like sort featured in the state constitutions of New Hampshire, Pennsylvania and Delaware. Magna Carta, clause 61, authorized a committee of barons to seize King John's castles if he should fail to observe the terms of the charter. Admittedly constitutional documents are rarely as weak-kneed as this. Later editions of Magna Carta omit the rebellion clause. The US constitution, unlike the Declaration of Independence, makes no mention of the right to rebel or secede. Hence at the time of the civil war the north could argue that the southern states had no right to break away, the latter on the contrary that they might lawfully do so. On the other hand the constitution of the German Federal Republic concedes to citizens, including officials, a right to resist any attempt to subvert the democratic foundations of the state. This explicit recognition of a right of resistance (*Widerstandsrecht*),[16] first by certain Länder, then by a constitutional amendment of 1968, was clearly prompted by reflection on the circumstances in which the Nazis had come to power. Obviously the means by which the private citizen or official exercises his *Widerstandsrecht* can and normally will involve the use of force. All the same, sovereign states can seldom be expected to admit the constitutional right of their citizens to rebel. The international order, though based on state sovereignty, is less constrained. It concedes, at least by implication, the right of a colony, dependent territory or subdivision of a state to rebel in the cause of self-determination.[17] More broadly, it sees a link between the denial of human rights and rebellion. Though the right to rebel is not listed in *UDHR*, the preamble to that document says that 'it is essential, if man is not to be *compelled to have recourse as a last resort to rebellion against tyranny and oppression*, that human rights [e.g. the right of freedom from arbitrary arrest] should be protected by the rule of law'. Of course this clause can be taken in more than one way. It could be meant simply to warn states how best to avoid rebellion. Indeed *UDHR* as a whole could be thus restrictively interpreted. It might, despite its terms, be intended to confer rights not on individual citizens but exclusively on states.

16 Grundgesetz art 20 (4). The right is available against those who undertake to destroy the constitutional (viz free and democratic) order, provided that other means of resistance (*andere Abhilfe*) are not available. It can be exercised only in order to preserve, not to change that order.

17 *Declaration on the granting of independence to colonial countries and peoples*, UN General Assembly Resolution 1514 (XV), 14 December 1960.

These would then be entitled to complain about the conduct of other states in disregarding what are misleadingly listed as human rights. So interpreted, the point of *UDHR* would be that the violation of the interests which it calls human rights is likely to provoke international unrest and so indirectly to threaten even those states in which the interests in question are respected.

But a different interpretation is more plausible. *UDHR* can be seen as declaring that subjects have certain rights against their governments. These rights are to be enforced, however, not directly by the subjects themselves but indirectly through other states and their citizens, who will bring pressure to bear on the offending state. As always when people who have interests are for some reason incapable of asserting them effectively, for instance because they are young children or detainees, their interests can only be interpreted as rights if there is someone in a position to assert those rights on their behalf.[18] Campaigns on behalf of detainees and dissidents often conform to this pattern.

But suppose the campaigns in favour of those who are denied human rights are ineffective. Surely the implication must be that the citizens to whom human rights are conceded and whom *UDHR* says may be *compelled* as a last resort to rebel are not merely to be excused when their patience snaps but are justified in rebelling. And if the moral justification for doing so consists in the fact that rebellion is the only means by which they can in the last resort assert their humanity, defend their way of life or vindicate their independence, does it not follow that they have a *right to rebel*? It is not merely that they regard themselves as justified because they see no alternative, or that the consequences of rebellion appear preferable to those of passive resistance, but that they have a right which others are bound to respect and which entitles them to the help, or at least the neutrality, of those who are not party to the dispute. Would it make sense to deny someone the right to do what he is compelled to do in the sense not of being coerced but of having no other means of vindicating his fundamental interests? Does not almost everyone, if the dilemma is presented, recognize such a right? To deny it would be to assert that people may be bound indefinitely to submit to conditions of life which we and they recognize as intolerable; that their interests may properly be disregarded and they themselves treated as unworthy of respect.

It seems to me, therefore, that in a proper case there *must* be a right to rebel. It will not generally be a formal legal right, but neither is it a purely informal right grounded in the conventional morality of the international community. It possesses an intermediate, semi-formal status. It is based, that is, both on a certain conception of human dignity and on an interpretation of the political norms of the international community, including the principles, embodied in documents, which members of that community have endorsed.

That the right to rebel is recognized at least in one class of case by the norms of the international society of states is suggested by the UN *Declaration on*

18 Honoré, *Making Law Bind* (1987), 251–5.

Principles of International Law (1970).[19] This claims to embody basic principles of international law and makes an appeal to states to be guided by these principles. Legally it constitutes, at the minimum, an aid to the interpretation of the UN Charter. Under it every state has a duty to refrain from organizing civil dissension and terrorist acts in another state. But the 'subjection of peoples to alien subjugation, domination and exploitation constitutes a violation of the principle' of equal rights and self-determination of peoples. Every state must therefore refrain from forcible action which deprives peoples of their right of self-determination. In resisting such forcible action in pursuit of the right of self-determination peoples are entitled to seek and receive support in accordance with the principles of the UN Charter.

The Declaration is careful to condemn the dismemberment of states which respect the principle of self-determination. But if they do not, it implies that the group which forms a unit of self-determination can resort to force to make good their right. It then becomes wrongful for the state against which the right of self-determination is exercised to use force to prevent its exercise. In plain words, which, to avoid embarrassment, the document sedulously avoids, the right of self-determination can be vindicated by rebellion. The right of a former colony to independence is a striking, but not the only, instance of a just claim which will in a proper case yield a right to rebel.

It therefore seems that the case for the right to rebel manages to surmount the hurdle of recognition. The international society of sovereign states indirectly but, in the case of self-determination, unequivocally concedes its existence.

III. WHAT AIMS CAN JUSTIFY REBELLION?

More difficult, though crucial, is question (a) viz whether there can sometimes be a justification for rebellion. Justification is needed both for the pursuit of certain aims and for the use of violent means to achieve them. The case for rebellion will fail if either the end or the means cannot be upheld.

I begin therefore with ends or aims, and first discuss the aim which is most clearly recognized in international political morality: (i) One aim of rebellion is to assert the autonomy of a group, its right to determine its own form of government and destiny. How to decide whether a group is entitled if it wishes to become a sovereign state, whether it constitutes a 'unit of self-determination', is a difficult matter. So far as colonies are concerned, it is generally recognized that they are, on the basis of self-determination, entitled to freedom *vis-à-vis* the colonizing power. In other instances the elements of self-determination are controversial. This is not the place to discuss them in detail, but only to sketch a paradigm of the unit in which this right inheres. A group which (i) consciously possesses a certain degree of separateness from its rulers or neighbours as

19 UN General Assembly, 24 October 1970.

regards language, culture, religion, ethnicity, history, topography and social mores, and in addition (ii) is geographically coherent, sufficiently numerous, economically viable and in general has the capacity to assume the responsibilities of a member of the international community, satisfies the paradigm. Often only some of these criteria will be satisfied. Both the degree of separateness of the group and its capacity to form a viable sovereign state are to some extent matters of degree on which judgments may properly differ. But, granted the existence of a unit of self-determination, all its members need appeal to, to establish their right to independence, is their wish to be autonomous. For example Scotland could clearly claim the right to form an independent state if the great majority of its inhabitants so wished. The Scots would not have to show that their existing form of government as part of the United Kingdom was oppressive, save in that it denied them autonomy. In other respects it might be a better government than the newly independent state was likely to enjoy. This is recognized in the case of ex-colonies, which accordingly have a right to independence irrespective of whether they would be better governed, autonomy apart, if the colonizing power remained in charge.

Why do some groups possess the right to self-determination while others, which, though culturally distinct, lack the capacity to act as viable sovereign states, do not? The explanation must surely reside in the judgment that, however distinct the group, the international community is entitled, before conceding the group's claim to sovereignty, to take account of the likely impact of the new state on the international community. If the new state would be unmanageable, or disruptive of international order, a source of misery to the group claiming freedom or to other states, the claim of the group to self-determination will properly be rejected. The existing members of the international society of sovereign states can refuse to admit new members who do not satisfy certain internal and external criteria of viability. The club can insist on qualifications for admission.

But the argument for a right to rebel is often not, or not merely, based on the aim of group autonomy. It may be predicated solely or mainly on misgovernment, oppression, tyranny or exploitation on the part of the rulers. Complaints on this score take one of two forms, conservative or radical.

I begin with conservative rebellion, since there is a connection between this sort of rebellion and rebellion on the score of self-determination. Groups often contemplate rebellion in order, as they see it, to preserve the status quo. It is in this way that Locke presents the case for the revolution of 1688. That event, he says, took place because the rebels perceived that James II and his government were conspiring by stealth to reintroduce Roman Catholicism ('that religion underhand favoured though publicly proclaimed against') as the state religion.[20] Again, the American Declaration of Independence took note of a train of abuses

20 *Second Treatise on Government* s 207, 210.

and usurpations by the British, pursuing invariably the same object, that of subjecting the colonists to 'absolute despotism'. Perhaps the colonists would have preferred to rely on the right of self-determination had that then been part of the political vocabulary. The southern states which seceded from the US in 1860–1 proffered similar arguments. The people of the north had assumed a revolutionary posture towards them, enticing away slaves and obstructing their return under the fugitive slave law. They permitted the open establishment of abolition societies. Again, as with the revolt of the American colonists, had the southern states been able to appeal to a right of self-determination they would have had a powerful case. It might no doubt have been answered by the argument that the common language and historical origin of north and south outweighed their cultural differences, or by the Burkean argument that a choice of government, once made, (e.g. in 1688) cannot be revised. But why should the right to choose a form of government be like a bee sting, which can be used once only? In any event, the creeping abolitionism of which the southern states complained parallels the creeping catholicism of James II and the creeping despotism of George III. Even today the cause of conservative rebellion is alive. Certain white groups in South Africa contemplate with dismay what they see as President Botha's creeping majoritarianism: a political programme which to them appears as a series of manoeuvres intended to edge the country towards the unavowed goal of black majority rule. While this paper was being delivered certain elements in the Argentinian army rebelled against what they perceived as the attempt of the civilian government to assert their subjection to the rule of law and in particular to try those officers who had tortured and murdered citizens during the period of military rule between 1976 and 1983. Whether or not these particular perceptions were accurate, the important question is whether the preservation of a status quo, oppressive to English catholics in 1688, American slaves in 1860, to black South Africans and civilian Argentinians in 1987, can justify rebellion.

The right claimed by conservative rebels is a right of collective self-defence, broadly conceived. If we provisionally accept that there may be such a right, analogy would suggest that its exercise is subject to two conditions. First, it is available only when less violent remedies are unavailable or have been exhausted. This is an important restriction because it is generally both incumbent on the potential rebels and possible for them to resort to a whole series of steps—peaceful protests, recourse to law, the exercise of civil rights, political propaganda, passive resistance and non-violent disobedience—before embarking on rebellion. It is true that the case for the exhaustion of peaceful remedies before there is recourse to violence cannot be pressed beyond certain limits. Account must be taken of whether some irreversible step, which would permanently change the character of the society, is in prospect. Thus, if the rulers are about to invite a foreign state to send in troops whom it will then be impossible to dislodge within the foreseeable future, the prospective rebels cannot be required to stand idly by while peaceful means of protest, illusory in the circumstances, are exhausted. But when nothing irreversible is in prospect the rebels have a duty to resort in the first instance to constitutional methods, or if these are unavailing, civil disobedience and passive resistance. In 1860 the southern states of the USA enjoyed a degree of legal protection which by itself must have invalidated their claim to be entitled to rebel in defence of a slave society. For they were in a position to bar any constitutional amendment proposed by the north and so could have defeated any constitutional attempt to abolish slavery. Had the north somehow circumvented these provisions Lincoln himself recognized their moral right to revolt.[21]

Secondly, in order to justify a conservative rebellion the rebels must show that the threat apprehended is grave and urgent or can reasonably be interpreted as such. In the present South African context the diagnosis which attributes to President Botha a programme of creeping majoritarianism is plainly mistaken. It does not represent a rational interpretation of his speeches and actions or those of his supporters. On that ground alone a hypothetical rebellion in aid of the white South African way of life can be stigmatized as unjustified. Of course those who wrongly conceive themselves to be threatened with unacceptable change or who overlook alternative remedies may in fact resort to rebellion. But the fact that rebellion may appear justified to the rebels does not give them the *right* to rebel. Their rebellion will be interpreted by the sympathetic but rational observer as the reaction, understandable but mistaken, of people who wrongly suppose that they have no other choice.

Grant, however, that in a given case the threat is a real one and that other remedies have been exhausted. Is the claim to a right of collective self-defence on behalf of a certain, perhaps privileged, way of life then morally convincing? Does its cogency depend on the sort of culture that is being defended? Must we, before deciding whether there is a right to rebel, first ascertain whether the rebellion is intended to preserve a nearly just or a notably unjust society?

It would be a mistake to shirk the issue of which rebellions are just and which unjust merely because the problem is politically so prickly. Why should a group not collectively have a right to defend the way of life to which it is used and which it values? Surely the right of self-defence must extend to all the main interests of the person seeking to defend himself. If so, it must extend to his membership of a society the special and distinct features of which may be central to his sense of identity. After all, the case for self-determination itself rests precisely on certain assumptions about the value of what may be called *collective domesticity*. The enduring strength of nationalism shows what weight most people attach to belonging to a coherent and distinct collectivity. If it is in order for a sufficiently distinct group, provided that certain criteria of viability

21 President Lincoln, First Inaugural: 'If by the mere force of numbers a majority should deprive a minority of any clearly written constitutional right, it might in a moral point of view justify revolution . . .'.

are satisfied, to claim as of right an independent society in which their separate culture can flourish, it must be equally in order for them to seek to preserve a distinctive way of life which is threatened with evisceration or extinction.

But does this give a group of whose culture the exploitation of others is a central feature a collective right of self-defence? Can a collective way of life be so oppressive to others (e.g. Catholics, slaves, black South Africans) that rebellion in defence of it, though understandable, cannot morally be justified? In defence of the oppressive society it can be argued that even the worst of men has a right to defend himself. When I argued that anyone who had the opportunity would have been justified in killing Hitler, I was not denying that Hitler would have been entitled to defend himself against assassination—though not of course against the loss of those powers which he had used to oppress others. Some elements of the right to defend one's life and basic interests are exempt from forfeiture, however evil one may be. Even the Hitlers and the Eichmanns are human beings, not things. That we judge this to be the case is reflected in the fact that in western legal culture those guilty of even serious crimes like murder are not bound to give themselves up, to preserve the evidence of their guilt or in general to make it easy for the state to secure a conviction. They are entitled, for example, to conceal their whereabouts, to hide from the police. If charged, they can insist that the prosecution prove its case. In some states they have a constitutional right against self-incrimination. Though they may ultimately gain credit for confession or contrition neither is a duty. On the contrary they retain the right to defend themselves as they see fit even though in doing so they violate the immediate interests of the society to which they belong.

But this limited right of self-defence does not extend to a right to use force against the lawful authorities. Though the right of self-defence continues in those who know themselves to be guilty, it is now limited in scope. It becomes a passive rather than an active right.

In like manner, though Hitler had a right to defend himself he did not have a right to exploit anyone else. He and his cronies were not entitled to continue their destructive rule. We cannot therefore solve the problem of conservative rebellion simply by saying that conservative groups have a right to defend their own way of life. We must distinguish, if possible, between those societies which it is legitimate to defend and those of which this is not true, since one of their central features is the exploitation of others. In the end there is no way of avoiding the intractable problem of what constitutes a destructive, tyrannical, oppressive, or exploitative regime. The answer will throw light on both conservative and radical rebellions, since the factors which make the preservation of an existing way of life indefensible are likely to be the same as, or very similar to, those which justify radical forms of rebellion.

It is exploitation or oppression that disqualifies conservative and qualifies radical rebellion. By common consent the exploitation or oppression must be such as to render life under the existing ruler, government or policy intolerable.

The exploited or oppressed may then, in the absence of an effective structure of legal, democratic and representative institutions, have little chance of securing tolerable reforms within the foreseeable future. Rebellion is then justified in order to secure a change of ruler and/or government and/or policy. But what counts as exploitation for this purpose? And who judges whether the situation is intolerable?

The question can only sensibly be discussed on the assumption that, contrary to Kant's view,[22] states have duties towards their citizens and citizens rights against their states. Kant's arguments against the existence of such rights and duties are weak. He thinks that citizens have no rights against the state, since only through submission to the universal legislative will can law and order be maintained. But in modern practice countries with Bills of Rights, and many without them, allow citizens to protect their interests by pursuing claims against the state.[23] In particular Kant asserts that for a sovereign to grant his subjects a right to resist is self-contradictory,[24] since it requires (i) that the supreme legislation should contain a provision to the effect that it is not the supreme legislation, and (ii) that subjects should be entitled to judge the authority to whom they are subject. But though it may be unwise for the supreme law of a state to grant a constitutional right of resistance, the notion is not incoherent. The constitution of the German Federal Republic, we saw, grants citizens a right to rebel against a threatened suppression of constitutional rule,[25] and the right to rebel in the cause of self-determination is implicitly recognized by most states, at least in their capacity as members of the international community.

Kant's third argument is that rebellion could be justified only if the rebels were as strong as or stronger than the Supreme Power, i.e. the lawful authorities.[26] In that case the rebels would already have displaced or be about to displace the lawful authorities. The rebels would in their turn have become the Supreme Power. This argument goes, however, not to the justification of the right to rebel, but rather to the wisdom of choosing a particular moment for a showdown with the lawful authorities. It assumes that there can be no right to rebel at the time when the potential rebels are building up their strength and trying to undermine that of the state. Kant is in effect arguing that Might is Right. He endorses resistance to authority, but only when it is already successful or on the verge of success. He does not explain why oppressed citizens who are not yet in a position to challenge the state head on are not

22 Op cit, 204. Kant does not say that states have no duties to their citizens but that they have no *mandatory* duties: *der Herrscher im Staate hat gegen den Untertan lauter Rechte und keine (Zwangs-) Pflichten*.

23 Good discussion in T. H. Green, *Lectures on the Principles of Political Obligation* (1882) ss 137–145: 'Has the citizen rights against the state?'.

24 Op cit, 205, 207.

25 Above n 16.

26 Op cit, 205.

justified in resorting to passive resistance or to a lesser degree of force, short of an all-out confrontation. Why should they not do this in order to win support and by degrees to build up their power so that in the end it equals or surpasses that of their opponents?

Assuming then that the state or community can have duties towards citizens, and that the right to rebel depends on a serious violation of these duties, how is the content of the obligation to be settled? The duties of the state to its citizens can be conceived either as contractual obligations embodied in an institutional framework or as duties inherent in the nature of a co-operative enterprise to which the institutional framework may give expression. Locke's contractual theory leads to a somewhat legalistic construction of the right to rebel. The citizen may oppose by force nothing but unjust and unlawful force on the part of the government.[27] It is true that 'unlawful force' in Locke's exposition includes breach of trust and the exercise of arbitrary power contrary to the laws enacted by the legislature. But this makes the legislature, which is assumed to be responsive to the interests of citizens, the ultimate arbiter of state duty. It leaves citizens unprotected against legislative tyranny. Whether subjects are oppressed or exploited cannot depend simply on whether the rulers have broken laws enacted by the legislature. It may be that the rulers have manipulated the legislature so that it has enacted tyrannical laws. This is not to deny that illegal conduct by the authorities often points to exploitation, which in turn justifies rebellion. But this will be because in violating the law the rulers breach duties laid, irrespective of legislation, on all those who rule towards those over whom they have power.

What are these duties? It is easier to answer if we think of the state as engaged with its subjects in a far-ranging cooperative enterprise which in modern conditions covers most aspects of human well-being. The state whose duties we are trying to elucidate is not a minimal Nozickian state, of which there are few or no examples at the present day, but one which commands a major part of the resources of the community and has assumed far-reaching responsibilities towards it. The duties of this type of state to its subjects can be thought of as analogous to those of parents who are charged with fulfilling the basic needs of their family and dealing justly with their children. These guiding notions of need and justice contain both fixed and variable elements. Though conceptions of both vary between and within societies, there are certain goods—enough food to eat—which in all communities represent basic needs and others—the equal claim to security in life, body and property—which reflect the minimum demands of justice. A state which neglects its duty to provide these goods runs the risk that there will come a point at which it is no longer entitled to the allegiance of its subjects or some of them. But when exactly is that point reached?

27 Op cit, s 204.

I have in an earlier essay[28] proposed that, to justify withdrawal or rebellion, the state's breach of duty must be *weighty, crucial and severe*. These words are chosen, however inadequately, to make the point that, to justify rebellion, the respects in which a citizen complains of the state's dereliction of duty must be important both to him and to the society of which he is part. The dereliction must, that is, relate to matters which (a) are important (weighty) in the society in question and which (b) are felt to be central (crucial) to his interests by the individual who suffers from being deprived of them. Besides this, he must also be affected (c) to a serious (severe) extent, so that in sum his situation becomes unendurable.[29] In some societies, for example, the military are not highly regarded, and it is no great hardship to be barred from becoming a soldier. In others a law which prevented a certain class of person from joining the army would obstruct access to the highest honour and esteem. But even if it did, some people would not care, or not much, that they or others were debarred from a military career. To them, in contrast with those who aspired to be generals, the bar would count as weighty, but not as crucial or severe.

These adjectives being unavoidably imprecise, it may help to express the thought which underlies them from a different angle. Sometimes a state in dealing with its subjects or some of them displays and is reasonably taken as displaying *sustained disinterest or contempt*, just because over a long period it discriminates against them in matters which are known to be weighty to them and to their fellow subjects. In that case it, and those who support it, in effect disclaim the idea that they and those so treated are partners in a common enterprise. A state which behaves in this way towards its subjects, can be said to *oppress* them; and if in addition it profits from their services, it *exploits* them. The existence of such oppression or exploitation can be tested in part by asking whether the disadvantages to which it exposes them are, to use the terms previously mentioned, sufficiently weighty, crucial and severe. If so, the state can be stigmatized for treating its subjects as mere tools to be used for the benefit of the exploiters rather than as persons each of whom is an object of concern both for his own sake and for his contribution to the welfare of others. This explanation is of course still incomplete. What it ultimately appeals to is the duty of the state, as representing the community, to show if not equal concern for all its subjects, at least that substantial concern which is the right of people who are jointly engaged with the rulers in a common enterprise. It is hardly possible to be more precise.

In the upshot it is oppression and exploitation that may justify rebellion and

28 *Making Law Bind* (1987), ch 12.

29 All three elements are present in the judgment, in a different context, in *Goddard* v *Goddard* 118 Atl 2d 906 (1955), where it is held that in a divorce action 'intolerable cruelty' has a subjective as well as an objective significance, and requires not only proof of acts of cruelty but also that in their cumulative effect upon the plaintiff such acts rendered the continuance of marital relations unbearable.

disqualify the defence of a tyrannical way of life. The analysis of these notions concludes our survey of the different aims which may possibly justify people in rebelling. We have in the end three sorts of aim which may qualify (i) the aim of a group which represents a viable political unit to become independent, (ii) the aim of a group which cultivates a distinct and non-exploitative way of life to preserve that way of life, (iii) the aim of citizens oppressed or exploited by their state to escape from an intolerable situation. The first two aims are connected. Both turn on the right of a sufficiently numerous and coherent group to choose and retain the mode of government, manner of life and culture which they prefer. What these two aims seek to protect is an interest in *collective domesticity*. The third aim is different. It seeks to protect the interest we all have in being treated with proper consideration by those who are engaged with us in a common enterprise rather than as tools to be used for their benefit. The interest which is here in issue is an interest in the recognition by the state and its officials that we are participants in the enterprise and as such entitled to a substantial degree of consideration. It is our interest in possessing a *participatory status*.

IV. VIOLENT MEANS

Having discussed the aims which can justify rebellion, I go on to treat of the means which rebels are justified in using. Although it is a matter of definition that in a rebellion the use of violence *may* be justified, it does not follow that those whose aims could potentially justify rebellion endorse, even conditionally, the use of violence. They may instead be (i) constitutionalists of various sorts, (ii) resisters of various sorts, or (iii) rebels who can secure their aims without violence. Of course potential rebels often move by stages from constitutional action to passive resistance and finally to the use of force.

(i) Constitutionalists are those who pursue independence, reform or resistance to change only by the use of constitutional means. Sometimes, as with the independence of Norway from Sweden in 1905 and some instances of decolonization, the constitutional means prove adequate to secure the desired change. Other constitutionalists seek not to secure change by peaceful means but to ensure that the existing constitution is enforced and that the rights listed in it are respected. In eastern Europe most dissidents fall into this class.[30] They engage in propaganda and protest to this end but confine themselves to lawful methods. Themselves lacking constitutional power, they try to exercise the 'power of the powerless'[31] by shaming the authorities, who appeal to the authority of the law, into observing it themselves.

(ii) Resisters go a step further. They are willing to break the law so long as the

30 Vaclav Havel and others, *The Power of the Powerless* (1985).

31 Havel, op cit, 67.

methods employed are non-violent. Their tactics include civil disobedience, passive resistance and non-cooperation. Kant speaks as if any resistance on the part of subjects was incompatible with law and order. But non-cooperation in certain matters is not inconsistent with continued cooperation in others. Resistance can sometimes be effective to secure reform in a society without destabilizing it. Resort to civil disobedience, for example by refusing to obey a call-up for military service, may be a good way of helping to bring an unpopular war to an end or discouraging the use of soldiers to repress the civilian population.

(iii) Some rebels are lucky enough to be able to realize their aim, for instance to escape from an intolerable situation, without the need to use force. A child who rebels against his family may in the last resort simply leave home. He need not set fire to the house or assassinate his parents in order to escape from their clutches. A dissident subject who wishes to be free of the political bonds which oppress him may emigrate; but of course some states forbid or obstruct emigration and some dissidents cannot afford to take the plunge. In any case dissident citizens often aim not at a new domesticity but the reshaping of the old one. So in the end we cannot escape the intractable issue, inherent in the etymological root of rebellion (*bellum*), of the right to make war on one's society. It is one thing to concede that, despite our prima facie duty to obey the law,[32] there are conditions in which we can properly refuse to cooperate and resort to passive resistance or civil disobedience. It is quite another to justify treating members of our society as enemies.

If there is ever a right to do this it must be the sort of right that I have elsewhere termed a *counter-social right*.[33] These rights are intermediate between positive and natural rights. They presuppose a breach of duty by a state or society to its members for which the remedy may take either a passive form like the evasion of military service or the active form of which rebellion presents the clearest example. The breach of duty by the state and its supporters is conceived as relieving the subject of his normal duty of obedience or allegiance either in relation to a particular matter or generally. The breach is the breach not of a contract but of a duty arising out of the common enterprise in which the whole community is engaged. But it possesses in common with contractual obligation the feature that breaches of the duty can be of various degrees of gravity which in turn justify recourse to different remedies. The special feature of the right to rebel as a counter-social right is that it is predicated on a breach of duty on the part of the state so *serious and sustained* that it can properly be treated by the subject, if he so chooses, as dissolving the bonds between them. The use of force then assumes a different aspect. While the bonds were intact the state had the right to define the conditions in which the use of force by either subjects or officials was lawful. The subject might use force either when the law

32 *Making Law Bind* (1987), ch 6.
33 Ibid, 245–251.

expressly gave him power to do so or when officials used force against him in violation of the conditions prescribed by law. But if the officials respected these conditions the subject had no such right. These platitudinous propositions are inherent in the notion of the rule of law.

But when, through a fundamental and sustained breach by the state of its obligations, the subject has the right to treat the bond between himself and the state (as opposed to that which binds him to his fellow subjects) as dissolved, it is no longer open to the state to define the conditions in which subjects may lawfully use force. For the subject in question, and those other subjects who by virtue of their membership of the society are entitled to and choose to make common cause with him, is no longer a participant with the state and its officials in a common enterprise. The moral basis for restraining their resort to violence has therefore disappeared. Hence the rebels are not bound to use force only when the law allows them to do so or when the state unlawfully uses force against them. To them *all state force is now unlawful force*. They may therefore treat it as hostile force, and meet it as they see fit, whether by way of defence, pre-emptive strike or counter-attack, while respecting the same restraints as they would be bound to observe if the rebellion were a war between states. They must do this because they are at war not with their fellow subjects who have broken no duty towards them but only with the state and its officials; and the fact that the same person may be both a fellow subject and a state official must not be allowed to obscure this distinction, though it sometimes makes it more difficult to respect in practice.[34] So, while they must direct their attacks only at the state and its officials, and not terrorize those who are innocent of denying them their rights, they are not debarred from using force because incidentally it may happen, as is inevitable in a war, that there will be some innocent victims.

That is my conclusion, no doubt dangerous, perhaps unpalatable, in the end a modified version of what Locke has said much better. No rational person lightly embarks on war, least of all civil war, the most disruptive of all forms of belligerence. No one has the right to do so if there are other means of securing within a reasonable period the justified aims which he and his fellow rebels are determined to secure. Even if he has the right to resort to violence, the rebel must weigh up the likely consequences of his action. This process will often and properly lead him to decide not to exercise his right to rebel or not to do so at the present juncture.[35] But sometimes it will not and should not. In the end the only guarantee of human dignity is that we would, if pressed too far, be prepared to rebel, and, if we did so, would have right on our side. It would then be the duty of other members of our community to support us.

34 Havel, op cit, 70, puts it as a condition of revolt involving violence that there should be a clear distinction between the usurpers of power and the subjugated population. In my view this is to set too stringent a condition, but the difficulty to which he draws attention is important.

35 Hook, *Revolution, Reform and Social Justice* (1974), 119. Havel, op cit, 71, has a good statement of the conditions in which resort to violent revolt is appropriate.

[22]

Sovereignty and Human Rights in Contemporary International Law

> **anachronism** . . . 1: an error in chronology; esp: a chronological misplacing of persons, events, objects or customs in regard to each other . . . 2: a person or a thing that is chronologically out of place; esp: one that belongs to a former age and is incongruous if found in the present . . . .
>
> *Webster's Third International Dictionary*

I.

Since Aristotle, the term "sovereignty" has had a long and varied history during which it has been given different meanings, hues and tones, depending on the context and the objectives of those using the word.[1] Bodin and Hobbes shaped the term to serve their perception of an urgent need for internal order. Their conception influenced several centuries of international politics and law[2] and also became a convenient supplementary secular

[1] *See* [Installment] 10 ENCYCLOPEDIA OF PUBLIC INTERNATIONAL LAW 397, 399 (R. Bernhardt ed. 1989) (discussion of historical evolution of term "sovereignty" from Aristotle to present).

[2] *Id.* at 401–02.

slogan for the various absolute monarchies of the time. Sovereignty often came to be an attribute of a powerful individual, whose legitimacy over territory (which was often described as his domain and even identified with him) rested on a purportedly direct or delegated divine or historic authority but certainly not, Hobbes's covenant of the multitude[3] notwithstanding, on the consent of the people.

The public law of Europe, the system of international law established by the assorted monarchs of the continent to serve their common purposes, reflected and reinforced this conception by insulating from legal scrutiny and competence a broad category of events that were later enshrined as "matters solely within the domestic jurisdiction."[4] If another political power entered the territory of the sovereign (whatever the reason) without his permission, his sovereignty was violated. In such matters, the sovereign's will was the only one that was legally relevant.

With the words "We the People,"[5] the American Revolution inaugurated the concept of the popular will as the theoretical and operational source of political authority. On its heels, the French Revolution and the advent of subsequent democratic governments confirmed the concept. Political legitimacy henceforth was to derive from popular support; governmental authority was based on the consent of the people in the territory in which a government purported to exercise power. At first only for those states in the vanguard of modern politics, later for more and more states, the sovereignty of the sovereign became the sovereignty of the people: popular sovereignty.

It took the formal international legal system time to register these profound changes. Another century beset by imperialism, colonialism and fascism was to pass, but by the end of the Second World War, popular sovereignty was firmly rooted as one of the fundamental postulates of political legitimacy. Article 1 of the UN Charter established as one of the purposes of the United Nations, to develop friendly relations between states, not on any terms, but "based on respect for the principles of equal rights and self-determination of peoples."

Any lingering doubt that use of the term "self-determination" might have amounted to a mechanical, or at best a deferential, carry-over from Wilsonian diplomacy, and not a radical decision that henceforth the internal authority of governments would be appraised internationally, was dispelled three years later. In the Universal Declaration of Human Rights, a document then describing itself as "a common standard of achievement" but now accepted as declaratory of customary international law, Article 21(3) provided that "[t]he will of the people shall be the basis of the authority of government; this will shall be expressed in periodic and genuine elections which shall be

[3] T. Hobbes, Leviathan (M. Oakeshott ed. 1946).

[4] Under Article 15(8) of the Covenant of the League of Nations, if the Council found a dispute between any two parties "to arise out of a matter which by international law is solely within the domestic jurisdiction of that party," the Council would refrain from making any recommendation as to its settlement. *See* League of Nations Covenant Art. 15, para. 8, *reprinted in* 13 AJIL 128, 134 (Supp. 1919).

[5] U.S. Const., Preamble.

by universal and equal suffrage and shall be held by secret vote or by equivalent free voting procedures."[6] Of course, there had been regional pacts based upon similar notions,[7] much as there had been holy alliances based on their antithesis. The significance of this statement in the Universal Declaration was that it was now expressed in a fundamental *international* constitutive legal document. In international law, the sovereign had finally been dethroned.

Unlike certain other grand statements of international law, the concept of popular sovereignty was not to remain mere pious aspiration. The international lawmaking system proceeded to prescribe criteria for appraising the conformity of internal governance with international standards of democracy.[8] Thanks to a happy historical conjunction, modern communications technology has made it possible to verify that conformity rapidly and economically and to broadcast it widely. International and regional organizational monitors now use the new technology in critical national elections so as to ensure that they are free and fair.[9] The results of such elections serve as evidence of popular sovereignty and become the basis for international en-

[6] Universal Declaration of Human Rights, GA Res. 217A (III), UN Doc. A/810, at 71 (1948).

[7] *See, e.g.*, Central American Treaty of Peace (Treaty of Washington), Additional Convention to the General Treaty, Art. I, 2 FOREIGN RELATIONS OF THE UNITED STATES 1907, at 696, 696, *reprinted in* 2 AJIL 229, 229–30 (Supp. 1908):

> The Governments of the High Contracting Parties shall not recognize any other Government which may come into power in any of the five Republics as a consequence of a *coup d'etat*, or of a revolution against the recognized Government, so long as the freely elected representatives of the people thereof have not constitutionally reorganized the country.

[8] See, for example, United Nations Declaration on the Elimination of All Forms of Racial Discrimination, GA Res. 1904 (XVIII) (Nov. 20, 1963); International Convention on the Elimination of All Forms of Racial Discrimination, *opened for signature* Mar. 7, 1966, 660 UNTS 195; International Convention on the Suppression and Punishment of the Crime of *Apartheid*, GA Res. 3068 (XXVIII) (Nov. 30, 1973); Convention against Discrimination in Education, Dec. 14, 1960, 429 UNTS 32; Convention concerning Equal Remuneration for Men and Women Workers for Work of Equal Value, June 29, 1951, 165 UNTS 303; Convention on the Elimination of All Forms of Discrimination against Women, GA Res. 34/180 (Dec. 18, 1979); Declaration on the Elimination of All Forms of Intolerance and of Discrimination Based on Religion or Belief, GA Res. 36/55 (Nov. 25, 1981); Convention concerning Forced or Compulsory Labour, June 28, 1930, 39 UNTS 55; Declaration on the Protection of All Persons from Being Subjected to Torture and Other Cruel, Inhuman or Degrading Treatment or Punishment, GA Res. 3452 (XXX) (Dec. 9, 1975); Convention against Torture and Other Cruel, Inhuman or Degrading Treatment or Punishment, GA Res. 39/46 (Dec. 10, 1984); Code of Conduct for Law Enforcement Officials, GA Res. 34/169 (Dec. 17, 1979); and Declaration of Basic Principles of Justice for Victims of Crime and Abuse of Power, GA Res. 40/34 (Nov. 29, 1985); as well as the numerous conventions on social welfare, marriage and the family and cultural rights. *See also* Resolutions Adopted by the General Assembly During its 20th Session, 20 UN GAOR Supp. (No. 14) at 53–65, UN Doc. A/6014 (1965) (series of resolutions adopted on non-self-governing territories).

[9] For example, in the recently concluded Namibia elections, the ballot counting and tabulation were overseen by 1,700 electoral supervisors, part of a United Nations Transition Assistance Group (UNTAG). *See* UN CHRON., March 1990, at 42. Similarly, a UN observation mission for the verification of elections in Nicaragua (ONUVEN) was set up there in December 1989 to observe and monitor the 1990 elections. *Id.* at 64.

dorsement of the elected government.[10] In functional terms, this process constitutes a new type of inclusive international recognition. Decisions to withhold recognition where the will of the people has been demonstrably ignored or suppressed have increasingly led to the next stage, the institution of international programs designed to permit or facilitate the realization of the popular will.[11]

II.

Although the venerable term "sovereignty" continues to be used in international legal practice, its referent in modern international law is quite different. International law still protects sovereignty, but—not surprisingly—it is the people's sovereignty rather than the sovereign's sovereignty. Under the old concept, even scrutiny of international human rights without the permission of the sovereign could arguably constitute a violation of sovereignty by its "invasion" of the sovereign's *domaine réservé*. The United Nations Charter replicates the "domestic jurisdiction–international concern" dichotomy, but no serious scholar still supports the contention that internal human rights are "essentially within the domestic jurisdiction of any state" and hence insulated from international law.

This contemporary change in content of the term "sovereignty" also changes the cast of characters who can violate that sovereignty. Of course,

[10] After the November 1989 elections in Namibia, the UN Security Council congratulated the people of Namibia and affirmed the election results; the Special Committee on Decolonization declared on December 4 that the Namibian elections had been held "in conformity with established UN standards of decolonization"; and Special Representative Ahtisaari declared that the electoral process had "at each stage been free and fair." *See id.* at 41–43.

[11] After Rhodesia's unilateral declaration of independence in 1965, the international community overwhelmingly denounced the action and refused to recognize Rhodesia as one independent state. *See generally The Situation in Southern Rhodesia: Resolutions Adopted by the General Assembly and the Security Council of the United Nations, reprinted in* 60 AJIL 921 (1966). For commentary, see McDougal & Reisman, *Rhodesia and the United Nations: The Lawfulness of International Concern*, 62 AJIL 1 (1968).

With respect to Namibia, the United Nations consistently refused to recognize South Africa's occupation of Namibia. *See, e.g.*, Marín-Bosch, *How Nations Vote in the General Assembly of the United Nations*, 41 INT'L ORG. 705, 705–06 (1987) (pointing out that Namibia was the subject of more resolutions than all other past decolonization issues combined). Indeed, by Resolution 2145 (XXI) of October 27, 1966, the General Assembly placed Namibia under the direct responsibility of the United Nations so as to enable Namibians to exercise their right of self-determination. It also established the UN Council for Namibia (by Resolution 2248 (S-V) of May 19, 1967) with the objective, inter alia, of obtaining the withdrawal of South Africa from Namibia. *See* Report of the United Nations Council for Namibia, 39 UN GAOR Supp. (No. 24) at 1, UN Doc. A/39/24 (1984). Other international programs eventually led to the independence of Namibia on March 21, 1990.

The South African situation has also gained the attention of the international community in the past few decades. *See, e.g.*, the Policies of *Apartheid* of the Government of the Republic of South Africa, GA Res. 3151 (XXVIII), 28 UN GAOR Supp. (No. 30) at 33, UN Doc. A/9030 (1973); GA Res. 39/72, 39 UN GAOR Supp. (No. 51) at 40, UN Doc. A/39/51 (1985); International Convention on the Suppression and Punishment of the Crime of *Apartheid*, GA Res. 3068 (XXVIII), 28 UN GAOR Supp. (No. 30), *supra*, at 75. Talks are currently under way to work out a form of representative government for a future South Africa. *See* Waldmeir, *ANC May End Armed Struggle*, Fin. Times (London), May 5, 1990, at 1, col. 7.

popular sovereignty is violated when an outside force invades and imposes its will on the people. One thinks of the invasion of Afghanistan in 1979 or of Kuwait in 1990.[12] But what happens to sovereignty, in its modern sense, when it is not an outsider but some home-grown specialist in violence who seizes and purports to wield the authority of the government against the wishes of the people, by naked power, by putsch or by coup, by the usurpation of an election or by those systematic corruptions of the electoral process in which almost 100 percent of the electorate purportedly votes for the incumbent's list (often the only choice)? Is such a seizer of power entitled to invoke the international legal term "national sovereignty" to establish or reinforce his own position in international politics?

Under the old international law, the internal usurper was so entitled, for the standard was de facto control: the only test was the effective power of the claimant. In the *Tinoco* case,[13] Costa Rica sought to defend itself by claiming a violation of its popular sovereignty. Tinoco, the erstwhile Minister of War, had seized power in violation of the Constitution. Therefore, the subsequent restorationist Costa Rican Government contended, his actions could not be deemed to have bound Costa Rica. But Chief Justice Taft decided that by virtue of his effective control, Tinoco had represented the legitimate government as long as he enjoyed that control.

The *Tinoco* decision was consistent with the law of its time. Were it applied strictly now, it would be anachronistic, for it stands in stark contradiction to the new constitutive, human rights-based conception of popular sovereignty. To be sure, there were policy reasons for *Tinoco*, which may still have some cogency, but the important point is that there was then no countervailing constitutive policy of international human rights and its conception of popular sovereignty.

Caudillos and their like appear to be susceptible to a megalomania that identifies their corporeal selves with the symbols of the nation and the state. They invoke a "'sovereignty' so grandiose and capricious . . . it might be supposed to be a deliberate caricature, save for the intensity of the sentiments that are mobilized around the symbol itself."[14] Happily, the international legal system in which declamations such as "l'état, c'est moi" were coherent has long since been consigned to history's scrap heap. In our era, such pronouncements become, at least for audiences at a safe remove, the stuff of refined comedy. They would be occasions for general hilarity, even in the countries where they are still staged, were it not for the endless misery that the dictators who grant themselves sovereignty always inflict upon the human beings trapped within the boundaries of the territory the dictators have confused with themselves.

[12] On the invasion of Afghanistan by the Soviet Union and the applicable norms of armed conflict, see generally Reisman & Silk, *Which Law Applies to the Afghan Conflict?*, 82 AJIL 459 (1988).

[13] Tinoco case (Great Brit. v. Costa Rica), 1 R. Int'l Arb. Awards 369 (1923), *reprinted in* 18 AJIL 147 (1924).

[14] McDougal, Lasswell & Reisman, *The World Constitutive Process of Authoritative Decision*, in M. S. McDougal & W. M. Reisman, International Law Essays 197 (1981).

III.

In many countries, the internal political situation is murky and constitutional procedures for the orderly transfer of power are nonexistent or ineffective. In a flurry of coups and putsches, both outsiders and insiders may be unable to ascertain the popular will, especially if the disorder or tyranny has prevented it from being consulted or expressed. Even in the absence of elections—indeed, even when there are "supervised" elections—it is often clear that the vast majority of the people detest those who have assumed power and characterize themselves as the government. It is more difficult, however, to say who the people would wish in their stead. They may not know, which is one of the reasons that international legal supervision of elections is designed to include an adequate period for candidacies to be developed and to allow campaigning, so that voters can make the informed choice that is at the center of free and fair elections.

But in circumstances in which free elections are internationally supervised and the results are internationally endorsed as free and fair and the people's choice is clear, the world community does not need to speculate on what constitutes popular sovereignty in that country.

When those confirmed wishes are ignored by a local caudillo who either takes power himself or assigns it to a subordinate he controls, a jurist rooted in the late twentieth century can hardly say that an invasion by outside forces to remove the caudillo and install the elected government is a violation of national sovereignty. Cross-border military actions should certainly never be extolled, for they are necessarily brutal and destructive of life and property. They may well be unlawful for a variety of other reasons. But if they displace the usurper and emplace the people who were freely elected, they can be characterized, in this particular regard, as a violation of sovereignty only if one uses the term anachronistically to mean the violation of some mystical survival of a monarchical right that supposedly devolves *jure gentium* on whichever warlord seizes and holds the presidential palace or if the term is used in the jurisprudentially bizarre sense to mean that inanimate territory has political rights that preempt those of its inhabitants.[15]

This is not to say that every externally motivated action to remove an unpopular government is now permitted, or that officer corps that feel obsolescence hard upon them can claim a new raison d'être and start scouring the globe for opportunities for "democratizing" interventions. Authoritative conclusions about the lawfulness of the unilateral use of force, no less than about any other unilateral action, turn on many contextual factors: e.g., the contingencies allegedly justifying the unilateral use, the availability of feasible persuasive alternatives, the means of coercion selected, the level of coercion used (the classic test of necessity and proportionality), whether the ob-

[15] *See* Stone, *Should Trees Have Standing?—Toward Legal Rights for Natural Objects*, 45 S. CAL. L. REV. 450 (1972); Tribe, *Ways Not to Think about Plastic Trees: New Foundations for Environmental Law*, 83 YALE L.J. 1315 (1974). For a cogent critique on this point, cf. Schwartz, *The Rights of Nature and the Death of God*, PUB. INTEREST, No. 97, 1989, at 3.

jectives of the intervener include internationally illicit aims, the aggregate consequences of inaction, and the aggregate consequences of action.[16] But it is to say that the suppression of popular sovereignty may be a justifying factor, not a justification *per se* but a *conditio sine qua non*. And it is to say that the word "sovereignty" can no longer be used to shield the actual suppression of popular sovereignty from external rebuke and remedy.

International law is still concerned with the protection of sovereignty, but, in its modern sense, the object of protection is not the power base of the tyrant who rules directly by naked power or through the apparatus of a totalitarian political order, but the continuing capacity of a population freely to express and effect choices about the identities and policies of its governors. In modern international law, the "unilateral declaration of independence" by the Smith Government in Rhodesia was not an exercise of national sovereignty but a violation of the sovereignty of the people of Zimbabwe.[17] The Chinese Government's massacre in Tiananmen Square to maintain an oligarchy against the wishes of the people was a violation of Chinese sovereignty. The Ceausescu dictatorship was a violation of Romanian sovereignty. President Marcos violated Philippine sovereignty, General Noriega violated Panamanian sovereignty, and the Soviet blockade of Lithuania violated its sovereignty. Fidel Castro violates Cuban sovereignty by mock elections that insult the people whose fundamental human rights are being denied, no less than the intelligence of the rest of the human race. In each case, the violators often brazenly characterize the international community's condemnation as itself a violation of their sovereignty. Sadly, some organizations and some scholars, falling victim to anachronism, have given them comfort.

In modern international law, sovereignty can be violated as effectively and ruthlessly by an indigenous as by an outside force, in much the same way that the wealth and natural resources of a country can be spoliated as thoroughly and efficiently by a native as by a foreigner.[18] Sovereignty can be liberated as much by an indigenous as by an outside force. As in the interpretation of any other event in terms of policy, context and consequence must be considered.

IV.

The international human rights program is more than a piecemeal addition to the traditional corpus of international law, more than another chapter sandwiched into traditional textbooks of international law. By shifting the fulcrum of the system from the protection of sovereigns to the protection of people, it works qualitative changes in virtually every component. Many of the old terms survive, but in using them in a modern context, one should bear in mind Holmes's lapidary dictum: "A word is not a crystal,

[16] *See* M. S. McDougal & F. Feliciano, Law and Minimum World Public Order, ch. 3 (1961).

[17] *See supra* note 11.

[18] *See* Reisman, *Harnessing International Law to Restrain and Recapture Indigenous Spoliations*, 83 AJIL 56 (1989).

transparent and unchanged; it is the skin of a living thought and may vary greatly in color and content according to the circumstances and the time in which it is used."[19]

When constitutive changes such as these are introduced into a legal system while many other struts of the system are left in place, appliers and interpreters of current cases cannot proceed in a piecemeal and mechanical fashion. Precisely because the human rights norms are constitutive, other norms must be reinterpreted in their light, lest anachronisms be produced. This process of "updating" or "contemporization" or *actualisation*, as French scholars call it, is not unknown to international law. In the *South-West Africa* opinion,[20] the International Court indicated the absurdity of mechanically applying an old norm without reference to fundamental constitutive changes, and national courts have often expressed the need and authority to actualize.[21] The same style of actualization is required with regard to the assessment of the lawfulness of human rights actions. When this is not done, legal arguments and judgments will be marked by anachronism.

In the debate over the U.S. action in Panama in the United Nations, the Nicaraguan Permanent Representative, whose Government had requested the meeting, opened it by proclaiming: "Once again an offence has been committed against our peoples. Once again an attempt is being made to make brute force appear to be law. Once again the principles which are the foundation of international relations have been violated."[22] The Permanent Representative proceeded to cite, chapter and verse, the United Nations Charter and the OAS Charter to establish "[t]his flagrant violation of Panama's sovereignty and territorial integrity."[23] No reference whatsoever was made to Manuel Antonio Noriega's suppression of popular sovereignty, or to the fact that both the internationally supervised election before the military action and the opinion polls after it indicated overwhelming support for the change that was realized.[24] These issues were swept away by indirection, when the Permanent Representative said that "no argument can possibly justify intervention against a sovereign state."[25]

[19] Towne v. Eisner, 245 U.S. 372, 376 (1918).

[20] South-West Africa—Voting Procedure, 1955 ICJ REP. 67, 77 (Advisory Opinion of June 7).

[21] M. S. McDOUGAL, H. LASSWELL & J. MILLER, THE INTERPRETATION OF AGREEMENTS AND WORLD PUBLIC ORDER, ch. 4 (1967).

[22] UN Doc. S/PV.2899, at 3–5 (Dec. 20, 1989). I treat this statement as made in good faith. It is not inappropriate to note, however, that those who invoke this argument frequently reserve for their governments a right of intervention for various revolutionary purposes, e.g., wars of national liberation. See, in this regard, Reisman, *Old Wine in New Bottles: The Reagan and Brezhnev Doctrines in Contemporary International Law and Practice*, 13 YALE J. INT'L L. 171 (1988).

[23] UN Doc. S/PV.2899, *supra* note 22, at 4.

[24] One of the more ironic aspects of the Panama affair was that all indications before and after the U.S. invasion were that while the vast majority of the Panamanian people viewed it as a liberation, the other governments of the region voted in the OAS to condemn it as a violation of Panamanian sovereignty. According to most news reports, the U.S. military action in Panama was met with overwhelming approval by the Panamanian people. *See, e.g.*, *After Noriega*, ECONOMIST, Jan. 16, 1990, at 37.

[25] UN Doc. S/PV.2902, at 7 (Dec. 23, 1989).

This is what Professor D'Amato, in his remarkable article, has called "the rhetoric of statism."[26] The anachronism here is effected by the *selective* use of the language of international law, carefully screening out everything that has been introduced by the human rights movement. It may be contrasted with the remark of Thomas Pickering, the United States Permanent Representative, that "the people, not governments, are sovereign."[27] That formulation, in turn, oversimplifies the decision calculus now required, for, as expressed, it could make that single variable determinative of lawfulness in all future cases. But at least it expresses the critical new constitutive policy in international law, which is completely absent from the Nicaraguan formula.

Under the Nicaraguan version, sovereignty is not international protection of the will of the people, but international protection for a group that calls itself the government against the wishes of the people. There is no international test of the legitimacy of a self-proclaimed government. The only test is internal naked power. Under this version, Panama's sovereignty is violated by the removal of the usurper and the establishment of conditions for the assumption of power by the legitimate government. That is an anachronism.

Anachronism can only be avoided in legal decision by systematic actualization, which considers inherited norms in the context of changed constitutive normative systems and makes sensitive assessments of the relative weight each is to be given and the various intensities with which each is demanded.

V.

The consequences of these changes are far-reaching. Some are clearly beneficial to the new values of the international system. Some hold the potential for destabilizing the system. On the credit side, international human rights puts current and erstwhile tyrants on notice that monarchical and elitist conceptions of national sovereignty cannot be invoked to immunize them from the writ of international law. Some have already grasped the implications of this development. Haiti, in July 1990, asked the United Nations to provide three hundred civilian officials to supervise its upcoming elections and forty military officers to ensure that the local armed forces would be part of the solution rather than part of the problem.[28] Haiti's provisional Foreign Minister, Kesler Clermont, said such a team would set "a powerful precedent" for UN monitoring of Third World elections "to certify their legitimacy."[29] Three of the seven Third World members of the Security Council opposed the request.[30] The princes may not like this, but for peoples languishing under despotism and dictatorship, the development promises, at least, the condemnation by international law of the violation of their sovereignty and the possibility, uncertain as it may be, of a remedy.

[26] D'Amato, *The Invasion of Panama Was a Lawful Response to Tyranny*, 84 AJIL 516, 518 (1990).

[27] UN Doc. S/PV.2902, *supra* note 25, at 8.

[28] Lewis, *Haiti Wants U.N. to Monitor Vote*, N.Y. Times, July 22, 1990, at 10, col. 6.

[29] *Id.*

[30] *Id.*

On the debit side, while the bite of human rights norms is extended, so, too, is systemic instability. In decentralized systems whose members themselves perforce make the decisions, the more the number of constitutive appraisal norms, the more the number of cross-border appraisals and the greater the possibility of cross-border meddling by various actors. The problem is contained, to an extent, when internationally supervised "free and fair" elections credibly and unequivocally indicate the wishes of a majority of the people. It is also contained when other nonelectoral indicators show the popular will, though without the clarity and freedom vouchsafed by secret ballot. When popular wishes are usurped violently, the confirmed expression of popular sovereignty tells everyone who the real usurper is and who should rightfully constitute the government, no matter how convincing the newspeak of the dictator's apparatus may be.

Unambiguous situations, however, may be exceptions. When the internationally supervised elections result in an absence of consensus on who should govern, *or* the integrity of the elections is doubtful, *or* there have been no elections, *or* a civil insurrection has left diverse groups vying for power, no one can be sure that the unilateral intervener from the outside is implementing popular wishes. To varying extents, the intervener will be shaping them. In some circumstances, the banner of popular sovereignty can become a fig leaf for its suppression by foreign intervention, especially when governments bent on intervention maintain stables of alternative local leaders who can be brought forward to authorize an invasion at the appropriate time.[31] In practice, therefore, there may be a factual "gray" area between unequivocal expressions of popular will through internationally supervised, observed or validated elections, on the one hand, and the atrocities that warrant humanitarian intervention, on the other. Situations falling into the gray area will simply not lend themselves to unilateral action.

The most satisfactory solution to this problem is the creation of centralized institutions, equipped with decision-making authority and the capacity to make it effective. But in the immediate future, that solution remains unlikely, and to make it a condition of lawful decision now only evades addressing the policies that the notion of popular sovereignty encapsulates. The given of contemporary international decision making is the absence of such institutions and the need to focus on regulating unilateral decision making. Because rights without remedies are not rights at all, prohibiting the unilateral vindication of clear violations of rights when multilateral possibilities do not obtain is virtually to terminate those rights.

It is no longer politically feasible or morally acceptable to suspend the operation of human rights norms until every constitutive problem is solved. In the interim, new criteria for unilateral human rights actions must be established. In addition, more refined techniques for their legal appraisal and more effective means for their condemnation when such actions are themselves unlawful must be developed. One contribution of our profession

[31] *See, e.g.*, Reisman & Silk, *supra* note 12, at 466–79 (discussion of factual situation in Afghanistan leading to "invitation" of Soviet armed forces by Afghan "government").

should be to develop methods for assessing popular will and making judgments about divergences.

The violation of sovereignty has heretofore largely been treated with passive strategies: absorbing those who have been obliged to flee their own countries. With the increasing refinement of transportation, domestic human rights pathologies now generate larger and larger numbers of refugees. But the welfare democracies of the world, which are the preferred refuge of those fleeing human rights violations in their own countries, have begun to reach the limits of their absorptive capacities. The passive strategy of dealing with violations of sovereignty will no longer work. An active strategy that addresses the pathology itself is required, both pragmatically and by the very conception of modern sovereignty.

VI.

Because human rights considerations introduce so many more variables into the determination of lawfulness, an even heavier burden of deliberation devolves upon international lawyers in assessing the lawfulness of actions. Matters become more complex and uncertain than they were in an international legal system that was composed of a few binary rules applied to a checkerboard of monarchical states and, most particularly, that lacked an international code of human rights. One can no longer simply condemn externally motivated actions aimed at removing an unpopular government and permitting the consultation or implementation of the popular will as *per se* violations of sovereignty without inquiring whether and under what conditions that will was being suppressed, and how the external action will affect the expression and implementation of popular sovereignty. The identification of what is clearly "externally motivated action" is itself an increasingly difficult task.

No one is entitled to complain that things are getting too complicated. If complexity of decision is the price for increased human dignity on the planet, it is worth it. Those who yearn for "the good old days" and continue to trumpet terms like "sovereignty" without relating them to the human rights conditions within the states under discussion do more than commit an anachronism. They undermine human rights.

W. MICHAEL REISMAN

Name Index

Acton, J.E.E.D. 494
Ago, Justice 78
Ajami, F. 56–7, 68–9
Alchourrón, C. 359–60
Alston, Philip xx, 3–29
Ames, R.T. 305
Amin, Idi 157, 479–80
An Na'im, A.A. xxii, 253–92, 363, 366–7, 368, 371, 377, 378, 380, 381
Aristide, Jean-Bertrand 444
Aristotle 303, 344, 364, 545
Asante, S.K.B. 151
Asbún, J.P. 57
Austin, J. 359–60, 445

Baumann xv
Bentham, Jeremy 152, 359–60, 405, 407
Berger, P. 66–8
Berlin, I. xvi
Bhutto, Benazir 267
Bhutto, Zulfikar Ali 266–7, 284
Binaisa, Godfrey L. 479–80
Bobbio, N. xvi, 358–9, 362–3, 367, 368, 369, 371, 380
Bodin, Jean 545
Bokassa, Jean Bedel 157
Botha, P.W. 535, 536
Boulware-Miller, K. 328
Brezhnev, Leonid Ilyich 424, 425–6, 427
Brownlie, I. 78
Buergenthal, Justice Thomas 93, 465, 481
Bulygin, E. 359–60
Burke, Edmund 152, 535
Burlatsky, F. 424–5, 427
Burrows, N. 335
Bush, George Herbert Walker 207, 472
Buultjens, R. 153

Camus, Albert 529
Carrio, G.R. 359–60, 369
Carter, James Earl (Jimmy) 7, 21, 57, 63–4, 65–6, 68, 207
Cassese, A. 6
Castro, Fidel 56, 551
Ceausescu, Nicolae 551
Chalidze, V. 153
Chen, L.-C. 12, 90

Chkhidvadze, V. 153
Clemenceau, Georges 450
Clermont, Kesler 553
Clinton, William Jefferson 204, 205, 207–8
Cojuangco, Eduardo 214
Confucius 236, 305–6, 311, 312

D'Amato, Prof. 553
Deng Xiaoping 214, 421
Diamond, S. 52
Dilthey, Wilhelm 346
Dochring, Prof. 93–4
Dominguez, J. 69
Donnelly, J. 4–5, 147–60
Dworkin, R. xvi, 148, 149, 302, 361–2, 374

Edwards, Justice Harry T. 77
Edwards, R. 304
Egorov, A.G. 154
Eisler, R. 333
El Saadawi, N. 324
Engle, Karen xxiv, 323–40

Falk, Richard xix, xx, 49–75
Franck, T.M. xii, xxiv, 443–88, 491–2, 493, 519
Friedman, Wolfgang xiii

Gadamer, Hans-Georg 346
Galey, M.E. 331
Gandhi, Indira 192
Gandhi, Mahatma 53
George III, King of England 535
Ghai, Yash xv, xxiii, 219–52
Gorbachev, Mikhail Sergeevich 421, 426, 427–9
Gough, K. 75
Gros Espiell, H. 508
Guggenheim, P. 9

Habermas, Jürgen xvii, 343–55
Hakim, K.A. 154
Hall, D.L. 305
Hampshire, S. 364
Harkin, T. 147
Harrington, James 348
Harris, M. 52

Hart, H.L.A. 149–50
Hassan II, King of Morocco 273
Hatch, Elvin xxii
Hegel, Georg Wilhelm Friedrich 364, 369, 371
Heidegger, M. 345
Henkin, L. xii, 29, 144, 298
Herndl, Kurt 89
Higgins, Rosalyn xii
Hitler, Adolf 526, 537
Hobbes, Thomas 301–2, 303, 317, 348, 407, 545–6
Ho Chi-Minh 131
Hohfeld, W.N. 307
Honderich, T. 529–30
Honoré, Tony xxiv, 523–43
Howard, R.E. 363, 366–7, 368, 377
Hume, David 446
Humphrey, J.P. 5, 12

Ishaque, K.M. 150

Jaenicke, G. 97
James II, King of England 534, 535
Jefferson, Thomas 446
Jennings, R.Y. 4

Kahn, P.W. 348
Kant, Immanuel 102, 140, 302, 309, 348, 352–4, 364, 371–2, 376, 485, 529, 538–9, 542
Kaufman, Justice 12
Kausikan, B. xxiii, 201–18
Keenan, E.L. 156
Kelsen, H. 9, 10, 81, 358, 359–61, 375
Khadduri, M. 151
Khomeini, Ayatollah Ruhollah 273
Kierkegaard, Sören Aabye 345
Kingsbury, Benedict xxiv, 489–521
Kirgis, F. 17
Kishwar, Madhu 194
Kiss, A. 12–13, 17
Koskenniemi, M. xiii, xiv, xv, xvi, xvii, xx, 31–47, 492
Kothari, Rajni 189–99
Kraprayoon, Suchinda 214
Kropotkin, P. 530

Lam, M.C. 503
Lande, C.H. 59
Lane, E. 22
Lansing, Robert 450
Lasswell, H. 90
Lauterpacht, Sir Hersch xii
Legesse, A. 147, 152, 155, 156
Leng, Shao-Chuan 152
Lenin, V.I. 424, 429, 433, 494
Lillich, R. 14
Lincoln, Abraham 536
Lo, Chung-Shu 152, 153
Locke, John 149, 301–2, 348, 349, 405, 446, 447, 534, 539, 543
Louis XIV, King of France 157
Lyons, D. 136

MacIntyre, A.C. 364, 366, 367, 368
Madison, James 446
Manglapus, R. 147
Manu 182
Mao Tse-tung 59, 297, 312–13
Marcos, Ferdinand Edralin 214, 446, 551
Marcos, Imelda 214
Marek, Prof. 96, 97
Marx, Karl 53, 144, 156, 171–2, 311–12, 424, 429, 433
Mawdudi, A.A. 250
Mazrui, Prof. 237
McDougal, M. 12, 90
McGoldrick, D. 458
McNair, A. 79
Menem, Carlos Saul 369
Meron, T. xx, 6, 14–15, 77–99, 464
Michelman, F. 343–4, 349
Mill, James 407
Mill, J.S. 303–4, 311, 405, 407, 479
Minogue, K.R. 494
Mohan, Inder 194
Mosler, Justice H. 94–5, 96, 97
Moynihan, D.P. 59, 65–6, 67
Muhammad 257–8

Nadvi, S.M. 150
Nandy, Vaskar 194
Nayar, K.M.G. 12
Nino, C.S. 361, 366, 369, 374, 376, 379, 380
Noriega, Manuel Antonio 462, 481, 486, 551, 552
Nozick, R. 302, 539

Obasanjo, Olusegun 55–6

Paine, Thomas 149
Panikkar, R. 161–88
Pankin, Boris D. 480
Panyarachun, Anand 214
Peerenboom, R.P. xxii, 293–321
Pickering, Thomas 553
Pincoffs, E. 308
Pinochet Ugarte, Augusto 131

Piscatori, J. 269
Plato 152, 303, 446
Pohl, Galindo 11
Pollis, A. 147, 157, 158
Pol Pot 157
Popper, K. 144, 145

Ramos, Fidel 214
Rawls, J. 135–6, 137, 302, 372
Raz, J. 510, 523–4
Reagan, Ronald Wilson 207
Reisman, W.M. xxiv, 449, 472, 545–55
Richardson, Elliot 469, 472
Rosemont, H. 301
Ross, A. 359–60, 369
Rousseau, Jean Jacques 234, 302, 344, 345, 348, 352–4, 405, 407
Rubin, A. 22

Said, A.A. 147, 151
Sandel, M. 364, 368
Sartre, Jean-Paul 345
Sawczuk, K. 153
Schachter, O. xii, xx, 6, 13–14, 16–17, 26, 80, 89, 101–7, 131
Schleiermacher, Friedrich Ernst Daniel 346
Schwab, P. 147, 157, 158
Schwebel, Justice 94
Sen, A.K. xviii, 248
Shapiro, I. xvii
Simma, Bruno xx, 3–29
Slack, A. 327, 328
Smith, Ian Douglas 551
Smith, W. 271–2
Somoza, Anastasio 'Tacho' 462, 486
Spivak, G.C. 325, 339–40
Stalin, Joseph 421, 432, 428, 435
Steiner, Henry J. xiv, xix, xxiv, 385–442
Suharto, Thojib N.J. 266, 267
Suy, Prof. 92

Tabandeh, S. 150
Taft, Chief Justice 549
Taha, M. 286
Tanaka, Justice J. 26
Taylor, C. 364, 365–6, 367, 368
Tesón, F.R. xxii, 117–46
Tinoco, Minister 549
Tocqueville, Alexis de 303–4
Tolley, H. Jr. 19
Turpel, M.E. 502, 503

Van Boven 82
Vance, Cyrus 63–4
Van Hoof, G.J.H. 6
Verdross, A. 22, 25–6, 96

Wafi, A.A. 262
Wai, D.M. 151–2
Walzer, M. 364, 372
Watson, J.S. 22
Weil, S. 52, 77
Weisburd, A.M. 22
Whiteman 91
Williams, B. 136–7, 139–40, 364
Wilson, Woodrow 450–51, 494
Wolf, S. 363

Yamani, A.Z. 155
Yeltsin, Boris Nikolayevich 443

Zia ul-Haq, Mohammed 266–7, 276, 284, 285

www.ingramcontent.com/pod-product-compliance
Lightning Source LLC
LaVergne TN
LVHW102107300926
849161LV00014B/3067